Excommunication in Thirteenth-Century England

Communities, Politics, and Publicity

FELICITY HILL

Great Clarendon Street, Oxford, OX2 6DP,
United Kingdom

Oxford University Press is a department of the University of Oxford.
It furthers the University's objective of excellence in research, scholarship,
and education by publishing worldwide. Oxford is a registered trade mark of
Oxford University Press in the UK and in certain other countries

© Felicity Hill 2022

The moral rights of the author have been asserted

First Edition published in 2022

Impression: 1

All rights reserved. No part of this publication may be reproduced, stored in
a retrieval system, or transmitted, in any form or by any means, without the
prior permission in writing of Oxford University Press, or as expressly permitted
by law, by licence or under terms agreed with the appropriate reprographics
rights organization. Enquiries concerning reproduction outside the scope of the
above should be sent to the Rights Department, Oxford University Press, at the
address above

You must not circulate this work in any other form
and you must impose this same condition on any acquirer

Published in the United States of America by Oxford University Press
198 Madison Avenue, New York, NY 10016, United States of America

British Library Cataloguing in Publication Data
Data available

Library of Congress Control Number: 2022930670

ISBN 978–0–19–884036–7

DOI: 10.1093/oso/9780198840367.001.0001

Printed and bound in the UK by
Clays Ltd, Elcograf S.p.A.

Links to third party websites are provided by Oxford in good faith and
for information only. Oxford disclaims any responsibility for the materials
contained in any third party website referenced in this work.

Acknowledgements

The research for this book was made possible initially by doctoral funding from the Arts and Humanities Research Council (via the University of East Anglia), then by fourth-year funding from the Scouloudi Foundation via the Institute of Historical Research. I was able to begin the process of turning the PhD thesis into this book as a Research Fellow at Corpus Christi College, Cambridge. I am enormously grateful to supervisors, colleagues, and friends from my undergraduate degree at Manchester, my MA at University College London, my PhD at UEA, my year at the Institute of Historical Research, my postdoc in Cambridge, and finally now to my colleagues at St Andrews. I have benefited throughout from encouragement and generosity without which I could never have produced this book. John Sabapathy has provided invaluable advice throughout the last decade, at each stage of this book's development. He generously read almost the entire manuscript; his comments have improved the text in a great many places. I am likewise grateful to John Hudson for reading a full draft and for his comments. Ian Forrest, who has revealed that he was one of the reviewers for OUP, provided me both with much appreciated encouragement and with helpful suggestions for improvements. The recommendations of the anonymous reviewers were also invaluable. John Arnold kindly read some chapter drafts. I have benefited a great deal from John's kindness and counsel in Cambridge and since. I would further like to thank my PhD supervisor Nicholas Vincent, who of course read the text in its earlier thesis form, for giving me free rein as a doctoral student, and for his help and guidance since. The process of turning the thesis into a book was greatly facilitated by the suggestions of my examiners, Sarah Hamilton and Tom Licence. Sarah has been generous with her time on numerous occasions. Ben Savill honoured the writing pact. David d'Avray, who piqued my interest in excommunication back in 2011, has been consistently kind and supportive throughout my studies and beyond. He helped a great deal with both appendices, providing editorial assistance with the second.

I am grateful to a great many more people with whom I had discussions, from whom I received advice, and who helped make the process of researching and writing a PhD then a book enjoyable. These include Sophie Ambler, Rob Bartlett, David Carpenter, Stephen Church, Peter Clarke, Emily Corran, Caitlin Ellis, Will Eves, Caroline Goodson, Julia King, Donald Logan, Stephen Mossman, Simon Parsons, Danica Summerlin, Alice Taylor, Emily Ward, Sarah White, the fellows of Corpus Christi College, and all my colleagues in the Department of Medieval History at St Andrews. Emily, Lesley, and Sam, as well as Caitlin, helped me to keep writing (about social isolation) through lockdowns.

In addition to various university libraries, the IHR, Warburg Institute, and British library provided indispensable resources. The estate of the late Jeffrey Denton kindly gave me many of his books, which have been much appreciated and used. Finally, I would like to thank my friends and family, in particular Gemma, my parents, and my grandmother, who sadly never got to see the book completed.

December 2021

Contents

Glossary of Automatic Excommunications referred to in the text — ix

Introduction — 1
Misuse, overuse, inefficacy? — 5
The significance of excommunication — 10
The purpose of excommunication — 11
Ab homine sentences and *latae sententiae* — 13
Layout of the book — 17
Quantitative data — 18

PART I. INDIVIDUALS

1. The Spiritual Effects of Excommunication: Instilling Fear — 29
Excommunication as medicine and legal sanction — 30
Excommunication in miracle tales — 36
Anger and legal procedure — 41
The rite of excommunication — 45
Words of excommunication — 51
'Nisi' clauses — 55
Conclusions — 57

2. Belief, Fear, and Conscience — 59
Dying excommunicate — 60
Unforced absolution — 68
Wariness of excommunication — 78
Divine retribution — 86
Living as an excommunicate — 90
Conclusions — 98

PART II. COMMUNITIES

3. Exclusion from the Community of the Faithful — 103
Exclusion and contagion — 104
Mitigations — 107
Loss of legal rights — 111
Exclusion from church — 114
Pretext for mistreatment — 115
Implications of a lack of evidence — 124
Prelude to physical force — 126
Conclusions — 136

4. Apathy, Rejection, and Divided Loyalties — 138
Problems with voluntary ostracism — 139
Punishment of communicators — 157
Unjust excommunications — 164
Mouldable sentences: *Latae sententiae* — 172
Royal interference — 176
Conclusions — 182

PART III. PUBLICITY

5. Publicity, Reputation, and Scandal — 185
Audience — 187
Public discords — 192
Fulmination — 195
Reputation, defamation, and denunciations — 198
Absolution and penance — 212
Excommunication and public unrest — 219
Violence against clergy using excommunication — 225
Conclusions — 228

6. Violence, Excommunication, and Dispute Settlement: Thame, 1292–94 — 230

7. Ecclesiastical Broadcasting in the Thirteenth Century: The Origins of the Great Curse — 259
A new practice — 261
Offences condemned — 263
Publication provisions — 271
Why publish *latae sententiae*? — 273
Implementation — 280
Reception — 287
Conclusions — 289

Conclusion — 290

Appendix I: *Ipso facto* Excommunications Promulgated via Thirteenth-Century English Ecclesiastical Legislation, with Provisions for Their Regular Pronouncement — 297
Appendix II: William of Pagula's *Oculus sacerdotis* (c.1320), Dextera Pars — 304

Bibliography — 309
Index — 333

Glossary of Automatic Excommunications referred to in the text

Clericis laicos (1296) Excommunicates clergy of any sort who pay or promise to pay laymen taxes of any kind without papal permission. Rulers of any condition, rank, or status who impose or receive such payments, or who seize ecclesiastical possessions, or those kept in church buildings, or who order such offences or in any way support them are likewise excommunicated.

Contempnunt exequi domini (1222, revised 1279) [1222] Excommunicates all those who by reason of profit, hatred, or otherwise maliciously, refuse to execute the mandate of the lord king enacted against excommunicates scorning the keys of the church. [1279] Adds those who impede their capture or unjustly procure their liberation, against the decree of ecclesiastical discipline.

Crimen imponunt alicui (1222) Excommunicates all those who, by reason of hatred, profit, or favour, or any other reason, maliciously impute a crime to someone, when they were not infamous amongst good and serious men, so that he must undergo purgation or is otherwise wronged.

Magna Carta sentence (1253) Excommunicates all those who henceforth knowingly and maliciously deprive churches of their liberties or who violate, infringe, diminish, or change the ancient approved customs of the realm, especially the liberties and free customs which are contained in Magna Carta and the Charter of the Forest, by any method or trick, openly or secretly, by deed, word, or counsel, in any article; likewise, all those who decree statutes against them, or who obey statutes thus decreed. Also all those who presume to disturb the peace of the king and the kingdom.

Quicumque abstrahunt violenter (1268, abridged 1279) Excommunicates those who violently extract criminals who have fled to a church, cemetery, or cloister for sanctuary, and those who forbid them to be provided with necessary provisions, and those who violently remove, or cause to be removed, goods belonging to others deposited in those places, or cause this to be done, or in any way support such things.

Quicumque de domibus (1268, abridged 1279) Excommunicates anyone who presumes to consume, remove, or handle anything from houses, manors, granges or other such places pertaining to archbishops, bishops, or other ecclesiastical persons, without the will or permission of the lords or their custodians. Satisfaction must be made before absolution can be granted.

Qui malitiose ecclesias (1222, revised 1279 and 1281) [1222] Excommunicates all those who maliciously presume to deprive churches of their rights or through malice and against justice strive to infringe or disturb their liberties. [1281] This includes three types of men: those who deprive churches of their rights; those who infringe ecclesiastical liberties; and and those who disturb them. Understood to include not only general liberties of the universal church, but also particular liberties, both temporal and spiritual. Especially includes those who use writs of prohibition in cases that pertain to the church. Other infringements of ecclesiastical liberties are not approved; the excommunication simply intends particularly to chastise the above offenders with due rigour. Also excommunicates all those who impede episcopal or archiepiscopal process with false exemptions and those who avoid discipline.

Qui pacem et tranquillitatem (**1222, revised 1279**) Excommunicates all those who presume injuriously to disturb the peace and tranquillity of the lord king and realm, and who strive unjustly to detain the rights of the lord king. [1279] Understood to include not only those who rouse the horror of wars, but equally all public thieves and plunderers and anyone who presumptuously attacks the justice of the realm.

Si quis suadente (**1139**) Anathematizes anyone who, at the devil's instigation, lays violent hands on a cleric or monk. Absolution is reserved to the papacy.

Introduction

Early in 1299, Adam le Warner sought absolution from excommunication, the medieval church's most severe sanction. His reconciliation with the church was fairly swift, for Adam had been excommunicated only a few weeks.[1] That of his contemporary, Juliana Box, was less so. She made peace with the church a fortnight before Adam, by which time she had been excommunicate for around ten months. Moreover, her remorse was short lived, for the following summer she was once again living under a sentence of excommunication.[2] These two individuals are unusual because their different attitudes and the events that prompted their absolutions are relatively clear. Adam had fallen deathly ill and was afraid to die excommunicate; Juliana had been captured and imprisoned by secular authorities as a result of her sentence. It was not excommunication itself that induced Juliana's reconciliation; absolution was her only way out of prison.

In the vast majority of cases, it is impossible to know why excommunicates acted as they did. Why did John, Richard, and Walter Irreby turn themselves in, seeking absolution from a sentence that no churchman apparently knew they had incurred?[3] Why did Sir Richard de Scholand die under his sentence rather than take pains, as Adam le Warner had done, to avoid that fate? What made John de Gravene and his wife Gunnora, who had been excommunicated for 'a long time', finally decide to seek absolution in 1303?[4] These individuals all lived in England at the turn of the thirteenth and fourteenth centuries and they all reacted to excommunication in different ways. To their number could be added many more names of people who lived with excommunication for a short while or for many years, who were excommunicated several times or only once. Offences for which an excommunication was imposed are not always known, and reasons for absolution—beyond the excommunicate having a 'change of heart'—are almost never explained in the extant sources.

The intention of this book is to discuss and analyze such experiences. What were the consequences for an excommunicate's soul, their social life, their reputation? In what ways was it damaging and why were these injuries often not enough to prompt a quick return to the bosom of the church? How did the use of excommunication affect those who were expected to enforce sentences, and

---

[1] *Registrum Antiquissimum*, ii, nos 499–500; *Reg. Sutton*, vi, 133–4. And below, 62–3.
[2] *Reg. Winchelsey*, i, 215–6, 230–1, 296, 390–1. And below, 145–6.
[3] *Reg. Swinfield*, 408–9, 431–2.   [4] *Reg. Winchelsey*, i, 458–9.

society more broadly? This is, therefore, a qualitative study that analyzes excommunication not only by looking at the intentions of churchmen who used it and the reactions of those sentenced, but also by considering excommunication's effects upon the wider population.

Excommunication was used often in the Middle Ages. A political struggle without at least the threat of excommunication during its course was a rare thing indeed.[5] It was also used routinely at lower levels, for a multitude of offences. Excommunication is thus perhaps overfamiliar to many medieval historians—ubiquitous to the point that its consequences are not always given due consideration. Moreover, there are many examples of high-profile figures treating their sentences with contempt (in the thirteenth century, most famously Emperor Frederick II), so it has become received wisdom that excommunication was overused and thus ineffective. Excommunication was far from an irrelevance, however. Its effects were extensive, even when it did not achieve the desired outcome.

Excommunication has understandably attracted a lot of attention from historians, producing a number of important and invaluable works. In particular, Elisabeth Vodola's 1986 monograph *Excommunication in the Middle Ages* and various works by R. H. Helmholz (from 1982 onwards) have illuminated the legal effects of the sanction.[6] The present study rests upon their shoulders, for they have made it possible to go beyond canon law, its commentaries, and its implementation. An understanding of canon law is fundamental to any study of an ecclesiastical sanction, but there are limitations to an approach that focuses upon prescriptive sources and legal procedures.[7] Popes, bishops, and canonists—and indeed excommunicates—are only part of the story. A number of other historians have illuminated specific aspects of excommunication. Donald Logan's 1968 study of the role of the secular arm in arresting recalcitrant excommunicates in England elucidates this aspect of the sanction (and provides an excellent overview generally). Christian Jaser has recently (in 2013) produced an in-depth exploration of the formulae of ritual excommunication.[8] The focus of Véronique Beaulande's 2006 study of excommunication in late medieval France is closer to that of this book. As in her *Le malheur d'être exclu?*, excommunication is here approached from a social and cultural perspective. Canon law is considered but is not the focus.[9] Nonetheless, she places greater emphasis than here upon the crimes for which excommunication was applied, and focuses upon how it worked as a penalty rather than how it was received. A plethora of excellent articles illuminate

---

[5] Cf. Edwards, 'Ritual excommunication', 3.
[6] Vodola, *Excommunication*; A selection of Helmholz's key works on excommunication: 'Excommunication as a legal sanction'; 'Si quis suadente'; *Spirit of Classical Canon Law*, 366–90.
[7] Barton, in 'Enquête, exaction and excommunication', makes a comparable point about *enquêtes*, considering them not as abstract principles but as providing valuable insights into human relationships and power dynamics.
[8] Jaser, *Ecclesia maledicens*.   [9] Beaulande, *Malheur*, 19–20.

specific uses of excommunication, but the most cited works on excommunication tend either to focus upon one particular genre of evidence or to cover several centuries and places.[10] In one sense, therefore, work on excommunication has been surprisingly narrow.[11]

This book thus provides a social, political, and cultural history of excommunication, addressing how it was used in practice and how it was received and perceived both by excommunicates and by the wider lay community. I will not provide an in-depth exploration of legal theory, procedures, or commentaries, or provide quantitative data, but rather seek to illuminate the human experience of excommunication. The book does this by focusing on one kingdom in one century, and by bringing into dialogue sources that are not usually considered together. The printed material available for thirteenth-century England is extensive and rich; the analysis thus relies upon edited texts, though it is occasionally supplemented with manuscript material. Episcopal and papal registers, chronicles, *miracula* and *exempla*, English ecclesiastical legislation, canon law, liturgy, court records, and secular governmental records are here all discussed alongside one another. They reveal a full picture of the actions and attitudes that characterize excommunication at a national and local level in this period.

The wealth of evidence is one reason to focus upon thirteenth-century England. It enables comparison between these different types of evidence to approach excommunication holistically, providing a social as well as a religious history. Papal registers survive continuously from the pontificate of Innocent III (1198-1216), a watershed pontificate in many ways, not least regarding the use of ecclesiastical sanctions. Episcopal registers containing memoranda were kept from the middle of the century in England, revealing attitudes and actions at the more local level. Governmental records, which similarly proliferate from the late twelfth century, provide another angle from which to approach the sanction. English ecclesiastical legislation experienced a golden age during the thirteenth century.[12] The thirteenth century is, moreover, often considered a turning point when it comes to the 'political' use of ecclesiastical sanctions. Innocent III is viewed as an innovator here, excommunicating Philip Augustus of France, the Holy Roman Emperor Otto IV, and King John of England.[13] This was then the high point of the 'papal monarchy', before the Great Western Schism irreparably altered papal authority. Canon law had expanded and developed in the twelfth century; further councils and decretals in the thirteenth century clarified and regulated excommunication. Excommunication was also central to several of the thirteenth-century English causes célèbres, notably Magna Carta and the

---

[10] It is not possible to cite them all in a single footnote, but those that consider the sanction within a specific context often work best. In addition to references below, see the Bibliography.
[11] Cf. Whalen, *Two Powers*, 244 n. 17: 'English scholarship on medieval excommunication and interdict is strangely limited, considering their importance.'
[12] As it did in France: Mazel, *L'évêque et le territoire*, 322–6.   [13] E.g. Clarke, *Interdict*, 2.

mid-century baronial rebellion. A somewhat limited geographical and temporal scope is necessary to provide a detailed study of practice rather than an overview of theory. Study of excommunication in England in this period should provide a valuable point for comparison, for the realm was free from (institutionally recognized) heresy. Excommunication and heresy were deeply intertwined, and there is much to be gained by studying them together. At the same time, however, the 'everyday' nature of excommunication can be occluded by these links; it is instructive to consider how Christians responded to the sanction when heresy was unlikely to be in the minds of either excommunicates or excommunicators.[14]

The proliferation of documents no doubt reflects real changes in society and practice.[15] Greater documentation and more systematic administration altered aspects of how excommunications played out, not least concerning publicity, which is a crucial theme in this book. Nonetheless, the new or newly-surviving documents may also lead to false assumptions about developments or indeed progress. To use Sarah Hamilton's phrase, there may be 'a trick of the evidential light' here.[16] Vodola, focusing on excommunication as a judicial sanction, notes that court procedures were 'divorced from their theological origins'; her emphasis on law courts comes at the expense of extra-judicial aspects of excommunication.[17] Amongst the many excellent articles written by R. H. Helmholz, which have done so much to clarify excommunication in the Middle Ages, one of his influential arguments cannot be sustained. In 1994–5, Helmholz argued that in a struggle between 'judicial sanction' and 'powerful curse', by the end of the twelfth century the former had won a victory, albeit one 'not immediate or unqualified'.[18] Excommunication was no longer wielded as a weapon, but 'had largely been "tamed" by acceptance of the emerging canon law's requirements' that sought to restrict how the sanction was used.[19] This 'judicialization' or 'canonical leap forward', he argued, meant that by the thirteenth century excommunication as a legal sanction had replaced excommunication as curse. Judicial process and the ability to appeal to the papal court had made excommunication more measured and procedural, so that 'sudden and ex parte excommunications, issued without formal citation or judicial process' largely died out.[20]

Helmholz undoubtedly overemphasized these developments. Most importantly, judicial procedures were expected far earlier than he allows, as Sarah

---

[14] For instance, living under a sentence of excommunication for a long period elsewhere in this century would provoke assumptions of heresy: Mansfield, *Humiliation*, 75.

[15] Florian Mazel has emphasized that the twelfth and thirteenth centuries witnessed significant changes in episcopal administration and bureaucratization. Episcopal control greatly increased (though bishops were ever more subject to the papacy). *L'évêque et le territoire*, ch. 5.

[16] Hamilton, *Practice of Penance*, 15.   [17] Vodola, *Excommunication*, 36.

[18] Helmholz, 'Excommunication in twelfth century England', 237.

[19] Helmholz, 'Excommunication in twelfth century England', 242.

[20] Helmholz, 'Excommunication in twelfth century England', and *Spirit of Classical Canon Law*, 370–6. 'Excommunication and the Angevin leap forward' is the same as 'Excommunication in twelfth-century England'; the latter is cited throughout.

Hamilton and Elaine Treharne have shown. Such processes had long been a key part of excommunication; any change was less drastic than Helmholz implies.[21] As Christian Jaser has noted, rejecting Helmholz's misrepresentation of earlier practice, part of the problem lies in the narrative sources that Helmholz used. Jaser observes that he did not look carefully enough at earlier practice to draw such a bold line. Moreover, *exempla* and narrative accounts look much the same in the later Middle Ages as the 'dramatic accounts' noted by Helmholz in the twelfth century.[22] Though Jaser acknowledges a turning point c.1200, he argues that the changes were slow and far from absolute. He also critiques the reliance of Alexander Murray—who likewise drew a (less absolute) line here—on theoretical sources, namely theology. Jaser instead argues that codification and systematization, rather than substantial change, was the significant development. Moreover, maledictions and solemn rituals continued to be used, albeit with somewhat gentler curses.[23] Helmholz provided various caveats to his core argument and acknowledged that certain abusive practices continued. Nonetheless, the misleading impression left by his article, and Vodola's seminal monograph, is that by the thirteenth century the sanction had become little more than a matter of procedure. As many examples throughout the following chapters show, there remained plenty of scope for dramatic sentences and for excommunication to be used for personal ends. Ritual excommunication, as Genevieve Steele Edwards and Jaser have shown, continued to play a part.[24] Rules and restrictions did not alter excommunication to the point that it became merely a dry legal sanction. The undoubtedly significant developments in the twelfth and thirteenth centuries relating to legal developments, as well as the proliferation of valuable legal documents that accompanied these changes, have perhaps caused a neglect of social history in thirteenth-century England. It is a time characterized by increased systematization and judiciousness, but one that is fascinating from a cultural perspective too.

Misuse, Overuse, Inefficacy?

Studies of excommunication have frequently—almost routinely—reached the conclusion that the sanction was overused so that it became ineffective. When

---

[21] Hamilton, 'Remedies for "great transgressions"'; Hamilton, '*Absoluimus uos*'; Treharne, 'A unique Old English formula'. Even in the *Life of St Hugh of Lincoln*, which Helmholz uses to show excommunication as a curse (the saint's victims are miraculously struck down as a result of his sentences), St Hugh's excommunications were in fact preceded by warnings. They thus included the most crucial requirement for a valid judicial sentence, even if the excommunicates subsequently suffered or died as a result of his sentences. It might be added that a hagiography was intended to show miracles performed by the saint, in this case to show the power of Hugh's curse, not procedural niceties. *Life of St Hugh*, ed. Douie and Farmer, ii, 31–32, 20–5.
[22] Jaser, *Ecclesia maledicens*, 303–5.
[23] Jaser, *Ecclesia maledicens*, 301–10; Murray, 'Excommunication'.
[24] Edwards, 'Ritual excommunication'.

Rosalind Hill asserted in 1957 that excommunication 'was imposed too freely so its impressiveness diminished', she made a crucial point.[25] The observation that it was used commonly and not always respected thus remains important, for it is necessary to dispel any sense that in this 'age of faith' excommunication must always have been taken very seriously. The popular perception is often that excommunication must have been treated with great reverence. By contrast, certain academics have rather too enthusiastically embraced the idea that excommunication was overused and therefore a damp squib. Hill's comment implying excommunication's feebleness has been absorbed as the standard view of excommunication in thirteenth-century England by those who do not work on it. In 1982, Helmholz pointed out that historians usually envisage a time in the past when the sanction 'worked', and that the move from effective to ineffective through overuse always mysteriously occurred in precisely the period under study.[26] His sensible conclusion that 'something is evidently wrong with a method of analysis which produces such results' has been too little heeded. The by-now meaningless aphorism 'ineffective through overuse' continues to be repeated, ad nauseam, in a way that risks dismissing the effects of excommunication entirely. Ironically, its own overuse means its usefulness to historical analysis has long since expired.[27]

There are many reasons why the maxim is reductive. Helmholz was right to question the concept of a 'golden age' of excommunication, as was Paul Dresch to similarly question the assumption that outlawry lost key powers that it had possessed at some hypothetical earlier time.[28] When, precisely, might this time have been? Helmholz questions the idea by citing works that place the 'breakdown in respect for the sanction' in the thirteenth, fourteenth, sixteenth, seventeenth and eighteenth centuries.[29] The idea that excommunication was overused or misused (concepts that are frequently conflated), with consequent diminishing of respect for it, is extremely widespread. Crucially, comments to that effect were made by contemporaries, who often made extreme statements such as that almost everyone in the realm had been sentenced at some stage (Abbo of Fleury, tenth century) or that half of all Christians were excommunicated (Marini Sanuti, fourteenth century).[30] It has been pointed out that Augustine worried about overuse undermining the sanction.[31] In the Merovingian period, excommunication was called 'antiquated'; the common opinion was that the sanction had lost its effect through excessive and unreasonable use.[32] There were similar complaints

[25] Hill, 'Theory and practice'.
[26] Accusations of overuse are deeply connected to abuse because the chief abuse is typically 'trivial' use.
[27] Helmholz, 'Excommunication as a legal sanction', 202–4. Beaulande noted the fondness historians have for received ideas about excommunication: *Malheur*, 7.
[28] Dresch, 'Outlawry', 122–4.   [29] Helmholz, 'Excommunication as a legal sanction', nn. 2–6.
[30] Goebel, *Felony and Misdemeanor*, 308–9; Lea, *Studies in Church History*, 417.
[31] Lea, *Studies in Church History*, 271–2.   [32] Keygnaert, 'Misbruik'.

under Charlemagne and Louis the Pious.³³ The late eleventh and early twelfth centuries equally generated criticisms of indiscriminate use of the sanction.³⁴ William of Malmesbury complained that excommunication, frequently used, failed to achieve much in twelfth-century England.³⁵ Gerald of Wales condemned his contemporaries' abuses.³⁶ French bishops in the thirteenth century worried about the numbers of excommunicates and how little people cared about their sentences.³⁷ In England, at the same time, bishops feared there were more excommunicates than anywhere in the world.³⁸ The papal Council of Vienne (1311–12) complained of increasing apathy as the penalty was imposed too often.³⁹ The archbishop of Armagh complained that excommunication was futile in the late fourteenth century.⁴⁰ Heretics and orthodox alike criticized use of the sanction in the late Middle Ages.⁴¹ Excommunication came in for particular vitriol during the Reformation.⁴² Yet Elizabethan reformers too complained of trivial usage leading to ineffectiveness.⁴³ Accusations that excessive use damaged excommunication's efficacy are indeed not unique to studies of the Christian ban. Precisely the same point has been made about the Jewish *herem* in late medieval northern Europe, Renaissance Italy, early modern Germany, and Poland-Lithuania, while a 'high number' of excommunications has been observed in early modern Amsterdam and Hamburg.⁴⁴ The only studies concerned with spiritual sanctions that appear to buck this trend are those on the Calvinists. Here historians are happy to state that excommunication was not used a great deal, albeit often citing a reaction to Catholic overuse as one cause for this restraint.⁴⁵ There are undoubtedly a plethora of examples not here cited.

Historians have, therefore, merely been following the comments and complaints of contemporaries. The first problem with both 'overuse' and related 'abuse' declarations is the simple human tendency to grumble about things going downhill, implying a better past.⁴⁶ The complaints should not be taken at

---

³³ Lea, *Studies in Church History*, 324–6, 331–5.
³⁴ Huysmans, 'Excommunication under discussion'.
³⁵ Lewandowski, 'Cultural expressions of episcopal power', 78.
³⁶ Helmholz, 'Excommunication in twelfth-century England', 243–4.
³⁷ Jaser, *Ecclesia maledicens*, 320; Lea, *Studies in Church History*, 399–400.
³⁸ *C&S*, 971.   ³⁹ Jørgensen, 'Excommunication', 65.
⁴⁰ Gundacker, 'Absolutions and acts of disobedience', 183.
⁴¹ Forrest, 'William Swinderby', 249–50, 255–8; Beaulande, *Malheur*, 157, 185, ch. 7, 257–8.
⁴² Lange, *Excommunication for Debt*, 227–39, 276; Thomas, *Religion and the Decline of Magic*, 502–3.
⁴³ Price, 'Abuses of excommunication', 111.
⁴⁴ Woolf, *Fabric of Religious Life*, 71 n. 239; Bonfil, *Rabbis and Jewish Communities*, 72–5; Hertz, 'Judaism in Germany', 753; Guesnet, 'Jews of medieval Poland-Lithuania', 807; Kaplan, 'Discipline, dissent and communal authority', 401; Kaplan, *Religion, Politics and Freedom of Conscience*, 20.
⁴⁵ E.g. Mentzer, 'Marking the taboo', 126–7; Todd, 'None to haunt'; articles by Chareyre, Murdock, and Bezzina in Mentzer, Moreil, and Chareyre (eds), *Dire l'interdit*.
⁴⁶ Beaulande also observes the wooliness of the idea of abusive excommunication: *Malheur*, 20.

face value.⁴⁷ Further, as Frederik Keygnaert states, respect for excommunication is far less likely to be recorded.⁴⁸ The second issue is the implicit value judgments that surround use of ecclesiastical sanctions more generally. Medieval clergy worried about overuse because they did not want their most powerful weapon to be devalued, but also because of the ties that excommunication had to cursing. Overuse complaints are so prevalent that the thought that spiritual sanctions will always be deemed overused, however frequently they are employed, is unavoidable. As a spiritual sanction, excommunication endangered souls; irresponsible usage was untenable. That was, of course, at the root of the complaints of the Protestant Reformers. Their criticisms continue to unduly influence perceptions of the sanction. The 'innate immorality' of excommunication as a whole, as Genevieve Edwards phrased it, still hangs over accusations of abuse.⁴⁹ The nineteenth-century historian H. C. Lea typifies the condemnatory attitude. Though his study of excommunication includes a great deal of valuable primary evidence (which clearly shows the continuity of contemporaries' worries about the sanction losing its power), it is peppered with judgmental asides. The very existence of a sanction that threatened eternal damnation 'is an exhibition of the worst and darkest side of human nature'. His final assessment lamented the lack of Christian charity, deploring the oppression, greed, abuse, and evil.⁵⁰ Catholic reformers shared some of this rhetoric: when the papacy cancelled the yearly general excommunication ceremony in 1770, the reason given was 'now is the time of kindness, not of anathemas'.⁵¹ Protestant contempt and Catholic embarrassment, ever since the early modern period, have combined to imply that excommunication was never a justifiable means of coercion. Thus while abuse is often alleged as a cause for criticism, 'correct' usage becomes an illusory concept if the sanction's very existence is deemed antithetical to Christian morals.⁵² Elsewhere (not least in informal conversations I have had with academics) there is perhaps some snobbishness, a sense that medieval clergymen were foolish. Did they not realise that they were devaluing their sanction? They did, of course, which is why concern was so often expressed in the Middle Ages.

It is clear that overuse as a concept bears little relation to actual numbers. The amount that excommunication was used cannot have been constant, yet the same conclusion is reached regardless of time and place, or indeed religion.⁵³ Overuse assertions also imply that there was such a thing as the correct frequency with which to pronounce excommunications. This is a nonsense. Just as Helmholz

---

⁴⁷ Jeffrey Denton similarly cautioned that contemporary complaints about illiterate clergy, made in the context of reforms, and bound to be critical, can 'be taken all too easily as social characteristics of the age': 'Competence of the parish clergy', quotation 275.
⁴⁸ Keygnaert, 'Misbruik', 33.   ⁴⁹ Edwards, 'Ritual excommunication', 5.
⁵⁰ Lea, *Studies in Church History*, 239, 520–1. Many more examples could be cited.
⁵¹ Jaser, *'Ostensio exclusionis'*, 358.   ⁵² Thomas, *Religion and the Decline of Magic*, 502–3.
⁵³ Pre-modern population numbers and numbers of excommunicates make comparison extremely difficult; I shall not attempt it. Beaulande, *Malheur*, ch. 5 shows how difficult it is to reach numbers.

rejected any imagined golden age when excommunication was effective, so too can we reject a 'goldilocks' hypothesis that it would have worked if only it had been used just the right amount. Certainly, it seems that use of excommunication did increase during the later Middle Ages. Alexander Murray is right that there are too many examples from the later period, even accounting for increased source material, to deny it. He consequently rejects the suggestion that contempt for excommunication remained steady; it surely increased.[54] Perhaps he is right, but there can be no doubt that simplistic claims that overuse and misuse devalued excommunication stultify analysis of its role in society and the effects that it *did* have.

Excommunication's impact was widespread and significant. It is worth mentioning that if it had been used less it would have affected far fewer people. Its prevalence makes it more, not less, worthy of study. In addition, clergymen evidently did see its value, so the modern tendency to discount its usefulness is a little puzzling. For all their complaints, contemporaries did not dismiss it. Privileges sought to be free from ecclesiastical sanctions, complaints about their injurious nature and contemporary observers' interest in sentences pronounced all further indicate that excommunication was far from worthless.

It must be stressed that studies of the sanction generally provide nuanced analyses that acknowledge the prevalence of the received wisdom about efficacy, endorsing it to an extent but also showing its limitations. Beaulande, for instance, admits that by the end of the Middle Ages the sanction was used very frequently. Yet she finishes her book by emphasizing excommunication's importance.[55] Brian Pavlac has revealed both ineffective and effective uses of the sanction. While he argues for overuse, he equally stresses that it was often a successful tool and a useful weapon.[56] Rob Meens points out that the fact that excommunication did not have the envisioned results does not mean that it had no results at all.[57] Richard Barton has recently observed the 'ubiquity' of excommunication in thirteenth-century Le Mans, but his analysis by no means suggests that it was ineffective. Instead, he carefully considers its consequences and how it functioned as a 'tool of lordship'.[58] Such balanced and careful analysis of *how* and to what extent abuses limited efficacy, however, needs to filter through to medieval historians more generally. At worst, those not focused on excommunication take the 'overuse so ineffective' maxim as licence to dismiss the sanction as insignificant. Excommunication should be carefully considered in each case's proper context, where its effects could be various and important. Sometimes its effects will have been negligible, but this must not be assumed. The exhausted

---

[54] Murray, 'Excommunication', 192–3. The increase chiefly relates to the use of excommunication for debt. See Lange, *Excommunication for Debt*, and Beaulande, *Malheur*, esp. 193–9.
[55] Beaulande, *Malheur*, 257–8. [56] Pavlac, 'Excommunication and territorial politics'.
[57] Meens, 'Uses of excommunication'. [58] Barton, '*Enquête*, exaction and excommunication'.

phrase must be retired, or at the very least end its reign as the only thing that certain historians (think they) know about excommunication.

The Significance of Excommunication

Efficacy is central to any study of excommunication. However, while assessing whether excommunication achieved precisely what churchmen wished is an obvious starting point for study, effectiveness should be approached from a broad perspective.[59] The question of efficacy is complicated, just as would be any attempt to answer whether the modern use of prisons, for instance, is effective.[60] There are a multitude of consequences, both positive and negative. Here the focus will be upon practice, looking at the sanction from the outside as well as from the perspective of those who used it. Paul Töbelmann has perceptively argued that answering 'Did it work?' need not depend on the understandings of those who were involved in a process.[61]

A broader perspective illuminates consequences that were not intended, not least how misguided uses affected respect for ecclesiastical authorities. If excommunication achieved the opposite of its intended consequences, this requires proper analysis.[62] Analyzing misuse, rather than emphasizing overuse, is especially central to addressing this question, and it is dealt with at various points in the following chapters.[63] Looking at practice also, however, reveals that churchmen used excommunication for purposes that were not discussed in canon law. In particular, excommunication was valuable for its public nature, which could be especially useful in political contexts. A sentence's impact was not limited to whether an individual sought immediate reconciliation with the church.

It is thus necessary to move study of excommunication away from individuals. Excommunication did not simply affect an excommunicate's relationship with the church. How excommunicates responded to their sanctions is important, but it is just as important to consider the sanction from an institutional perspective.[64] How everybody else reacted was just as crucial and affected relationships between clergy and between clergy and laity.[65] Much more than an individual's soul was at stake. A focus on 'spiritual terrors' marginalizes the equally important social aspect of excommunication; if 'external' pressure forced an absolution, this was the

---

[59] A point also made by Paul Töbelmann, 'Excommunication', 102–3.
[60] Pavlac made an analogy with drunk driving legislation: 'Curse of Cusanus', 199–200.
[61] Töbelmann, 'Excommunication', 102.
[62] Vincent, in *Holy Blood*, undertakes a similar exercise. Clarke's chapter in *Interdict* on the 'Interdict in action' brings out interdicts backfiring wonderfully.
[63] In greatest depth in Chapter 4.
[64] Ian Forrest has recently argued for histories of the 'social church': *Trustworthy Men*, 4.
[65] Björn Weiler, too, has emphasized the importance of witnesses, who participated in and gave legitimacy to ceremonies: 'Symbolism and politics', esp. 27.

sanction working, for it was always dependent upon communal enforcement. Conversely, if a sentence failed to coerce a sinner, it was because their compatriots did not enforce it, as much as because the individual was not afraid.[66]

Specific uses of and reactions to excommunication reveal a great deal about attitudes and society. A key argument of the book, advanced in Part III, is that excommunication's public nature requires emphasis. Part of excommunication's importance is that it involved a great deal of communication. Its impact on society was thus profound, affecting individuals' reputations of course, but also communicating political events and much more down the social strata of medieval society. As David d'Avray has shown in a different way, mass communication did not begin in the early modern period.[67] This social and religious study of excommunication in thirteenth-century England intends to provide a fresh discussion of many cross-cutting themes that will be of interest to those who study a host of other topics, periods, and areas. Excommunication is an important subject; the study of it offers new perspectives on medieval piety and beliefs, sin and penance, government and strategies of social coercion, communities and solidarity, cursing, slander, and mass communication.

The Purpose of Excommunication

The point of excommunication was ostensibly to force an offender to make amends. It dealt primarily with public offences and scandals, which had to be corrected in public (rather than in confession, for example) so that those who set bad examples were not seen to go unpunished. However, excommunication is complicated because it sought to induce reconciliation in various ways. It provoked fear of hell, it cut off social contact, it prompted shame, and it removed legal rights.[68] It was 'caught somewhere between canon law and liturgy'.[69] 'The purposes of the sanction were too complex' even for canonists to have imagined that it would immediately bring excommunicates to obedience.[70] The following chapters will show that there were also secondary motives, for instance to defame individuals or to spread a certain political narrative. Social, political, legal, and spiritual effects were all inextricably linked. If its 'legal meaning' won, there were 'always loose ends, ambiguities and contradictions'.[71] Part of the complexity of

---

[66] The burden placed on communities was noted by Hyland in 1928: *Excommunication*, 40–1.
[67] D'Avray, *Medieval Marriage Sermons*.
[68] Töbelmann writes that it was 'effective in the ritual sphere, the sociological sphere, and the spiritual sphere', 'Excommunication', 102–3.
[69] Hamilton, 'Interpreting diversity', 157.
[70] Helmholz, 'Excommunication as a legal sanction', 218.
[71] Helmholz, *Spirit of Classical Canon Law*, 374; cf. Murray, 'Excommunication', 165.

excommunication is that it was simultaneously medicine and the church's 'spiritual sword'. It was both a weapon and a treatment.[72]

Excommunication's centrality to pastoral care is easily forgotten. It requires emphasis here also because it is rarely in evidence in specific cases against individuals. Excommunication had always been central to the pastoral responsibility for souls, yet it is hardly what springs to mind when historians think of the cure of souls (*cura animarum*).[73] Vodola may have stated that the sanction's ordinary function was to enforce legal procedures and that it had only an 'artificial' link to sin, but the fact that it came under the umbrella of the sacrament of penance should not be forgotten.[74] Correcting sinners was a key duty for those with cure of souls. Certainly, legal procedures intended to curb misuse meant that excommunication's use was restricted, so that it was not strictly a matter for the penitential forum (except for sentences incurred automatically) but required legal processes. The theory that excommunication was imposed not for sin but for contumacy—refusing to be corrected by ecclesiastical authorities—further broke the link. Yet the pastoral need is clear. Clergy who did not fulfil their duty to use ecclesiastical censures were to be punished.[75] Bishops expressed fear that they would be accused of negligence for failing to correct subjects.[76] If fear of God did not recall someone from evil, clergy had a duty to chastise them.[77] There was great danger in leaving one crime unpunished, for this might lead to more.[78] Moreover, it was hardly an incentive to be obedient if those who were contemptuous were not reprimanded.[79] The emphasis placed upon excommunication in pastoral manuals in the later Middle Ages is also striking, and further demonstrates the centrality of the spiritual sanction to the *cura animarum*.[80]

The medicinal aspect of excommunication, the fact that it was not *supposed* to be a punishment, must be borne in mind. The idea was in practice certainly contravened, as will become clear in Chapter 1 and beyond, but the fact that the goal was redemption and not punishment was central to its function.[81] It had important implications for how and to what effect it could be employed. Excommunication's medicinal purpose meant that it was not intended to be permanent, nor was it meant to be difficult to secure absolution. This impermanence had a multitude of

---

[72] Beaulande wrote that the punishment involved two 'antithetical' forms: *Malheur*, 7. An edited volume on shame addresses similar issues about its being at the centre of several spheres: Sère and Wettlaufer (eds), *Between Punishment and Penance*.

[73] Hamilton, 'Law and liturgy', 189.

[74] Vodola, *Excommunication*, 35-6. On the distinctions between sin and crime, see Fossier, *Bureau de âmes*, 261-78.

[75] *C&S*, 575.

[76] *Reg. Gandavo*, i, 8-9; *Royal Letters*, app. v, no. 34. Chapter 7 contains more examples of this sentiment.

[77] *Reg. Halton*, i, 239-40; *Reg. Winchelsey*, i, 2-3.   [78] *Reg. W. Giffard*, 180.

[79] *Records of Antony Bek*, ed. Fraser, 66.   [80] See Chapter 7.

[81] Helmholz, 'Excommunication as a legal sanction', 217; Helmholz, *Spirit of Classical Canon Law*, 376-8; Forrest, 'William Swinderby' on Wyclif's criticisms, 260-2.

consequences. It weakened the sanction in one sense, but also made it useful in different ways.⁸²

Ab Homine Sentences and *Latae Sententiae*

Excommunication was divided into two types: major and minor. This book deals predominantly with the former, which (in theory) entailed complete exclusion from Christian society. Minor excommunication was most commonly incurred by associating with someone sentenced with major excommunication. It suspended someone from reception of the sacraments and entry to churches but did not separate them from all intercourse with their fellow Christians. Minor excommunication was associated with interdict, which usually suspended sacraments in a geographical area.⁸³ Major excommunication had far more dire consequences, which are explored thematically in the chapters below.

Sentences of major excommunication could be pronounced against individuals by individuals. These sentences were *ab homine*. Only higher clergy could excommunicate. A cleric must have jurisdiction, so that a bishop, abbot, or dean could not excommunicate someone unless he or she was under his care.⁸⁴ The pope alone could excommunicate anybody.⁸⁵ Women were never permitted to excommunicate.⁸⁶ The question of who could excommunicate was complicated by the fact that judges in ecclesiastical cases could have jurisdiction even if they were not in other circumstances able to excommunicate. Their power came not from holy orders but from their position as judge, so that even a layman might be able to excommunicate. More usually, the bishop's official or his archdeacons were delegated the authority to pronounce sentences. A parish priest was not permitted to excommunicate a person by name, nor to announce that someone was excommunicated, without the permission of his superior.⁸⁷ He could, however,

---

⁸² For instance making it a tool for dispute resolution, for instance: Hamilton, '*Absoluimus uos*', 209–10.

⁸³ See Peter Clarke's monograph: *Interdict*. He discusses the different types of interdict in ch. 2.

⁸⁴ The specifics were not fully settled, for Raymond of Peñafort's section on the matter includes different opinions: Peñafort, *De Poenitentia*, 397–8; Aquinas, *Summa Theologiae*, Bk III-Supplementum, q. 22, a. 1. Who could excommunicate in the earlier middle ages is discussed at length in Péricard, 'L'excommunication dans le royaume franc'. Peter Clarke's *Interdict* deals with who had the power to excommunicate and interdict in the thirteenth century, providing full references to canon law, 86–103.

⁸⁵ C.9, q.2, c.1; Chobham, *Summa*, 200.

⁸⁶ For example, the papal penitentiary made clear that an abbess, as a woman, had no authority to excommunicate ('sexus conditio auctoritatem excommunicandi non habeat'): *Formulary of the Papal Penitentiary*, ed. Lea, no. LXIX.

⁸⁷ Chobham, *Summa*, 210–11; Chanter, *Summa*, 395, 398–9. Peter observes that the custom is 'mirum' since priests had the power of binding and loosing.

pronounce minor excommunications.[88] Parish priests may, of course, have sometimes broken this rule.[89] Absolution was supposed to be granted by the cleric who had imposed a sentence, or his successor or superior, though any parish priest could absolve if the excommunicate was *in articulo mortis*.[90] Appeals could only be lodged on the grounds that procedure had not been followed—for instance if insufficient warning had been given or the excommunicator did not have the right to sentence the individual—and not on the grounds that the sentence was unjust. Since excommunicates did not have legal rights they could not lodge appeals, so those who wished to appeal were provisionally (*ad cautelam*) absolved; they would revert to their excommunicate state after a year, or if the appeal failed.[91]

Latae sententiae were distinct from *ab homine* sentences in that they were pronounced against 'whoever' committed a certain offence.[92] The excommunicator was not an individual, as in *ab homine* sentences, but the law; these sentences were thus *de jure*, *a jure*, or *ipso jure*. Although the nature of these excommunications has led to assumptions that *lata* means 'broad' or 'concealed', both of which fit well with the niceties of these sentences, in fact *lata* comes from *fero, ferre, tuli, latum*.[93] Used with the noun *sententia*, *ferre* is the verb most often employed in relation to excommunication (used far more than *excommunicare* by itself), and in *lata sententia* the perfect passive participle of this standard verb is used to distinguish it from sentences that should be pronounced (*ferendae sententiae*, also known as *dandae sententiae*). It is difficult to settle upon the best way to translate *lata sententia*, for the verb has a plethora of meanings; thus it is best kept in the Latin here rather than translated. *Lata sententia* literally means 'sentence that had been given' (*data sententia* was occasionally used as a synonym), but perhaps declared, established, decreed, issued, or pronounced give a better sense. The crucial thing is that the sentence had *already* been pronounced. A person could commit an offence for which they were liable to be excommunicated—this would be a *ferenda sententia*—or they could commit an offence for which they *were* excommunicated, the moment they did it—a *lata sententia*. The automatic nature of these sentences meant that people were said 'to incur' a sentence ('incurrere sententiam') or 'to fall into' it ('incidere in sententiam'). These verbs emphasize that the excommunicate

---

[88] A priest could excommunicate for tithes unjustly detained, which clearly injured him, in English legislation: *C&S*, 137, 387; Flamborough, *Liber Poenitentialis*, 146–7.

[89] Murray, in 'Excommunication', provides some examples of lower clergy using the sanction for personal revenge: 186–7.

[90] Logan, *Excommunication and the Secular Arm*, 137–9.

[91] Helmholz, *Spirit of Classical Canon Law*, 378–80; 'Excommunication as a legal sanction', 209–11; Logan, *Excommunication and the Secular Arm*, 117–19. Inability to appeal unjust sentences is discussed below, in Chapters 2 and 4.

[92] For the development of this type of excommunication, see Huizing, 'Earliest development of excommunication latae sententiae'; Vodola, *Excommunication*, 28–35; Helmholz, *Spirit of Classical Canon Law*, 383–90.

[93] Murray, 'Excommunication', 178–9 ('broad sentence'); Forrest, 'William Swinderby', 247 ('concealed verdict'); Pavlac, 'Curse of Cusanus', 200 ('latent excommunication').

was excommunicated as soon as they committed the offence—*ipso facto*—without need for intervention from any authority to confirm the sentence. A sentence could subsequently be publicized, and in that sense confirmed by an authority, but the law remained the legal excommunicator. Throughout this book, *latae sententiae* will also be referred to as *ipso facto* and *de jure* sentences—both medieval synonyms— and as automatic sentences.

Although there was initially some concern voiced by canonists and decretalists about automatic excommunications and their absence of warnings—Gratian was a notable dissenter—they quickly became an accepted part of canon law.[94] They have been widely recognized and discussed, but *latae sententiae* have sometimes been presented as an oddity or as a special case, separate from the day-to-day function of excommunication. Their value and importance have been overlooked. Vodola, in particular, places automatic excommunication in opposition to the sanction's 'ordinary' function: 'excommunication *latae sententiae* was a very specialized application of excommunication'.[95] This book will demonstrate, however, how fundamental such sentences were to quotidian life in high and later medieval England. Many individuals incurred these sentences; offences that incurred them were constantly advertised to the laity. Understanding how they worked—often a complicated task—is important.[96] The absence of specific warning before an excommunication took place, the fact that someone could be excommunicated without anyone knowing about it, and many more peculiarities related to this type of sentence, had important implications. For instance, Thomas Becket suffered criticism from his contemporaries for excommunicating without warning, notably at Vézelay in 1166. Yet if he had acted in the same way a century later, he would have been able to argue, quite reasonably, that he had done nothing wrong.[97] The possessions and rights of his church of Canterbury had been violated.[98] These rights were, from 1222, protected by the *ipso facto* sentence *Qui malitiose ecclesias*. Becket could have claimed that he was not himself excommunicating anyone: the malefactors against whom he acted had been excommunicated by the law—Becket himself was merely denouncing them. In 1282, for instance, John Pecham declared that he had not excommunicated anyone (the king had complained he had), but he had pronounced a general sentence against those who infringed his rights. Various people had then been

---

[94] Huizing, 'Earliest development of excommunication latae sententiae', 292-4; Vodola, *Excommunication*, 28-35.

[95] Vodola, *Excommunication*, 35.

[96] Helmholz admitted that *latae sententiae* supply an exception to his judicialization argument—'In some sense, a new name was put on an old practice, changing the practice in the process and bringing it within the law's control' (*Spirit of Classical Canon Law*, 383-9)—but argues that even this 'non-judicial' excommunication was judicialized. See 'Excommunication in twelfth-century England', 251-2.

[97] As Helmholz points out in 'Excommunication in twelfth-century England'. Becket did argue this anyway, but Helmholz judges that Gilbert Foliot *et al.*, who had complained, 'had a point'.

[98] E.g. *Correspondence of Thomas Becket*, ed. Duggan, i, 78-81, 310-11, 314, and letter 262.

denounced as falling into this sentence: 'Sir, take notice that denunciation does not excommunicate anyone unless he is rightly excommunicated'. If they were under the ban, they had been excommunicated *a jure* not *ab homine*. The archbishop had only publicized the fact.[99] The subtleties of these sentences, and the opportunities they provided for clergy to use excommunication legally and yet without legal process, are of great importance. The consequences, uses, and value of understudied *ipso facto* sentences are under constant scrutiny throughout the following chapters.

The best known and most frequently invoked *lata sententia* protected ecclesiastical persons from attack, and is known by its incipit, *Si quis suadente*. Though heresy had long been assumed to incur automatic separation from the church, *Si quis suadente* was the first official *lata sententia*, promulgated by the second Lateran Council in 1139. *Latae sententiae* could be pronounced by the papacy, but were also advertised in local legislation, applying to particular ecclesiastical provinces or dioceses. There are a number of important automatic sentences in English legislation. Because some of them are frequently referred to in the following chapters, I have assigned them titles based on their incipits, like *Si quis suadente*. This was not medieval usage, but it seems preferable to referring to a sentence as '1222 Council of Oxford, c. 1' and so on, not least because the sentences were adapted and expanded in later councils.[100] The Glossary provides these names and summaries of the contents of these (select) sentences, while Appendix I includes many more English *ipso facto* sentences. Archbishop Stephen Langton's 1222 Provincial Council at Oxford was the most significant council here. Not only did Langton provide a list of *latae sententiae*, the remarkable aspect was its placement. He began his council with a striking statement of ecclesiastical liberties in the form of automatic sentences, which he ordered to be regularly publicized.[101] Top of his 'most wanted' list were those who infringed the liberties of churches.[102] The other significant councils for *latae sententiae* were the papal

---

[99] *Reg. Epp. Pecham*, i, 178, 392s, 180, 392t; cf. *Parliament Rolls*, i, 163–5.

[100] In the Middle Ages, c. 5 of the Oxford council was known as 'Auctoritate dei patris'. Although this was medieval usage, it is unhelpfully general because this incipit introduced all seven excommunications and indeed pronouncements of individual sentences. See Helmholz (ed.), *Select Cases on Defamation*, xiv. Because cc. 5 and 7 start so similarly, it was necessary to use words beyond their incipits to identify them. The identifying phrases for the two clauses in the glossary from Ottobuono's 1268 legatine council are taken from the more extensively disseminated 1279 council of Reading, which incorporated and abbreviated them.

[101] Langton was probably asserting himself as archbishop: though he had been primate for well over a decade, he had first been prevented from taking up the position by the king, was then suspended, and was finally dwarfed by papal legates. See Vincent, 'Stephen Langton', 99–105, 110. Langton could now exercise control and show, among other things, his displeasure about the terms under which the interdict was lifted in 1214. *SLI*, no. 70; Cheney, *Pope Innocent III*, 332–7, 348–55; Sayers, *Papal Government and England*, 162–7; Vincent, 'Stephen Langton', 90–2.

[102] It is perhaps surprising that Langton did not use the phrase *libertas ecclesie* (as he had in c. 1 of Magna Carta), since before becoming archbishop Langton had been 'the most prolific theologian in the schools of Paris', where the mantra was 'accepted doctrine' (Baldwin, 'Master Stephen Langton', 811,

legate Ottobuono's 1268 council and two provincial councils held by John Pecham in 1279 and 1281. The excommunications pronounced at these councils were frequently invoked (to varying degrees).

Layout of the Book

The chapters focus on what happened after a person had been sentenced with excommunication and are arranged thematically. The book is split into three sections, on individuals, communities, and publicity. Chapter 1, using largely normative sources (unlike the remaining chapters), discusses the implications of excommunication for an individual's soul, arguing that churchmen encouraged the belief that hell was the ultimate destination for those who failed to seek absolution. Ritual excommunication remained an important aspect of the sanction. Chapter 2 attempts to answer the difficult questions of whether this belief was accepted and how far fear of damnation affected the actions of excommunicates. The ever-present possibility of absolution, however, dampened the effect of fear of hell. Chapter 3 begins Part II by setting out the requirements for communal shunning of excommunicates, then analyses occasions when shunning was performed. It finishes by considering extreme consequences of excommunication, such as deposition of rulers and political crusades. Chapter 4 then deals with the apparent fact that communities did not routinely ostracize excommunicates. This chapter makes comparisons with discussions of ostracism in other contexts, as well as using thirteenth-century English material, to explore the complex issues surrounding communal enforcement. Part III develops the book's central argument, which emphasizes excommunication's public nature. Chapter 5 discusses the impact it had upon individuals' reputations and its ability to provoke shame and indignation, as well as the wider implications of broadcasting both general and *nominatim* sentences so extensively. Chapter 6 is a case study of a particularly well-documented and venomous dispute over an ecclesiastical benefice in Thame. It looks at this case in detail in order to illuminate the various mechanisms discussed in earlier chapters. While a number of significant aspects of excommunication are apparent here, the value of excommunication for its publicity—as a motive in its own right—is especially clear. Chapter 7 builds upon the role of excommunication as a means of mass communication, discussing how the church used *latae sententiae* to publicize which crimes it took most seriously. These sentences were a form of ecclesiastical public broadcasting. Pastoral care and canon law necessitated that they be explained to the people in the vernacular,

---

833). Thomas Becket, by whom Langton was greatly influenced, had consciously and publicly asserted that he suffered for the ideal. *Correspondence of Thomas Becket*, ed. Duggan, ii, 1080–1. See Chapter 7 below for more on Langton's council and intentions.

with important implications for the knowledge of lay society and its perception of the church, as well as for church-state relations.

Quantitative Data

The book's focus on the aftereffects of excommunication makes it necessary to provide some basic background information here. The conflicts focused upon throughout the book are both national and local, and the nature of excommunication—expecting communal enforcement and well-publicized—means that the wider population is part of the story even in 'high political' cases. The data provided here are intended to give a flavour (rather than a complete picture) of how and why excommunication was imposed, before the remainder of the book focuses on its aftereffects. Although some of my extrapolations are deliberately speculative, that speculation provides a useful potential scale for giving a sense of the phenomenon which this book analyzes. The following has been mined solely from one of the fullest and best edited episcopal registers. The memoranda of Oliver Sutton, bishop of Lincoln 1280-99, survive in his register (edited by Rosalind Hill) from May 1290 to April 1299.

Numbers of Excommunicates

I have already shown my doubts about putting too much emphasis upon numbers of excommunicates, without claiming that how many excommunicates there were is irrelevant. It is not, but unfortunately the extant sources for thirteenth-century England provide no clear answers. Most excommunications happened at administrative levels for which records do not survive. It is also difficult to determine whether numbers increased or decreased, because the better records at the end of the century—episcopal registers—do not survive from the earlier period. The following, using information concerning the diocese of Lincoln (the biggest English diocese, comprising c.2000 parishes), is intended to provide no more than a rough idea. How great or small a proportion this is of the total number of excommunicates in the years discussed is impossible to say, but it is perhaps better than nothing.[103] Since the rest of the book provides qualitative analysis, this provides a quantitative and general empirical introduction.

---

[103] Alexander Murray discusses the value of statistics in *Suicide*, i, 348–51. I am something of an 'unbeliever', to use his terms. Beaulande, who had far better data for late medieval France than is available for thirteenth-century England, nonetheless conveys how frustrating an experience trying to piece together numbers can be: *Malheur*, ch. 5.

In the period between May 1290 to April 1299, we can be sure that a little under 200 individuals were excommunicated by name in Oliver Sutton's diocese.[104] The majority of these known excommunicates appear in writs for capture (the process by which the secular arm arrested and imprisoned those who had been excommunicated for at least forty days): the bishop ordered 132 people to be arrested (these include names found on original writs surviving in the National Archives).[105] A further five people complained about or appealed their sentences, and one man had his annulled. The remainder were noted as excommunicates in other contexts, usually orders to publicize their sentences. Two orders to release men imprisoned by the secular arm show that they too must have been excommunicated by name.

It is remarkably rare that we are able to follow an individual through the various statuses. Three men are mentioned in the register as both excommunicated and absolved, though several of the imprisoned excommunicates were to be released (or not captured if they had not yet been attached) so were presumably absolved. Only one man, Nicholas Miller, occurs as an excommunicate in the register, and as someone to be arrested by the secular arm, and as an absolvent.[106]

In addition to excommunicates who we can be fairly sure were sentenced by name, a further sixty individuals sought or received absolution from excommunication (or, if clergy, asked for a dispensation). Some of these had probably been judicially sentenced by name, but others undoubtedly sought absolution from an automatic sentence into which they had fallen. That fact was not necessarily known to others.[107] We have, therefore, c.250 known excommunicates in the Lincoln diocese during the last decade of the thirteenth century. Yet some of the sixty absolvents were never publicly denounced, and without official confirmation their sentences would not have stood up in court. Though their souls were imperilled, there would have been no obligation that others shun them, nor would they be barred from legal acts and so on. Thus these people, though excommunicated no less than those who had been sentenced by name, are certainly a different category of excommunicate.

---

[104] I have counted 189, but there is some room for manoeuvre: some were not named as such ('kinswoman of Ela countess of Warwick', for instance), or were known via their position only ('rector of' etc.), or the register is damaged where the name would have appeared. There is debate to be had about what evidence proves that someone was, without a doubt, judicially excommunicated by name. People who were not in the diocese of Lincoln are also mentioned, notably the bishop of London and the Prior of Lewes.

[105] Fifty-five writs are known to have been issued in this period—fifty-four of these are in Sutton's register and forty-four originals are extant in London, TNA, C 85/101. Five of those named appear in more than one writ. There is evidence that eight of those to be captured were ordered to be released (or were not to be imprisoned if not yet attached). Sixteen of the excommunicates in total were recorded as having been absolved, though three of the sixteen were re-excommunicated and remained so at their last mention.

[106] *Reg. Sutton*, v, 36, 90, 106.

[107] Beaulande notes more absolutions than excommunications for the same reason: *Malheur*, 96.

That many more people were excommunicated than the surviving sources reveal is implied by the fact that only three of the people requested to be captured appear in the register as excommunicates before any writ ordering their arrest was issued. Someone had to be excommunicated by name, and to have remained in this state for at least forty days, before the king's help could be requested. Most excommunicates did not suffer arrest by the secular arm, so the bishop had no reason to note their excommunications. Consequently, we do not know about them. The original excommunicator, noted in the writs, was typically an archdeacon or his official. It was only when it was deemed necessary to coerce the excommunicate by his or her body that the bishop became involved, since only he could issue the request. Occasions when the bishop intervened hint at excommunicates unknown to us. For instance, the bishop stepped in to suspend the dean of Gartree's excommunication of the servants of Sir William of Swineshead's chaplain.[108] Presumably these servants had been named as excommunicates, but because Oliver Sutton did not here list them we cannot know how many there were. The point is that the bishop only mentioned the case at all because he wished their sentences to be relaxed while matters were settled. It is possible that the bishop was notified about all excommunicates in his diocese and that he and his administrators (as in other dioceses) did not bother to add lists of excommunicates to the register. Certainly lists exist elsewhere and were possibly kept on loose sheets.[109] On the other hand there would have been no practical reason to inform the bishop in most cases, so the bishop himself may not have been aware of each excommunicate in his diocese. His involvement was necessary in some cases: recalcitrant excommunicates, appeals and accusations of misconduct, disputes that escalated, runaway excommunicates, and cases that required publication beyond a local area are the sorts of instances where names make it into the records available to us.

While excommunicates that the bishop of Lincoln ordered to be captured by the secular arm in this decade must be the tip of the iceberg of total excommunicates, it seems likely that we do at least have an almost complete list of these excommunicates. Writs for capture were routinely kept by royal government. Since some original writs were lost, it is more important to note that only two individuals appear in original writs in the archives but *not* in Sutton's register.[110] It is clear, therefore, that the writs were typically enregistered and that this is the more reliable source. Indeed, one of the extant writs not in the register was revoked; this revocation was enrolled by Sutton's registrar and probably explains the absence of the writ itself. As already noted, very few of these people appear elsewhere in the register. This perhaps indicates that clergy did not resort to the

---

[108] *Reg. Sutton*, vi, 120–1.   [109] For an early example see Allen, 'Earliest known list'.
[110] There are three writs not in the register: TNA, C 85/101/36, 44, 47. The last two concern the same man, Johannes dictus ad ecclesiam de Brincton (Brington). I have no explanation for why these two writs, from April and September 1297, are missing from the register. The two men in C 85/101/36 both appear elsewhere in Sutton's register as excommunicates.

secular arm for most excommunicates, presumably (but not necessarily) because they sought absolution before it seemed necessary to coerce them physically. If we arbitrarily guessed that around a tenth of excommunicates were ordered to be captured, we would have *c.*1,300 excommunicates in the diocese of Lincoln during the last decade of the thirteenth century. The diocese had *c.*2000 parishes, so this would amount to less than one excommunicate per parish in these ten years (though because people were often sentenced for the same crime together, if these figures are at all correct—which I doubt—the spread would not be even).[111] Even a surely excessively low estimation that the secular authorities were called upon in only one hundredth of excommunication cases would mean that there was less than one excommunicate per parish per year. Writs for capture, unlike the register, allow some comparison to be made with an earlier period. Across a similar extent of time forty years earlier, no significant change in the number of excommunicates/excommunicates-to-be-captured is indicated. The extant writs 1240 to 1258 number seventy, containing *c.*167 names, about seventeen of which are female.[112] Writs for the earlier part of this period are irregular, indicating that survival may be patchy. When they become more constant, there is far less of a difference to the end of the century, especially considering (as noted above) that the rate of attrition is higher in the archives than the register (which did not yet exist mid-century).[113] From August 1246 to March 1256 there are *c.*120 names in fifty-two writs. August 1248 to August 1258 reveals 101 names in forty-six writs.

Though some of these numbers are seriously speculative, it is worth noting that neither extreme quite corresponds with the assumption that excommunication was overused so ineffective. If a full ten per cent or more of excommunicates required coercion by secular power, this would mean that the total number of excommunicates was quite small. Rosalind Hill, who edited this register, concluded that 'the people who were excommunicated formed a very small proportion of the inhabitants of the diocese'.[114] If, on the other hand, the number of excommunicates was far greater, and only one per cent of them was ordered to be arrested, then the sanction was more common, but must have been more effective in its own right than is often assumed because the secular arm was so rarely needed. One thing can be stated with certainty: witnessing excommunication denunciations that publicized either names of excommunicates or *latae sententiae* would have been a common experience.

---

[111] Groups of people excommunicated together for infringing sanctuary, for instance.
[112] The earlier writs are more frequently damaged, making it necessary to guess how many names might fit into a certain space; dates are not always legible. Proportions of men and women cannot be determined for the same reason.
[113] The very earliest register does not contain general memoranda.   [114] *Reg. Sutton*, iii, xlix.

Who and for How Long?

Twenty-nine of the 189 people known to have been judicially sentenced in the last decade of Sutton's episcopate were women (fifteen in writs for capture) and two of the absolvents. Three of these excommunicates and one of the absolvents were nuns. Laymen and clergy at all levels alike were sentenced. A whole host of rectors was excommunicated in 1296 for failing to pay the clerical subsidy to the crown. Various monks and canons and many clergy, several of them masters, were also subject to the ban. The remainder were apparently laymen (there is one indecipherable name on a damaged writ). The excommunicates appear to have been from a range of social classes. Around ten men are designated 'dominus'. Lady Isabella de Mortimer was apparently the only noblewoman. Most of the remaining men are given some sort of surname, often along with a place of origin. As ever, it is impossible to say whether those with professional surnames worked in that occupation. Vintner, Miller, Warenner, Apothecary, Butcher, Reeve, and Fuller all appear. However, sometimes professions were specifically noted, for instance, John of Cowley, tailor, Peter de Marue, cook, Roger Sewall of Aylesbury, baker, and Walter, under-bailiff of Oxford. Matilda of Wycombe was a burgess of Oxford. Many were merely designated 'of' a place and sometimes 'wife/widow of' or son of a father (or, in the case of Hugh son of Emma of Stamford, a mother).[115]

Though the vast majority of people noted in the context of excommunication are mentioned only once, a few individuals' situations can be known in a little more detail. John of St Lys persuaded the bishop to order John's rector to stop molesting him, unless the latter could prove that John indeed deserved the excommunication pronounced against him for stealing the goods of a late William of Houghton. The following year, however, John admitted to embezzling goods worth 6d. from a will (whose is not noted) and was absolved: the rector's suspicions were probably well founded.[116] John of Heyford had been absolved for fornicating with a nun, Christina, but was re-excommunicated when he refused to carry out the penance enjoined upon him (three beatings around the marketplace).[117] Though there is no information about their offences, there appear to have been some slippery characters. Matilda of Wycombe was included in writs for capture no fewer than four times between 1295 and 1299. It seems most likely that she was absolved each time but reoffended.[118] Emma of Bradley was to be captured as an excommunicate, appealed (presumably unsuccessfully) and was later absolved, but was then re-excommunicated and contumacious in October

---

[115] Cf. Beaulande, *Malheur*, 200–5 for late medieval France.　　[116] *Reg. Sutton*, iv, 107, v, 49.
[117] *Reg. Sutton*, vi, 73, 93–4.　　[118] *Reg. Sutton*, v, 97, 198, vi, 72, 141.

1297. In May 1299 another *captio* was issued, this time claiming she had been obdurate for over a year.[119]

The case of Eustace de Bingham, in particular, introduces some of the difficulties inherent in the church's use of excommunication. Eustace was excommunicated for failing to pay the executors of a will 36s. belonging to the deceased man. Initially Eustace moved parishes, allegedly to avoid the bishop's coercion. He then pleaded inability to pay and was absolved on the condition that he make satisfaction when he was able. Having taken an oath to this effect, when he failed to repay the money for two years he was again excommunicated now for perjury as well as for his original offence. Again he was absolved, then for the third time excommunicated when once again he failed to meet the conditions. All this is relayed in a letter of September 1292. In 1298 the situation was just the same: a payment plan 'amicably' arranged so that instalments be paid to the executors in 1296 and 1297 had not helped, and Eustace was, for at least the fourth time, under a sentence of excommunication. Judging by his behaviour, Eustace was keen to avoid the consequences of excommunication, first trying to run away, and subsequently seeking absolution. The churchmen who had sentenced him had little choice but to absolve him. If he was unable to pay, it would be cruel to leave him thus imperilled. Moreover, Eustace might have argued fairly that he would never be able to earn any money if everyone was forbidden to have contact with him. An oath from Eustace was sufficient to allow him to be absolved on the condition he did pay. Excommunication was, then, an insufficient threat to force Eustace to repay the money, yet it was sufficiently arduous that he did not want to live as an excommunicate. The problem was that a sanction intended to be medicinal and coercive rather than punitive could not be fairly wielded against someone who promised he was trying to find the money he owed. One wonders whether Eustace ever repaid the patient executors.[120]

Why?

Those excommunicated by name committed various offences. There are far too many potential causes of excommunication to list here. Peter Clarke groups causes of interdict into thirty-six categories in his monograph. Aside from the first of these, which relates to supporting major excommunicates (this would result in minor excommunication), his categories could apply also to excommunication.[121] Beaulande emphasizes violence and marriage cases as the principal causes of excommunication in late medieval France.[122] The variety will emerge as individual cases are discussed in the chapters below, though the broad category of infringing

---

[119] *Reg. Sutton*, vi, 35, 179.   [120] *Reg. Sutton*, iv, 33–4, 86–7.
[121] Clarke, *Interdict*, 112–16.   [122] Beaulande, *Malheur*, ch. 3.

ecclesiastical liberties features heavily. In Sutton's register, failing to execute wills properly was the most common cause for sentences, with five certain examples. Donald Logan noted that this was the most common identifiable offence in writs for capture (until the Reformation).[123] Apostasy of nuns, monks, and canons, if taken together, have more cases—three nuns, one monk, two canons. There are a small number of cases of theft, infringing rights or tithe obligations, adultery, assaulting a cleric, and stealing items from churches. Writs for capture rarely state the offence committed, merely specifying contumacy and manifest offences. There are occasional exceptions: many rectors failed to pay a moiety due to the crown; Thomas Browning had not paid his tithes of fish. Two writs, including that concerning Lady Isabella de Mortimer, mention roles as executors of wills. Since this was a common cause of excommunication, their failings as executors were probably the cause of their sentences.

In addition to excommunications against individuals, Sutton's register contains a large number (c.210) of general excommunications, where an offence had been committed but the malefactors were unknown. Here, unlike sentences against individuals, we probably have all or almost all the general sentences pronounced in the diocese in these years. The bishop generally reserved the right to pronounce general sentences and, since the perpetrators were unknown, his officials would conduct an investigation alongside the general denunciations. Some of these alleged that an offence had been committed against which a *lata sententia* had been pronounced; this allowed an excommunication to be proclaimed even where names of the malefactors were not yet known. In other cases, the denunciations initially merely threatened excommunication if no amends were made. About a quarter of these general sentences reacted to theft (usually, but not always, from clergy), including poaching or killing another's animals. Charters were the most common item (seven instances of theft), hidden in one instance, a whole box stolen in another. Finding a dropped breviary and failing to return it was a reason to be threatened with excommunication. Documents and records of debts and books also feature, generally stolen but in one case forged. Animal theft was frequent—horses, rabbits, swans, oxen, deer, and tithe-lambs all appear. Trees are mentioned four times, as well as timber in another entry.[124] Money, corpse-candles left after burial services, and materials to repair a bridge were all also stolen. Wasting land, burglary, and failing to return lost goods were also dealt with by excommunication. The victims were usually clergymen of some sort, but not invariably.

The next most common cause of general sentences was violence against clerics (*Si quis suadente*), of which there are over thirty cases. Failure to properly execute wills or related abuses also resulted in over thirty general sentences. Sanctuary violations account for six. Many general sentences related to the failure to pay

---

[123] Logan, *Excommunication and the Secular Arm*, 51 n. 38.   [124] Cf. Beaulande, *Malheur*, 140.

tithes or other church dues, or otherwise preventing their collection. Disputes over ecclesiastical benefices were also often a cause for offences incurring excommunication. In one case, miscreants had been drinking in a vacant church and using it for other insalubrious activities.[125] A particularly intriguing case is a general sentence pronounced against those who had bought a baby boy and rebaptized him in order to pass him off as someone else's heir. The parents, who had accepted the money because of poverty, had admitted the crime but the excommunication sentence indicates the affair had become a local scandal. As is so often the case, nothing more about the case survives.[126]

The victims of these offences were almost always clergy or religious institutions, except in cases concerning execution of wills and violation of sanctuary (where both the church and the fugitive were harmed). Occasionally, however, a layperson was aided. When Adam of Ferriby, a paralytic, was burgled, the bishop stepped in to threaten the (unknown) thieves with excommunication.[127] Alan and Emmicena of Holland, thrust into poverty by the killing of two oxen, were helped in the same way.[128] Sutton was willing to excommunicate the poachers who had taken beasts from the land of Sir Ralph Pyrot and rabbits from the warren of Sir John Birthopre.[129] A widow, Petronilla Sutton, was unable to obtain her dower right after a charter testifying to the purchase of seven and a half acres was stolen; the evildoers were therefore threatened with excommunication.[130] The law did not allow for the immediate excommunication of these malefactors; because the victims were not clergy, warnings had to be given beforehand. By contrast, in a comparable case, following the theft of the goods of Hugh of St Martin, vicar of All Saints Stamford— who was known to be insane—a general sentence could immediately be publicized.[131]

Those seeking absolution had most often injured a cleric and thus incurred *Si quis suadente*. Others had drawn blood in a churchyard, attacked a church, or extracted fugitives from sanctuary. Christina of Heyford, a nun, had committed fornication with a married man.[132] John Garland was absolved from excommunication for fornicating with Cecily Drayton, and Roger of Acre with Ivetta; both women were nuns.[133] Clergy had the presumption to attend civil law lectures at Oxford, and one to teach there after he had been ordained.[134]

Excommunication thus affected men and women throughout society, who had committed a wide variety of offences and who reacted to their sentences in different ways. It was familiar, whether as a personal experience or as a spectacle, at all levels of society. Its affects were wide-ranging in many different spheres. The rest of the book will focus upon the aftereffects of excommunication.

---

[125] *Reg. Sutton*, iv, 178–9.   [126] *Reg. Sutton*, v, 127–8.   [127] *Reg. Sutton*, iv, 8–9.
[128] *Reg. Sutton*, iv, 149–50.
[129] *Reg. Sutton*, iv, 62–3. The king's justices were, however, dealing with the poachers as well; see vi, 91.
[130] *Reg. Sutton*, vi, 170–1.   [131] *Reg. Sutton*, vi, 132.   [132] *Reg. Sutton*, vi, 73, 93–4, 109–10.
[133] *Reg. Sutton*, iv, 40, vi, 5.   [134] *Reg. Sutton*, iv, 96, v, 76, iv, 133–4.

PART I
INDIVIDUALS

1
The Spiritual Effects of Excommunication

Instilling Fear

One does not have to look far to find descriptions of excommunication implying it was a sentence to hell. Too much credence has been given to the 'official line' of the church, which stressed the medicinal purpose of excommunication, insisting that it did not *automatically* result in eternal damnation. Beliefs that contradicted the protestations of canonists and theologians were not occasional anomalies or misconceptions based on antiquated ideas about excommunication. Though extant sources present numerous difficulties of interpretation, it is clear that harsher views of the ecclesiastical censure remained prevalent. They were not held by misinformed laity, but propagated by churchmen within the ecclesiastical hierarchy. We should not share Elisabeth Vodola's surprise that 'as urbane a scholar as the canonist Johannes Andreae (d. 1348) wrote that excommunication hastened sickness and death'.[1] Such ideas remained current at various levels. Although there was friction between the justifications of excommunication carefully worked out by scholars, who therefore mollified the sanction, and other presentations of excommunication, this is not a question of elite versus popular or folkloric ideas.

Excommunication has been unduly de-dramatized. The overall impression of literature based within a legal framework is that excommunication, by the thirteenth century, was centred around courts, judges, and legal procedures. Contradictory statements and practices have been treated as relatively unimportant deviations from the norm. The more prominent English-language studies by Vodola, Helmholz, and Logan all note the potentially damnatory results of being solemnly excluded from the church, but because their focus lay elsewhere it forms only a small proportion of their combined works. Christian Jaser's recent German monograph *Ecclesia maledicens* has been an important contribution to the field, focusing as it does on the ritual across the Middle Ages. The legal processes of excommunication are important, but sources which reveal excommunication as a legal sanction obscure the fact that it remained a dramatic penalty. Miracle stories

---

[1] Vodola, *Excommunication*, 46. Cf. Edwards, 'Ritual Excommunication', 113, which also counters Vodola.

dealing with excommunication, the ritual ceremony, and contradictions regarding the sanction within legal sources have not gone unnoticed. The ceremony, in particular, requires integration with analyses of other facets of the censure.

Excommunication continued to be presented as a curse, and was sometimes used as one. The faithful were actively encouraged to be afraid of excommunication. In terms of practice, there was, indeed, an increased emphasis on following 'correct' legal procedures from the twelfth century. Yet judicial process had always been an aspect of excommunication. It would be unrealistic to argue that the practice of excommunication in the thirteenth century differed in no important respects from that of the earlier Middle Ages. However, the emphasis hitherto placed on the legal aspects of excommunication has perhaps highlighted differences rather than continuities.

Excommunication as Medicine and Legal Sanction

Developments in canon law and theology were no doubt important, having significant effects on the use and understanding of the church's spiritual sanctions. Yet for the majority of people living in thirteenth-century England, as elsewhere, it is likely that the information they received regarding excommunication encouraged the belief that it was indeed a curse affecting both body and soul. While the law emphasized due process and fairness, theologians (and indeed legal texts) stressed that excommunicates were not damned. Yet definitions of excommunication continued to indicate that it resulted in damnation. Miracle stories described the horrible fates of excommunicates; the ritual denunciation of excommunicates verbally and symbolically seemed to condemn such people to hell. As Alexander Murray has observed, it was not uncommon throughout the Middle Ages for churchmen and laymen to believe that excommunication resulted in 'misfortune in this world and damnation in the next'.[2] They were repeatedly encouraged to believe it.

The problem with excommunication was that it was 'quaedam maledictio', as the problem was introduced in the Supplement to Thomas Aquinas's *Summa Theologiae*.[3] Maledictions, or curses, were forbidden in the Bible (Romans 12:14[4]), and were hard to reconcile with New Testament teachings that emphasized love and forgiveness.[5] The church was thus forced to justify excommunication, and to counter arguments against its use. The Dominican writer of the Supplement justified the use of excommunication in a number of ways, in a *quaestio* asking

---

[2] Murray, 'Excommunication', 177.
[3] Aquinas, *Summa Theologiae*, Bk III-Supplementum, q. 21, a.2.
[4] 'Bless them that persecute you: bless, and do not curse.' (*Benedicite persequentibus vos: benedicite, et nolite maledicere*).
[5] Murray, 'Excommunication', 170-9.

whether it ought to be used at all.⁶ First, he argued, excommunication could be found in the Bible, in 1 Corinthians 5:5 and Matthew 18:17.⁷ More importantly, the purpose of excommunication was to shame the sinner to return to the bosom of the church, not to separate him from it irreparably. There were two types of curse. In the first, the evil inflicted was the sole intent. This type of curse was forbidden in every way. But in the second, the medicinal quality of the sanction was emphasized. Cursing with good intentions was licit and salutary, as when a doctor inflicted pain in order to cure a man.⁸ Provided the intent was medicinal and not punitive, excommunication was good and necessary. Bonaventure used the same medical analogy (an extremely common and by no means a new one). Excommunication, he declared, supplies medicine to a rebellious person because it cures the disease of rebellion, just as surgery supplies treatment for an abscess even though it causes pain. Bonaventure also stated that whilst an excommunicate was separated from the sacraments and from corporal communication, no one was separated from spiritual communion.⁹

Thus the severity of excommunication, in spiritual terms, was played down by the theologians.¹⁰ Yet their justifications were problematic: the only thing that distinguished a 'good' curse from a 'bad' curse was the intent. As Peter Abelard observed, the action itself was not forbidden. The Bible merely forbade *wanting* to curse ('nolite maledicere').¹¹ This was a rather dangerous position. Pronouncing a curse in order to harm the sinner would harm only the one pronouncing it.¹² Conscience, therefore, might prevent a cleric excommunicating with malicious intent, that is, cursing. Nonetheless, whether or not someone was cursing was impossible to police, since a person's intention cannot be definitely known. There was nothing external to prevent cursing.

Canon law sought to deal with this problem by insisting that clerics used excommunication sparingly, and with the right intentions. Clergy who were permitted to use the sanction were limited.¹³ Just as theologians stressed the importance of intent, canon law endeavoured to ensure that those who excommunicated

---

⁶ The Supplement, though based on Aquinas's writings, was composed after his death.

⁷ '[I...have already judged] to deliver such a one to Satan for the destruction of the flesh, that the spirit may be saved in the day of our Lord Jesus Christ.' 'If he will not hear the church, let him be to thee as a heathen and publican.'

⁸ Aquinas, *Summa Theologiae*, Bk III-Supplementum, q. 21, a.2. Excommunicates themselves were often described as being infected with a contagious disease, notably leprosy. See Chapter 3 below.

⁹ Bonaventure, *Commentaria in quatuor libros*, d. 18. p.2 a.1 q.1. For a fuller discussion of theological developments, see Murray, 'Excommunication', 170–9; Vecchio, 'Légitimité et efficacité', 352–61.

¹⁰ It should be noted, however, that separation from the Eucharist—which was essential to salvation—was itself a serious matter. See Macy, *Theologies of the Eucharist*; d'Avray, *Medieval Religious Rationalities*, 45–7.

¹¹ Vecchio, 'Légitimite et efficacité', 358 and n. 35.

¹² Vecchio, 'Légitimite et efficacité', provides a full discussion of the development of the idea that an unjust malediction or excommunication injured whoever pronounced it (354–7).

¹³ See Introduction, 13–14.

acted with the right motives. This was chiefly done by insisting they follow proper procedures. Expectations of judicial process were longstanding, as Sarah Hamilton and Elaine Treharne have shown, but legal procedures were increasingly emphasized. Clergy who flouted these compulsory requirements were to be punished.[14] Sentences pronounced spontaneously were apt to be unjust, so preventing such sentences was the focus. The 1215 Lateran Council issued an important decree (c. 47), which insisted that warnings had to be given, in the presence of witnesses, before a sentence could be pronounced.[15] Before a sentence of excommunication was declared, an excommunicate would thus have demonstrated his scorn for the sanction and for authority (that is, been contumacious), by refusing to avoid it in the first place.[16]

In 1245, Pope Innocent IV emphatically asserted at the First Council of Lyon that 'excommunication is medicine not death, discipline not annihilation'.[17] The canon, known as *Cum medicinalis*, reflected conclusions reached by theologians: excommunication was justifiable if it was used to rehabilitate a sinner, it was not a curse, and it would not send a person to hell. This was an important decree, described by Vodola as 'the most momentous change of all' in the law of excommunication.[18] Following its initial emphasis on the medicinal purpose of excommunication (which quoted Augustine and was therefore innovative not in content but rather by cementing the view in an ecumenical council), Lyon I decreed that a sentence should be provided in writing, with its cause clearly explained.[19] The excommunicate was to receive a copy if he or she requested one.[20] This made it impossible to issue a legal sentence without reasonable cause; to do otherwise would result in appeals and ultimately sanctions against the cleric who had acted hastily or unjustly. *Cum medicinalis* exerted considerable influence, and was duly incorporated into the 1298 canon law collection known as the *Liber Sextus* (VI 5.11.1). It was frequently cited. The medicinal purpose of excommunication as expressed in the canon was contravened in practice; clerics might issue sentences in the wrong spirit, but no one maintained that this was acceptable, so far as I am aware. Complaints against those who had acted in contravention of these decrees were voiced long after they were promulgated, but there is good reason to suppose they did affect practice.[21]

Scholars have acknowledged that ideas that excommunication resulted in damnation continued to be held in the later Middle Ages, yet nevertheless they

---

[14] Hamilton, 'Remedies for "great transgressions"'; Hamilton, '*Absoluimus uos*'; Treharne, 'A unique Old English formula'; Jaser, *Ecclesia maledicens*, 305.

[15] The canon thus reflected the verses in Matthew 18: 'But if thy brother shall offend against thee, go, and rebuke him between thee and him alone. If he shall hear thee, thou shalt gain thy brother. And if he will not hear thee, take with thee one or two more: that in the mouth of two or three witnesses every word may stand. And if he will not hear them: tell the church. And if he will not hear the church, let him be to thee as the heathen and publican.' Tanner, *Decrees*, i, 255.

[16] The same insistence on warning applied to interdicts. As Peter Clarke has pointed out, this effectively denied the right of appeal. Clarke, *Interdict*, 103–6.

[17] Tanner, *Decrees*, i, 291; VI. 5.11.1.   [18] Vodola, *Excommunication*, 42.

[19] Keygnaert, 'Misbruik', 20.   [20] Tanner, *Decrees*, i, 291.   [21] *Cal. Pap. Reg.*, 399.

often treat continued beliefs in excommunication as a curse as outdated survivals or outliers rather than a key and fundamental part of how the censure worked and was understood. Thus though Vodola conceded that excommunication continued to be 'burdened with great ambivalence', she also boldly stated that by the early thirteenth century 'it was evident...that major excommunication concerned only the punishment (*poena*) that detained a soul in purgatory, not the guilt (*culpa*) that consigned it to hell'.[22] R. H. Helmholz carefully noted the links between excommunication and cursing long after the thirteenth century, but still argued that following a competition during the twelfth century between two concepts of excommunication—judicial sanction versus powerful curse—by the end of the century the former had won a (qualified) victory.[23] The tension and complexity here has been explored most fully by Alexander Murray in his 1991 John Coffin Memorial lecture.[24]

Damnatory consequences were in fact implied in legal, narrative, didactic, and liturgical sources throughout the Middle Ages, contradicting the assertion that excommunication was neither death nor annihilation. For a full understanding of the implications of excommunication in the thirteenth century, these sources must be given as much weight as canonical and theological sources. The Lyon decree perhaps influenced perceptions of the sanction less than it might have done. Moreover, there was an important 'unless' to the assurance of *Cum medicinalis*, making it far closer to the 'older' views than it first appears: excommunication was not death, provided that ('dum tamen') the excommunicate did not treat it with contempt. It was the consequences for those who did not seek reconciliation with the church, glossed over in this canon, that many other sources dealing with excommunication highlighted. Many of these sources do not in fact contradict *Cum medicinalis*. Excommunication was not an irreversible and automatic condemnation to hell, for there was always the possibility of redemption for those who sought it. All that *Cum medicinalis* did was emphasize that a sentence was reversible for those who did not scorn it; the fate of those who did is implicit. The reverse emphasis is more common: excommunication would cause you to suffer horribly (in this life or the afterlife, or both), but such a fate could be avoided. For those who remained bound by a sentence, hell seems to have been the ultimate, if not the immediate or inevitable, destination.

The intention behind excommunication canons in the Lateran and Lyon councils was that excommunication be treated with caution and due consideration, since it was a serious matter. *Cum medicinalis* was supposed to deter clerics from issuing sentences unless truly necessary, that is, once it was clear that there was no other

---

[22] Vodola, *Excommunication*, 45–6.
[23] Helmholz, 'Excommunication in twelfth century England', 235–53; Helmholz, *Spirit of Classical Canon Law*, 366–76.
[24] Murray, 'Excommunication'.

means by which the person at fault might be corrected. This was equally the intent of a canon from the 845 Council of Meaux, which had nonetheless declared 'anathema is damnation of eternal death'. This canon was included in Gratian's *Decretum*; its definition was often used in relation to excommunication thereafter (C. 11, q. 3, c. 41).[25] Though this definition was at odds with that of Innocent IV, the aim of the 845 canon as a whole aligns with that of its successor. It was intended to ensure that anathema be used only for mortal sins. Like *Cum medicinalis*, it was supposed to curb use of the sanction. It differed only in its means of persuasion. Long after 1245, prelates continued to impress upon their subordinates that excommunication was so severe that it had to be handled carefully and in accordance with law. This might be done by stating that it did indeed endanger the salvation of those sentenced, and, if used unfairly, of the cleric pronouncing the sentence.[26]

English legislation, like the universal canon law, endeavoured to ensure that excommunication was used properly. Yet *Cum medicinalis*, however great its significance more generally, was given no particular prominence.[27] Many statutes provided no definition of excommunication, but we find John Pecham, in the provincial statutes of Lambeth (1281), observing that excommunications incurred through ignorance plunged people into a 'pit of danger'; excommunication 'struck down' wicked men, and those who absolved excommunicates when they had no legal right to do so were bringing back to life souls that did not live.[28] Oliver Sutton, in a mandate ordering promulgation of automatic sentences, referred to the danger of being separated from God and the faithful, and of being 'released to the possession of hell'. He encouraged those who had fallen into such sentences to repent and to in future abstain from excesses and 'the bonds of eternal damnation'.[29] Rather than stressing the importance of medicinal intent, both prelates emphasized the serious consequences for souls if the law was not followed by clerics with a duty of care.

A clause contained in the 1289 diocesan statutes of Exeter, given the rubric 'De excommunicationum sententiis cum deliberatione promulgandis', demonstrates the point. Bringing together various canons dealing with excommunication, the clause repeatedly stresses that the sanction was a serious matter and needed to be handled accordingly. Thus, those who wield St Peter's keys of binding and loosing should be aware of how great that power is, since they have this honour through Christ. Since excommunication is damnation of eternal death, it should be imposed only for mortal sins, and only on those who cannot otherwise be

---

[25] Raymond of Peñafort, the compiler of the *Liber Extra*, used the 'damnation of eternal death' definition in Peñafort, *De Poenitentia*, 410–11.

[26] Cf. Helmholz, 'Excommunication as a legal sanction', 214–15.

[27] *Cum medicinalis* is referenced in the Statutes of Wells, *C&S*, 621; the Statutes of London I, *C&S*, 631–2; the Statutes of London II, *C&S*, 650–1; the Statutes of Exeter II, *C&S*, 1040–1. *Reg. Pontissara*, i, 292–3, 297–8, cites the medicinal rather than the deadly nature of excommunication with reference to specific sinners.

[28] *C&S*, 898–9.   [29] *Reg. Sutton*, vi, 24–7.

corrected (C. 11, q. 3, c.41). Provident deliberation and maturity are needed, since an unjust excommunication injures him who issues it rather than him who is sentenced (C. 11, q. 3, c. 87). Sentences should be imposed only with reasonable cause, following three warnings issued in the presence of witnesses (Lateran IV, c. 47; X 5.39.48). The cause of a sentence should be expressly written down and a copy be given to the excommunicate within one month if requested (*Cum medicinalis*; VI 5.11.1). Parish priests should publish their names and the causes of their sentences, using candles and bells, to ensure that nobody communicate with them through ignorance of their excommunicate status.[30]

This Exeter constitution thus promulgated the substance but not the definition of *Cum medicinalis*. However, despite employing a definition of excommunication that contrasts starkly with *Cum medicinalis* and the tenets of theologians, its purpose aligns with both. It sought to counter abuse of excommunication. The only real difference between the Lyon and Exeter decrees is the argument used. Instead of emphasizing the medicinal rather than the vengeful purpose of excommunication, the Exeter clause underlines its severity, continually urging carefulness and restraint. The Exeter canon may have used the earlier definition simply because it was a compilation, in chronological order, of various canons. Its definition, derived from Gratian, came from a source earlier than Lyon (1245), and rendered a second definition obsolete. Yet this might also have been part of a calculated strategy. The clause sought to curb excommunication's use. As a result, underlining the idea that excommunication sent people to hell was perhaps a better means of persuading clergy to 'use with care' than stressing that excommunication was medicine *not* death.

Instilling fear was useful, even if clergy making such claims knew the theoretical denials. Whether or not this supplies an explanation for such supposedly antiquated usages, it is certain that in legal texts primarily intended for clergy there was a degree of ambiguity about what excommunication meant for the afterlife. Perhaps the idea that excommunication had hellish consequences was simply too ingrained to be dismissed. Certainly, the idea that it resulted in damnation was not expunged. Robert Grosseteste quoted Numbers when he warned the dean and chapter of Lincoln not to 'go down to hell alive' by incurring excommunication.[31] In 1232 (so before *Cum medicinalis*) Pope Gregory IX described the sanction as 'the chain of excommunication, which thus separates the contumacious and rebellious from the fellowship of the faithful and the unity of the faith, so that life is a torture for them, and their conscience, wary of the sin committed, strikes fear of eternal damnation into them even while sleeping'.[32] Gregory was well aware that no excommunicate was sent to hell automatically, and that

---

[30] *C&S*, 1040–1; cf. The Statutes of Wells, *C&S*, 621. The social consequences of excommunication will be discussed in later chapters.
[31] *Grosseteste Letters*, 308; Numbers 16:30.   [32] *Ann. Burton*, 240.

absolution and thus salvation was always possible. But it was in many ways advantageous—necessary, even—to stress that hell was the eventual consequence of living and dying excommunicate. Such an emphasis was more beneficial for the church in most contexts than one that played down excommunication's spiritual consequences.[33]

Excommunication in Miracle Tales

Miracle stories dealing with excommunication described both how excommunicates suffered after death and how they were tormented while living. Such tales were an important means through which ideas were communicated to medieval society. Excommunication miracles were included in saints' lives and chronicles, and were incorporated into lists of *exempla* which preachers could draw upon in order to liven up their sermons. They are thus likely to have reached a wide audience of both clergy and laity, whether they were believed or not.[34] For Jaser, such *exempla* were the primary means by which, from the twelfth century, congregations were informed about the existential consequences of excommunication.[35] For the laity in particular (and probably for many clergy), they would have been a far more significant means of learning about excommunication than theology or canon law.

Numerous excommunication miracles survive, generally demonstrating the sanction's potency. Some collections of sermon *exempla* were comprised of thematically organized sections and contained a series of excommunication tales preceded by a definition of the censure. Thus the *Speculum laicorum,* composed in England some time during the reign of Edward I, described excommunication as a spiritual sword that divided men from the unity of the church, just as a limb from a body or a branch from a tree-trunk. An excommunicate was to have the burial of an ass (Jeremiah 22:19): as the skin of a dead ass is used by men, its body eaten by dogs, and its intestines played with by ravens, so an excommunicate's possessions are given to his heirs, his body to vermin, and his soul to demons.[36]

Some stories describe curses inflicted upon inanimate objects or animals. One particularly common miracle involves a sceptic being convinced of the powers of excommunication when a cleric excommunicates some bread. Immediately upon being excommunicated, the white bread turns black. When absolved, the bread reverts to its original white form, thus also demonstrating the virtue

---

[33] See also Forrest, 'William Swinderby', 268–9.   [34] *Friars' Tales*, ed. Jones, 14, 24–6.
[35] Jaser, *Ecclesia maledicens*, 321.
[36] *Speculum laicorum*, ed. Welter, 56. See also Stephen of Bourbon, *Anecdotes Historiques*, a contemporary but not English collection.

of absolution.[37] Others described the cursing of fleas and flies. In the *Liber exemplorum,* a thirteenth-century British collection created for Franciscan friars, the value of such miracles is explained by a quotation from Gerald of Wales: 'For if a curse has such great power over...snakes and tiny creatures, whose animal nature excuses them from sin, should not legitimately imposed excommunication... be greatly feared by men endowed with reason who knowingly commit sins...?'[38] In the bread miracle, equal weight is given to the powers of excommunication and absolution. Though the severity of the sanction's effects upon the soul are proved to the sceptic, he is also shown that it is reversible if he makes amends. The Gerald of Wales quotation emphasizes that excommunication should be terrifying when it was just, because those on the receiving end had brought its severe effects on themselves. Demonstrating excommunication's dire consequences was thus not incompatible with legitimacy, nor did it necessitate claiming that its potency was irreversible.

Exempla involving those who suffered excommunication publicized the idea that those who died under a sentence would suffer terribly in the afterlife, and even that excommunication could cause death or otherwise afflict the living.[39] One tale, set in the reign of Henry III, describes how a matron walking through a graveyard heard moaning coming from a grave. When asked the cause of its groaning, the unquiet spirit replied that an excommunicate was due to be buried with it in the same grave later that day, 'and thus my bones will have no peace until Judgement Day'.[40] The reader (or listener) is told to consider 'how the souls of excommunicates are disturbed in hell'.[41] Other stories reflected a common trope that the bodies of excommunicates did not decay. The *Speculum* describes the grave of an excommunicate filled with foetid and boiling water, containing a bloody corpse (which demonstrated the benefit of absolution by dissolving into dust when absolved): 'Therefore everyone should pay attention to how his soul boiled in hell, when his body had so boiled in the grave'.[42]

One story, apparently composed in England in the second half of the thirteenth century, can be taken to represent local attitudes to excommunication and is worth describing in detail. It was later abbreviated by John Bromyard, and turned into a Middle English poem by John Lydgate (here the original Latin text is used),

---

[37] For some (undoubtedly not all) occurrences of this miracle, see: *Index exemplorum,* ed. Tubach, no. 754; *Catalogue of Romances,* ed. Herbert, 446, 615, 719; Stephen of Bourbon, *Anecdotes Historiques,* no. 308; *Lanercost,* 132–3.

[38] *Friars' Tales,* ed. Jones, 108; Gerald of Wales, *Gemma Ecclesiastica,* 161.

[39] For the latter, see Hill, '*Damnatio eternae mortis*', 43–4; Murray, 'Excommunication'; Jaser, 'Ritual excommunication'. The tales here discussed are mostly confined to those found in English sources, for the sake of space. Many more are discussed by Murray and Jaser.

[40] Since excommunicates were not supposed to be buried in consecrated ground, for this reason, it is unclear whether a rule was being broken or if the excommunication was not public.

[41] *Speculum laicorum,* ed. Welter, no. 280.

[42] *Speculum laicorum,* ed. Welter, no. 281. See also *Index exemplorum,* ed. Tubach, no. 1924.

and thus it circulated widely in the late Middle Ages.[43] Despite the date of its composition, the lengthy narrative is set in Oxfordshire in the time of St Augustine of Canterbury, shortly after the Anglo-Saxon conversion to Christianity.[44] The purpose of the story was first to convince people to pay their tithes, and second to impress upon them the power of excommunication.

In Augustine's day, a village priest, having failed to convince his local lord to pay his tithes, threatened him with excommunication. Informed of this, Augustine summoned the knight and quizzed him about the matter. When the lord refused to accept that he owed tithes, he was duly excommunicated by the saint. Augustine then went to church to celebrate mass, commanding excommunicates to leave before he did so. At this, a body was seen to rise from its tomb and leave the church. After mass, the 'pious shepherd' with his 'terrified sheep' approached the 'foul and deformed cadaver' in the cemetery, who explained that angels had expelled him when Augustine had ordered 'stinking flesh [i.e. excommunicates] to be thrown out of the church'. The corpse was discovered to be that of a Briton who had been excommunicated (before the pagan Anglo-Saxon invasion) because he never paid his tithes. Having died under this sentence, he explained that he had thus hurled his soul into 'the infernal confines to be tortured continually in the fires'.[45] Augustine then performed a miracle, resurrecting the British priest who had excommunicated the man. The priest confirmed the cause of the sentence, insisting that he had reason, since the man was always a rebel and a retainer of tithes. He too described how the man had been 'enclosed in the dark prison' and had 'sustained hellish punishments'.[46] The resurrected priest then imposed penance on the excommunicated corpse, which, once absolved, crumbled into dust and ash. The priest firmly declined Augustine's unappealing invitation to give up the 'delights of eternal life' to return to 'the laborious suffering' of temporal life to preach the gospel. Before the story ends with the lord of Augustine's own time seeing the error of his ways, the narrator interjects to quash any doubts amongst his audience that Augustine could have performed such a miracle, observing that 'there is no doubt that the stiff necks of the English were never accustomed to be subjected to the yoke of Christ except through great miracles'.

Ostensibly, these tales seem to propagate the idea that the souls of excommunicates suffered in hell, not purgatory. If a strict, Le Goffian, emphasis is placed on the importance of words, then the fact that neither 'purgatorium' nor related words are used, but hell ('infernus'), and related adjectives ('infernalia', 'iehennales') as well as more ambiguous terms such as fires ('incendia') and tortures

---

[43] Nine MSS survive containing the original text. These have been collated by E. Gordon Whatley, who discusses the story's later history in 'John Lydgate's Saint Austin at Compton'. See also Whatley, Thompson and Upchurch (eds) *Saints' Lives in Middle English Collections*, 215–19.

[44] Its account of this period is anachronistic.

[45] 'animam ad claustra infernalia iugiter cruciandam incendiis emisi'.

[46] 'tenebroso relusa in carcere, penas sustinuit iehennales'.

('cruciare', 'torquere') are used to convey the fates of these excommunicates is significant.[47] On the other hand, the Briton cannot have been in hell proper, for he was absolved and thus relieved from his suffering: hell itself was inescapable.[48] In 1199, Innocent III confirmed that posthumous absolution from excommunication was possible.[49] This meant that purgatory, not hell, must be the immediate destination for those who died excommunicate. Purgatory, whether 'born' in the twelfth century, or having developed gradually, albeit with less certain terminology, was an idea of considerable importance in the thirteenth century. People were now informed that they could continue to work towards salvation after death, by suffering purgatorial, or cleansing (as opposed to punitive), fires. Purgatory provided hope for the faithful because heaven was an eventual possibility even for those who had sinned.[50]

The sufferings described in these tales can have been purgatorial; 'hellish', but not of hell itself. Only if they were purgatorial were they escapable. These descriptions perhaps represent the 'infernalization' of purgatory, whereby writers used purgatory to induce not hope but fear.[51] Interestingly, John Lydgate's fifteenth-century Middle English version of the Augustine tale ('Saint Austin at Compton') does specify purgatory as the place where the Briton has been for 150 years.[52] The *Speculum*'s matron passing through the graveyard is informed that the dead man will suffer for his proximity to an excommunicate until Judgement Day, perhaps indicating that there would be a second judgement for both the deceased.[53] These descriptions can be reconciled with the notion that excommunication resulted in purgatory, not hell.[54]

Yet there was conceptual looseness here, one that benefitted the church. The neat categories of theologians and lawyers cannot and should not be imposed upon the actual thinking of medieval people. As we have seen, 'eternal' remained a word associated with an excommunicate's condemnation. These miracle stories are not easily interpreted, but the fact that they *can* be made to fit into thirteenth-century ideas of purgatory does not mean they were interpreted as such by the masses.[55] Though a number of tales make clear the impermanent nature of

---

[47] Le Goff, *Birth of Purgatory*; Edwards, 'Purgatory: "Birth" or evolution?'.
[48] Watkins, *History and the Supernatural*, 176; Le Goff, *Birth of Purgatory*, 195–6.
[49] X 5.39.28. The ruling enabled families of excommunicates to make satisfaction on the deceased's behalf.
[50] Le Goff, *Birth of Purgatory*: Kabir, *Paradise, Death and Doomsday*; Foxhall Forbes, *Heaven and Earth in Anglo-Saxon England*; Watkins, *History and the Supernatural*, 170–201; Watkins, 'Sin, penance and purgatory'.
[51] Le Goff, *Birth of Purgatory*, 310–15, 346.
[52] 'Saint Austin at Compton', l. 304. The earlier Latin version, not mentioning purgatory, continued to be copied.
[53] Gurevitch, *Historical Anthropology*, 72–7. The implication is that an excommunicate who was not the beneficiary of a miraculous resurrection allowing him to undergo penitentiary flagellation, like the Briton, would escape a Judgement Day condemnation to hell.
[54] Cf. Jaser, 'Ritual excommunication', 136–8.
[55] Cf. Watkins, *History and the Supernatural*, 173–5.

excommunication, provided that absolution took place, understanding that the destination for those who had not (yet) been absolved was purgatory requires a good understanding of doctrine. It was not explicitly stated. Certainly, the equation between hell and purgatory present in many writings is visible in excommunication miracle stories.[56] The language of hell is far more prevalent, perhaps misleadingly so. 'Dark prison' was associated with hell, and Gehenna (whence gehennalis/iehennalis) was almost always used with reference to eternal hell without redemption. If excommunication miracles were intended, by men well aware of purgatory, to educate about the 'official' beliefs of the church, it is uncertain how far they would have succeeded.[57] Alternatively, some may have been written by men who had not fully internalized the church's newer doctrines. Theological niceties reached the greater proportion of the population only slowly and in highly simplified form.[58]

Whether these stories intentionally blurred the lines between hell and purgatory or were ambiguous through lack of clear understanding, it is obvious why they continued to be popular with clergy throughout the Middle Ages. The Augustine story, for example, was presumably prompted by the reluctance of certain thirteenth-century parishioners to pay their tithes; the need for miracles to convince people is explicitly stated. Although it demonstrates the value of absolution, this is only made possible through a saint's miracle. The moral of the story was no doubt that it would be better to pay tithes than to risk suffering in the fires after death. Though posthumous absolution was legal, clergy would undoubtedly have preferred their parishioners to make amends in life. This was desirable from a pastoral perspective, since it was safer for their souls. It would also mean that clergy would receive their tithes or other recompense immediately, because satisfaction was required before absolution could be granted. Satisfaction as a condition of absolution made dying excommunicate problematic, for the dead relied both upon being proved to have died repentant and upon their heirs making amends on their behalf.[59] There are many more miracle tales dealing with excommunication. The key point is that they urged people to be afraid of the sanction. As with legal sources discussed above, excommunication miracles were designed to prevent excommunications, this time aimed at those who might suffer a sentence rather than those who issued them. They did this by making excommunication terrifying.

---

[56] Le Goff, *Birth of Purgatory*, 303–20; Gurevitch, *Historical Anthropology*, 86.
[57] Watkins, *History and the Supernatural*, 20–1.
[58] Watkins, *History and the Supernatural*, 187–93; Watkins, 'Sin, penance and purgatory', 7–33.
[59] Watkins, *History and the Supernatural*, 179, 199, and his ch. 5 *passim*. Links can be drawn with the emergence of revenant stories in which the undead asked the living to put their souls to rest by making amends.

Anger and Legal Procedure

Whilst these miracles implied hell, they did not contradict the ideal that clergy must not issue sentences with the intention of cursing. The severe consequences for excommunicates in these tales were the results of their own refusals to return to the church. The intention behind the excommunications might still be described as medicinal, even if the ultimate result was fatal. Even those tales which described excommunicates suffering while living reflected 1 Corinthians 5:5, which qualified the extreme statement that flesh was 'handed over to Satan to be destroyed' with the clarification 'so that the spirit might be saved'.

In practice, unlike miracle tales, excommunications were issued in anger, even with intent to curse. Whilst such practices did not adhere to the teachings of theologians, they could occur perfectly well within the limits of legal procedures associated with excommunication. Canon law was designed to minimize the possibilities for such occurrences, chiefly by preventing sentences being pronounced in the heat of the moment, but in fact left plenty of scope for them. One final miraculous excommunication, from a rather different source, involved a curse without medicinal intent. This story, told by Matthew Paris in his *Chronica Majora*, provides a link between excommunication miracle tales and thirteenth-century practice.

Paris described the excommunication of William Marshal, the great knight who had acted as a regent for the minor King Henry III. The story was included in Paris's chronicle under the year 1245 to explain the failure of the Marshal's dynastic line, for the last of the Marshal's five sons died that year. None had left male heirs. The events described took place in 1219, the year the Marshal died. Surely fabricated in light of later events, the story is nonetheless revealing.[60] Paris attributed the death of the Marshal's five childless sons to the excommunication of their father. While in Ireland, the Marshal had seized two manors belonging to the bishop of Ferns.[61] William, who argued he had legitimately gained these manors through war, refused to return the manors or to heed the bishop's warnings. As a result, he was excommunicated. The Marshal died under this sentence, having neither repented nor returned the manors. He was buried at the New Temple in London, despite the fact that, as an excommunicate, he ought to have been buried in unconsecrated ground.[62] Upon hearing of his death, Bishop Ailbe of Ferns travelled to England and informed the eleven-year-old king that his former regent had died excommunicate, and asked that Henry arrange the return of his property so that he might absolve William. Henry, saddened ('contristatus') by the news,

---

[60] *CM*, iv, 492–5. Crouch, *William Marshal*, 144, 176.
[61] For the background to this dispute, and references, see Flanagan, 'Ó Máelmuaid, Ailbe [Albinus O'Molloy]'.
[62] The burial of excommunicates is discussed in Chapter 2, 61–65.

asked the bishop to absolve the Marshal, promising that he would personally make satisfaction. Speaking to the tomb as if it to a living person, the bishop absolved the earl:

> O William, who lies here buried, entangled in the chains of excommunication, if those things which you injuriously stole from my church are restored by the king, or by your heir... with competent satisfaction, I absolve you; but otherwise I confirm that sentence, so that always bound by your sins you remain condemned in hell (*in inferno*).

The king was angry at the bishop's 'immoderate vigour', but Ailbe only replied that he should not be surprised, for the church of Ferns had been despoiled of its greatest assets. Despite the king's persuasions, the Marshal's sons subsequently refused to return the manors, the eldest claiming that he held them by right because his father had obtained them through war. This younger Marshal declared that if the 'old and delirious' bishop pronounced an unjust sentence, 'let his curse be turned on his head', reflecting the idea that an unjust sentence only hurt the one uttering it.[63] The young king was unable to do anything further, and the bishop's anger remained unabated. Unable to secure the return of his possessions, the bishop is said to have declared:

> What I said, I said; and what I wrote, I wrote indelibly. For the sentence stands, a punishment is inflicted upon the malefactors by the Lord, and the curse which is written in the Psalms is imposed as a heavy burden on earl William, of whom I complain. *His name will be destroyed in one generation* [Ps. 108:13]; and his sons will have no share in that blessing of the Lord, *Increase and multiply* [Gen. 1:28]; and some of them will die with a lamentable death, and their inheritance will be scattered.

These things the king would come to witness while still in the prime of life. The bishop's words, which left the Marshal bound by anathema, Paris explains, were spoken 'in cordis amaritudine': with a bitter spirit. Moreover, they all came to pass, so that Paris treated the speech as a prophecy. Further proof of the earl's cursed state was revealed in 1240 when the New Temple was rededicated and his body was found, intact but putrid.

Matthew Paris's account of William Marshal's excommunication is important for several reasons. Not only does he portray the bishop issuing a curse, but it is presented by the monk as having been effective. Its consequences were certainly more severe than was generally considered acceptable by theologians. Most

---

[63] Mary Mansfield discusses the issue of property not returned by heirs and subsequent excommunications of dead culprits in *Humiliation*, 87.

importantly, the bishop violated the fundamental rule that excommunication must not be used with the intention to curse. Paris used a phrase—'in bitterness of heart'—often used in the context of excommunications, seemingly to convey reluctance and sadness that such a step was necessary.[64] Yet the circumstances here hardly suggest medicinal intent, not least because the Marshal was already dead. It is clear that the bishop's primary concern was retrieving his properties (he should not, in fact, have absolved the earl without proof that he had died repentant, something not mentioned, yet was willing to do so if his manors were returned to him). As later chapters will demonstrate, Ailbe's preoccupation with his own material interests was not exceptional. Many others used excommunication with similar aims.

Yet if in spirit the bishop flouted accepted doctrine, his actions in no way contravened canon law.[65] The details of Paris's account should perhaps be doubted, but the way the chronicler presented his narrative makes clear that he believed the bishop was acting justly and in accordance with proper procedures. Writing in 1245, after he had included the canons of the Council of Lyon in his chronicle, Paris was certainly aware of the church's official stance on excommunication. It may be that this is why he took such pains to emphasize that the bishop's sentence was fair. First, he noted that the Marshal had acted violently and injuriously, responding impudently to the bishop's frequent admonitions and contumaciously retaining the manors. For this he was sentenced deservedly ('non immerito'). Scorning ('contempnens') this sentence, the Marshal piled injuries upon injuries. After his death, the bishop again told King Henry that the sentence had been pronounced 'non immerito'. In his second speech, the bishop mentioned that his sentence had also been recorded in writing, indicating that there was at least some kind of legal procedure. The most crucial things here are the bishop's warnings before any sentence was pronounced, and the assertion that the Marshal was behaving contumaciously ('contumaciter'): the two most fundamental prerequisites for a valid sentence of excommunication. Phrases such as 'piling injury upon injury' were commonly used before a sentence was 'aggravated' (for instance by interdicting lands).[66] Paris thus made use of legal terms associated with excommunication, yet the bishop's spirit and the consequences of his actions are a long way from a purely judicial sanction.

However many restrictions canon law tried to impose on the use of excommunication, provided procedure was followed a cleric could act with vengeful intent.

---

[64] Cf. *Reg. Greenfield*, i, no. 301; *Reg. Epp. Pecham*, ii, 477; Heidemann, no. 29e; *Foedera*, II.i.41–2. These examples are all later than Paris's account.

[65] One possible justification for the bishop's curse is indicated by Paris's treatment of it as a prophesy. As Silvana Vecchio has shown, some Church Fathers took the view that maledictions were acceptable because they were prophesies which announced a future condemnation by God, and did not in fact influence Him. See Vecchio, 'Légitimité et efficacité', 352–3.

[66] On aggravation of excommunication see Jaser, *Ecclesia maledicens*, 311–18; and below, 158–9, 200–201.

Such procedures made it more difficult for a cleric to sentence someone without reasonable cause or to pass sentence without warning (though many appeals indicate that both 'faults' continued to arise on a frequent basis[67]). Even so, they did not preclude use of excommunication as a curse. If the anger expressed was just, as it was later proved to be in the Marshal's case, the curse was more likely to work.[68] The bishop of Ferns's sentence might be aptly described as a 'judicial anathema', as too might other sentences pronounced in thirteenth-century England. The law, which insisted upon adequate warnings, prevented sentences being pronounced on the spot. But this requirement hardly stopped clerics issuing sentences in cases where their anger was prolonged through personal interests. Like the bishop of Ferns, clergy might be protecting their own rights yet have a just cause. They could act legally, nonetheless using excommunication to their own advantage, potentially with the intent to curse. Vengeful and partisan use of excommunication, however, even if perfectly legal and impossible to appeal, was one reason why medieval communities treated the censure with disrespect.

Furthermore, *latae sententiae*, so common in thirteenth-century England, in particular allowed for sentences pronounced in anger. These sentences frequently protected clerics and their rights, in England especially via *Qui malitiose ecclesias*. Thus the offences that were most likely to provoke anger were those that allowed the pronouncement of excommunications without additional warnings (frequent publication of such sentences served as the warning). Certainly not every cleric was permitted to declare someone automatically bound, but many clerics could indeed excommunicate without procedure. The development of *ipso facto* sentences thus perhaps reversed any trend towards increased judicialization. Once again it must be stressed that *ipso facto* sentences were not anomalies but very common.

The law of excommunication put restraints upon clergy using the sanction. While these limits prevented a spur of the moment excommunication declared in a rage, they could not stop excommunication being wielded by those who were angry. They merely required sustained, rather than impetuous, anger. Once an individual had behaved contumaciously by failing to alter their behaviour, the censure was legitimate. Moreover, the wait for contumacy was not always necessary, especially where ecclesiastical rights were at issue. The prevalence of *latae sententiae* meant clerics were *more* rather than *less* able to excommunicate immediately when their own rights were at stake.

---

[67] The phrase used in such complaints is 'non monitos, non confessos, non convictos, absque causa rationabili, et contra statuta concilii generalis', or similar.

[68] Cf. Thomas, *Religion and the Decline of Magic*, 505.

The Rite of Excommunication

The liturgical ritual of excommunication was the final means by which people were informed of the spiritual dangers of excommunication. This is true for the thirteenth century as well as the earlier (and later) Middle Ages. Donald Logan's assertion in the *Dictionary of the Middle Ages* that sentences were pronounced in courts, with a simple 'I excommunicate you', and not with the solemn ceremony, is technically correct.[69] It is nevertheless misleading. The original pronouncement of a sentence against a named individual was indeed usually done in this way, but it was also required that excommunicates subsequently be denounced in local churches, to ensure that knowledge of their state reached everyone. This was done with candles and bells. Moreover, every parish priest was to solemnly publish certain *latae sententiae* four times a year.[70] When a crime covered by an automatic sentence was committed, but the perpetrator unknown, general excommunications would be ritually pronounced against whoever had committed the offence while investigations were on-going.[71] Thus, to parishioners in the thirteenth century, the excommunication ceremony would have been a familiar spectacle. Just as it had been in the eleventh century, ritual excommunication was an important aspect of parish life.[72]

That excommunication ceremonies of some kind took place on a frequent basis throughout England in this period is indisputable. It is less clear, however, precisely what they involved. It is reasonable to conclude, with Roger E. Reynolds, Edwards, Jaser, and Hamilton, that there was much continuity between the tenth and fifteenth centuries.[73] However, the ceremony was so common that mandates and legislation often specify merely that it was to be conducted in the usual way—with bells ringing and candles burning and extinguished. Normative sources reveal relatively little. Nevertheless, it is certain that candles and bells were routinely used to denounce excommunicates (which might be compared with trumpets and black candles used in the Jewish equivalent, *herem*).[74] Hundreds, possibly thousands, of references to this ceremony could be cited, from sources of many different kinds (including canon law, legislation, papal and episcopal registers, records of court proceedings, chronicles, and chancery rolls). So crucial was the use of candles that when the legate Pandulf wanted

---

[69] Logan, 'Excommunication'.   [70] See Chapter 7 and Appendix I.
[71] Edwards claims that ceremonial pronunciation was, by the fourteenth and fifteenth centuries, largely for these general sentences: 'Ritual excommunication', 129–30.
[72] Hamilton, 'Remedies for "great transgressions"', 101. Jaser shows that the more elaborate ritual did not disappear, *Ecclesia maledicens*, 319–20.
[73] Reynolds, 'Rites of separation'; Edwards, 'Ritual excommunication'; Jaser, *Ecclesia maledicens*; Hamilton 'Interpreting diversity', esp. 133–4.
[74] The Jewish *herem* ceremony involved 'opening of the Ark, blowing of the shofar, and the lighting of black candles', Katz, *Tradition and Crisis*, 85; Kaplan, *Religion, Politics and Freedom of Conscience*, 6–7.

to excommunicate those who sought to hang a felonious clerk (on King John's orders), Pandulf's response was immediately to flee and look for a candle (the king was successfully recalled from his intention).[75]

The essential form of excommunication is provided by Gratian's *Decretum*, in its second recension:

> Twelve priests ought to stand around the bishop, and hold burning candles in their hands, which in the conclusion of the anathema or excommunication they should throw to the ground and tread on with their feet.[76]

The 'conclusion of the anathema' came after an individual and their crime, or the crime that incurred an automatic sentence, had been announced. Though most English sources from the thirteenth century merely note extinguishing candles, there are occasional references to stamping them out in the early fourteenth century, despite this no longer being included in Durandus's 1290s pontifical.[77] As the gesture was performed, some version of the phrase 'thus his soul is extinguished in hell' was uttered. As Thomas of Chobham explained in his *Summa confessorum*, this meant that 'his soul is obscured in infernal darkness, namely lest he sees the light of the grace of God, until he comes to emendation'.[78] Variations of this phrase could be more severe, though formulae include an 'unless clause'. For instance, one formula from a thirteenth or early fourteenth-century manuscript has 'And thus these lights are extinguished, so let their souls remain in hell with the devil and his angels, unless they come to their senses'.[79]

As the Gratian prescription makes clear, this was a staged spectacle. The ceremony was designed to induce fear, achieving this with a solemn setting, candles, bells, and explicit condemnations to hell. While anger or charisma might make the ceremony more terrifying, it did not rely upon them. As Lester Little noted, discussing monastic curses, 'this was not the stuff of passion'.[80] Thus whilst Helmholz makes the case that the earlier 'powerful curse' was 'dependent for its efficacy upon the spiritual power of the person who issued it, as well as upon

---

[75] *Ann. Burton*, 217. For the history and significance of candles in this context, see Jaser, *Ecclesia maledicens*, 222–9.

[76] C.11, q.3, c.106; Winroth, *Making of Gratian's Decretum*, 115. The ceremony was based on earlier practice. See Hamilton, 'Anglo-Saxon and Frankish evidence', 173. Though Gratian does not mention bells, they were nonetheless already associated with excommunication. See Little, *Benedictine Maledictions*, 29, 43, 139, 168–70. It does appear, however, that bells were not included in formulae, leading Edwards (who studied the formulae) to claim that 1253 was the first time bells were associated with excommunication: 'Ritual excommunication', 116.

[77] E.g. *Reg. Gandavo*, i, 395–8 (1311); Jaser, *Ecclesia maledicens*, 296; *Pontifical Romain*, iii, 612–15.

[78] Chobham, *Summa*, 253.

[79] London, BL, Additional MS 15236, f. 25r. For the above see also Jaser, 'Ritual excommunication', 125–6. Jaser notes that the devil in this context is passive, suffering with excommunicates: *Ecclesia maledicens*, 214–16.

[80] Little, 'Anger in monastic curses', 32; Little, *Benedictine Maledictions*, 40. Jaser also criticizes Helmholz's charisma argument: *Ecclesia maledicens*, 304.

the justice of his cause', the significant event was less the original pronouncement but instead the later denunciation.[81] The staging necessary prevented this being spontaneous, whether we are discussing a period before or after a supposed 'judicialization'. Moreover, the proportion of clerics with a sufficiently saintly reputation can surely not have been high enough, at any time, for the efficacy of the sanction to depend on sanctity alone.

It is important, nonetheless, to acknowledge that by the thirteenth century the ceremony was merely publicizing something that had already happened; it did not itself enact the excommunication sentence. This was not an Austinian speech-act.[82] Thus in general the phrasing was 'we announce that X is excommunicated' rather than 'we excommunicate'.[83] Though the excommunication was already in force, it was the (repeated) public denunciations that notified the community and provided an opportunity to damn the excommunicate and impress upon others the dangers of the sanction. There would thus be a short interval between the declaration of the sentence and its denunciation on Sundays and feast days. An unusual example, concerning a general sentence pronounced to confirm an agreement about the boundary between the dioceses of Hereford and St Asaph, clarifies the distinction, emphasizing that the public announcement was the more important event. On 22 November 1288, an agreement was reached. An excommunication was issued by clerks present against anyone who infringed it. Then, in the presence of a great multitude of noble men and others, 'two of the clerks stood up and promulgated the sentence of excommunication which they had issued while sitting'. This they did in both English and Welsh. Then they stood up (here the series of events becomes a little unclear) and confirmed the sentence, clothed in stoles and with burning candles in their hands, in the presence of the clergy and people.[84]

The dramatic ceremony could evidently have a profound effect, with the words mirroring the action. Robert Winchelsey, archbishop of Canterbury (1294–1313), explained (here discussing *ipso facto* sentences) that the ceremony using candles and bells was crucial because the laity paid more attention to this solemnity and were more likely to fear excommunication because of it.[85] The audience, however, was the community rather than the excommunicates themselves.[86] An excommunicate sentenced *ab homine* would not usually be present since he or she would already be banned from church, where such rituals typically (but not

---

[81] Helmholz, 'Excommunication in twelfth century England', 237–8.
[82] Austin, *How to Do Things with Words*.
[83] Töbelmann describes it as a 'meta-ritual', in that it affected other rituals. It was unnecessary for excommunicating someone, but it had many other effects: 'Excommunication', 106–10.
[84] *Reg. Swinfield*, 207–8.
[85] *C&S*, ii, 1194: 'faciatis [sententias]...publicari...pulsatis campanis et candelis accensis, ut propter solempnitatem huiusmodi, quam laici magis quam effectum huiusmodi sententiarum attendunt, amplius timeatur'.
[86] Beaulande, *Malheur*, 33–4; Töbelmann, 'Excommunication', 101.

exclusively) took place. Witnesses of the excommunication ceremony were used to 'audio-visual effects' used in religion, such as when bells were rung and candles were lit at the elevation of the host or when the host was carried to the sick.[87] Here, however, such positive uses of candles and bells were inverted, intended to strike fear not adoration into the hearts of those present. Christian Jaser has shown that the papal Maundy Thursday general excommunication made use of disordered bell ringing. According to the ceremony book from the 1270s this, in contrast to the ordered bell ringing of usual worship that gathered believers, instead 'scatters the unbelievers'.[88] Other sources note that bells were rung slowly; no source from thirteenth-century England indicates which might have been the practice.[89] According to Matthew Paris, during the Magna Carta excommunication in 1237, once the candles were thrown down, the smoke and smell generated caused offence to bystanders, with smoke getting in their eyes and choking their nostrils. At this point Edmund of Abingdon, archbishop of Canterbury (1234–40), declared 'thus let the condemned souls of those who violate the charter be extinguished, smoke and stink'. In the ceremony of excommunication staged to confirm Magna Carta in 1253, Boniface of Savoy, archbishop of Canterbury (1241–70), declared 'thus let those who incur this sentence be extinguished and stink in hell', and bells were then rung.[90]

Paris's descriptions add weight to Sarah Hamilton's assertion, discussing the practice of extinguishing candles and the accompanying phrase in earlier formulae, that the 'vividness of this allusion to the sulphurous smells of the inferno reminds us how rites relied on more than mere words to convey their message'.[91] The gist of what was going on was clear, even if the words were not heard or understood. Thus when an excommunication was the subject of witness depositions in the case of Thame (Chapter 6), one witness explained that

> the bishop of Lincoln, dressed in pontificals, had a chaplain attending him read the names of those occupying the church of Thame; and when the names were read, the bishop taking up a candle proclaimed the words of excommunication on them, as was publicly said by all present, and he threw (*proiecit*) the candle to the ground saying "fiat, fiat, amen".[92]

The importance of the ritual is well demonstrated by this witness: he was 'unlettered', and he had therefore been unable to understand the words of the excommunication pronounced in Latin. He was told by others that they were words of excommunication, but he presumably understood what was taking place

---

[87] Rubin, *Corpus Christi*, 58, 78. [88] Jaser, 'Ostensio exclusionis', 377–8.
[89] Beaulande, 'Force de la censure', 259. [90] *CM*, v. 360–1, 377.
[91] Hamilton, 'Interpreting diversity', 136.
[92] *SCC*, 585. This quotation is the editors' calendar of the testimony, but they have included most of the Latin.

nonetheless. The concluding words of a sentence often involved the participation of the whole congregation, who were to join in with the final 'fiat fiat, amen amen' (so be it, so be it, amen amen).

Though the trio 'bell, book and candle' is traditionally associated with the excommunication ceremony, if a third key element should be added to 'bell and candle' it should not at this time be 'book' but solemn dress.[93] Descriptions of clergy pronouncing sentences mention solemn robes, white pontificals,[94] albs, and stoles. The Lanercost chronicler, for example, specifically noted that when the bishop of Worcester excommunicated Robert the Bruce in 1306, he removed his ordinary robes and put on his pontificals.[95] Sometimes a cross being held erect is also mentioned.[96] An unusually full description of a sentence pronounced against infringers of the liberties of St Alban's describes the abbot and the full convent in a solemn procession, with bells and candles, and with stoles placed around the shrine, the cross, and around the neck of every monk.[97] When a new archbishop was to be elected in 1228, the prior of Canterbury (pre-emptively) excommunicated anyone who conducted themselves badly in the matter, in the presence of reliquaries (wood from the Cross, the veil of the Virgin, and the 'corona' or skull relic of Thomas Becket) which had been brought in to terrify the chapter.[98]

These were the essentials of the ceremony of excommunication. The extinguishing of candles gesturally and orally condemned a soul to hell in a manner closely allied to cursing. Though candles and bells were fundamental in ceremonies of any size, the full ritual anathema was supposed to be the preserve of bishops but not of lesser clergy.[99] A full contingent of twelve priests was clearly impractical for every excommunication and denunciation, and many involved much less spectacle. A mandate ordering denunciations in 1293, for example, stated that this should be done with the full twelve priests assisting at least once, implying that on other occasions (every Sunday and feast day, as was standard) a lesser ceremony could take place.[100] Another mandate from the same episcopal

---

[93] I have found only a few mentions of 'books' in this context. Two appear in vernacular sources: *Robert of Gloucester* has 'boc & candle' (l. 10370); *Chronicle of Pierre de Langtoft*, ed. Wright, has 'lyvre et chaunaylle' (248). The vicars of Whyton and Hayton had the book and candle ('librum et candelam') snatched from them when they pronounced a sentence in 1302: *Register of Thomas of Corbridge*, ed. Thompson, ii, 13; Borthwick Institute, Abp Register 6, f.196v. The Becket Leaves (see cover image) show Thomas Becket reading from a book and holding a candle.

[94] However, in 1268 the legate apparently wore red when he excommunicated the rebels in Kenilworth Castle: *Robert of Gloucester*, ii, 772.

[95] *Lanercost*, 206. Vestments were important, too, for solemn absolution: the Anonymous of Béthune asserts that Prince Louis was not absolved from excommunication on the same day that he made peace, in 1217, because the clergy did not have their vestments with them: *History of the Dukes of Normandy*, trans. Shirley, 188.

[96] e.g. *Annales Londonienses*, 74–5; *Reg. Sutton*, v, 103.
[97] *Gesta abbatum*, ed. Riley, i, 316–17.   [98] *Gervase*, 120.
[99] E.g. Peñafort, *De Poenitentia*, 397–8.   [100] *Reg. Sutton*, iv, 70–2. See Chapter 6 below.

register instructed a priest to recruit four or five nearby parish chaplains, dressed in alb and stole, to pronounce a sentence.[101] On the other hand, in 1243, Robert Grosseteste was reportedly excommunicated by fifty or more monk-priests. In 1273, all the priests of the city of Winchester were gathered to excommunicate the monks of St Swithun's.[102] It is evident that the number of clergy involved was important: chroniclers frequently noted how many had been gathered for a particular denunciation, often citing a specific number, or stating that all the priests from a city or area had been gathered, or merely asserting that there was 'a multitude' of clergy. It is equally clear, from these examples and others, that the number of priests or bishops involved in an excommunication ceremony varied a great deal. There is also evidence that laymen could participate more actively than by merely joining in with the final 'fiat fiat, amen'. In 1237 and 1258 (but not 1253), Henry III held a candle, both at the Magna Carta excommunication and at that supposedly pronounced against infringers of the Provisions of Oxford.[103] In 1221, the earls of Chester and Salisbury threw candles to the ground along with the bishops when Willian de Forz was excommunicated.[104] That the ritual was intended as spectacle is also indicated by the emphasis placed, in mandates and chroniclers' reports, upon there being a large audience to stand witness.[105]

Ritual excommunication was unquestionably a visually memorable and possibly terrifying spectacle, even if the variety in specifics makes generalizations ill advised. The number of people present is particularly significant for the argument of this book. Many clergy would, presumably, have made the event more solemn, imposing, and terrifying. Increasing the solemnity in this way also, however, made the excommunication more striking and thus more memorable. Thus, as later chapters discuss, excommunication was a useful means of communicating information to communities. The emphasis on large crowds reinforces the impression that excommunication was used to influence public opinion in this way. Part of this was because the workings of excommunication required it—people had to be informed who they were supposed to shun and be convinced to do so—but it came to be a reason for using excommunication in its own right.

---

[101] *Reg. Sutton*, iv, 35–6.

[102] *CM*, iv, 248; *Annales Monasterii de Wintonia*, 116. For Grosseteste's excommunication see Morgan, 'Excommunication of Grosseteste in 1243'.

[103] *CM*, v, 360–1; *Guisborough*, 186; *Robert of Gloucester*, ii, 734; *Documents of the Baronial Movement*, ed. Treharne and Sanders, 259. However, as Sophie Ambler has argued, the 1258 sentence possibly never took place: *Bishops in the Political Community*, 108–12. Moreover, David Carpenter doubts that Henry held a candle in 1253: *Henry III*, 46 n. 150.

[104] *Ann. Dunstable*, 63–4, and *Coventry*, 247–8.

[105] This is discussed in greater depth in Chapter 5.

Words of Excommunication

Beyond those that accompanied the dashing of candles, it is difficult to determine what words were used in excommunication denunciations. However, as with the visual aspects of excommunication, there must have been great diversity in practice.[106] Unfortunately, only a handful of records of precise sentences survive, compared to mandates ordering publication, which survive in droves. Unlike a twelfth-century letter sent by the bishop of Norwich, discussed by Nicholas Karn, thirteenth-century orders for publication do not usually provide words to be used in the solemn denunciation.[107] What was said when these mandates were fulfilled might have been quite different to the contents of the mandates themselves, though it is likely that the description of the crime as contained in mandates was used. Clerics probably had a good deal of opportunity to improvise, and to use whatever formulae they had to hand. As Sarah Hamilton has observed, the 'liturgy for excommunication (as opposed to the canon law) was simply not subject to the same prescriptive forces of regulation and correction as those which existed for other rites'. Formulae were likely to be ad hoc and did not necessarily follow prescriptions for rites contained in pontificals and sacramentaries.[108] For general sentences, as is demonstrated in ecclesiastical legislation, the 'Auctoritate Dei' formula was certainly used. Sentences based on this model invoked the authority of the Trinity, and a variable number of other spiritual authorities.[109] The Magna Carta sentence, for instance, invoked Almighty God, the Son and the Holy Spirit, followed by the Virgin, SS Peter and Paul and all apostles, St Thomas Becket and all martyrs, St Edward the Confessor and all confessors and virgins, and all the saints of God.[110] Varying the length of the list of authorities was one way in which sentences differed in terms of solemnity. For general sentences, it appears that the formula would be 'By the authority of God [etc.] we excommunicate all those who [commit a certain crime]'. For individual sentences, evidence indicates that the crimes of perpetrators and their names were described first, often at great length, using highly condemnatory language. Only then did the 'Auctoritate dei' formula begin.[111]

How 'maledictory' a sentence could be certainly varied. It must be admitted, however, that the (very limited) evidence surviving from thirteenth-century England contains remarkably tame sentences compared to those found by others

---

[106] Cf. Hamilton, 'Interpreting diversity', for variation in the tenth and eleventh centuries.
[107] Herbert Losinga's 1110 letter: Karn, '*Textus Roffensis*', 52–9.
[108] Hamilton, 'Medieval curses and their users', 44. Hamilton is discussing an earlier period, but the observation holds true for the thirteenth century. Formulae were often written onto flyleaves of commonplace books and similar, for instance.
[109] See Edwards, 'Ritual excommunication', 19–21, and ch. 4 of her thesis *passim*.
[110] C&S, 477–8.
[111] See the form of a sentence pronounced by Boniface of Savoy, as recorded in a letter of Innocent IV: *CM*, vi, 197–200.

working on both earlier and later material, in England and on the continent. They were shorter and to the point.[112] There is no reason to imagine that sentences of excommunication were uniform. The Romano-German tradition contains five excommunication texts, of varying length and severity, from which the most appropriate could be chosen.[113] Circumstances dictated how elaborate a sentence was. Unfortunately, excommunication forms definitely in use in England during this period are hard to find, largely due to the lack of surviving pontificals. Some denunciations were probably fairly quick and perfunctory, perhaps resembling the 'Excommunicatio brevis' included in some manuscripts in the Romano-Germanic pontifical tradition, or the form of excommunication (more correctly, of denouncing someone already excommunicate, as discussed above) contained in the episcopal register of John le Romeyn, archbishop of York (1286–96):

> Since therefore we bound A. of B., because of their contumacies and offences, with a sentence of major excommunication with ordinary canonical authority, we announce them to you, by the tenor of the present, to be thus excommunicated; ordering that, out of reverence for God and the church, you strictly avoid them in congregations, assemblies, and all legitimate acts, until s/he deserves to obtain the benefit of absolution after fitting satisfaction.[114]

At the other end of the scale, a concise but forceful text transcribed by Véronique Beaulande from a thirteenth-century Cambrai manuscript is plausibly similar to those in use in England in the same period:

> By the authority of Almighty God the father, and of the son, and of the holy spirit, and of Peter, prince of the apostles, and of all the elect of God, we excommunicate those wrong-doers, and damn and anathematize them, and exclude them from the threshold of the holy church of God, and sequester them from the fellowship of Christians. So that, struck by the sword of the holy spirit, they descend living to hell with Dathan and Abiron, and are handed over to the devil and his angles with whom, tormented, let them be tortured

---

[112] Excommunication and malediction formulae have been described by a considerable number of historians, including Hamilton, 'Interpreting diversity'; Lea, *Studies in Church History*; Little, *Benedictine Maledictions*; Gurevitch, *Medieval Popular Culture*, 213; Lange, *Excommunication for Debt*, 67–73. Jaser discusses the change here specifically, *Ecclesia maledicens*, 301–3.

[113] *Pontifical romano-germanique*, i, 308–17. For the difficulties with this edition, see Parkes, 'Questioning the authority'. Not all MSS contain these formulae, but only one MS has one of these without the others; four have all five excommunications in the same order: database.prg.mus.cam.ac.uk.

[114] *Pontifical romano-germanique*, i, 314; *Reg. le Romeyn*, i, 53: 'Cum itaque A. de B., propter ejusdem contumacias et offensas, majoris excommunicacionis sentencia auctoritate ordinaria canonice innodaverimus, ipsum sic excommunicatum vobis tenore presencium nunciamus; rogantes quatinus, ob reverenciam Dei et ecclesie, ipsum in congregacionibus, colloquiis, et omnibus actibus legitimis, tam in judicio quam extra judicium, arcius evitetis, donec post satisfaccionem congruam absolucionis beneficium meruerit optinere'.

without end and be destroyed in eternity. And as these lights are extinguished, thus let their lights be extinguished in the midst of darkness, and let them be cursed in the eternal fire unless they come to their senses and make satisfaction to the church of God. So be it, so be it.[115]

This formula is tame compared to formulae found elsewhere. It does not, as both earlier and later examples do, curse individual actions and body parts. Thus although roughly contemporary manuscripts contain excommunication texts with phrases such as 'maledicti sint manducando, bibendo, vigilando, dormiendo, sedendo, stando, ambulando' ('let them be cursed while chewing, drinking, waking, sleeping, sitting, standing, walking'), there is no way of linking such litanies of curses to any particular event in thirteenth-century England.[116] Edwards suggests that canonists and theologians ('high culture') were abandoning such practices in the twelfth century, but that clergy of 'middle culture' remained interested in 'Auctoritate dei' formulae and curses.[117] Since malediction formulae survive from both earlier and later, in Latin and in Middle English, continuity of use must not be ruled out.[118] Such curses ought not to be viewed as archaisms. It is possible that they were known to and used by English churchmen without leaving evidence, which would fit with Edwards's proposition.[119] Nonetheless, lack of evidence advises caution. Such indications as there are suggest that excommunication formulae used in the cases discussed in the remainder of this book were likely to be mild relative to the corpus of such formulae as a whole.

There are, however, hints that elements of the more severe anathemas continued to be used. The excommunication of William Marshal, though not a ritual ceremony (the bishop was alone, without candles, bells, or assistants), made use of Psalm 108. This psalm, in the words of Lester Little, is 'perhaps the most maledictory of all psalms', and the 'psalm most renowned for its curses, cited

---

[115] Beaulande, *Malheur*, 271: 'Auctoritate Dei Patris omnipotentis et Filii et Spiritus sancti et beati Petri apostolorum principis et omnium electorum Dei, excommunicamus et dampnamus et anathematizamus et a liminibus sancte Dei ecclesie excludimus et sequestramus a consortio Christianorum illos maleficos. Quatinus transverberati gladio Spiritus sancti descendant cum Dathan et Abiron vivi in infernum et tradantur diabolo et angelis ejus cum quibus cruciati torqueantur sine fine et in eternum pereant. Et sicut extinguntur lucerne iste, sic extinguantur lucerne eorum in mediis tenebris, et sint maledicti in ignem eternum nisi resipuerint et ecclesie Dei satisfecerint. Fiat, fiat.'

[116] For example, a late thirteenth or early fourteenth-century English manuscript contains a formula with such maledictions: London, BL, Additional MS 15236, f. 25r. The MS is a collection of medical and other tracts. See Edwards, 'Ritual excommunication', 124, for how often formulas in this period were written in a wide variety of MSS, usually not pontificals.

[117] Edwards, 'Ritual excommunication', 127.

[118] Cf. the formula with, for example, 'Excommunication formula, about 900' and '"Pope Leo" excommunication formula, 937' in appendix C of Little, *Benedictine Maledictions*, 255–8, and with the Middle English form in Carruthers 'Great Curse', 45–59. Edwards, 'Ritual Excommunication', also contains appendices with numerous formulae demonstrating the prevalence of such phrases. There is continuity right up to the nineteenth century: Gallant, 'Peasant ideology', 493.

[119] Her suggestion was, however, based on the fact that such curse formulae were regularly copied in the twelfth century, not the thirteenth.

frequently both in full and in part'.¹²⁰ As Thomas Hardy was later to remind readers of *The Mayor of Casterbridge*, it provided ample material for cursing enemies.¹²¹ Excommunications pronounced against those who attacked the church of Thame in 1293 (Chapter 6) also made use of this Psalm. In 1296, the Lanercost chronicle reported that the Scots excommunicated the king of England and the English, reciting Psalm 108.¹²² That year, a certain chaplain from Edinburgh, Thomas, was arrested and delivered to the archdeacon of Lothian because, 'in contempt of the lord king', he had excommunicated the king of England, publicly with bell and candle. Richard Guile, who had rung the bell, was similarly charged. Their excommunication, then, may well have involved a reading of Psalm 108.¹²³ Such references to thirteenth-century use of Psalm 108 are exceptional. But it is not implausible that the Psalm text was used more frequently than the evidence implies.¹²⁴ It can hardly be claimed that clergy were ignorant of the Psalms.

Excommunication rites often ended by condemning the excommunicates along with various biblical villains, such as Judas, Caiaphas, Pilate, Ananias and Sapphira, and particularly Dathan and Abiron.¹²⁵ There is some (limited) evidence that such phrases remained in use. Thus the sentence pronounced against the Thame attackers declared that the guilty parties were to share in the fate of Cain the fratricide, and of Dathan and Abiron, who were swallowed alive for their crimes.¹²⁶ Dathan and Abiron, who in the Book of Numbers were swallowed alive by the earth for contesting Moses's authority, certainly continued to be associated with sinners.¹²⁷ For example, John Pecham justified his excommunication of the bishop of Hereford, Thomas Cantilupe, by describing him as acting in the spirit of the two biblical sinners.¹²⁸ He similarly believed that certain schismatics deserved to be punished with Dathan and Abiron, and ordered their excommunication.¹²⁹

There is much we cannot know about how sentences were pronounced in thirteenth-century England. But it should at least be considered that such ceremonies were more dramatic than much of the evidence suggests. It is thus important to acknowledge that there were grades of ritual force, both gesturally and verbally, within the broader category of excommunication.¹³⁰ Though Vodola

---

[120] Little, *Benedictine Maledictions*, 23, 63.
[121] See Little, *Benedictine Maledictions*, 63–7; Jaser, *Ecclesia maledicens*, 178–85; Reynolds, 'Rites of separation', 405–33.
[122] *Lanercost*, 175–6.
[123] 'A plea roll of Edward I's army', ed. Neville, no. 115. I am grateful to Sophie Ambler for this reference.
[124] Parts of the psalm occasionally appear in other excommunication-related contexts, such as when people who had remained excommunicated were described as 'drinking up curses like water' (*Reg. Bronescombe*, no. 1175).
[125] Jaser, *Ecclesia maledicens*, 204–12. [126] *Reg. Sutton*, iv, 117–18.
[127] See Jaser, *Ecclesia maledicens*, 183, 204–8; Edwards, 'Ritual excommunication', 84–5, 93. For earlier usage, see Little, *Benedictine Maledictions*, 65–8.
[128] *Reg. Epp. Pecham*, ii, 394. [129] *Reg. Epp. Pecham*, i, 183.
[130] See also Jaser, 'Usurping the Spiritual sword', 509.

has argued that there was no theological distinction to be drawn between major excommunication and anathema, a tripartite division of excommunication (minor, major, anathema) remains helpful in understanding practice.[131] Thus the Durandus pontifical, written on the continent in the 1290s, included separate rituals for excommunication and anathema. The latter was far more elaborate.[132] For particularly serious cases the full anathema, making use of Old Testament maledictions from the Psalms and Deuteronomy, could be used. In practice, it is difficult to judge whether an individual sentence was a major excommunication or an anathema (and no attempt will be made to do so in the remaining chapters). But acknowledging that there were grades of solemnity is helpful when considering how excommunication was carried out.

If it were not for chroniclers, we would not know that the archbishops declared that infringers of Magna Carta would stink in hell, or how the smell of the extinguished candles affected the audience. We would not know that Edward I was anathematized via Psalm 108 (however applied) in 1296. Chronicle evidence is erratic. Most excommunications were not noted, and those that were, often only briefly. Beaulande, too, has argued that bishops in thirteenth-century France probably used the spectacular ritual even if they did not specifically call it 'anathema'. The term, while difficult to apply to individual events, remains useful.[133] It is thus possible, if impossible to prove, that some of the excommunications discussed in this book were pronounced using language akin to cursing. If we err on the side of caution and conclude, through lack of definite evidence, that the more severe maledictions were not in use in thirteenth-century England, the final condemnation with candles remained in any case the most explicit indication of what would happen to an excommunicate's soul.[134]

'Nisi' Clauses

Although the words that accompanied candles being thrown to the ground were dramatic, formulae made clear that this condemnation to hell, the eternal fires, or to join the devil and his angels, was escapable. Formulae invariably include a clause which states that this eventuality was only unless ('nisi') the excommunicate refused

---

[131] Vodola, *Excommunication*, 14–16 and notes. Jaser, similarly noting the difficulties of distinguishing 'excommunication' from 'anathema' favours 'ritual excommunication' to indicate the 'ultimate, high-end sanction...an orally and gesturally performed excommunication': 'Ritual excommunication', 121. The problem with this terminology is that there was a ritual used in announcing all excommunications. The variation lies in how dramatic this ceremony could be. For intensification of excommunications (following ongoing contumacy) he uses 'feierliche Denunziation', *Ecclesia maledicens*, 320.

[132] *Pontifical Romain*, iii, 10, 612–15. See also discussion in Jaser, *Ecclesia maledicens*, 290–6.

[133] Beaulande, 'Force de la censure', 258–60.

[134] Though it was always made clear that this was only unless the sinner came to their senses.

to make amends and return to the church.[135] If excommunication was severe, it was clear that anyone who eventually succumbed to an eternity in hell because of it had brought this fate upon themselves. An excommunication formula thus ended with a statement of hope: redemption was possible for those who saw the error of their ways. The medicinal nature is evident in such phrases.[136] We have here again excommunication presented as a condemnation to hell in a dramatic fashion, but which was reconcilable with theology because it was not irreparable or automatic. In fact, this would do little to make excommunication itself less terrifying. Once again it hammered home the necessity of absolution.

The 'nisi' clause encapsulates the key difference between the intent behind curses and excommunications. An 'effective' curse was one that successfully afflicted its victim; an excommunication might also afflict the person sentenced, but it was 'effective' only when the affliction caused the victim to return to the bosom of the church. Excommunication had essentially failed if the excommunicate refused to come to their senses. Even when clerics used excommunication in anger, it seems likely that, for many, their desire was to force excommunicates to make satisfaction rather than simply to make them suffer.[137] The distinction between effective curse and effective excommunication is a crucial one.

It is therefore noteworthy that Matthew Paris's descriptions of the two Magna Carta excommunications include no such 'nisi' phrase. If he reported the words spoken correctly, then this indicates that, whatever formulae intended, clergy could omit this final hopeful phrase. Perhaps skipping the phrase was more common for *latae sententiae*, as the Magna Carta sentence was. Alternatively, Paris decided that his narrative was more dramatic if he had the archbishops end with the forceful statement, since the 'nisi' clause undoubtedly weakens the sentiment. A final possibility is that the archbishops did include the standard 'nisi' phrase, but this was barely noticed by those present (as Paris was), who still had the mention of hell, smoking candles, and bells ringing in their ears, distracting them from paying attention to these words. It is in fact difficult, from a written text, to see where these words would best fit. The candles had to be thrown down in conjunction with the 'thus their souls' phrase, and it seems that the bells were rung afterwards. There could then have been a pause while this was happening, then the 'nisi' clause, followed by the communal 'fiat' and 'amen'. If there was no such pause, this 'unless' could easily have been lost in the commotion, perhaps even drowned out by the bells if these were rung before the 'nisi' clause rather than after it. In at least one Middle English text, the 'nisi' clause was replaced with a reiteration of the curse. *Jacob's Well*, a fifteenth-century penitential sermon, includes a malediction, cursing the sinners wherever and whatever they were

---

[135] See Hamilton, 'Anglo-Saxon and Frankish evidence', 169–70 and *passim*.
[136] Jaser, *Ecclesia maledicens*, 229–35.
[137] Inevitably, occasional exceptions to this will have existed.

doing, and ends '& as þe candele schal departe fro his ly3t, so þei are departyd fro þe ly3t of saluacyoun to therknes[138] of dampnacyoun, tyl þei come to dampnacyoun! ffiat! ffiat! Amen'. Just where the 'nisi' clause would typically be, this formula reinforces the idea that excommunication will send people to hell.[139]

The omission by Paris and the difficulties of reconstructing the ceremony, as well as this later evidence, all suggest that a 'nisi' clause could have gone unuttered or unheard. Both law and theology required that all excommunicates be given chances to repent; hell was not an inescapable consequence of excommunication. Yet what people heard and understood is another matter entirely. It was in the interests of churchmen to emphasize the serious consequences. The lived experience of excommunication, how it was represented to the broader population and how it was perceived by the people, was plausibly further away from theological and legal niceties than has always been acknowledged.

Conclusions

Certain points made in this chapter ought to be highlighted. Superficially, many sources present a harsh view of excommunication as a sanction that punished sinners by condemning them to hell. In fact, most of these presentations can be made to fit into the church's doctrine of medicinal excommunication. Excommunicates were given plenty of opportunity to avoid an eternity in hell: excommunication was neither an automatic nor an irreversible condemnation to the inferno. Purgatory rather than hell was therefore logically the immediate destination of those who did die excommunicate. However, the surface reading of these texts is important. The immediate impression is likely to have been the one that stayed with people. The nuances and mitigations are generally revealed only through in depth and often learned analysis. Certainly, clergy wished their subjects to be aware that excommunication could be undone. Yet they did not, in so doing, wish to imply that it was a light matter. Excommunication was the clergy's most potent weapon. It was the spiritual sword. Propagating the idea that the sanction was no serious matter was against their interests. The kinder views of excommunication were to some extent confined to the intellectual sphere. Finally, the ritual of excommunication, with bells and candles, was common and well known. There was much variation in the drama with which such ceremonies were enacted, but they happened regularly and throughout the country. They were useful for terrifying people, and for publicizing information.

---

[138] I.e. darkness.
[139] *Jacob's Well*, ed. Brandeis, 63. Elsewhere in the same text, an inverted 'nisi' clause appears, emphasizing what happens if the sinner does not repent: 'In þis cursyng, who-so deye vnrepentaunt, schal haue a dredeful end', 9. See Carruthers, *'Great Curse'*, 53, and Work, 'Echoes of the anathema', 428.

Excommunication was a legal sanction governed by rules and procedures; its practice could be systematic, routine, and governed by due process. Yet it was also supposed to be frightening.

> In a spirit of fervent anger [Gregory IX] solemnly excommunicated the emperor Frederick...handing him over to be terribly possessed in destruction [of the flesh] [1 Cor. 5:5]. And using the same words, as if thundering in a roar of fury, he vehemently compelled all those listening to terror.[140]

Thus Matthew Paris described the dramatic effect that the pope's 1239 excommunication of Frederick II had upon the audience. For all the legal and theological developments, inducing fear remained at the core of excommunication's potential power. It was beneficial for the church to present it as spiritually severe. Developments in canon law merely exacerbated the tensions inherent in the sanction, which, despite many changes, involved many continuities. In one sense there are contradictions between theory and practice. The sanction cannot be made neat and easily intelligible; inconsistencies cannot be explained away as anachronisms or abuses. The theology emphasizing medicine, the rules enforcing due process, sentences pronounced in anger, the implication of hell, all these were all aspects of excommunication, experienced differently by different people. These different facets must all be recognized.

The fact that excommunication continued to be associated with hell and misfortune is important for the next chapter, which discusses to what extent people were afraid of excommunication. It will be useful to keep in mind throughout the book the potentially serious consequences of excommunication for the afterlife: many of the cases discussed deal with churchmen using excommunication in anger or at least for personal gain. Acknowledging the visual and rhetorical force of the solemn rite is also crucial for assessing how people reacted to sentences, and thus excommunication's efficacy. The ceremony's role was significant not only because it might be frightening, but because of the part it played in publicizing excommunications. As Part III will emphasize, excommunication was an effective way to spread information, and the drama and intelligibility of its ceremony was a crucial part of this.

---

[140] *CM*, iii, 533; cf. Innocent's own letter, *CM*, iii, 571–2.

2
Belief, Fear, and Conscience

They 'declared that they were excommunicates, and that they would prefer to go to hell than submit in the matter of taxation'.[1] Thus the Dunstable Annalist claimed that, in 1229, the excommunicated townsmen of Dunstable refused to desist from the 'fury and malice' they had begun during their dispute with the priory. Though the townsmen's forceful assertion is apparently unique—such explicit desires to suffer eternal damnation for the sake of worldly ends are, unsurprisingly, rarely recorded—in many ways the townsmen's beliefs and actions were unexceptional.[2] First, their declaration reflects an assumption that remaining under their sentence of excommunication would send them 'ad infernum'. This acceptance of the idea that excommunication resulted in damnation appears to have corresponded with the majority of their contemporaries' beliefs. Second, believing that damnation was the consequence of excommunication nevertheless did not cause them to seek immediate reconciliation with the church. Finally, and despite their explicit determination to persevere in their cause, their obstinacy did not last. Like the vast majority of excommunicates, they subsequently made peace with the church. As in most cases, it is impossible to know from the annals' evidence why they gave in, but there is little to indicate that fear of hell was a prime concern.[3] Immediate practical considerations probably mattered far more.

It is extremely difficult to separate spiritual fears from temporal ones, and indeed a central argument of this book is that excommunication's potency relied on far more than engendering fears of damnation. Nevertheless, excommunication was evidently supposed to be terrifying; its spiritual implications were a fundamental part of its power. Assessing to what extent the church succeeded in making the faithful afraid of excommunication, and how such fear affected behaviour, is therefore important. The discussion in this chapter necessitates a somewhat arbitrary distinction to be drawn between 'temporal' and 'spiritual' concerns. Use of 'spiritual' is here strictly limited to issues surrounding the state of the soul, separation from God, and supernatural punishment while living. What did the faithful believe were excommunication's spiritual effects? Were they afraid of it? How did their beliefs and fears (or lack thereof) affect their responses?

---

[1] *Ann. Dunstable*, 122: 'sed profitebantur se esse excommunicatos et se velle potius ad infernum descendere quam in causa tallagii succumbere'.
[2] That is, in thirteenth-century England; comparable examples can be found elsewhere.
[3] The dispute and agreement are described in *Ann. Dunstable*, xii–xiv, 110–11, 118–24; *Annals of Dunstable Priory*, trans. Preest, 71–2, 78–82.

Concerns cannot be divided into neat categories. Fear of damnation, ostracism, loss of reputation, arrest by royal officials, and many other worries might all feature, inseparably, within 'fear of excommunication'. However, if temporal fears are more easily identifiable, fear for the soul should be neither discounted nor overlooked. We can never know what people felt in the past, but neglecting to consider whether individuals were afraid of excommunication because of epistemological difficulties would be to ignore an important part of excommunication's coercive potential.[4]

Dying Excommunicate

The clearest evidence of the fear excommunication generated is the fact that few people were willing to risk dying under a sentence. As others have also observed, excommunicates seem almost always to have sought absolution eventually. Véronique Beaulande found that belief that the sanction was an obstacle to paradise was widespread. One example of a parishioner denying that excommunication endangered souls is, she notes, exceptional. I have found no comparable examples.[5] Those who were not suffering serious temporal consequences and who were indifferent to other aspects of religious life—such as receiving the sacraments—could, as Beaulande notes, remain excommunicated provided death was not imminent, but closeness to death could conquer their resolve.[6] Absolution suddenly became a priority, after a long time excommunicated, because a sentence was an obvious bar to salvation. Though it is impossible to tell what village worshippers felt, representations of hell were plentiful. As J. H. Moorman long ago observed, 'The possibility of being condemned to such an existence was constantly in men's thoughts.'[7] Not constantly enough, perhaps: for some, it took a health scare for excommunication's power to affect their actions.

It was not the church's intention that excommunicates would die still bound by a sentence. Such an eventuality would signify failure: not only was a soul lost, but the church would have received no satisfaction for the offence committed. Even Pope Clement IV, who harboured deep resentment against the baronial rebels as a result of his time as legate, lamented that many of them had died excommunicate at the Battle of Evesham (1265). Though Clement himself had pronounced the sentence against the rebels, he expressed 'profuse grief' that they had died mindful neither of God nor themselves.[8] Sentences were meant to induce offenders to return to the church, not condemn them for eternity. As a result, the church was generous when it came to deathbed absolutions: any priest could absolve someone

---

[4] A similar point has recently been made by Ian Forrest in *Trustworthy Men*, 64.
[5] Beaulande, *Malheur*, 241–2.   [6] Beaulande, *Malheur*, 238.
[7] Moorman, *Church Life in England*, 74–5.   [8] Martène, *Thesaurus*, no. 148.

from excommunication *in articulo mortis*.⁹ Even those who showed signs of repentance before death but who died without absolution were, from 1198, to be considered absolved.¹⁰ Deathbed absolutions from simple priests had some conditions, however. If the sinner recovered, they would have to make appropriate satisfaction and do fitting penance (for those already dead, satisfaction would be fulfilled by their families, and they would receive penance in purgatory).¹¹ If the conditions were not met, the excommunicates would fall back into their original sentences.

Excommunicates who died unabsolved were deprived of Christian burial.¹² Excommunication was considered contagious in death as in life, so those under the ban were forbidden from entering churches while living. Denial of ecclesiastical burial was not restricted to excommunicates; interdicts also prevented burial in sacred ground. As Peter Clarke has observed, this deprivation was 'perhaps the most feared effect of an interdict, distressing not only to the dying but also to their family and friends'.¹³ Yet the majority of those who died under interdict were denied Christian burial through no fault of their own. By contrast, excommunicates brought it upon themselves; their ignominious burial was indicative of their damnation. When Robert Winchelsey lifted the interdict on Dover in 1299 (imposed early the previous year, after townspeople acting with the mayor's consent violently and publicly assaulted two rectors), he judged that bodies which had been buried in consecrated ground illegally during the interdict need not be exhumed. They were to have no grave markings, however, which indicates they had previously been given such insignia. If so, this would help with the difficult task of identifying the correct bodies. Winchelsey reserved the right, however, to exhume bodies of townsmen who had directly caused the interdict and who were thus excommunicated.¹⁴ The illicit burial of bodies in cemeteries demonstrates the importance placed on burial in this sacred and communal space.

---

⁹ Similarly, during interdicts, giving the viaticum to the dying was permitted: Clarke, *Interdict*, 148–50.

¹⁰ As Innocent III informed the prior of St Andrews: X 5.39.28; Vodola, *Excommunication*, 38–9. This countered the earlier maxim that the church can bind and loose the living but not the dead: C.24, q.3, c.2. See also Clarke, *Interdict*, 156–7, 164–5.

¹¹ Chobham, *Summa*, 202–3; Clarke, *Interdict*, 240–1.

¹² The rule was based on the Old Testament. See Jaser, *Ecclesia maledicens*, 197–9; Jégou, 'La sepulture de l'âne'; Schmitz-Esser, *Corpse in the Middle Ages*, 501–15, though the latter focuses on political figures who often achieved proper burial eventually. Criminals and excommunicates being given ignominious burials is evident in the Anglo-Saxon period. See Blair, *Church in Anglo-Saxon Society*, 464; Crawfield, 'Differentiation in the Later Anglo-Saxon Burial Ritual', 94; Reynolds, *Anglo-Saxon Deviant Burial Customs*, 25, 214.

¹³ Clarke, *Interdict*, 161. The implications here have been discussed at greater length by Clarke in relation to interdict, *Interdict*, 160–6; Vodola, *Excommunication*, 156–8.

¹⁴ *Reg. Winchelsey*, ii, 885–90. See also i, 222–3, 225–9, 237–8, 240–2, ii, 884–5; Graham, 'An interdict on Dover'. Cf. Clarke, *Interdict*, 164; Beaulande, *Malheur*, 220–1.

The rule precluding Christian burial for those under sentences of excommunication appears to have generally been followed.[15] Thus an unknown baronial supporter who died in the Battle of Lincoln (1217) was buried outside the city at a crossroads as an excommunicate.[16] Baronial adherents who died in the Battle of Evesham (1265) suffered a similar fate.[17] A more drastic requirement was exhuming those who had died and were only later discovered to be excommunicates.[18] In 1305, Winchelsey ordered that Hugh le Blake of Canterbury, who had died excommunicate but was buried in a cemetery 'amongst faithful Christians' by certain clerks 'led by the sin of cupidity', should be disinterred and placed in 'a profane or unconsecrated place'. The clerks had perhaps been bribed by friends or family, once again showing burial's importance for those who outlived the deceased.[19] In 1273, Pope Gregory X ordered that the bodies of citizens of Norwich, if any had died excommunicated and been buried in an ecclesiastical cemetery, should be 'exhumed . . . and cast aside far away from Christian burial'.[20]

It was, therefore, safer not to wait until the deathbed to secure absolution. Going through official channels was preferable if everyone was to be made aware that absolution had been obtained, not least in order to secure ecclesiastical burial. Not only did this guarantee that the absolution was legal and properly documented, but the penitent could ensure that restitution was completed. If the conditions for an absolution, for example returning stolen goods or otherwise making compensation, were not fulfilled, the absolution would be invalidated.

In 1299, Adam le Warner of Bolingbroke, parishioner in the prebend of Asgarby, chose the safer option, securing absolution before he died. He did so explicitly because he had fallen ill.[21] Adam had incurred *Qui malitiose ecclesias* for illicitly erecting a sheepfold in Asgarby parish and for 'other injuries' inflicted on the prebend's rights. He had been 'judicially convicted through legitimate process' and been publicly announced to be excommunicated.[22] A proctor, Henry de Langton, subsequently appeared before the bishop of Lincoln on Adam's behalf because Adam was at death's door. Henry supplicated the bishop to impose the benefit of absolution on Adam, especially since the latter was in such great danger, 'lest he, prevented by death, die with risk of damnation, without having obtained absolution'. Adam was prepared to make full satisfaction and offer guarantees that he would obey mandates. Though he could not be present because he was 'debilitated by grave infirmity', Adam submitted himself to the dean and chapter as a penitent. As proctor, Henry recognised that Adam had no right to erect a sheepfold in the parish without the prebendary's licence, renouncing Adam's and

---

[15] As Clarke has also shown for interdicts: *Interdict*, 161–2.   [16] *CM*, iii, 23.
[17] *Lanercost*, 77.   [18] Flamborough, *Liber Poenitentialis*, 158.
[19] *Reg. Winchelsey*, i, 488–9. Clarke notes the extreme example of a revolt in Dax (south-west France) sparked by refusal to provide ecclesiastical burial to an excommunicate: *Interdict*, 219.
[20] *Cotton*, 425.   [21] *Registrum Antiquissimum*, ii, no. 499.
[22] Adam's original sentence is in *Reg. Sutton*, vi, 133–4.

his successor's rights to make any such claim. In this way, Adam obtained absolution, with the proviso that henceforth he did not presume to erect a sheepfold or do anything else to the prejudice of the prebend's liberties. If he did, he would *ipso facto* fall back into his earlier sentence, be denied Christian burial after death, and incur perjury and infamy. In a separate document, Adam renounced his claim to the incumbent prebendary of Asgarby, thereby ensuring all conditions of absolution were fulfilled.[23]

Adam le Warner therefore left nothing to chance or for his heirs to execute on his behalf. He could die secure in the knowledge that his absolution was approved (provided he lived long enough for Henry to report on his audience with the dean and chapter). Adam had not in fact been excommunicated very long, probably about six weeks.[24] It is evident, nevertheless, that his submission directly related to his illness; his fear of damnation was explicitly noted. It is further significant that deprivation of Christian burial was specifically threatened if Adam broke the conditions for his absolution. Though this was a standard consequence of excommunication, it was not routinely noted, and was presumably an added threat with reference to his ill health.

In a comparable case documented in the Curia Regis Rolls (1226), the excommunicate similarly had to renounce a claim on behalf of his heirs in order to secure absolution. During a dispute over land between the abbot of Thorney and a certain Walter de Trayly, the latter had been excommunicated for refusing to give the abbot a charter assigning him forty acres of land, as per their prior agreement. However, Walter subsequently fell ill. His parents were concerned that he might die under this sentence (the editor plausibly suggests that *morari* be corrected to *mori*), so at the beginning of Lent Walter made a charter assigning the abbot the land. He died on the vigil of Palm Sunday. Walter's son, who subsequently attempted to recover the land, lost his case because his father had assigned it before his death. Walter had conceded his right in order to avoid dying excommunicate; as a result, his family lost the land in perpetuity.[25]

In both these cases, the sanction's spiritual terrors were effective. Excommunication had secured legal documents confirming the rights and liberties of those who had made use of it, ensuring that no reversals in situation or attitude would profit the excommunicates. John Arnold, for instance, has described how a certain Pierre Isarn, excommunicated for fifteen years in southern France (1270s), fell gravely ill and received absolution. When he subsequently recovered, however, Pierre refused to cooperate with the authorities and was re-excommunicated.[26] As

---

[23] *Registrum Antiquissimum*, ii, no. 500. The charter is very damaged.
[24] The memorandum of Adam's absolution is dated 11 February 1299. The dean and chapter had asked the bishop to have Adam's excommunication denounced locally on 3 January 1299. Adam is likely to have been excommunicated shortly before this. Bishop Sutton ordered the relevant deans to publicize Adam's sentence. *Reg. Sutton*, vi, 133–4.
[25] *CRR*, xii, no. 1815.   [26] Arnold, *Belief and Unbelief*, 167.

Walter's son found, the charter meant he was unable to pursue his claims. Had he recovered, Walter himself would have been similarly incapacitated. In comparison, the heirs of William Marshal, who reportedly died excommunicated, refused to return the lands he had stolen from the church so that their father was posthumously confirmed to be excommunicated rather than absolved.[27] The Marshal's case, and perhaps that of Walter de Trayly, shows that it was prudent not to leave fulfilment of conditions in the hands of others, who might choose worldly gain over their relative's salvation. Greedy relatives might imperil salvation by refusing to obey the church's mandates, a concern both for those seeking absolution and for churchmen seeking to secure permanent rights.

Others might, of course, have been happy to make sacrifices for their relatives' souls. As Peter Clarke has noted, families could be compelled to make satisfaction for their deceased heirs when ecclesiastical burial was denied them.[28] This is perhaps what happened in the case of Sir Richard de Scholand, who died excommunicate in 1301. Richard had been excommunicated for committing sacrilege (it is unclear when). There is no way of knowing whether he intentionally failed to reconcile with the church or if a sudden death prevented him from doing so. His friends, however, sought to persuade the archbishop of Canterbury of the latter, corroborating Clarke's observation that family and friends were distressed by refusal of a deceased person's Christian burial.[29] Robert Winchelsey was petitioned to provide a remedy because Richard remained unburied as an excommunicate. Wanting to remove the shame ('opprobrium') of both the deceased and his friends, who were suffering through this delay, Winchelsey ordered the dean of Shoreham to investigate whether Richard had repented before death.[30] If it was established that he had made evident signs of repentance while alive and had been prevented from receiving absolution by death, the dean was to absolve him posthumously.[31] The dean was not to hand over the body for ecclesiastical burial, however, until either his heirs, the executors of his will, or other friends, made satisfaction for the 17*l*. 10*s*., oblations, damages, and expenses Richard owed.[32] It may be hoped that the 'friends' of Richard who had sought this remedy did not balk at paying these costs.

Not all excommunications related to finances, however. There were no financial repercussions for Simon de Montfort's family when they sought to secure proper burial for the deceased earl. The Annals of Osney report that, after Simon was

---

[27] *CM*, iv, 492–5, and see Chapter 1 above, 41–4.   [28] Clarke, *Interdict*, 161.

[29] The document mentions the suffering of Richard's friends ('amicorum suorum') rather than his family.

[30] *Reg. Winchelsey*, i, 402–3.

[31] See X 5.39.28 for Innocent III's ruling on posthumous absolution. Cf. Chobham, *Summa*, 261, where he explains that those who died in tournaments (participation in which incurred excommunication), if found with their hand 'with three fingers erect as if to make a cross on the forehead', were deemed penitent and could be buried within a cemetery.

[32] *Reg. Winchelsey*, i, 403–4.

killed at Evesham, his body was exhumed and thrown into a remote and hidden place by certain men who still felt vengeful towards him. They asserted that, bound by a sentence of anathema and infected by the leprosy of treason, he did not deserve a Christian burial.[33] Two years later, in 1267, Simon's son Amaury petitioned the pope to sanction an ecclesiastical burial for his father, who Amaury claimed had sought and obtained absolution *de facto* before his death.[34] It is uncertain whether the legate Ottobuono, who was instructed to discover the truth, ordered that Montfort be reburied. But it is likely he did: several chroniclers report that he absolved Montfort and his supporters at the Council of London in 1268.[35] If approaching death prompted absolutions, these examples indicate that fear of being deprived ecclesiastical burial was a significant element here. Profane burial induced shame at the same time as it represented a physical barrier to salvation.

Where no specific rights had to be renounced to secure absolution, the chances of *volte-faces* were perhaps higher. Thus certain baronial supporters were re-excommunicated by Pope Clement IV in 1265 because they had obtained absolution 'in true or simulated sickness'. Leaving aside, for the moment, the suspicion that some of these men had gained absolution by feigning illness, the absolved had failed to fulfil the conditions for their absolutions and were thus subject to their original censure. No charters or similar were relevant here; they had simply been required, and failed, to shun Simon and his supporters as heathens and publicans (Matthew 18:17). The legate was told to warn them to correct their ways (again), entirely abandoning support for the rebels, within one month of becoming well (or from obtaining absolution if they had been faking).[36] Sent less than a month before several of these (unnamed) men presumably died at Evesham, as Clement later mourned, the letter almost certainly failed to reach England in time for any of them to have been made aware of its contents.

The case of Sewal de Bovill, archbishop of York (1256–58), who also sought absolution when ill, necessitated renouncing something quite different to Adam and Walter. Sewal did not have to give up any possessions or rights, but rather his conviction: he believed his sentence to be unjust. The narrative is recounted by Matthew Paris. Sewal had been excommunicated by the pope for objecting to a papal provision in his diocese. Acting in a manner reminiscent of his contemporary Robert Grosseteste, Paris observed, Sewal objected on the grounds that the Italian being promoted was unknown in England, ignorant of English, and utterly unworthy. Remaining steadfast in this conviction, the archbishop refused to accept that the pope's excommunication against him was just. However, when Sewal fell ill and 'sensed his death was undoubtedly near', he reconsidered. Paris described his thought-process thus, 'lest from contempt of the papal sentence,

---

[33] *Annales Monasterii de Oseneia*, 174–8. [34] *Reg. Clement IV*, no. 452.
[35] *C&S*, 746–7. [36] *Reg. Clement IV*, no. 122.

although unjust, it becomes just, I, having been ensnared, humbly pray to be absolved from such chains [of excommunication]'. The archbishop knew that obedience to the mandates of the church was required, regardless of their perceived injustice.[37] Although Paris notes that Sewal had suffered various injuries as a result of the excommunication, in particular to his reputation, he presents the archbishop's impetus for seeking absolution as a response to the illness that would soon kill him.[38] Sewal's submission to the papacy was reluctant—he forcefully condemned the pope's unjust actions, appealing to the 'supreme and incorruptible Judge', with heaven and earth as witness to his harassment at the pope's hands— but his imminent death meant he had little choice but to submit.[39]

A final example demonstrates the change of attitude proximity to death could precipitate. Even King Edward I, who was never sentenced with excommunication, was not immune to the concern about the sanction that illness generated. Perhaps the indulgences he had received as a crusader encouraged him to have confidence in his own salvation, for (unlike his father) he demonstrated little concern about the possibility that he was excommunicated. Though Edward sought, in 1284, to clear his conscience ('ad serenationem conscientie domini regis') about offences committed during the Welsh wars and the civil war, there is little evidence of comparable worry until 1301.[40] This date is notable because it was four years after he had probably incurred excommunication during the *Clericis laicos* dispute.[41] Upon the clergy's refusal to grant him a tax without papal consent (as Boniface VIII's bull forbade on pain of *ipso facto* excommunication), Edward removed the clergy from his protection and seized their lands and possessions. He then allowed them to buy back his favour and their possessions, thereby receiving the money he desired. The bishop of Lincoln, for one, strongly implied that Edward had incurred not only the excommunication specified in *Clericis laicos*, but also *Quicumque de domibus* and *Si quis suadente*. Thus Oliver Sutton publicized these sentences in 1297:

---

[37] For the rule that an unjust sentence became just if scorned, see below, 93.
[38] For reputation in this case, see Chapter 5, 201-202.   [39] *CM*, v, 692.
[40] A letter of Pope Martin IV declares that Edward, 'solicitously thinking about his health and that of others, humbly supplicated us that, since he is believed to be manifoldly guilty, we take care to provide about this'. The letter makes no mention of specific absolution granted to the king, however. Carefully denying that homicides perpetrated in churches or cemeteries had proceeded from his will, Edward duly made various restitutions to the church and the poor to clear his conscience. *Foedera*, I.ii.641, 642; cf. *Reg. G. Giffard*, 248. Nevertheless, Archbishop Pecham wrote to the king ten days later, warning him about his conscience in relation to offences committed against ecclesiastical liberty during the war, and specifically stating that the king could not excuse himself from the damages inflicted on churches, ecclesiastical persons, and the innocent. If the king had been severe on perpetrators of such injuries from the start, most would never have occurred (*Foedera*, I.ii.643; Douie, *Archbishop Pecham*, 260-1). Nor did Edward care about Pope Nicholas IV's 1290 warnings concerning his salvation for various infringements of ecclesiastical liberty (Odoricus Raynaldus, *Annales*, ed. Mansi, iv, 87-8). For Edward's piety see Prestwich, 'Piety of Edward I' and *Edward I*, 111-14.
[41] See Denton, *Robert Winchelsey*, 80-136; Prestwich, *Edward I*, 412-18.

If perhaps [the king] believes in all conscience that he has excuse for his mandates and is not alive to the peril to souls which could ensue, or perhaps thinks himself protected by some privilege or reason which, he supposes, saves him from having incurred the sentence in question, we do not intend any prejudice to him by our declaration and publication.[42]

The bishop added that the king's son was certainly innocent.[43] Sutton specifically referred to the king's assumption that he was immune from excommunication. Edward either assumed he was protected, or did not care if he incurred the excommunication, provided he avoided public denunciations.

Only in 1301 was Edward absolved from any possible excommunication. The reason for the king's sudden desire to deal with his guilt in these matters, nearly four years after the *Clericis laicos* dispute had come to a head, and after a thirty-year reign, is made clear. Pope Boniface VIII absolved Edward from any excommunication he might have incurred, 'noting that you are now declining into old age and because of this intending salubriously to provide for your salvation'. The king, now in his sixties, was thinking about what might happen to him after death. He asked the pope to provide for his salvation because he had, as a result of wars, disturbances, and scandals, harmed churches and clergy through 'illicit impositions and exactions'. This surely refers primarily to the *Clericis laicos* dispute.[44] Boniface did not state that Edward had certainly incurred excommunication. Absolution was simply a precaution.

The second time that Edward received papal absolution from excommunication was the year before his death, on 5 August 1306.[45] Edward, according to Clement V's letters, had 'humbly supplicated' that he and his supporters be provided with a salutary remedy for various offences—including arson, sacrilege, and plundering (*rapina*)—committed while fighting against rebels and the kingdom's enemies (presumably in the Scottish wars). Clement absolved the king from any sentences of excommunication, suspension, or interdict that he had incurred. He did not want the king's 'gnawing conscience' to cause him disquiet ('nec te aliquatenus remordens conscientia inquietet'), but he also advised that it would help his salvation if he were generous in granting immunities, freedoms, and other gifts to churches and other places that had been burnt or destroyed. Financial consequences were here optional, rather than conditions for absolution. The timing is again significant: Edward was ill in the summer of 1306. Though he

---

[42] *Reg. Sutton*, vi, 25; the translation is Jeffrey Denton's in *Robert Winchelsey*, 156–7.
[43] Hill's belief that this section of Sutton's speech was never published, 'to spare the king public offence and humiliation' (*Reg. Sutton*, vi, 23 n.1), cannot be accepted. Both Denton (*Robert Winchelsey*, 156–6 and n. 243) and David Burton ('Politics, Propaganda and Public Opinion', 247) have also doubted it.
[44] *Foedera*, I.ii.931. Philip IV of France received a similar absolution in 1305 (Brown, 'Moral imperatives and conundrums of conscience', 11–14).
[45] *Foedera*, I.ii.994.

recovered in the autumn, he was again to fall ill and die the following year.[46] It is therefore likely that the king, concerned to ensure his salvation, was insuring himself against the real possibility of death in the summer of 1306. After Edward I's death, Edward II (potentially on his father's wishes) made a similar request to Clement, who provided the new king with absolution but declined to absolve Edward I again since he had done so before his death.[47]

The unwillingness of excommunicates to die under a sentence is the greatest proof that, in general, its spiritual consequences were believed and feared. Some excommunicates did die under their sentences, but most were absolved before they died. Even those who had previously shown contempt for sentences, or who believed them to be unjust, seem to have reconciled with the church eventually. A few figures bucked this trend, either by accident or through conviction. Even then, friends or relatives sought to provide for posthumous absolution. Certainly, part of the desire for absolution in such circumstances related to standing within the community and the shame associated with profane burial, but no small part of it must be judged to relate to fear of damnation (for oneself or others). No prayers for the souls of excommunicates would, of course, take effect. Given that the church permitted any priest to perform deathbed absolutions from all excommunication sentences, it is likely that many more sought absolution in such circumstances. Few were willing to risk jeopardizing salvation by remaining separated from God and from the community of the faithful in death.

Unforced Absolution

For the most part, when excommunicates sought absolution there is no indication whether they were ill or dying. Without imminent death as part of the equation, it is less persuasive to argue that spiritual fears drove desires to have sentences lifted. It certainly should not be assumed, in the absence of information, that those who sought absolution did so primarily because of spiritual fears.[48] Whilst eventual damnation may have been a factor, more immediate issues linked to social exclusion, loss of legal rights, and loss of reputation are likely to have been more immediate concerns. Death and the hellish eventualities linked to excommunication would have seemed a long way off.[49]

---

[46] Prestwich, *Edward I*, 507, 557.   [47] *Foedera*, II.i.74.

[48] Tyler Lange, for example, in his recent book *Excommunication for Debt*, discusses evidence provided by registers recording sentences and absolutions. His monograph focuses on economic developments before the Reformation, but he nevertheless tends to revert to the assumption that these absolutions should be attributed to spiritual fears, leaving anxieties about reputation and social exclusion largely undiscussed.

[49] John Arnold notes that the tendency of people to think this way meant the church sought constantly to remind them about death: *Belief and Unbelief*, 167.

There are requests for absolution, however, that were made in circumstances that allow emphasis to be placed on conscience rather than external pressures. In some cases, people sought absolution from excommunications although they had not been publicly and judicially excommunicated. They worried they had incurred a *lata sententia*. Excommunication imposed as a judicial sanction belonged to the external forum, which dealt with crimes and offences against public order tried in court, and imposed *poenae*.[50] However, many excommunications were incurred but never publicly announced or legally confirmed. These came under the aegis of the internal, penitential forum, which dealt with private sins and imposed *poenitentiae*. Absolution from such excommunications could be received in the penitential forum. The distinction between fora was nonetheless not absolute.[51] If a crime was not manifest, it would in fact be impossible to prosecute it publicly; the matter would have to be dealt with privately.[52] Though what took place under the seal of confession tends to leave no record, evidence for absolutions sought from *latae sententiae* survives because of the considerable overlap between sentences incurred *ipso facto* and excommunications for which absolutions were reserved.[53] Most *latae sententiae* excommunications required absolution from either the papacy or, in England, the archbishop of Canterbury (depending on who had issued the excommunication in the first place). Those who sought absolution therefore petitioned these authorities, leaving written records. As has recently been shown by Peter Clarke, Patrick Zutshi, Ludwig Schmugge, and Arnaud Fossier, the papal penitentiary was concerned with matters of conscience.[54] From the twelfth century, the church increasingly urged that every Christian examine their conscience. The Fourth Lateran Council (c. 21) famously required yearly confession from every Christian. In the thirteenth century, *latae sententiae* and general sentences proliferated, and were regularly publicized so that people were aware of them. Given this environment, it is perhaps understandable that people considered it prudent to seek absolution voluntarily if an automatic sentence was thought to have been incurred.[55]

---

[50] Clarke, *Interdict*, 86.

[51] See Fossier, 'Le for "interne"'; Fossier, *Bureau de âmes*, 439–43, 448–66, and Goering, 'Internal forum', which discuss the relationship between the judicial and penitential fora. They were 'two interrelated spheres of the church's authority' (Goering at 380). See also Beaulande, *Malheur*, 91. Mary Mansfield pointed out that the fora were further blurred by the fact the many offences that incurred *ipso facto* excommunication required public penance, even if they had been confessed secretly: *Humiliation*, 121–4.

[52] Publicizing a crime that had hitherto been private might generate scandal. See below, 203. Also Beaulande, *Malheur*, 251–2.

[53] Although see Murray, 'Confession as a historical source', particularly 53–7; Longère, 'Les évêques et l'administration'; Fossier, *Bureau de âmes*, 415–24.

[54] Clarke, 'Central authority and local powers'; Clarke and Zutschi, *Supplications from England and Wales*; Schmugge, 'Towards the medieval conscience'. They all discuss fifteenth-century petitions.

[55] Beaulande, *Malheur*, 93–4.

There were obvious practical difficulties with *latae sententiae* and general sentences. It was up to an unknown excommunicate to confess their crime—though general sentences also launched investigations—and many probably did not (or perhaps did so only on their deathbeds, like Edward I). The issue is amusingly and aptly demonstrated by a miracle tale included in Peter of Cornwall's *Book of Revelations* (*c*.1200). In the parish of Borden near Sittingbourne, some time before 1170, an old man was forced to sell his wood. Being old and housebound, he delegated the task to his son. The son, however, was greedy, and defrauded his father of most of the money he had received from the sale. Knowing he had been tricked but not suspecting his son, the old man asked the parish priest to bind with anathema whoever had cheated him. Despite denunciations being made by the priest in church, with the guilty son present, the adolescent admitted his guilt neither publicly nor privately. After he had dissembled in this way, unrepentant and taking no account of Satan's possession of both his body and his soul (cf. 1 Corinthians 5:5), while asleep one night—wearing nothing but a cloth nightcap—he was dragged through the wall by two malignant spirits calling 'you are ours, you are ours, and you are coming with us'. Only his nightcap was found, but the spirits forced sailors to carry them and their naked prisoner across the Thames 'for no other reason, I suspect, than that what had happened should afterwards be made known by them'.[56]

Until he was dragged away by demons, the son was 'getting away with' his crime. This was precisely why divine intervention was needed, and why it was necessary that the sailors witness it and spread the word. The story is testimony of the problem inherent in sentences aimed at unknown criminals and in *latae sententiae*: how could guilty people be persuaded to return to the church through any of the usual means if they had incurred excommunication without anyone else knowing? Some were discovered through investigations launched by bishops. If the guilty were discovered, matters could proceed much as they would for an *ab homine* sentence.[57] Many others, however, like the son in Peter's tale, must have kept quiet about their guilt and continued as normal, going to church and receiving the Eucharist.[58] The story itself was presumably aimed at such people (though it is only extant in one manuscript), and is testament to their existence. Whether or not influenced by miracle stories, evidence indicates that some people felt sufficient unease that they sought absolution from sentences that were never publicly proclaimed.

In theory, there were no temporal advantages to reconciling with the church if the excommunication had not been publicly pronounced. Sentences needed to be judicially confirmed in order for individuals to be denounced by name, to be publicly shunned, or to suffer loss of legal standing or invocation of the secular

---

[56] Peter of Cornwall, *Book of Revelations*, ed. Easting and Sharpe, no. 2897.
[57] See Hill, 'General excommunications'.   [58] *Reg. Sutton*, iii, xliv.

arm. These excommunications were nonetheless as valid as any other: the souls of such excommunicates were imperilled. Yet they might be able to carry on living just as they had before. They had only to contend with their consciences and their private fears for their souls. In all the cases discussed below, it is possible to argue that more temporal considerations, not revealed in the evidence, prompted these absolutions being sought. They might, for instance, have been victims of social exclusion and loss of reputation as a result of common knowledge of an offence rather than official promulgation. However, any such treatment would not have been authorized by the church as with public excommunications.[59]

Whilst these possibilities should be acknowledged, the argument advanced here is that absolutions sought by 'unrevealed' or 'unknown' excommunicates indicate that the sanction plagued people's consciences and induced them to seek reassurance.[60] As Christian Jaser has noted, putting pressure on individual consciences in order to induce a self-denunciation was, to a large extent, the aim of these automatic sentences.[61] Documents relating to the absolution of people privately believing themselves to be excommunicated, in this period usually extant in episcopal registers, use language of conscience rather than chastisement. The implication is that these were people afraid for their spiritual wellbeing. Though unrevealed excommunications generated practical difficulties, absolutions from them perhaps get us closer to the 'internal' feelings of excommunicates than any other source. However we interpret the cases below, and there is a good deal of room for differing opinions, the excommunicates were not facing any *legal* consequences of excommunication.

A particularly curious example of a man seeking absolution from a sentence he had incurred automatically is found in the register of Archbishop Winchelsey. Simon, son of Gilbert of Walsoken (Norwich diocese), had petitioned the papal penitentiary about an excommunication he had incurred for laying violent hands on the local rector (*Si quis suadente*). The archbishop supplied notification of his absolution from this sentence, enjoining (unspecified) penance on Simon.[62] The fact that the papal penitentiary was involved immediately indicates that this was a matter of conscience rather than law, and that no legal measures had been taken against Simon. The letter is notable for another reason, however: according to certain legal exceptions, Simon was not in fact excommunicated. The circumstances of Simon's assault are detailed in the notification. He had found the rector, Stephen, with his wife, both naked ('nudum cum nuda').[63] This was one of the

---

[59] See Mansfield, *Humiliation*, 118–22, and below, Chapters 3–5.

[60] These terms are not ideal, but such excommunications must be distinguished from those publicly pronounced and subject to legal procedures. Sentences incurred *ipso facto* could be made public (see Chapter 6 in particular), so using this term will not suffice.

[61] Jaser, *Ecclesia maledicens*, 369; Jaser, 'Ostensio exclusionis', 364. Beaulande observes that there are more absolutions recorded than excommunications for *Si quis suadente* because it was a *lata sententia*: *Malheur*, 96.

[62] See Fossier, *Bureau de âmes*, 367–8, for the penitentiary absolving in such cases.

[63] *Reg. Winchelsey*, i, 340–1.

exceptions to *Si quis suadente*. Someone laying violent hands on a cleric found 'shamefully' ('turpiter') with his wife, mother, sister, or daughter, was not excommunicated or compelled to go to the apostolic see (X 5.39.3). A serious assault might still require absolution from the papacy, but it is carefully noted that Simon had not even drawn blood. Further, those excommunicated for lesser violence ('pro levi manuum iniectione in clericum'), even without another exception, could be absolved by a bishop (X 5.39.17). Simon in theory need not have taken his case to the papal curia at all.

There is probably more to this story than we can know. In a further letter, the archbishop instructed the bishop of Norwich (probably not previously involved because he had only just been elected) to take control of the satisfaction to be enjoined upon Simon.[64] The bishop was to ensure it was just, in case the injured rector made himself 'excessively difficult' about it.[65] Simon may therefore have petitioned the curia because he was worried that he would not receive fair treatment closer to home. Stephen cannot have been pursuing Simon for the assault in the judicial forum (surely a bad move, given it would reveal his own offence), because in such circumstances Simon would not have been able to circumvent the proceedings by petitioning the penitentiary. Similarly, if this was a roundabout way for Simon to incriminate the adulterous rector, against whom he harboured justifiable anger, this would not have been a standard, or perhaps even a possible, route to having him reprimanded.[66] Winchelsey made no mention of admonishing or investigating the incontinent rector. Both offence and dispensation were supposed to be, and to remain, secret.[67] It is conceivable that Stephen was refusing to cooperate with Simon for fear of being discovered, and that Simon was forced to approach the highest authority to secure the absolution he desired. *Si quis suadente* was the best-known *lata sententia*, and it is more than plausible that he knew his actions typically incurred a sentence but was less well versed on the exceptions which excused his case. The standard advice, if someone was in doubt whether they had incurred a sentence, was that they consult the pope.[68] It remains odd that no one, at any point in this process, pointed out that the circumstances and nature of Simon's assault exempted him, since these exceptions were hardly unknown to churchmen.[69]

---

[64] Simon had apparently not acted alone: here Ralph 'the Gardiner' is introduced as his accomplice.
[65] *Reg. Winchelsey*, i, 341–2.
[66] Waiting for the bishop's visitation was one option, or going to the bishop directly, as did certain men from the diocese of Salisbury, accusing the prior of St Guthlac of incontinence (he pleaded defamation): *Reg. Swinfield*, 406–7.
[67] Fossier, 'Le for "interne"', 66.
[68] E.g. Peter the Chanter counselled that if someone doubted whether or not he had incurred *Si quis suadente*, he should consult the pope because it might be more dangerous to do nothing: *Summa*, 400.
[69] The exceptions of *Si quis suadente* were noted in many widely circulated texts, such as Raymond of Peñafort's *De poenitentia* (Book 3), Robert Grosseteste's *Templum Dei* (VII.8), and Robert of Flamborough's *Liber Poenitentialis* (157). Cf. a case in Sutton's register, where someone was judged not to have incurred *Si quis suadente* on the grounds of another exception: *Reg. Sutton*, iii, 126–7.

Simon's absolution is testament to the extra-judicial pressures exerted by excommunication. Any compulsion he felt to seek absolution cannot have been imposed on him by churchmen acting within the legal system of the institutional church. No legal process preceded his petition. Unrecorded social pressures may have affected him—perhaps he was being shunned by locals who were aware of the incident—but it is not at all clear that there was any provision for publicizing such an absolution, or that the penitent would receive it in a written document.[70] It is equally possible that the thought of being excommunicated caused him disquiet. It does not seem likely that Simon felt much guilt for his actions.

Examples of such petitions to ecclesiastical authorities seeking absolution from unrevealed excommunications are far rarer from laymen than they are from clerics and monks. The overwhelming majority of cases in a thirteenth-century papal penitentiary formulary, of which there are many, deal with clergy.[71] It could be argued that men in orders were more pious than laymen, or that they knew the law better, but the issue is complicated by the fact that if a clergyman discharged his divine offices while excommunicated, all his acts were irregular. Nor could an excommunicated cleric be promoted to higher orders. There was therefore a risk that, if it later became known that a monk or priest had fallen into a sentence of excommunication many years before, his career would be impeded, and he would be deemed 'irregular'. Papal dispensation was required to lift suspension in such instances, in order that a particular individual could proceed to promotion.[72] Clergy may therefore have been as concerned with their temporal livelihoods as with their salvation.[73]

In 1292 a subdeacon, Thomas of Codicote, consulted the papal penitentiary because he was concerned about the joy he had felt at the capital punishment of certain murderers who had killed his brother-in-law, which might impede his progression to higher orders.[74] The reply from the penitentiary, included in Oliver Sutton's episcopal register, carefully noted that Thomas had not provided 'counsel, help, or favour' to the capture or sentencing of the murderers.[75] Excommunication is never explicitly mentioned, but Rosalind Hill credibly suggested that Thomas was seeking absolution from an excommunication or

---

[70] Those absolved in the external forum could expect to receive absolution in writing: Clarke, *Interdict*, 246. Mansfield, *Humiliation*, 119, notes shaming of rumoured sinners (not necessarily excommunicates).

[71] See *Formulary of the Papal Penitentiary*, ed. Lea. There are hundreds of petitions, but most mention that the petitioner is a cleric or regular of some sort.

[72] See for instance Flamborough, *Liber Poenitentialis*, 141.

[73] Schmugge, 'Towards the medieval conscience', 221–3, discusses the issues at stake for a cleric, and possible motives to approach the penitentiary.

[74] Cf. Peñafort, *De Poenitentia*, 427–8: discussion whether someone incurs excommunication for rejoicing at the news that a cleric who has harmed him has been wounded (he does not incur a sentence).

[75] *Reg. Sutton*, iii, 191–2.

suspension incurred because of his inappropriate joy.[76] It is difficult to see how this could have been used against him in any legal sense. Only he could know whether he had been 'gavisus', though others might deem that he appeared joyful. Perhaps he had been threatened—his petition mentions that he is supplicating lest a competitor use it against him—and the church was particularly cautious in such matters. Even if the truth could not be proved, he could have been in trouble. However, it was also stated that he appealed 'for the greater security of his conscience', so that apostolic mercy might supply 'a remedy of salvation'. The circumstances thus allow the interpretation that Thomas was concerned about his conscience and salvation as well as his career.

The bishop of Moray in 1255 expressed his doubt that he had incurred any sentence but was nevertheless afraid that he had incurred excommunication for opposing the promotion of a man to dean. The man in question had a papal provision that threatened all those contradicting it with excommunication; the bishop had acted in order to avoid perjury. Regardless of his doubts, he needed dispensation for irregularities he had incurred for exercising his episcopal office while excommunicated, and the pope therefore provided for his 'conscience'.[77] Similarly, in 1213 a scholar realized that as a teenager he had fallen into *Si quis suadente* for using too much force while teaching—not with enthusiasm for educating his students (which would have excepted him from the sentence), but to extort things from them—but had subsequently forgotten about his excess. He had since taken minor orders without first receiving absolution, which he now humbly sought.[78]

Laymen are more commonly found seeking absolution before the bishop. These cases were not in the penitential forum, they were public, but they were nonetheless spontaneous absolutions not driven by legal processes. These voluntary absolutions were usually prompted by general sentences (like that on behalf of the old man deceived by his son). Thus four foresters voluntarily came to the bishop of Hereford, Thomas Cantilupe, 'fearing that they were bound by the sentence of excommunication' pronounced against those impeding his liberty. They evidently felt they had incurred this, and 'humbly sought' the gift of absolution.[79] In a similar case, John Cros, Peter of Dean, and Walter Edmund admitted to entering the archbishop of Canterbury's chase at Southmalling, Sussex, thereby incurring an excommunication recently pronounced against such infringers of the archbishop's rights. They did so 'fearing' the excommunication pronounced and admitting to their actions, 'asserting that their consciences were injured on account of that wickedness'. They thus sought absolution,

---

[76] *Reg. Sutton*, iii, xlii. Mention of 'counsel, help or favour' supports this, since excommunications often stated that whoever had provided such support was equally bound by the sentence.
[77] 'teneri te vinculo dubitabas', *Les Registres Alexandre IV*, ed. Bourel de la Roncière, i. no. 1015.
[78] *Letters of Innocent III*, no. 913 (appendix).   [79] *Reg. Cantilupe*, 227–8 (undated).

'humbly and devotedly, on bended knees as if with an effusion of tears'. Rejoicing at their contrition, the archbishop absolved them in form of law.[80] Two and a half months later, at the start of 1299, a host of men were cited to appear before the archbishop for the same offence. Their appearance was not voluntary, their names likely discovered via an investigation.[81] John, Peter and Walter, and others who 'humbly' sought absolution in comparable circumstances, might merely have been pre-empting this eventuality by handing themselves in, their talk of consciences and signs of repentance a covering for more practical concerns.[82]

A case with the opposite series of events is thus even more interesting. In June 1305, the bishop of Salisbury had issued a general sentence against certain unknown malefactors who had illicitly cut down many trees in the bishop's wood at Ross and subsequently 'violently, notoriously and publicly carried them away', thus incurring *Quicumque de domibus*.[83] Following an investigation into the names of those responsible, fourteen men 'humbly imploring the benefit of absolution' made satisfaction to the bishop and were enjoined penance. These men were found by the investigation, and it may be suggested that their supposedly humble supplication was not entirely voluntary.[84] Nine months following the original excommunication, however, John, Richard, and Walter Irreby came forward in different circumstances. By this time, it seems likely that the bishop, having punished the malefactors, was no longer investigating the case. The memorandum recording the Irreby brothers' submission does not obviously follow from any investigation by the church. Instead, it describes a voluntary (albeit fairly public) confession, and the vocabulary used is that of conscience. On 8 March, the three brothers went to the bishop's manor at Ross because of the transgressions they had made against him in cutting down and removing his trees.

> Considering that they were bound by the chain of excommunication, with conscience dictating, they sought from the lord bishop in chapel that the benefit of absolution be imposed on them.[85]

The bishop, accepting the men as 'penitent and contrite', accordingly absolved them and imposed penance.[86] The brothers also promised to stand by the mandates of the church, a standard condition for absolution. Their confession was of course recorded by churchmen, and to some extent this language is formulaic. However, it is possible that their consciences were nagging at them

---

[80] *Reg. Winchelsey*, i, 287–8.   [81] *Reg. Winchelsey*, i, 304–5.
[82] Cf. Mansfield, *Humiliation*, 121–2.   [83] *Reg. Swinfield*, 407–8.
[84] *Reg. Swinfield*, 408–9.   [85] *Reg. Swinfield*, 431–2.
[86] They were to visit the church of Hereford and make oblations there before the images of the Virgin and of St Ethelbert; to pay 100s. for the fabric of the church; to restore the damages caused to the wood, and prevent others from doing this in future. The men previously given penance for this crime had been told to return the wood taken, and process around the church and market of Ross in their underclothes (the ringleaders were given harsher punishment than the rest).

(at the start of Lent[87]) because they felt guilt that their accomplices had been given public penance, which they would have witnessed, while they remained undisciplined. More cynically, local knowledge that they had been involved but had escaped without punishment had forced them to come forward. If so, presenting themselves to the bishop as voluntary confessors was undeniably the wise choice. That anxiety about being excommunicate had driven them to seek out the bishop is certainly the implication of the memorandum as we have it, and if medieval belief and piety are taken seriously it was at least one cause of their supplication.

Further concern amongst laymen about incurring *ipso facto* excommunications can be found, surprisingly, in royal records. In 1306, the bishop of Carlisle and three abbots (St Albans, Waltham, and St Mary's, York) were granted full power by Clement V to absolve those of the king's subjects who feared they had incurred excommunication or clerical irregularity through crimes committed while striving to protect the king's peace during the Scottish wars. In the course of their efforts, many had killed or injured rebels, and damaged churches and ecclesiastical property. The sheriffs of England, a letter recorded in the Close Rolls reveals, were ordered to make a public proclamation in cities, boroughs, and other places, that those who felt they needed absolution or dispensation ('qui hujusmodi absolutione seu dispensatione se sentiunt indigere') should go to the bishop or one of the abbots to request and receive it. The letter written to the sheriffs states that the pope had granted this power at the king's request; the king also wrote to the bishop of Carlisle asking him to fulfil this commission.[88]

The phrase used, 'sentiunt se' ('believed themselves'), suggests men being conscious of their sins and wanting remedy. William Prynne, who printed the letters in 1668, believed that the king was acting here having been 'informed by some of his superstitious Prelates and Clergy'. Edward may indeed have been advised by prelates, but they in turn were perhaps responding to popular demand. It is entirely plausible, given the publicity afforded to *latae sententiae*, that those who fought for Edward were aware that they needed papal absolution for laying violent hands on clergy.[89] Though Prynne noted that he had found no examples of such absolutions (hysterically adding that it was anyway licit to kill the perfidious Scottish traitors, 'yea to burn their churches'), it is highly unlikely that these absolutions would be documented. Royal intervention in such cases was not unprecedented. In 1234, Louis IX of France had begged remedy (seemingly of his own accord but possibly with input from ecclesiastics) for those who might still be bound by Guala's sentence against the followers of his father Louis in the invasion of England (1215–17). Gregory IX accordingly ordered the bishop of Paris to absolve such men.[90] In 1284, Martin IV similarly commanded the

---

[87] Lent began on 3 March; this memorandum is dated 8 March.
[88] *CCR 1302–07*, 435; Prynne, *Records*, 1136–7; *Reg. Halton*, i, 261–2.   [89] See Chapter 7.
[90] *Reg. Gregory IX*, i, no. 1688.

bishops of Worcester and Bangor to absolve those who had committed various injuries to churches during the Welsh wars, if they sought absolution and made satisfaction.[91] Such mass desire for absolution could hardly be prompted by legal action.[92]

Complaints made by Pope Urban IV (in 1264) and John Pecham (in 1281) further indicate that laypeople desired absolution from unrevealed excommunications. Unscrupulous clergy were apparently absolving people from various *latae sententiae*, when they did not, *de jure,* have the right to do so.[93] Even if they were unaware that these absolutions were invalid, such penitents were concerned about excommunications they had incurred automatically, for which they had not been prosecuted. Since there were strict rules governing who could absolve any judicially pronounced sentences, these people were presumably asking friars for absolution of their own accord.

There was thus certainly an appetite for absolutions from unrevealed sentences of excommunication amongst both clergy and laity. Seeking absolution from sentences that were not public demonstrates that the effects of excommunication were not confined to its legal consequences. None of these men (they were all men) was found guilty through any sort of process, and their absolutions were provided in the penitential forum or in a liminal space between the internal and external forum.[94] Even if some of them were advised by their priests to consult the papal penitentiary, seeking advice from clergy closer to home indicates concerns of conscience. Accusations from others would have resulted in a judicial inquiry, not a petition to the penitentiary.

That some combination of external pressure and internal guilt drove absolutions from unrevealed excommunications seems plausible in many cases; these are far from mutually exclusive. However precisely these documents are interpreted, they demonstrate that the church's teachings on excommunication had been effective enough to convince that it was wise to deal with the sanction. Absolutions sought in the internal forum of the church are evidence of the sanction's power. It was not wholly reliant upon public shame, or the secular arm, or legal penalties. Excommunications incurred *ipso facto,* never confirmed or revealed by the authorities, may have been the weakest form of excommunication. Yet these sentences were just as perilous for the soul as any other, and as such they

---

[91] *Foedera,* I.ii.641.

[92] The papal registers contain many privileges granting faculty to absolve large groups of people. Many, for instance, had incurred *Si quis suadente* during the baronial rebellion. Though the papal chaplain, master Leonard, was given permission to absolve some of these, others had to go to Rome for absolution (*Cal. Pap. Reg.,* 380. See also *Cal. Pap. Reg.* 114, 437, 454, 523, 613; *De Antiquis Legibus Liber,* ed. Stapleton. 65–7).

[93] *Reg. Urban IV,* iii, no. 1562; *C&S,* 898–99, cf. *Reg. Epp. Pecham,* iii, 909–10. According to Urban's letter, these religious claimed that they had been granted these faculties while the king's peace was disturbed.

[94] Mansfield notes while discussing similar absolutions in the bishop's court that it is difficult to make clear distinctions: *Humiliation,* 121–4.

could generate disquiet. It is easy to discount a sentence that was never confirmed by authorities, but the evidence of thirteenth-century clergy and laity shows that they did not disregard incurred sentences. An important part of excommunication's ability to successfully alter behaviour targeted individual consciences.

Wariness of Excommunication

A number of accounts, predominantly from chronicles, make claims about how people responded to the threat of excommunication. These are often difficult to interpret. There are two main issues here. The first is how far the viewpoints and interpretations of the overwhelmingly clerical authorship of these texts can be taken as indicative of those of the wider population. It is significant that the only explicit evidence for belief in supernatural consequences of excommunication during life, such as bad luck or hastened death, are found in chronicles and *miracula*. The second problem is how far to trust accounts attributing statements, motives, and beliefs to excommunicates. Claims that excommunicates themselves expressed feelings about their sentences are particularly noteworthy, but they may reflect authors' prejudices rather than the excommunicates' own thoughts. In addition, even if narratives are taken to be accurate, the general assumption that excommunication ought to elicit fear meant that claiming to be cowed by the sanction, whatever other circumstances influenced a decision, was tactically sensible. The contumacious were routinely condemned in ecclesiastical sources as unafraid to incur a sentence; the jibe was typically used to suggest that excommunicates were not thinking of their souls. To fear excommunication and to act accordingly was laudable; attributing a *volte-face* to fear of excommunication was thus perhaps a way to save face, whatever the 'real' motives were. Despite the problems inherent in interpreting what people in the past felt, there are a number of cases which merit discussion.

Chroniclers' accounts tend to show better the interplay between spiritual fears and more practical difficulties than do episcopal registers (which couch decisions to seek absolution in formulaic terms). Thus Roger of Wendover, explaining King John's submission to the papacy in 1212, stated that the king was greatly confused and perturbed in his mind for four principal reasons. The first cause of John's mental disturbance was the only one that concerned John's chances of salvation, but also the only one in which one of the verbs *metere, timere,* or *vereri,* (all meaning 'to fear'), was *not* used: the king had been excommunicated for five years and was despairing ('desperabat') of the state of his soul. The other three fears were more pragmatic. John feared a French invasion, he feared that the English magnates would abandon him, and he feared the loss of his temporal kingdom in addition to loss of the eternal kingdom. John reportedly feared loss of his realm above all else.⁹⁵ Mutinous barons and an aggressive French prince provided much to worry him.⁹⁶ Alarm about damnation featured in the king's calculations, but Wendover plausibly laid greater emphasis on John's fears about excommunication making his position on earth weaker.

Eagerness to avoid excommunication, as presented in narrative accounts, reflects similar calculations. In 1225, Falkes de Bréauté sought to explain why certain letters he had apparently directed to Henry III the previous year had never reached the king. These letters, sent during Falkes's rebellion, had supposedly sought a safe conduct to approach the king, accepting whatever punishment Henry saw fit to inflict upon him for his offences. Falkes wrote that he had charged a cleric, Robert of Leicester, with delivering the letters. However, having heard about the excommunication against Falkes and all who supported him, Robert was consequently afraid to incur this sentence ('timens ne...sententia ligaretur') and Falkes speculated that he had either suppressed the true letters or presented different ones to the king. Falkes's *Querimonia*, in which he made this claim, should be treated with caution. Written to the pope in 1225 to exonerate Falkes, the complaint provides a highly coloured account of events. Falkes may have calculated that the intended papal recipient would be particularly receptive to this excuse. Even if Falkes fabricated this whole event, his account is nonetheless of interest: he would surely not have chosen this particular defence if it was wholly implausible that Robert had been deterred by excommunication.⁹⁷ Falkes, a layman, was also not claiming such pious fears for himself, but attributing them to a clergyman.

Other accounts of refusals to incur excommunication are equally interesting. The monks of St Albans explicitly used spiritual fears as an excuse for being uncooperative, though their refusal to incur excommunication was rather convenient. In 1258, Simon Passelewe was busy extorting cash on the king's behalf for the Sicilian business. The king, having a hard time raising these funds, enlisted Simon to shake down monastic houses. According to Matthew Paris (himself a monk at St Albans at the time), the monks refused to give any money, on the grounds that they had documents forbidding, under pain of excommunication and interdict, anyone from burdening their church. Their argument was theologically sound: they would prefer, they said, to incur the earthly king's indignation than offend the King of Heaven by contradicting a papal prohibition, and thus be bound by the chain of anathema.⁹⁸ Simon tried to push the issue by warning them that they thus spurned the king's protection, and by assuring them

---

⁹⁵ *CM*, ii, 540–1.
⁹⁶ Cf. the Anonymous of Béthune: 'Terror seized King John... —he was in so many difficulties—he knew that he was excommunicated, he knew too that everyone in his land hated him, he also knew that the king of France was coming to attack him...he saw clearly that if the pope did not rescue him, no rescue would there be', *History of the Dukes of Normandy*, trans. Shirley, 128.
⁹⁷ *Coventry*, 266.   ⁹⁸ Cf. Clarke, *Interdict*, 170.

that the pope had granted a Franciscan who accompanied him faculty to absolve anyone who incurred such a sentence. The monks countered that this did not seem 'healthy' ('non sanem videtur'), since agreeing to incur excommunication on the grounds that they could be absolved would be like agreeing to have a leg broken on the promise that the best surgeon could be provided to mend it.[99] The monks' argument was surely a good and pious one, yet it might be taken with a pinch of salt; it cannot be denied that it was in their interests to refuse Simon payment. These motives are not, however, mutually exclusive. It was foolish and dangerous to incur a sentence knowingly at the same time as it was in the monks' fiscal interests.

Forty years later a remarkably similar argument was again used to resist the king's extortions. In this case, it can be reasonably accepted that Robert Winchelsey, archbishop of Canterbury, and his followers were acting on principle and not merely out of self-interest. Following Boniface VIII's 1296 bull *Clericis laicos,* which forbade clerical grants of subsidy to lay rulers without papal consent, on pain of excommunication, King Edward nonetheless insisted on ecclesiastical subsidies. When he subsequently put clergy who refused him outside his protection and seized their property, essentially outlawing them, many more gave in to his demands than resisted him. They paid to receive the king's protection and their property, in effect paying the tax originally demanded. The archbishop, however, stood firm. He asserted that the clergy had two lords, and that they owed greater allegiance to their spiritual than their temporal master.[100] When a number of clergy relented, the archbishop himself 'chose rather to incur the king's anger than the sentence of excommunication'.[101] The chronicler of Bury St Edmund's wrote: 'The assembly feared the Eternal King more than he who was king for a time, and the peril of their souls more than the hazards of worldly affairs'.[102] This is much the same argument the monks of St Albans had made. Certainly the political circumstances were very different, and the *Clericis laicos* dispute had more serious implications, but the two events indicate that some religious men, at least, put their salvation and their principles above their temporal safety.

In other cases, excommunication was instead used to support extortion of money. Such practices were condemned and detested; use of a spiritual sanction to achieve temporal ends was particularly blameworthy. Criticism indicates both that excommunication could be an effective threat and that it was so because of its spiritual coercive power. Matthew Paris thus complained about the 'insatiable avarice' of papal money collectors, who wrung money from the 'wretched English

---

[99] *CM,* v, 685–7.
[100] Cf. Matthew 6:24. Used in a comparable context by Stephen Langton: Clarke, *Interdict,* 170.
[101] *Guisborough,* 288; *Cotton,* 322–3; Denton, *Robert Winchelsey,* 126–31; Clarke, *Interdict,* 226.
[102] *Chron. Bury,* 137–8.

church' by interdict and excommunication in 1241.[103] Four years later, he complained about various actions of the legate Martin, noting that his use of excommunication and interdict against those who contradicted him led to 'great crisis and peril of souls'.[104] Archbishop Boniface provoked similar criticism when, in 1248, he extracted money from vacant churches, citing a papal privilege that excommunicated all those who contradicted it. Paris noted that the king and his family were excepted from this sentence, which caused him to be suspicious that Henry III had sanctioned such extortion. He later wrote that the archbishop's mandate caused widespread indignation, not only because of the 'avid extortion of money', but also because of the king's consent.[105] Indeed, the king had been implicated in such immoral extortions as early as 1229, when his minister, Stephen of Seagrave (dismissed in 1234 as one of Henry's 'evil counsellors'), was given papal authority to excommunicate anyone who prevented him collecting Gregory IX's tenth (to fund war against the excommunicate Frederick II). The prelates had consented to this tenth, 'fearing to inflict upon themselves a sentence of excommunication or interdict if they opposed the apostolic mandate'. So effective was the 'shameless' Stephen's extortion that clergy were forced to pawn their sacred vessels to pay him.[106]

In 1237, such methods were again fruitful. Lamenting the state of the kingdom, Paris complained against simony, usury, and illiterate men 'armed' with papal bulls extorting whatever they wished, by immediately excommunicating anyone who opposed them. Thus, 'not by prayer, not canonically, but by imperious exaction, they despoiled the common people (*simplices*)'.[107] Paris and Falkes thus indicate that the sanction was effective, but a comparable complaint by the French king Louis IX (in a 1245 letter to Innocent IV preserved by Paris), suggests the opposite. Louis repeatedly deplored the unscrupulous methods of the Roman Church, explicitly noting the 'remarkable sentiment', which Gregory the Great had condemned: 'Give me so much, or I will excommunicate you'.[108] Louis was concerned that there was now an infinite multitude of people excommunicated for their failure to comply with papal demands.[109]

These examples might be contrasted with excommunication used to force participation in religious activities. Thus Robert Grosseteste (with what appears to have been obsessive pastoral care), according to a complaint in the Close Rolls, compelled his diocesan subjects to gather together on pain of excommunication, forcing them to confess their private sins. Since they should have

---

[103] *CM*, iv, 137.
[104] *CM*, iv, 443, cf. vi, no. 69. The English magnates also complained to the pope: *Foedera*, I.i.262.
[105] *CM*, iv, 636–7; v, 36–7; *Flores Historiarum*, ii, 341–2.
[106] *CM*, iii, 187–9.   [107] *CM*, iii, 389.
[108] '"Da mihi tantum vel excommunico te"; quod mirabilis sententia, cuius effectum editum contra prolatores talis sententiae verbum beatissimi patris nostri Gregorii denuntiat invalidum esse'; *CM*, vi, 101. See also 102, 107, and 112. Cf. Campbell, 'Attitude of the monarchy', 536–7.
[109] *CM*, vi, 112.

been working in the fields at the time, protested 'magnates and others', he caused them impoverishment. The letter forcefully condemns the 'unusual and undue vexations' because of the labour consequences and dangers of perjury. Excommunication, nonetheless, seems to have played a key role in getting people to comply before they complained.[110] Matthew Paris's assumption that the threat of excommunication was an effective means of coercion is further demonstrated by a miracle story included in his *Chronica Majora*. In 1235, the pope sent friars to preach the cross throughout Christendom, according to Paris instructing them to compel attendance at their sermons on pain of anathema. Thus a Franciscan, Roger of Lewes, was preaching at Clare in Suffolk that year. A paralyzed woman 'fearing the punishment of excommunication' gave her last pieces of silver to a neighbour so that he would carry her to the sermon on his shoulders. While preaching, Roger was forced to stop and ask the woman why she was groaning. She answered that she had been brought there by fear of excommunication, upon which Roger told her to go home, not knowing that she was unable. Learning of her paralysis, the friar cured her.[111] The tale (which was at least meant to sound credible) supplies a rare example of an individual coerced to action through fear of the punishment, and nothing more.

Henry III, by contrast, was undoubtedly motivated by excommunication's potential impact on his status as well as his soul. The king's reluctance to incur excommunication and fears he had incurred it are particularly well documented. Rulers had more to lose from excommunication than the average layperson, and no doubt Henry had in mind the difficulties faced by his father as well as by his contemporary, Frederick II. Henry's marked anxiety—far more evident than his father's or son's—indicate he was worried about not only temporal effects but also about his spiritual health. Given Henry's well-known piety, and his self-image as a pious king, this ought to come as no surprise: excommunication was to a large degree dependent upon the personality and religiosity of those against whom it was used.

Henry demonstrated his concern about incurring excommunication several times during his reign.[112] Like many noblemen, and following in the footsteps of his father, he received privileges from the papacy that provided that only the apostolic see could excommunicate him.[113] There are an unusually high number of extant privileges for Henry III.[114] We have already seen the account of his

---

[110] *CR 1251–53*, 224–5.   [111] *CM*, iii, 312–13.

[112] David Carpenter discusses Henry's piety at length in *Henry III*: ch. 6. 276–9 are especially relevant here; cf. ibid., 55, 601–2.

[113] Religious houses also frequently obtained these. Clarke, *Interdict*, 124–6, discusses privileges from interdict and excommunication.

[114] King John: 15 April 1214 (*SLI*, nos 66 and 63); Henry III: 15 May 1226 (*Royal Letters*, app. v, no. 25); 27 May 1227 (*Foedera*, I.i.185), 28 February 1228 (*Foedera*, I.i.189), 20 January 1231 (*Foedera*, I.i.199), 7 November 1262 (*Foedera*, I.ii.422); Edward I: 1 January 1306 (*Foedera*, I.ii.979). There is some variation in the terms of these privileges. Generally they prevented clergy pronouncing any general or

youthful worry on behalf of his deceased regent, William Marshal, as described by Matthew Paris. According to a disgraced Hubert de Burgh in 1232, it was 'fear of the sentence' that had convinced the king to return Bedford Castle to its rightful owner in 1224.[115] Roger of Wendover's account of the 1234 political crisis, provoked by Henry's reliance on Peter des Roches, who had instigated the ousting of Hubert de Burgh, assigns a clear role to excommunication. Michael Prestwich, indeed, claims that this was the only time the threat of excommunication was effective in thirteenth-century English politics.[116] Des Roches and other unpopular counsellors had been excommunicated by several bishops, who warned the king that if he failed to dismiss these advisors he risked a sentence himself by associating with them. Once Edmund of Abingdon had been consecrated archbishop, Henry could no longer prevaricate. The new archbishop again threatened excommunication; led by repentance, 'the pious king' humbly agreed to obey the prelates' advice in everything and forbade Peter des Roches to meddle in the kingdom's affairs.[117] In 1236, Henry feared ('sententiam...se metuit incurrisse') that he had incurred the sentence of excommunication binding all those who provided help or support to the excommunicated heretic Count Raymond VII of Toulouse. Henry had supplied Raymond with money and therefore humbly sought the counsel of Gregory IX. In a letter couched in terms of salvation and repentance, Gregory ordered Edmund of Abingdon to absolve the king (subject to suitable satisfaction and penance).[118] Six years later, Henry promised to help Raymond against the king of France in any way he could, even if Louis IX entered Raymond's land on the pope's orders. The sole reason Henry was able to back out of their agreement was if he was forced to by a sentence of excommunication.[119] In 1237, Henry sought absolution, this time from the *lata sententia* attached to Magna Carta.

---

special denunciation of excommunication or interdict against the king, his chapel, or his close family members, without special papal mandate. In 1244, the archbishop of Canterbury was permitted, at Henry's request, to absolve the king from *Si quis suadente* should he incur it and the injury not be serious. The indult was limited to four years (*Foedera*, I.i.252). Cf. a comparable grant to his half-brother, William de Valence (*Bullarium franciscanum*, ed. Sbaraleae, ii, no. 82). The 1262 privilege was also time-limited, to five years.

[115] Hubert de Burgh, deposed in 1232, was accused, amongst other things, of wrongly giving Bedford Castle to William de Beauchamp, from whom King John had confiscated it during the baronial war. Hubert countered that the peace agreed after the war provided that everyone be restored to their seisins as held at the start of the war, so Beauchamp was the rightful holder, and that Henry had backed down because the legate Guala had pronounced excommunication against those who infringed the agreement. *CM*, vi, 67–8. See Carpenter, 'Fall of Hubert de Burgh', and Vincent, *Peter des Roches*, 303–20.

[116] Prestwich, *English Politics in the Thirteenth Century*, 75–6.

[117] *CM*, iii, 268–72.

[118] *Reg. Gregory IX*, ii, no. 3331. Cf. the sentence pronounced against Raymond in 1225: *Diplomatic Documents*, ed. Chaplais, no. 191. In 1226, Honorius III warned the king not to risk putting a stain on the purity of his faith and incurring excommunication by assisting Raymond, since he and his supporters were excommunicated: *Royal Letters*, app. v, no. 22.

[119] *Foedera*, I.i.248–9; Powicke, *Henry III*, 194–5.

> From that excommunication the lord king and the barons, because they feared that they had fallen into the same excommunication... urgently sought absolution from the venerable father, Archbishop Edmund, who absolved them to the effect that if in future they were to violate the charter, they would *ipso facto* relapse into their previous state of excommunication.[120]

Henry had incurred this sentence, Matthew Paris reported, by relying on bad counsel.[121] It is interesting that Paris describes Henry actively participating in the 1237 Magna Carta excommunication ceremony by holding a candle: if the king subsequently felt himself guilty of infringing the charter, his extinguishing a candle might have struck him as, in effect, cursing himself. In 1253, Henry refused to participate in this way.[122]

There is not here space to analyze each of these episodes in detail, but the evidence shows that the king was deeply affected by the threat of excommunication. According to his actions and the (somewhat less reliable) accounts of the St Albans chroniclers, he took decisive steps to ensure that he was not and would not be excommunicated. In 1228 he even used a *lata sententia* he remembered had been pronounced by Stephen Langton against tourneying as an excuse to postpone a tournament in Northampton.[123] Henry was responding to crises in his kingdom and often (though not necessarily always) acting upon advice. Nor did he seek absolution so much as might be expected: he was repeatedly accused of infringing Magna Carta, for instance, but never again sought absolution from the sentence.[124] Nonetheless, his behaviour was markedly different from that of his predecessor and successor, neither of whom demonstrated such trepidation at the prospect of spiritual sanctions.

The most striking indication of the extent to which Henry III was perturbed by excommunication is supplied by his behaviour during the so-called Sicilian business. Henry's reaction to the real prospect of being sentenced demonstrates clearly both the spiritual and temporal consequences of excommunication that made it so disturbing. The terms of the agreement with Pope Alexander IV, set out in a letter dated 9 April 1255, stated that prince Edmund would receive the kingdom of Sicily if he defeated the Staufen ruler Conrad IV. However, if Henry did not fulfil his part of the bargain, which included paying the pope 135,000 marks, providing 300 knights, and being present in Sicily by October 1256, he and

---

[120] *Grosseteste Letters*, no. 72*, 253–4, Mantello and Goering's translation slightly altered, using the text in *Grosseteste Epistolae*, 231.

[121] *CM*, iii, 382–3.

[122] *CM*, v. 360–1, 377–8. However, as Carpenter notes, Paris's original description of 1237 (*CM*, iii, 382–3) mentions no candle: *Henry III*, 46 n. 150.

[123] Carpenter, *Henry III*, 76–7.

[124] See Gray, 'Church and Magna Charta'. Carpenter discusses the apparent tension between Henry's piety and his infringements of ecclesiastical rights and Magna Carta: *Henry III*, 434–5.

his heirs would *ipso eo* be excommunicated and 'stained with the blemish and sin of perjury'.[125]

David Carpenter, who has described the provisions as 'horribly targeted at the pious Henry', is surely right to link Henry's repeated attempts to delay or avoid ecclesiastical sanctions with the king's piety.[126] On 6 October 1256, Alexander IV agreed to extend the deadline by which the king's money was due, assuring Henry that meanwhile he would 'by no means incur sentences of excommunication', nor would his kingdom be interdicted.[127] In the summer of the following year, Henry asked that the threat of excommunication and interdict be entirely lifted, and 'more tolerable conditions' be imposed. If the pope was unwilling to do this, he was asked to at least defer the deadline.[128] On 12 December 1257, the pope notified Henry that he had sent his nuncio, Arlot, to deal with the matter: chroniclers plausibly noted that Arlot threatened the king with excommunication.[129] The pope assured Henry, nevertheless, at the insistence of the king's messengers but also as a result of his own concern, 'that you have by no means incurred a sentence of excommunication' and would not do so before the new deadline.[130] He declared that he was being cautious for the king, both with regard to 'consciencia' and to 'fama', particularly so that Henry was not assumed to be stained ('maculatus') by the crime ('reatu') or the 'nota' of perjury. The pope was thus reassuring Henry that he need not be concerned about the state of his soul, either through having incurred excommunication or as a result of perjury (a mortal sin). Yet the pope was equally keen to ensure that nobody could accuse Henry of being a perjurer or excommunicate: his reputation (*fama*) must remain untainted.[131]

Each time Henry was forced to plead for an extension, he also sought to reassure himself that he would not fall into a sentence of excommunication. Alexander responded directly to the king's concerns. Matthew Paris also noted that the pope's threats of excommunication caused Henry to pay 500 marks to defer the sentence, because he was 'confused in mind'.[132] Yet Henry's barons too needed reassuring, for Alexander wrote to them directly, informing them that the king was not excommunicated.[133] Alexander's emphasis on reassuring Henry that he was neither an excommunicate nor a perjurer, nor in any immediate danger of becoming one, indicates that the king was preoccupied with this idea. Being separated from the church spiritually and physically was a significant threat to

---

[125] 'respersi et notati labe ac reatu perjurii', *Foedera*, I.i.316–18.
[126] Carpenter, 'Henry III and the Sicilian affair', 6. Henry would 'never' have risked excommunication: *Henry III*, 448. Discussing another event, Carpenter notes that excommunication was a 'horrific prospect for Henry, if not for his father': ibid., 438. Clanchy, *England and its Rulers*, 243–7.
[127] *Foedera*, I.i.350.   [128] *Foedera*, I.i.360.
[129] *Ann. Dunstable*, 208; *Ann. Tewksbury*, 162–3.
[130] Nor was his kingdom under interdict, Alexander assured him.
[131] *Foedera*, I.i.366; *Les Registres Alexandre IV*, ed. Bourel de la Roncière, no. 2379.
[132] *CM*, v, 666.   [133] *CM*, vi, no. 208.

Henry's religious practices as well as to his salvation and his reputation. It might also leave him vulnerable to rebellion, though there is no evidence aside from the letter sent to the barons that this possibility was raised at the time. A final letter, sent to Arlot on 19 January 1258, again made clear that until 1 June the king was in no danger of incurring any of the punishments laid out in the terms agreed. The pact as a whole, however, remained in force: it was not to be understood that the pope had annulled it.[134] Henry's foolish decision to proceed with this agreement was one of the key causes of the baronial rebellion in 1258. Henry's fears were driven by the fact that he was unable to fulfil its terms so was bound to incur the sanctions attached. Only in 1263 was he formally freed from the terms negotiated in 1254.[135]

Eagerness to avoid excommunication could be motivated by many factors, for the consequences of the sanction were manifold. One of these factors was, however, that the soul and salvation were endangered. The desire to avoid this, especially by those who considered themselves devout and who wished to appear as such, ought to be taken into consideration alongside the more tangible results of ecclesiastical censures.

Divine Retribution

Evidence for the specific fear that excommunicates who refused absolution would suffer bad luck or even death as a result of their obstinacy, which the church encouraged primarily via miracle tales, is more elusive. It is often reflected in monastic chronicles and annals, but not elsewhere. Chroniclers found numerous examples of divine vengeance exacted against excommunicates. If public figures were excommunicated and subsequently fell victim to anything that could be deemed unfortunate, this bad luck was generally attributed to excommunication. The fate of William Marshal's sons is one example.[136] A particularly popular and dramatic cautionary tale told by a number of thirteenth-century English chroniclers concerned the plagues and death experienced by Leopold V, Duke of Austria, excommunicated for capturing and imprisoning Richard I in 1192.[137] When Robert de Guagi, excommunicated in 1218 for occupying the castle of Newark, died the same year (though having returned the castle), the Dunstable annalist wrote that he had been 'struck by infernal fire'.[138] Far more examples could be cited.[139] However, these stories do little to inform us about how the majority of people interpreted these events, or whether excommunicates were afraid such disasters would befall them.

---

[134] *Foedera*, I.i.369.   [135] Weiler, *Henry III of England*, 156–7.
[136] *CM*, iv, 492–5. See above, 41–4.
[137] The story originates in Howden and was repeated by many later thirteenth-century chronicles. *Chronica Magistri Rogeri de Hovedene*, ed. Stubbs, iii, 274–6.
[138] *Ann. Dunstable*, 54.   [139] See also Murray, 'Excommunication', 174–5.

Chroniclers were possibly reacting to scepticism about excommunication's supernatural effects amongst the laity. *Miracula*, discussed in Chapter 1, indicate that laypeople needed persuading. One of the commonest miracles explicitly acknowledged the existence of doubters: it describes a sceptic who is convinced of the powers of excommunication and absolution when bread is anathematized.[140] A story related in the *Gesta Abbatum* of St Albans describes similar cynicism. Ralph Chenduit (a persecutor of St Albans abbey) boasted that, despite being excommunicated for three years, he had grown so fat that his saddle could not hold him. According to Matthew Paris, upon saying this, cackling ('cachinans'), Ralph immediately fell mortally ill (though he managed to make amends to the wronged monks through the intercession of St Alban before he died).[141] Writing from St Albans abbey, apparently so mistreated by Chenduit, Paris evidently felt that Chenduit had got what he deserved, interpreting his death as divine retribution. On the other hand, mocking excommunication's power must have been an obvious impulse for anyone who had heard the miracle tales propagated by the church, but who witnessed excommunicates living healthily. A remarkably similar observation was made by Martin Luther about his own sentence three centuries later.[142] As Alexander Murray observed, that excommunication was so often scorned shows that such *exempla* were insufficiently persuasive: 'supernatural punishment, even if it was sometimes available... was not available in sufficient *quantity* to win respect for the church's sentence'.[143] Ralph Chenduit may thus represent a 'type'. Churchmen may have held these beliefs, but they were responding to scepticism by writing cautionary tales, trying to bolster respect for the sanction. As Murray notes, they could choose their examples.

In one particular area, however, political and religious considerations were especially intertwined. In warfare, the danger of being struck down by bad luck or worse was particularly acute. Pope Gregory VII had asserted that an excommunicate could not obtain victory in battle.[144] There were a number of conflicts in thirteenth-century England in which one side or the other was excommunicated. Going into battle when God was against you made a loss more likely; losing as an excommunicate meant that dying excommunicate and consequent eternal damnation and profane burial were a real prospect. Men engaged in military enterprises may thus have been especially susceptible to beliefs in the supernatural consequences of excommunication.[145]

---

[140] See 36-7.
[141] *Gesta Abbatum*, ed. Riley, i, 319-20; *CM*, iv, 262. See also Weiler, 'Matthew Paris on the writing of history', 267-8.
[142] Jaser, 'Ostensio exclusionis', 380.
[143] Murray, 'Excommunication', 174-5 (Murray's italics).
[144] Lea, *Studies in Church History*, 348-9.
[145] Some canonists argued that anyone going on pilgrimage or crusade had reason to fear death and could be absolved as though dying: Clarke, *Interdict*, 157.

In this context, belief in excommunication's supernatural effects was reportedly expressed by laymen themselves as well as by clerics reporting on events. The most significant excommunication-related military loss in thirteenth-century England concerns Louis, son of King Louis VII, who invaded England during the barons' war in 1216. Following the death of King John, the French prince had the support of many English barons and had only to contend with a nine-year-old as his rival for the crown. He was, for a time, in control of a significant proportion of the kingdom. So when he was defeated by an inferior force at the Battle of Lincoln, the continuator of Walter of Coventry treated this as a miracle. 'The reason is obvious', he pointed out, 'because the hand of God was not with him, as one might expect for someone who came there [to England] against the prohibition of the holy Roman church, and delayed there under a sentence of anathema'.[146] For the Melrose chronicler, Louis's men, 'oppressed by the weight of excommunication', had been miraculously captured and imprisoned by only a few.[147] According to Wendover, Louis himself viewed the events in much the same way: he lamented that his misfortune at the Battle of Lincoln had been inflicted upon him 'by God rather than men'.[148] Meanwhile the English barons, hitherto Louis's supporters, are described by Wendover's successor, Matthew Paris, as being driven back to Henry by the excommunication pronounced against them.[149]

The belated trepidation purportedly experienced by Louis and the barons is plausible partly because they initially ignored their sentences. When first excommunicated, instead of ceasing his campaign, Louis went on to take Winchester.[150] Propagation of excommunication's detrimental temporal effects had not been effective enough to deter Louis from entering battle in the first place. His victories strengthened his position, increasing his chances of negotiating an absolution at a later date. Only when things had begun to go badly, against the odds, did he begin to question whether God was against him. Following Lincoln, excommunication was merely one of Louis's problems. As David Carpenter has shown, this loss obliged Louis to negotiate. He was losing militarily and losing his support base.[151] The barons, meanwhile, also had both practical and religious concerns. Carpenter accepts that a change in the religious circumstances affected the barons' decision to return to their 'natural lord', but argues that it 'confirmed and strengthened, rather than instigated, the decision to desert Louis'. The crucial change here was the fact that, back in 1215, the barons had called themselves the army of God, and presented their rebellion as a religious undertaking. In 1217, the legate Guala had launched a crusade against them, drastically undermining their ability to present their cause as just. In addition, Louis's ability to offer the barons anything worthwhile was increasingly in question, particularly considering his need to

---

[146] *Coventry*, 239.   [147] *Melrose*, 131.   [148] *CM*, iii, 25.
[149] *Flores Historiarum*, ii, 163; *History of the Dukes of Normandy*, trans. Shirley, 162–3.
[150] *Coventry*, 230.   [151] Carpenter, *Minority*, 35–49.

cater for both his French and English followers.¹⁵² Wendover further noted that Louis was eventually driven to treat with King Henry because the legate Guala's sentence was to be confirmed by the pope. Papal endorsement would, indeed, mean the excommunication could no longer be ignored as invalid.¹⁵³

By submitting when he did, Louis demonstrated his piety and his acceptance of papal authority. It was a politically sensible move. The possibility that excommunication might occasion adversity had not been enough, on its own, to deter Louis. It is believable, however, that it factored alongside his other troubles when he chose to leave England. Indeed, if it was believed that excommunication caused his difficulties, it cannot be separated from them. Political and religious motives are not mutually exclusive, and indeed often worked together. Louis's and the barons' decisions were affected by both.¹⁵⁴

We can compare Louis's situation with that of Ranulf, earl of Chester, six years later. Again according to Wendover, when the earl and his accomplices in his rebellion against the young Henry III realized their forces were no larger than the king's, they were 'afraid to enter uncertain battle', fearing that they might soon be excommunicated by name (a general sentence having already been pronounced).¹⁵⁵ The earl therefore surrendered the castles he had unjustly occupied.¹⁵⁶ Here the practical and religious motives attributed to Ranulf were deeply connected: his inferior forces and his excommunicate status both meant he was more likely to lose in battle. Had he commanded greater military strength, perhaps he would have weighed his options differently. Louis and the rebel barons had had good reason to expect to win at Lincoln, and it is possible that his unexpected loss had been widely attributed to his excommunicate status. In 1223, Ranulf was already in the weaker military position, and would have been aware of the additional perils brought by excommunication.

Those who fought against excommunicates might, on the other hand, receive a morale boost from the status of their enemies. Thus before Lincoln, Hubert de Burgh reportedly used the sentence against Louis to encourage his men, declaring 'we should oppose them boldly, since God is with us because they are excommunicated'.¹⁵⁷ Even more strikingly, William Marshal's biographer has him make a speech to his troops, rousing them before the battle:

> And, if we beat them, it is no lie to say
> that we will have won eternal glory...
> And I shall tell you another fact
> which works very badly against them:
> they are excommunicated

---

[152] Carpenter, *Minority*, 27–31.   [153] *CM*, iii, 13.   [154] Arnold, *Belief and Unbelief*, 8.
[155] *CM*, iii, 83; *Oxenedes*, 150.   [156] Carpenter, *Minority*, 316–27, particularly 326.
[157] *CM*, iii, 28.

> and for that reason all the more trapped.
> I can tell you that they will come to a sticky end
> as they descend into hell.
> There you see men who have started a war
> on God and Holy Church.
> I can fully guarantee you this,
> that God has surrendered them into our hands.[158]

The Marshal's biographer was of course writing after the victory at Lincoln, and the speech itself is surely fabricated, but its arguments are interesting, particularly since they do not come from an ecclesiastical source. Part of the Marshal's (or rather his biographer's) point was that the French were in a weak position precisely because they were excommunicated. Such ideas were at least sufficiently well known that they could be expected to resonate with readers or listeners of the Anglo-Norman verse *History*. If the Marshal did say anything of this sort, it could well have had a strong effect upon the army. Wendover indicates that it would have been inspiring, claiming that there was 'an ardent desire to fight against the excommunicated French'.[159] In situations of heightened tension, beliefs in the ability of excommunication to affect the fortune of those sentenced might have mattered. Nevertheless, it must be concluded that, despite the best efforts of churchmen to convince that excommunicates would suffer terribly in life, as Murray observed, too often such eventualities patently did not take place (even if they occasionally did). This would have been all too evident to people, and there is little more to indicate that excommunicates sought absolution as a result of them.

Living as an Excommunicate

Excommunication's weakness lay not in any failure to convince the faithful of its impact on salvation, but in its lack of urgency. If the assumption that excommunication ultimately resulted in hell was a widespread one, it nevertheless enabled absolution to be put off until such a time as death seemed imminent. In the short term, other concerns trumped fear of hell. That excommunicates often remained under sentences for long periods demonstrates that most did not live in fear that their sentences would supernaturally afflict them before death. The issue is not simply one of belief versus disbelief, or of piety versus impiety. These things played a part: there were sceptics, while pious individuals were more likely to be influenced by the spiritual punishment, not least the inability to attend church or

---

[158] *History of William Marshal*, ed. Holden, ii, ll.16295–307.
[159] *CM*, iii, 18–19; cf. *Oxenedes*, 142.

receive the sacraments. The majority of people who chose not to seek immediate absolution can mostly be divided into two (not mutually exclusive) categories: those who calculated that it was advantageous to suffer a sentence for the time being, and those who believed that they were not truly excommunicated. Neither implied a rejection of excommunication *in toto*. Particularly for those who fell into the latter category, their refusal to submit to the church does not preclude genuine piety or fear of a justly imposed sanction.

Disrespect for excommunication was often followed, however belatedly, by absolution. Thus John de Beaupré, a knight, declared in 1275 that he had persisted in a state of excommunication for nearly three years, rejecting the 'oft-repeated admonition... with hardened heart, scoffing at the said sentence'. His assertion, however, was part of his public notification of the terms of his absolution (preserved in the episcopal register of Walter Bronescombe, bishop of Exeter): 'At last I came to myself, humbly and devoutly recognizing my offence, by the intervention of sons of peace who urged the salvation of my soul'. It is probable that this text, despite use of the first person, was composed by the bishop's administration. The terminology and phrasing correspond with that found in other ecclesiastical sources. John may not, therefore, have viewed his actions in these terms. Nonetheless, whether or not John truly 'scoffed' at his excommunication or instead felt justified in his defiance, his delay hardly demonstrates strong respect for the sanction.[160]

Rejections of excommunication need not be emphatic. Considering the conditions attached to it, delaying absolution was simply advantageous for many. Making satisfaction often involved monetary recompense; public penance was intentionally humiliating. It was against the spirit of excommunication ever to deny absolution, so the only risk of delaying lay in sudden death (even then, it might be hoped relatives would arrange a posthumous absolution). We cannot know why all those people, discussed by Donald Logan, who remained excommunicated and who were therefore threatened with arrest by the secular arm, gambled on remaining obdurate, but their behaviour need not imply that they did not 'believe' in excommunication's effects.[161] Instead, they acted in their own interests and sought absolution when it suited them.

The citizens of Dunstable, with whom this chapter opened, demonstrate the point. They neither denied the efficacy of excommunication nor disputed the validity of the sentence against them. They did, however, refuse to succumb to the monks' demands, seemingly concluding that their current dispute was more important than their salvation. The Dunstable Annalist's assertion that they

---

[160] *Reg. Bronescombe*, no. 1085. John was obliged to pay the bishop 200 marks, in installments. If he fulfilled this, an obligation to pay a further 200 marks was waived. Guarantors shared his obligation and sealed the letter.

[161] See Logan, *Excommunication and the Secular Arm*, particularly ch. 2.

'declared that they were excommunicates, and that they would prefer rather to descend to hell, than to succumb in the cause of tallage', however rhetorical, shows their insistence on standing their ground. Before the matter was settled, they threatened to leave the town altogether. Yet mediation, and a final concord, settled the dispute. Like John de Beaupré, they made peace with the church. The Dunstable example is unique because the men were not appealing their sentence, and did not, apparently, believe that it would prove invalid in the afterlife. They emphatically declared that they were willing to go to hell. The townsmen perhaps did not 'mean' that they were willing to go to hell, yet, significantly, they were in no doubt as to excommunication's effects: it meant damnation.

Delaying absolution could be a well-chosen policy. Paying fines, or giving up rights or (stolen) possessions were often conditions of absolution (dependent, of course, upon the offence committed). The afterlife was too far off to trump such worldly consequences, which could be more severe than mere loss of wealth. Thus, though Archbishop Winchelsey and a number of other resolute bishops refused to incur the *Clericis laicos* excommunication, most clergy capitulated to the king rather than face outlawry. As Jeffrey Denton observed, 'At least in this world, the consequences of the temporal ban were far more severe than those of the spiritual ban'.[162] Again, it was preferable to put off absolution and seek it later.[163] The bishop of London, Fulk Basset, similarly prioritized temporal over spiritual matters. Fulk was excommunicated by the archbishop of Canterbury, the queen's uncle Boniface of Savoy. He sought absolution from Boniface, Matthew Paris claims, not because he feared the excommunication, but because he feared the king's wrath. Although the sentence was reportedly widely considered unjust, Fulk sought to avoid royal anger.[164]

This last example brings us to excommunicates who believed their sentences unjust: not only did people often disrespect their sentences, it was also believed that sometimes they *should* ignore them. Paris states that Fulk was criticized and questioned not for disobeying the church, but for submitting to it. This demonstrates a fundamental problem with excommunication. Those who imposed sentences were fallible. As discussed in the last chapter, legal restrictions did far less than might be imagined to prevent *ex parte* excommunications. It is therefore hardly surprising that excommunication was not so terrifying as to cause people who had hitherto believed they had done nothing wrong to suddenly and meekly accept they were at fault. The church could not stamp out conviction. If clerics used excommunication vengefully or unjustly, people were bound to reject the doctrine that whoever was bound on earth was bound also in heaven (Matthew 18:18).

---

[162] Pollock and Maitland, *History of English Law*, i, 480; quoted in this context by Denton, *Robert Winchelsey*, 134.
[163] Both the papal registers and Winchelsey's register are filled with absolutions from the canon.
[164] *CM*, v, 206. See also Chapter 4 below, at 170. Carpenter, *Henry III*, 557–9.

The law regarding unjust sentences was clear: even if a sentence was unjust, the person sentenced should humbly submit to it. Thomas of Chobham discussed the issue, introducing the proposition that Matthew 18:18 appears false 'because many foolish priests unjustly and unwisely bind someone who has no fault, and such a person is not bound in heaven because God does not approve that binding'. Not so, answers Chobham: God does consider such a person bound, because he wants them to obey that sentence, not to destroy the unity of the church. Chobham then quotes Gratian's *Decretum*: 'The sentence of a priest, whether just or unjust, should be feared' (C. 11, q. 3, c. 1). The only exceptions were extreme cases in which a priest expressed an obvious error, such as 'I excommunicate you if you believe in God'.[165] Sentences could be unjust in three ways, Chobham explains: in cause (*ex causa*), in spirit (*ex animo*), or procedurally (*ex ordine*). Sentences unjust in judicial procedure, for instance where someone was not properly cited or convicted, could be appealed. However, a sentence 'is unjust in cause when the person bound committed nothing; it is unjust in spirit when someone excommunicates because of anger or jealousy; and in both cases the sentence must be held, although it is unjust'. Scorning an unjust sentence was a mortal sin and automatically made the sentence just.[166] Provisional absolution had to be given before sentences could be appealed, since excommunicates could not act in court (X 5.39.40).[167]

Despite the clear rules, for every Sewal de Bovill (who submitted to his unjust sentence lest it became just through his contempt), there were many more who refused to accept their excommunications. The church's position on the matter made sense: to have allowed the laity to question the judgements of churchmen would have been to irreparably weaken the sanction.[168] Individuals' responses to this position are equally understandable. Many appear to have believed that excommunication, in their circumstances, would not damn them utterly.[169] God would rectify errors perpetrated on earth. Refusing to submit to the church in such situations demonstrates contempt for ecclesiastical authority, but it does not necessarily imply disdain for the entire concept of excommunication.[170] People do not, in general, like to be punished for something of which they consider themselves innocent, or do not agree is wrong.

It cannot be claimed that those who contested sentences were invariably irreligious. Indisputably pious men, trained in canon law, such as bishops Robert Grosseteste and Thomas Cantilupe, refused to accept that excommunications

---

[165] Cf. Innocent III's ruling in *Per tuas* (X 5.39.40).
[166] Chobham, *Summa*, 173, 201–2. Cf. Flamborough, *Liber Poenitentialis*, 154; Peñafort, *De Poenitentia*, 406, 412–14, 414–15; Helmholz, 'Excommunication as a legal sanction', 210.
[167] Clarke, *Interdict*, discusses the rules regarding appeals at 251–9. [168] C.11, q.3, c.1.
[169] Jacob Katz made the same point about Jewish excommunication: 'those who transgressed the *herem* did not deny its power and did not mock it in principle; rather, they found some way to justify their actions by arguing that the *herem* did not apply to their specific deed': *Tradition and Crisis*, 85.
[170] Logan, *Excommunication and the Secular Arm*, 15, made a similar point.

against them were valid. Cantilupe, although he died excommunicate in 1282 (while in Rome to appeal Archbishop Pecham's sentence), was in due course even canonized.[171] If such exemplary prelates could not bring themselves to submit, why should others behave more obediently? Moreover, there was an argument that would excuse disobedience to excommunication: if obedience to the terms of absolution would incur sin, an excommunication should be borne.[172] This tension between conscience and authority has been discussed at greater length by Alexander Murray. Twelfth and thirteenth-century theologians stressed the importance of obeying one's conscience; in the end, conscience ranked higher even than the pope's *plenitudo potestatis*.[173] It was therefore possible to argue like Innocent III that, in certain situations, it would be worse to submit to the church. The emerging emphasis on conscience in the twelfth and thirteenth centuries again plays a role here. While conscience might cause people to seek absolution from secret excommunications, it could also justify disobedience if someone felt they did not deserve their sentence.

The ambiguity of certain *ipso facto* sentences provided further scope for arguments that people were not truly excommunicated. What precisely constituted disturbing the peace of the realm (*Qui pacem et tranquillitatem*) was open to interpretation.[174] What one man considered disturbing the peace, another believed was in order to achieve that peace. The argument was open to dissimulation, but it could allow people to feel that they had not, in good conscience, incurred an excommunication, even when they were being denounced as excommunicates.

The thought process was most eloquently described by Llywelyn, prince of Wales, in a 1224 letter to Henry III. Following the rebellion and outlawry of Falkes de Bréauté, Llywelyn had been forbidden from helping or receiving Falkes. Llywelyn responded to this angrily, pointing out that Wales was as free as Scotland, and the kings of Scotland were able to take in English outlaws with impunity. He defended the actions of Falkes, pointing out how well he had served the king in the past. Finally, he declared that while Falkes was excommunicated for disturbing the peace, in reality it was the king's advisers who were the

---

[171] For this venomous quarrel over jurisdiction see Finucane, 'Cantilupe-Pecham controversy' and Douie, *Archbishop Pecham*, 192–217; Powicke, *Thirteenth Century*, 488–90. Susan Ridyard's forthcoming edition of Cantilupe's canonization process will no doubt illuminate much about excommunication as well as sanctity and devotion. For Grosseteste's excommunication by the monks of Canterbury, see *Grosseteste Letters*, no. 110; Morgan, 'Excommunication of Grosseteste'.

[172] X 5.39.44. Innocent III wrote that if a spouse, but not the church, knew of a marriage impediment, excommunication should be suffered: paying the marital debt in such a marriage would be worse. See also Murray, 'Excommunication', 194–6, and Clarke, *Interdict*, 44.

[173] Murray, 'Excommunication', 187–97, provides a fascinating and nuanced discussion; Helmholz, *Spirit of Classical Canon Law*, 378–80; Helmholz, 'Excommunication as a legal sanction', 210–11; Hill, 'Theory and practice', 5–6.

[174] Complexities of interpreting *ipso facto* sentences and differing opinions are discussed further in Chapter 4.

true disturbers. Thus Llywelyn wrote 'we do not believe that he [Falkes] is excommunicated as far as God is concerned'. Llywelyn refused to act against his own conscience, even if this meant incurring excommunication himself: 'We prefer to be excommunicated by man, than to do anything against God, with our conscience condemning us.'[175] He did not reject excommunication in principle, but believed that this particular sentence would not be upheld by God. Whether or not Llywelyn truly believed his argument, if his conscience urged that he would sin by submitting to the excommunication, he made a theologically sound one, endorsed by Innocent III.[176]

Falkes de Bréauté himself argued that the excommunication against him was not only unjust, but also invalid. Thus he wrote that the archbishop and bishops had excommunicated him 'not cited, not confessed, not convicted'. They had been pretending to act with pious intent, when in fact they had acted through malice. Moreover, they were 'proved to have proceeded from hatred rather than to have wanted to save souls with zeal for justice'.[177] Falkes's first complaint implied that the sentence contravened canon law, invalid *ex ordine*; the second meant it was unjust in spirit, *ex animo*. As we have seen, Falkes was only permitted, in theory, to complain about the first fault. His complaint about the injustice of his excommunication clearly shows why he rejected it, even if churchmen would merely condemn this as a mortal sin. Llywelyn, however, was making a valid theological argument, rendering his disobedience not only justified but vital.

Llywelyn's letter is an especially lucid example, but there is evidence that others reacted similarly. The abbot of Westminster and prior of Canterbury were excommunicated in 1216, after objecting to Henry III's coronation at Worcester by the bishop of Winchester, because it infringed their respective liberties. But they 'did not consider themselves excommunicates' because they had appealed, and did not withdraw their appeals.[178] The clergy who submitted to Edward I when he withdrew his protection argued that necessity excused them from the pope's *Clericis laicos* excommunication. Edward himself argued that he was forced to burden his people with levies: if clergy believed Edward's demands were necessary to protect the kingdom, their consciences would have been clear.[179]

The problem that death seemed a long way off is shown again by those who expressed willingness to remain excommunicated for the time being. In 1232, when the crops of various Roman clergy were stolen and the pope ordered that the perpetrators be punished, Roger of Wendover noted that the ringleader protested openly. This Robert had done it because he hated the Romans, who had despoiled him of his church by fraud. He declared that he had a just cause, announcing that 'he preferred to be excommunicated unjustly for a time (*ad tempus*) than to be

---

[175] *Royal Letters*, no. 201; Carpenter, *Minority*, 74.   [176] X 5.39.44.   [177] *Coventry*, 171–2.
[178] *Melrose*, 124–5 ('ipsi tamen nec pro excommunicatis se habuerunt').
[179] *Cotton*, 322–3. *Necessitas* has always supplied a powerful argument to justify exceptions.

despoiled of his benefice without justice'.[180] The idea that an unjust sentence was preferable 'ad tempus' was also voiced by the French prince Louis. According to Wendover, Louis rejected the pope's assertion, in 1215, that he had incurred excommunication for aiding the excommunicated English barons, insisting that he was not supporting them but rather seeking his own rights. 'Louis did not, and could not, believe that the pope or the council would excommunicate anyone unjustly.' He had sworn to help the barons, and he would therefore 'prefer to be excommunicated by the pope temporarily, than incur the accusation of falsehood'.[181] Again, the implication is that both men were acting as they believed was right, but that they did not intend to stay excommunicated.

Finally, a most emphatic belief in the righteousness of a cause, even in the face of excommunication, was upheld by the baronial reformers between 1258 and 1266. The programme of reform had the support of a number of bishops and other churchmen. It was enforced by oaths and excommunication. Moreover, the Montfortian army fought with white crusader crosses on their shoulders both at Lewes and at Evesham.[182] After Montfort's death at Evesham, miracles were ascribed to the martyred earl, and his cult was propagated by the Franciscans.[183] Abigail Hartman has shown the strength of feeling amongst those who supported Montfort after his death by looking at the various poetry that venerated him as a saint. Ignoring his excommunicate status while emphasizing the justice of his cause and his use of violence, they believed God was on their side.[184] There is no doubt that many of those who fought against the king did so in the conviction that their cause was just. It appears, indeed, that the mutually contradictory excommunications pronounced by both sides facilitated rejection of sentences pronounced against either party. The rebels demonstrated their contempt sacrilegiously. According to the chronicler Robert of Gloucester, at the siege of Kenilworth in 1266 the legate Ottobuono excommunicated all those in the castle, along with their supporters and helpers. Far from being terrified by this sentence, the rebels staged their own mock excommunication against the royalists. They dressed up their surgeon as a mock legate ('wit legat'), in a mock cope ('cope of wit'), he then stood on the castle wall and cursed ('amansede') the king, the legate and all their men.[185]

---

[180] *CM*, iii, 217–19. For the context of these riots, see Vincent, *Peter des Roches*, 303–9.

[181] *CM*, ii, 662, 653. Hanley, *Louis: The French Prince*, 97–9, discusses the prince's reaction to excommunication.

[182] The *Song of Lewes*, trans. Kingsford, written between the battles of Lewes and Evesham by a friar in support of the baronial cause also provides much detail of how the rebels viewed their own cause as moral, just, and religious. For crusader crosses see Maddicott, *Simon de Montfort*, 247 n. 91, 271 n. 192.

[183] See Valente, 'Simon de Montfort'; Maddicott, *Simon de Montfort*, 347–8.

[184] Hartman, 'Poetry and the cause of Simon de Montfort'.

[185] *Robert of Gloucester*, 772. Christian Jaser has discussed the phenomenon of lay 'counter-excommunication', with reference to the fourteenth century: 'Usurping the spiritual sword'.

The following year, an exchange is reported by William Rishanger's chronicle. Though a fourteenth-century account, John Maddicott has argued for the chronicle's value for its account of the barons' wars.[186] The disinherited hiding in the Isle of Ely were warned by the legate's messenger to return to the faith of the church, to the obedience of the Roman Curia and to the king's peace, to receive absolution from the sentence of excommunication, and finally to make restitution for robberies perpetrated and commit no more. Their responses were emphatic. First, they firmly held the same faith that they had learnt from the holy bishops St Robert (Grosseteste), St Edmund (of Abingdon), St Richard (Wych), and other Catholic men.[187] They believed in the articles of faith, the Lord's Prayer, the gospels, and the sacraments, and for the sake of this faith they were prepared to live and die. Second, they owed obedience to the Roman Church as head of all Christianity, 'but not to all the arbitrary lusts and demands of those who ought to control the same [church] and king'. Third, the legate had been sent to make peace but instead 'he fosters more war, because he manifestly supports and favours the king's party'.

> To the fourth they say that the first undertaking and the first oath were for the utility of the realm and the whole church, and all the prelates of the kingdom fulminated a sentence of excommunication on all contradictors, therefore to this they stand firm in the same will, and are prepared to die for the same oath. They encourage the legate to revoke the sentence; otherwise they appeal to the apostolic see and also to the general council, or, if necessary, to the Highest Judge.[188]

These men were not heretics. They were not impious. On the contrary, they were avowedly devout and accepted that they owed allegiance to the Roman Church. What they questioned was the judgement of the legate in their particular circumstances. Excommunication had already been pronounced in support of their enterprise and they could not obey another such sentence declared with the opposite intent. They were willing to take their chances with God rather than submit to a sentence they did not accept.[189]

There is no evidence of Montfort's personal reaction to his excommunication. He was certainly aware of the dangers of publicity, threatening to kill the legate, Gui Fouquois, should he land in England to publish his sentence, and to decapitate anyone who dared carry, read, or publish letters of interdict or excommunication against those observing the Provisions of Oxford.[190] John Maddicott has sketched

---

[186] Maddicott, *Simon de Montfort*, 87–90, 245–6.
[187] Respectively, Bishop of Lincoln (1235–53), Archbishop of Canterbury (1234–40), Bishop of Chichester (1244–53). Attempts to have Grosseteste canonized were in fact unsuccessful.
[188] *Chronicle of William de Rishanger*, ed. Halliwell, 62–3. They also answered the other points.
[189] See Knowles, 'Resettlement of England after the barons' war', for how the disinherited were eventually reconciled.
[190] Gilson, 'Parliament of 1264', 501. See Chapter 5 below, at 225–7.

Montfort's spiritual influences and personal piety with admirable clarity. Montfort's close relationship with bishops and friars meant that he was well versed in matters of conscience, even lecturing Henry III on the futility of confession without penance and satisfaction. He also demonstrated his 'exceptionally fastidious conscience' through pious devotional practices. Most notably, he wore a hair shirt. If the earl's piety rendered him more likely to be perturbed at the prospect of damnation, his learning and understanding of the fundamental importance of conscience make it eminently plausible that he was one of those who believed his conscience excused him. He was not concerned about the legate's sentences of excommunication because he believed that he was fighting for justice.[191] 'For him the issues were ones of religion and conscience, and the battle that he faced was "God's battle".'[192] The actions and words of his followers after his death reinforce the idea that Montfort did not believe that God had condemned his actions. As Maddicott observes, 'Pride of place must be given here to Montfort's conscience, for in the last phase of his life it supplies us with one key to our understanding of his actions'.[193]

Many more who lived under sentences of excommunication surely felt similarly that they were being unfairly treated by the churchmen who imposed sentences on them. For the vast majority, the extant evidence does not permit certainty about this. Perhaps some were irreligious or sceptics. Questioning ecclesiastical authority could, however, certainly come from those who were both pious and orthodox. There is little to suggest that excommunicates were, as a group, impious or disbelieving. Certain men excommunicated in the diocese of Hereford, though 'scorning the keys of the church, to the detriment of their salvation and our church...do not fear the sentence of excommunication', were nonetheless attending divine services and receiving the sacraments.[194] The language used here by the bishop is typical in mandates of this sort and presents the offenders as wicked. Attending mass and receiving the sacraments while excommunicate certainly demonstrates disrespect for their sentences (the bishop launched an investigation into where they had been going), but also shows a clear desire to involve themselves in ecclesiastical practices.[195]

Conclusions

Excommunication was supposed to encourage absolution partly by instilling fear that the soul was imperilled. Warnings that divine retribution might strike down excommunicates had power only in limited circumstances and were in general

---

[191] Maddicott, *Simon de Montfort*, 84–96; Ambler, *Song of Simon de Montfort*, 288–9.
[192] Maddicott, *Simon de Montfort*, 271.   [193] Maddicott, *Simon de Montfort*, 84.
[194] *Reg. Cantilupe*, 97–8. Three villages, Chastroke, Aston, and Muliton, claimed by both Llywelyn of Wales and the bishop, were the cause of this dispute. Ibid., xxviii, 10, 29, 31, 42, 97–8, 103–4.
[195] Cf. Beaulande, *Malheur*, 217–18; Vodola, *Excommunication*, 55–6.

little heeded, but the idea that hell was the ultimate destination for those who failed to secure absolution was accepted. Yet reactions varied from fearful to indifferent to defiant. The indifferent, who were too little disturbed by deprivation of the sacraments and church, judged that they would benefit from delaying absolution. Nothing indicates that there was any widespread scepticism about excommunication's effects. No doubt elsewhere, for instance in areas where Cathars or Waldensians were plentiful, such individuals would have been accused of heresy. But in thirteenth-century England the link between such contempt for ecclesiastical authority and heresy was weaker and did not necessitate such suspicions. Nor did the defiant reject the power of excommunication *in toto*. Clergy were fallible, so some simply rejected the validity of their own individual sentences, questioning such sentences' ability to imperil their salvation. They disregarded the church's unequivocal teaching that scorning an unjust sentence rendered it a just one, but could still believe in the spiritual perils of valid excommunication. Even the pious might refuse, at least temporarily, to accept a sentence pronounced against them by someone they believed was acting unjustly. *Ipso facto* or *de jure* sentences, by contrast, were incurred rather than judicially imposed. There was no unreasonable clergyman to rail against. Instead, the excommunicate had to contend with their own conscience (and perhaps accusations), provoking a different type of disquiet. These internalized fears, in which guilt from sinning and worries about being separated from God surely featured, sometimes did cause requests for absolution from those who had never been publicly excommunicated.[196]

The issue was not that the spiritual terrors inflicted by excommunication were too weak, but rather that they took effect too slowly. These effects provided an important part of the sanction's potency. Yet it is clear that only in certain circumstances were they enough to impel a swift absolution. The afterlife was something to worry about later. Spiritual effects provided an incentive to reconcile with the church or to avoid excommunication in the first place, but alongside social and other worldly and immediate repercussions. As Peter Clarke found in his study of interdict in the thirteenth century, in general the inconvenience of ecclesiastical sanctions eventually caused its victims to come to terms.[197] As a means of *quickly* driving sinners to make satisfaction, fear of hell alone was not enough. In the case of deathbed absolutions, which are unfortunately difficult to quantify, excommunication might have been very effective. For the healthy, however, loss of salvation was of less immediate concern than temporal repercussions. For all the criticisms (medieval and modern) that excommunication was morally questionable, and despite the damnatory rhetoric, the medicinal purpose

---

[196] Though it ought to be noted that there was often less to lose than when submitting to the church in a public case.
[197] Clarke, *Interdict*, esp. 234.

of excommunication triumphed. That excommunication was not intended to be permanent was well understood. Ease of absolution (especially when *in articlo mortis*), Véronique Beaulande has observed, is one cause of the indifference provoked by ecclesiastical censures.[198] The sanction was undeniably weakened by New Testament principles of charity and forgiveness, which compelled churchmen to grant absolution when it was sought and to make the process very easy indeed for the dying. Excommunication was almost always effective if judged by its medicinal intent, since most excommunicates eventually returned to the church. For an individual's soul, the timing did not matter. Practically speaking, for those who wanted recompense, retribution, or repentance, it did. The relative absence of spiritual risk inherent in deferring absolution precluded fear of hell being the most effective way to coerce timely submission.

---

[198] Beaulande, *Malheur*, 205.

PART II
COMMUNITIES

3
Exclusion from the Community of the Faithful

'You should avoid the said Reginald, so that he whom fear of God does not recall from evil, subtraction of human social interaction induces and compels more quickly to make due satisfaction'.[1] This order, sent by the bishop of Carlisle to his subjects in 1300, demonstrates that clergy did not rely upon spiritual terrors to coerce excommunicates. Communities, having participated in the excommunication ceremony by collectively declaring 'so be it' ('fiat, fiat') at its culmination, were expected to avoid excommunicates or themselves risk becoming 'infected' with excommunication. Ostracism, unlike the danger of hell in the afterlife, might be a pressing concern. Being 'outside the community of the faithful' should have made it impossible for an excommunicate to function in an overwhelmingly Christian society. If we are to consider the effectiveness of excommunication, we must look at the communities charged with enforcing it.

The effectiveness of the sanction relied less upon the reaction of the individual excommunicated than upon that of the wider community expected to perform ostracism on a day-to-day basis. Though an excommunicate's opinion about his or her sentence (for instance that it was unjust and would not be upheld by God) might affect how others perceived a sentence, an excommunicate's belief that a sentence was unfair was irrelevant if friends, neighbours, or enemies properly enforced it. Some of the ways in which excommunicates were excluded from the Christian community relied upon authorities: the prohibition to enter church or receive the sacraments would be enforced by clergy; exclusion from legal proceedings was carried out by both ecclesiastical and secular authorities; the more extreme measure of arresting and imprisoning excommunicates was performed by royal agents. For the most part, however, churchmen using excommunication were dependent upon the general population to implement their sentences.

Records are far more likely to note failure to ostracize the condemned; when excommunicates were treated as canon law demanded there was no need for further action or for comment from ecclesiastical sources. In one sense, therefore, it is to be expected that examples of shunning are harder to find. This perhaps led Rosalind Hill to conclude that 'the excommunicated person, if his name were

---

[1] 'Subtractio communionis humane', *Reg. Halton*, i, 131–2. Reginald de Cumbredal had been excommunicated for over forty days (though the bishop did not request his arrest).

known, was generally avoided'.² Nonetheless, recorded instances are markedly rare compared with examples of illicit communicating. It must be concluded that excommunicates were not routinely or consistently shunned by the wider community as a whole. The numerous and complex reasons for this are discussed in Chapter 4, which should be read alongside this chapter. A lack of persistent shunning does not, however, mean that excommunicates had nothing to fear. Excommunicates were placed in a vulnerable position. The danger was that the sanction could be used as a pretext to justify mistreatment. Those in power were left particularly exposed, not least because excommunication was a steppingstone to deposition and even crusade. Excommunication thus remained a useful tool for both clergy and laity, but it was not necessarily under the control of the clergy who pronounced sentences.

Exclusion and Contagion

The Christian imperative to avoid excommunicates can be traced back to the Bible. In Matthew 18:15-17, Jesus taught that a brother who offended should first be rebuked in private, then before witnesses, and then reported to the church. If he still remained recalcitrant, 'let him be to thee as a heathen and a publican'. In 1 Corinthians 5, Paul wrote that 'a little yeast corrupts the whole batch of dough'. He urged Christians not to keep company with fornicators, the covetous, extortioners, or idolators, instructing: 'do not eat with such a one'.

Use of this particular method of censure and means of altering behaviour hardly requires explanation, for ostracism is a natural human impulse. Social scientists Margaret Gruter and Roger D. Masters noted in a 1986 interdisciplinary special journal edition devoted to ostracism that 'the process by which some individuals are...excluded from interaction with other members of a social group' is not only common to almost all known human societies, but can even be observed amongst animals.³ Groups of children can use exclusion to punish unacceptable behaviour, without any need for an explicit collective decision to do so.⁴ The psychologist Kipling D. Williams observed that it is unnecessary to ask *whether* someone has experienced a form of ostracism; simply asking *when* suffices, since everyone will have been exposed to 'the silent treatment', 'ghosting', or some other form of social exclusion.⁵ It can be performed by individuals or groups informally, such as when people express their anger with silence or discipline children by sending them to their rooms, for example. It can also be formal, imposed upon others by institutions, as in the case of medieval

---

² *Reg. Sutton*, iii, xlix.
³ Gruter and Masters, 'Ostracism as a social and biological phenomenon', 150.
⁴ Barner-Barry, 'Rob: Children's tacit use of peer ostracism'.   ⁵ Williams, *Ostracism*, 1–2.

excommunication and other organized religions (the clearest non-Christian parallel is the Jewish *herem*). As an institution, the medieval church thus sought to harness a powerful social impulse, paralleled throughout history.[6]

The idea that sin was contagious was present from the time of the early church, as Paul's letter shows.[7] This rhetoric became an important part of how excommunication was described.[8] The language, used to convince the faithful to shun excommunicates, closely resembles that used about heretics, lepers, and other deviants considered dangerous to Christian morals and health, as discussed by R. I. Moore, though one cannot talk of any 'persecution' of excommunicates *qua* excommunicates.[9] Gratian's *Decretum* incorporated Julianus Pomerius's fifth-century assertion that

> Those who for a long time do not want to be corrected ought to be cut off by the sword of excommunication as rotten parts of the body. Just as the flesh, dead from illness, corrupts the health of the remaining flesh with the contagion of its rottenness if it is not cut off, thus those who disdain to be corrected and persist in their illness, if they remain in the society of the holy, kill them with the example of their perdition.[10]

The idea was reflected in normative sources from thirteenth-century England. Thus Thomas Chobham wrote, 'major excommunication . . . is like leprosy and it therefore pollutes someone communicating with it'.[11] The common law treatise Bracton's *De legibus* noted 'as there may be leprosy in the body so there may be in the soul, and as the communion of mankind is denied a leper, so it is to an excommunicate'.[12] The rhetoric was not unique to Christianity. Jewish excommunication, the *herem*, made use of similar language regarding infection and contagion, requiring similar treatment.[13]

One purpose behind the shunning that was supposed to accompany excommunication was therefore to protect others from being polluted by contact. Stephen of Bourbon's preaching aid sought to emphasize the dangers of contact by recounting a miracle story in which the devil boasted that a single excommunication in a parish could lead to his gaining many souls: if parishioners continued to associate with the excommunicate, the devil had them all in his net.[14]

---

[6] Robert Parker speculates that apparently spontaneous ostracism in ancient Greece might have been the survival of an earlier formal institution: *Miasma*, 194.

[7] Though as Rosalind Hill noted, there were similar pre-Christian practices, for instance amongst the Druids: 'Belief and practice', 2.

[8] See also Rosemblieh, 'Limiter la contagion', 62.

[9] Moore, *Formation of a Persecuting Society*, 58–9, particularly addresses the language of infection. Vodola notes that heretics were 'scrupulously differentiated' from other excommunicates: *Excommunication*, 32.

[10] C.24, q.3, c.18.   [11] Chobham, *Summa*, 248.   [12] Bracton *De legibus*, iv, 292–3.

[13] Kaplan, *Religion, Politics and Freedom of Conscience*, 9–10.

[14] *Anecdotes Historiques*, no. 307.

Excommunication's dangerous contagiousness meant that it was a commonplace, expressed in innumerable texts of different types, that those under the ban were to be avoided ('evitari'). Robert of Flamborough defined excommunication as 'separation from any licit and honest communication with the faithful'.[15] Canon law (and a common mnemonic verse) decreed that Christians were not to communicate with excommunicates in speaking, eating, drinking, or kissing.[16] Knowingly communicating with an excommunicate, even to say 'hello' ('ave'), was forbidden.[17] A tract on confession that circulated with the 1224 × 1237 Coventry Statutes is concise: avoid excommunicates 'at table, in prayer, greeting, the kiss of peace, and conversation'.[18] Bishops often added that buying from and selling to an excommunicate was forbidden.[19] In 1270, William de Nevill was even to be denied fire and water.[20]

Fear of contagion was articulated in practice as well as in normative sources. In 1268 the parishioners of Honyburn were told to shun the chaplain Henry de Norton 'as one infected with a contagious disease'.[21] Excommunicates were a danger to others, for they might 'infect healthy sheep with their contagion'.[22] The seriousness with which infection was taken is reflected in the concern that the innocent might be infected unknowingly. Innocent III sought to stop unknowing communication with excommunicated Rouen merchants who were travelling to England on business.[23] The bishop of Salisbury wrote to the abbess of Wilton, expressing concern that the nuns might unwittingly communicate with the excommunicated Martin de Bridecumbe, formerly a chaplain at the chapel pertaining to their monastery.[24] Runaway excommunicates and those who pretended they had been absolved likewise posed threats to those with whom they interacted, 'by which the Lord's flock is blemished'.[25]

These last examples express concern that the ignorant might 'catch' excommunication without realizing. In fact, the law excepted those who communicated with an excommunicate through ignorance so that they were not infected. The emphasis on protecting the flock conceals the worry that communication, whether ignorant or not, undermined the impact of excommunication. The doctrine and rhetoric of infection, even while the latter emphasized shielding the faithful from this spiritual leprosy, was surely originally motivated by the need to persuade the

---

[15] Flamborough, *Liber Poenitentialis*, 145.
[16] 'Si pro delictis anathema quis efficiatur: / os, orare, vale, communio, mensa negatur'. 'If someone is afflicted with anathema for their offences, / they are deprived of the kiss [of peace], prayer, greeting, communion, and meals'. The verse was widespread, see for example Thomas Aquinas' *Summa Theologiae*: Bk III-Supplementum, q.21, a.1; Peñafort, *De Poenitentia*, 406-7. See also Hyland, *Excommunication*, 38.
[17] C.11, q.3, c.17; C.11, q.3, c.110. There are, however, a plethora of canons concerning the rules about communicating with excommunicates in C.11, q.3; Rosemblieh, 'Limiter la contagion', 62.
[18] *C&S*, 226. [19] E.g. *Reg. Pontissara*, ii, 588-9.
[20] *SCC*, 331-3; cf. Dresch, 'Outlawry', 101. [21] *Reg. G. Giffard*, 32.
[22] *Reg. Gandavo*, i, 147-9. [23] *Letters of Innocent III*, no. 29 (appendix).
[24] *Reg. Gandavo*, i, 116. [25] *Foedera*, I.i.369-70; *Reg. Bronescombe*, no. 1025 (quotation).

populace to perform ostracism. Avoid this person or *you* will be at risk. There was, then, a pastoral imperative to urge avoidance since excommunication spread and endangered souls. But more practically important was the fact that without the compliance of the faithful, excommunication's social impact was a dead letter.

The primary purpose of the exclusion itself, as John de Halton's warning to his subjects shows, was to drive the excommunicate back into the bosom of the church and to right his or her wrongs. Exclusion would cause numerous practical difficulties, while the social stigma was supposed to humiliate excommunicates: 'so that...covered with shame he might be compelled...to due obedience'.[26] Thus Thomas of Chobham instructed, 'we cannot say "hello" [to an excommunicate], but we must always respond with a bitter word whence he or she may have shame, such as "may God correct you" or "may God make you such that I can greet you"'.[27] Juliana Box was supposed to be shunned so that 'through removal of social intercourse...she returns more quickly to the bosom of the church, embarrassed with shame'.[28] Indeed, a stern reception from friends and neighbours would have been unpleasant and humiliating, and certainly a reason to seek reintegration with the community through absolution.

Mitigations

The ostracism associated with excommunication was in fact less severe than the principle of complete separation from the community implies, both when compared to other forms of ostracism and because of various mitigations introduced during the Middle Ages. Studies of ostracism indicate that social exclusion can be a powerful tool, with biologically and psychologically severe effects. Even mild social ostracism can produce physiological symptoms on the person ostracized.[29] Indeed, the impact of social exclusion can be more severe than that of physical means of ostracism, such as exile.[30] Individuals who have suffered long-term ostracism report extreme feelings of worthlessness and depression, as well as issues with their physical health.[31] But excommunicates were spared some of the worst effects of social ostracism identified by psychologist Kipling D. Williams. Many of his interviewees, excluded informally rather than as a result of an official judgement, were most distressed by not knowing the cause of their shunning and

---

[26] *Parliament Rolls*, 590. Before this, the importance of preventing him contaminating the flock with 'his pestilential communion' is noted, as is the failure of fear of God to restrain this excommunicate, the bishop of Durham.
[27] Chobham, *Summa*, 248. [28] *Reg. Winchelsey*, i, 390–1.
[29] MaGuire and Raleigh, 'Behavioral and physiological correlates of ostracism'.
[30] Williams, *Ostracism*, 49–50.
[31] Williams, *Ostracism*, 30–1, 230–9. Unable to recreate such experiences via scientific experiments, Williams relied on a self-selecting group willing to discuss their experiences.

their consequent inability to do anything about it.[32] By contrast, excommunicates knew why they had been sentenced (whether or not they considered their sentence fair). Similarly, the means to stop any ostracism they were suffering was clear: repent, make amends, seek absolution, and return to the Christian community. Even the advice to urge excommunicates to repent might have provided some relief: Williams found that individuals who were shunned for long periods began to feel invisible, even preferring physical abuse to this emotional withdrawal by those closest to them.[33] Perhaps such twentieth-century accounts do not correspond with reactions in the Middle Ages, but in any case medieval excommunicates were spared some of the potentially most unpleasant characteristics of social exclusion suggested by Williams's study, even when treated as ecclesiastical authorities expected. Excommunicates were not supposed to be treated as invisible by those amongst whom they lived; nor were they ignorant of the reason for their mistreatment.

Excommunication was also far gentler than outlawry, with which excommunication has a superficial similarity. Both sanctions sought to exclude individuals from the community, and were accordingly linked in Anglo-Saxon law codes.[34] An association remained in thirteenth-century England; Matthew Paris noted that Falkes de Bréauté was subject to both censures: 'the archbishop and the other bishops there... excommunicated Falkes and those complying with him, decreeing him outlawed (*ipsum utlagari decernentes*)'.[35] However, the effects of outlawry were harsher than those of excommunication. Though by the thirteenth century outlaws were not to be killed by anyone who came across them, they nevertheless faced loss of legal status, property, and safety.[36] The most important difference to excommunication was that outlawry was intended to be a permanent state. In fact, pardons became more common during this period, but were far from an integral part of outlawry as absolution was for excommunication.[37] In theory, abjuration— leaving the realm within a fixed time—was a fugitive's only option other than living outside the law (which is why outlaws living in the woods were a feature of medieval England, made famous by Robin Hood). Those harbouring outlaws faced loss of life and limb along with the outlaw himself, without exception for close relatives.[38] In-lawed outlaws did not recover their property or rights but were 'reborn' as a new person (though if an outlawry was deemed void, they returned to their prior state).[39] This was in stark contrast to excommunication, which, as a

---

[32] Williams, *Ostracism*, 21–3, 56–7, 96.   [33] Williams, *Ostracism*, 26–7, 49, 233–4.
[34] Pollock and Maitland, *History of English Law*, i, 478.
[35] *CM*, iii, 89; Sartore, *Outlawry*, 137–8.
[36] Dresch, 'Outlawry', 108–9; Pollock and Maitland, *History of English Law*, i, 480.
[37] Stewart, 'Outlawry', 42–3; Sartore, *Outlawry*, 204–5, 214.
[38] Stewart, 'Outlawry', 45–6. Women could be 'waived' but not declared outlaws: *Bracton De legibus*, ii, 353–4.
[39] Pollock and Maitland, *History of English Law*, i, 477; *Bracton De legibus*, ii, 357–8.

function of its medicinal claims, was designed to be temporary and without consequences after appropriate contrition had been shown.

That excommunication was less severe than its secular equivalent is perhaps to be expected. Even within its own terms, however, excommunication was increasingly tempered. As mentioned above, complete ostracism was not required: it was licit to talk or to preach to excommunicates in order to convince them to return to the church.[40] Excommunication's social effects were mitigated by canon law, particularly from the eleventh century. In *Quoniam multos* (1078), Pope Gregory VII declared his concern that the severe rules governing communication with excommunicates caused many to perish (spiritually). Therefore, those who knowingly failed to appropriately shun excommunicates were *ipso facto* 'infected', but only with minor excommunication. This excluded them from the sacraments but not the whole Christian community.[41] We may note again how much milder this was than the capital punishment faced by harbourers of outlaws.[42] Minor excommunication was not contagious, so excommunication did not spread to a third person. Those who had specifically helped the excommunicate in their crime were not included in this reprieve, however, and could expect a major sentence.[43]

Gregory VII thus accepted the reality that the rules regarding the avoidance of excommunicates were often disregarded, since no epidemic would ensue if excommunicates were appropriately shunned. In the same bull, he exempted those who communicated with excommunicates through ignorance, simplicity, fear, or necessity. He further ruled that excommunicates' wives, children, servants and other dependants, and travellers forced to buy food from excommunicates, were not bound by minor excommunication for communicating.[44] Though ignorance had always implicitly been an excuse for contact, Gregory's other exceptions were novel, and considerably lessened excommunication's infectious nature. In the fifteenth century, the prevalence of *ipso facto* excommunications made further mitigations necessary. Reformers during the Great Western Schism sought to limit the contagion of excommunication only to sentences that had been publicized, with the canon *Ad vitanda* (1418).[45] The motive for lessening the infectiousness of excommunication was supposedly pastoral, intended to prevent the loss of souls: Gregory referred to an 'epidemic'. Elisabeth Vodola observed that Gregory may have felt that 'matters had gone too far', for the pope himself had

---

[40] E.g. Aquinas, *Summa Theologiae*, Bk III-Supplementum, q. 23, a. 1; X 2.25.2; X 5.39.43.
[41] Peñafort, *De Poenitentia*, 396–7.   [42] Cf. *Bracton De legibus*, ii, 361–2.
[43] X 5.39.29.   [44] C.11, q.3, cc.102, 103. Further explained in X 5.39.31.
[45] This reform did not prevail long-term. See Rosemblieh, 'Limiter la contagion'. As Rosemblieh notes, contagion had always been dependent upon communicating knowingly, but it was now specified that knowledge depended upon promulgation of a named sentence: ibid. 64–5; Vodola, *Excommunication*, 142–4; Beaulande, *Malheur*, 41, 44–5; Hyland, *Excommunication*, 40–1. However, there was earlier controversy about avoiding *ipso facto* excommunicates. See Vodola, *Excommunication*, 29–32.

issued many excommunications.[46] Providing immunity from contagion for those who had no choice but to communicate or did so unknowingly was certainly a kindness. Indeed, Innocent IV declared in Lyon I (1245) that failing to warn communicators invalidated a sentence.[47] Exempting those most likely to flout the doctrine that forbade communication may also, however, have been a practical attempt to limit overt contempt for ecclesiastical law. The more people who refused to shun excommunicates, the weaker the sanction appeared. By Gregory VII's time, it had perhaps become clear that enforcing the rule of contagion—introduced to strengthen the custom of voluntary avoidance—too stringently was impossible, making it both impractical and pastorally irresponsible. It was better to revise the regulation to ensure that the infection did not spread indefinitely. Though Gregory's mitigations were viewed by some contemporaries as a threat to the unity of the church, *Quoniam multos* was quickly absorbed into canon law collections.[48]

By the thirteenth century, exceptions limiting the severity of excommunication's contagiousness were well known, though Vodola states that ignorance remained the only universally valid excuse.[49] Robert of Flamborough noted six types of licit communication:

[1] By just ignorance (*justa ignorantia*), because if you communicate with any excommunicate while unaware that s/he is excommunicated, you are not excommunicated unless your ignorance is stupid and crass (*bruta et grossa*). [2] By domestic necessity (*domestica necessitate*), because, through the exception of Gregory [VII], a father legitimately communicates with his son and vice versa, and man with wife and vice versa, and servant with his master and vice versa. [3] By external necessity (*adventitia necessitate*) because, if a pilgrim cannot avoid an excommunicated castle, if s/he communicates with the men of the castle s/he is not excommunicated. [4] *By number* (*numero*) because excommunication does not cross to a third person. [5] *By humanity* (*humanitate*) because, if an excommunicate lacks the necessities of life, you are bound to assist them. [6] *By rebuke* (*correptione*) because you will communicate with an excommunicate in matters which relate to chastisement.[50]

A mnemonic verse once again summarized these rules.[51] Elsewhere, additional cases in which it was excusable to have contact with an excommunicate were

---

[46] For *Quoniam multos*, see Vodola, 'Sovereignty and tabu Part I', and Vodola, *Excommunication*, 24–7. Cf. Kaplan, *Religion, Politics and Freedom of Conscience*, who writes of an 'epidemic' of Jewish excommunication in early modern Amsterdam, 9–10.
[47] Tanner, *Decrees*, i, 291–2; VI 5.11.3; Clarke, *Interdict*, 105.
[48] Vodola, 'Sovereignty and tabu Part I', 44–5.   [49] Vodola, 'Sovereignty and tabu Part I', 49.
[50] Flamborough, *Summa poenitentialis*, 155–6.
[51] Utile, lex, humile, res ignorata, necesse / Haec anathema quidem faciunt ne possit obesse: Peñafort, *De Poenitentia*, 407–10. See also Hyland, *Excommunication*, 39.

posited. Thus since excommunicates were not to profit from their sentences, it was reasonable to recover debts, or to seek tithes or oblations from them.[52] It was permissible to repay a debt to an excommunicate, though Raymond of Peñafort implied this was still up for debate in the 1230s.[53] Innocent III permitted enforcing a contract with an excommunicate. However, Vodola argued that the ruling was not generally adopted by canonists: 'the *ius commune* to all appearances dictated that excommunicates should be avoided entirely in extrajudicial matters'.[54] Peñafort clarified the potential repercussions of the duty to rebuke, stating that if someone accidentally relayed information which might profit an excommunicate in the course of an admonition, they would not thereby incur a sentence.[55]

Robert Grosseteste's diagrammatical instructional manual also added detail to the basic principles. It states that sons who no longer lived at home, for example, were obliged to ostracize their fathers. But if a father was supported by an excommunicated son, he could converse with him (this presumably came under 'necessity'). Only servants who had been adherents before their lord's excommunication were allowed to communicate. A lord could address an excommunicated servant, but the excommunicate him or herself was not permitted thus to communicate. Perhaps most interestingly, Grosseteste claimed that the wife of an excommunicate could communicate with her husband in all matters. By contrast, the husband of an excommunicate was to communicate with her in 'necessary ministrations' and in returning the (marital) debt. That is, he could have sex with her. This discrepancy between the sexes does not appear to have been universal, but it perhaps demonstrates a fear that excommunication could be a cause of fornication if enforced too strongly.[56]

Loss of Legal Rights

Perhaps the most consistently enforced practical consequence of excommunication in England was loss of legal rights. Though excommunicates were not, like outlaws, placed outside the law—a much more serious disadvantage—their loss of legal status perhaps links the two sanctions. Because the legal consequences of excommunication were discussed at length in Elisabeth Vodola's 1986 monograph, which demonstrated that the exception of excommunication was upheld in England, they will not be covered here in great depth. She described them, not

---

[52] Chobham, *Summa*, 249; Robert Grosseteste, *Templum Dei*, VII.9. See also Helmholz, 'Excommunication as a legal sanction', 211–12.
[53] Vodola, *Excommunication*, 148; Peñafort, *De Poenitentia*, 416–18.
[54] Vodola, *Excommunication*, 132–5 151–3. Quotation 135.
[55] X 5.39.54; Peñafort, *De Poenitentia*, 418–19.   [56] Robert Grosseteste, *Templum Dei*, VII.9.

unreasonably, as 'the most palpable form of ostracism'.⁵⁷ Loss of legal rights was, no doubt, a powerful incentive to seek absolution.

'Every legal act is forbidden one who is excommunicated, so that he cannot sue or summon anyone, though he may be sued by others...lest he profit by his own wrong'.⁵⁸ Thus Bracton, the common law legal text, described the 'exception of excommunication'. This exception prevented excommunicates acting as plaintiff in both secular and ecclesiastical courts. The person who put forward the exception would need to have proof of the excommunication claimed, however, or the exception would be rejected.⁵⁹

> William Devereux, lord of Lyonshall...incurred a sentence of excommunication issued by our authority...therefore we ask you to separate him from your communion, not permitting the same to act or depose his lawsuit in your presence until...he deserves to obtain the benefit of absolution.⁶⁰

This mandate, sent to the king's justices by the bishop of Hereford in 1290, exemplifies how excommunicates were expected to be treated. William, who had reportedly been excommunicated 'for a long time' for detaining tithes, received absolution only three weeks after the bishop wrote to the justices. His change of heart may then be attributed to his excommunicate legal status.⁶¹

Numerous examples in the *Curia Regis Rolls* show that the exception of excommunication was routinely upheld in English courts, despite the fact that the church relied on secular officials.⁶² The rule was so well followed that many cases probably never made it to court, since excommunicates knew they would never get anywhere while they were under the ban. In 1231, for example, the prior of Worksop was required to respond to a certain Adam de Creteling to explain why he had pursued a plea about a fief in ecclesiastical, rather than secular, court. Adam complained that the prior, Robert, had excommunicated him, through which he suffered damages. Robert in turn pointed out that 'he should not respond to [Adam], because he is excommunicate, and as an excommunicate, every lawful act is denied him'. Robert provided letters patent from the bishop of Coventry, which stated that the archdeacon of Derby had excommunicated Adam; Adam failed to show any evidence that he had been absolved, so the case was dismissed and Adam instructed to seek absolution.⁶³ Edith of Gleddun's plea three years later against the abbot of Titchfield was likewise dismissed. Although she claimed that her arrest and imprisonment had followed the false suggestion of the

---

⁵⁷ Vodola, *Excommunication*, 70.   ⁵⁸ *Bracton De legibus*, iv, 326.
⁵⁹ *Bracton De legibus*, iv, 326–7.   ⁶⁰ *Reg. Swinfield*, 242–3.   ⁶¹ *Reg. Swinfield*, 243.
⁶² See Vodola, *Excommunication*, 159–63 and 189.   ⁶³ *CRR*, xiv, no. 1358.

bishop, the latter proved that Edith had indeed been sentenced for refusing to marry the man to whom she was betrothed.[64]

Most cases ended in much the same way, with the excommunicate being told to seek absolution.[65] The validity or justice of the sentence was irrelevant; it was a complete bar to being heard in court. As Vodola noted in her discussion of the apostate nun Alice Clement, this could result in something of a catch-22. Alice sought to regain her inheritance but, as an excommunicate, was unable to seek legal remedy. Her only choice was to seek absolution. However, since her excommunication claimed she had wrongly left her monastery, which she denied, the only way to secure absolution would have been to admit that she had wrongly renounced her vows and return to her monastery. She would then automatically be unable to inherit. After a struggle lasting over thirty years, spanning the reigns of Henry II to Henry III, Alice was forced to give up her cause.[66]

Excommunicates were also denied legal rights beyond court. A valid will could not be held by an excommunicate. Thus in 1282 certain 'sons of iniquity' maliciously and falsely claimed that Master Omer of Canterbury had died 'excommunicated, namely intestate'. In this case, those who thus slandered Omer's memory were perhaps simply jealous, possibly greedy, since there was no evidence he had ever been so sentenced. Being excommunicate would evidently have precluded his having a valid will, since claiming he had died as an excommunicate automatically threw his inheritance into doubt.[67] However, like the concerns for the afterlife discussed in Chapter 2, the dangers affecting inheritance could be ignored while death seemed far off.

Any excommunicate who found themselves in a position that necessitated recourse to legal processes would find themselves unable to do so. Occasionally, excommunicates might even plead that they had been excommunicated by their clerical opponent with the specific aim of preventing them being heard in court. When an adversary refused to respond to Richard Scottus because he was excommunicated, Richard complained that this should not injure him because the bishop (of Worcester) who had excommunicated him, William de Blois, was his opponent in the suit.[68]

In England, at least, there is no reason to believe that this exception of excommunication was regularly undermined or disregarded. The only anomaly was the fact that there had to be proof of an excommunication for the exception to

---

[64] CRR, xv, no. 1360.
[65] In addition to the printed *Curia Regis Rolls*, see Vodola, *Excommunication*, app. 5.
[66] Vodola, *Excommunication*, 102–110, particularly 109–10; CRR, v, 79–80, 123, 171, 183–6; vii, 109–9, 180, 246; viii, 173, 184; ix, 381–2, 385.
[67] *Reg. Pecham*, ii, 173–4. Lateran IV declared, in a clause on heretics, that excommunicates who refused to make satisfaction for over a year could not be elected to office, make wills, or inherit: Tanner, *Decrees*, i, 234.
[68] CRR, ix, 78–9. In a later entry about the case, no excommunication is mentioned, perhaps because Richard had been absolved in the meantime: 380–1.

be applied. This meant that someone who had incurred a *lata sententia,* but had not been officially denounced, would retain their rights. However, automatically incurred sentences could be, and were, confirmed by ecclesiastical authorities. It is not therefore true, as Vodola implies, that excommunicates who had fallen into *latae sententiae* were typically spared this powerful means of enforcement.[69] It might not, however, be clear in later records that their original excommunication had been automatic.[70]

Exclusion from Church

Excommunicates were forbidden to receive the sacraments or enter churches. Such enforcement thus relied upon clergy rather than the wider populace, potentially making these rules easier to enforce. Clerics were, however, just as capable of flouting ecclesiastical sanctions as the laity. There are, in particular, records of their illicit celebrations of divine services during interdicts. Though some excommunicates undoubtedly did attend church services, whether by going elsewhere (so unknown to the local clergy), forcing their way in, or through collusion with clergy, there are only a few accounts of such occurrences.[71] There are many more accounts of excommunicates interacting with the community more generally. Since clergy who admitted those banned from church into the building or gave them the sacraments were undoubtedly more blameworthy than an average layman who failed to shun an excommunicate, it is difficult to believe that this was a serious problem. Bishops would deal harshly with such disobedient clergy and, presumably, record their reprimands. There is thus little cause to suppose that many excommunicates were spared this central consequence of their sentences.

On the other hand, there is no direct evidence that excommunicates *were* excluded from church. Conspicuous absence from religious services ought to have been an important inducement to seek absolution. We might expect there to have been social stigma associated with non-appearance at mass. But the rich records from thirteenth-century England fall short here. While there is little evidence that excommunicates were illicitly admitted to church or to the sacraments, there is almost none that proves their exclusion, much less how people felt about it. In later medieval France, Beaulande and Tyler Lange both found evidence that excommunicates were more likely to seek absolution before religious feasts, particularly Easter. This, of course, implies that appearance at Easter mass was felt to be important, perhaps for both spiritual and reputational reasons.[72] The

---

[69] Vodola, *Excommunication*, 80, 99, 180–2. [70] Hill, 'General excommunications'.
[71] See below, 158–60; *Reg. Cantilupe*, 97–8.
[72] Beaulande, *Malheur*, 246–8; Lange, *Excommunication*, 138, 142, 163, 172.

absence of evidence for this book is thus frustrating, since how excommunicates reacted to being deprived of the sacraments has implications for how socially important attendance at mass was, and more besides.

It is worth noting that in France, from the central Middle Ages, long-term excommunication and long-term absence from mass led automatically to suspicion of heresy.[73] Similar behaviour in thirteenth-century England would not have had the same connotations. Thus early the next century (1309), people from the borough of Wallingford had apparently no qualms about associating with Nicholas, who had failed to receive the sacraments for three years and subsequently been excommunicated for it.[74] It might tentatively be suggested that non-attendance at religious services had fewer social repercussions in this context, in which heresy was not a prime concern amongst the local populace.

This is not so for ecclesiastical burial, the final means of exclusion for excommunicates. As Alexander Murray has shown in his study of suicide, burial mattered a great deal.[75] Moreover, in thirteenth-century England there is evidence that the exclusion of excommunicates in death as well as in life was upheld by clergy.[76] However, once again this particular type of ostracism was not an urgent incentive to seek reconciliation unless a person was on his or her deathbed. It was not something that necessitated, for most people, a prompt change in behaviour.

Pretext for Mistreatment

Work

Episcopal registers, so richly informative about many aspects of excommunication, provide little information about successful ostracism. There was no reason to note when a sentence was enforced as it should be.[77] When excommunicates sought absolution, their decision was invariably ascribed to the fact that they had 'come to their senses' ('resipiscere'). It is therefore difficult to use such sources to judge the degree to which social exclusion drove absolutions. Therefore we must, for the most part, turn to narrative sources and to documents associated with the royal court to find indications of how excommunicates were treated. As a result, the majority of examples concern figures in more or less public roles rather than typical parishioners. This is important, for the stakes differed considerably depending on the position of an excommunicate. Anyone needing to perform

---

[73] Lateran IV, c. 3 (X 5.7.13); Logan, 'Excommunication'; cf. Beaulande, *Malheur*, 234–40; Vodola, *Excommunication*, 32, 164–80, 190.
[74] *Reg. Gandavo*, i, 346–8.   [75] Murray, *Suicide*, ii, 454–61.   [76] See Chapter 2, 61–65.
[77] Peter Clarke notes that violation of interdict was more worthy of comment that observance: *Interdict*, 134.

official duties or command others would be more adversely affected. Reputation also perhaps mattered more to those in higher social positions, though surely anyone can smart at public shaming.[78]

Despite the scarcity of evidence for how communities enforced sentences, it is clear that excommunicates remained at risk of abuse from fellows who wished to take advantage of an excommunication. They did have cause to fear social and practical repercussions as a result of their sentences, but ostracism was not necessarily performed by 'good Christians' dutifully carrying out ecclesiastical orders, but rather by those to whom it offered benefits. Excommunication was not simply the cause of mistreatment, but a convenient justification. Churchmen employing the sanction, therefore, had only limited control over how sentences would play out.

> I do not at all believe that I am bound in any way by these sentences. Nevertheless, so that no one may out of spite be able to cite the sentence of excommunication against me... I ordered a proctor of mine to obtain for me an adequate remedy against this possibility from the lord pope.[79]

The use of 'malignitas' by Robert Grosseteste, bishop of Lincoln, here is crucial. He did not consider the excommunication, pronounced against him by the monks of Christ Church Canterbury (exercising vacancy rights), to be valid.[80] He was, however, worried that the sentence would be used against him because of others' malevolence. He sought absolution not for fear of spiritual consequences but because of the vulnerable position in which excommunication placed him.

One of the biggest dangers of enforced excommunication was that it would affect the victim's ability to work. Grosseteste was worried about being unable to carry out the duties of his office. Secular officials were equally constrained by excommunication. Indeed, kings claimed the privilege (not always obeyed) that their officials could not be sentenced without the king's consent.[81] The difficulties faced by Thomas fitz Adam, a bailiff in Ireland, demonstrate the potential difficulties. In 1220, he wrote to Henry III to complain about his excommunication by the archbishop of Dublin, Henry of London, in the midst of a dispute over forest jurisdiction. The archbishop had objected that the bailiff did not possess the right to arrest men on his land, responding to Thomas's arrest of a purported malefactor first by imposing an 'ambulatory' interdict on the bailiff.[82]

---

[78] Mansfield, *Humiliation*, 267. She also argued that public penance was rarely suffered by the lower classes: ibid. ch. 8, esp. 252.

[79] *Grosseteste Letters*, 342; *Grosseteste Epistolae*, 324.

[80] During the interregnum between archbishops Edmund of Abingdon and Boniface of Savoy. For Grosseteste's dispute with them, see *Grosseteste Letters*, nos 94 and 110; Morgan, 'Excommunication of Grosseteste'.

[81] See 177-9.   [82] See Clarke, *Interdict*, 82-4.

When the bailiff did not return the prisoner, the archbishop proceeded with the excommunication he had threatened, notwithstanding Thomas's appeals to both the archbishop and the pope requesting a period of grace to discuss the matter with the justiciar. Throughout the land, the people were forbidden to communicate with Thomas. He was unable, for instance, to attend the assizes at Dublin. When the archbishop was informed of the king's right to be consulted before excommunications of his bailiffs, 'he responded that he would believe that privilege when he saw it, not before'. Thomas asked the king to arrange that he be absolved by someone else, believing that the archbishop would keep him excommunicated until he acquiesced entirely (which was, of course, the whole point of excommunication).[83]

The archbishop's own letter to the king, justifying his actions, states that Thomas experienced a change of heart, and sought absolution.[84] The excommunication had apparently fulfilled its purpose. Though the archbishop carefully excluded the king from blame, he ended his letter by asking that the king stop molesting him and allow the liberties due to his church. He was certainly out of royal favour, for he wrote to the dean of Lichfield and the king himself, complaining that he had been blamed unfairly and had only ever been acting in the king's interests. He intended to come to England himself to prove his innocence.[85] The archbishop's concern here invites the possibility that he had been pressured to absolve the bailiff. The archbishop's assertion that Thomas had changed his mind and now deserved absolution may well obscure the truth, as might comparable phrases in many more cases. In any event, Thomas had been prevented from performing his office.

It is not difficult to envisage the advantages of performing ostracism against an official so that he could not function. Thomas fitz Adam was not alone in facing such difficulties. Falkes de Bréauté complained that his bailiffs were unable to collect the king's debts because, when they tried, their targets complained to deans and chaplains who excommunicated and interdicted the debt collectors.[86] In 1290, a certain Richard de Loges complained in parliament about the injuries caused by excommunication. The bishop of Coventry and Lichfield had excommunicated him and caused him to lose High Cannock, while the bishop of Chester had previously prevented the 'regarders' of the forest of Cannock from exercising their office through a sentence of excommunication.[87]

---

[83] *Royal Letters*, no. 72. For this dispute, which was more complicated than is here worth detailing, see Margaret Murphy, 'Ecclesiastical censures'. A letter sent by the citizens of Dublin a few months later claimed a 'great controversy' had arisen between them and the archbishop over the latter's liberties. Many citizens, now excommunicated, asked the king for advice: *Royal Letters*, no. 91.
[84] *Royal Letters*, no. 73.   [85] *Royal Letters*, nos 74, 84.
[86] London, TNA, SC 1/1/26 (no date).   [87] *Parliament Rolls*, i, 305.

Provisions

A form of ostracism more serious than the inability to work was that which prevented victims even from accessing provisions. It was a measure occasionally included in ecclesiastical orders. While the barons were in control in the 1260s, the papal legate repeatedly forbade the transfer of arms, horses, grain, wine, and other victuals to England.[88] In 1272, Henry III was preparing to travel to Norwich following a serious incident there. He was perturbed to discover, however, that the ecclesiastical interdict imposed on the city had been extended to include anyone who carried supplies there. He ordered the interdict to be lifted so that he could enter Norwich (and, presumably, eat and drink well while there).[89]

Monastic houses seem to have been particularly affected by such deprivation. Interrupting access to provisions is of course an effective coercive tactic, and links with the rule that people should not dine with excommunicates. However, since feeding a starving excommunicate was permitted, things were clearly not meant to go too far. Yet the prior and convent of Great Malvern complained that they were unable to buy food as a result of the excommunication decreed against them by the archbishop of Canterbury and their own bishop of Worcester.[90] The prior and monks of Durham similarly alleged that the bishop, having excommunicated them, had confined them in their dwellings, prevented food from reaching them, cut the waterpipes, and broken the mill dams. Their complaint unsurprisingly reached Pope Boniface VIII in 1301. Hunger and thirst were amongst the tribulations allegedly suffered by these monks. Evidently this was all part of a particularly spiteful dispute between the bishop and the Benedictine house in Durham.[91]

The canons of St Oswald's Priory, Worcester diocese, were on the receiving end of such treatment at several points across a twenty-five-year period. Their refusal to accept the visitation of Archbishop Pecham (1279–90) caused him to forbid Christians to 'eat, drink, buy, sell or communicate with them in any way'. In 1300, the same issue prompted the complaint that they were prohibited from buying or selling wine, bread, ale, or any other provisions, making many of them ill. The king, who was involved because the priory was a royal foundation, duly ordered the excommunication imposed by the bishop of Worcester to be lifted. Yet two years later the priory faced the same treatment, and in 1304 the bishop was forced to appear before the king to explain his actions, which the prior claimed had cost him £200. The king himself claimed contempt of the fantastic sum of £10,000.[92]

---

[88] Heidemann, nos 20q, 44a, 50a; *Foedera*, I.i.447–8. [89] *CCR 1268–72*, 572.
[90] *Reg. G. Giffard*, 211–12. [91] *Cal. Pap. Reg.*, 589.
[92] *Reg. G. Giffard*, 309–10; *Reg. Epp. Pecham*, ii, 547; *CCR 1296–1302*, 411, 526; *CCR 1302–07*, 87–8, 191, 224–5; *SKB*, iii, 138–44. What was at stake is discussed more fully in Page (ed.), *Victoria County History... Gloucester*, 84–87, which provides full references.

The prevalence of monastic complaints about access to food and drink could be an issue of records: monks were more able and thus likely to complain about their plight. The separated nature of their dwellings would, however, have made policing their reception of provisions easier than controlling how an individual obtained sustenance. This, combined with the acrimonious relationships monastic houses often had with their bishops, might have made them more likely to suffer this particular treatment.

Shunning and Insults

Some occasions when excommunicates were shunned might be taken at face value. In 1283, Archbishop Pecham mentioned in passing that Ralph of Fremingham had been excommunicated and that Edward I had consequently removed him from service.[93] Henry III refused to see Hugh de Lacy, excommunicated in Ireland by Henry of London, for eight days after he arrived in England. Only once he was absolved did the king receive him.[94] In 1265, in a letter close, Hervey de Boreham was told to keep away from court and other business of royal administration because he was excommunicated and should be 'strictly avoided by all'. It would be 'shameful and unsafe' if he involved himself in anything that pertained to the royal ministry.[95]

Taking such instances as simple obedience to the rules of excommunication is misguided, however. In many more instances (discussed in Chapter 4), the crown was quite willing to ignore or even actively impede excommunications. The shunning of Hervey de Boreham is particularly ironic. This fell in the period when Simon de Montfort was in control of England, having won the Battle of Lewes against the royalist army in 1264. The king was king merely in name, in reality Montfort's prisoner. Montfort was himself at the time excommunicated by the pope for his part in the rebellion. Indeed, Paul Brand suggests that Hervey was excommunicated for his part in the Battle of Lewes, further compounding the insincerity of the intent of this letter, sent in the king's name only.[96] Perhaps Montfort, whose excommunication was never published in England, was trying to bolster his reputation for piety by ostracizing Boreham in this way.

Self-interest is even clearer in other cases. In 1295, Edward I asserted that it was not 'licit or honest' to communicate with Madoc, the excommunicated Welsh leader, until he had been absolved. He therefore asked that Archbishop Winchelsey provide authority to certain (named) men that they might absolve

---

[93] *Reg. Epp. Pecham*, ii, 766–7. [94] *Ann. Dunstable*, 91–2.
[95] *CR 1264–68*, 51–2. [96] Brand, 'Boreham, Hervey of'.

Madoc, in order to allow peace talks.[97] Edward's sudden fastidiousness against associating with excommunicates, insisting that he would not treat with Madoc until he was absolved, allowed him to demonstrate power over his rival. Moreover, as Sarah Hamilton points out, lifting an excommunication was as significant an act of power as imposing such a sentence.[98] The king would not, of course, personally absolve Madoc, but he held control over this absolution. The safe conduct issued by the king's regents to protect the excommunicate Falkes de Bréauté when he travelled to Northampton in 1224 to be absolved might be viewed in a similar light. It also, however, potentially indicates that an excommunicate without a safe conduct was in danger of abuse.[99] Falkes indeed claimed that his (reluctant) decision to seek absolution from the archbishop, since he was unable to approach the pope, was taken lest he be handed over to his enemies.[100]

The excommunications of both Falkes and Hugh de Lacy were pronounced during Henry III's minority, during which time the government made frequent use of ecclesiastical censures to bolster the young king and rein in overmighty subjects. During the years of political instability following John's death, excommunication was used against those who, like Falkes, illicitly detained castles.[101] In 1218, the sheriffs of Canterbury and Essex were instructed to proclaim throughout their bailiwicks that 'all clerics who were excommunicated because they adhered to Louis or his supporters, and who are still not absolved, should leave our realm ... and whoever such are found should be captured'.[102] This was not a routine enforcement of an excommunication, but excommunication exploited in order to punish clerics who had not supported the king.

In the same period, tournaments were viewed as threats to the peace; the papal sentence prohibiting them was repeatedly enforced. In 1219, therefore, earls, barons, and freeholders were instructed by the regents not to provide counsel or favour to William de Forz, earl of Aumale, who had held a tournament. They were to avoid the earl, in no way communicating with him and his accomplices as excommunicated and disobedient to the king. If any disregarded the order to shun him, their bodies, lands, and tenements would be taken.[103] This was typical use of excommunication during the minority of Henry III (by contrast, though Edward sought to curb armed gatherings amongst his nobles several times in the 1280s, he did not employ excommunication) and reflects the way that the censure could be

---

[97] *Reg. Winchelsey*, i, 4–5. Cf. a cancelled 1271 memorandum telling chancery clerks not to communicate with the archbishop of Canterbury's excommunicated official: *CCR 1268–72*, 418.

[98] Hamilton, 'Absoluimus uos', 209–10.

[99] *PR 1216–25*, 461. Cf. safe conducts issued so that excommunicated Welsh leaders could attend various meetings: *PR 1225–32*, 475; *CPR 1232–47*, 461; *Foedera*, I.i.149.

[100] *Coventry*, 268.

[101] *Royal Letters*, app. v, no. 19. Carpenter, *Minority,* 360–3. Philip of Oldcotes was ineffectually told, on pain of excommunication, to surrender the castle of Mitford: *PR 1216–25*, 224–6.

[102] *Rotuli Litterarum Clausarum*, 377a; *Royal Letters*, 56–8.

[103] *Royal Letters*, no. 47; *PR 1216–25*, 257–8.

used to the advantage of an individual or administration.[104] Aumale was once again excommunicated in 1221, for seizing and holding royal castles, and for taking up arms against the king.[105] In 1222, the Crowland chronicler records that Archbishop Langton, pitying the king's youth and weakness, responded to rumours of plots implicating the earl of Chester by threatening to excommunicate those who disturbed the kingdom or assaulted the king.[106]

While those in power recognized the value of excommunication when it suited their interests, they could equally have it used against them. In 1256, King Alfonso X of Castile threatened to invade Henry III's lands in Gascony, arguing that the king had broken a peace treaty made with the Gascons (Alfonso had been mediator). He declared, according to Matthew Paris:

> I am sorry to be allied with the king of England, who guards neither his words nor even charters inviolate, nor blushes to transgress oaths, or to be thrust into the given sentence (*precipitari in latam canonem*). Therefore I may not and ought not observe a peace undertaken with one not observing faith.[107]

Canon, especially used with the verb *fero* as here, is a standard term for an automatic excommunication, typically a penalty for breaking a peace treaty.[108] The king of Castile was accusing Henry III of incurring the sentence, thereby justifying his own actions (though the English king was able to appease the Castilian). Excommunication was hardly the cause of his bad faith, but it provided a justification.

Social shunning between individuals is even more difficult to find than such political uses. The best example of the sort of interaction described by Thomas Chobham, in which an excommunicate is straightforwardly shunned and humiliated, concerns Henry III and Simon de Montfort in 1238 and is described by Matthew Paris. The king refused to allow the earl of Leicester and his new wife, the king's sister, to attend Queen Eleanor's churching. According to Paris, 'the king called him an excommunicate' ('rex eum excommunicatum vocavit'), and forbade him or his wife, whom Simon had 'wickedly and secretly defiled' before marriage, to be present at this purification ceremony following childbirth. Moreover, when Montfort tried to return to his lodgings, the king ordered that the couple be forcibly ejected. According to Paris (who is, admittedly, not to be relied on here) the king then declared that he had given his sister to Simon in marriage

---

[104] *Foedera*, I.ii.503, 674, 685, 709, 710, 711–12.   [105] *Coggeshall*, 188; *Ann. Dunstable*, 63–4.
[106] *Coventry*, 251. Many examples could be cited. See Hill, 'Excommunication and politics', 25–7. The political narrative of Henry's minority is given at length in Carpenter, *Minority*, chs. 3–9. See also Vincent, *Peter des Roches*, chs. 5–6; Powicke, *Thirteenth Century*, 16–37.
[107] *CM*, v, 585.
[108] Usually *sententia* would also appear. Indeed, *latam* and *canonem* do not agree—the feminine *sententiam* would have been more correct.

unwillingly. The earl, whose new wife had previously taken a vow of chastity, stood accused of bribing the papacy to allow the marriage. Finally, unpaid debts (for which Montfort had made the king guarantor without his knowledge or consent) meant that Simon 'deserved to be bound by a sentence of excommunication'.[109] The phrasing indicates that the king was suggesting Montfort *should* have been excommunicated—and was in the king's eyes—but that he had not, in fact, been condemned by the church.[110] If Paris fabricated this exchange and the king's words, it is certainly true that the Montforts did not attend Eleanor's churching.[111]

The chronicler twice noted Simon's shame—he was 'confusus' and 'erubuit'. Montfort's disgrace and distress is indicated by his immediate departure for the continent, and further implied by a letter from Robert Grosseteste, in which the bishop noted the 'weight of [Montfort's] suffering', advising him to bear it with patience and to gain strength from it. He also offered to plead before the king on Simon's behalf.[112] Excommunication was not the only accusation levelled by the king, and Montfort was no doubt shamed both by the king's accusations and by his treatment. The king's shunning of the earl, however, was based on the accusation that he was excommunicated. Henry had not simply used harsh words, but he had publicly forbidden Simon to participate in the 'festive solemnities', evicting him from the bishop of Winchester's palace where he was staying. The earl's apparent status justified the exclusion; the king was using excommunication to make the earl's disfavour abundantly clear both to his court and to Montfort himself.[113] Björn Weiler has noted that Montfort's fall from grace was made public by the king's rejection of Montfort here, but does not mention that Henry was using an accusation of excommunication to treat the earl this way.[114] The usefulness of excommunication in social relationships, rather than its direct effects, is evident.

Henry III, in Paris's narrative, also appears to have used excommunication as something of an insult. In a dispute recorded in the register of Godfrey Giffard in 1283, Peter de Altaribus, prior of Wotton, was accused of laying violent hands on the monk Roger, by hitting him on the nose and drawing blood. Though the prior claimed Roger had hit himself in the face in order to blame Peter, many witnesses had seen the assault. During the preceding quarrel, the prior had called Roger a 'leprous peasant' and peasant he had bitten his finger. Several witnesses

---

[109] *CM*, iii, 566–7; Maddicott, *Simon de Montfort*, 21–9.

[110] John Maddicott notes it is impossible to know whether the threatened excommunication ever took place, but it is unlikely that Grosseteste would have written to an excommunicated Montfort, as he did shortly after this confrontation. Maddicott, *Simon de Montfort*, 24, 28 (this incident more generally, 21–9).

[111] Carpenter, *Henry III*, 207.   [112] *Grosseteste Letters*, no. 75.

[113] The king was, of course, capable of refusing to see people without the involvement of excommunication, e.g. Carpenter, *Henry III*, 397, 436, 509.

[114] Weiler, *Kingship, Rebellion and Political Culture*, 113.

noted, however, that before being punched Roger had accused the prior of being excommunicated. Peter was a drunk, but Roger was 'quarrelsome', and had in fact 'provoked the aforesaid prior to violence, publicly asserting that he [Peter] was excommunicated by his abbot'. Both men were subsequently absolved from major excommunication, for assaulting one another.[115] Despite the accusation, Roger had no qualms about sleeping in the same dormitory as the alleged excommunicate, as the prior himself pointed out.[116]

This bizarre episode hardly informs us about typical treatment of excommunicates. In this instance, excommunication was not used to justify violence but rather provoked it. Excommunication appears to have been used as an insult, but it was one that triggered a strong response (albeit from a drunk). Excommunication used as a slur may have been common; Véronique Beaulande has found examples also in France.[117] In this case it did not, however, lead to shunning.

The leprous peasant argument and Henry III's treatment of Simon de Montfort have one significant thing in common: both involved accusations of excommunication, but no sentence appears to have been confirmed by an ecclesiastical authority. Alfonso's accusation is the same. This does not mean that none of the three men was excommunicated; *ipso facto* sentences were 'real' even if they had not been publicized. However, there is a definite trend towards excommunication used to insult, or to justify mistreatment, in instances where sentences had been (supposedly) incurred. Given the few examples of shunning, this is noteworthy.

Some of these cases make it into the records precisely because the victim denied they were excommunicated. In 1283, certain canons of Malton, near York, complained that they had been imprisoned and maltreated by Agnes de Vescy and his men. Their livestock was taken, and they were detained without food so that 'the greater part' died of hunger. The attackers announced in public that nobody should communicate with the malefactors or provide them with victuals. In spite of this abuse, the canons insisted that they had not been excommunicated, evidently the excuse given for their treatment.[118] A remarkably similar episode was reported before the king's bench. The word excommunication is not used; instead, Reginald the Clerk complained that he had done nothing for which he should be 'separated from the community of the burgesses of Bristol', yet the mayor had proclaimed that no one should sell victuals or have intercourse with Reginald in any way. This could potentially refer to either excommunication or outlawry, but it suggests an explanation analogous to that given by the attackers of

---

[115] *Reg. G. Giffard*, 129-32, 133. This edition is a calendar, but here a very full one. The Latin for leprous peasant is 'rusticum leprosum', See Worcestershire Archives and Archaeology Service, Register of Godfrey Giffard (b.716.093-BA.2648/1 (i)), modern pagination 221-3, old foliation 115r-116r.

[116] The prior said that Roger should not sleep in the dormitory with him because he had called him an excommunicate. It is not clear whether the prior meant 'you should be avoiding me' or was simply indicating his anger.

[117] Beaulande, *Malheur*, 251.   [118] CPR 1281-92, 76.

the canons in Malton.[119] In a late case (1321) discussed by Rosalind Hill, certain English parishioners claimed that others were refusing to sell them food and other necessities because they had incurred excommunication for communicating with the excommunicated Scots (this, the victims claimed, they had been forced to do).[120]

In each of these cases, the accusations and consequent treatment related to particular circumstances and relationships. The most easily interpretable is Hill's example, which undoubtedly relates to English animosity towards the Scots during the Anglo-Scottish wars. Perhaps the victims here were disliked for other reasons. They *would* have incurred an automatic excommunication for dealing with Scots at this time; the accusation was apparently accurate. But in none of these cases can the behaviour be adequately explained by the simple statement 'they shunned them because believed they were excommunicates'. The decision to enforce sentences stringently is likely to have had more to do with how doing so might benefit the ostracizers, and rather less to do with how excommunicates were treated *qua* excommunicates. In some instances, churchmen were actively encouraging such treatment via public pronouncements. In others, people saw fit to enforce sentences that may not have existed at all. These examples span the social hierarchy and concern religious and laity. Everyone saw the advantage of excommunication-related mistreatment, whether or not the church had ordered it against these specific individuals. They coopted excommunication for their own ends.

Implications of a Lack of Evidence

The relative dearth of records that describe avoidance of excommunicates makes it difficult to assess the extent to which the population enforced excommunication. Rosalind Hill's assumption that most people did so cannot be substantiated.[121] Evidence presented in Chapter 4 suggests that communities frequently made up their own minds: there was certainly no universal willingness to unquestioningly obey orders to shun. There are simply too many examples of illicit communication, and not enough of avoidance, to conclude that excommunicates as a group were routinely shunned. On the other hand, as has already been noted, we would not expect many sources to record proper enforcement of these rules. It is conceivable, for instance, that those men whom Clement IV suspected of faking illnesses in order to obtain absolution during the baronial war were being shunned. Even though they seemingly had no intention of changing their behaviour, they evidently judged there to be an advantage to obtaining absolution.[122]

[119] *SKB*, i, 15–16.   [120] Hill, 'Belief and practice', 138.   [121] *Reg. Sutton*, iii, xlix.
[122] *Reg. Clement IV*, no. 122. See above, 65.

Excommunicates who ran away from their homes perhaps provide rare indications of effective shunning. Some runaways were trying to avoid the secular arm, but in other cases there is no reason to suppose that the possibility of arrest led them to abscond.[123] Alexander IV, urging English bishops to help one another, described how excommunicated clerks and laymen left the cities and dioceses in which they had committed their offences, and subsequently 'do not fear to communicate with others'.[124] This practice is visible in 1301, when the bishop of Winchester informed the bishop of London about a renegade, who was now 'wickedly infecting the flock' in his diocese.[125] John, vicar of Kedington, was never to be seen again after his excommunication in 1275; N., excommunicated in Wiltshire in the 1280s, went to Berkshire; Eustace de Bingham tried to move parishes.[126] Christiane Hirdeman reportedly fled Bristol, abandoning her two daughters, when she was excommunicated.[127]

Shunning might have encouraged excommunicates to seek absolution even if it was not performed universally. Equally, it would be possible to live as an excommunicate while some, but not all, fellows performed ostracism. Whichever way the balance tipped, the response of the excommunicate would surely depend upon which people shunned as much as how many. This balance might change quite quickly. Thus John de Stonegrave sought absolution six days after an investigation was launched into who had been communicating with him; these people were now also excommunicated with a major sentence.[128] Though John was simultaneously threatened with arrest by the secular arm, perhaps these additional measures meant that several people who had previously socialized with John changed their minds. If the majority of the community were then avoiding him, his perseverance would have become untenable. In other contexts, it is possible that an excommunicate's persistence convinced others that a sentence had been unjust, or simply caused them to tire of chastising their fellow, so that after a while they stopped avoiding him or her, further enabling this contumacy.

Without further evidence, nothing certain can be determined. It is significant, however, that the accounts above do indicate that how excommunicates were supposed to be treated was common knowledge. This is not surprising given the constant orders to avoid those under the ban, but it does make obedience to the

---

[123] Anabilia Brown was probably fleeing to avoid the secular arm in 1277: *Calendar of Inquisitions Miscellaneous*, i, no. 1092. See also: *Fine Rolls*, 38 Henry III, no. 366 (m. 8); *Rotuli Litterarum clausarum*, 540b, 561b; *CR 1247–51*, 97; Logan, *Excommunication and the Secular Arm*, 95.

[124] *Foedera*, I.i.369–70.

[125] *Reg. Pontissara*, i, 111–12. Cf. a similar request from the bishop of Salisbury to the official of Winchester in 1304: *Reg. Gandavo*, i, 155–6.

[126] *Rotuli Ricardi Gravesend*, ed. Davis, i, 76; Hill, *Ecclesiastical Letter-Books*, 117; *Reg. Sutton*, iv, 33–4. See also *Reg. Sutton*, iii, xliv.

[127] According to her daughters' uncle, answering charges before the king's bench that he and others had beaten Christiane, taken her goods, and abducted her daughters. He claimed he was rescuing his nieces, who were wandering about town unprotected: *SKB*, i, 134–5.

[128] *Reg. W. Giffard*, 142–3, 161–2. And see below, 160.

rule more likely. The examples above, especially considering that several of them concern cases where it is uncertain whether the victims of mistreatment were excommunicated at all, might be the tip of the iceberg. They might indicate that this treatment was typical and only recorded in these instances because there was no sentence to enforce. In any case, excommunicates were vulnerable, and at the mercy of the opinions of their neighbours. The sanction was enforced when it suited people.

Prelude to Physical Force

The Secular Arm

Excommunicates were not only vulnerable to mere avoidance. In England, excommunicates were at risk of being arrested and imprisoned by their sheriff, at a bishop's request. Of this possibility they were frequently reminded: the automatic excommunication against officials who failed to execute a writ (*Contempnunt exequi domini*) was frequently publicized in churches.[129] The property of those arrested could also be taken by royal officials while they were imprisoned.[130] Donald Logan's 1968 monograph on the subject remains the authority for the procedure for capturing excommunicates.[131] The latter's existence alone shows that social ostracism did not routinely work, though it is by no means the case that *most* excommunicates ever suffered arrest.

Like social ostracism, the custom of invoking the secular arm could be abused. In 1241, Henry III made Andrew of Brittany prior of Winchester, apparently through violent means. This imposter proceeded to excommunicate those members of the convent who contradicted him, after forty days invoking the secular arm. Though calling upon the secular arm was an ordinary response, the 'quasi-prior' told the king's ministers to 'go and avenge the injury to us and the king on our rebels, for they are excommunicates, and it is no offence to lay violent hands on them'. Matthew Paris, who wrote this account, went on to itemize the various offences committed against the monks, including torturing them with hunger and cold.[132] We may doubt Paris's account, but the prior was here reportedly using excommunication with the express purpose of taking revenge against his enemies. His supposed claim that laying violent hands on excommunicates was acceptable was a stretch, yet the monks were no longer part of the church, and the special protection given to them by *Si quis suadente* as religious could hardly still

---

[129] See Chapter 7.
[130] *Rotuli Litterarum clausarum*, 563; *CR 1254–56*, 27; *Fine Rolls*, 25 Henry III, no. 715 (m. 2). In France, property of excommunicates who remained under their sentences for a year was seized: Campbell, 'Attitude of the monarchy', 541–3.
[131] Logan, *Excommunication and the Secular Arm*. [132] *CM*, iv, 159–60.

apply. Violence against them, as opposed to against a monk who had not been expelled from the church, was comparatively unobjectionable.

In 1237, excommunication was used after the fact to show certain Londoners' questionable actions in a more positive light. The mayor and others were required to explain why they had arrested and imprisoned certain mariners, who had set up kidels (wooden fish traps) against the city's privileges. The mayor and others gave four reasons for their actions: the mariners were acting against God and in detriment to the realm; they were acting against the king's dignity; they were acting against London's confirmed liberty, and, finally, they had incurred excommunication for violating Magna Carta.[133] Needless to say, although excommunicates could be arrested, anyone who wished to secure the arrest of an excommunicate would have to go through official channels, after they had remained under a sentence for forty days. In this case, the Londoners were using the mariners' automatically incurred excommunication to strengthen their case for making an arrest. Excommunication did not cause this violence, but arguably excused it.

King John

Of the three thirteenth-century English kings, only King John was excommunicated by name.[134] The way that his excommunication played out demonstrates clearly what was at stake for a ruler but also how reliant the church was upon others. The king's rejection of Stephen Langton as archbishop of Canterbury resulted in an interdict over England from 1208 to 1214, and the excommunication of the king from 1209 to 1213. The interdict, though generally executed, did not have the desired effect of turning the people against their king, nor of compelling him to capitulate to the pope's demands. John's excommunication, a response to the failure of interdict to compel submission to Innocent's demands, was never fully enforced. Although most of the episcopate (with the exceptions of the bishops of Norwich and Winchester) felt they must go into exile after the excommunication was pronounced, the majority of regular and secular clergy remained in England.[135] John's barons continued to communicate with their excommunicate king, who was able to rule for three and a half years while separated from the church.[136] Robert Fitzwalter's claim that he had left England

---

[133] *Liber Albus*, ed. Riley, i, 500–2; c. 23 of the 1225 charter forbade erection of kidels in the Thames and the Medway.
[134] On excommunication of kings see also Demangel, 'L'excommunication du roi'.
[135] Innocent ordered these to be suspended: *SLI*, no. 47.
[136] Sentences imposed: *SLI*, nos 30, 31, 36. For the interdict and John's excommunication, see Cheney, 'King John and the papal interdict'; Cheney, 'A recent view of the general interdict'; Cheney, 'Alleged deposition of King John'; Cheney, 'King John's reaction'; Cheney, *Pope Innocent III*, 303–25;

because John was excommunicated, as reported by the Anonymous of Béthune, is likely to have been disingenuous. He was later one of the king's most prominent baronial opponents.[137]

Many have taken a dim view of the efficacy of John's excommunication. The traditional interpretation is that it failed to achieve its ends, and that this was largely because the sanction had lost its spiritual terrors. Excommunication's apparent weakness was thus explained by W. L. Warren: 'the clergy had unfortunately used it too often for frivolous reasons for it to be seriously regarded by any but the most pious.'[138] R. V. Turner states that 'the church's overuse of the ban as a political weapon was making it less frightening to the faithful'.[139] Stephen Church, more recently, is not so dismissive.[140]

John's excommunication had its desired effect. John sought absolution; the interdict was lifted; Langton became archbishop. The king subsequently granted a charter of free elections to the church, and declared himself a papal vassal.[141] Certainly, John's excommunication cannot be claimed as an ideal working of the sanction, for it took too long to work. Yet both Warren and Turner focus on excommunication's spiritual terrors for the individual, when much more important was the collective response. It misses the point to state that John 'only' succumbed to papal pressure because his position as king had become precarious. Churchmen using excommunication were *always* at the mercy of the those who were supposed to enforce their sentences, in this case John's subjects, particularly his barons.

By the time John sought absolution, his excommunication had become too great a liability. It could be used against him by his increasingly mutinous barons; the French king might use it as a pretext for invasion. John Maddicott rightly places a great deal of emphasis on the pressures imposed by excommunication in his discussion of the 1209 Oath of Marlborough, a measure taken by John to sure up his position.[142] The king's reaction was not yet to seek absolution, but to take hostages from those he distrusted and to require an oath of allegiance from every man in his kingdom. The excommunication was not published in England, which perhaps limited its impact.[143] Nevertheless, the ability of those who opposed the king to use his excommunication against him made the sanction dangerous indeed. By the time John made peace with Innocent III, these dangers had increased. Roger of Wendover attributed his submission, amongst other factors, to the danger of a French invasion and the fear that he would be abandoned by his

---

Sayers, *Innocent III*; Maddicott, 'Oath of Marlborough'; Warren, *King John*, 154–73; Turner, *King John*, 109–27; Clarke, *Interdict*, 169–71, 180–2; Harper-Bill, 'King John and the Church of Rome', 304–15; Vincent, *Peter des Roches*, 74–88.

[137] *History of the Dukes of Normandy*, trans. Shirley, 130; Strickland, 'Fitzwalter, Robert (d. 1235)'.
[138] Warren, *King John*, 169.   [139] Turner, *King John*, 121.
[140] Church, *King John*, 179–80, 189–91.   [141] *C&S*, 38–41.
[142] Maddicott, 'Oath of Marlborough', esp. 287–92; Cheney, 'Alleged deposition of King John'.
[143] Maddicott, 'Oath of Marlborough', 312–13. See Chapter 5 below for the importance of denunciation.

nobles and subjects in those circumstances.[144] The chronicler explicitly claims that the nobles refused to follow their king on an expedition to the continent until he had been absolved.[145]

John's sentence thus demonstrates a key point: spiritual fears aside, the efficacy of excommunication depended upon factors over which the church had limited control. Innocent III's pontificate is generally viewed as the 'height' of papal monarchy. It is unlikely that there was ever a time when the sanction generated automatic respect.[146] Yet the expectation that those under a sentence should be avoided, disobeyed, or even abused, exposed excommunicates. John was compelled to remove the vulnerability that accompanied excommunication as his popularity declined. His relationship with the barons was central to whether or not Innocent would achieve his aim. Rulers were simultaneously better able to weather excommunication, if they had support or were able to exert sufficient (physical) pressure, and more at risk of it being used against them.[147]

John's mind will have been focused, in addition, by a possible aggravation of excommunication: deposition. Dethronement as a consequence of excommunication made a good deal of sense: if no one was to communicate with an excommunicate, how could he possibly lead his men?[148] Clauses in Gratian's *Decretum* justified refusing to serve an excommunicated master: Gregory VII and Urban II had both declared that fealty to excommunicates need not be observed.[149] Nonetheless, excommunication neither immediately absolved subjects from fealty nor deposed a monarch. Thus Llywelyn the Great was first excommunicated, then threatened with interdict over his lands, and finally his subordinates would be announced absolved from their homage and fealty if he did not make satisfaction within six months.[150] Deposition was an extreme measure.

As Christopher Cheney showed, there is no official record that Innocent III ever went so far as to declare John's subjects released from oaths of fidelity.[151] Yet John had good reason to fear deposition. He would have been aware of eleventh and twelfth-century depositions pronounced by popes, particularly against German emperors. The most famous example was Emperor Henry IV, and the most recent Otto IV, John's own contemporary. Later in the century, the deposition of Frederick II would be a considerable scandal for the papacy.[152] For these rulers, too, the principal danger was that excommunication might supply a pretext for insurrection.[153] It is, nevertheless, significant that chroniclers reported that John had indeed been deposed. Their accounts may reflect a common misconception

---

[144] *CM*, ii, 540–1.   [145] *CM*, ii, 549–50.   [146] See Introduction, 5–11.
[147] Cf. Whalen, *Two Powers*, 180; Clarke, *Interdict*, 61.
[148] Vodola, *Excommunication*, 22–7; 67–9; Helmholz, *Spirit of Classical Canon Law*, 381–3; Ullmann, *Growth of Papal Government*, 299–30; Ullmann, *Principles of Government and Politics*, 75–8; Clarke, *Interdict*, 49.
[149] C.15, q.6, cc.4–5. See Vodola, 'Sovereignty and tabu Part I'.   [150] *Royal Letters*, no. 191.
[151] Cheney, 'Alleged deposition of King John'.   [152] See Whalen, *Two Powers*, esp. chs. 6 and 7.
[153] Reuter, 'Contextualising Canossa'; Keygnaert, 'Meaning of ecclesiastical exclusion', 771.

that the king had been removed from power. Even rumours might have provided an excuse. Chroniclers' false reports are as significant as the fact that Innocent did not take this step. The possibility, or perhaps an assumption that John had already been deposed, armed the French king and the discontented barons with more ammunition. The prospect of a French invasion brings us to perhaps the most extreme consequence of excommunication: crusade.

Military Force and Crusade

The launching of a crusade against excommunicates was far from an expected eventuality. Only in exceptional cases, and crucially as a response to long-term recalcitrance, would the extreme measure to sanction military attacks on excommunicates be taken. Yet the thirteenth century saw numerous crusades launched against heretics and excommunicates. These 'political crusades' were often controversial, but the practice came to be established.[154] Attacks against excommunicates had an entirely different character from attacks on fellow Christians (the links between heretics and excommunicates are probably significant in this context). Those who, burning with zeal for the church, had killed excommunicates, Urban II wrote to the bishop of Lucca, were not murderers (though they were still required to do penance).[155] Robert Grosseteste reportedly (almost certainly spuriously) declared that war against heretics, who were suspended and excommunicated, was sanctified.[156]

As Charlotte Lewandowski has observed, discussing the reign of King Stephen, bishops were required to use excommunication in response to violence 'but also as a prelude to violence and force'.[157] There was more than one occasion on which thirteenth-century England played host to armies claiming to fight a crusade against excommunicates on behalf of the church. Some of these ventures were launched by the papacy; others were self-proclaimed 'crusades', supported only by a few maverick clergy. The benefits of appropriating crusading terminology were clear: 'the crusade provided a readily acceptable ideology of legitimate warfare'.[158] Crusades drummed up support and boosted morale, transforming rebellions into religious enterprises. An enemy's excommunication made all this possible.

The first such crusade in thirteenth-century England was linked to the supposed deposition of King John supplying a pretext for a French invasion. According to Wendover, Innocent not only deposed John, legitimizing rebellion against him, but offered Philip Augustus of France the English throne. Foreign

---

[154] Strayer, 'Political crusades of the thirteenth century'; Whalen, *Two Powers*, 186–7.
[155] C.23, q.5, c.47.   [156] *CM*, v, 401.
[157] Lewandowski, 'Cultural expressions of episcopal power', 80–1.
[158] Tyerman, *England and the Crusades*, 133.

knights who helped Philip secure the throne were to receive the same indulgences as those who took the cross and went to Jerusalem.[159] Wendover presents John's decision to seek absolution as being significantly influenced by imminent invasion. The chronicler further reports that Philip was irate when told not to invade, having spent a good deal of money as instructed by the pope.[160] Though none of this ever happened, Cheney observed that Innocent might well have had these plans 'up his sleeve', giving Philip reason to believe his invasion would be supported by the church. The French king cannot, therefore, have been pleased 'to find that a crusade against an excommunicate had turned, overnight, into an attack on a vassal of the pope' following John's submission to the papacy.[161]

The air of legitimacy that John's excommunication lent the French king's invasion was now eliminated. Suddenly it was John's barons, who in 1215 'had taken the mantle of God and the church' led by the self-styled 'Marshal of the army of God and Holy Church', who were excommunicated by the pope.[162] In 1217, the Crowland annalist noted that those who had called themselves the 'army of God' and claimed to be fighting for the liberties of church and realm were now reputed to be the sons of Belial and compared to infidels.[163] No attempt to claim that the baronial rebellion and Louis's invasion were religious undertakings could be maintained. Instead, Innocent sanctioned war against Louis, Philip's son, and the rebellious barons. The pope wrote to the barons in 1215, threatening excommunication. Their actions were particularly 'nefarious and absurd' because they had supported the king while he was excommunicated, yet, now that he was reconciled with the church, they sought to eject him from the kingdom.[164] Innocent instructed the barons to help the king against the rebels, in remission of sins.[165] Six months later, the pope wrote to the archbishop of Bourges, his suffragans, and probably the other ecclesiastical provinces of France,[166] ordering them to:

Persuade the princes, knights, and barons of your diocese, ... for the remission of sins, to furnish immediate help and support to the king, ... showing clearly by this action how valiantly for Christ's name they would range themselves against the Saracens ... in battle: for they have as neighbours men who in this respect are worse than Saracens, because, having taken the sign of the Cross, they now seem renegades working to fulfil the pagans' hopes by hindering such a magnificent venture for the Holy Land.[167]

---

[159] *CM*, ii, 536–7; *Oxenedes*, 127.   [160] *CM*, ii, 540–1, 549–50.
[161] Cheney, *Pope Innocent III*, 338–41.
[162] Carpenter, *Minority*, 28; Carpenter, *Magna Carta*, 290, 333.   [163] *Coventry*, 236.
[164] After John had submitted to the pope but before he had received absolution, the barons said they would not follow him until he was absolved, to avoid helping him regain his continental territories: *CM*, ii, 549–50.
[165] *Letters of Innocent III*, no. 1013 (appendix).   [166] *SLI*, 226 n. 1.   [167] *SLI*, no. 87.

Innocent never used the word 'crusade', but if he never made a formal declaration of a crusade against the rebels, he came 'perilously close to it'.[168]

Procuring an excommunication attached moral weight to any military campaign taken against enemies. This could also be good for morale. As discussed in Chapter 2, war was one situation in which the idea that God was against excommunicates might be more potent. An excommunicate was perhaps more likely to lose. For those fighting against excommunicates, the opposite logic applied: they surely had God on their side. Thus before the Battle of Lincoln in 1217, the earl Marshal is said to have roused his men by arguing that their rivals' excommunication would undoubtedly cause their demise. They were 'all the more trapped' because of it, and would end up in hell.[169]

> There you see men who have started a war
> on God and Holy Church.
> I can fully guarantee you this,
> that God has surrendered them into our hands.[170]

Likewise, Hubert de Burgh used the sentence against Louis to encourage his men, declaring 'we should oppose them boldly, since God is with us because they are excommunicated'. Indeed, Wendover's testimony indicates that such exhortations would have been inspiring. The chronicler claimed that there was 'an ardent desire to fight against the excommunicated French' as well as for England ('pro patria'). Before the battle, the legate ritually excommunicated Louis and his supporters. The king's army was then promised eternal salvation, blessed, given absolution, and fortified by receiving the Eucharist.[171] Many of the chronicle accounts note that the royalist forces wore crosses on their chests, generally describing the conflict in the language of crusades.[172] Wendover himself wrote that there should be no doubt that Louis's misfortune was down to 'just judgement of God' as a result of his excommunication.[173] The excommunication of the French and rebels thus bolstered the royal army's claim to have a just cause, protected by God.[174]

Excommunication could also provide a pretext for more unscrupulous behaviour. Thus after the Battle of Lincoln, the cathedral church was plundered. This was because, according to both the Crowland annalist and Wendover, the legate had excommunicated the clerics of the city who had supported the rebels. Even the women and children who fled to the church were excommunicated by contagion, since the churches of the city had been contaminated by condemned

---

[168] Lloyd, 'Political crusades', 115.
[169] *History of William Marshal*, ed. Holden, ii, ll.16295–303.
[170] *History of William Marshal*, ed. Holden, ii, ll.16304–7.   [171] *CM*, iii, 28.
[172] *Coventry*, 235; *Ann. Dunstable*, 49; *Annales Monasterii de Waverleia*, ed. Luard, 287; *Gervase*, 110; Lloyd, 'Political crusades', 114, provides further references.
[173] *CM*, iii, 25.   [174] *CM*, iii, 18–19; cf. *Oxenedes*, 139–40.

clerics. If the legate indeed ordered this plunder, the point is not whether pillaging excommunicates was a legitimate act, but that the sanction was being used to excuse it.[175] It justified rather than caused violence.

In the tumultuous 1220s, when excommunication was frequently employed against rebels who threatened the crown, chroniclers once again claim that the sanction spurred people on to fight against these rebels. In early 1221, William de Forz, earl of Aumale, was solemnly excommunicated by the legate Pandulf, acting together with a large number of bishops at St Paul's.[176] The earls of Chester and Salisbury participated in the ceremony by throwing down candles along with the clergymen, indicating that the earls were deeply involved in the decision to sentence de Forz.[177] The excommunication offered an important prelude to raising arms against the earl. The Dunstable annalist claimed that after the ceremony, by common council, 'they declared against him', and immediately commenced military campaigns at the castles of Fotheringay and Bytham.[178] The king sent for military assistance, explaining that William, 'excommunicated by the lord legate... along with all his supporters, accomplices, and adherents', had 'seditiously and furtively captured the castle of Fotheringay' and was disturbing the peace.[179]

According to the Crowland annalist, the use of excommunication to inspire armed resistance against the earl was successful. The earl of Chester, who had been present at the council,

> was enraged in many ways when he heard the excommunication of the earl and his obstinacy and violent plundering of both rich and poor, both because he saw his lord king held in contempt because of his youth, and because of the fraudulent occupation of the castle of Fotheringay... Whence he faithfully promised... that he would put forth all his men to destroy the aforesaid earl and his men.[180]

Subsequently, many nobles followed the earl's lead, 'because the excommunicated earl and his men were long held in contempt by many men (*a multo tempore exosi habebantur*)'.[181] At the siege of Bytham, the legate renewed his sentence 'in the presence of the whole army', and afterwards urged them 'strongly and faithfully to exert themselves in this matter for the honour of the church and the tranquillity of the realm', in remission of sins. The castle was duly captured and burnt to the ground, an event that the Dunstable annalist compared to the Fall of Jericho.[182]

---

[175] *Coventry*, 238; *CM*, iii, 23.
[176] Either seven or eleven bishops: cf. *Ann. Dunstable*, 63–4, and *Coventry*, 247–8. See also Carpenter, *Minority*, 165–7, 227–34 and Turner, 'William de Forz', 238–42.
[177] For the causes of his sentence see *Ann. Dunstable*, 63–4.
[178] *Ann. Dunstable*, 64. Although Carpenter has shown that de Forz's seizure of Fotheringay Castle was after the excommunication, and therefore not a cause of it: *Minority*, 230 n. 12.
[179] *Royal letters*, no. 145; London, TNA, SC 1/2/34.   [180] *Coventry*, 248.
[181] *Coventry*, 248.   [182] *Ann. Dunstable*, 64.

Excommunication did not cause the siege of Bytham Castle. In all probability it did not affect how events unfolded. However, it may have caused the king's men to fight more enthusiastically, simultaneously deflating the morale of those inside the castle. Most importantly, it altered how the events of 1221 were perceived: quashing the excommunicate rebels became a religious enterprise.[183]

Three years later, Falkes de Bréauté was himself occupying a castle, Bedford, against the king's wishes. Falkes's *Querimonia* relates that as he was besieged there, the legate and other bishops promulgated a sentence of excommunication against him. This sentence was then published throughout the kingdom with indulgences offered to those who aided the king's cause 'so that the castle would be captured more quickly'. Falkes was particularly angry that the bishops collected funds to be used against him. Again, excommunication was used to provide the violence needed to defeat Falkes with a religious tint. Falkes bitterly noted that 'so great was the desire, or lust, for capturing the castle', that some of the bishops even blessed the stones thrown during the siege.[184]

Yet if all these excommunications added weight to use of military force, and despite the fact that indulgences were offered to those who took part, the language of crusading ('crucesignatus' and so forth) was rarely used to describe them. With the exception of the campaign against Louis and his men, those who fought against excommunicates in thirteenth-century England could not expect to be called *crucesignati*, nor to receive all the benefits that such a title implied. In the 1260s, however, a crusade *was* preached throughout Europe against the rebellious English barons. Clement IV also absolved all oaths and promises made to Montfort and forbade vassals from obeying him (a deposition if Montfort had had any legitimate claim to power).[185]

The decision to publish a crusade against Simon de Montfort and his supporters was undoubtedly taken in desperation. Up to this point, excommunications pronounced against the rebels had had no effect. Quite the reverse: the rebels themselves had launched a self-proclaimed crusade against those who did not uphold the Provisions of Oxford.[186] Before the Battle of Lewes, Bishop Walter de Cantilupe of Worcester had provided indulgences for the baronial forces, who wore white crosses on their shoulders and chests.[187] Many sources from the period presented the baronial cause as just and holy. To cite merely one example, the

---

[183] Cf. Edward I's presentation of his Scottish campaigns as a holy war against excommunicates, presenting the Scots as Godless people, while the English carried saints' banners; Burton, 'Politics, propaganda and public opinion', 340–4.

[184] *Coventry*, 265–6. Excommunication was again an important prelude to Henry III's Welsh campaign in 1231. See *CM*, iii, 202.

[185] *Reg. Clement IV*, no. 232.

[186] See Tyerman, *England and the Crusades*, 144–51; Lloyd, '"Political crusades"', 116–17; Stacey, 'Crusades, crusaders', 148–50.

[187] *Oxenedes*, 221–2; *Flores Historiarum*, ii, 494–5; *Chronicle of William de Rishanger*, ed. Halliwell, 31; Maddicott, *Simon de Montfort*, 271.

baronial tract the *Song of Lewes,* written before Evesham, described the royalists as 'the enemy of the English and the whole realm... Perchance too of the church, therefore also of God'. Montfort, because of his 'wholly singular religion' was England's one hope; his victory at Lewes was God-given.[188] The barons exercised a monopoly on religious as well as secular propaganda.[189] Clergy and friars preached on behalf of Montfort's cause, while the papal excommunications against them were never published in England.[190]

Excommunication alone therefore had little impact upon Montfort and his men. But what excommunication might provoke was still to be feared. The Tewksbury annalist recorded a letter of anonymous advice given to the barons in 1263 (unfortunately the manuscript ends abruptly halfway through this letter). It explains the dangers posed by the papal legate:

> If they admit him [to the kingdom], the nobles will gradually be perturbed, and become weak. If they do not admit him, they will be excommunicated, and the land interdicted, and afterwards the secular arm will be called against them.[191]

Later the letter asserts 'it is believed that the king of France is very given to invading England', and claims that the church enjoined this on Louis IX. The barons were advised to ensure that they could gather a large army by uniting Ireland, Wales, and Scotland against their enemies. The warning was indeed relevant, for Urban IV instructed the legate, in 1263, to launch an army against those who opposed his mission, and shortly afterwards to preach a crusade against them. Those who helped the pope's cause would receive the same indulgences as accompanied crusade vows to the Holy Land.[192] The faithful were even to receive indulgences merely for attending crusade preaching.[193] When the legate himself became pope, as Clement IV, he pursued his predecessor's policy with even more vigour. His successor as legate, Ottobuono, was to raise an army and preach a crusade in England, Scotland, Wales, Ireland, Denmark, Norway, Gascony, Brittany, Normandy, Flanders, Picardy, the Saintonge, and Germany.[194] Even after the death of Montfort at the Battle of Evesham, Ottobuono was instructed to preach the crusade in other parts of Europe, if he were unable to land in England.[195]

---

[188] *Song of Lewes,* trans. Kingsford, ll. 373–4, 266–8, 392; cf. Hartman, 'Poetry and the cause of Simon de Montfort'; Maddicott, *Simon de Montfort,* 255.
[189] See Leidulf Melve's discussion of how the baronial movement sought to influence public opinion: 'Public debate'.
[190] Maddicott, 'Politics and people', 11; Carpenter, 'English peasants in politics', 338–9.
[191] *Ann. Tewksbury,* 179–80.   [192] *Cal. Pap. Reg.,* 397.
[193] *Cal. Pap. Reg.,* 398–9, 428; *Reg. Clement IV,* no. 58.
[194] *Reg. Clement IV,* no. 44; *Diplomatarium Norvegicum,* ed. Unger and Huitfelt, vii, no. 23.
[195] Martène, *Thesaurus,* no. 148.

The crusade against the rebels never materialized, although for few months in 1264 a French invasion was a real and highly disturbing possibility.[196] That it never took place does not negate the fact that excommunication could have drastic consequences. In such high-stakes disputes, those against the will of the pope risked a crusade being launched against them. If there were those who disagreed with the pope's judgement, others would be happy to assume the role of crusader without having to travel to Jerusalem. Still more worrying was the possibility that an enemy would exploit the situation, in England a danger that came primarily from the king of France.

Conclusions

The church emphasized the contagious nature of excommunication, urging its members to cut off those who were infected with it. Though this principle was mitigated in various ways, social exclusion ought to have been a key factor in decisions to seek absolution. Yet evidence that excommunicates were shunned by communities is remarkable by its scarcity. It bears repeating that compliance with the law was unlikely to have been noted by ecclesiastical sources. Records are likely to obscure social pressure, especially since shunning would be complying with ecclesiastical mandates. Nevertheless, whilst it is difficult to argue from absence of evidence, the lack of routine shunning of excommunicates visible in available sources is striking. It is in stark contrast to both considerable explicit evidence that communities continued to associate with excommunicates (Chapter 4), and that publicity was a detrimental consequence of the sanction (Chapter 5). If those under the ban were frequently excluded from their communities, and if this was one of the sanction's worst effects, we would expect more indications of such treatment.

This does not, however, mean that excommunicates had nothing to fear when it came to the temporal results of a sentence. First, there is a spectrum of social consequences. It is possible, indeed quite likely, that *some* Christians did routinely shun excommunicates. Absolutions sought without explanation in records might have been driven by, or partially driven by, the shunning faced by excommunicates. That the population was well aware of how excommunicates were supposed to be treated seems clear. Second, excommunicates left themselves open to attack from those who only required an excuse to take advantage of the sanction. The faithful did not necessarily attack those under sentences simply because they were excommunicated, but excommunicate status could provide a pretext for abuse. With or without official ecclesiastical support, excommunication could be used to

---

[196] Maddicott, *Simon de Montfort*, 290–1.

launch such attacks because the church sometimes did sanction them. Often it must be concluded that instances of ostracism and related treatment tell us more about the circumstances and individuals involved in a particular case than about excommunication as a whole. It remains the case that while excommunicates frequently, perhaps usually, avoided complete ostracism, they were at risk of maltreatment. There was no guarantee that social consequences would be negligible. For those in positions of power, the stakes were higher. Excommunication was a step towards deposition, religiously justified violence, and even crusade.

4
Apathy, Rejection, and Divided Loyalties

There is both implicit and explicit evidence that excommunicates in thirteenth-century England were not consistently ostracized. The simple fact that many excommunicates lived with their sentences for prolonged periods of time, which they would have been unable to do if appropriately shunned, is an example of the former. Records and complaints that the faithful were intermingling with excommunicates provide specific examples. As I stated at the start of this book, the reasons why excommunicates sought absolution are usually obscure. We cannot rule out that many did so because of social shunning. Nevertheless, there is sufficient evidence that communities often failed to comply with orders to ostracize excommunicates that consideration must be given as to why. Studies of excommunication and ostracism in other societies, as well as close analysis of thirteenth-century English documents, provide valuable insights.

The reasons why the church was unable to ensure such treatment require analysis, even if on one level it is not altogether surprising that excommunicates were not consistently treated as contagious lepers. It is all too easy to blame lack of compliance on clerical misuse or overuse of the sanction. Both abuse and overuse, without a doubt, contributed to resistance and apathy towards excommunication. Yet so too did many other factors. The difficulties faced by the church in thirteenth-century England included both long-standing obstacles and more recent developments. The sanction's medicinal purpose, and consequently the way it was supposed to work and be enforced, was one insurmountable issue. Another was the simple fact that a great burden was placed on communities, even without accusations of overuse. Attempts to mitigate this burden by limiting contagion and providing exceptions, though both merciful and practical, undermined the rhetoric of contagion, particularly from the eleventh century. The proliferation of *latae sententiae*, and the ambiguity that often accompanied them, was an even newer problem. Active attempts by rival authorities, here usually royal government, to undermine clergymen's use of excommunication were rather less novel. Consideration of these problems will accompany discussion of 'misuse'. Misuse and overuse of excommunication helped undermine respect for the sanction, but they are far from the sole causes of refusal to avoid excommunicates.

The enforcement of the vast majority of excommunications depended upon ordinary men and women, both clerical and lay. To paraphrase Ian Forrest, historians have not hitherto appreciated how far the regulation of sin rested upon collaboration between clergy and laity.[1] Laypeople rarely had the opportunity to influence judgments, yet they were nonetheless tasked with carrying out this penalty. They seldom have a 'voice' in our sources but voted with their feet. Higher-profile excommunications, which inevitably generated more evidence, allow greater discussion of the potential reasons for resistance, though less well-documented cases might have been subject to many of the same social and political factors at a local level. While indifference was no doubt the cause of some communal (in)action, in other cases there is evidence of considered opposition. In still others, conflicting information and mutual excommunications necessitated choosing a side. Collective action lies at the heart of sanctions such as excommunication. In the absence of force to ensure conformity, collective action relies upon unity of intention and judgment. Though the medieval church exerted pressures on communities to coerce them to obey excommunication's requirements, chiefly interdicts, these were insufficient. Excommunication, a sanction which removed an offender from Christian society, was most effective when the *communio fidelium* acted as a unified body. It could not be expected to do so.

Problems with Voluntary Ostracism

The Burden of Enforcement

Ostracism is neither a passive nor an easy activity. The determination needed to maintain social shunning necessitates either anger towards the deviant individual, conviction that they need to be removed from the community, or such forceful social pressure from others that associating with the target would harm the communicator. As an institution, the church sought to create anger with forceful denunciations of individual excommunicates. Although these invectives had important effects, they did not apparently provoke widespread ostracism, so are discussed separately in Chapter 5. The idea that excommunicates must be removed for the good of the rest of society was put forth in the language of contagion. This was linked to sanctions used to punish communicators, who incurred (or rather were infected by) minor excommunication when they made contact. Interdicts were further used to punish communities that failed to enforce sentences of excommunication. It is clear that the rhetoric proved insufficient to invariably induce voluntary ostracism.

    A standard episcopal mandate, initially directing subordinates to publicize an excommunication, would not necessarily make use of the language of infection. Such orders typically state merely that the excommunicate ought to be strictly

---

[1] Forrest, *Trustworthy Men*, 308. He is discussing, more specifically, the alliance between bishops and local elites.

avoided by all. The rhetoric of contagion is stronger and more prevalent in episcopal missives seeking to deal with communities flouting the doctrine, indicating that greater care was taken to persuade when illicit communication had already taken place.

> Ralph de Honilane, vintner, once executor of the will of the now late Thomas le Lyndraper, citizen of London, was previously rightly and legitimately bound by a sentence of major excommunication, by authority of our court of Canterbury. He has damnably sustained the same sentence for three years and more with a hardened heart, as a son of disobedience, and still he pertinaciously persists in the sentence, not without heretical depravity, scorning the keys of the church. Therefore, he was for a long time solemnly publicised to be excommunicated, along with those communicating with him, through the whole city of London. Yet even more obdurate, he throws himself in with the communion of the faithful, staining others with his contagion, and many degenerate sons, forgetful of their own salvation and scorning the vigour of ecclesiastical discipline, do not fear to be bound by the snare of the same sentence with him by impudently communicating with the same. We do not want to hide such great causes of offence to God and mankind, which are contrary to the Catholic faith, under the cloak of connivance and dissimulation, lest the blood of those erring, whom we are held to recall to the way of life, is required from our hands by the terrifying Judge [Ezek. 18:19]. Therefore, we explain to you all...the danger of such dreadful communication, which we want to be hidden from nobody through deliberate ignorance, ordering you, in virtue of holy obedience and under threat of eternal malediction,... diligently to take care to avoid the said Ralph in all your discussions and convocations as a putrid limb of the church and a representative from the devil. We also strictly forbid on account of the health of souls lest anyone presumes illicitly to communicate with the same Ralph by eating, drinking, buying, selling, hiring, employing, trading, speaking or in any another way, knowing that the corrective hand will not be delayed against rebels found in this matter.[2]

No more is heard of Ralph the wine merchant following this letter, addressed to the mayor and community of London by the archbishop of Canterbury in 1300. It is impossible to know why he remained part of the community for at least three years despite his excommunication, or whether Robert Winchelsey's threats against communicators, here unusually made directly to the mayor, had their desired effect. Perhaps Ralph's sentence was considered unjust. Perhaps he was popular amongst his neighbours. Perhaps people were unwilling to forego their

---

[2] *Reg. Winchelsey*, i, 394–5.

wine. What is clear is that those who associated with Ralph had been unable or unwilling to treat him as canon law demanded.

The simplest explanation for the failure of Christians to shun excommunicates is that the process asked too much of them. The fact that excommunicates in general continued to live in their communities increased the burden of enforcement for their fellows. Though excommunication may be compared to other forms of ostracism such as exile and outlawry, in this respect it was quite different. Exile and banishment, in particular, though intended to remove deviants from the community like excommunication, extracted them from their homes and homelands.[3] Exile could be difficult for the friends and families of the excluded, but did not require the social shunning, and the daily effort and resolve required by it, that was essential to an effective excommunication. Thomas of Chobham's instruction to respond to an excommunicate's greeting with 'may God correct you' or other bitter words, is harder than it sounds.[4] If confronted with an individual in person (in contrast to our own society, in which communication via technology is common), rebuffing them is far more difficult than communicating with them, especially if they seek to engage. Ignoring them might be deeply unpleasant or, at the very least, awkward. Only in the case of monks and nuns did excommunication necessarily entail a kind of exile, since an excommunicated religious could hardly continue to live amongst those who had taken holy vows, though occasionally lay excommunicates also ran away from their homes, imposing exile upon themselves.[5] On other occasions, excommunication and banishment were linked. In 1225, a papal legate was sent to ask the king of France if he would accept the excommunicated Falkes de Bréauté until he was reconciled with Henry III and absolved.[6] The excommunications of clerics who had supported Prince Louis's invasion were in 1218 effectively commuted into outlawries: such clerics were instructed to leave the realm or face capture.[7] Matthew Paris described William Lupus, the excommunicated archdeacon of Lincoln, who had been forced to traipse around England to avoid arrest, as 'a fugitive, a sort of exile'. He eventually went to Rome to appeal the archbishop of Canterbury's excommunication, securing a 'remedy' from the pope but dying on his way home after so many 'tribulations'.[8] Other excommunicates were supposed to go to Rome in order to secure absolution directly from the pope, usually for having incurred *Si*

---

[3] For exile and outlawry see Van Houts, 'Vocabulary of exile and outlawry'; Dresch, 'Outlawry'. Milani, 'An ambiguous sentence', provides a useful introduction to political banishment in the thirteenth century.
[4] Chobham, *Summa*, 248. See above Chapter 3, 107.
[5] See Hicks, 'Exclusion as exile'. For runaways, see Chapter 3, 124–5.
[6] *Cal. Pap. Reg.*, 124. [7] *Rotuli Clausarum*, 377a.
[8] *CM*, v, 412–13. Laura Napran has discussed self-imposed 'exile' to avoid capture in her discussion of excommunicated noblewomen: 'Marriage and excommunication'.

quis suadente, thus potentially suffering a sort of temporary exile.[9] In general, however, excommunicates were not exiles at all, but continued to live where they had before. The lack of 'geographic' exclusion might well be more traumatizing: 'to live among people and yet lack all human solaces'.[10] It also asked more of communities.

Outlawry had more in common with excommunication than had exile or banishment, for communities were required to enforce it (though did not always do so).[11] Outlaws were also permitted to abjure the realm, thereby becoming exiles. Outlawry could be difficult for the closest associates of the excluded, since they would have to overcome the natural desire to harbour their friends or relatives. Yet secular authorities had far more coercive means of ensuring obedience, even if studies note that outlawry became less effective as the thirteenth century progressed. Crucially, harbouring an outlaw incurred outlawry. It was a capital offence, a far greater and more immediate risk than associating with an excommunicate. Excommunicates, by contrast, would continue to live with their close relatives, who were excepted from contagion. Outlawry was also designed to be permanent. Mistakes occurred, so that outlaws were sometimes in-lawed.[12] In principle, nevertheless, outlaws were never coming back.

The key difference between secular exclusionary sanctions and excommunication lay in the purpose of the latter. Whether seeking to alter behaviour or to drive out the target, ostracism's essential purpose is to strengthen group cohesion.[13] There is, however, a big difference between ostracism that 'purifies' by driving a member out altogether, and ostracism that is intended to force a change in behaviour, emending rather than expelling the deviant. Perpetual banishment was an example of the former.[14] Religious exclusion usually intends the latter, and medieval excommunication certainly did. Whatever the motives of individual clerics—and there were certainly those who used excommunication punitively—the sanction's ostensible purpose was medicinal. Its function was to induce a sinner to make amends so that they could be reintegrated.[15] Clergy were to lead erring sheep back to the flock with warnings and terrors, as Gregory IX urged the English prelates in 1232.[16] Those who failed to deal with offenders were being

---

[9] Though as Helmholz notes, the requirement was often waived in practice: Helmholz, 'Si quis suadente'. Penance might similarly require an extended absence, if pilgrimage was a condition for absolution. E.g. *Reg. W. Giffard*, 280: William Driffield was to go to the Holy Land or else donate half his goods in its aid.

[10] From a fourth-century imperial constitution on apostasy, quoted by Elisabeth Vodola, *Excommunication*, 47. Beaulande also observes that remaining in the same place might be more traumatic: *Malheur*, 43.

[11] Stewart, 'Outlawry', 39

[12] Pollock and Maitland, *History of English Law*, i, 477; Stewart, 'Outlawry', 45.

[13] Williams, *Ostracism*, 11.

[14] Beaulande contrasts this with excommunication's purpose in *Malheur*, 95.

[15] The same applies to interdict: Clarke, *Interdict*, 259.   [16] Ann. Burton, 243.

negligent pastors.[17] The result was that excommunication was designed to be short-lived, not to uproot those sanctioned. An excommunicate should be reincorporated into the community the moment he or she made amends for their offence.

The medicinal purpose of excommunication may, therefore, have made enforcement more difficult for those expected to ostracize. In one respect, the ideal of a short sentence would have lightened the burden, since shunning might not have to be carried out for long. Yet temporary exclusion meant that before, during, and after an excommunication, excommunicates continued to live alongside their would-be ostracizers. People could, certainly, be excommunicated in a group, for instance when an offence was committed by several people. But, generally, an excommunicate was an individual and not part of a group to be ostracized as a whole. The mental leap required to view a sinner as suddenly a dangerous source of infection, and then to just as quickly forgive them, was very—perhaps too—great. On the other hand, one possible consequence of successfully convincing the faithful to ostracize was that they might continue to shun an excommunicate after absolution, something about which clerics occasionally expressed worry.[18] No idea of 'once an excommunicate, always an excommunicate' was intended.[19] If forms of ostracism generally seek to create a scapegoat for the remainder of a community to define themselves against, excommunicates' constant presence and speedy rehabilitation did not aid this.[20] Nor were excommunicates visually identified by badges or other marks, as could be Jews, lepers, and heretics, emphasizing their separation, though they were regularly announced to be excommunicates.

Moreover, the church's own mitigations hardly helped the rhetoric of infection, not least because rules with many exceptions are harder to have confidence in, to understand, and to follow. Thus, as noted in Chapter 3, close family members were excepted from the requirement to ostracize. The church had to be merciful, unlike secular authorities. The idea of contagion was even further undermined by advice that if someone was believed to be excommunicate (if they had incurred an *ipso facto* sentence) but their status was not publicly known, they ought to be shunned only privately and not in public (though this remained a grey area until 1418's *Ad vitanda*).[21] Such a doctrine undermined the idea that excommunicates were dangerously contagious and risked implying that *latae sententiae* were not

---

[17] See Introduction, at 12.
[18] *C&S*, 774, c. 28; *CM*, vi, no. 96; *Foedera*, I.i.275. 'Local opinions about reputation were certainly in dialogue with official pronouncements, but were not governed by them': Forrest, *Trustworthy Men*, 340.
[19] Cf. Helmholz, 'Excommunication as a legal sanction', 214.
[20] A point made by Randolph Starn, discussing exiles in medieval and renaissance Italy: *Contrary Commonwealth*, 7.
[21] Vodola, *Excommunication*, 34, 48–9. *Ad vitanda* confirmed that only publicized excommunications were contagious.

'real' excommunications.[22] Here bureaucratization, alongside practical and pastoral concerns, was fighting against the rhetoric and principles of the practice. Whilst these exceptions and rules were practical, they cannot have done much to help the faithful treat excommunicates like lepers, since the 'disease' was supposedly only infectious in some circumstances. Real lepers, unlike metaphorical lepers, could not be cured.

A Disparate Group

The difficulty of inducing the shunning of excommunicates as a group was compounded by the fact that Christians could be excommunicated for a great many offences. One obvious explanation for the lack of routine shunning was that excommunication was too commonplace; generating sufficient communal anger against each and every excommunicate was an impossible task. Excommunicates had little in common with one another; they were a difficult group to 'other'. It is noteworthy that, although excommunicates were described by ecclesiastical authorities in much the same language as heretics and lepers, they barely feature in R.I. Moore's *Formation of a Persecuting Society*. Indeed, several of the persecuted groups discussed by Moore were also excommunicates: heretics, sorcerers, sodomites. Jews were of course not part of the Christian community in the first place (though they were, on occasion, excommunicated by Christian authorities nonetheless).[23] No 'constructed persona' can be attached to the heterogenous group excommunicates, any more than we could attach a persona to all people who go to prison.[24]

Scorn for ecclesiastical authority was all that excommunicates shared. The only characteristic that was generally attributed to excommunicates was 'hardness of heart' because, officially, all excommunications were the result of contumacy. It is evident that the mere fact of not treating ecclesiastical mandates with the utmost respect was not enough to generate widespread ill will towards excommunicates. Though the vehemence in the language used in excommunication denunciations varied, as did the solemnity of the publication rite, in terms of social consequences, major excommunication was one size fits all. This, however, was despite the fact that the offence that initially drew excommunicates to the attention of church authorities could be minor or serious. It would be foolish to assume the

[22] Vodola, *Excommunication*, 99.
[23] Meyer, 'Making sense of Christian Excommunication of Jews', provides references to the debate between William Jordan and Joseph Shatzmiller, broadly agreeing with the latter that the practice was not merely an anomaly introduced by a (deliberate) misinterpretation.
[24] Moore, *Formation of a Persecuting Society*, 153. It is true, of course, that these groups could not be described as homogenous either, but it was easier to group them together as the essential offence was the same.

original offence did not matter to people simply because all excommunicates were sentenced for the all-encompassing crime of contumacy. The excommunicates who had incurred sentences by interacting with the Scots were shunned, for instance, but this treatment tells us more about early fourteenth-century nationalism than it does about feelings against excommunicates as excommunicates.[25]

Unfortunately, scant examples of shunning performed against excommunicates preclude easy answers about whether certain crimes that incurred excommunication *were* taken seriously when others were not. We have so few records of performed ostracism that there is a danger of assuming that examples of illicit communicating prove that certain crimes were tolerated by communities. In the 1220s, Agnes de Hayford refused to return to the priory of Kattedy, where she had lived as a religious for two years, but was nevertheless able to stay 'sometimes in her father's house, sometimes elsewhere'.[26] Those who harboured her could have felt that apostasy was not too serious a sin, or else they simply wished to help their relative or friend, or both.[27]

Ralph the Vintner, introduced above, was apparently sentenced for his failings as executor of the will of the late Thomas le Lyndraper. Should we therefore conclude that Londoners continued to associate with Ralph because they did not consider this to be a shunnable offence?[28] Certainly it did not make him dangerous other than in a spiritual sense. Or did their communicating have more to do with Ralph's personality and place in the community? The difficulty of assessing how seriously crimes were judged is increased by the complexity of personal relationships. Perhaps some initially did exclude him from contact, but as time went on fewer and fewer people were able to maintain this harsh treatment. It seems likely both that Ralph's associates liked him or benefitted from his companionship, and that they did not judge his fault to have been especially horrendous. The two explanations are not mutually exclusive.

We know a little more about Juliana Box, who was excommunicated for the same offence, also in London, at the same time as Ralph. In 1300, the archbishop of Canterbury asserted that Juliana 'indifferently integrates herself with the community of the faithful every day, and many communicate with her knowingly, against our inhibition, to the danger of their souls'. He ordered these communicators (once discovered) to be sentenced with major excommunication.[29] Juliana had in fact been sentenced two years earlier, seemingly for maladministration of her late husband's estate, of which she was executor. She had subsequently been imprisoned by the secular arm and had therefore sought absolution. The sentence

---

[25] Hill, 'Belief and practice', 138; Reynolds, *Kingdoms and Communities,* 253; Forrest, *Trustworthy Men,* 79–81.
[26] *Rotuli Hugonis de Welles,* ed. Phillimore and Davis, ii, 233.
[27] The desire of friends and family to protect their loved ones is an unsurprising phenomenon, noted also in Vodola, *Excommunication,* 59–67, and Beaulande, *Malheur,* 231–2.
[28] On execution of wills see Forrest, *Trustworthy Men,* 273–5.   [29] *Reg. Winchelsey,* i, 390–1.

she was under in 1300 was thus at least her second excommunication. What is interesting about Juliana is that, though her sentence seems to have related only to her role as executor, she had also contracted a *de facto* marriage with Richard of Louth, a subdeacon.[30] Richard was himself excommunicated for his illicit relationship with Juliana and for his fornication and adultery with Margery Skip and Johanna wife of Richard Peyforer.[31] Three years earlier, he had been accused of mistreating his wife, as well as fornication and adultery with other women.[32] Juliana seems not to have been a paragon of virtue by contemporary ecclesiastical standards, yet she evidently had numerous people who were willing to communicate with her. Her common law marriage (or fornication, depending on whom you asked) with Richard seems to have done her no harm.[33] Her fellows may have supported this relationship, though Richard's public adultery, fornication, and abuse make this suggestion harder to sustain. Juliana's frustratingly incomplete history provokes more questions than it answers. Alongside Ralph of Honilane's case, the idea that failure to execute wills properly was not considered worthy of ostracism by lay Londoners is supportable. But it is by no means conclusive. It is entirely plausible that others excommunicated for the same crimes were shunned and so sought absolution promptly, and thus had no reason to be recorded in the register.

Another problem is that, though we know many excommunicates lived bound by their sentences for prolonged periods of time, the specific reason for their excommunication is usually obscure. Thus writs for the capture of recalcitrant excommunicates who had been sentenced for forty days or more merely recite the formula that the wrongdoer had committed 'manifest offences and contumacy', hiding whatever misdeed or accusation thereof had originally brought them to the attention of the authorities. Unless records elsewhere fill in the gap, it is not possible to explain failure to shun as indifference towards a particular crime. Thus if Nicholas from Wallingford was ordered to be arrested by the secular arm, as the bishop of Salisbury threatened 'so that he whom fear of God does not induce to return, at least bodily coercion will bring back, and his spirit...may be saved on Judgement Day', the writ would not have stated, as did the threat, that the original cause of his sentence was his failure to receive the Eucharist and refusal to confess for three years. Nor would it have specified that, by 1309, he had been able to live with his excommunication for over a year because the people of the borough, though aware of his sentence, did not fear to communicate with him. In addition

---

[30] The only letters that concern Juliana alone do not state the cause of her excommunication. However, everyone who sought to conceal her late husband's property was excommunicated. Juliana was certainly guilty of this: *Reg. Winchelsey*, 215–6, 230–1, 296. See also 234–5 and 335.

[31] *Reg. Winchelsey*, i, 236.

[32] *Reg. Winchelsey*, i, 45–7. No record of these other women being sanctioned for their affairs with Richard is extant.

[33] Cf. Forrest, *Trustworthy Men*, 195.

to the threat of capture, the bishop, desiring that 'those who exist in filth through such communication are not made more filthy', ordered re-publication of Nicholas's sentence and that those who communicated incurred a major (as opposed to the standard minor) sentence. Nicholas and all his communicators were cited to appear before the bishop, Simon of Ghent, which is perhaps why there is no record of the sheriff being invoked.[34]

Once again, however, Nicholas's case does not allow the conclusion that the boroughs ignored the sentence because lack of engagement with the sacraments was considered broadly acceptable. Missing mass may not have been exceptional, though to omit Easter Eucharist and confession for three years would surely have raised eyebrows in areas where such actions would provoke suspicions of heresy. Nicholas's case could, then, demonstrate that attendance at church and reception of the sacraments was not widespread, so that failure either went unnoticed or had no stigma attached.[35] Yet such a conclusion is too audacious; there are too many other possibilities that the records do not allow us to explore.

The fact that there was such a range in the nature and seriousness of offences that excommunicates had committed is of course related to the supposed overuse of excommunication. It is clear that, while I have already questioned the value of thinking in terms of 'overuse', the sanction was used to punish a wide variety of actions, many of them far from atrocious. Excommunication for debt, a well-known and widely condemned phenomenon in the later Middle Ages, is perhaps the most famous example of the routine use of excommunication for relatively minor offences.[36] There is no escaping the idea that a common sanction, used even for minor offences, is less likely to be taken seriously.[37]

However, it is important not to over-stress the effect of frequent use of excommunication when it comes to community enforcement. Margo Todd has shown that excommunication was rarely used in the Reformed Scottish Kirk at the close of the sixteenth century. She explains that this was partly a reaction to excommunication's overuse by Catholic clergy (the criticism continues to affect attitudes towards medieval excommunication). Yet even in this culture, in which excommunication was used so rarely and reluctantly, she has found that 'neighbours, masters and clients regularly flouted excommunication orders and socialised with them'. Decrees that forbade contact were frequently renewed, indicating that communicators continued to be common. Todd attributes this flouting to the 'obligations of neighbourhood and kinship' that were so important in Scotland, arguing that they also contributed to the sparse use of excommunication, since

---

[34] 'qui per communionem huiusmodi in sordibus existunt in hac parte amplius non sordescant': *Reg. Gandavo*, i, 346–8; quotation 347.

[35] Cf. Rieder, 'Implications of exclusion'; Beaulande, *Malheur*, 257.

[36] See Lange, *Excommunication for Debt*; Jørgensen, 'Expulsion from heaven and earth', 65. Hill, 'Theory and practice', also notes excessive use of the sanction.

[37] Cf. Monter, 'Consistory of Geneva', 484.

disobedience undermined both the session's authority and the sanction's efficacy.[38] The importance of neighbourliness in early modern Scotland may well have contributed to the flouting described by Todd, but her study perhaps indicates just as much that, however scantly employed, excommunications imposed by authorities are always a tough sell to the communities expected to carry them out. Véronique Beaulande has indeed argued that communication with excommunicates should be interpreted as an expression of how deeply important communal life was felt to be, rather than as contempt for the church.[39]

The Difficulties of Collective Action

Had excommunication been used less often and for fewer offences, a perhaps even bigger obstacle would have remained. Effective ostracism requires collective action, a remarkably big ask for an act as arduous as social ostracism. On an individual level, social shunning is no small task. Kipling D. Williams's psychological study suggests that performance of social ostracism—emotional withdrawal in the presence of the target—can be far more difficult than physical ostracism, when the one ostracized is removed from society (banished, for instance). Performing social ostracism might even be as challenging as suffering exclusion.[40] Yet social dynamics, what we might call peer pressure, are surely crucial here. If the majority of a group are ostracizing someone, it might be easier to shun than not. Conversely, if most people are continuing to associate with someone condemned by the church, great willpower would be needed to persevere in ostracizing that individual.

In a case discussed by Margaret Gruter, an Old Order Amish community in 1940s Ohio performed *meidung* (shunning) on a member so successfully that he won damages in the state court, where he had pleaded his civil rights had been violated. The severity of the ostracism suffered by Andy Yoder, who had purchased a car to drive his ill daughter to frequent hospital appointments, required unity from his community. He believed he was 'right' to buy a car in his circumstances, but if others agreed they were too afraid of the social and economic injuries they themselves would suffer (Yoder was awarded $5000 in damages) if they were ostracized for associating with him. Yoder was isolated because he threatened to contaminate others. The danger he posed was the 'spread of individual decisions conflicting with the laws of the group'. This case is a striking example of the power of social ostracism when performed by a tight-knit group. If there was any dissent, the group mentality was strong enough to prevent it being

---

[38] Todd, 'None to haunt', esp. 230–3. [39] Beaulande, *Malheur*, 233.
[40] Williams, *Ostracism*, 17. Long-term ostracizers questioned by Williams almost all described themselves as stubborn: 235–6.

expressed. Winning his secular legal case did nothing to end Yoder's separation from his erstwhile community.[41] This was how excommunication was supposed to work.

While the possibility that excommunication could function this way should not be dismissed, the lack of evidence is remarkable. Nor need we assume that shunning need be so complete as in the Amish case; partial ostracism might produce results too. Shame and humiliation might be generated and prove quite effective. Nonetheless, if the balance tipped too far in the other direction, so that only a minority avoided an excommunicate, the sanction might fail to provoke a change of heart.

Social regulation achieved by shunning thus works best in close communities with shared values. Collective shunning will take place if there is a consensus that someone has contravened accepted morals or practices; ostracism's effects are weaker without combined effort. It is often observed that 'pollution' is a mechanism of self-defence and that exclusion serves to protect group identity.[42] Communities are defined by who is in and who is out. Émile Durkheim argued that outrage against an offender can generate or increase group solidarity. A deviant act provides a focus for group feeling, bringing together its members in common anger leading to tighter group solidarity.[43]

The premise of excommunication was that Christians constituted a community or fellowship with shared values. Excommunicates were separated from the *communio fidelium*. *Communio* can mean communion, social interaction, fellowship, and a great many other things. Community, however, seems to be the sense in this phrase, encompassing all the above ideas within it. But what precisely bound this community, or society, together besides faith and worship? In a society where religion is something everyone has in common, other values might assume greater importance. It is not surprising that a 'community' encompassing over 99 per cent of the population of thirteenth-century England did not, in fact, share unbreakable solidarity or cohesion.[44] Religion was a given; it was not a primary unifying force. There was therefore a fundamental problem that opinions would differ within this massive group of 'the faithful' as to what acts merited shunning, making collective ostracism unlikely in all but extreme circumstances. As Vincent Challet and Ian Forrest observe, 'Affective community—feelings of common interest and identity—can only be based on interaction'. All Christians were members of this huge community, but they would simultaneously belong to

---

[41] Gruter, 'Ostracism on trial', quotations at 129 (277).
[42] E.g. Murray, *Suicide*, 426–8; Moore, *Formation of a Persecuting Society*, 94–5. Both citing Douglas, *Purity and Danger*.
[43] Erikson, *Wayward Puritans*, 3–11; Moore, *Formation of a Persecuting Society*, 100–1.
[44] The biggest group of non-Christians was Jews, who represented c.0.25 per cent of the population (even less following the 1290 expulsion), as estimated in Vivian Lipman, 'Anatomy of medieval Anglo-Jewry', 65.

many more overlapping groups. Geographical, social, and institutional communities closer to home—parishes or villages, towns or factions within them, local friendships and alliances, even allegiance to a kingdom—might be more likely to influence opinions and behaviour than the nebulous idea of a unified Christendom.[45] Whatever values bound such groups together might or might not align with those of churchmen who used excommunication to censure offences deemed to be against the church's precepts. Peter Clarke, for instance, has discussed a case where an Italian commune performed 'the secular equivalent of excommunication' against clergy as countermeasures against ecclesiastical sanctions. This community was united, but locally, and *against* churchmen and their censures.[46]

Gruter talked about the 'laws of the group' in her Old Order Amish case. This Amish community in Ohio were likely, however, to have based their solidarity on their separation from and difference to the rest of society, though this is not a point Gruter makes. The relative smallness of Jewish communities was similarly important for the *herem*. The community represented 'an undifferentiated whole'—the whole rather than individuals cast members out.[47] By contrast, the medieval Christian *communio* from which excommunicates were 'sequestered' was too big, however much excommunication rituals were designed to emphasize its boundaries. Community is notoriously difficult to define; it cannot be controversial, nevertheless, to state that the entirety of Western Christendom, or even merely Christians in England, was too large to fit to any definition.[48] Practically speaking, much smaller pockets of the Christian community would be expected to shun excommunicates—the parish is the most relevant community—but that does not mean that what united even a cohesive community was Christian values. Christianity would not be what differentiated one parish from the next. Elisabeth Vodola noted that the earliest legal expressions of the contagion of excommunication appeared in the fourth century, when 'the custom of voluntary avoidance of sinners that usually obtained in the early church was breaking down'.[49] As the Christian community grew, tacit agreement and solidarity disintegrated, making it necessary to enforce shunning with penalties against communicators. Thirteenth-century Roman law commentators and canonists themselves recognized that communities were unlikely to reach an agreement on collective action.[50]

---

[45] Challet and Forrest, 'The masses', 283–7, quotation 285.   [46] Clarke, *Interdict*, 213–14.

[47] Woolf, 'Communal and religious organisation', 385; Kaplan, 'Discipline, dissent and communal authority', 404–5. Yosef Kaplan, discussing the role excommunication played in maintaining boundaries, notes that the Sephardic Jewish community in early modern Amsterdam strove to mark the boundaries of its separate identity: *Religion, Politics and Freedom of Conscience*, 14–15.

[48] E.g. Alan Macfarlane's 1977 discussion: 'History, anthropology and the study of communities', 631–5. Parker, *Miasma*, 278–9 and Murray, *Suicide*, ii, 481–2, provide interesting discussions of communities in comparable contexts. Susan Reynolds has argued that 'kingdoms were the highest form of secular community that there was', *Kingdoms and Communities*, 330.

[49] Vodola, 'Sovereignty and tabu Part 2', 582. Cf. Moore, *Formation of a Persecuting Society*, 11.

[50] Clarke, *Interdict*, 22, 25, citing Azo and Zoën Tencarius.

The pervasiveness of medieval Catholic Christianity was a blessing and a curse. The pope, as the ultimate ecclesiastical authority, unified Christians.[51] The potential advantage was that there was nowhere for excommunicates to run if their fellow parishioners did ostracize them. They were, in theory, expelled from the majority of western Europe and had little choice but to seek reconciliation. There were conceivably other options. Heretical sects were one possibility (remaining excommunicate for over a year itself led to suspicions of heresy).[52] Studies of excommunication elsewhere in Europe may reveal conversions to other religions. But in thirteenth-century England there were fewer possibilities, and I am unaware of any excommunicates converting to Judaism. By contrast, studies of both Jewish and Christian excommunication in the early modern period have argued that it could have been ineffective simply because religious toleration provided alternatives. Rather than forcing a sinner to make amends with their communities, excommunication drove excommunicates to a rival religion or denomination, whether that be Catholic, Quaker, Anglican, or Baptist.[53] Yosef Kaplan observed that choosing to live outside the Jewish community was not usually an attractive option, but that choice nevertheless weakened the potency of excommunication.[54]

Here the purpose of excommunication must once again be stressed. If an individual left the community, ostracism was effective in the sense of maintaining a community's purity, as in the Amish case. But the goal of religious sanctions, including medieval excommunication, was altering behaviour and inducing compliance. Excommunicates were not scapegoats expelled for the good of the rest.[55] For all the talk of pollution, the sanction was not, in fact, only about preserving group solidarity but also about saving individuals' souls. An excommunication that drove a sinner permanently from the church would be considered a failure.

Clergy and Laity: The Absence of Collective Decision Making

The difficulties surrounding collective action were compounded by the fact that excommunication was imposed from above.[56] The masses were tasked with enforcing the sanction, yet their consent was in no way sought or acquired. Instead, the decision to exclude a sinner was taken by ecclesiastical authorities,

---

[51] The Great Western Schism irreparably undermined this, see Flanagin, '*Extra ecclesiam*'.
[52] Lateran IV, c. 3 (X 5.7.13); Logan, 'Excommunication'; cf. Beaulande, *Malheur*, 234–40; Vodola, *Excommunication*, 32, 164–80, 190.
[53] Brown, 'Keys of the kingdom', 559–62; Chareyre, 'Maudit est celui qui fait l'œuvre du seigneur lâchement', 66; Bezzina, 'Consistory of Loudun', 265; Kaplan, 'Discipline, dissent, and communal authority', 403–5.
[54] Kaplan, *Religion, Politics and Freedom of Conscience*, 15–19.
[55] Cf. Parker, *Miasma*, 258, 269; Malkopoulou, 'Ostracism and democratic self-defense'.
[56] Cf. Reynolds, *Kingdoms and Communities*, 23, 154.

who did not necessarily have the same concerns or reach the same conclusions as those (including other members of the ecclesiastical hierarchy) expected to carry out their judgements. This is not simply a question of clergy versus laity; 'community' could cut in many directions, not necessarily 'along lay and clerical lines'.[57] Clergy were as likely to disobey excommunications pronounced by their fellow members of the ecclesiastical hierarchy as the laity. The point, however, is that not only was the community too big to be cohesive, but that sentences were not products of collective decision-making, or anything close to it. Jacob Katz, discussing the *herem*, observed that 'This type of sanction was typical of a weak governmental structure that had not the means to execute punishments on its own', noting that its 'powers of enforcement thus depended...upon the entire community's identifying with its purpose and decisions'.[58]

Though some members of the community might play a role in the process that led to an excommunication in thirteenth-century England—for instance the *fidedigni* recently discussed by Ian Forrest might aid investigations that resulted in excommunications—on the whole, the wider population was not involved.[59] People might, for any number of reasons, have sympathy with those sentenced, disagreeing that the excommunicate deserved to be excluded and voting with their feet. Whether excommunicates would be treated as such was decided on a case-by-case basis, by those who were supposed to eschew them. It has been observed that ordeals sometimes allowed communities to make collective decisions through interpretations of the results of these ordeals, providing a means by which matters could be settled.[60] Excommunication did not provide for such judgments, despite the effectiveness of the sanction being dependent on communal behaviour.

Although the nature and quantity of evidence does not permit a thorough discussion of individual offences and how they were viewed by communities, it is surely relevant that excommunication above all protected the church, its property, and members of the ecclesiastical hierarchy. Even if in individual cases locals sometimes influenced the judgments made by authorities, the general population had no say in what *sort* of offence merited excommunication.[61] Alexander Murray has shown interestingly that suicide *was* considered dangerous by communities, who desired rigorous enforcement of the law. In this instance there was a general desire to be protected from this behaviour collectively judged deviant—it was

---

[57] Clarke, *Interdict*, 225.
[58] Katz, *Tradition and Crisis*, 108; Cf. 80 on the *parnasim* being perceived as representatives of the community. Sartore explains that a similar view has been taken of outlawry: *Outlawry*, 8.
[59] E.g. *Reg. Gandavo*, i, 280–2. See Hill, 'General excommunications'. Cf. quite different inquisition processes discussed by John Sabapathy, who notes that audiences needed to accept decisions, and thus the processes by which decisions were reached needed to be approved too: 'Making public knowledge'.
[60] Moore, *Formation of a Persecuting Society*, 117–23. He provides references to the many works on the topic.
[61] Forrest, *Trustworthy Men*, 99–105 and more generally chs 6 and 7. Cf. Sartore on secular juries influencing outcomes: *Outlawry*, 89.

authorities (and families of suicides) who sometimes tried to mitigate the harsh consequences (deprivation of ecclesiastical burial), but never communities. The latter might even protest that a death had been judged natural when they believed it had been a suicide.[62] But excommunication was in general a self-interested punishment enacted by the church, only disguised as a communal medicine imposed by the community. The church failed to generate consensus that excommunicates needed to be removed to protect the rest or that they were inherently dangerous and needed to be avoided. Sentences failed when communities called the church's bluff.[63] Top-down persecution was not achieved here.[64] Instead, excommunications were matters for discussion.[65]

From the period of Gregorian reform onwards, the separation of lay and clerical society was increasingly emphasized; excommunication was often used to enforce this. *Si quis suadente* (1139), for example, protected clergy from assault; it explicitly placed them in an elevated position.[66] English *ipso facto* sentences almost all protected the rights and liberties of the church. If ostracism is effective in small communities keen to protect their values, it will not be if in practice the sanction tends to protect elite members of the group. Though individual excommunications might be 'unjust' (discussed below), they did not need to be in order for laity simply to shrug their shoulders about an offence committed. Excommunication, which relied on the support of the laity to be effective, was used to the advantage of churchmen and not necessarily everyone else.[67] It is interesting, in this context, to note contemporary Jewish decrees in Speyer, Worms, and Mainz, which prevented rabbis excommunicating without the knowledge and consent of the community.[68] Examples of petty quarrels involving excommunication throughout medieval Christendom discussed by others are too numerous to cite. There was considerable potential for conflict of interest.

There are certain categories of offence which, even without explicit indications in the sources, could clearly have provoked divided loyalties, leading the laity in particular to ignore the excommunications of their fellows or even retaliate against clergy.[69] It is understandable that public opinion might sometimes side with an offender when clerical interests were detrimental to parishioners. For instance, *Si quis suadente* allowed for the possibility that violence performed against a clergyman might be excusable. If someone injured a priest or monk in self-defence, if the injured man was not dressed properly so his status was not obvious, or if he had been caught in a compromising position with a female relative, the assaulter

---

[62] Murray, *Suicide*, 452–71. [63] I am grateful to John Sabapathy for his thoughts here.
[64] Moore, *Formation of a Persecuting Society*, 186–7 and *passim*.
[65] Cf. Melve, 'Even the very laymen', 37. [66] Helmholz, 'Si quis suadente', 425, 434.
[67] Cf. ancient ostracism of anyone who citizens considered a threat to the city: Antonopolou-Treckli, 'Continuité et ruptures', 339–44.
[68] 'Takkanah', *Jewish Encyclopedia*; Zimmer, *Harmony and Discord*, 28, 106–7, 217 n. 14; Finkelstein, *Jewish Self-Government*, 63–4, 222, 242–3.
[69] See Clarke, *Interdict*, 116–17, 191–2, 221.

did not incur the sentence.[70] Many who incurred this sentence, however, might have had support for their assault simply because the victim was unpopular or 'had it coming' for another reason not accepted by canon law. Failure to pay tithes could also have generated sympathy, especially in times of hardship (though law-abiding parishioners, who struggled to pay their tithes but did so nevertheless, may equally have resented their tax-evading neighbours).[71] Excommunications pronounced against infringers of ecclesiastical liberties often concerned theft from church lands. Pilfering of trees, for instance, was quite often the cause of excommunications. Yet while trees were a valuable commodity—not a petty theft—their removal, or the poaching of rabbits, might have been supported when the church appeared so rich compared to parishioners.[72] Poaching and claims to wood were always fiercely contested, resulting in alternative ideas about who held rights to lands.[73] Support for such thieves might have been expressed by a refusal to treat them as outcasts. Laypeople's loyalties might lie with their excommunicated compatriots, alongside whom they lived, rather than the abbots and bishops who protected their own interests.

Even more problematic for churchmen using excommunication were cases when the ecclesiastical sanction competed with other jurisdictions. Individual occasions when secular powers attempted to hinder the enforcement of excommunication are discussed elsewhere, but canon and common law did not always function seamlessly. Sanctuary is the obvious example here.[74] Secular law required communities to raise the hue and cry and pursue felons. But sanctuary gave fugitives an opportunity to abjure the realm.[75] Felons were in danger of state-sanctioned violence unless they sought sanctuary on ecclesiastical ground, where they could not be touched: those who attacked sanctuary-seekers were excommunicated as committers of sacrilege. Moreover, the violence perpetrated against fugitives often involved the shedding of blood on holy ground, polluting the sacred space. Harming those who had sought sanctuary was explicitly forbidden both in canon law and in English synodal legislation (*Quicumque abstrahunt violenter*).[76]

The two jurisdictions were thus at odds—the logical conclusion of secular law was ill-treatment of fugitives, wherever they were. Laypeople were *expected* to take the law into their own hands, even if they were not, by the thirteenth century, to kill fugitives. Local sympathy could, not unreasonably, have lain with those who

---

[70] E.g. *Reg. Sutton*, iii, 126–7, where the assailant claimed the clerk he injured was brawling and wearing striped clothing, obscuring his clerical status. The sentence was quashed. Cf. ibid. 13–14.

[71] Oliver Sutton's register, for example, contains many cases where tithes were resisted. Cf. Gallant, 'Peasant ideology', 501, who discusses clergy pronouncing sentences for crimes that most nineteenth-century Ionian villagers (then subject to British rule) would not have considered illegal or wrong.

[72] *Reg. Pontissara*, ii, 541.   [73] Thompson, *Whigs and Hunters*, esp. 260–1.

[74] Cf. Forrest, *Trustworthy Men*, 129–30, 315–16.

[75] Swanson, *Church and Society*, 153–7, gives an overview of sanctuary.

[76] C.17, q.4, c.20; C.17, q.4, c.35; By the legate Ottobuono in 1268: *C&S*, 764.

attacked or starved a murderer, even if the attackers were excommunicated. Gervase Rosser discusses the fact that the operation of sanctuary, like excommunication, was dependent upon the local community. Its power depended on collective action, which might result in the fugitive being reconciled following compurgation, escaping (if the community had sympathy with the fugitive), being guarded until they left the realm, or mob justice.[77] The last option was when conflict with ecclesiastical law arose. A community that had been persuaded to treat a fugitive as secular authorities demanded was less likely to punish by ostracism someone who had harmed such a fugitive. The frequently gory nature of these assaults might have meant that men found guilty and excommunicated were deemed to have gone too far and were indeed avoided. As Rosser notes, local societies would have been divided on these issues.[78] Yet these men (they were usually men) were attacking felons, albeit violating sacred ground as they did so. As Henry Summerson points out, emotions were likely to have been high amongst those guarding felons (to prevent them absconding rather than abjuring the realm as they ought).[79] Excommunication sought to create an 'us' and a 'them', but local group solidarity might lie with perpetrators rather than victims in sanctuary-violation cases.

Churchmen were compelled to punish such malefactors quite often, as episcopal registers show. Some of these committed outright assault or even homicide. In other cases, the fugitives were simply starved out of their havens.[80] Often these offences resulted in general sentences, so locals would have been involved in aiding churchmen discover who amongst them had committed these crimes. In a particularly gruesome example, the hands of certain felons, clinging onto St Paul's as their assailants tried to drag them out of the protected area, were cut off. Later so were their heads.[81] The prevalence of this offence is indicated by a letter sent by the bishop of Salisbury in July 1300, which responded to two separate (presumably related) incidents. Although 'those who flee to the bosom of the church ought to remain secure and defended under the firm protection of ecclesiastical liberty', fugitives at Sparsholt church had had the necessities of life removed, and were being detained in fetters and denied opportunity to confess. A couple of miles up the road, Alan at Wood had been dragged from sanctuary in Fawler chapel. The perpetrators, initially unknown, had automatically incurred *Quicumque abstrahunt violenter* through their acts and an investigation was launched into their names. A month later, the perpetrators had been discovered, confessed to their offences, and been given penance as a condition of their absolution.[82]

---

[77] Rosser, 'Sanctuary and social negotiation', esp. 61–70.
[78] Rosser, 'Sanctuary and social negotiation', 66–7.
[79] Summerson, 'Structure of law enforcement', 322–3.
[80] Jordan, 'A fresh look at medieval sanctuary', 24–5. *Reg. Pontissara*, i, 252–3; *Reg. Sutton*, iii, 172–4.
[81] *Reg. G. Giffard*, 169–70.
[82] *Reg. Gandavo*, i, 24–8. Though the incidents were probably related, the perpetrators were not the same. See Hill, 'General excommunications'.

Disobeying excommunications was not, however, only the preserve of the laity. As will be evident in the remainder of this chapter, clergy often sided against one another, flouting ecclesiastical sanctions in the process. Clerics were frequently excommunicated themselves. Local clergy may have felt greater loyalty towards the parishioners they lived with than with their bishop, archbishop, or the pope.[83] It should be remembered that excommunication was also not the right of all clergymen; parish priests could not wield the 'sword' of excommunication (though may have illicitly done so). And, of course, laity could benefit from ecclesiastical censures. The bishops of Lincoln, for example, protected their tenants from unjust exactions and infringements of their rights.[84] In political disputes, prelates frequently took sides and bolstered a cause with their sanctions. Thus while in some circumstances excommunication separated the interests of clergy and laity, in others—particularly disputes rather than excommunications of individuals—clergy and laity could together resist the expectations attached to ecclesiastical sanctions imposed by other churchmen.

There was, therefore, insufficient unity of purpose and opinion to ensure voluntary ostracism, even if some people shunned excommunicates some of the time. The masses had little control over whether an individual was sentenced with excommunication, and none over when he or she would be absolved. The way excommunication was used—often and for a broad range of offences that more often than not protected 'the church'—exacerbated these problems. This last issue might provoke charges of overuse and of clergy being self-serving. However, such an accusation would be unfair, failing to recognize the limited options available to clergy.[85] Certain acts might have provoked widespread condemnation, but the church's jurisdiction was limited. It did not in general deal with serious offences such as murder, and was instead restricted to infractions of canon law and ecclesiastical rights.[86] While churchmen were often using excommunication in their own self-interest, it is difficult to argue that this an unreasonable response, for they sought to right wrongs that no one else would correct. It was inevitable that many or most of these were in the church's own interest. Excommunication was the obvious tool. Alternatives were limited. Moreover, clergy had a duty to correct sin. The proliferation of *latae sententiae* meant that offenders were already excommunicated, making it a good pastor's duty to publicize the fact and urge contrition. Both the use of excommunication for so many offences and the persistent declaration of new *ipso facto* sentences may seem ill advised, but by this time it was too late to rethink the entire remit of excommunication. The

---

[83] Forrest, *Trustworthy Men*, 341. They might also be more trusted by the locals: Gallant, 'Peasant ideologies', 487–8.
[84] *Reg. Sutton*, iv, 53. This was a general sentence pronounced occasionally.
[85] Rosalind Hill argued for overuse, but against any condemnation of bishops' motives; they were too thorough: 'Theory and practice', 10–11.
[86] See Swanson, *Church and Society*, 148.

inability of excommunication to provoke voluntary shunning of all excommunicates was to a large degree the result of the way society was structured and the way the sanction had developed. To imagine thirteenth-century England without these obstacles is impossible. It would necessitate an inconceivable number of changes in how and why excommunication was used, and in the nature of governance and jurisdiction. Excommunications deemed unjust in particular circumstances, to which we shall return, aggravated these problems, but they would have existed regardless.

Punishment of Communicators

Ensuring voluntary shunning of excommunicates was an impossibly tall order, but churchmen did not rely upon it. Indeed, explicit evidence of illicit communication with excommunicates comes chiefly from attempts to deal with the problem by imposing sanctions on communicators. The contagion of excommunication began in the fourth century, when voluntary exclusion was becoming less likely as the church expanded.[87] Individuals and communities that refused to treat excommunicates as they ought could expect to suffer excommunication or interdict, respectively.[88] Minor excommunication was an automatic consequence, immediately excluding such rebels from the sacraments without official intervention. This penalty could be increased to major excommunication by authorities if it seemed necessary.[89] Since collective excommunication was banned, at least from 1245 (only individuals have souls), interdict, which suspended all the sacraments and Christian worship except baptism, was used when a larger number needed to be coerced or punished.[90] Nevertheless, it is likely that resources were only directed towards punishing communicators in particularly egregious or enduring cases.

Those who associated with excommunicates were blameworthy because they were failing to correct sin. As Susan Kramer has argued, the rhetoric attached to infection in the Middle Ages did not exempt communities from fault. The infected were corrupted by their own weakness.[91] In the case of Ralph de Honilane, Archbishop Winchelsey left little doubt that, whilst he wanted to protect the souls of those under his care, they had been wilfully ignoring the church's orders and the principles of Christian society. The danger this posed was clear. Ralph himself had little incentive to make peace with the church if his fellow citizens were happily associating with him. All those who did so were endangering their own souls and Ralph's. However, the very fabric of society and the church, it is implied, were at stake. Their refusal to shun Ralph, along with the latter's own

---

[87] Vodola, 'Sovereignty and tabu Part 2', 582.
[88] Cf. the (harsher) punishments against those harbouring outlaws, Stewart, 'Outlawry', 39, 45.
[89] VI 3.5.11; cf. X 5.39.29, X 5.39.30; Chobham, *Summa*, 249.   [90] Clarke, *Interdict*, 25–7, 127.
[91] Kramer, 'Understanding contagion', esp. 153–7.

contumacy, were offensive (literally 'obstacles', 'offendicula') to God and to all humankind. Three years earlier, in 1297, Winchelsey had threatened those who communicated with John de Moresdenne, facilitating his lengthy excommunication, with major excommunication, 'lest the diseased sheep infects the Lord's flock or the accustomed rebellion of excommunicates, who do not fear irreverently to throw themselves in with the communion of the faithful, increases the number of the damned'.[92] The potential for contagion was no small matter.

Individuals thus merited punishment for their consent to sin. Interdicts were more complicated, however. Clarke demonstrates clearly that a great deal of time was spent justifying their use, which seemed to punish the innocent for others' sins.[93] Yet Clarke observes that the most frequently cited cause of interdicts was consent to the wrongs of others.[94] When interdict was used as an aggravation of excommunication, as it so often was, there is a clear case to be made that the communities were not innocent at all.[95] Communicating with an excommunicate was an active choice; such malefactors had 'scorned the vigour of ecclesiastical discipline' by keeping contact with the excommunicate. If they had acted properly, the excommunicate would have been forced to make amends with the church. There might have been individuals within communities who shunned excommunicates as the church required and were therefore innocent, but canonists 'thought in terms of collective responsibility rather than collective guilt'. Tacit consent within a community was all that was needed for this lesser punishment to be incurred. Explicit, active consent and help would earn those individuals major excommunication.[96]

Interdict as an aggravation of excommunication made sense, related as it was to minor excommunication. The two censures in fact almost amounted to the same thing: minor excommunicates were unable to participate in ecclesiastical services; interdicts suspended all such services.[97] The terminology was blurred here: both minor excommunication and interdict were referred to as 'suspension'.[98] An individual could be suspended from church and divine services; divine services in a city or district could be suspended. Early in the dispute between the priory and townsmen of Dunstable (who would rather go to hell than submit to ecclesiastical discipline in a tax dispute in 1228–9), the excommunicated ringleaders had the support of their neighbours. The people continued to communicate with

---

[92] *Reg. Winchelsey*, i, 192–3. [93] Clarke, 'Innocent III'; Clarke, *Interdict*, ch. 1.
[94] Clarke, *Interdict*, 116.
[95] Whole communities could be judged to be at fault: so many people from Beverley had participated in an attack on the church that 'the whole community of the town' was reckoned to have been present. The archbishop of York consequently placed a general interdict on the entire town. *Reg. W. Giffard*, 151.
[96] Clarke, *Interdict*, 37–8, 46, 63.
[97] Clarke, *Interdict*, 59–85, describes the different types of interdict, and how they related to excommunication.
[98] On blurred distinctions see also Clarke, *Interdict*, 76; Keygnaert, 'Prohibition of church services'; Keygnaert, 'Meaning of ecclesiastical exclusion', 774–7.

them, while the excommunicates themselves were entering churches with the people. This resulted in a *de facto* interdict, where the convent and parish priest stopped celebrating mass for over two months.[99] Similarly, in 1274 there was concern that excommunicates were hearing mass in Bodmin when they went to the shire court held there (indicating no avoidance from the laity present), so the bishop ordered services to be celebrated only in hushed tones.[100] A large number of excommunicates, major or minor, might necessitate suspension or private celebration of services, even without the imposition of an official interdict.[101]

The immediate threat, requiring action from the authorities, was that an excommunicate might be able to persist in his or her contumacy. Sanctions sought to coerce ostracism. But the rejection of ecclesiastical authority inherent in refusal to shun merited punishment even after this danger had passed.[102] Thus Pope Innocent III, on the same day (during the English Interdict) that he permitted Stephen Langton to absolve Fulk de Cantilupe and Reginald of Cornhill, ordered an investigation into the 'certain people, both clergy and laity, greater and lesser men', who had been 'everywhere and knowingly' communicating with the two men. Even if the original excommunicates had come to their senses, the disobedience of others had to be reprimanded, for it threatened to 'dissolve the nerve of ecclesiastical discipline'.[103] Clergy were particularly culpable in such situations. For years after King John had been absolved, clerics who had remained in England suffered repercussions for failing to enforce his sentence. Many clergy were sent to Rome to seek absolution, though 'less guilty' clerks could be absolved by the legate.[104]

The barons, who Roger of Wendover observed spent Christmas with John at Windsor in 1210, 'communicating with him, notwithstanding the sentence by which the king was bound', later faced wrath from Innocent III for their hypocrisy: these men, Innocent III fumed, had assisted the king when he was 'offending God and the church'. Yet now the king was a papal vassal they rebelled against him. Unlike the clergy who had associated with John, Innocent would probably not have admonished the barons for their earlier association with an excommunicate if they had not subsequently provoked the pope.[105] They were so condemnable because after John had made peace with the church and taken the Cross they had dared to instigate a rebellion against him, thereby impeding the business of the crusade. Innocent defended the king by annulling conspiracies and plots against him; the barons were told to make peace or they would be excommunicated within

---

[99] *Ann. Dunstable*, 110. See above Chapter 2, 59, 91–2.   [100] *Reg. Bronescombe*, no. 979.
[101] Celebration behind closed doors was frequently permitted during interdicts.
[102] Clarke, 'Innocent III', 95.
[103] *Letters of Innocent III*, nos 825 and 826; *Patrologiae Latinae*, ed. Migne, 215, 1530. For their excommunication, incurred for detaining church lands, see *Letters of Innocent III*, no. 764.
[104] *Coggeshall*, 167; *Letters of Innocent III*, nos 903 and 930.
[105] Clarke observes that penalties for violation of interdicts were aimed mainly at clergy: *Interdict*, 195.

eight days.[106] This excommunication indeed took place, for the barons were entirely unwilling to back down.

While an excommunicate remained at large, putting pressure on their neighbourhood was a logical tactic, though it is important to note that additional measures were neither immediate nor automatic. Presumably limited resources necessitated that only long-term or egregious cases were subject to further action. When such steps were taken, those who had harboured no ill feelings towards an excommunicate might begin to resent the latter once their own life was affected. The desire to persuade the excommunicate to reconcile with the church would be greatly increased if their sentence meant nobody could go to church. Such tactics might tip the balance towards avoidance in the community. In 1269, the archbishop of York, Walter Giffard, ordered the arrest of John de Stonegrave by the secular arm. In the meantime, he placed an ambulatory interdict on the excommunicate (which suspended services wherever John went), excommunicated all communicators along with him, and launched an investigation into the names of those who presumed to communicate with him. John had hitherto been persisting in his contumacy, 'hurling himself into the communion of the faithful, while he labours with an illness so contagious, he does not cease to stain the Lord's flock'. He had also been hearing divine services, thereby 'damnably profaning' various places. Six days after the archbishop took these measures, however, John 'humbly' sought absolution. It is possible that the threat of arrest prompted John's change of heart (the arrest itself was unlikely to have happened so quickly). Yet this was Walter's second request, indicating that the secular authorities were being uncooperative and that John had not been cowed by the earlier threat of imprisonment. John's decision might therefore have been the result of the archbishop's increased pressure on those around John. Anywhere John went was deprived of ecclesiastical services; anyone who had previously been associating with him was now liable to the same penalty. The loyalty of communicators was undoubtedly tested by these measures.[107]

Censures introduced in response to illicit communication with excommunicates could nevertheless backfire. A distinction should be drawn here: if people were communicating because they were simply indifferent, further sanctions were more likely to alter behaviour; by contrast, where individuals were communicating because they thought the excommunicate was being treated unfairly, they might only aggravate the situation. As Clarke has shown, the idea of interdicts was to harness communal pressure and bring it to bear against the original excommunicate (King John's excommunication, which took place only after the interdict had been laid over England, was thus unusual). But both interdict and

---

[106] *CM*, ii, 528; *Letters of Innocent III*, no. 1013 (appendix).

[107] *Reg. W. Giffard*, 142–3, 161–2. John's excommunication related to a dispute over a benefice. See ibid. 44, 46 and 206 for this case.

excommunication were ineffective when communities sided with 'wrongdoers' against the church.[108]

Disobedient Clergy

Supporting malefactors against 'the church' was not the preserve of laity. When Louis (later VIII), son of the king of France, invaded England to take the throne in 1216 he was excommunicated. The first extant episcopal register, that of Hugh of Wells, bishop of Lincoln, indicates that numerous laypeople had been 'bound by the general sentence because [they] stood with the barons against the king'.[109] But these sentences were not taken any more seriously by clergy. The Melrose chronicler noted that the interdict and excommunications were not observed in England, and not even announced in Scotland, where the king had been sentenced for supporting Louis.[110] Roger of Wendover claims that various clergy in London refused to publish the sentences against the barons and knowingly participated in divine services with them. These assisters, particularly the dean of St Martin's-le-Grand, Geoffrey of Buckland, were to be named alongside the barons in the sentence of excommunication.[111] The Anonymous of Béthune, even more remarkably, contains the accusation that four of Louis's clerks preached in London that 'the king's people were excommunicated, that Louis and his men were good and the pope was wrong to excommunicate them'. For this behaviour, they were reportedly excluded from the absolution granted to Louis and the rest of his men.[112] In 1216 the monks of Worcester Cathedral Priory were excommunicated (possibly with only a minor sentence) for celebrating divine services with Louis.[113] Honorius III censured the canons of Carlisle, who had presumed 'publicly to communicate with the capital enemies of the king' and to celebrate divine offices in interdicted places.[114] Louis's own clerks, having celebrated divine offices with the excommunicated Louis and his accomplices, were condemned by the pope for their presumption and contempt for the Apostolic See.[115] Many more clergy were suspended and deprived of benefices.[116] As with King John's

---

[108] Clarke, *Interdict*, 168–87, 192; Clarke, 'Innocent III', 80–2; Beaulande, *Malheur*, 230–3; Beaulande, 'Contester l'excommunication', 258–60; Beaulande, 'Force de la censure', 267–9.
[109] *Rotuli Hugonis de Welles*, ed. Phillimore and Davis, i, 37. Numerous similar examples are recorded throughout the register.
[110] *Melrose*, 124–5. [111] *CM*, ii, 648–9.
[112] *History of the Dukes of Normandy*, trans. Shirley, 183, 188: Simon Langton, Gervase de Howbridge, Robert of St Germain, Master Helyes, a clerk of the archbishop of Canterbury.
[113] *Ann. Worcester*, 406–7.
[114] *Foedera*, I.i.147. The pope's letter was a response to the regents' complaint: *PR 1216–25*, 111.
[115] *Royal Letters*, app. v, no. 1.
[116] *Letters and Charters of Guala*, ed. Vincent, xli–xliii, lxi–lxvi and notes.

communicators, scorners of these sentences were dealt with later, even after Louis had left the kingdom, absolved, in 1217.[117]

Archbishop Stephen Langton notoriously failed to stand fully with the king in 1215. He refused, crucially, to excommunicate the barons by name.[118] Before the interdict had been lifted, he threatened John with excommunication if he dared to wage war against his nobles (at the time a successful threat).[119] Langton certainly had sympathy with the barons' cause. He was accused, with some justification, of supporting the rebels.[120] He claimed that excommunications might hinder rather than help his efforts to make peace, and he sought personal communication with the pope before pronouncing any sentence against the rebels. Not unreasonably, he argued that the pope was misinformed.[121] Nevertheless, his pleas were ignored, and he was suspended from office.

It is evident, as Clarke has argued, that interdicts tried not only loyalties, but also 'the authority of ecclesiastical superiors over clergy'.[122] The same can be said of excommunications.[123] A considerable challenge for clergy using ecclesiastical sanctions was the fact that the institutional church was not a unified body any more than was the rest of society. Clerics were frequently on opposing sides of disputes, whether as protagonists or as supporters on different sides in a clash between laymen, as in the baronial war above. For example, when the cathedral chapter of Christ Church Canterbury were excommunicated in the late 1230s, both the laity and the clergy of the city appear to have supported the monks rather than the archbishop who had excommunicated them, flouting both excommunications and interdicts.[124] Archbishop Winchelsey expressed his anger in 1298 that the 'mayor and community' of Dover had persevered under interdict for over a year and a half. The clergy were complicit here too, for the community had procured divine services to be celebrated (or 'rather profaned') in interdicted places.[125] Such cases show that local clerics could display greater allegiance to the people amongst whom they lived than to their archbishop.

To return to the larger stage of the major political struggles in thirteenth-century England, certain clergy sided with rebels during the period of reform and rebellion 1258–1267. The 'Montfortian' bishops were vehemently chastised for continuing to associate with Simon de Montfort and failing to publish his sentence when he was excommunicated by the pope.[126] In 1265 Clement IV

---

[117] *Coggeshall*, 174, 186; *Melrose*, 129–30. *CM*, ii, 629–30, 633–4; *Oxenedes*, 134; *Foedera*, I.i.129; *SLI*, nos 75, 82, 84; *Letters of Innocent III*, no. 1026.
[118] *Coggeshall*, 174.   [119] *CM*, ii, 551–2.
[120] See Vincent, 'A New Letter of the Twenty-Five Barons'; Vincent, 'King John's diary and itinerary', 25–31 January 1215, 24–30 May 1215, and 31 May–6 June 1215.
[121] Cheney, *Pope Innocent III*, 379–81, 389–90.   [122] Clarke, *Interdict*, 191.
[123] See also Beaulande, *Malheur*, 221–30.
[124] E.g. *Gervase*, 176, but see below, 206–12, where this case is discussed in depth.
[125] *Reg. Winchelsey*, ii, 885–90, here 886; Graham, 'An interdict on Dover'.
[126] For these bishops see Ambler, *Bishops in the Political Community*, esp. ch. 5.

wrote to the legate Ottobuono, suspending the bishops of London, Worcester, and Winchester.[127] His condemnation of the rebellion and its episcopal supporters was categorical, his letter full of vitriol. Before the Battle of Evesham, when they had spoken to Clement (then Gui Fouquois acting as legate) at Boulogne, the bishops were accused of having masked the 'bitterness of bile with sweetened speeches'. Not only presumptuous but notorious transgressors, they had subsequently presumed to profane divine services, and had not shunned excommunicates or observed interdicts. They had refused to appear before the pope, persevering in their iniquity, their hearts hard as stone like a blacksmith's anvil. As for Montfort himself, he had denied the legate entry, 'exercising his tyranny... with others whom he infected under semblance of simulated piety'. Clement proclaimed himself amazed at the infamy of Montfort and his supporters, especially the prelates.[128] The source of Clement's anger is clear: the bishops had disobeyed his direct instructions, and his authority was at stake.[129] They had treated him badly when he was legate (he was never able to enter the kingdom), and they continued to do so after he had become pope. Calling them before him in 1266, Clement charged that the bishops 'knowing that the earl and his supporters were bound by sentence of excommunication by authority of the highest pontiff... communicating with the said excommunicates, were bound by a similar sentence, according to the words of the canons'. Despite thus knowing themselves to be excommunicates, they incurred irregularity by not abstaining from divine services.[130] In 1267, Clement wrote to the bishop of Lincoln, Richard Gravesend, asking why he was familiar with those he knew to be cut off from the church: 'How can you touch tar without us seeing that you have been blackened by it?'[131]

The bishops' failure to publish the excommunication of Montfort and his accomplices was, they claimed, the result of force and threats. The bishops were indeed captured at Dover when they returned from their audience with the legate at Boulogne.[132] They were apparently threatened with death if they dared to publish anything from the legate's letters of excommunication, which were torn up and thrown into the sea. The royalist chronicler Thomas Wykes, however, suggested that they may have been captured on purpose by the rebels they in fact supported.[133] According to Wykes, Clement IV was later unmoved by their excuses, citing Matthew 10:28: 'Do not fear those who kill the body, but cannot

---

[127] Richard Gravesend, bishop of Lincoln, had already been suspended by Pope Urban IV in 1264: *Reg. Urban IV*, ii, no. 647.
[128] Martène, *Thesaurus*, no. 190. [129] Cf. Beaulande, 'Force de la censure', 269.
[130] Wykes, 185–7.
[131] Martène, *Thesaurus*, no. 463. 'Quomodo picem tangere valeas & ab ea non infici non videmus?'
[132] For precedent under Henry II, see Duggan, 'Henry II, the English Church, and the papacy', 175.
[133] *Wykes*, 155. For the bishops' failure to publish these sentences see *Wykes*, 155–7, 185–7; *De Antiquis Legibus Liber*, ed. Stapleton, 83–4; *Ann. Londonienses*, 64–5; *Flores Historiarum*, ii, 500–2; *Gervase*, 238–42; *Ann. Dunstable*, 233; Rishanger, *Chronica*, 47; *Chronicon Petroburgense*, ed. Stapleton, 19; *Foedera*, I.i.461; *Reg. Clement IV*, no. 237; Martène, *Thesaurus*, no. 190; *Registres de Grégoire X*, ed. Guiraud, no. 25.

kill the soul'.¹³⁴ Their continued communication with the rebels was justified by no such threats, the bishops' excuses evidently judged specious. Their actions throughout this period do indeed indicate that they were acting of their own free will.

Nevertheless, clergy acknowledged that not all failures to enforce ecclesiastical censures were malicious or even voluntary. Anyone might be compelled by force or other pressures to disregard ecclesiastical sanctions.¹³⁵ Those in positions of power, the obvious example here being King John, had the clout to forbid compliance with their excommunications.¹³⁶ Henry III, unlike the Montfortian bishops, was excused from blame for illicit associations with the excommunicated reformers. As legate, Gui Fouquois excommunicated with a major sentence anyone who dared to help the barons, but excepted the king and the clergy attending to his chapel. Gui did not believe that these men, though they communicated with the barons, supported them intentionally.¹³⁷ In this instance—Henry was after all essentially a hostage—the communicators were not at fault.

Unjust Excommunications

Frequent use of excommunication for relatively minor offences could no doubt generate apathy towards the sanction and its enforcement. However, the refusal of both clergy and laity to enforce sentences was in some circumstances more considered and deliberate. Just as individuals sometimes believed judgements against them were unfair, so too could their compatriots deem these excommunications unjust. Those who supported the barons in either of the wars discussed above were surely not being wilfully negligent. Instead, their behaviour reflected their assessment of the matter at hand.

Explicit assertions of a belief that a sentence was unreasonable tend to concern clerical disputes. This is partly because our sources were overwhelmingly written by churchmen of some sort, and partly because churchmen did not have (licit) recourse to more physical means of coercion, so often resorted to excommunication. Chronicles are often particularly informative here, remarking as they did upon recent events, though their comments inevitably concern major disputes rather than parochial dynamics. Episcopal and royal documents additionally suggest thoughtful rejection of excommunications. Through the enforcement, or

---

¹³⁴ *Wykes*, 186.
¹³⁵ Those excommunicated for interacting with the Scots in 1318 claimed they had been forced to do so: Hill, 'Belief and practice'.
¹³⁶ Clarke, *Interdict*, 191. Those communicating with the earl of Surrey, John de Warenne (sentenced for adultery), in 1311 might have felt compelled, or been actively forced, to communicate with so powerful a man, for instance. *Reg. Gandavo*, i, 414–17. See also Pavlac, 'Curse of Cusanus', 213.
¹³⁷ Heidemann, nos 20q; 50d, 52: 'mente tamen ipsis non credimus adhaerere'.

not, of excommunications, it is therefore possible to perceive public opinion at work. Few sources contain the words of laypeople in this period. But if actions speak louder than words, failures to shun certain excommunicates inform us when people did not consider the church's sanctions worth enforcing. This might be because ostracism required too much effort or seemed excessive, as discussed above, or the excommunication might be considered unfair.

Unjust sentences were inevitable, and the medieval church admitted that God would not uphold these. However, there was no appeal process; unjust sentences were to be treated with the same reverence as any other excommunication. As R.H. Helmholz observed, the object here was to avoid undermining the judgements of churchmen: 'the validity of a sentence of excommunication could not be left to the unstable and self-interested interpretation of the person involved'. Obedience was paramount.[138] But since excommunication relied on collective action, the lack of an opportunity to appeal increased the likelihood that communities would make their own judgements and act accordingly. It is again worth comparing the thirteenth-century Jewish ordinances that, requiring communal consent, sought to prevent rabbis from misusing the *herem*.[139] Such rules would have been impossible in the disparate Christian community of the thirteenth century. But the same misuses that prompted these Jewish ordinances are evident elsewhere.

Resistance to censures and restrictions is natural and unavoidable. It is important that criticisms made before and during the Reformation are not taken as evidence that sanctions were newly abused in the later Middle Ages. While excommunication for debt was a newer phenomenon (probably as debt itself became more common) and generated criticism and indignation, it was far from the only petty use of excommunication. As Véronique Beaulande has pointed out, use of the sanction was rejected in other circumstances; there is no need to focus on resistance to excommunication for debt.[140] The thirteenth-century papacy's use of censures, and the criticism this provoked, does permit an argument for a degree of novelty at the highest level in the thirteenth century, however. Clarke has shown that the papacy's use of interdict 'to bolster its own temporal power' generated resistance.[141] Likewise, the excommunication pronounced against Emperor Frederick II was famously rejected by many, who

---

[138] Helmholz, 'Excommunication as a legal sanction', 209-10; Helmholz, *Spirit of Classical Canon Law*, 368-9, 378-9; Logan, *Excommunication and the Secular Arm*, 116-18. See also Beaulande, *Malheur*, 221-6; Murray, 'Excommunication', 187-8.

[139] 'Taḳḳanah', *Jewish Encyclopedia*; Zimmer, *Harmony and Discord*, 28, 106-7, 217 n. 14; Finkelstein, *Jewish Self-Government*, 63-4, 222, 242-3. A similar order was passed in Ferrara in 1554, which Robert Bonfil has argued weakened the ban's power as a means of imposing personal authority: *Rabbis and Jewish Communities*, 67-75.

[140] Beaulande, 'Contester l'excommunication', 258. On excommunication for debt see Lange, *Excommunication for Debt*; Brunner, 'Disorder, debts and excommunication'.

[141] Clarke, *Interdict*, 117.

considered the pope's campaign against him to be ungrounded and unjust. Matthew Paris noted such cynicism several times in his chronicle—the pope's 'avarice' caused many not to support him; rectors in Berkshire stated that Frederick had not been proved a heretic, though he was excommunicated, and thus refused to provide funds to the papal legate for use against the emperor; a French priest publicly excommunicated Frederick as he had been told, but added that he did not know why he had been excommunicated or which party was at fault.[142] Haakon, king of Norway, rejected Innocent IV's call to crusade on the grounds that he wanted to fight the church's enemies, not the pope's.[143] But the papacy was not the only authority using sanctions, and there is little reason to suppose there was increased abuse at the provincial level.

Susan Taylor Snyder and Melissa Vise have recently (independently) discussed a fascinating case in Bologna at the close of the thirteenth century in which an ecclesiastical sentence was roundly criticized by the community. The locals rejected the judgement of the inquisitor that their compatriots (particularly one Bonpietro, who was burnt), whom they considered to be good people, were heretics. As a result they rioted, claiming that the *true* heretics were the Dominican inquisitors, who were acting out of greed, ambition, or other inappropriate intentions. As Snyder argues, there was room for communal judgements in such cases, ones that did not align with ecclesiastical authorities' decisions.[144] Similar questioning can be found in excommunication cases in thirteenth-century England.

Llewelyn the Great asserted that he preferred to follow his conscience than do anything against God, even if that meant he was excommunicated by man.[145] He was, in fact, responding to an order forbidding him to receive the excommunicated Falkes de Bréauté. Llywelyn stated that he did not believe Falkes to be truly excommunicated, evidently considering the rebel's actions to have been reasonable in the circumstances.[146] Falkes himself felt that he was the victim of Archbishop Langton's vendetta; the sense that clergy used excommunication for their own ends was a problem for communal enforcement just as it was for individual fear.

Alice Clement, fighting to recover her inheritance (ultimately unsuccessfully), undoubtedly considered her excommunication to be unjust.[147] She was sentenced for apostasy, but claimed that she had been placed in the care of the nuns of Ankerwic by her brother when she was just five. As a child, she had asked to

---

[142] *CM*, iii, 608, iv, 39, 406–7.   [143] Whalen, *Two Powers*, 206.
[144] Synder, 'Orthodox fears'; Vise, 'The women and the inquisitor'.   [145] See 94–5.
[146] *Royal Letters*, 229–30; cf. an eleventh-century expression of a similar point in Huysmans, 'Excommunication under discussion', 46, 56; and a fifteenth-century example in Pavlac, 'Curse of Cusanus', 206–7.
[147] Elisabeth Vodola used Alice's case to show vigorous enforcement of the 'exception of excommunication'. For full references to the case see above Chapter 3, 113.

become a nun, 'as she was taught', but left the habit when she reached the years of discretion.¹⁴⁸ During the course of her long case—Alice was first excommunicated in the 1180s but the case was only resolved in the 1220s—she had support. In particular, she had a 'receiver, support and helper' in her 'error' in a certain W. de Bidun, who was told to stop this communication and support.¹⁴⁹ How Alice knew this W. is uncertain, but the individual was perhaps persuaded by Alice's own assertion that she was not excommunicated.

In the 1270s, the monks of St Swithun's, Winchester, expressed a similar sentiment to Llewelyn's. They continued to support their deposed and excommunicated prior, Andrew of London, asserting 'we are all compelled, as our consciences demand of us, to adhere to him'. They refused to accept the new prior or that the sentence imposed on the deposed prior was valid, and accordingly deemed that imposed upon his communicators also to be unmerited.¹⁵⁰ In this case there were, evidently, different opinions about who ought to be prior, which impeded proper enforcement of the bishop of Winchester's sentence.

Local Rivalries

The monks' support for their excommunicated prior instead of the rival candidate is indicative of a common problem. Disputes over ecclesiastical positions and benefices were commonplace, frequently involving violence and usually excommunication (Chapter 6 discusses one such dispute in detail). In these matters, where two rival candidates vied for a position, locals often took matters into their own hands. Locals were deeply involved in their churches and clearly had strong views about who ought to hold positions.¹⁵¹ Violent occupation of churches appears with some regularity in episcopal registers in the late thirteenth and early fourteenth centuries. The perpetrators of these illicit possessions were of course excommunicated, but it was inevitable that there would be gossip about rival candidates. Any excommunications pronounced would be bound up with this, so that whether a sentence was thought fair and whether it should be enforced were up for discussion.

In 1304 the bishop of Salisbury deposed the archdeacon of Wiltshire. Fifteen laymen subsequently occupied the church and manse of Minety, which were attached to the archdeaconry, on behalf of the deposed Thomas of Savoy. Excommunicated for consuming and removing church property, and for 'wickedly excluding Master William de Chadeleshunt, their true lord' by force, six

---

¹⁴⁸ *CRR*, v, 79–80.   ¹⁴⁹ *CRR*, v, 185–6.
¹⁵⁰ *Reg. Pontissara*, ii, 645–6. See also 643. Page 400 n. 1, gives a full account of this dispute.
¹⁵¹ For the investment laity had in the local churches and their staffing, see Hoskin, 'By force and arms'.

weeks later they remained in Minety church. The church itself had been placed under interdict, 'since it is not right to celebrate divine offices in the presence of excommunicates, lest the same excommunicates infect healthy sheep with their contagion'.[152] Yet evidently people were providing them with provisions while they squatted. The bishop thus ordered an investigation into the names of communicators. It seems clear that there was support for these men, and presumably for the former archdeacon for whom they acted, so that the excommunication was disregarded.[153]

There was pre-emptive concern in 1301 that locals would support Robert de Lacy as prebendary of Leighton Manor rather than the man appointed to the position by Pope Boniface VIII. Robert had been excommunicated (a sentence he appealed) for his 'intrusion, rebellion and manifest resistance'. That is, he had attempted to secure the prebend for himself. The bishop's letter shows that trouble was expected: any rebels resisting the induction of the papal candidate, Master Philip Barton, were to be excommunicated, anathematized, and sequestered from the threshold of the holy mother church until they left him and his possessions in peace. 'Each and every tenant of the prebend and manor' was to be warned not to obey Robert de Lacy as prebendary. Names of anyone who treated him as prebendary rather than as an excommunicate were to be reported to the bishop.[154]

In such cases, the issue may have been less that 'everyone' supported Robert, but rather that certain influential locals did. The challenge for the bishop was convincing these bigwigs, who had the weight to cajole or threaten others perhaps rather more than the bishop had. Ian Forrest has recently illuminated these local power dynamics. Forrest demonstrated that bishops placed a great deal of trust in these locals, but the latter may equally have been more able than the bishop to control whether or not an excommunication was enforced.[155] Even if they were unable to secure the prebendary they wished, they could have used their local influence to prevent subsequent ostracism of those excommunicated in the conflict.

The controversy of papal provisions to benefices, evident at Leighton Manor, was discussed by Matthew Paris half a century earlier. When Pope Alexander IV excommunicated Sewal de Bovill, archbishop of York, for refusing to bestow benefices on unsuitable foreigners, the chronicler reports that 'however much he was cursed at the pope's command, so much more was he blessed by the people (although silently, because they were afraid of the Romans)'.[156] Though Sewal himself submitted to the pope on his deathbed, according to Paris he had had the support of the laity, because they, like him, believed his actions had been right.

---

[152] Parishioners were instructed to attend another local church instead.
[153] *Reg. Gandavo*, i, 135–40, 145–51.
[154] *Reg. Pontissara*, i, 96–104. Robert's appeals appear to have come to nothing.
[155] Forrest, *Trustworthy Men*, 432–3 and ch. 7. [156] *CM*, v, 653.

When Boniface of Savoy published an excommunication against anyone who prevented his attempts to secure money from vacant benefices throughout England 'in every church', Paris claimed that this 'generated indignation in the hearts of many'.[157] In the instances narrated by Matthew Paris, the resentment he attributes to 'the people' or 'many' aligned with his own prejudices. Björn Weiler argues that in Paris's works people of a lower social status, in which we might include unnamed masses as well as lowly individuals, 'were used to testify not to the course of an event, but its moral meaning'.[158] Paris may have been seeking to bolster the legitimacy of his viewpoint by ascribing it to the masses. There is no corroborating evidence that they failed to adhere to sentences with their actions. Nevertheless, in both cases, superior clergy (the pope, the archbishop of Canterbury) were, supposedly, impoverishing local communities with their sentences. In the first case, Sewal refused to appoint men unsuitable for the cure of souls, for which he was punished. In the second, the local impoverishment was monetary. It is certainly believable that the loyalties of people did not lie with the powerful men using excommunication, and that their sentences were, accordingly, questioned.

Mutual Sentences

Disputes often involved excommunications pronounced by both sides. In such disputes, where clergy were fulminating sentences of excommunication against one another, it would have been evident to everyone that there was no unity within the ecclesiastical hierarchy.[159] The Great Western Schism, the greatest medieval example of two sides mutually using excommunication against one another, was yet to come.[160] During the Schism, support was decided largely along national lines. But in thirteenth-century English cases, there was no simple way of choosing who to support. In theory, before the Schism, once the pope had stepped in it was clear which side the institutional church had taken, but this did not ensure individual clergy would toe the line, nor that the laity would accept the pope's judgement. Indeed, though R.H. Helmholz argued that the judicialization of excommunication prevented *ex parte* sentences, when it came to papal uses of the sanction there were no such procedures. Only the requirement for warnings applied in these cases. The papacy's judgements were by no means universally accepted. Matthew Paris (who was, admittedly, very anti-papal) even deplored the

---

[157] *CM*, v, 36–7.
[158] Weiler, 'Matthew Paris and the writing of history', 263 and *passim* for the importance of Paris's authorial intentions.
[159] Deborah Hertz argued that in early modern Germany the people became indifferent to the Jewish *herem* and cynical about warring rabbis: 'Judaism in Germany', 753.
[160] See Beaulande on the repercussions for excommunication: 'Force de la censure', 266–7.

'new custom' whereby warring nobles—he cites Daffyd Prince of North Wales as an example—could apply to the papacy to have their opponents excommunicated. This way the papacy secured the eternal obligation of the triumphant party.[161]

Both sides could not be right, nor both excommunications be valid, so communities had to decide which faction had the better case. This inevitably meant scorning one of the sentences. A story related again by Matthew Paris, in 1251, perfectly sets out the issues at stake here. In a dispute between the dean of St Paul's and the archbishop of Canterbury over visitation rights, both parties claimed to be acting with papal authority.[162] Thus those the pope absolved were immediately excommunicated by their enemies, by authority of the pope ('ex parte papae'), for a different reason: 'Thus their quarrel appeared ridiculous to the laity, and no wonder'.[163] Elsewhere, Paris observed of the same dispute that 'a shameful scandal arose', precisely because of these mutual sentences of excommunication.[164] Archbishop Boniface's excommunication of the bishop of London, Fulk Basset, who had become involved in support of the canons of his cathedral church, inspired equal contempt. The bishop sought absolution because, finding himself 'ground between two millstones', he decided that submitting to Archbishop Boniface rather than confront the wrath of Henry III was the lesser of two evils. This he did despite believing that he was unjustly sentenced.[165] According to Paris, the people supported Fulk to such an extent that 'many' wondered that he did not fear the threat 'Woe to you who justify an impious man' (Isaiah 5:22–3).[166] Supposedly the wider populace here even condemned the excommunicate's decision to seek absolution, believing that he ought to have stood up to the archbishop's oppression. The chronicler certainly condemned it.

The cult of Simon de Montfort and the miracles attributed to him provide evidence for the popular belief that he was not truly or justly excommunicated.[167] We have already seen the papal anger directed at the disobedient Montfortian bishops for failing to execute the excommunication of Montfort and his allies. Their belief in the cause, despite its condemnation by the papacy, was shared by others in the kingdom.[168] Montfort, though he died excommunicate, was considered by many to have been a saint. This was partly because of his violent death, and the dismemberment of his body. He was made a martyr. The Lanercost chronicle, written within a Franciscan milieu, observed that men continued to

---

[161] *CM*, iv, 548. [162] See Cheney, *Episcopal Visitation*, 138–9. [163] *CM*, v, 229.
[164] *CM*, v, 217–18. 'Ortum est igitur turpe scandalum, dum nunc ab his denuntiabantur excommunicati in his, nunc in aliis ab his partibus absoluti.'
[165] For this dispute see Franklin, 'Basset, Fulk (d. 1259)'; Carpenter, *Henry III*, 557–9.
[166] *CM*, v, 206.
[167] Maddicott, *Simon de Montfort*, 346–7, 367–8; Valente, 'Simon de Montfort'; 'Lament of Simon de Montfort', in *Thomas Wright's Political Songs*, 124–7; Hartman, 'Poetry and the cause of Simon de Montfort'.
[168] Why the bishops took the barons' side, and how they justified this, has been discussed by Sophie Ambler in *Bishops in the Political Community*, chs. 6 and 7. See also Hoskin, 'Natural Law, protest and the English episcopate'.

honour those who died excommunicated at Evesham. Though they had been buried outside the cemetery as excommunicates, 'they proved themselves not to be in error, through signs from God'.[169] The disobedience of Montfort's supporters was not unthinking, and once again excommunication was used by both sides in the struggle. Even if no excommunication was pronounced in favour of the Provisions of Oxford in 1258, as Sophie Ambler has argued, the reformers did make use of Magna Carta and its excommunication to legitimize their actions.[170] It was possible to argue that anyone contradicting Montfort was an excommunicate. Since the pope had annulled the provisions and the oaths to enforce them in 1261, this was hardly the pope's view. Nonetheless, the final supporters of the reforms referred to this sentence and were unwilling to act against it. When they were besieged (and again excommunicated) at Ely in 1267, they said they would take their chances with God, if necessary.[171]

Whether major political struggles such as that between the papacy and the empire or the king and the barons, or more local clashes concerning ecclesiastical positions, instances of rival clergy, often using excommunication against the opposing side, were perhaps common enough to evoke a sense amongst the populace that all excommunications merited individual judgement. In these cases, one of the sentences was necessarily wrong; why could more run-of-the-mill excommunications not also be erroneous? Self-interest rather than moral rectitude could influence resistance just as much as it could affect authorities' uses of sanctions. Locals might simply prefer 'their man' for a position, without necessarily considering his excommunication to be innately invalid. Nevertheless, such decisions were not merely the result of indifference to excommunication. Lower down clergy were charged with publishing sentences and enforcing excommunications and interdicts, without themselves having the right to excommunicate. While failure to obey sentences should not be overstated, the complicity of clergy and laity against sentences of other members of the clergy suggests conviction rather than apathy. Though political use of excommunication was unsurprising and had always existed, it is nevertheless important that such uses of the ecclesiastical weapon at least in theory conflicted with the intention behind it, that is to correct sinners. Unlike political exile in Italian city-communes, for instance, where politics and factionalism were integral to how and why banishments were ordered, overtly partisan uses of excommunication risked damaging the authority of clergy and the sanction itself.[172] Both clergy and laity could resent and question the judgements and sentences of (typically senior) ecclesiastics.

---

[169] *Lanercost*, 77.
[170] Ambler, *Bishops in the Political Community*, 108–12; Ambler, 'Magna Carta'. If no sentence was pronounced, this remains surprising.
[171] See Chapter 2, 96–7.   [172] See Milani, 'An ambiguous sentence'.

Mouldable sentences: *Latae sententiae*

The problem of clergy pronouncing excommunications in favour of opposing sides in quarrels was compounded by the use of *latae sententiae*. General and automatic sentences were often ambiguously phrased, so that it was possible for each party to claim the other had incurred the same sentence. Even in cases where only one person had purportedly fallen into such an excommunication, there was plenty of room for uncertainty, though some argued that such individuals need not be shunned until they were publicly named as excommunicates.[173] There were legal solutions to this difficulty. Only confirmed excommunicates were to be shunned and to be excluded from courts and other legal matters. The practical difficulties were therefore largely resolved. There nevertheless remained the fact that automatic sentences were *discussable*. A similar difficulty is apparent in the Bologna heresy case noted above: there was disagreement between the authorities and the citizens about what constituted heresy, which was, as John Arnold put it, 'in the eye of the beholder'.[174] Heresy was less of a hot topic in thirteenth-century England, but who was to say who was 'disturbing the peace of the realm' (*Qui pacem et tranquillitatem*), for example? The prevalence of *ipso facto* sentences meant such discussions were likely to have been commonplace, and again led to the inevitable feeling that all excommunications were subjective, and thus open to question.

Which actions might incur *Si quis suadente*, and what circumstances might mean it was not incurred, were discussed at length by canonists and theologians.[175] Peter the Chanter, for instance, dedicated some time to addressing theoretical circumstances in which someone injures a priest, answering whether or not the injurer would thereby incur excommunication. Thus if an untonsured cleric was injured, and he was not known to be a cleric, the injurer did not fall into the canon. Hitting a cleric while drunk was no excuse, however. He was undecided about clergy who attended tournaments and were accidentally injured there, since tournaments were (at this time) forbidden by the church: clergymen should not be there anyway. Hitting a cleric in the face with urine during the Feast of Fools celebrations, 'as many there are hit', probably would not incur a sentence.[176] If a cleric was injured during a game, provided that the rules of the game were followed and the injury was not serious, no excommunication was incurred. Hitting a clerk during a snowball fight would not necessarily incur excommunication unless, Peter argued, a layman hardened the snow into ice and thereby

---

[173] See Vodola, *Excommunication*, 28–32; Rosemblieh, 'Limiter la contagion'.
[174] Arnold, *Belief and Unbelief*, 193.
[175] See much discussion of *Si quis suadente* in Peñafort, *De Poenitentia*, Book 3. Helmholz, 'Si quis suadente', 426–30 deals with interpretations of the canon.
[176] Unless the injury was enormous.

injured a priest. This was not playing fair.[177] Cases where there might be doubt about whether an individual had incurred the canon were endless.

Latae sententiae that were specific to English provinces did not have commentaries discussing when the sentences were incurred, yet their phrasing was just as ambiguous. R.H. Helmholz spends fifteen pages discussing every aspect of the wording of the 1222 Council of Oxford's fifth clause (*Qui crimen imponunt*).[178] 'Maliciously' (*malitiose*) is used in five of the Oxford sentences; Helmholz notes that the word is impossible to define precisely, and that it was used in more than one sense in canon law. Certain characteristics appear to have been associated with it, such as perseverance (rather than passing anger), but it defied clear definition.[179]

The first two excommunications pronounced at the 1222 Oxford Council, in particular, were notably unspecific. These declared 'we excommunicate all those who maliciously presume to deprive churches of their rights, or through malice and against justice strive to infringe or disturb their liberties' (*Qui malitiose ecclesias*), and 'we bind with a sentence of excommunication all those who presume to disturb the peace and tranquillity of the lord king and his realm, and who unjustly strive to detain the king's rights' (*Qui pacem et tranquillitatem*).[180] Later councils sought to clarify what offences might be covered by the clauses, but they erred on the side of coverage, not specificity. Thus John Pecham in 1281 emphasized that liberties, great and small, were protected by *Qui malitiose ecclesias*, as were both temporal and spiritual possessions and rights. He stressed the broad coverage of the excommunication, even adding that he did not intend in any way to limit its application by his specific additions.[181]

These vague clauses left room for different interpretations. Though we might imagine that such discussions occurred at all levels of society, the consequences of the ambiguities of these *ipso facto* sentences are particularly evident in high politics, for chronicles observed such divergences of opinion. Often these opposing understandings of general sentences might be understood as prevarication, pretence, or posturing. In other circumstances, the differing opinions were perfectly valid. High-profile examples occur particularly in the reigns of King John and Henry III. In both reigns, excommunicates were not ostracized as they were meant to be, but there were reasonable cases to be made that the excommunications invoked did not apply.

Innocent III's sentence against the barons who rebelled against John in 1215 was initially a general excommunication in which they were not named. It was

---

[177] Chanter, *Summa*, 395–6. Handbooks for priests noted that one of the exceptions to *Si quis suadente* was 'playful levity', e.g: Peñafort, *De Poenitentia*, 389–90; Flamborough, *Summa poenitentialis*, 156–7; Robert Grosseteste, *Templum Dei*, VII.8.
[178] *Select Cases on Defamation*, ed. Helmholz, xxvi–xli.
[179] *Select Cases on Defamation*, ed. Helmholz, xxxii.   [180] *C&S*, 106–7.   [181] *C&S*, 905–6.

pronounced against 'all disturbers of the king and kingdom'.[182] The problem with this was that the rebellion against John was not without cause. As a result, the Crowland annalist observed, 'many interpreted that... [the sentence] fell on the king's head, because he, they said, was disturbing the kingdom and expelled himself with his deeds'. However, the chronicler noted that many others interpreted the sentence in the opposite way: whoever was striving to expel their lord was excommunicated.[183] The second interpretation was of course the one Innocent intended, but who exactly was 'disturbing the realm' was by no means universally agreed. Everyone claimed that he was acting for the good of the kingdom, and could accordingly accuse the opposing side of falling into the pope's sentence. As discussed, many individuals—clergy and laity—were guilty of failing to shun Louis and the barons. The potential for debate that these sentences invited perhaps puts their disobedience into a different perspective. Their defiance was not merely an issue of belief that a sentence was 'unjust', let alone wanton insubordination, but could have stemmed from a genuinely held different interpretation of an ambiguous phrase.

The ambiguity of excommunication against disturbers of the realm was once again an issue under Henry III. The bishops and the king with his counsellors had different opinions about who was 'disturbing the peace'. In 1233, Henry faced rebellion from Richard Marshal, earl of Pembroke, in an episode that highlights dissension between papal and episcopal attitudes. The full background here was complicated, though the earl was not alone in taking exception to the influence at court of certain counsellors, in particular of Stephen Seagrave, Robert Passelewe, and Peter des Roches. Peter, it was alleged, had denied the magnates access to the king, whom they wanted to resolve their disputes. Arms were their only option— the Marshal took the castle he was owed by force.[184] At the same time, the bishops' response was to threaten the king's principal advisors with excommunication, pronouncing a general sentence against those who influenced the king against native Englishmen, or who disturbed the peace of the realm. In the bishops' eyes, the disturbers of the peace were not the Marshal, but Henry's foreign advisors, who had turned the king away from his English magnates. Henry, nevertheless, sought episcopal sentences for his own ends. When the Marshal took the castle of Usk, Henry asked the bishops to excommunicate him by name. They refused, arguing that the castle was rightfully the Marshal's.[185]

The fallout demonstrates the danger posed by ambiguous sentences. The bishops, particularly Alexander Stainsby, were accused of supporting a challenge to the throne and of excessive familiarity with the Marshal. They responded to this

---

[182] *SLI*, no. 80.   [183] *Coventry*, 224.
[184] Weiler, *Kingship, Rebellion and Political Culture*, 28. See also Vincent, *Peter des Roches*, 399–428; Carpenter, *Henry III*, 140–50.
[185] *CM*, iii, 251–2.

charge by generally excommunicating all who intended iniquity against the king. They also excommunicated, according to the later testimony of Matthew Paris, all those who had accused them of supporting these conspiracies, since they were in fact 'wholly concerned with the king's health and honour'. Their acts had been to protect him and his kingdom.[186] The bishops, nonetheless, were reprimanded by the pope. Henry complained to Gregory IX that they had refused to excommunicate disturbers of the peace, despite the pope's earlier letter, and despite the various homicides, fires, invasions of castles, and other disturbances perpetrated by the king's enemies. The bishops' arguments were judged spurious and disingenuous. Gregory sternly warned them to disregard their frivolous excuses and to restrain disturbers of the peace with ecclesiastical censure. Peace was to be restored, and the king to be shown love and honour.[187]

The bishops, in turn, pressed their point. They argued that the councillors could not personally profit through peace, and so were creating dissension and disinheriting others to their own advantage. The English magnates, by contrast, had been dismissed from court. They warned the king that, since his advisors had perverted the law of the land, itself confirmed by excommunication (the Magna Carta sentence), 'it is to be feared that they are excommunicated and you also for communicating with them'. If he did not dismiss such men, the bishops would proceed against him with ecclesiastical censure. They awaited only the consecration of Edmund of Abingdon, archbishop-elect of Canterbury.[188] The Marshal himself had made a similar argument: Stephen Seagrave (the king's chief justiciar, one of the chief 'bad counsellors') had sworn to observe just laws, but had instead corrupted them and introduced new ones. Surely both he and his accomplices were consequently excommunicated? He continued by stating that the pope loved the king and kingdom, so excommunicated the enemies of the kingdom, whom he identified as 'those who give counsel to the king against justice... because peace and justice go hand in hand'.[189] Henry balked at the idea he should dismiss his counsellors so suddenly and pleaded for time, but capitulated following the archbishop's consecration and renewed threats that, unless he correct his errors, he and all those who disturbed the peace along with him would be excommunicated.[190] Peter des Roches was dismissed from court and told to attend to cure of souls in his diocese.[191]

The account of these events in the chronicle of St Albans (written at first by Roger of Wendover, thereafter by Matthew Paris), on which the above is based, should not be taken at face value. Nicholas Vincent and Björn Weiler have both

---

[186] *CM*, iii, 268; Vincent, 'Master Alexander Stainsby', 631–2. [187] *Royal Letters,* app. v, no. 34.
[188] *CM*, iii, 269–71.   [189] *CM*, iii, 260–2.
[190] On Edmund's consecration, and the unity of the bishops against des Roches at the ceremony, see Vincent, *Peter des Roches,* 435 and n. 30.
[191] *CM*, iii, 269–71.

dissected the issues in far greater depth than is possible here.¹⁹² The significance of the episode, however, is first the different policies of the English episcopate and the papacy. The former sought to use excommunication against the king's advisors and against his wishes, while the latter wished to protect the king's interests with the sanction. Though no significant rift occurred, the lack of ecclesiastical unanimity is clear. Second, the two sides had different opinions on who within the kingdom were truly 'disturbing the peace'. The bishops and the Marshal considered Henry's recent bad decisions, inspired by his evil counsellors, to be a threat to the kingdom. Just rule was a fundamental principle that could not be thus ignored. The king felt, not unreasonably, that the Marshal's occupation of a castle by force threatened the peace. There was evident reluctance to pronounce sentences against named individuals. Reliance on these general sentences left room for divergence. The bishops suggested that Henry might have incurred excommunication by associating with his excommunicated counsellors, but the king had little incentive to shun his advisers while they were not named excommunicates.

In the reign of Edward I, it was the king himself who sought to twist interpretations of *latae sententiae* in his own favour. *Clericis laicos*, promulgated by Boniface VIII in 1296, excommunicated anyone who imposed or paid lay taxes on clergy without papal consent. Edward I did not react well to this prohibition, forcing the English clergy to contribute the following year. He argued, amongst other things, that he was impelled by urgent necessity. He invoked a bull of Clement IV, issued in his father's reign, that excommunicated disturbers of the peace.¹⁹³ He thus sought to argue that *not* helping him would incur a sentence. As Jeffrey Denton remarked, however, 'in 1297 it was not those who disturbed the peace that were under a papal ban of excommunication, rather it was those who supported the crown by contravening "Clericis laicos"'.¹⁹⁴ The ambiguity of *Si quis suadente*, *Qui malitiose ecclesias*, *Qui pacem et tranquillitatem*, and other general sentences all encouraged arguments—genuine or specious—about who and what actions incurred sentences.

Royal Interference

Excommunication was also actively sabotaged by secular government. Often this involved failure to fulfil requests to arrest and imprison excommunicates. Clerical

---

¹⁹² For these events see Weiler, *Kingship, Rebellion and Political Culture*, particularly 159–61 for the bishops' involvement; Vincent, *Peter des Roches*, 399–438; Carpenter, *Henry III*, 140–50; Ambler, *Bishops in the Political Community*, 49–50, 62–6, 79–81.

¹⁹³ *Foedera*, I.ii.873. Edward was citing either *Foedera*, I.i.469–70 or *Reg. Clement IV*, 483. These in turn referred to the sentence published when Clement was legate (Gui Fouquois): Heidemann, no. 50; Denton, *Robert Winchelsey*, 147–9.

¹⁹⁴ Denton, *Robert Winchelsey*, 149.

gravamina noted sheriffs not capturing excommunicates at all or else releasing them before absolution had been granted.[195] Langton's seventh *ipso facto* excommunication from his 1222 provincial council (*Contempnunt exequi domini*) was directed at such abuses.[196] There are examples in practice of royal officials impeding it.[197] Nevertheless, though the reluctance of officials to use bodily coercion lessened the threat of excommunication, the problem was not endemic, whatever clerical complaints to the king implied.[198] Likewise, though clergy complained that the exception of excommunication was not applied, Vodola concluded that the exception was in fact enforced for the most part consistently in England.[199]

More detrimental to the functioning of excommunication was the understanding that royal officials could not be excommunicated without the king's permission. This was claimed since at least the time of William the Conqueror.[200] In 1231, Henry III complained to Gregory IX, obtaining a letter from the pope forbidding archbishops and bishops to 'presume to promulgate a sentence of excommunication against the said justices, sheriffs and bailiffs, without manifest and reasonable cause' and requiring them to give appropriate warning beforehand.[201] The king had complained that bishops' sentences had been unjust, hasty, and derogatory to royal right. The pope did not specify that the king's permission should be sought, but this is surely the implication of this 'privilege', as the pope called it. Asserting that he wished to preserve the king's justice undiminished, it is otherwise difficult to understand what privilege Gregory was granting: all excommunications required just and reasonable cause and warning.

However, exemption from excommunication for royal officers was not clear cut. Vodola argued that one consequence was that the legal exception of excommunication in courts was resilient in England (by contrast to France) because 'the constant excommunications of royal agents that so exasperated the French *parlement*' did not take place in England.[202] Yet it is evident that the English Church

---

[195] *C&S*, 541 (c. 11), 576–7 (c. 6), 1213 (c. 18); *Reg. Halton*, i, 172.   [196] *C&S*, 107.
[197] *CR 1234–37*, 13; *CRR*, xi, no. 1823; *Fine Rolls*, 25 Henry III, no. 715 (m. 2); London, TNA, SC 1/13/168; *Reg. Epp. Pecham*, ii, 606–8; *Reg. Pecham*, ii, 210; *Reg. Pontissara*, ii, 522–3; *CM*, v, 109–10; Logan, *Excommunication and the Secular Arm*, 79–80, 87–9, 101–4. For France see Campbell, 'Attitude of the monarchy', 536, 541–3.
[198] Logan, *Excommunication and the Secular Arm*, 110–12, 148–55. In France, especially under Louis IX, there was much more questioning of excommunications by the king. See Campbell, 'Attitude of the monarchy', esp. 537.
[199] Vodola, *Excommunication*, 159–63 and 189.
[200] *Select Charters*, ed. Stubbs, 96. The instruction was reiterated in the Constitutions of Clarendon, c. 7: *Councils & Synods* I, ed. Whitelock, Brett and Brookes, 864, 880. See also Hill, 'Theory and practice', 4–5, and Vodola, *Excommunication*, 189; Pollock and Maitland, *History of English Law*, i, 478–9. Use of the secular arm against excommunicates also dated to the Conqueror: Logan, *Excommunication and the Secular Arm*, 18–19.
[201] *Foedera*, I.i.200.
[202] Vodola, *Excommunication*, 189. In fact, in 1205 Philip Augustus had claimed a similar right in Rouen: Campbell, 'Attitude of the monarchy', 537, 551. See also Logan, *Excommunication and the Secular Arm*, 102–4.

did not take this privilege seriously. Ecclesiastical legislation frequently provided for the excommunication of the king's men. Thus *Contempnunt exequi domini*, published four times a year in parish churches, automatically excommunicated 'all those' who failed to execute writs for the capture of excommunicates. Since royal officials would be given such a task, the sentence can only have been directed at them.[203] Other statutes similarly show no acceptance of any exemption for the king's men. One set of diocesan statutes (1222 × 1225) specifically threatened constables, castellans, or bailiffs with anathema if they should molest ecclesiastical persons or possessions.[204] Winchester statutes (c.1247) commanded that sheriffs, foresters, and bailiffs who hosted 'scotales' be bound with excommunication *ipso facto*.[205] Sheriffs and bailiffs were again singled out for offences against the church in the 1258 Merton council, and threatened with excommunication in several of the constitutions.[206] The Oxford sentence, in particular, was repeated from synod to synod and received a good deal of publicity. Archbishop Pecham was made to withdraw the sentence in 1281 (to no long-term effect).[207]

Bishops' failure to acknowledge any privilege enjoyed by royal officials in their statutes was reflected in their actions. Certainly there are examples of clerics stopping short of excommunicating officials by name, perhaps indicating that they expected resistance.[208] Yet on many other occasions clergy did excommunicate royal officials, albeit sometimes only with a general sentence. The fact that these examples almost all come from royal rather than ecclesiastical sources shows that the king's response was inevitably one of indignation, but that clergy were not deterred from excommunicating in the first place.[209] Henry III apparently referred to his privilege from Gregory IX in 1233, complaining that the bishop of Rochester had contravened it by excommunicating 'certain nobles'.[210] In 1254, Henry 'marvelled' at the excommunication of an official by the archbishop of Bordeaux, with the king 'ignorant and unasked', citing his apostolic privilege (evidently the privilege applied in the king's continental lands).[211] But on other occasions no specific mention was made of the privilege, though royal anger remained. In 1236 Henry III wrote to the bishop of Winchester's official, having heard of the sentence pronounced by the prior of St Swithun in a dispute over a 'royal fish' (possibly a whale), claimed by the priory. The king declared himself amazed that the prior had claimed such a fish but did not note that he had no right

---

[203] *C&S*, 107.   [204] *C&S*, 150. Unknown diocese.   [205] *C&S*, 416.
[206] *C&S*, 582, 574. They were to be denounced excommunicated for infringing Magna Carta c. 1, 576–7.
[207] *C&S*, 856–7; Hill, 'Magna Carta'. See also Chapter 7 below.
[208] E.g. *Reg. Epp. Pecham*, i, 13–14, in which it is hinted that a bailiff had incurred *Qui malitiose ecclesias* but was not yet denounced as such. He also excommunicated all those who had procured the release of an imprisoned clerk, surely likely to include the responsible royal officials: *Reg. Pecham*, ii, 210. cf. *Reg. Epp. Pecham*, ii, 538.
[209] See also Gray, 'Magna Charta', 34. E.g. *CRR*, 13, nos 2236, 2605.   [210] *Royal Letters*, 413–14.
[211] *CR 1253–54*, 246.

to excommunicate royal bailiffs.²¹² Equally, in 1262 he rebuked the chancellor and university of Oxford for sentencing bailiffs in a dispute over arrested clerks. Henry remarked that they had done so in contempt of himself, but again mentioned no privilege.²¹³ Even during the *Clericis laicos* turmoil, when Edward I forbade excommunication of his ministers on pain of forfeiture, he did not mention any papal privilege.²¹⁴

The king interfered in sentences of excommunication, forcing clergy to back down, on many occasions.²¹⁵ Usually the cases involved his own men or were perceived to infringe royal rights in some way (frequently both). On the one hand, it is evident that the king could and did, as clerical *gravamina* complained, undermine excommunications. Writs of prohibition, which were issued to prevent bishops calling people to their courts in cases deemed to belong to secular jurisdiction, were another important point of conflict. In 1285, clerical complaints even cited prohibitions as the reason why 'it should probably be feared that...there are more excommunicated today in England than in any land of the world': those who used such prohibitions in cases where they should not were bound by a major excommunication.²¹⁶ Yet clergy who disobeyed these writs, often by excommunicating those who failed to appear before them when cited, faced the king's ire.²¹⁷ Precisely this problem was voiced in a letter in 1261 from Urban IV to Henry III. The pope wrote that laymen secured writs via justices and bailiffs forbidding judges to issue sentences of excommunication.²¹⁸ After such prohibitions, 'the said layman is not shunned as an excommunicate, because the said justices and bailiffs prohibit it'.²¹⁹

On the other hand, the number of cases reveal not only Henry III's and Edward I's willingness to intervene in sentences, but also that their frequent interference did not deter clergy.²²⁰ Many clergy went ahead with excommunications of royal officials without informing the king, regardless of any privilege supposed to protect officials, even if they later faced repercussions. Vodola's observation that the exception of excommunication was enforced in England because it did not affect royal officials is important.²²¹ It is possible that clergy did not bother to claim that an excommunicated official should not plead in the king's court. If they had tried to press for the exception of excommunication against royal officials, it would probably have been quashed because of their supposed exemption from the

---

²¹² *CR 1234–37*, 378–9. Cf. *CPR 1232–47*, 183.   ²¹³ *CR 1261–64*, 106–7.
²¹⁴ *Foedera*, I.ii.875.
²¹⁵ *CR 1242–47*, 353; *CR 1247–51*, 525; *CR 1253–54*, 314; *CR 1254–56*, 167–8; Prynne, *Records*, 1285; *CPR 1232–47*, 441; *SKB* ii, 80–1; *Parliament Rolls*, i, 162–5; *CCR 1296–1302*, 532; *CCR 1302–7*, 326. Royal clerks were also excommunicated, incurring royal wrath: *CR 1242–47*, 477–8; *CCR 1296–1302*, 215. See also the issues involving St Oswald's, a royal foundation, above at 118–19, and below, 181. See also Carpenter, *Henry III*, 533 n. 108, 560.
²¹⁶ *C&S*, 971 (c. 10).   ²¹⁷ E.g. *CR 1268–72*, 575.
²¹⁸ Clashes over writs of prohibition were common. See Flahiff, 'The writ of prohibition' I and II; Douie, *Archbishop Pecham*, 313–17; Helmholz, 'Writ of prohibition'.
²¹⁹ *Foedera*, I.i.411.   ²²⁰ Fewer records for John's reign obscure his practices here.
²²¹ See also Logan, *Excommunication and the Secular Arm*, 61.

sanction. Similarly, it would have been foolish to attempt to have them arrested by the secular arm. However, plenty of damage could be done without either of these measures by publicizing an excommunication, as will be fully explored in Chapter 5. Lay officials purposefully sought to undermine the ostracism of excommunicates. Though there is plenty of evidence that they were excommunicated, the number of examples across the century are not so numerous that cases can be said to have been common. The theoretical immunity that officials enjoyed may thus have led them to feel emboldened to disregard clerical mandates and infringe the key principles of excommunication.

The greatest impediments linked to the crown were failure to shun excommunicates and active attempts to encourage the same behaviour from others. Failure to enforce writs for capture of course undermined excommunication, but if an excommunicate needed to be coerced by his or her body, communally enforced ostracism had already failed. By contrast, ordering the faithful to associate with those under the ban struck at the root of excommunication's social effects.

'The lord king, his justices and bailiffs everywhere and indifferently communicate with excommunicates', complained the clergy in 1257. Furthermore, they observed, the king ordered in his letters that excommunicates should not be avoided, even though they were being publicly denounced.[222] His bailiffs were also at fault for communicating with Jews who had incurred excommunication for not wearing signs to distinguish them as Jews (as Lateran IV ordered).[223] These complaints, repeated the following year, are very general, giving little indication of the sorts of cases in which they might have applied.[224] The first complaint, asserting as it does that the king and his men communicated 'passim et indifferenter' with excommunicates in divine and judicial matters, indicates that it was widespread. In 1285, the clergy even claimed that the king forced people to communicate with excommunicates, his ministers announcing that sentences were void ('non tenere').[225] Prone as they are to hyperbole, such complaints should not be taken entirely seriously. Although these accusations were denied by Edward I, there is evidence that they were not unjustified.[226] The crown certainly contradicted orders to shun excommunicates in particular cases.

Contradictory information was thus not only promulgated when clergy were at odds. Secular powers could fuel gossip and debate about whether a censure should be obeyed, as Clarke has shown also in relation to interdicts.[227] As in instances when clergy pronounced opposing sentences, royal counter-proclamations invited communities to make their own judgements about whether or not an excommunication was valid. The problem was not common, but it further demonstrates the difficulties posed by the communal enforcement of excommunication. The king

---

[222] C&S, 541 (cc. 12, 13).   [223] C&S, 545 (c. 33).   [224] C&S, 576–7 (c. 6).
[225] C&S, 958, 960–1. See also Douie, *Archbishop Pecham*, 305–7.   [226] C&S, 958, 963.
[227] Cf. Clarke, *Interdict*, 177–8, 190, 221.

appears, in fact, to have ordered people to communicate when they were forcefully carrying out the requirement to shun. His orders provide some of our few examples of successful ostracism.

During a dispute between the prior of Great Malvern and the bishop of Worcester, the king wrote to the sheriff of Gloucester, in 1283, ordering him to proclaim in the county court that everyone was allowed to communicate with the prior and convent. Edward I's order, preserved in the bishop of Worcester's register, claimed that the monks of Malvern had been unable to buy and sell anything as a result of their excommunication. They were, apparently, starving.[228] Some account was taken of the king's wishes, for when his treasurer, Richard de Ware, incurred excommunication for seizing the priory's temporalities, Giffard did not publish the sentence, out of reverence for the king.[229] Similar announcements, telling citizens to communicate with the monks of St Oswald's priory, and to provide them with victuals, were made in the early 1300s, also in Gloucester. The bishop of Worcester was told not to forbid this; subsequently the sheriff was commanded to proclaim that people were to ignore the bishop's prohibitions. It might be noted that, in this case, the king's efforts to influence the community do not seem to have been any more effective than the bishop's: the first letter was sent in 1300, the last in 1304.[230]

The bailiff of Fécamp, excommunicated in 1283, was able to take advantage of his position by broadcasting that he was not sentenced. Throughout the diocese of Chichester, the bailiff and his accomplices proclaimed that those who supported and adhered to him were not bound by excommunication. Archbishop Pecham complained to the bishop of Chichester about this, noting that the excommunication was not being enforced and that his order to publish it had not been carried out everywhere. The bishop was to make it publicly known that everyone who supported the bailiff in any way was equally bound, except the king and his family.[231] Nor did the king only order his own men to make counter-proclamations. In 1256, Henry III ordered the official of Canterbury, Hugh de Mortimer, to announce that a sentence pronounced by various bishops against Roger, abbot of Glastonbury, was 'invalid and inane' because the case between the abbot and the bishop of Bath and Wells 'manifestly touches the honour and dignity of our crown'. If the bishops did not stop making denunciations, the official was to defend Roger, who had appealed to Canterbury.[232] The church relied on publishing excommunications to inform the faithful as to whom they were obliged to shun. Perhaps such active attempts from secular authorities to counteract these orders were rare, but, where they did take place, these counter-proclamations posed a considerable problem.

---

[228] *Reg. G. Giffard*, 211–12; J. W. Willis-Bund and William Page (eds), *Victoria County History ... Worcester*, ii, 136–143, and n. 37.
[229] *Reg. G. Giffard*, 186.
[230] *CCR 1296–1302*, 411, 526; *CCR 1302–07*, 225–6; Prynne, *Records*, 857, 1026; *SKB*, iii, 138–43.
[231] *Reg. Epp. Pecham*, ii, 604.   [232] *CR 1254–6*, 404.

Conclusions

The regulation that excommunicates were to be removed from all social interaction with other Christians ought to have been the most immediate impetus for those under the ban to seek absolution. However, getting all Christians, or even a sufficient proportion within the relevant area, to treat excommunicates as heathens and publicans was an impossibly tall order. There were a myriad of reasons for this, but it is hard to sustain an argument that using the sanction less would have made any significant difference. Shunning is no trivial undertaking; it asks a lot of the ostracizers. Although ostracism of various sorts is common to most societies, the problem here was perhaps the routine nature of its use and the fact that it did not occur naturally because individuals or groups wished to punish or correct behaviour but because the church did. Any sanction imposed by only a select group within a community but that is to be carried out by all is bound to face difficulties.

This is not to deny that excommunication was sometimes used for trivial offences, undermining the seriousness with which it might be received. Yet here again clergy had limited options; it is easy to see why they resorted to it so often and for their own gain. The development and proliferation of *latae sententiae* only added to this problem, for clerics were obliged to deal with those who had already incurred one of these sentences. Unjust sentences were another matter, but no legal system is free from such abuses. The issue, once again, was that everyone, rather than a select few who worked in 'law enforcement', was tasked with imposing the penalty. This was not unique, in medieval legal practices, to excommunication, but it was certainly a key part of why excommunications proved less coercive than the ideal. The absence of appeals, though understandable from the perspective of an institution that could not afford to have its judgments questioned, again added to the sense of injustice that individuals and communities felt.

Excommunication's weakness in this respect is thus not surprising. It does not, however, mean it was a worthless sanction. Even without complete acceptance amongst the population it could have deleterious effects. Moreover, its reception by communities reveals a good deal about medieval society—how communities functioned and where loyalties lay. In particular, the way that clergy and laity alike made up their own minds—in the face of threats of contagion and sanction—is evident. Excommunication was automatically a matter that invited gossip. Sentences had to be publicized or they would not be enforced. The consequences of the inevitable discussion of sentences are evident in this chapter. The publicity attached to excommunication was in fact its most important aspect. It was damaging to individuals and used by clergy in ways that affected communities considerably. The remainder of the book focuses on the public nature of excommunication and its consequences.

PART III
PUBLICITY

5
Publicity, Reputation, and Scandal

The publicity associated with excommunication is perhaps the most striking aspect of the sanction. It is prominent in sources of all kinds. A person was not simply excommunicated; they were excommunicated and subsequently publicly announced to be excommunicated. To publish ('publicare') in this period usually meant to have something pronounced orally, often several times in a variety of places.[1] Though it is difficult to assess how many people suffered excommunication in this period, it can be suggested with confidence that everyone would have witnessed excommunication denunciations in the course of his or her life.[2] This need not involve his or her own neighbours being sentenced, for excommunications were promulgated over considerable distances, while *latae sententiae* were supposed to be announced on a regular basis.[3]

The public nature of excommunication had important consequences for individuals and communities that went well beyond the functions of excommunication articulated in canon law and other normative sources. Excommunications needed to be published, otherwise nobody would shun those sentenced and the sanction was unlikely to be effective. Moreover, sentences were designed not only to inform communities whom they ought to avoid, but also to convince them to do so. As we have seen, a community's judgement was fundamental to how and whether an excommunication was enforced.[4] The purpose of publication was to communicate ideas, and to influence public opinion and thereby communal behaviour.[5]

During an excommunication denunciation, crimes committed could be described in vigorous and condemnatory detail (often in the vernacular) so that the audience understood why the excommunicates had been so condemned. The ceremony that accompanied these condemnations, as described in Chapter 1, was meant to be striking and memorable. Excommunication should thus be included in discussions of medieval mass communication.[6] Sentences were promulgated on

---

[1] Sometimes, documents were posted on doors etc., but it is clear that publishing usually meant public speaking.
[2] As was similarly the case for public penance: Mansfield, *Humiliation*, 130. See Introduction for a sense of how many were sentenced.
[3] See Chapter 7 for publication of *latae sententiae*.   [4] See Chapter 4.
[5] Cf. Melve, 'Even the very laymen', 27.
[6] See for example d'Avray, *Medieval Marriage Sermons*; publication of excommunication does not quite count as 'news': see Birkett, 'News in the Middle Ages', 28–32.

Sundays and feast days by parish priests; no section of church-going society was excluded from hearing them.

Practice indicates that this publicity became, in its own right, a reason to use excommunication. Though publication was a natural and essential element of excommunication, necessary if clergy were to have any hope of getting parishioners to ostracize excommunicates, how long and how geographically extensively sentences were promulgated varied.[7] Administrative developments that took place during the twelfth and thirteenth centuries undoubtedly facilitated the promulgation of excommunication sentences. Though publicity of excommunications was by no means new, greater oversight of bishops over their subordinates, increasingly sophisticated channels of communication within dioceses, and ever-growing records inevitably made it easier to ensure that sentences were widely publicized at the local level. As the population steadily increased until the early fourteenth century, so too did the number of administrators in the bishop's household. More officials to issue written orders and to follow up on whether such orders had been executed perhaps made it ever easier to manipulate and exploit the publicity that had always been a fundamental part of excommunication.[8]

Denunciations were not governed by strict rules in the way that imposing a sentence in the first place was. Rather than being a side effect of excommunication's functions, denunciation was a key part of excommunication's usefulness. Efforts to publicize sentences, both those pronounced against named individuals and *generaliter,* were often more stringent when personal grievances were held by clergy wielding the 'sword of excommunication' against their enemies or rivals. Excommunication sentences devised to influence public opinion were extremely advantageous for those pronouncing them (or for those who had procured the excommunications). Bad publicity could simply be another way to put pressure on excommunicates to make peace with the church, but it could also be an end in itself. This point should cause a reconsideration of what excommunication was intended to achieve, and therefore how we assess its efficacy in particular situations.

For many who were censured with excommunication, the publicity that accompanied their sentences seems to have been what they found most offensive. As we have seen in Chapter 2, excommunicates were often able to put aside fear of spiritual consequences. Equally, excommunicates were not always ostracized as

---

[7] An interesting comparison might be made with defamatory paintings used in medieval Italy. These paintings originally resulted from a punishment but became part of the punishment of exclusion itself (the secular ban). They similarly sought to influence public opinion and prompt anger. Milani, 'Ban and the bag'.

[8] Cheney, *English Bishops' Chanceries*; Cheney, *From Becket to Langton*, 145; Swanson, *Church and Society*, 2; Clanchy, *From Memory to Written Record*, 75–8; Kemp, 'Informing the archdeacon'; Hamilton Thompson, 'Diocesan organization'.

the law required. The damage that excommunication could do to reputations, however, was more problematic. Public denunciations were injurious to everyone, regardless of whether or not they thought their sentences were just. Indeed, for those who denied that they deserved to be excommunicated at all, this slander was particularly provoking. Clergy who disagreed with their superiors' sentences and refused to carry out orders to publish them demonstrate the significance of publication. Not publishing sentences, or preventing clergy from publishing them through threats or force, did not change the fact that someone was excommunicated in spiritual terms. It merely prevented others from learning of the fact, and from being fed a potentially untrue or one-sided versions of events.

The impact of denunciations varied. The ability to excommunicate, or having clergy who were willing to excommunicate on one's behalf, could undoubtedly be profitable. Rivals' reputations could be damaged. Sentences attacking individuals or causes could turn communities against people and their causes, and even provoke civil unrest. Yet publication of sentences that the faithful deemed self-serving or based on false or exaggerated accusations could backfire, bringing clergy who used them into disrepute. This affected not just the individuals and the particular dispute involved, but risked causing respect for the sanction in general to dwindle. Excommunication could publicize the fact that the church was not united, airing its dirty laundry in public. Nevertheless, this was evidently a risk worth taking, and there are cases where it appears that opinions and actions were affected by the content and promulgation of sentences of excommunication.

Audience

Canon law makes clear that excommunications had to be publicized. Gratian's *Decretum* stated that, following an excommunication ceremony, a letter containing the names of excommunicates and the cause of their sentences should be sent through the parishes.[9] Elsewhere, a canon emphasized that sentences should be announced in a public place ('in celebri loco') before the doors of churches, in both the excommunicate's own parish and nearby parishes.[10] These measures were required because the enforcement of excommunication depended upon communities, who were supposed to ostracize excommunicates. There was both a pastoral need to inform people, since excommunication was contagious and would cause those who communicated with an excommunicate to incur minor sentences, and a practical one, since ignorance was a legitimate excuse for associating with excommunicates. If people did not know whom they were supposed to shun, or even if publication was sufficiently limited that they could reasonably claim they were unaware of a sentence, excommunication might not

[9] C.11, q.3, c.106.   [10] C.11, q.3, c.20.

be enforced.[11] The secular penalty of outlawry, analogous to excommunication in some ways, similarly required proclamations to be made lest people could allege ignorance.[12] English ecclesiastical statutes frequently decreed that excommunicates be publicly denounced until they made satisfaction. The unusually full diocesan statutes of Exeter (1289) ordered parish priests to make the names of excommunicates, the causes of the sentences, and the authority by which they were bound, known to all. The denunciations were to be made with bells ringing and candles burning when 'a greater multitude of people is present in churches'.[13]

Practice confirms that the law's instructions regarding publication of excommunication were followed. Like public penance, excommunication required an audience.[14] Mandates ordering sentences to be published usually specified that denunciations should be made publicly and solemnly, during solemn mass, in the presence of clergy and people. Sentences could be pronounced relatively locally, or throughout the whole of Christendom, or anything in between (cities, archdeaconries, dioceses, provinces, kingdoms, or several kingdoms). Often promulgation depended upon the severity of the crime committed and the status of the excommunicate (a ruler's excommunication was inevitably relevant to more people than that of a peasant labourer).[15]

Publicity could also depend upon the anger of the excommunicator and the obstinacy of the excommunicate: increasing publication was a way of aggravating a sentence. Excommunications were customarily pronounced in church on Sundays and feast days, when attendance would be greater.[16] In 1294, the bishop of Carlisle ordered that silence should be established so that this great crowd would be able to hear and understand the sentence.[17] Nevertheless, excommunications could be pronounced outside the setting of the parish church, for instance 'through all the churches and schools' of Oxford.[18] Many mandates added that denunciations might be made 'wherever you consider it expedient', but there is usually no way of knowing where might have been so considered.[19] From

---

[11] Thomas Coleman, for instance, communicated with Matilda Wlnoch, claiming he was unaware of her status (as Matilda herself also claimed). He was able to purge himself with three compurgators. See Gransden, 'Some late thirteenth-century records', 67.

[12] Summerson, 'Structure of law enforcement', 318–19, 324; Dutour, 'L'élaboration', 144, 152.

[13] C&S, 1041. Cf. Lange, *Excommunication*, 64 n. 130, which describes the sheets of names that circulated in late thirteenth-century France, and Beaulande, *Malheur*, 49–50, on late medieval French registers of excommunicates.

[14] Mansfield, *Humiliation*, 130.

[15] Brett Whalen notes the necessity of publishing sentences, and remarks that in the case of Emperor Frederick II's excommunication, 'the "parish" constituted the entirety of Christendom', *Two Powers*, 25, 13.

[16] Attending mass on Sundays and feast days was expected but nonetheless not necessarily standard practice. See Tanner and Watson, 'Least of the laity', 408–10; Murray, 'Piety and impiety', 92–5; Rider, 'Lay religion', 336–7.

[17] *Reg. Halton*, i, 19. [18] *Reg. Epp. Pecham*, i, 169.

[19] Secular orders regarding proclamations could be similarly worded. See Dutour, 'L'élaboration', 145–6; Maddicott, 'Politics and people', 10.

chroniclers, we know that the general sentence attached to Magna Carta was published, in 1253, in secular courts and 'wherever people gathered'. Priests wielded hand bells so that they could properly enact the ritual.[20] Two years later, the same sentence was to be published 'in county, hundred and other public meetings and places, wherever there may be opportunity... distinctly and plainly' in both English and French. According to the Burton annals, this was done.[21] Robert the Bruce's excommunication (in 1318) was even to be fixed to cathedral doors. Rosalind Hill, however, judged this to be exceptional. Certainly there is little to indicate that this was common practice in the thirteenth century.[22]

Publication was intended to ensure that the faithful cooperated with the church by treating excommunicates appropriately, but publication itself required the cooperation of other clergy.[23] Once an excommunication was declared, mandates were sent out to appropriate priests, ordering them to announce it in their own churches. There were certainly instances when clergy were disobedient, negligent, or physically unable to carry out these orders.[24] Difficulties arose in contentious circumstances, when clergy were not necessarily on the same side as one another. It is likely that local clergy were sometimes less diligent than their superiors expected, perhaps publishing sentences less often than they were supposed to, or even not at all. Archdeacons were probably tasked with punishing negligent clergy, and unfortunately we do not have records for their activity in this period.[25] Absence of evidence proves nothing, but there is no reason to believe there was any significant issue here. It was common for bishops to request confirmation that their mandates had been carried out, and remarkably few repeat requests are recorded.[26] Véronique Beaulande similarly observes that clergy were sometimes

---

[20] *CM*, v, 500–1; *C&S*, 477.   [21] *Ann. Burton*, 320–2.
[22] Hill, 'Belief and practice', 137. In 1279, Magna Carta and lists of *ipso facto* sentences were ordered to be posted in churches (the king immediately caused the order to be revoked); it is not inconceivable that this was done for individual sentences. See Chapter 7 below and Hill, 'Magna Carta'. Earlier practice might also have included attaching announcements to church doors. See Keygnaert, 'Meaning of ecclesiastical exclusion', 771 and Allen, 'Earliest known list', 397.
[23] The same was true of interdicts, which equally required other clergy to publicize them and see that they were observed: Clarke, *Interdict*, 88.
[24] Some examples of clergy not announcing sentences as instructed can be found in *C&S*, 1151, 1192–6; *Cal. Pap. Reg.*, 124; *Reg. Epp. Pecham*, i, 367–9, 352, ii, 422–3. *Reg. Pontissara*, i, 17–18. See also Chapter 4 above, at 161–4.
[25] Cf. Statutes for London Archdeaconry, c. 22: *C&S*, 337. The constitution expected archdeacons to punish clergy who failed to publish general sentences. In 1270, the archdeacon of Canterbury confirmed he had excommunicated several men as instructed, a rare use of the verb form 'excommunicavi': *SCC*, 333.
[26] It was standard practice for mandates to request replies explaining how they had been executed. Such confirmations survive but are uncommon, probably because the clergy who requested confirmations did not bother to record those they received. Thus the archbishop of Canterbury ordered the monks of Great Malvern Priory to be denounced in 1283, asking for confirmation that his suffragans had executed the mandate (*Reg. Epp. Pecham*, ii, 568–70). The bishop of Winchester recorded his confirmatory reply, but the archbishop's own register does not document it (*Reg. Pontissara*, i, 268–70). Repeat requests are sometimes recorded when excommunicates continued to be contumacious (rather than because clergy had been negligent).

negligent or considered sentences unjust, refusing to publish them, but she also stresses that such cases are rare: clergy in later medieval France probably executed their duties appropriately.[27] There is reason to be optimistic about the quarterly publication of *ipso facto* sentences in this period.[28] Thus, unlike lay refusal to shun excommunicates, there does not seem to have been any endemic problem with clergy routinely neglecting or refusing to pronounce sentences.

Our main sources for dissemination of excommunications are, overwhelmingly, letters sent by popes and bishops ordering publication. If it cannot be confirmed that all such orders were carried out, there is little cause for pessimism. Occasionally bishops' letters mention that sentences had indeed been published throughout a certain area, for example when complaining that people continued to associate with those under the ban. Thus, despite having been denounced 'in every church of [the] deanery', the bishop of Hereford's tenants continued to have dealings with others.[29] Similarly, the prior of Great Malvern and various other monks of the priory did not capitulate, even though the archbishop of Canterbury had caused their excommunication to be announced 'in each and every church and in all solemn places in the diocese' of Worcester. The bishop of Winchester subsequently confirmed that he had fulfilled the mandate to publish this sentence in all solemn places and in 'every cathedral, conventual or collegiate [and] parish church' in his own diocese.[30] Other sources further confirm that sentences against individuals were extensively published, for instance, 'through every church in Leicester', 'through the whole county of Buckingham, in every deanery and public place', 'through every parish church in our province [of Canterbury]', or 'through every church in the realm'.[31] In this respect, the theory of excommunication was sometimes carried out more strictly than necessary. The average English parishioner was unlikely, for instance, to bump into Emperor Frederick II. They did not therefore *need* to be informed that Frederick had been excommunicated by Gregory IX in 1239, yet the pope ordered that the emperor be denounced throughout England. The required publications were apparently carried out by the legate Otto.[32] Frederick was of course a special case, but his experience was mirrored by many others, albeit on a smaller scale.

Narrative sources confirm that excommunications were not only pronounced far and wide, but that large crowds were sought to witness them. Ensuring an

---

[27] Beaulande, *Malheur*, 226–8. [28] See Chapter 7. [29] *Reg. Cantilupe*, 97–8.

[30] *Reg. Epp. Pecham*. ii, 568–71; *Reg. Pontissara*, i, 268–70. The prior's excommunication was recorded in the Annals of Worcester, which state that he had usurped the name of prior against justice: *Ann. Worcester*, 487.

[31] *SKB*, ii, 80–1 (king's bench records); *SCC*, 336 (Canterbury court records); *Gervase*, 176 (archiepiscopal letter preserved in a chronicle); *Coventry*, 265 (excommunicate's complaint). Some of these and further examples will be discussed during the course of this and the next chapter.

[32] *CM*, iii, 545, 568–73. Gregory's 1229 sentence had also been published in England: *CM*, iii, 145, 184–5; *Flores Historiarum*, ii, 192; *Ann. Tewkesbury*, 73; *Oxenedes*, 151, *Ann. Dunstable*, 111–12. Whalen, *Two Powers*, 25.

adequate audience was in any case the reason why the usual days for publication were those when church was better attended. But in some cases particular efforts were made to guarantee bigger audiences, such as when the 1253 Magna Carta sentence was published 'wherever people gathered'.[33] In 1238, the bishop of Winchester and the abbots of Evesham and Abingdon published a sentence (pronounced against those who had killed the legate Otto's cook and besieged the legate in Osney Abbey) 'with the clergy and people convoked, with great solemnity at St Frideswide's Oxford'.[34] The bishop of Salisbury selected the feasts of Pentecost and Holy Trinity in 1304 to have a sentence announced in Salisbury Cathedral 'when a greater multitude of people' would be present.[35] Clement IV wrote that he had confirmed the sentence pronounced against Simon de Montfort and other rebels while he was legate, in Perugia 'with a huge crowd of the faithful standing there'. He had earlier commanded the sentence to be published in France and elsewhere 'in a public place, with clergy and people convoked, publicly and solemnly with the clergy and people assisting'.[36] The excommunication of Llywelyn in 1231, immediately preceding Henry III's invasion of Wales, was pronounced in Oxford in the presence of the whole nobility of England, both clerical and lay.[37]

These examples are not necessarily representative. They were sentences involving political struggles; for this reason, there is greater evidence surrounding them than we have for excommunications in less high-profile cases. It is nevertheless possible that similar efforts were made more locally, on a smaller scale, when clergy were themselves involved and particularly when personally injured.[38] In such circumstances, excommunication was being used as a way to disseminate political material, specifically that which condemned individuals and their causes. Clergy generally exerted due diligence in promulgating excommunications as far as the law required, but it was easy to disseminate them further if there was something to gain.[39] Perhaps chroniclers would have made less of the struggle following the murder of Otto's cook if an excommunication had not been publicized, making the homicide a notorious event. Excommunication brought matters to the attention of a wider public. It should be included in discussions of other symbolic communications through which political messages were conveyed to the public.[40]

---

[33] *Ann. Burton*, 320–2.
[34] *Flores Historiarum*, ii, 224–5. For this clash see *C&S*, 260–1 and notes, and Vincent, *Peter des Roches*, 477; Weiler, *Kingship, Rebellion and Political Culture*, 135. The king also instructed the archdeacon and chancellor of the university to publicly denounce clerks who fled as a result of this incident: CPR, 1232–47, 226.
[35] *Reg. Gandavo*, i, 138–40. For this dispute following an archdeacon's deposition, see above, 167–8.
[36] *Foedera*, I.i.459; *Reg. Clement IV*, no. 122; Heidemann, no. 52.   [37] *CM*, iii, 202.
[38] Discussed in this chapter at 203–12 and in Chapter 6, esp. 240–2, 247–8.
[39] Similarly, interdicts might be enforced more strictly than canon law required: Clarke, *Interdict*, 207–8.
[40] Cases discussed in greater depth below provide further examples. Björn Weiler, in 'Symbolism and politics' and *Kingship, Rebellion and Political Culture* (esp. 105–50) has discussed medieval

Public Discords

In excommunication the church had a powerful publicity tool at its disposal, and its use in 1252 by Boniface of Savoy, archbishop of Canterbury, demonstrates how it could be exploited in personal disagreements. This example also, however, shows that such usages were not always in the interests of clergy who used them and were certainly not advantageous for the church as a whole. During a dispute over the priorship of St Thomas' Southwark, Boniface excommunicated one of the candidates nominated by the bishop-elect of Winchester, Aymer de Lusignan.[41] Following the procedure that contumacious excommunicates could be arrested after forty days, Aymer's nominee was arrested and imprisoned at Maidstone.[42] This arrest, however, was made violently. Men from Aymer's *familia* responded by committing numerous injuries in Maidstone and subsequently launching an attack on the archbishop's palace at Lambeth. There they looted the archbishop's possessions and abducted his official, Eustace of Lynn, who was taken to Farnham. Though Eustace was later freed, 'vilely and abjectly expelled', Boniface responded by excommunicating the perpetrators of these enormities. This excommunication is of much value for understanding how excommunication could be practiced in thirteenth-century England. Though the specifics of how this dispute fitted into the politics of court and exacerbated anti-foreign sentiments prevalent in England at this time do not concern us here, it is important to note that there was a good deal of personal animosity behind these events. 'The affair quickly escalated into a sharp political confrontation at Court between the Savoyard faction and the rising power of the Lusignans.'[43] Boniface was the queen's uncle, a Savoyard; Aymer was Henry III's half-brother, a Lusignan.

The events were described by Matthew Paris, who also preserved a copy of Boniface's letter to his suffragans in which the archbishop ordered his excommunication to be published. The fact that Paris had a copy of this mandate itself demonstrates that Boniface was intent upon having his sentence disseminated. Although some of Paris's narrative is likely to have been influenced by the contents of this letter, it is equally clear that he had additional information, some of it perhaps first-hand. Paris moved in political circles and was thus better informed than the vast majority of his contemporaries, as demonstrated by the documents to which he regularly had access (contained in the Book of Additions to his *Chronica Majora*). Nonetheless, if his account of this excommunication is

---

audience and the importance of symbolic communication for conveying political messages to the public. Leidulf Melve ('Even the very laymen') and D.W. Burton ('Politics, propaganda and public opinion') have both noted excommunication's value in this context.

[41] See Carpenter, *Henry III*, 560–1.
[42] For this procedure see Logan, *Excommunication and the Secular Arm*.
[43] Ridgeway, 'Ecclesiastical career of Aymer de Lusignan', 165–6; Carpenter, 'What happened in 1258?', 191–2. Carpenter, *Henry III*, 485–8, provides the background to Aymer's election.

correct, many others were well aware of these events. Paris's interest in this excommunication and its promulgation was probably generated by Boniface's strenuous efforts to spread its contents.

The archbishop took extraordinary steps to publicize his excommunication. According to Paris's narrative, the archbishop himself pronounced the sentence 'in the presence of innumerable people'. This great crowd had been called to the church of St Mary le Bow by a crier ('voce preconia') advertising thirty days' remission of sins granted to those coming to witness the excommunication.[44] Nicholas Vincent's slightly facetious remark that an indulgence was here being used as 'an early form of rent-a-crowd' perhaps understates the gravity with which the archbishop was treating the matter.[45] Boniface was using all methods at his disposal to ensure a large audience for his striking denunciation of these attackers in order to influence the communal perception of events. Adorned with pontifical robes, the archbishop pronounced the sentence, along with the bishops of Hereford and Chichester, 'excessively menacingly and solemnly'.[46] Subsequently, Boniface went to Oxford to publish the sentence, again personally, 'in the presence of all the clerks, whom he had caused to be gathered for this by ringing the common bell'.[47] Paris explained that the archbishop had gone to Oxford so that the scholars there, who were from all over the world, would spread news of the crime to diverse nations.[48] There are, as yet, no other examples of either indulgences or bells being used to gather people to witness excommunications, nor of using a university's international connections, though it is possible that such measures were employed elsewhere. Boniface's final measure—sending a letter to his suffragans telling them personally to publish the sentence in their cathedrals and to have it published throughout their dioceses, with bells ringing and candles burning, every Sunday and feast day—was entirely commonplace.[49] Paris's account thus indicates that Boniface's sentence, both as pronounced by the archbishop himself (a striking, indeed fear-inspiring, spectacle), and as published by his subordinates, was heard by a great many people.

The narrative condemning the acts of excommunicates contained within sentences provided an opportunity to convince the audience of how reprehensible an excommunicate was, and to impress upon them the severity of the crime committed. Boniface's own letter contains the words that were likely used to denounce the men who had committed this crime. These demonstrate the vehement language often used in sentences, further making them an effective means of

---

[44] *CM*, v, 351.
[45] Vincent, 'Some pardoners' tales', 38 and n. 57. Like excommunication, indulgences' effectiveness depended upon them being widely publicized.
[46] 'horribiliter nimis et sollempniter'.
[47] The town bell was used to summon town assemblies: Reynolds, *Kingdoms and Communities*, 188.
[48] *CM*, v, 353-4.
[49] *CM*, vi, 222-4. Paris records that the bishop of Ely sent this letter to his archdeacon, so it was enforced by at least one bishop.

spreading a particular narrative. Boniface described the 'great enormities' of Aymer's men. They were 'sons of Belial' who, 'with horses and arms in a spirit of fury' had laid sacrilegious hands on Eustace of Lynn and others, 'violently tearing them from the horn of the altar to which they had fled, in insult to God, ignominy of the clerical order, and contempt and disgrace of us and our church, and also of the whole of England'. They carried Eustace off, forcing him to walk through the mud, beating and striking the other captives. These enormities had been perpetrated not just against the church of Canterbury but against the universal church. The malefactors were declared to have incurred *Si quis suadente, Qui malitiose ecclesias,* and had disturbed the peace, 'having disregarded fear of God and cast aside reverence for the prince'. They were denounced by authority of the Father, Son and Holy Spirit, blessed Mary mother of God, the holy martyr Thomas, St Edmund the Confessor (*sic*), and all saints. All of this would, of course, have been followed by the ceremony described in Chapter 1. The fourteen named men ('and many others of whose names we are ignorant') were thus publicly denounced in a rhetorical and visually arresting ceremony. Years later, Paris claimed that the baronial embassy to Rome in 1258 noted the excommunication's promulgation throughout the whole province of Canterbury and in the presence of all Oxford, remarking that everyone who heard about the attack on the cook was dumbfounded.[50]

Boniface's attempts to further his agenda against Aymer, using excommunication as a means to broadcast his own narrative, did not necessarily cast the archbishop himself in a good light. Paris reported that neither party in the matter came off well—some people favoured neither party and both the Savoyard and Lusignan factions were defamed. Boniface did not, it seems, successfully convince everyone that Aymer and his men were out-and-out villains. This is another case in which excommunication was devalued by being used by both sides in a dispute. Aymer was forced to counter the bad publicity he was receiving by ordering the dean of Southwark and others to announce publicly that the archbishop's sentence was null, 'rather, inane and frivolous'.

Thus the people of Southwark and potentially further afield were receiving contrary information, and could use their knowledge to pick a side. Excommunication sowed divisions as it provoked discussion in the public sphere. These political factions were vying in public, with excommunication providing a chief means through which their clash played out. Nonetheless, it is interesting that, although fault was found with both parties, Paris claimed that the Poitevins (Aymer's faction) were more widely condemned. Paris himself of course had a copy of the sentence, and it is therefore unsurprising that his description of the attack on Eustace of Lynn resembles that in the excommunication (though it is certainly not

---

[50] *CM*, vi, 405–6. They sought to show the justness of their grievances against Aymer de Lusignan.

identical).⁵¹ Six years later, jurors in the Hundred of Brixton remembered the event in detail, attributing the attack to three men who were the first (of fourteen) named in Boniface's excommunication. The jurors provide other details, not least the names of those attacked not included in the 1252 excommunication.⁵² The attack was serious and public—the archbishop himself noted that it had happened in sight of the people ('in conspectu populi')—and was certainly not well known only through the archbishop's sentence.⁵³ Yet the vehement public denunciations would no doubt have increased the event's notoriety and cemented it in the consciousness of the locals. Boniface's use of public excommunication as a sort of propaganda may be judged effective if others also absorbed that narrative and consequently turned against the Poitevins.

The archbishop had an advantage because he had the means to have his side of the story broadcast—using every trick he had up his sleeve. Ensuring people heard material did not necessarily mean, as Björn Weiler has pointed out, that they would believe whatever they were told. Ian Forrest has similarly emphasized the importance of audience reception in generating meaning—a message's meaning was created by its reception as well as by its distribution. Nevertheless, whether they rejected or opposed an official narrative, such excommunications created the potential for public debate.⁵⁴ Excommunication used in this way was neither new nor rare. As Leidulf Melve has demonstrated, during the Investiture Contest the sentence against Emperor Henry IV was read out in the localities and became a topic of public discussion.⁵⁵ Excommunications were designed to influence wide audiences and contained rhetoric that was designed to be persuasive, or perhaps divisive. They might provoke sympathy with the church or have the opposite effect, but understanding the public aspect of the sanction is fundamental to understanding its importance and its consequences.⁵⁶

Fulmination

It is worth briefly citing various other examples to demonstrate how forcefully excommunications could decry the acts that had provoked them. Boniface's sentence contains features that occur again and again. Excommunicates were frequently called sons of Belial. They were limbs of the devil, sons of iniquity,

---

⁵¹ *CM*, v, 349–52.   ⁵² *1258–9 Special Eyre*, ed. Hershey, no. 163; Carpenter, *Henry III*, 561.
⁵³ *CM*, vi, 224.
⁵⁴ Forrest, *Trustworthy Men*, 345–6; Weiler, 'Symbolism and politics', 18, discussing royal proclamations; Melve, 'Even the very laymen', 26–31.
⁵⁵ Melve, 'Even the very laymen', 36–7.
⁵⁶ See also Whalen on the papal excommunications of Frederick II and attempts to spread accusations across Christendom: *Two Powers*, 25–7, 174, and elsewhere throughout the book.

wicked degenerates, and angels or satellites of Satan.[57] Fear of God was thrown aside, salvation forgotten, and acts committed in contempt of the church and of God, and to the scandal of many. More specifically, narratives often described crimes in graphic detail, presumably in an effort to arouse the anger, outrage, and disgust of those listening. Thus in 1273, certain clerics were 'atrociously wounded, flogged and hurled to the ground', blood was spilled in church, priestly garments were defiled and the priests' horses were mutilated, having their ears and lips cut off, and injured 'so as to lay bare the bone'.[58] In 1295, Archbishop Winchelsey excommunicated the Welsh, describing (amongst many other crimes) how they had committed massacres of the English, discriminating neither by age nor sex, leaving bodies unburied to rot, exposed to be torn to pieces by birds and reptiles.[59] Elsewhere, the rectors of Saltwood and Cheriton were 'notoriously', 'shamelessly' and 'inhumanely' assaulted before a great crowd at Dover. Archbishop Winchelsey could not leave unpunished 'an offence to God so horrendous and pernicious'.[60] Many more examples, using similar language, could be cited.

Some of these offences were undoubtedly horrific, but they may not have been as bad as the excommunications claimed. Denunciations sought to manipulate perceptions of events and people. In Giuliani Milani's words, 'they were able to change the reality they were representing'.[61] Sometimes stronger language was used to describe crimes whose perpetrators were unknown. These sentences urged people who had any information about the crime to come forward; descriptions were vivid to persuade people that the malefactors deserved to be punished.[62] Such condemnations were not limited to violent crimes (though these were the most strongly worded): the Welsh were often described as treacherous, for instance. There is, however, a definite trend towards strong language being used when the church or its property had been injured. In 1308, certain 'sons of iniquity', 'haters of ecclesiastical privilege', deserved to have their 'detestable audacity' and 'nefarious presumption' remedied. They had, 'forgetful of their salvation', in their 'savage cupidity' through 'too great malice and temerity', had the nerve to uproot some trees belonging to the church of Canterbury.[63] In 1283, Pecham excommunicated the sacristan of Westminster because, 'transformed into an angel of Satan', he had

---

[57] It is sometimes possible to detect a preference for turns of phrase by certain bishops (Winchelsey was fond of 'degenerate' for instance). Sentences often use one or more of these phrases to describe malefactors.

[58] *Reg. Bronescombe*, no. 1429; Miller, 'Knights, bishops and deer parks', 211–14.

[59] *Reg. Winchelsey*, i, 1–3.   [60] *Reg. Winchelsey*, i, 222–3; Graham, 'An interdict on Dover'.

[61] Milani, 'Ban and the bag', 119. He is discussing defamatory paintings.

[62] It is often assumed that sentences pronounced generally against unknown persons were futile, but they could prompt successful investigations into names. See Hill, 'General excommunications'.

[63] *Reg. Winchelsey*, ii, 1090–1. This incident was deemed so important that notes were written in the margin declaring 'Vide litteram istam' and 'nota bene contra abscindentes arbores etc.'. The culprits were unknown in this case. Cf. *Reg. Swinfield*, 407–8 for a similar incident described in much the same language.

committed a 'horrendous crime' when he 'rashly and violently threw a great and hard scroll in our face'.[64]

Vehement denunciations might have caused the audience to feel the desired outrage but could equally have been considered excessively melodramatic in some cases. They perhaps produced eye-rolls or shrugs amongst audience members who had heard rather too many condemned as 'sons of Belial'. On the other hand, episcopal registers demonstrate that there was much diversity in the acerbity of the language used. While many examples of harsh language survive, such excommunications would not have been a weekly spectacle. In particular, it is important that the severest language was used when perpetrators were not yet known; individuals were not typically subject to the same vitriol.[65] This, in combination with the fact that variation was possible in how widely sentences were published, for how long, and in the bombast of their language and ritual, meant that communities were not necessarily excessively over saturated with such hyperbole.[66] If the most dramatic excommunications were reserved for special cases, they could retain their impact on the audience when an especially contentious event had taken place. Responses varied, but the potential for generating public attention was undiminished.

In so far as they were trying to manipulate public opinion, excommunications were propaganda. Both churchmen and laymen sought to capitalize on the sanction's public nature. Rhetorical sentences were an effective means of disseminating information, whether this was simply in order to rebuke sinful Christians who needed to be corrected, or because they wished to discredit their rivals or punish their enemies. For although there were rules governing how and why a sentence should be issued, how it should be enforced and publicized was not subject to the same regulation.[67] It was therefore up to a cleric to decide what words to use to rebuke sinners, and whether a sentence should be pronounced merely for three Sundays and feast days in excommunicates' own parishes and a few nearby parishes, or instead throughout an archdeaconry, diocese, country, or even more widely, for a much longer period of time.[68] The sanction was a powerful force that could be exploited, but also abused.

The idea that excommunication could be intended primarily to influence public opinion rather than to change the behaviour of excommunicates is particularly clear when whole realms or territories were sentenced during military campaigns. Thus those who excommunicated the Welsh, the Scots, and the French are unlikely to have seriously believed that they would alter the conduct of these

---

[64] *Reg. Epp. Pecham*, ii, 617–18.
[65] Chapter 6, 247–8, provides an example of softened language after names had been discovered.
[66] Cf. Chapter 1, 45, on the excommunication ceremony.
[67] I am grateful to John Hudson for helping me clarify this point.
[68] Cf. Dutour, 'L'élaboration', 147–8, who makes a similar point about secular material. How it was publicized depended on the subject matter and its importance.

nations. Instead, they sought to increase support for campaigns against them by publicizing their evil misdeeds and their separation from the Christian faithful. Such sentences were probably aimed more at the English than the excommunicates. Edward I in particular seems to have utilized excommunication's value here. He sought the church's support, asking that his campaigns against the Welsh and the Scots be aided with public prayers and excommunications against his enemies.[69] He set out to conquer Wales in 1276, completing the venture in 1283.[70] In the intervening years, the English bishops pronounced several sentences against the Welsh.[71] Edward asked, for instance, in 1282, that the Welsh be denounced through every diocese because they had incurred the sanctions of the 1222 sentence *Qui pacem et tranquillitatem*.[72] The faithful of every diocese in the realm were informed that the Welsh were getting no more than they deserved. When John Comyn was murdered in 1306, the papal excommunication of the assassins (that is, Robert the Bruce) was publicized through England and Scotland, Ireland, and Wales. The Lanercost chronicle confirms that the sentence was 'denounced for a long time throughout all England', especially in the north.[73] In these conflicts, the king was therefore attempting to harness the powerful ecclesiastical tools of excommunication and public prayer to inspire hatred for the Welsh and Scots amongst his own subjects. The mediums were ideal for the dissemination of polemical accusations and attacks, having potentially long-lasting consequences for attitudes towards, in particular, the Scots.[74]

Reputation, Defamation, and Denunciations

As a result of the publicity and vehemence given to excommunication sentences, those receiving such treatment could feel victimized. In some extreme circumstances that was precisely what was happening, but even in routine cases an individual was condemned and their crimes described before all their friends and neighbours. Certainly, many sentences contained in episcopal registers

---

[69] Excommunications had also been pronounced against the Welsh in the reign of Henry III. For public prayers, see Burton, 'Requests for prayers'; Barrow, 'Clergy in English dioceses', 22. *Reg. Gandavo*, i, 9-10 includes a nice example of prayers for Edward's 1297/8 Scottish campaign, describing the massacres, rapes, arson, and so on that the Scots had purportedly committed.

[70] For Edward's Welsh campaign, see Prestwich, *Edward I*, 170-232; Prestwich, *War, Politics and Finance*.

[71] *C&S*, 821-2; *Foedera*, I.ii.536-7, 541; *Willelmi Rishanger Chronica*, ed. Riley, 99; *Wykes*, 290; *Reg. Epp. Pecham*, i, 324, 352, 403, 422-3. Cf. sentences in 1295 following a revolt in 1294-5 (see *Reg. Winchelsey*, 1-3), which were to be pronounced in Wales, presumably in order to remove support for the rebellion. Burton, 'Politics, propaganda and public opinion', 380-4. Cf. the Scottish campaign and excommunication used in a similar way: ibid. 386-7.

[72] *Foedera*, I.ii.603; *Reg. G. Giffard*, 150; *Guisborough*, 218-19.

[73] *Foedera*, I.ii.987; *Lanercost*, 206.

[74] Ian Forrest discusses later medieval attitudes towards the Scots in England, which started in the 1290s: *Trustworthy Men*, 79-81.

were gentler than those just described, but they were nonetheless a categorical denunciation of the excommunicates, who were decreed to be no longer part of the Christian community.[75] As we have seen in Chapter 4, many excommunications failed to convince sufficient people that they should ostracize excommunicates. Yet in a society where reputation was of the utmost importance, such public rejection could only be damaging.[76] From the church's perspective this was 'good defamation' which was intended to affect social opinion, creating public pressure through which recalcitrant sinners might be persuaded to change their behaviour.[77] Véronique Beaulande, similarly observing that public denunciations injured excommunicates' honour, provides an example of a man who hit the priest about to denounce him, saying that he was lying.[78] For an excommunicate, denunciation was often the most harmful aspect of a sentence, and could be deemed by both victims and communities to be unjust or excessive.

The 'bad press' with which public excommunicates had to contend affected those who believed their sentences to be unjust even more than those who recognized that they deserved their sentences. This point was articulated by Guillaume de Nogaret, a leading minister of the French king Philip the Fair (1285–1314), who, for his attacks upon the papal court, was excommunicated for seven years. Nogaret understood what was at stake. A man must look after his reputation; conscience might excuse an innocent person before God, but that was of little use amongst men on earth. Even if one believed that God would not uphold a sentence, scandal had to be avoided.[79] Similarly, a late fifteenth-century man denied that excommunication posed any danger to the soul but admitted the shame it provoked amongst people.[80] There is no evidence of a refusal to believe in the effects of excommunication upon the soul in thirteenth-century England except in unjust cases. Nonetheless, these examples show that the public aspect of excommunication was troubling even if individuals believed their soul was not endangered.[81] The rector of St Mary's, Marlborough, was aggrieved about the damage his reputation was suffering as a result of an excommunication denounced throughout the town. The accusation of incontinence, he alleged, was made by his enemies. Through the unjust sentence, which was

---

[75] See Forrest on the importance of reputation: *Trustworthy Men*, 77–83.
[76] Although, as Mansfield has indicated, some would undoubtedly suffer from public shame more than others. Merchants were particularly vulnerable to public opinion: *Humiliation*, 74, 254.
[77] Forrest, 'Defamation', 148–58; Lemeneva, 'Do not scandalize thy brother', 27.
[78] Beaulande, *Malheur*, 253, and more generally 251–8.
[79] Brown, 'Moral imperatives and conundrums of conscience', 23, 34.
[80] Beaulande, 'Contester l'excommunication', 260.
[81] Bartholomew Cotton claimed (adding to Matthew Paris's contemporary account) that the monks of Winchester were vexed by Aymer de Lusignan in 1255, who 'monachos...diffamando excommunicavit'—defamation and excommunication are here again inextricably linked. *Cotton*, 132.

suspended on his appeal because he was refused a copy, this defamatory charge was broadcast through his locality.[82]

Evidence suggests that many excommunicates felt more aggrieved about this publicity than about any of the other consequences of excommunication. The negative publicity associated with the censure was an important part of its ability to induce people to return to the church. Shame was integral to excommunication. Those who sought absolution from ostensibly secret excommunications because their consciences compelled them (as discussed in Chapter 2) may in addition have been worried about gossip and rumours that they had incurred a sentence and thus wished to have their names cleared. But they were not forced to deal with the public announcements of their statuses, undeniably the route through which reputations were generally damaged by excommunication.

The importance of publicity as a separate issue to any spiritual consequences is shown by the concern people expressed about being excommunicated 'by name'. This, of course, made no difference to the spiritual effects of the sentence, but it did ensure that everyone knew that a particular individual had been condemned.[83] The importance of sentencing people by name is demonstrated by Wendover's report of the excommunication of the rebellious barons in 1215: 'But the magnates, because none of them had been expressed by name in the pope's decree, not observing the said sentence, considered it invalid and null'.[84] Later, Innocent did sentence the barons by name.[85] Excommunication *nominatim* could thus be used as a way of aggravating a sentence.[86] We still use the phrase 'to name and shame', and it is obvious that a sentence pronounced generally would be less effective than one in which the perpetrator's name was publicized. This is one reason why *latae sententiae* have often been dismissed by historians as ineffective, but, as will be shown in Chapter 6, general sentences did have some advantages. Nevertheless, Langton's refusal to excommunicate the barons publicly, only doing so privately, demonstrates the importance of the public nature of excommunication. He was worried not for the barons' souls, but for their reputations and for the effect such bad publicity might have upon their cause.

In situations where increased publication of excommunications was a means of aggravating sentences, publicity was no longer primarily about ensuring that an excommunicate was shunned. It was instead an effort to bring the

---

[82] *Reg. Gandavo*, i, 189–91. Failing to provide a copy infringed Lyon I, c. 21. See also Chapter 6, 249–50.

[83] Robert of Flamborough had an interestingly broad definition of *nominatim*. He considered both 'I excommunicate Peter' and 'I excommunicate whoever stole that horse', if Peter had stolen it, to be excommunication by name: Flamborough, *Liber Poenitentialis*, 154.

[84] *CM*, ii, 630.   [85] *SLI*, no. 85.

[86] The king of Scotland's counsellors were similarly sentenced generally in 1257, and threatened with excommunication by name if they remained contumacious (this eventuality happened): *Melrose*, 182–3. Wendover claimed that John had been concerned, in 1208, that Innocent III would aggravate the interdict by excommunicating the king by name: *CM*, ii, 523.

excommunicate's name into disrepute, to force them to capitulate. The publicity of excommunication could be exploited for vengeful purposes. Rather than merely following the law, clerics sought to defame and harass their opponents, though of course official pronouncements might not be accepted by audiences.[87] Exploiting the public nature of excommunication in this way resembles uses of public penance found by Mary Mansfield. She noted a particularly elaborate penance performed in a dispute in Reims, observing that it was so extensive because the canons 'wanted the humiliation of their enemies publicized' across a vast swathe of France.[88] Though similar use of excommunication was not, of course, an expressly stated motive, it is one implied by contemporary accounts. Like Mansfield's Reims case, the political and social context often dictated how widely an excommunication was publicized.

In 1257, Pope Alexander IV ordered the archbishop of York, Sewal de Bovill, to be 'excessively ignominiously' excommunicated throughout England. This was, according to Matthew Paris, an aggravation of his sentence, intended 'to weaken his resolve'.[89] The archbishop was not perturbed by this 'papal tyranny', however, believing his sentence to be unjust. He was, nevertheless, apparently greatly troubled by his treatment. In the (presumably fabricated) speech attributed to the archbishop by Paris, Sewal is made to declare that the pope had unjustly attacked him and slandered ('scandalizavit') him in many ways. Paris went on to describe the archbishop's letter to the pope, which listed the ways in which he had been injured. Innocent IV had harassed him by suspending him, banishing him from church, taking his cross from him, horribly and openly excommunicating him through the realm, and by 'denigrating his reputation in diverse ways, not without great temporal injury'.

Sewal was the hero in this story, which fits perfectly into Paris's strongly anti-papal narrative. Sewal's excommunication was the result of resisting a papal provision to his diocese, a practice to which Paris vigorously objected. Because of his strong belief in the justness of his cause, and influenced by Becket and St Edmund, Sewal did not succumb to such pressure. He reportedly appealed against the pope before the 'supreme and incorruptible Judge'.[90] In this case, it was imminent fear of death rather than reputation which forced Sewal's capitulation.[91] Here again, this publicity did not cause support for the excommunication. In the *Chronica Majora*'s narrative, the people of England were as opposed to the pope as Paris himself was.[92] Those tasked with publicizing the sentence through the kingdom apparently did so unwillingly. Even if part of Paris's aim here was to malign the pope, both for the unjustness of his sentence and for the

---

[87] Forrest, *Trustworthy Men*, 340.   [88] Mansfield, *Humiliation*, 269–77, quotation 275.
[89] *CM*, v, 653: 'jussitque eum ignominiose nimis in tota Anglia excommunicari...ut tali terrore ac tanto suam constantiam enervaret'.
[90] *CM*, v, 692, 653.   [91] See Chapter 2, 65–6.   [92] *CM*, v, 653. And see above, 168–9.

unreasonable way he enforced it, it is significant that Paris did so by emphasizing the effects of the sentence's publicity. Sewal is reported to have suffered considerably as a result of his excommunication, and it is clear that no small part of this injury was public defamation. Moreover, if Paris was exaggerating the actions of the pope he nevertheless did so by alleging a misuse of excommunication that was recognizable.

The same chronicler's comparable presentation of the treatment suffered by Frederick II is confirmed (and was perhaps influenced) by the emperor's own complaints. Paris wrote that Gregory IX caused the emperor to be excommunicated in many regions, scandalized him as much as he could, and 'unceasingly denigrated his name and reputation'. Nothing, the chronicler noted, was more damaging than that.[93] The *Flores Historiarum* even assert that when Frederick was excommunicated for the final time, and deposed in 1245, Innocent IV caused it to be published through England and France 'so that the infamy of his name would stink more through Christendom'.[94] In 1238, Frederick wrote to his brother-in-law, Henry III of England, to express his anger that the king had allowed the unjust sentence against him to be published in his kingdom. Frederick wrote that the sentence brought injury, shame, and damage to his empire.[95] To the English barons, he wrote that the pope had acted with 'carnal hatred', and the sentence, which was published through the whole kingdom of England, contained defamation of his name and honour.[96] Clearly, Frederick had far more to be concerned about in relation to his excommunication, particularly in his own lands. In England, however, there was less at stake, though one serious cause for alarm was that money was being collected by the papacy for use against Frederick. Part of the role of excommunication denunciations was presumably to aid this money-raising effort.[97] Both pope and emperor were taking part in what T. C. Van Cleve termed a 'war of propaganda'. These sentences were one of the cannons in the papacy's arsenal in this 'war'. Frederick was forced to counter the pope's slanders, writing in his own defence that the pope was fickle, volatile, a father of mendacity, a wolf in sheep's clothing, a so-called vicar of Christ, a schism-stirrer, and a friend of dissension.[98]

An equally prejudiced but informative account is provided by the rebellious baron Falkes de Bréauté, who wrote a complaint to Honorius III about his treatment at the hands of various enemies, particularly Stephen Langton. This

[93] *CM*, iv, 122. See also Whalen, *Two Powers*, 33, on publicity attached to earlier excommunication.
[94] *Flores Historiarum*, ii, 286.   [95] *Foedera*, I.i.237.   [96] *Foedera*, I.i.237–8.
[97] To the barons, Frederick wrote that allowing his sentence to be published before the king and through the kingdom was unacceptable, but that it was even worse that money had been raised there for use against him.
[98] *Foedera*, I.i.238; *CM*, iii, 582, 585; Van Cleve, *Immutator Mundi*, 429. For further discussion of the propaganda of both the papacy and Frederick, see Van Cleve, *Immutator Mundi*, 199–201, 428–38; Morris, *Papal Monarchy*, 564–5. Whalen, in *Two Powers*, discusses the propaganda war repeatedly, but see particularly 104–8.

Querimonia should not be taken as an accurate representation of events, but it is an invaluable account of Falkes's own view of his excommunication (incurred for his rebellion and detention of castles during Henry III's minority). Towards the end of his complaint, Falkes explained that the sentence against him was unjust, had been issued contrary to law, and arose from hatred rather than desire for justice.[99] As a result of this unjust sentence and through the bishop's hatred, he complained, he had suffered many injuries, including being stained with 'serious infamy', and becoming notorious ('clarueram') amongst his neighbours. He had been deprived of his wife and family, and finally suffered exile.[100] Earlier in his complaint, Falkes observed that the bishops had promulgated a sentence against him 'to show affection' for the king. This sentence had been published 'through every church in the realm' within a week, with indulgences offered to those who provided help towards the capture of Bedford.[101] These wrongs cannot all be ascribed to the bishops' excommunication, for secular involvement also played a part. But if they were the result of the sentence, as Falkes implied, his was a highly unusual case: most people who were excommunicated would not be in a position to suffer such losses, and those who were would not expect to be so gravely persecuted. But that was Falkes's point. The bishops had behaved reprehensibly, causing him to suffer unduly. Falkes was not alone in feeling that his excommunication had slandered his name.

Scandal

Falkes's complaint introduces another important aspect of excommunication: scandal. It is a word often associated with excommunication, but it permits various interpretations.[102] It is most commonly found in relation to excommunication in sentences themselves, which responded to scandals. Scandal was understood in theology and canon law as something that led others to sin.[103] Anything that damaged the authority of the church or of clergymen might cause the laity to lose respect for it. Walter Giffard, for instance, threatened to excommunicate a parishioner, Robert de Balliol, because he had mendaciously been 'disparaging . . . our name and reputation . . . in offence to God and our church and also scandal of the common people'.[104] The archbishop of York's personal reputation had implications for the church as an institution: someone slandering the archbishop in

---

[99] For Falkes's treatment and an analysis of his claims in what follows, see Carpenter, *Minority*, 351–5, 360–70.
[100] *Coventry*, 272.   [101] *Coventry*, 265.
[102] Jaritz, 'Varieties of *scandalum*', discusses the various meanings of the word in the Middle Ages. See also Lecuppre, 'Le scandale', esp. 187. Fossier, *Bureau de âmes*, 467–501, discusses scandal at length.
[103] Helmholz, 'Scandalum in the medieval canon law', 260.   [104] *Reg. W. Giffard*, 299–300.

public needed to be corrected in public, even if the archbishop himself, as he claimed, was not personally worried. Public sins were more likely to be scandalous, since they were openly visible to others and might set a bad example. They thus required public censure, and, as a public punishment, excommunication was the natural choice. Conversely, excommunication for a sin committed in private might well be the wrong choice, since it would unnecessarily publicize a sin, potentially itself causing scandal by inciting others to sin. Whichever was the best course to avoid endangering souls was the right one.[105]

Though it was usually a response to scandal, excommunication could also cause scandal. In the cases of Falkes, Frederick II, and Sewal de Bovill, one part of the word's use appears to equate roughly with slander.[106] Though Falkes appealed his sentence, he had earlier sought absolution, having been told by the archbishop of Canterbury and the bishop of Chester that it would be 'a fitting opportunity to avoid scandal'. Their words were, apparently, fraudulent, for when Falkes went to Northampton as instructed, he was unable to obtain absolution.[107] Certainly, all three as well as Guillaume de Nogaret seem primarily to have been referring to their reputations when they used the word. Scandal arising from their sentences was the public vilification they received.

However, clergy could bring the church into disrepute by their misconduct. That is, when excommunications were considered unjust, as they were by Falkes, Frederick, and Sewal, there is an implication that they were themselves scandalous. Clerical misconduct in such a public way *ipso facto* brought the church into disrepute, thereby inciting disrespect and ultimately provoking sin.[108] People could be corrupted by those who were supposed to behave unimpeachably; anticlericalism or even heresy was a dangerous consequence of scandalous clerical conduct.[109] This was the sort of scandal caused when excommunication was used for trivial matters, as Martin Luther was later to condemn.[110] Both Falkes and the Canterbury monks, discussed below at 206–212, claimed that the actions of the archbishops of Canterbury (Langton and Edmund of Abingdon respectively) had disgraced the church of Canterbury.[111] Scandal was generated when the archbishop and the dean of St Paul's both used excommunication at cross purposes, claiming papal authority. This caused the whole matter to be judged ridiculous by the laity. Matthew Paris described this affair as a 'scandal' three times, the first

---

[105] Bryan, 'Scandale is heaved sunne', 75–9; Lemeneva, 'Do not scandalize thy brother', 27 and *passim*; Helmholz, 'Scandalum in the medieval canon law', 262–3, 266–8; Mansfield, *Humiliation*, ch. 2.
[106] Cf. Bryan, 'From stumbling block to deadly sin', 15–16; Helmholz, 'Scandalum in the medieval canon law', 270–1.
[107] *Coventry*, 267. [108] Bryan, '*Periculum animarum*'; Nemo-Pekelman, 'Scandale et vérité'.
[109] Fossier, *Bureau de âmes*, 475–9; Forrest, *Trustworthy Men*, 340.
[110] See Beaulande, *Malheur*, ch. 7 and 262; cf. Helmholz, 'Excommunication in twelfth century England', 243.
[111] *Coventry*, 268–9; *Gervase*, 166 (see below).

time calling the scandal 'shameful' and the last time 'manifold'.[112] Thus it was not only individual reputations that were slandered by the conspicuousness of excommunication; instead a widespread scandal that harmed the church itself might be created by it.[113]

Cases in which clergy were contending with one another, both making use of ecclesiastical sanctions, publicly aired disputes between churchmen. They were dangerous because they weakened the value of excommunication by undermining the objective unity of the church. Such simultaneous sentences could hardly be just and were often mutually exclusive; thus they allowed people to reason that their own sentences might be unjust. In 1275, Thomas Cantilupe, the newly elected bishop of Hereford, was forced to reprimand his subordinates for the 'enormous quarrels', 'many scandals', and 'manifold contentions' that were then taking place.[114] Two rival claimants to the deanery were the cause of these quarrels, which were in danger of causing sin. Both were acting as dean, excommunicating and suspending people (or rather 'confounding everything with confusion'), and each had appointed his own sub-dean. Great danger of souls resulted from this, 'and ever greater and greater cause for offending will be given to malefactors'. A second letter, sent a month later, made excommunication's significance even clearer. Its misuse was far from the contenders' only crime, for they were also 'moving arms' against one another. But again it should be emphasized that the public nature of excommunication is crucial. Cantilupe observed that, although they had been warned, the rival claimants

> nevertheless, daily accumulating evils upon evils, hurl ever greater and greater scandal at the people and clergy, while one of them excommunicates the supporters of the other, and vice versa... From which it happens that the authority of the church is vilified, and [the authority] of a priest is cared about no more than that of a jester (*scurra*). And it can probably be feared that in that city, within a short time, many will become as heretics, in which city there were previously good and stable Christians.... You [the chapter of Hereford] should warn them... to desist from excommunications, violent attacks, and other mutual injuries, from which scandals arise...[115]

The scandal here was generated not only by the squabbling and mutual sentences, but by the fact that it was all happening in a very public manner.[116] This created

---

[112] *CM*, v, 217–18, 229 ('turpe scandalum', 'scandalum exortum est' (rubric), 'pro scandalo multiplici jam per archiepiscopum exorto'). See also above, 170.
[113] Scandal could not exist without publicity: Leveleux-Teixeira, 'Le droit canonique médiéval et l'horreur du scandale', 201. Cf. Clarke, *Interdict*, 195, on the scandal of publicly disobeyed interdicts.
[114] *Reg. Cantilupe*, 2–3.
[115] *Reg. Cantilupe*, 4. For the background to all this see *Reg. Cantilupe*, xxii–xxiii.
[116] Helmholz, 'Scandalum in the medieval canon law': 'Discord and public debate among the people was then considered a serious wrong. Causing it was a criminal offence' (260).

the danger that the faithful would learn from their 'bad examples'; Cantilupe was obliged to protect those under his care by bringing the matter to a close.

The Monks of Christ Church versus Edmund of Abingdon

The dispute in the late 1230s between Edmund of Abingdon, archbishop of Canterbury, and the monks of Christ Church, Canterbury, is a final example of how the publicity of sentences could be exploited and result in considerable scandal. Like the actions of the rival deans in Hereford, the implication is that use of excommunication in this situation was making the church look bad (though it was here only used by the archbishop[117]). The main source for this dispute is highly prejudiced, written in the first person by a monk from Christ Church. It is of all the more interest for that reason. There was a great deal of personal acrimony on both sides, which contributed considerably to how the dispute played out, and to how excommunication was enforced.

The quarrel, supposedly, began with the foolish decision of the monks to rewrite a 'charter of St Thomas the martyr' containing the liberties of Canterbury, whose seal had been damaged: the so-called 'Magna Carta Beati Thome', a notorious forgery. It was subsequently diverted to their election of a new prior without the archbishop's permission (after the prior at the time of the forgery had resigned, and the sub-prior had been deposed).[118] The forgery caused the monks to be suspended; the election was the cause of their excommunication. However, as C. H. Lawrence (Edmund's modern biographer) has written, this was 'a purely personal squabble' greatly exacerbated by an underlying issue: the archbishop's attempts to erect a prebendal church at Hackington or at Maidstone (strongly opposed by the monks). Thus the 'petty incident' of monastic forgery, which had provoked open hostility, 'offered their adversary a handle'. More serious complaints soon followed.[119] The archbishops of Canterbury and their monastic chapter were regularly at odds, and the full background to their rivalry is not worth detailing here. This particular clash was long-drawn-out and tedious (the Canterbury account fills over fifty pages in the Rolls Series edition), as everyone who has studied the matter seems to agree.[120] One can only endorse Lawrence's conclusion that 'The manner in which the dispute was conducted reflects small credit on either the chapter or the archbishop'.[121] Things ended

---

[117] Until after his death, when the chapter took their revenge.

[118] The seal of the original papal document was ripped, so a new one was drawn up and the old seal attached. The document was later destroyed, but was probably the forgery discussed by Cheney, 'Magna Carta Beati Thome': pages 95–102 address this part of the charter's history; *Gervase*, 130–1; the election 146–9; *Reg. Gregory IX*, iii, no. 5388.

[119] Lawrence, *Archbishop Edmund*, 163–8, quotations at 167. See also Sayers, 'Peter's Throne and Augustine's Chair', 255–6.

[120] *Gervase*, xx–xxi.   [121] Lawrence, *Archbishop Edmund*, 168.

abruptly when the archbishop went into 'exile',[122] and the monks were absolved by the pope without further ado.

The monks were certainly not innocent in the matter. Stubbs, the chronicle's editor, described the dispute as being 'chiefly interesting for showing how impossible it was for the best of archbishops to manage his captious and litigious chapter'.[123] Matthew Paris (who wrote a hagiography of St Edmund) complained that the monks were judicially excommunicated rebels, whom the legate Otto 'impudently and irreverently' absolved after the archbishop's death.[124] Nevertheless, it is difficult to sympathize with Edmund's uncompromising and unrelenting enforcement of the monks' excommunication. He was indeed 'over-aggressive', and his efforts had a profound effect on the city of Canterbury as well as on the monks.[125] There is evidence that, on the whole, the monks had more support than the archbishop. They were absolved promptly after his death; the townspeople did not enforce the sentence against them; the other bishops sought to make peace, seemingly blaming Edmund more than the monks for an inability to compromise.

The archbishop's actions may be characterized as abuse of excommunication, but this conclusion is debatable. Edmund was probably acting against the principle that excommunication should only be used medicinally, but he broke no laws. He certainly provided adequate notice before excommunicating the monks. Edmund sent numerous warnings (though the monks argued he had not waited for them to respond), and later letters referred to these warnings.[126] Although the account was written from the monks' point of view, it includes numerous original mandates sent by the archbishop, his official, and others.

What comes across clearly from the Christ Church account is that the monks were particularly concerned about the denunciations that accompanied excommunication, as a separate issue to excommunication itself. Following the monks' contumacy and resulting sentence, the archbishop ordered (on 22 January 1239) standard solemn denunciations to be made, every Sunday and feast day, that the monks had been excommunicated.[127] The monks' subsequent appeal was to prevent these: 'they appealed against the denunciations, so that they would not take place'.[128] This is significant because legally, and in terms of the monks' salvation, denunciation changed nothing. They were excommunicated regardless. All it did was make that fact public. According to our source, the archbishop's mandates were carried out by chaplains reluctantly: 'although grieving'. The official of Canterbury, 'in tears' as he denounced the monks, sought to limit the sentence's effects by adding that only those who had been directly involved in

---

[122] As claimed by his hagiographers. See Lawrence's rejection of claims that Edmund had been forced into exile: *Archbishop Edmund*, 168–81.
[123] *Gervase*, xx.   [124] *CM*, iv, 72–3.   [125] Lawrence, *Archbishop Edmund*, 172.
[126] *Gervase*, 149–50 (the warnings are mentioned numerous times at 134–51).
[127] *Gervase*, 151.   [128] 'contra denuntiationes, ne fierent, appellarunt'.

the election of the new prior, Roger de la Le, were excommunicated, and not the whole chapter.[129] Edmund was later forced to correct this: he had in fact sentenced the whole chapter. Despite the appeals, the archbishop cited certain of the monks to appear before him, and denunciations were made throughout Canterbury and beyond the city.[130]

Various orders to denounce the monks were sent in the meantime, and the monks appealed. But in early March Edmund raised the stakes by ordering that all the bishops (gathered in London for a convocation) denounce the monks in their own dioceses.[131] This was thus an aggravation of the sentence. The bishops of Rochester and Chichester, and the elect of Armagh, tried to convince the archbishop to delay his intention 'because of the scandal that would follow'. When they were unsuccessful, they asked the papal legate, Otto, to intervene. The denunciations were successfully delayed.[132]

It is clear from this account that the prelates and legate did not agree with the archbishop's actions. Their concern that it might provoke scandal implies that they were worried about how the matter would appear thus publicized. This does not necessarily mean that they actively supported the monks, but they certainly wanted peace. They were able to stop only the denunciations, not the excommunication itself. The elect of Armagh went to Canterbury in an effort to make peace. Unfortunately, the elect's mission failed. He wrote, with perceptible frustration, that although he had found the monks willing to reach agreement, neither the archbishop nor anyone to act for him had appeared.[133]

The injuries alleged by the monks before the elect of Armagh reveal that the denunciations were injurious, in addition to excommunication in and of itself, because the monks were defamed with false allegations (as they saw it). They complained that they had been suspended twice, been excommunicated, that denunciations had been made, and that false crimes had been alleged ('criminibus falsitatem interpositis').[134] Later, another convocation of bishops was held in London, causing the monks to write to the prelates asking them not to proceed with denunciations. These, they argued, would be to the shame of their mother church ('ad confusionem suae matricis ecclesie').

The monks thus seem to have been arguing that Edmund was acting unjustly and that the scandal following would be because people would recognize this.[135] The bishops assented to the monks' request that they should not make these denunciations, perhaps agreeing that this quarrel should not be further aired in public.[136] Edmund nevertheless persevered in Canterbury, having denunciations made throughout the city. It was at this point that the wider community became

---

[129] *Gervase*, 152.   [130] *Gervase*, 153. Matters continue in a similar vein for the next few pages.
[131] *Gervase*, 159.   [132] *Gervase*, 159–60.
[133] *Gervase*, 165–6. The elect's own letter is included in the chronicle.
[134] *Gervase*, 161–6 (for the monks' complaints, see 163).
[135] Cf. Bryan, 'Scandale is heaved sunne', 77.   [136] *Gervase*, 166.

involved. The archbishop ordered that the denunciations—which included the whole chapter—forbid anyone to choose burial with the monks, follow funeral processions to their church, be present at their sermons, or celebrate divine services with them. The order was prompted by the fact that a certain Jordan 'salsarius'[137] had been brought to the monks for burial 'by the greater part of the city'. The citizens had thus, as yet, not properly enforced the sentence commanding them to avoid the excommunicated monks.[138] The citizens of Canterbury were getting caught in the cross-fire.

Many denunciations followed, in the school of theology, in parish churches, and at the priory of St Sepulchre, where the archbishop preached before a 'multitude of people'. The monks continued to appeal against denunciations and complained of the enormous injury all this was causing them. Edmund had contrived to have them suspended for one cause and excommunicated for another: 'a remedy for us seemed very remote and our shame (*confusio*) miserable and intolerable'.[139] The dispute continued at length, and here need only be briefly summarized. Frequent denunciations continued; the monks repeatedly appealed. Edmund eventually wrote directly to the sheriff and all the people of Kent, forbidding them to communicate with the monks and telling the authorities to deny hearing to anyone who continued to communicate with them despite the denunciations made 'through every parish church in our province'.[140] In a report sent to Rome in October, the monks begged for a remedy 'because so many and such great confusions threaten us, that our life is painful and miserable'. They would rather die than live thus, believing that Edmund had the king's support for his schemes to build a prebendal church.[141] In fact, the king eventually took the monks' side, and ordered his sheriffs to publicly forbid anyone to help erect this new college at Maidstone.[142] This prompted Edmund to find a new way to 'molest and injure' the monks, excommunicating anyone who presumed to enter the fiefs of Christ Church on account of any writ. He forbade the convent to alienate its possessions.[143] When the matter was finally over (after the archbishop's death), the convent took its revenge against the archdeacon of Canterbury, Master Simon Langton (brother of the late archbishop Stephen), who had played a crucial part, by themselves excommunicating him.[144]

The details of the lengthy quarrel are monotonous, but the parts concerning the wider community are remarkable.[145] Despite the archbishop's mandates following the burial of Jordan 'salsarius', he was once again forced to forbid burials at Christ

---

[137] Sauce-maker or salt-merchant.   [138] *Gervase*, 167.   [139] *Gervase*, 167–8.
[140] *Gervase*, 176. Writing to sheriffs was not unheard of: cf. *Reg. Pecham*, ii, 119–20.
[141] *Gervase*, 174, and n. 3. For the twelfth-century background, see Gelin, 'Gervase of Canterbury, Christ Church' and Sweetinburgh, 'Caught in the cross-fire'.
[142] *CR 1237–42*, 234; Carpenter, *Henry III*, 215.   [143] *Gervase*, 176–8.
[144] *Gervase*, 180–2. Using their vacancy rights.
[145] Cf. the 1285 rift between archbishop Pecham and the citizens of Canterbury: Douie, *Archbishop Pecham*, 75–7.

Church. Yet when the monks held an Ascension Day procession, a large crowd followed them. Services were suspended in two churches that allowed the procession to pass through.[146] Denunciations were then made, on 26 May 1239, that anyone who had followed the procession was also suspended. These denunciations were greeted with resistance: 'not without much grumbling amongst the people'.[147] In addition, inquisition was to be made into the names of the contumacious.[148] The archbishop's measures were supposed to turn the innocent against the guilty, but, as Peter Clarke noted in his discussion of interdict, 'might turn the innocent against the Church'. Indeed, the suspension of various churches and minor excommunications of many of the citizens meant that Canterbury was effectively under an interdict. Here, too, resentment was aroused against the church rather than against the supposed offenders.[149]

Edmund was within his rights to take such measures. The community had not ostracized the monks as it was bound to do, and those who had disobeyed the church incurred minor excommunication *ipso facto.* Increasing publication of original malefactors, and then their supporters in response to such disobedience, was acceptable. The community was not entirely innocent here, since its members had cooperated with excommunicates.[150] The future saint was far from the only cleric to order investigations into names in order to punish those scorning his mandates. Yet it is evident both that he did not have the support of the people— probably to be expected since the monks of Canterbury were far more involved with the city than the archbishop—and that his stringent measures caused them consternation, both spiritually and temporally. They were perhaps punished more than their guilt deserved, as will become clear. It ought to be noted that, while the archbishop certainly did issue the orders described, there is no evidence to corroborate the reactions of the citizens. It is possible that the chronicler (correctly) judged that sympathy for the monks' cause was best generated by explaining the collateral damage caused by the archbishop's methods. Nevertheless, the narrative, although exaggerated, rings true. That the citizens were worried about the lack of ecclesiastical burial, 'perhaps the most feared effect of an interdict', is certainly plausible.[151]

The collateral damage suffered by the community shows that the archbishop's actions were excessive. Following the suspension of those who had followed the Christ Church processions, many from the city were afraid for themselves ('sibi timentes'). They therefore went to the Dominicans and Franciscans for counsel. They asked that they should not be denied the sacraments, nor, if they died, ecclesiastical burial. Meanwhile, the chaplains who had been excommunicated claimed that they had been greatly injured by the denunciation, declaring that,

---

[146] *Gervase*, 169–70.   [147] 'non sine magno murmure in populo'.   [148] *Gervase*, 172.
[149] Clarke, *Interdict*, 182, 171.   [150] Cf. Clarke, *Interdict*, 20–8, 46. See also above, 157–161.
[151] Clarke, *Interdict*, 161.

through loss of oblations, they were unable to live. The archbishop's policy was less defensible here. He had reserved absolution to himself or his archdeacon, but neither was present. Later, when crowds attended the funeral procession of one of the monks and were excommunicated, 'many were scandalized' because no penitentiary or friar could absolve them. Here the verb can be understood to equate to how we use 'scandalized' today, that is, shocked and appalled. However, it might also entail an accusation that the archbishop was endangering souls, since he had, in effect, precluded the absolution of the citizens. His use of excommunication, albeit minor not major excommunication, was here punitive rather than medicinal. He was not taking measures to provide for their spiritual wellbeing. This was scandalous in more ways than one.[152]

The final mention of scandal in the Canterbury monk's account concerns the publicity and controversy that the affair had generated. The citizens were not only troubled by their suspension. They also complained that, because of the 'scandal' that had arisen—'both in England and in nearby provinces'—the merchants and pilgrims who usually flocked to the city had withdrawn themselves. The once populous city now lay as if desolate. The citizens, along with the monks, were crying and wailing, pleading 'Lord, save the city and monks of Canterbury, lest we are ruined (*pereamus*)'.[153] This dramatic outcry should be treated with a degree of scepticism. No other source confirms that Canterbury was avoided in this way, though the contemporary Waverley Annalist, based in Yorkshire, was aware of the dispute. He noted in late 1238 that the monks had elected a prior without the archbishop's assent and that they 'did not care greatly about the excommunication or interdict', continuing to celebrate the divine office.[154] The monks' lament may well have reflected a basic truth. Given how extensively the sentences were publicized, it is not inconceivable that visitors, particularly pilgrims, heard about and discussed this affair, choosing to give Canterbury a wide berth. Such a venomous dispute between the country's primate and the monks of his cathedral church might be expected to cause a scandal.[155]

The dispute between Christ Church and Edmund of Abingdon demonstrates a number of important features. First, it is clear that Edmund was acting with personal enmity, and that he took far greater steps to enforce his sentences than would be expected in more routine cases. He never acted against the law, yet he

---

[152] Cf. Clarke, *Interdict*, 171, which discusses unfair treatment and scandal during the interdict in 1213.
[153] *Gervase*, 173.   [154] *Annales Monasterii de Waverleia*, ed. Luard, 320.
[155] Some of the Canterbury account is corroborated by Gregory IX's letter absolving the monks and righting other wrongs, although the facts as presented by the pope would of course have been based on the monks' appeals: *Reg. Gregory IX*, iii, no. 5386. The Annals of Dunstable (*Ann. Dunstable*, 156) recorded the absolution of the monks, and Matthew Paris notes both the dispute and the absolution (*CM*, iii, 527–8, iv, 72–3). However, it was the abbots of St Albans and the prior of Dunstable who were instructed to announce the monks absolved. It is possible that this was how the writers came to know about the matter, not through denunciations: *Reg. Gregory IX*, iii, no. 5386; cf. no. 5387.

was nonetheless able to exploit the sanction and use it vengefully. That he was essentially acting as judge in his own case was apparently widely noticed, so that his sentences were called into question by both the clerical and lay communities. Second, excommunication was a public matter. It affected those who were excommunicated, those who lived in proximity to them, and also those who were further removed but heard about affairs through denunciations. Like cases described above, and as Lawrence noted, in all likelihood the matter made neither party look good. Finally, the monks' repeated complaints against denunciation rather than simple excommunication shows that they were more concerned about the publicity than they were about possible spiritual effects. Nor was the issue that simply being excommunicated was detrimental to reputation; it was rather that excommunication provided an opportunity to disseminate defamatory (in the monks' own view) material about them. When the monks were absolved, the pope provided, as they had asked, that thereafter neither their reputation nor their innocence were damaged in any way: only three monks had been guilty of the forgery and they had all been transferred to other monasteries.[156] The monks of Canterbury, it seems, were keen to ensure that their innocence was made known, and that their names were cleared.[157]

Absolution and Penance

The purpose of publicizing excommunications was not purely so that the faithful would ostracize those sentenced. It was also, as we have seen above, so that public crimes were seen to be punished by the church. Additionally, the publicity and the shunning itself were intended to humiliate the excommunicate.[158] A potential justification for some of the above publicity, which bordered upon misuse or even abuse of excommunication, was that it was to shame the recalcitrant excommunicates and cause them to make peace with the church. Numerous mandates articulated this idea. Certainly excommunicates did sometimes feel shame about their status. Simon de Montfort was reportedly humiliated when the king refused to interact with him.[159] According to the (admittedly questionable) testimony of Wendover, in 1215 the English barons returned to King John's allegiance for this reason. They fell into great anguish of body and mind because they were excommunicated every day, and were 'deprived of all earthly honour'.[160]

---

[156] *Reg. Gregory IX*, iii, no. 5388: 'nullum exinde incurrat fama vestra dispendium vel innocentia detrimentum'.
[157] Innocent IV confirmed this absolution in a letter concerning the election of Boniface of Savoy as archbishop, which was sent to the monks, the bishops of the province, the archbishop-elect, and the clergy of the city and diocese: *Reg. Innocent IV*, i, no. 116.
[158] See Chapters 3 and 4.   [159] See above, 121–2.   [160] *CM*, ii, 667.

The humiliation associated with excommunication did not end as soon as an excommunicate had a change of heart and requested absolution. Public shame was also part of the process of absolution. Absolution from major excommunication, like excommunication itself (but unlike interdicts), involved a solemn liturgical ritual. Robert of Flamborough described how major excommunicates were to be solemnly absolved before the doors of church. They would first swear to obey the church's mandates and provide guarantors for any pecuniary penalties. They would then be beaten, 'naked and bowing down in the sight of the people', with Psalm 51 (*Miserere mei Deus*). Women were not to undress but were to be beaten on their hands or otherwise punished.[161] The penitent was then received back into the church with prayers and acts of reconciliation.[162]

Absolution itself might thus have aroused shame in those who were forced to undergo it. Falkes de Bréauté complained of his 'shame and disgrace' when, before he was absolved in London, he was stripped and the archbishop preached a sermon which included 'infinite blasphemies'. This was, Falkes claimed, to the dishonour of the church of Canterbury. Before Falkes was absolved, he reported that Langton referred to him as the 'scourge of the earth', the 'affliction of the natives', and that he insulted him in various ways. If Falkes's account is accurate, he was indeed treated unfairly, since after his absolution he claimed to have been imprisoned for nine weeks, still naked.[163] Langton's sermon, however, fits with the practice that excommunicates' crimes be published before the people before absolution was granted, even if Langton's words were unusually strong. It is less certain how standard was the letter Falkes had to distribute, stating the terms of his absolution and publicizing his agreement that should he fail to fulfil them he would automatically fall back into his sentence.[164] Falkes's letter survives in the chancery rolls, which do not appear to contain other letters of this sort. However, there are similar letters recorded in the register of Walter Bronescombe, bishop of Exeter, in which knights publicized both the crimes for which they had been excommunicated and the terms of their absolutions.[165]

A degrading absolution rite was not the end of the matter, however. Penance was enjoined prior to absolution but could be completed after it (failing to complete it would result in being re-excommunicated). For major excommunication, solemn public penance was recommended, although the details would vary

---

[161] 'nudus et prostratus in conspectu populi cum *Miserere mei Deus*'. Flamborough, *Liber Poenitentialis*, 148. This solemnity was unnecessary for minor excommunicates. Early modern Jewish excommunicates were subject to similarly or indeed even more humiliating ceremonies, also involving whipping, in which they begged forgiveness: Kaplan, *Religion, Politics and Freedom of Conscience*, 7–8; Kaplan, 'Discipline, dissent and communal authority', 401.
[162] See Hamilton, 'Remedies for "great transgressions"'; Hamilton, '*Absoluimus uos*'; Hamilton, 'Anglo-Saxon and Frankish Evidence'.
[163] *Coventry*, 268–9.   [164] *CR 1227–31*, 228–9; cf. *PR 1225–32*, 210–11.
[165] *Reg. Bronescombe*, nos 1085, 1156. For Beaupré's excommunication, see Miller, 'Knights, bishops and deer parks', 212–13.

from case to case.¹⁶⁶ Public penance could be prescribed for sins separately from excommunication, but links between public penance and major excommunication were so strong that it can prove impossible to distinguish between the two (despite the best efforts of canonists). Excommunication might even have been used as a way to ensure that someone was made to undergo public penance.¹⁶⁷ Fear of the latter might, correspondingly, have been a reason to be afraid of excommunication.

As Thomas of Chobham wrote, 'he who sins publicly ought to satisfy God... and the church... so that the whole church sees his penance'. Since everyone was informed of excommunicates through denunciations, it followed that the excommunicate would have to display contrition and humiliation in public.¹⁶⁸ Just as scandals had to be visibly punished, a sinner's remorse also had to be publicly visible. Penance made an example of sinners, as did secular public punishments of criminals.¹⁶⁹ Penance is a vast topic in its own right, and there is not space here to address its complexities.¹⁷⁰ It is enough to note that it was often associated with absolution from excommunication, and that it was a further means by which excommunicates were shamed and their sins publicized. In many cases it is impossible to know what penance was enjoined on those who sought absolution from excommunication, since the only surviving evidence is a mandate ordering another cleric to enjoin fitting penance. A form of absolution from excommunication in John of Pontoise's register indeed warned clergy against imposing too harsh penances, because sinners might fail to carry out such penances and thus fall more easily back into sin.¹⁷¹ Despite the decree in the 1257 Statutes of Salisbury that those who fell into any of the 1222 Oxford sentences should be publicly whipped as many times as seemed expedient, there were not in general specific rules that governed what penance was given.¹⁷² Rather, penance lay at the discretion of individual clergy.¹⁷³

It was common—especially for violent crimes—for people to be publicly whipped, while their crimes were read out.¹⁷⁴ Chobham advised that noble men

---

¹⁶⁶ Peñafort, *De Poenitentia*, 404–6. Excommunicates did indeed fall back into their sentences, e.g. *Reg. Gray*, 262. See also the case of Eustace de Bingham in the Introduction, page 23.

¹⁶⁷ Hamilton, 'Penance in the age of Gregorian reform', 48; Hamilton, 'Remedies for "great transgressions"', 93, 99; Mansfield, *Humiliation*, 51, 114.

¹⁶⁸ Chobham, *Summa*, 213, 259. Cf. Mansfield, *Humiliation*, 51–8. The humiliation of penance might also be counter-productive, inducing people to remain excommunicate rather than to face it: Helmholz, 'Excommunication as a legal sanction', 216–17.

¹⁶⁹ On secular use of pillories, etc., see Masschaele, 'Public space of the marketplace', 400–6.

¹⁷⁰ See Hamilton, *Practice of Penance*, for an in-depth study and for references to the literature, and Mansfield, *Humiliation*, and Hill, 'Public penance' for this period.

¹⁷¹ *Reg. Pontissara*, ii, 573–4. ¹⁷² *C&S*, 561.

¹⁷³ See, for example, *Formulary of the Papal Penitentiary*, ed. Lea, no. 17. Although, see also a commission in Winchelsey's register that contains almost tariffed penances: fornicators known through *publica fama*—two beatings in church and two in markets and a procession; adulterers convicted through inquisition—three beatings in the market and three in church; simple fornication—three around the church; those convicted of sorcery—six around church and six through the market; usurers—three around the church and one through the market.

¹⁷⁴ See Hill, 'Public penance', for more examples.

and women should not be whipped on bare flesh, but instead should be covered with a thin material, so that they would still feel the scourge through it.[175] It is impossible to tell whether beatings were meant to hurt physically as well as to provoke shame, although the insistence on thin clothing even when nakedness was deemed indecent might point to the former.[176] As Rosalind Hill noted, public figures could sometimes be spared the harsher aspects of penance, such as a knight in Oliver Sutton's register who was let off his penance because it would injure his dignity and cause unnecessary civil disorder.[177] Nevertheless, this was by no means standard procedure. The register of Godfrey Giffard, bishop of Worcester, records that a knight, Osbert Giffard, was to be beaten on three feast days and three Tuesdays in several (specified) churches and markets. He was to serve in the Holy Land for three years and was not to wear knightly accoutrements unless he received permission from the king. When he was first taken to the door of the church on Ash Wednesday for absolution, his crime (raping and abducting nuns) was to be solemnly published before the people.[178] Prince Louis was forced to walk ungirded and barefoot to pray for absolution from the legate in 1217.[179] There were of course famous precedents in the penances undertaken by Emperor Henry IV at Canossa, and, following Becket's murder, Henry II of England. Evidence from chronicles describing events from the first half of the century equally confirms that penance involving public beatings and barefoot processions took place in order for absolution to be granted.[180]

Episcopal registers extant from the second half of the thirteenth century provide similar examples. A man from the diocese of Lincoln was absolved from the excommunication he had incurred for assaulting a priest, and was to be beaten on five Sundays, to make offerings on three of them, and to kneel before the altar from the end of the gospel until after the elevation of the host.[181] Hugh of Berwick, told he must treat his wife better, was to be beaten as an excommunicate in the church doorway on three separate days, unshod and ungirded, 'before the whole procession'.[182] A sub-bailiff was to undergo six beatings—three in Oxford market and three around the church.[183] A man of the diocese of Canterbury was to make a solemn procession—in only his shirt and breeches—through the market on three Sundays and feast days, and in the church where he had violently removed tithes and obventions, for seven Sundays, and in two other markets nearby. He was to be publicly beaten, with his crimes exposed before the clergy and people, and was not to be announced absolved from his excommunication

---

[175] Chobham, *Summa*, 259. Cf. Mansfield, *Humiliation*, 126–7.
[176] Masschaele, 'Public space of the marketplace', 409, notes that beating may have been merely symbolic.
[177] Hill, 'Public penance', 221–3.   [178] *Reg. G. Giffard*, 278–9.   [179] *Melrose*, 130–2.
[180] *Melrose*, 130–2, 132–4; *Flores Historiarum*, ii, 224–5; *Ann. Worcester*, 430–1.
[181] *Reg. Sutton*, iii, 40–1.   [182] *Reg. Gray*, 269.   [183] *Reg. Sutton*, v, 12–13.

until he had completed this penance.[184] Several people who had unlawfully communicated with the excommunicated prior of Great Malvern were to do penance with bare feet, in their underwear and with uncovered heads, with priests publishing their deeds before the people.[185] The crime of these men and women was relatively trivial, however, so they were spared public beatings. Painful or not, public penance carried out in churches and marketplaces ensured that a wide audience of acquaintances and strangers would have been witness to such humiliations.[186]

Absolutions were also publicized separately, alerting others that an excommunicate had been reconciled with the church. Publication of such information was, of course, necessary partly so that people ceased to shun those who had returned to the church or who had been judged wrongfully sentenced. Mary Mansfield observed that public penance was attractive partly because it was less severe and more adaptable than other forms of punishment. The severest secular punishments, in particular, were often both more extreme and irreversible.[187] Excommunication had similar advantages. Though it was the church's harshest penalty, and despite all the injuries potentially suffered by those under the ban, their suffering need not last. Once someone had been absolved, they were not to suffer any further prejudice.

It is clear that individuals were extremely keen on having such information spread.[188] The importance of publishing absolutions so that reputations were not further damaged is made plain in the legatine Council of London (1268), which asserts that this should be done so that no one be avoided by others 'to their indignity and scandal'.[189] The same was done in the secular sphere when sentences of outlawry were annulled.[190] It is unsurprising that when archbishop Winchelsey was absolved from excommunication, he took pains to ensure that this fact was well publicized. He thus sent letters to every bishop in his province (or to the officials in vacant sees) asking that they publish his papal absolution, 'so that, with infamy transformed into good renown (*infamia in bonam famam conversa*), all scandal and suspicious wavering concerning the damage of our status is deleted

---

[184] *Reg. Winchelsey*, i, 76–8. Some respite was provided, however, since only the penance ordered to take place in the offended church and the two nearby markets was to be done fully. The penance that was to take place in the church and market of Canterbury was to be held in suspense.

[185] *Reg. G. Giffard*, 186.

[186] Masschaele, 'Public space of the marketplace', 406–12, provides an excellent discussion.

[187] Mansfield, *Humiliation*, 266. Mansfield notes that public penance was useful because it was not governed by jurisdictions. This does not apply to excommunication.

[188] The absolution of Ymbert de Yenna, which the king had urged, was to be announced throughout the Isle of Wight: *Reg. Pontissara*, i, 281. A failed attempt at securing a public absolution: *Reg. Pontissara*, i, 287. See also a continental example in Clarke, *Interdict*, 245.

[189] 'in sui contumeliam vel scandalum': *C&S*, 774. On defamation in medieval England in general, see Helmholz, 'Introduction' to *Select Cases on Defamation*; Helmholz, *Oxford History of the Laws of England*, 565–89.

[190] The annulment of Hubert de Burgh's outlawry, for instance, was to be proclaimed throughout the county of Berkshire: *Royal Letters*, 443–4.

from the minds of Catholics'. The archbishop would understandably want his absolution publicized following public excommunication—the London annals, for instance, stated that his sentence had been denounced 'through all the churches of the city of London'—and he had the means to ensure this was achieved.[191] He knew that his authority, spiritual and secular, was undermined by any rumours of his excommunication. In one instance, the archbishop of York even asked Edward I that the absolutions of various men be publicly proclaimed in the king's jurisdiction.[192] Likewise, the monks of St Alban's, who had been sentenced by the bishop of Durham, were to be announced absolved throughout the bishopric.[193]

Mandates ordering publication of revocations are also common. Particularly strong efforts in these cases make sense, since the excommunicates would have been unjustly defamed by their sentences. A clear example of how excommunication affected reputation can be found in the parliament rolls from 1293. Master John of Pilsdon had been publicly excommunicated, by the bishop of London, in the presence of the justices in eyre and other nobles. John had, however, procured a letter from the official of Canterbury, which would be read out 'to clear his reputation and status, and to show the court and the lord king's lieges that the aforesaid bishop's sentence did not bind him in any way'. The letter, however, was seized from John before it could be read, and taken away by a clerk. Although the bishop originally claimed that, as the letter had been addressed to him, he could keep it without contempt to the king, he later admitted that the letter had been intended to clear John's reputation (*fama*) and status, and that he should not have prevented him from having it. The letter was to be given to John, and the bishop was 'liable to punishment for the aforesaid trespass at the lord king's pleasure'. Anything done by the bishop to John's injury, or against the terms of the letter, was to be annulled.[194] This whole dispute, then, had been about the loss of reputation resulting from excommunication, and the necessity of correcting this. When John was prevented from clearing his name, he took the matter to the king. This case may be compared with the complaints of Thomas fitz Adam, the royal bailiff excommunicated in Ireland in 1220. When the archbishop of Dublin was informed that he was not allowed to excommunicate royal bailiffs without the king's permission, he was also reprimanded because he had 'greatly defamed' fitz Adam.[195]

When the pope ordered that archbishop Boniface's excommunication of the monks of Holy Trinity and the canons of St Paul's, London, be declared null, he wrote that they should not be considered bound by any chain 'nor through its

---

[191] *Reg. Winchelsey*, ii, 763–5. For Winchelsey's excommunication and its causes (a dispute over the church of Pagham), see Denton, *Robert Winchelsey*, 273–4 and nn. 6–7. Cf. *Register of Walter Langton*, ed. Hughes, no. 470.
[192] *SKB*, i, 46.   [193] *CM*, vi, 382.   [194] *Parliament Rolls*, i, 567–9.
[195] *Royal Letters*, no. 72. See above, 116–117.

denunciation be notorious or avoided'.[196] Nearly two years later, at the complaint of the same, who asked that the pope 'provide for them over excommunication and denunciation', Innocent IV wrote to the archbishop, ordering him to cease making any further denunciations and to declare the targets of these sentences absolved in convenient places.[197] A sentence potentially brought against the dean of Stamford was not to be published, and was to be publicly refuted, because the archdeacon of Westminster had exceeded his authority in the matter in hand.[198] In 1280 a dispute in parliament between Archbishop Pecham and the king's bailiff ended with the archbishop promising to revoke a sentence of excommunication in all the churches where the denunciation had been made.[199] An injured party might even have control over how their name was cleared. The Court of Canterbury ordered that, if any sentences had been promulgated against a certain William de Bernham, the archdeacon of Huntingdon was to declare them null and void wherever he was requested to do so by William.[200]

In most cases, mandates for revocation state merely that a sentence had been declared null and should be announced as such. We cannot know, in contrast to sentences of excommunication, how these revocations were worded in practice. A letter sent by archbishop Pecham, in 1281, supports the possibility that, in the case of publication of annulments, the negative publicity against the wronged excommunicate might be counteracted with equally strong words against those who had unfairly sentenced them. Pecham described how the friars of Scarborough had been invalidly sentenced by the abbot of St Albans. The abbot had been 'led, or rather seduced, by more perfidious counsel', and had 'against all reason... struck down the Friars Minor at Scarborough, not from the authority of the keys but with the key of enflamed rage'. He was unable to do this legally, so this 'furiaca sententia', which 'opposes God and favours the devil', was not to harm the friars in any way. The recipients of the letter, the deans of Pickering and Ryedale and the vicar of Scarborough, were themselves threatened with excommunication if they were negligent in announcing that the sentence did not stand.[201] Whether the deans and vicar were supposed to declare the sentence's nullity using Pecham's text, or if they did so, is uncertain. But if the friars' reputations had suffered, the vehement condemnation of the abbot would have gone a long way towards clearing their names.

These examples further demonstrate the role that excommunication denunciations had in damaging the names of excommunicates. Allowance should be made for the fact that there was greater tension behind some of these excommunications

---

[196] *CM*, vi, no. 96; *Foedera*, I.i.275. They had been excommunicated for denying him right of visitation.
[197] *Ann. Burton*, 304.   [198] *Reg. Sutton*, iv, 55–6.   [199] *Parliament Rolls*, i, 163–5.
[200] *SCC*, 112–18. *Reg. Swinfield*, 29–30, provides a comparable example.
[201] *Reg. Epp. Pecham*, i, 246–8. Pecham was himself a Franciscan, and it is possible that this strongly worded letter reflects his anger at the ill-treatment of members of his order, and is not representative.

than there would have been for an average sentence. The nature of the surviving evidence obscures the experiences of excommunicates with less power and influence. It was standard practice that absolutions from excommunications were announced, but those without connections (many of the above were themselves clerics or otherwise able to exert influence) would perhaps have had less control over how and where their names were cleared.[202] On the other hand, the average excommunicate was perhaps less likely to be ill-treated through excommunication if there was no reason for clergy in power to feel personal anger towards them. Excessive publicity was not necessarily the common experience of excommunication. As Véronique Beaulande observed, there are differences between *les grands conflits* and local excommunications.[203] Nevertheless, the typical excommunicate was not spared the denunciations and public penance. The scale may have been smaller and the vitriol less, but excommunication and absolution was a humiliating and damaging experience for all.

Excommunication and Public Unrest

In times of conflict, the publicity given to sentences of excommunication could potentially exacerbate existing tensions, posing a real threat to an established regime. Rulers had more to be concerned about than just their reputations. Those who held positions of power only tenuously might well dread the publication of sentences. The issue was not simply that people might be given an excuse to rebel (as discussed in Chapter 3), but that public excommunication, in itself, might stir up trouble. In the same way that preaching might be feared for its ability to persuade and spread information detrimental to those in power, the rhetorical force of excommunication, manipulable by political enemies, was a cause for concern.[204]

For kings of England, there was concern that scandal and unrest would be provoked by the sanction. Henry III was concerned about his conscience and his *fama* when threatened by Alexander IV during the Sicilian Business.[205] In times of peace, an excommunication publicized against the king would be a great scandal, potentially damaging his reputation. Even so, it would not necessarily endanger his ability to rule. Complaints that excommunication—of both the king and his ministers—would disparage the king can be found expressed regularly during the century. But during periods in which the kingdom was in turmoil,

---

[202] Penances and absolutions of seemingly ordinary men, ordered to be announced, can be found for example in *Reg. Sutton*, iii, 12–14.
[203] Beaulande, *Malheur*, 12.
[204] Leveleux-Teixeira, 'Le droit canonique médiéval et l'horreur du scandale', 202–3.
[205] See Chapter 2, 84–6.

excommunication potentially posed a considerable threat to royal power. What was at stake varied a great deal from case to case.

Kings were often aggrieved by the excommunication of their officials or of religious houses under their protection. The desire to preclude excommunication of royal officials was partly to prevent government grinding to a halt if they were unable to perform their duties. But complaints that a king's privileges had been infringed also noted that his reputation was at stake. Thus in 1244, when the mayor and bailiffs of Winchester were excommunicated by the local diocesan, against the terms of the king's papal privilege, the complaint was that the king's *fama* had been blackened.[206] Henry was also annoyed, in 1233, when certain nobles of his kingdom were to be excommunicated by the bishop of Rochester, Henry of Sandford. Even though they alleged that it had been too dangerous for them to appear before papal judges delegate, and although they sent a proctor to obtain absolution, the bishop nevertheless wished to denounce them throughout the entire realm. The king felt that this would disparage his papal privilege.[207] His letter does not specify which nobles were in danger of suffering denunciation, and it is therefore unclear precisely what was happening here. In all likelihood, these were repercussions of the arrest of Hubert de Burgh and the ongoing tensions resulting from the regime of Peter des Roches. It is obvious, however, that while he may have feared contamination from them, the king in particular objected to public proclamation of the bishop's sentence.[208]

So keen were English kings to be free from excommunication's public effects that they insisted that general sentences include a clause specifying that the sentence did not include the king. Thus in 1293 the archbishop of York was reprimanded for excommunicating the bishop of Durham. The Bury chronicle states, 'the king was furious with the archbishop... partly because the bishop of Durham was his familiar, and partly because he and his sons were not excepted, it was said, from the sentence pronounced, against the privilege granted to him by the Roman curia'.[209] The previous year, the sheriff of Buckinghamshire and Bedfordshire complained before the king's bench. He noted that an excommunication against certain of the king's men, who had distrained the archdeacon of Buckingham's beasts, was promulgated 'throughout the whole county of Buckingham in every deanery and public place', but that the sentence had not excepted the king's men or even the king himself, as was customary. This was injurious to the crown and against the king's dignity, particularly because the king had given the orders from which the excommunication resulted. It was a further scandal that the king's ministers could be punished simply for executing his commands.[210]

---

[206] *CPR 1232–47*, 438–9.   [207] *Royal Letters*, no. 341.
[208] For contamination see Chapter 3, 104–7.   [209] *Chron. Bury*, 116–17.
[210] *SKB*, ii, 80–1.

The fact that the king insisted on being excepted from such sentences is odd. When an excommunication explicitly stated that the king and his family were not to be included in the sentence, as so many did, the king was nonetheless implicated. There was no need to state that a sentence was not intended to incriminate the king unless he was involved in some way. Given the publicity afforded to sentences of excommunication, it is difficult to see how excepting the king from general sentences did much good. On the contrary, it might be thought to have done harm by specifically associating the king with the offence committed. Oliver Sutton, for one, used such means to condemn the king's treatment of the clergy in 1297: 'however much the bishop had tried to soften the blow, the king stood accused'.[211] Nonetheless, it was certainly the accepted custom.[212] The king's response to the sheriff of Buckingham and Bedfordshire's complaint is unknown, since it was decided that the matter required the presence of Master Richard, the archdeacon who had pronounced and published the excommunication. It is clear, however, that although the king must be exempt from sentences of excommunication to have his orders executed as he desired, this particular case posed no real threat to the kingdom's tranquillity.

King John, though the only king in the century to be excommunicated, was in fact not subject to the publicity attached to the sanction. John's is a special case. His excommunication came only after England was placed under interdict, meaning that his sentence could not have been publicized in the usual way, in churches during mass. Wendover noted that his excommunication was not published by the few clergy who remained in England, though he claimed the news spread nevertheless.[213] Although John's sentence became a severe threat when combined with baronial unrest, he was not confronted with excommunication denunciations used as propaganda against him.[214] By contrast, both Henry III and Edward were given cause to fear precisely this.

In 1259, and therefore after the challenge to Henry III's authority that resulted in the Provisions of Oxford, the king was again threatened by Alexander IV, via his penitentiary, Velascus. The pope insisted, on pain of excommunication, that Aymer de Lusignan (also known as Valence), bishop of Winchester, be restored to his see. The king, however, argued that he could not allow this without provoking crisis and overturning the laws of the kingdom. Aymer (Henry's half-brother) was

---

[211] For Sutton's accusation, see Chapter 2, 67. This quotation is from Denton, *Robert Winchelsey*, 157.

[212] Some further references to the king being excepted from general sentences (in chronological order): *CM*, iii, 201; *Ann. Dunstable*, 150; *Flores Historiarum*, ii, 342; *Cal. Pap. Reg.*, 233; *CM*, iv, 636–7, v, 36–7, 351–2, vi, 222–5; *Foedera*, I.i.447–8; *Reg. Bronescombe*, nos 1024, 1429 (Richard of Cornwall only excepted); *Cotton*, 158, 335–6; *Reg. Epp. Pecham*, i, 147–50, ii, 604, 606–8; *Reg. le Romeyn*, i, no. 127, no. 553; *Reg. Sutton*, iv, 104–5, 107–8; cf. *Cal. Pap. Reg.*, 160. See also Hill, 'Theory and practice', 7, and Douie, *Archbishop Pecham*, 104.

[213] *CM*, ii, 526–7; Cheney, *Pope Innocent III*, 320; Clarke, *Interdict*, 179–81.

[214] Cheney, *Pope Innocent III*, 320–7; Maddicott, 'Oath of Marlborough', 288–90, 313.

so unpopular that he had been expelled from England by the same baronial coup that imposed the Provisions. As a result of the king's refusal, Velascus threatened to promulgate sentences of excommunication and interdict against him and his lands. Thus, wrote Henry, the pope's representative had no thought for the danger that might ensue, or the scandal it might rouse throughout the kingdom, amongst both clergy and people. The king contended that the customs of his realm did not permit Velascus, as a papal nuncio, to make such threats or promulgate such sentences.[215] In the turbulent climate of 1259, the king could ill afford excommunication and interdict. He clearly felt that Velascus threatened not only the king's reputation, but his very position. In these circumstances, the spiritual aspects of the sanction were the least of Henry's worries.

In 1297, Edward I was concerned that excommunication and rumour-mongering were uniting clergy and laity against him. In the midst of Scottish rebellion, and with his own nobility murmuring their discontent, he may also have been worried about opposition to his proposed war in Gascony.[216] This was perhaps the first time in his reign that Edward faced serious disquiet amongst his nobles. He had taken exception to excommunications in the past, notably in his dealings with archbishop Pecham, both in individual cases and when he ordered Pecham to revoke various general sentences pronounced at the provincial council of Reading.[217] In these earlier instances, the king's anger seems to have been roused by the perceived infringement of his rights and jurisdiction, by the prospect that the sentences might hinder his officials, and, possibly, because sentences might influence public opinion. The concerns about excommunication in the first twenty-five years of his reign, however, were distinct from those of 1297. Certainly he was still concerned about his dignity. But he was also concerned about scandals that might threaten his realm. In 1297, the dispute ignited by *Clericis laicos* led the king to seize grain and other goods from the clergy, by necessity, as he claimed. This in turn led the clergy to threaten those who had seized such grain on royal orders. The king wrote to the archbishops and bishops, forbidding them to excommunicate his ministers, which would 'redound in grave and enormous injury to our royal dignity and crown'. He added, however, that it would also result in 'more apparent scandal of the people, so that from this, destruction of the church (in England), and destabilisation of the entire kingdom might very plausibly (*verisimiliter*) follow'.[218] Public clerical hostility to this war might cost him valuable support from other parts of society.[219]

---

[215] *CR 1256–59*, 490–2.   [216] Denton, *Robert Winchelsey*, 116–18.
[217] Hill, 'Magna Carta', and Chapter 7.
[218] Denton, 'Crisis of 1297', 571 (27 February 1297); *Foedera*, I.ii.875 (19 August 1297). The letters are very similar, but only the latter mentions 'scandalum populi'; it also provides greater justification for Edward's actions.
[219] Burton, 'Politics, propaganda and public opinion', 235–41.

Earlier in the year, Edward had ordered a commission that made clear that excommunication, and clergy who promulgated sentences, were seen as threats to the kingdom's peace. The commission was to inquire into disturbers of the peace who spread news and slander, those who disturbed the execution of his commands, those who issued sentences of excommunication, those who published sentences previously pronounced (almost certainly *latae sententiae*), those who promulgated sentences against his ministers or subjects enforcing his commands, or those who did anything through which the peace and tranquillity of the realm might be disturbed. These malefactors were to be imprisoned.[220] That the first malefactors condemned were gossip-mongers ('troveurs de novelles'), coupled with the emphasis on promulgation of sentences, both general and against individuals, shows that the publicity of excommunication was dangerous. The 1275 Statute of Westminster had forbidden the publication of false news or stories through which discord or slander could arise between the king and his people.[221] In 1297, the king was stating that excommunication could do just that. Edward could not risk the widespread dissemination of accusations damaging to himself and his officials. He was genuinely concerned about the scandal such dissemination might create, and about the unrest it might provoke. He had always felt aggrieved by the excommunication of his servants, but he had never before been so worried by the civil unrest such sentences might rouse. As far as the king was concerned, publishing sentences was itself a subversive act.

Edward's fears about dangerous consequences of excommunication when he was already facing opposition can be compared to those of his old enemy Simon de Montfort. Nearly half a century earlier, during his ill-fated time acting as the king's deputy in Gascony, Montfort was excommunicated by the archbishop of Bordeaux. His position in Gascony was precarious, and his reaction demonstrates the threat public excommunication posed. The archbishop claimed (apparently falsely) that the earl had captured him and laid violent hands on him in the process.[222] Montfort appealed to the pope: not only had the archbishop made false assertions and caused Montfort to be publicly announced as an excommunicate, but he had contravened the exemption granted to Montfort that forbade anyone in Gascony promulgating a sentence of excommunication against him for two years. In fact, this privilege might have expired by the time Montfort was excommunicated, since it was granted on 28 January 1251. The papal letters concerning his excommunication date from late March and early April 1253. Nonetheless, the pope ordered the bishop of Clermont to inquire. In the meantime,

---

[220] *CPR 1292–1301*, 239; *Foedera*, I.ii.875. I am grateful to Simon Parsons for his help with translating the Anglo-Norman.
[221] *Statutes of the Realm*, i, 3 Edw. I, Statute of Westminster I (1275); Helmholz, 'Scandalum in the medieval canon law', 260.
[222] For Montfort's disastrous time as Henry III's lieutenant in Gascony between 1248 and 1254, see Maddicott, *Simon de Montfort*, 106–24.

denunciations were to cease entirely. If the bishop found Montfort's account true, he should announce the sentences to be null. If Montfort was found culpable, the bishop was to absolve him, after securing adequate satisfaction and enjoining fitting penance.[223]

Montfort had been in Gascony for more than two years before soliciting his exemption, which he did apparently at the height of his troubles, caused by opposition from the Gascon nobility. At the same time, Innocent IV had ordered the bishop of Agen, with the help of the archbishops of Bordeaux and Auch, to make peace between Montfort and his opponents. The bishop was empowered, if necessary, to absolve the nobles from any oaths made in connection with conspiracies, and from any sentences of suspension, interdict, or excommunication that they would incur for breaking them. He was to restrain them through ecclesiastical censure.[224] This letter, dated 31 January 1251, was clearly associated with Montfort's privilege, dated three days earlier. In these circumstances, Montfort saw the value of being immune from excommunication. It was in this period that Montfort was forced to return to England to ask for more money from the king, who also sent royal commissioners to Gascony, in January, to settle the disputes.[225] Whether Montfort was facing excommunication in 1251 is unclear, though the bishop of Agen was also told to investigate and punish 'clerks stirring up violent discords and such wars', suggesting that Montfort was facing problems from clergy as well as laity.

Montfort's privilege specifically forbade promulgation of any sentence against him, indicating that Montfort's primary concern was publicity.[226] It protected him from the various consequences of the censure, including the possibility that it could be used by rebels to justify their dissension. This is logical, given the mention of clerks 'stirring up' wars, since a venomous sentence publicized throughout Gascony would have been an effective means of rousing sedition. Public denunciations would have made his already precarious position even worse. In 1253, Montfort's complaints also focused on promulgation. No specific mention is made of the injuries suffered by Montfort. It is merely stated that he experienced 'no small detriment' as a result of announcements that he was excommunicated.[227] The pope's responses centre on the promulgation and public denunciations of his sentence. Not only were these to be relaxed (if they were indeed based on false assertions), but proclamation was to be made that the earl was not bound by such sentences.

---

[223] *Reg. Innocent IV*, iii, no. 6503, no. 6500, ii, no. 5019.   [224] *Reg. Innocent IV*, ii, no. 5016.
[225] Maddicott, *Simon de Montfort*, 113-14.   [226] *Reg. Innocent IV*, ii, no. 5019.
[227] *Reg. Innocent IV*, iii, no. 6500.

Violence against Clergy using Excommunication

Publications of excommunications, just like interdicts, were prevented by any means necessary, demonstrating the threat they posed.[228] Considering the publicity given to sentences of excommunication, and the strength of the sentiments expressed in such sentences, it is to be expected that people sometimes considered preventing publication to be their best option. The souls of anyone who took such measures were nonetheless imperilled, since the ceremony did not issue a sentence but only publicized it.[229] When such attempts to prevent denunciations were successful, excommunication could be rendered (temporally, though not spiritually) ineffective. Perhaps the most striking example of this can be found in the efforts of the Montfortian regime to prevent the legate, Gui Fouquois (later Clement IV), either from landing at Dover or from publishing his sentences in England. Montfort's position was by no means secure; he could not risk the damage that such sentences would do to his cause and his name. Perhaps he had learnt from his experiences in Gascony the previous decade. He felt forced, therefore, to obstruct the legate's mission (which in itself resulted in a sentence of excommunication in canon law).[230]

Public denunciations of the earl and his cause would clearly have proved detrimental. First, by 1264, Montfort relied a great deal on popular support. Many of his fellow nobles had returned to the king's allegiance by the time of the Battle of Lewes, and Montfort therefore needed to retain the wider support he had attracted. In the summer of 1264, he also needed to raise an army to defend England against an imminent French invasion (that never materialized).[231] Second, Montfort's cause was presented as a religious one. This would be severely undermined if churchmen up and down the country were to proclaim their condemnation of the earl and his principles, pronouncing all those who supported them cut off from the church.[232] Third, Montfort had the backing of a number of churchmen who publicly garnered support. The friars in particular helped him by preaching. Clergy who had helped Montfort in this way were roundly condemned by Clement IV in 1265. As well as alleging that they had given incentive to Montfort's malice, the pope told his legate that such clergy should publicly retract their previous statements in the places they had made them, and to urge nobles, barons and local communities to withdraw their support for Montfort.[233] If the clerics working for Montfort had been as effective as this letter implies, in 1264 the earl maintained a crucial if precarious monopoly over ecclesiastical attempts to influence popular opinion.

---

[228] Clarke, *Interdict*, 175–80.
[229] This point is clearly articulated in Flamborough, *Liber Poenitentialis*, 144: 'denunciation is nothing except notification of excommunication'.
[230] D.94, c.2; *Foedera*, I.i.447–8. [231] Maddicott, *Simon de Montfort*, 290–1.
[232] Cf. Hartman, 'Poetry and the cause of Simon de Montfort'. [233] *Foedera*, I.i.461.

If the legate had been allowed to enter England, the excommunications he pronounced would have challenged the narrative preached by clergy who favoured the baronial cause. It is likely that, as with the sentences discussed at the beginning of this chapter, excommunications against Montfort and his followers would have been phrased in extremely vitriolic language. The 1263 sentence pronounced by archbishop Boniface (also never published in England) condemned the sacrilege of various named men, declaring Montfort 'most responsible'. His supporters were declared to be sons of iniquity; their heretical depravity and nefarious daring was condemned. The cause of their excommunication, however, was merely their infringement of *Si quis suadente*. Though the sentence would have undermined the presentation of the Montfortian cause as religious, since Simon and his supporters had committed a number of offences against the church, as listed by Boniface, there was no mention of the reform movement.[234]

By contrast, if his later letters are anything to go by, Gui Fouquois would have condemned not only the means but also the ends.[235] When he became pope, Gui (now Clement IV) described Montfort as a tyrant who had infected others with his false piety. Clement warned his successor as legate, Ottobuono, about Montfort's cunning, claiming 'nothing can please God... unless the said pestilent man with all his progeny is torn from the kingdom of England'.[236] Following the Battle of Evesham, in which Montfort was killed, Clement detailed the magnates' 'seditious presumption' at length. His condemnation was unrelenting. If an excommunication describing Montfort and his enterprise in such terms had been disseminated, it would have 'undermine[d] the whole moral and religious foundation for [his] enterprise'.[237] Montfort could not risk it.

When Gui's envoy, the friar Alan, landed at Dover he was informed that if he carried a single letter that might injure the kingdom, he would lose his life.[238] Montfort and his supporters were already excommunicated; what had to be stopped were the denunciations, lest Montfort's dwindling supporters were persuaded that they were acting against the wishes of the church and of God.[239] The legate's complaints are attested by several chroniclers. Thomas Wykes reported that the legate was constantly denied entry into the kingdom, the rebels intending to kill him if he came to interfere in any way. He also noted that the archbishop, Boniface of Savoy, at this time exiled in France, was so afraid of the barons he 'feared for his skin'. When the legate ordered the bishops of Worcester, London, and Winchester to excommunicate the barons and to interdict London and the

---

[234] Oxford, Bodley MS 91, f. 136r-v.
[235] Gui's legatine register (Heidemann) includes a large number of letters condemning the barons and ordering that excommunications be published, but it is not here possible to discuss them at length. See also Ambler, *Bishops in the Political Community*, 147–69.
[236] Martène, *Thesaurus*, nos 190, 106. [237] Maddicott, *Simon de Montfort*, 291.
[238] Heidemann, no. 12a.
[239] Heidemann, no. 19. Ambler, *Bishops in the Political Community*, 169–83.

Cinque Ports, his letters were torn up and thrown into the sea upon their arrival at Dover. Wykes, a royalist, was unsure whether these bishops had been captured willingly or unwillingly, but he nevertheless noted that they were threatened with death if they should publish anything contained in the letters.[240] The same incident was noted by the *Flores Historiarum*.[241] The London Annals similarly recorded that no sentences were published, and the legate could not enter England, 'for fear of the barons'.[242]

The danger in 1264 was that the sanction could work as propaganda. The language that would have been used, accompanied by the ritual, threatened to persuade people to change their minds about the religious legitimacy of the baronial reform enterprise. Public religious condemnation could have deprived Montfort and his accomplices of desperately needed support. Adherents might have thought twice about supporting excommunicates and of incurring excommunication themselves. The unqualified need to prevent excommunications being published against the barons in England in 1264–1265 is clear. As we have seen, the reform agenda remained popular despite excommunication, perhaps in part because the sentences were never widely promulgated within the kingdom.

Sentences of excommunication were not only prevented from being published in such significant disputes. Clerics' attempts to pronounce sentences were also thwarted in more local disputes, for example in the great cause at Thame (Chapter 6 below). Some attacks on clergy pronouncing sentences perhaps indicate anti-clericalism: at Ecton, candles were snatched from the hands of priests proclaiming the 1222 Oxford sentences, as were the documents from which they read them.[243] These were general sentences, and though it is possible that the malefactors had incurred one of them and were afraid of people realizing this, they may have simply chosen a particularly solemn occasion to express their contempt for clerical authority. For their assault they were, inevitably, excommunicated. In other cases, revenge was perhaps a motive. In Guthmundham, the book and candle being used by the vicars of Whyton and Hayton in an excommunication ceremony were torn from their hands.[244] Clergy were never given the opportunity to denounce Jordan, a man from the Channel Islands, because he snatched the letters containing his sentence from a woman named Matilda. Jordan was brought to the attention of secular authorities, accused of obtaining an abortion for Matilda. Rather depressingly, he was pardoned because it was found that he had

---

[240] *Wykes*, 155–7.   [241] *Flores Historiarum*, ii, 500–2; see also *Gervase*, 238–9.
[242] *Annales Londoniensis*, ed. Stubbs, 64–5. The sentences were published in France: Heidemann, no. 52.
[243] *Reg. Sutton*, iv, 35–6.
[244] *Register of Thomas of Corbridge*, ed. Thompson, ii, 13. The malefactors had invaded a prebendal church, expelling and beating the proctor of the rightful prebendary.

not done so; rather Matilda had miscarried as a result of his assault. Again, Jordan sought to prevent others finding this out about his sentence.[245]

Violence might likewise be used to punish clergy who had pronounced sentences. The problem was sufficiently common that it was addressed in the Council of Lyon II (1274). This declared anyone who ordered clergy to be killed, captured, or molested for promulgating excommunications against public figures *ipso facto* excommunicated.[246] Such attacks would in many cases have been reactions against the publicity given to excommunication. Frederick II, who was excommunicated by the papacy three times, reportedly imprisoned the erstwhile legate in England, Otto, because he had published Frederick's sentence in England and 'to no moderate degree defamed' the emperor.[247] According to Matthew Paris, certain people of his diocese, both clergy and laity, objected to Grosseteste's orders that the Magna Carta sentence be unceasingly renewed by priests, parish by parish. As a result, they inflicted abuses on these priests (which of course caused them to be *ipso facto* entangled in the chain of anathema).[248]

Conclusions

The importance, efficacy, and potency of excommunication should be judged in a broader context that fully acknowledges the effects of the publicity attached to sentences. Publicity was one of the most potent forces of excommunication. Though promulgation was fundamental to the sanction's ordinary functions, it proved valuable: it could be used to damage reputations, to inspire shame, and even to provoke public unrest. Publication sought to influence behaviour—both of the excommunicate and the community—but even when it did not, it could play an important role in society. Excommunication of an enemy or opponent was desirable not only because they might be shunned and their souls be imperilled, but also because the wider populace would be informed both of their guilt and of the church's opinion on the matter. The next chapter, through a detailed study of one local case contested towards the end of the century in Oxfordshire, demonstrates the impact of public excommunication, how the sanction's mechanisms worked, and the effect of its use on legal processes and local society.

In certain circumstances, influencing public opinion might have been the sanction's primary purpose. The church was certainly aware of the value of excommunication in this context. If there was a personal element at work,

---

[245] *CPR 1301-07*, 303; *CCR 1302-07*, 231.   [246] Tanner, *Decrees*, i, 331.
[247] *CM*, iv, 170. Otto did have Frederick's sentence publicized throughout England: *CM*, iii, 545, 568–73. Frederick complained to Henry III and the English nobility about the publication of his excommunication in England, calling it 'intolerable', and saying it brought injury, shame, and damage to his empire, and contained defamation of his name and honour: *Foedera*, I.i.237–8.
[248] *CM*, v, 400.

denunciations were likely to be more potent and to be promulgated far more broadly. This is of crucial importance when it comes to interpreting requests for absolution. Excommunicates who sought to reconcile with the church often had most to lose, in the short term, from the temporal consequences of absolutions. Their disadvantage lay not in the simple fact that being an excommunicate was precarious, but rather in excommunication's mechanism for promulgation of derogatory material. If excommunication itself was not always viewed particularly negatively, as failure of ostracism shows, excommunication afforded an opportunity to decry offences and to discredit individuals so that, particularly if the (alleged) faults were serious, public opinion might be turned against excommunicates.

Dissemination of sentences was frequently the most valuable aspect of the sanction for clerics. Sentences that were 'ineffective' in other ways might still nevertheless be effective in terms of public involvement. When the church gave its support to an enterprise through excommunication, this does not have to be seen as a meaningless gesture.[249] However, the publicity that might be so advantageous to churchmen could also backfire upon them. When they were engaged in petty squabbles, ad hominem attacks, or other unbecoming behaviour, their use of excommunication ensured that this was evident to everyone in the vicinity. As such, a sanction designed primarily to protect ecclesiastical authority could end up damaging it. Controversial implementations of sentences certainly risked the reputations of individual clerics, but also of the influence of excommunication itself. Mutual sentences were especially risky. In fact, though individual sentences were mistrusted, as Chapter 2 showed, there was no general rejection of the spiritual potency of excommunication. It was, however, dependent on how and by whom it was used; it did not inspire unquestioning or inevitable awe.

Excommunication thus shows that political culture descended into the localities. Sentences were designed to reach the ears of everyone and did so. As a result, the masses were informed about local and national events, about divisions between nobles, and about conflicts within the church. Disputes may often have been between elites in society, but they affected local culture a great deal. The publicity given to sentences is testament to the fact that those at the top of the political hierarchy saw the value of influencing public opinion. The implications of this for how not only specific disputes but also both secular and ecclesiastical authorities as a whole were viewed by parishioners in towns and villages is considerable. Moreover, the people were expected to take action, whether active or passive, and it is possible to ascertain points of view from the collective behaviour following excommunications. Churches, marketplaces, and no doubt homes and roads, were places for political discussion, just as were courts.

---

[249] Gray, 'Church and Magna Charta', 35.

6
Violence, Excommunication, and Dispute Settlement
Thame, 1292–94

On the Saturday before the feast of St Laurence, almost two hundred satellites of Satan, most eagerly ready to attack the church, entering its cemetery with furious daring as if invigorated by a diabolic spirit, wickedly constrained the guards of the said church so that they could not freely escape and leave, and encircled the said sacred place on every side. Next, they made holes in the church in many places on its western side, so that they had the ability to shoot arrows inside even as far as the great altar. Not content with this, having piled an abundance of straw in the church's side chapel, they damnably presumed to proceed to burn the church, notoriously in the custom of infidels. Finally, having entered the said church that had been set on fire, the aforesaid sacrilegious sons of Belial atrociously wounded two clerks who were amongst the other guards there, staining and foully profaning the church by shedding blood, and presuming to have mass celebrated *de facto* in the place that had been profaned in that way, to the irreverence of God and the prejudice of ecclesiastical liberty, to the injurious disturbance of the lord king and realm as much as was possible, in violation of the immunity of the said sacred place and to the great danger of their souls and the vehement scandal of many.[1]

This dramatic attack on the church of Thame, Oxfordshire, took place on 8 August 1293. It was the climax of a dispute between Thomas Sutton (a relative of the bishop of Lincoln) and Edward St John (a royal clerk) over the prebend of Thame. By this time, the struggle had been ongoing for almost a year, and it would continue for another before it was finally settled. The narrative above is taken from an excommunication sentence pronounced, in Latin and English, in the cathedral church at Lincoln a week after the event.

---

[1] *Reg. Sutton*, iv, 104–5.

This lengthy dispute is the subject of this chapter, providing a case study through which various of the themes discussed in previous chapters (in particular Chapters 1, 4, and 5) can be brought together. The detail provided by this well-documented local case allows a close look at the mechanisms of excommunication and how the sanction worked alongside other legal and social practices. During the course of the dispute, the two rival parties each made use of violence, excommunication, and ecclesiastical and secular courts, and appealed to both the pope and the king. The dispute as a whole was conducted in the public forum. Excommunication's role in all this was significant. The quarrel illuminates, in particular, the value of public excommunication, the technicalities, importance and usefulness of *latae sententiae*, and how the personal involvement of churchmen in cases affected their use of the sanction. The extent of publicity and force of anathema are particularly noteworthy, showing how excommunication could be adapted to specific situations, all within its legal limits. However, it was not excommunication that brought the matter to a close. It was finally settled through the arbitration of King Edward I in the summer of 1294, rather than by any of the court proceedings. Although excommunication was viewed as injurious, neither side capitulated to its pressure. Instead, it was used tactically, alongside other strategies, and its main value here was perhaps its potential to influence public opinion. The short-sightedness of basing assessments of ecclesiastical sanctions upon narrow definitions of efficacy is thus well demonstrated by this case. Their failure to resolve the dispute does not necessarily mean that the excommunications pronounced during the case should be judged ineffective, and they were certainly not worthless.

The Thame dispute was undoubtedly a particularly acrimonious affair, but it is likely to have been similar to many other contests over benefices.[2] Its most striking feature is that it was unusually well documented. Its narrative can be pieced together from a number of different sources, although aspects of it do remain unclear.[3] Due to the case's complexity but relative obscurity—though it has been discussed by Rosalind Hill and Andrew Miller (whose forthcoming book will help this case achieve its deserved fame)—this chapter is structured mostly chronologically, so that the events and their significance are clear.[4] The *dramatis personae* are as follows: Master Thomas Sutton, archdeacon of Northampton, eventually

---

[2] The register's editor, Rosalind Hill, noted that 'spectacular as it was, the attack on Thame was not an isolated instance of lawlessness': *Reg. Sutton*, iii, xli.

[3] Its chief records are contained in the episcopal register of the bishop of Lincoln and in witness depositions recorded by the Court of the Arches at Canterbury. Additional information is provided by the plea rolls (from the court of the king's bench), the patent and close rolls, and the parliament rolls. Our two principal sources only provide information that favours one party or the other. Some balance is nonetheless restored by the information provided by the other sources.

[4] Hill, 'Public penance', 219; Hill, *Reg. Sutton*, iii, xxxiii, xl–xli; Miller, 'To "frock" a cleric'; Miller, 'Knights, bishops and deer parks'. Unfortunately, while I was alerted to Miller's two articles—for which I am grateful to John Arnold—before redrafting my PhD thesis version of this chapter for the book,

the successful claimant to the benefice of Thame; Oliver Sutton, bishop of Lincoln and Thomas's uncle;[5] Master Edward St John, Thomas's rival as prebendary, a royal clerk and member of a prominent local family with close connections to the king (Sir John of St John, Edward's father, was a knight in the royal household and close to the king);[6] Master Thomas de Lewknor, a papal chaplain and royal clerk who acted on Edward St John's behalf on a number of occasions;[7] King Edward I, who may in fact have been a relative of St John.[8] Both Sutton and St John had considerable local support, as is indicated by the numbers of men who took up arms on their behalf, and by witnesses who testified for them in the court of Canterbury. Neither the pope nor the archbishop of Canterbury played any part in this dispute, for it took place during interregna in both Rome and Canterbury.[9] This fact is of undoubted significance and probably explains the evident desperation shown by the Sutton party. As their connections indicate, Thomas seems to have had the better ecclesiastical connection, Edward St John the better secular.

Thame itself was a benefice, without cure of souls, in the diocese of Lincoln.[10] Its desirability is easily understood: it was valued in the great *Taxatio* of 1291 at £112, and was therefore one of the richest benefices in the diocese.[11] Some fifty years earlier, it had been the subject of a similar dispute involving the bishop of Lincoln, Robert Grosseteste, and the royal clerk John Mansel, which was settled by King Henry III.[12] Thame's attractiveness is further shown by the fact that Edward

---

I did not find out about Miller's own 2003 PhD thesis, '*Carpe Ecclesiam*: Households, Identity & Violent Communication', which discusses the case at length, until a much later stage. (He will soon publish a microhistory with Routledge: *Patronage, Power, and Masculinity: A Microhistory of a Bishop's and Knight's Contest over the Church of Thame*). As a result, I have not amended the main text or added references throughout, but I address key differences here. There are many points of overlap not only in content but also in interpretation, as might be expected. Miller provides a detailed narrative in ch. 3, and in chs. 5 and 6 he analyzes aspects of the case, as well as providing appendices of events and texts. I have delved more deeply into the technicalities of excommunication, while Miller gives far more prosopographical information. He shows clearly Edward St John's royal connections, in particular arguing strongly that the king's brother, Edmund, earl of Cornwall, was 'continually lurking in the background' of the entire dispute (quotation 97). Moreover, he ties a number of other events and bouts of violence in the diocese around this time to this dispute. Miller brings out very well the importance of publicity in Oxford (255–6). Where I have stressed the vacancies in Canterbury and Rome as a cause of the overblown nature of this dispute, Miller places the case in the context of 'bastard feudalism' and the growing power of royal government and the waning of episcopal authority from the reign of Edward I onwards (ch. 6). He is surely right to have put a great deal of emphasis, as I have not, on the fact that Edward I needed to resolve this dispute as he was on the brink of war. Many of those involved would have fought for the king.

[5] *SCC*, 567 nn. 2–3 provides biographical references.
[6] *SCC*, 567 n. 4; Vale, 'St John, Sir John de (*d.* 1302)'.   [7] *SCC*, 567 n. 8.
[8] Prestwich, *Edward I*, 281; *CCR 1288–96*, 358.
[9] Pope Nicholas IV died on 4 April 1292. He was succeeded by Celestine V, who was consecrated on 19 August 1294, though he resigned before the end of that year. Archbishop John Pecham died on 8 December 1292, and although his successor, Robert Winchelsey, was elected at the beginning of 1293, he was not consecrated until 1294, and did not return to England to perform his duties until 1 January 1295.
[10] That it did not involve cure of souls is mentioned several times.
[11] *Fasti Ecclesiae Anglicanae 1066–1300*, iii, 102.
[12] *Registrum Antiquissimum*, i, 181–3; *CPR 1232–47*, 257; *CM*, iv, 152–4; *Ann. Dunstable*, 158. See Liu, 'Matthew Paris and John Mansel', 161–2. As in 1292–94, the royal clerk's claim eventually failed, but Mansel subsequently received another valuable benefice.

St John's claim in 1292 was preceded by another. A certain Peter of Savoy was instructed by Bishop Sutton to resign his false claim, which he was asserting by taking the church by force. Local chaplains were instructed to forbid their parishioners from receiving him as prebendary.[13] Since nothing more is heard of Peter, he presumably abandoned his claim. Edward St John, by contrast, was persistent. Although his claim to the prebend was ultimately unsuccessful, his efforts to secure it over the course of two years were not unrewarded.[14] Thanks to the king's intercession, he was promised a benefice worth 110 marks, considerably more than the value of Decem Librarum, apparently St John's rightful prebend, which was valued at £6 13s. 4d.[15]

The first phase of the dispute, following the death of the incumbent of the prebendary of Thame, William Ferre, was chiefly characterized by attempts to demonstrate rightful ownership of the prebend through direct acts, public appeals, and excommunications.[16] These took place in the autumn and winter of 1292–3 and are known largely from depositions made at the court of Canterbury in January 1293. The court proceedings arose as a result of appeals, made by both parties, against the obstruction of their respective collations. Shortly after the death of Ferre, the bishop exercised his right to collate a successor, and on 16 September Thomas Sutton was accordingly publicly assigned a stall in the choir and a place in the chapter of Lincoln.[17] Immediately, the Suttons had to contend with the counterclaim of Peter of Savoy. This, however, was dealt with quickly.[18] Edward St John's claim took longer to become apparent. Although St John's men claimed that he was inducted to Thame in late September in Basing (Hampshire), it was several weeks before news was heard of his contention.[19] St John's claim was based on a papal provision granted by Nicholas IV. It is reasonably clear, however, that the terms of this provision were that St John should receive the next vacant prebend in the diocese, but that several had fallen vacant between the granting of this provision and the end of August when Thame became vacant.[20] Thomas de Lewknor had, apparently, already collated St John's proctor to Decem Librarum in July.[21] Nevertheless, news reached the Suttons that Edward St John was travelling

---

[13] *Reg. Sutton*, iv, 37–8.   [14] Cf. Smail, *Consumption of Justice*, 23.
[15] *CPR 1292–1301*, 390; *Fasti Ecclesiae Anglicanae 1066–1300*, iii, 65–6, 102. For Decem Librarum's undesirability see Burger, *Bishops, Clerks, and Diocesan Governance*, 183.
[16] William Ferre died in possession. *Fasti Ecclesiae Anglicanae 1066–1300*, iii, 102.
[17] *SCC*, 573.
[18] The dean of Thame was instructed to order the clergy and people not to receive Peter as prebendary, since he claimed the prebend on false pretences and was occupying it unjustly. Threatened with ecclesiastical sanctions if he and his men did not abandon their position, Peter is not heard of again (*Reg. Sutton*, iv, 37–8).
[19] *SCC*, 585, 605–7.   [20] *SCC*, 605, 589, 598. The provision itself is not extant.
[21] *SCC*, 572, 579.

from the king's court at Berwick with the intention to invade the prebend.²² St John's immediate intention was thus to take the prebend by force if he could.

The Suttons' response to this threat was to induct Thomas's proctor into corporal possession of the prebend, since their previous actions had all taken place in Lincoln. 'Medieval clerics also needed to be present in a church to take complete possession of the benefice.'²³ Oddly, this seemingly important act of establishing possession was later only mentioned by one witness in the Canterbury proceedings.²⁴ On 12 November, the Suttons appealed simultaneously to Rome and Canterbury.²⁵ By the time St John's men arrived in Thame, the Sutton party was able to prevent them, for the time being, from taking possession. Lewknor nonetheless attempted to assert St John's purported right, and witness depositions made in early 1294 imply that he was inducted (possibly unsuccessfully). Lewknor certainly contended that he had made the assignment and asserted that those who opposed it were excommunicated according to the terms of St John's papal provision.²⁶

The publicity that accompanied the attempts to secure physical control of the prebendal church requires stressing. In November 1292, Thame and nearby Oxford (*c*. thirteen miles away) were bombarded with mutually contradictory claims about who was the rightful prebendary. Such attempts to control *publica fama* would be important in future legal proceedings. The Sutton party made public appeals against St John on 14, 15, 17, 23, 26, and 30 November. Appeals were made in the cemetery of Thame, the Oxford churches of both the Franciscans and the Dominicans, and in the churches of St Peter and St Mary in Oxford. The appeal at Thame had been made in the presence of the parishioners. That at St Mary's was made in Edward St John's presence and was read, in Latin, 'before the clergy and people in a great crowd'.²⁷ The bishop also ordered St John and his supporters to be excommunicated in the churches of Oxford, Thame, Cuddesdon, and Waddesdon (both less than 10 miles from Thame).²⁸ These public assertions in Oxford were necessary, for the original Sutton appeal had been made far away in Spaldwick (Huntingdonshire), where the bishop had been staying, while there is evidence that St John had the support of a number of Oxford clerics. Thus, having publicly ordered Thomas Sutton's followers to leave the church of Thame on 14 November, Thomas de Lewknor travelled to Oxford. There he published his assignment of the prebend to St John and excommunicated Oliver and Thomas Sutton, on either 17 or 18 November. On 19 November, the same assignment and excommunication were published in the four schools of canon law and theology, by one of St John's clerks.²⁹

---

²² Whether St John himself would have described his intention as 'to invade' is unlikely, but he was presumably aware of the probable opposition.
²³ Hoskin, 'By force and arms', 162.   ²⁴ *SCC*, 592.   ²⁵ *SCC*, 578.
²⁶ *SCC*, 595, 607–8.   ²⁷ *SCC*, 573, 572, 576, 577, 572 (quotation).
²⁸ *Reg. Sutton*, iv, 47–9.   ²⁹ *SCC*, 572, 576.

Both Sutton and St John were thus trying to influence the *publica fama* surrounding the contested prebend of Thame. If the case was ever to be heard in court, which by this point it evidently would as a result of the appeals being made, it was important to control how the community perceived events. Reputation and rumour could alter outcomes in a legal system based upon oral testimony.[30] On the one hand, the two rivals sought to influence public understanding of the dispute by making attempts to have their agents seen to be inducted and seen in possession of the church. These were public 'direct acts' intended to create a local consensus. A claim would hardly be effective if no attempt was made to take possession of the benefice and to act as its incumbent. It was necessary to stake a claim.[31] On the other hand, they did so by publicizing in Oxford what had taken place in Thame. Each party attempted to legitimize its own claim, and also to make it known that they, in accordance with the law, rejected the other's as illegitimate. Alongside appeals against the other claimant, both those acting on behalf of Thomas Sutton and those supporting Edward St John asserted that their rivals had incurred excommunication. Possibly because both men were using the sanction, there is no evidence that the community or the courts enforced the sentences being pronounced. Although surely all the various consequences of excommunication would be of value in this context, it was undoubtedly here being used as a way to discredit the other's case.

St John excommunicated Sutton on the grounds of his own papal provision, which presumably stated that anyone who opposed the provision was excommunicated (as was usual). St John was thus able to announce that the Suttons were bound by a sentence of excommunication with apostolic authority.[32] It is impossible to know the precise contents of the sentences against the Suttons, but according to one of Thomas Sutton's witnesses, the publicity given to them was sufficient that he heard rumours ('rumores') about these excommunications when he arrived in Oxford a few days after their pronouncement.[33] As we might expect, the Suttons countered St John's sentences with their own public announcements. It is equally impossible to know the contents of their appeals, but it was important to make known that they were appealing to the papacy, since St John's claims were made on the strength of a papal provision.

Oliver Sutton's excommunication sentence condemning St John survives in his register, and it is therefore possible to appreciate how this struck at the root of St John's assertions and actions. The bishop began by setting out how he had rightly and legally collated the prebend to Thomas, explaining that he had been assigned a stall in the choir and a place in the cathedral chapter at Lincoln. He then explained the false position of St John, who claimed the benefice 'pretending'

---

[30] Vallerani, *Medieval Public Justice*, esp. 75 and ch. 2 *passim*.
[31] Wickham, *Courts and Conflict*, 216–22, 85; Wickham, '*Fama* and the law', 15–26.
[32] SCC, 572, 576, 603–4, 606.   [33] SCC, 572.

a provision from Pope Nicholas IV. On the 'pretext' of this provision St John had threatened to occupy and detain the prebend. In so doing, he was suppressing the truth, and his provision was invalid. The bishop was therefore forced by his conscience to excommunicate St John, desiring to defend Sutton's collation with the spiritual sword against those who presumed illicitly to impede, invade, occupy, or detain it 'with nefarious daring'.[34]

The bishop's sentence thus laid great emphasis on the legal validity and procedural rectitude of Thomas's collation, contrasting it with the fraudulent nature of St John's claims and his illicit attempts to occupy the prebend. Bishop Sutton's orders for promulgation specified that the sentence be published, alongside churches generally in the area, in the church of St Mary's, Oxford, with the full cohort of twelve priests assisting with the publication. The same was to be done in the church of Thame. This excommunication ritual, using candles and bells, was to be performed on Sundays and feast days for three weeks, and the sentence was to be explained in the vernacular ('vulgari ydiomate plenius exponendo').[35]

Testimony resulting from the Suttons' appeals indicate that there was much local discussion about the case.[36] Events were described as public and notorious, and many witnesses admitted that they did not know about events except through *publica fama*.[37] Others had been present at public events that were intended to be witnessed by crowds. The evidence clearly indicates that Thomas Sutton had the better claim to the prebend, though it must be qualified by the fact that the witnesses were all supplied by the Suttons, and therefore present a one-sided view. St John's actions, even if illicit, may have been more reasonable than the testimony implies.[38] By contrast, the Sutton faction was not innocent: the first casualty in this dispute was in fact Peter de Wryesdale, a yeoman of St John, who was murdered in Thame towards the end of 1292. An inquest was accordingly begun at the end of December, though this never intersected with any of the other legal proceedings in this case.[39] Significantly, it was concluded in 1294, ten days after the king had finally declared the Thame case settled.[40] Probably this murder

---

[34] *Reg. Sutton*, iv, 48.

[35] We can be fairly sure his orders were obeyed, for he requested reports to be sent to him by 13 December. Subsequent sentences mention that this had been published widely.

[36] SCC, 569–79. When the appeals lodged by Oliver and Thomas Sutton reached the Court of Canterbury in January 1293, witnesses were asked about the assignments, installations, appeals, and so on, that had been made the following autumn. The premise of the questions was evidently that St John was impeding Thomas Sutton's rightful collation. No judgement was made as a result of these proceedings.

[37] Such phrases are present throughout the testimony.

[38] Some witnesses described St John trying to invade the prebend with an armed force (SCC, 572, 578–9). Although they claimed such facts were 'notorious', their prejudiced nature means it is not possible to use them as evidence that the bishop's public condemnations had been effective.

[39] CPR 1292–1301, 44–5.

[40] CPR 1292–1301, 97, 116; CCR 1288–96, 370. Ten men were pardoned for the crime.

took place when St John's men first arrived at Thame and attempted to force their way into the church. It is a significant corrective to the Sutton party's presentation of Thomas's rightful and peaceful collation and possession.

Following the unresolved proceedings at Canterbury in January 1293, St John's men launched a more successful attack. On the second day of Lent, the men who were guarding the church of Thame on behalf of Thomas Sutton were evicted by 'certain knights and others in a great crowd'.[41] Throughout the spring of 1293, Sutton was deprived of the manor and appurtenances of Thame, though whether control of the church was in the hands of St John for this period is unclear.[42] Whilst St John was unable to appeal to the papacy to support his provision, the Suttons' appeals to the king fell on deaf ears. Oliver Sutton sent the writ *De vi laica amovenda*, asking to have the armed force occupying the prebend removed, four times between February and May.[43]

Five weeks after the attack, in March, the bishop again employed his ability to excommunicate. This is a long delay considering that he asked the king for help four days after the attack—it perhaps indicates that Oliver did not consider excommunication the best course of action in this situation but was left with few options. The excommunication reiterated the description of Thomas's rightful collation and St John's illicit provision, but it went on to detail the more recent crimes committed on St John's behalf. The manors of Thame, which Thomas had held peacefully and calmly, had been presumptuously invaded, rashly despoiled, and nefariously occupied. The perpetrators had not feared the earlier sentence of excommunication.[44]

It is evident that the illicit occupiers had supporters. Thus, like various examples in Chapters 4 and 5, the malefactors condemned by churchmen were not condemned by everyone else in the community. The sentence included what might be viewed as a more practical tactic, an attempt to force out the trespassers by threatening those who had been helping them. Excommunication was threatened against all those who communicated with the occupiers by eating, drinking, buying, selling, or praying with them. Sutton was expressly forbidding anyone to help the intruders in their squatting. The latter would be forced to leave if unable to acquire food, a particularly desirable outcome for the Suttons considering the king's silence. Often excommunication sentences only specified these automatically forbidden things if people had indeed been communicating with the

---

[41] *SCC*, 592.

[42] The bishop asked that a force be removed from the church, but evidence from the Canterbury court, and some of the bishop's letters, indicates it was only the prebend's appurtenances. So too does the fact that the sheriff found no force in the church: *SCC*, 591–2, 594; *Reg. Sutton*, iv, 70–2, 74; *Parliament Rolls*, i, 585–6.

[43] The words of the first letter, dated 16 February, were deemed 'deficient'. Further letters were sent on 2 March, 31 March, and 15 May: *Reg. Sutton*, iv, 64, 67, 74, 84. For this writ see Hoskin, 'By force and arms'.

[44] *Reg. Sutton*, iv, 70–2 for this and the following three paragraphs.

malefactors. Even the king was considered partially culpable for the state of affairs, for the bishop declared that his sentence was not intended to extend to the king or his family. This is an early indication that Edward I was thought to be complicit in St John's actions.

Once again Sutton sought to ensure that the sentence was well publicized. It was to be pronounced through all the schools of Oxford, in every church of the deanery of Cuddesdon, and in Thame and its dependent chapels on Sundays and feast days for three weeks. Buckingham, Waddesdon, and Wendover were added in a separate mandate.[45] Each publication was to be performed with bells ringing and candles extinguished, and in the churches of Thame and St Mary, Oxford, at least once with twelve or more chaplains dressed in white. Given that such denunciations were supposed to happen simultaneously in every church in a given area, the full contingent of priests was clearly impractical for each ceremony: Sutton was therefore ensuring that there was at least one particularly solemn and noteworthy spectacle in both Thame and Oxford. The value of public solemn excommunications is clear.

This sentence mentioned Edward St John, but he was not explicitly named as having incurred the sentence, which excommunicated 'all those who' invaded it in his name. It is a technical point, but a significant one. St John was probably not present at the armed invasion, and the sentence publicly discredited St John and his alleged right to the prebend without excommunicating him. Indeed, nobody was excommunicated by name in this sentence. Instead, it initiated a legal process by ordering the bishop's official and the archdeacon of Oxford to investigate the names of the offenders, who would subsequently be cited to appear before the bishop. In this way, though this sentence was surely intended to influence public perception of events, it also relied upon *publica fama* and the local community producing the names of the guilty (though at this stage no names appear to have been discovered).[46]

The king, meanwhile, had continued to be of no help to the bishop. It appears that he had in fact acted upon the request to have the lay force removed, for the sheriff of Oxford was told, on 28 May, to remove it.[47] Unfortunately for the Suttons, St John's men were able to fob off the sheriff merely by informing him that St John was the prebendary and that they were there rightfully. The sheriff found the church itself to be empty. The writ had specified the church, and the gang in the houses of the parsonage asserted 'clearly in the presence of many trustworthy people' that they would not leave until the sheriff was instructed to

---

[45] *Reg. Sutton*, iv, 72.

[46] For the relationship between bishops and their subjects in comparable contexts, see Forrest, 'Trust and doubt', 170–86; Forrest, *Trustworthy Men*, esp. ch.7. For investigations initiated by general sentences see Hill, 'General excommunications'.

[47] According to this mandate, the sheriff had already been instructed to do this, but it is unclear when.

remove them from the church's houses. When Thomas and Oliver Sutton went to parliament about the matter, they left with nothing more than advice to ask for a writ of *novel disseisin* with regard to the houses, lands, and tenements, since there appeared to be nothing then hindering Thomas from exercising spiritual offices in the church. This they admitted. The narrative they relayed before the king, which broadly corresponded to that in the excommunication sentence but also laid emphasis on disturbance of the king's peace (something not mentioned in the March excommunication), had thus achieved little. In any case, by the time they secured a writ, events had intervened.[48]

On 8 August 1293, the attack with which we began took place. An enormous crowd of armed men took the church of Thame by force, in the process wounding some of the men who had been guarding it. Subsequently, they continued to occupy the church. Though it might be doubted whether a full two hundred men appeared, it is evident that St John had secured a large following, either because he had support in the community, or simply because he was able to pay thugs to act for him. If the former, the Suttons' earlier attempts to convince that St John's claim was invalid had been unsuccessful, or else the latter's adherents supported him regardless. The narrative in the excommunication that followed the attack indicates that it was a carefully planned and well-thought-out assault (and, considering that the church was being guarded, an expected one). It was far from mindless violence, but rather an acknowledgement that St John's right could not be asserted unless he was seen to have possession of the church itself.[49] Chris Wickham has argued that, in comparable disputes, 'the more violent end of the scale to some extent represented that much more public and committed a claim'.[50] The mass said in the church on St John's behalf should probably be seen as a public ritual that confirmed his purported status as prebendary.[51] 'It was the public audience...that was intended to register, accept, and legitimize direct action.'[52] Although the excommunication implies that the mass took place in the desecrated church immediately after the attack, it is likely that there was a gap between the two events. Following the church's capture, performance of ecclesiastical rituals confirmed St John's role as prebendary.

The Suttons thus had a great deal of incentive to counter and delegitimize St John's actions. The way in which he had taken control of the benefice might well have been accepted. No help was forthcoming from the king, and from Rome came only silence.[53] The excommunication that followed the attack of 8 August was a forceful condemnation of the acts performed on behalf of Edward St John.

---

[48] *Parliament Rolls*, i, 585–6, Roll 6 appendix, no. 35.i. In parliament, the Suttons no longer claimed that St John's men were in the church itself. They got a writ after Michaelmas.
[49] White, 'Politics of anger', 150–1.   [50] Wickham, *Courts and Conflict*, 216.
[51] Wickham, *Courts and Conflict*, 270–85.   [52] Wickham, *Courts and Conflict*, 283.
[53] Once again, the king was implicated in the ensuing excommunication. Edward and his children were carefully excluded from the part of the sentence that bound those who helped the malefactors in

The sentence described the 'horrendous crime' in full, so that the 'cruelty of the sacrilege' would be more shocking to those listening, and they, with zeal for the honour of the church, would rise up against its perpetrators at the pressure of divine malediction.[54] The bishop took steps to ensure such outrage was felt by those who heard this excommunication, by causing it to be pronounced in both English and Latin, and by using rhetorical language. Some of the language used in the sentence is relatively common in this context; phrases such as 'satellites of Satan' and 'sons of Belial', for example, were often used to describe malefactors. But there is a notable multiplication in the language of outrage in this text, partly as a result of the length of the narrative. The damnatory asides ('invigorated by diabolic spirit'; 'in the custom of infidels') and condemnatory adverbs used to describe the main events ('atrociously wounded'; 'foully profaned') both added to the impression of the severity of the crime and made what was being said in the spoken declaration more memorable. Great emphasis was laid by the bishop upon the wounding of the clerks inside the church. No doubt this was partially because injuring churchmen and spilling blood on sacred ground were especially serious crimes and should be expected to provoke the highest outrage from the bishop. The emphasis, however, made it clear that the church had been defiled and contaminated. Until the church was reconciled, no religious ceremonies could be conducted there. Any mass celebrated since the attack through which St John might endorse his position was invalid: that spoken by his men was *de facto*, not *de jure*.

This sentence of excommunication was given considerable publicity throughout the diocese of Lincoln. It was originally pronounced by the bishop in Lincoln, but mandates were subsequently sent to the archdeacons of Oxford, Buckingham, Huntingdon, and Bedford, who were instructed to pronounce the sentence in their archdeaconries. This they were to do on every Sunday and feast day until further notice, in every church, via their rectors, vicars, or chaplains, and also in all convocations and synods. The archdeacons of Oxford and Buckingham were to personally go to Thame to anathematize the transgressors ('so that they are especially struck down by the horror of divine malediction'), along with a suitable number of clergy.[55]

Even for a serious crime such as that committed by the offenders at Thame, this was a wide area through which to have the sentence published, considering it remained a local rather than a national matter. The bishop's personal involvement

---

any way. Yet the acknowledgement that the king was 'immune' from *culpa* implies that he was none the less culpable. There is a sense that the bishop was protesting too much. See Chapter 5, C5.P73–C5.P74, for the practice of excepting the king from general sentences.

[54] *Reg. Sutton*, iv, 104: 'Ut autem hujusmodi crudelitas sacrilegii facti pupplicationem auribus audiencium amplius inhorrescat, et sancte matris ecclesie zelantes honorem ad impressionem maledictionis divine in autores ipsius sacrilegii nobiscum animocius insurgant'.

[55] *Reg. Sutton*, iv, 107–8.

in the dispute must surely in part account for this extensive publication. St John was not in fact named in this sentence, not even in the context of the attack being made in his name, as he had been in previous sentences. By this time, however, the matters at issue must have been well known (and certainly were if witness depositions are to be believed). Thus Oliver Sutton, in an effort to bolster the collation he had made to his nephew, was able to use his power to excommunicate to spread a version of events that condemned St John's methods of asserting his rights.

Via excommunication, Bishop Sutton was thus attempting to manipulate the meaning of the attack at Thame within the diocese.[56] Sutton had something of a monopoly over this particular tactic: despite the excommunications against the Suttons in the autumn of 1292, there is no further evidence of sentences from St John's side. His uncle had control over innumerable subordinates across the diocese of Lincoln. Whatever clerical support St John may have had in Oxford, it could hardly compete with that. The violence used by St John's men would not necessarily have been seen negatively by locals.[57] St John's supporters would not have viewed it as illicit. Sutton could, however, try to influence neutral observers and control how events were received.[58] Thus an attack arguably justifiable as an attempt to secure what was rightfully St John's was converted into a sacrilegious (a word used no less than eight times in the excommunication[59]) act that polluted a church and injured clergymen. An attempt to celebrate mass in his own church, thereby confirming St John's position as prebendary, became an illicit act carried out in a desecrated—so no longer consecrated—church.[60] Direct acts potentially justifiable from St John's view were thus rewritten as shameful, atrocious, and utterly deplorable.[61] Excommunication's efficacy in this context should be judged according to how effective it was at influencing perception of events. As will be seen, it was by no means entirely successful, but this more than anything can be deemed its main purpose.

The St John party recognized the power of public excommunication here, for the next violence carried out by them was to prevent publication of the sentence just discussed. While the attack on the church of Thame can be seen as a defensible strategy to secure the benefice, the next attack can hardly be viewed in this way. By this stage, the dispute had perhaps assumed aspects of a feud.[62] When numerous clergy assembled at the church of Long Crendon and the abbey

---

[56] Wood, *Memory of the People*, 25–6.

[57] White, 'Politics of anger', 150–1; Wickham, 'Conclusion' to *Moral World of the Law*, ed. Coss, 245. A case discussed by Jacek Maciejewski in fourteenth-century Cracow shares many similarities with this dispute: 'Making war and enormities'.

[58] Wickham, '*Fama* and the law', 22–3. [59] Describing both the perpetrators and their acts.

[60] On comparable lay invasions and the significance of having possession of the church building, see Hoskin, 'By force and arms', 161–3.

[61] Cf. Gundacker, 'Absolutions and acts of disobedience', 195–6.

[62] Cf. Hyams, 'Nastiness and wrong', 195–218; Hyams, *Rancor and Reconciliation*, 252.

of Notley (both not far from Thame), to execute the bishop's mandate to publish his excommunication, they were attacked. These excommunications might have been particularly noteworthy spectacles, for 'many chaplains' reportedly congregated from nearby and diverse places to carry out the bishop's mandate. There would be little use in stopping two of the denunciations when so many more were taking place regularly, so the malefactors 'extorted a promise under oath' that the denunciations ordered by the bishop would not be executed in future.

The assailants were demonstrating their contempt for ecclesiastical authority and perhaps for the bishop's partisan position by humiliating the clergy doing his bidding.[63] According to the subsequent excommunication, they explicitly uttered their contempt for episcopal authority.[64] During the attack, the clergy had the hoods and sleeves cut off their robes. As Andrew Miller has observed, during an excommunication ceremony they would have been dressed as impressively as possible. The attackers were thus conducting 'a counter-performance of their own', in which they humiliated and emasculated ecclesiastical authority. A 'chilling message of violence' was thus sent to the clergy and the bishop, whilst the audience who had gathered to witness the excommunication ceremony instead viewed the clerics' degradation. Such attacks were powerfully symbolic and humiliating acts of disrespect.[65]

The excommunication which resulted from this second violent attack was given even broader publicity. Every archdeacon or his official in the diocese of Lincoln was instructed, on 29 September, to publish the sentence in every church and synod.[66] If these orders were fulfilled (and there is every reason to suppose that the bishop took pains to ensure they were[67]) then, by Richard Southern's estimation, about one fifth of the population of England would have heard it pronounced.[68] Causing excommunications to be denounced throughout an entire diocese was not routine. For instance, an incident in which the church of Claybrook was occupied and turned into a fortification, complete with a siege engine, and in which the chaplain of Nuneaton was assaulted, provoked Oliver Sutton to have the perpetrators denounced only throughout the deanery.[69]

The content of the September excommunication was no less remarkable than the level of its exposure. The sentence began by rehearsing the excommunication that had followed the August attack, almost verbatim. The king was again declared

---

[63] Cf. *Reg. Bronescombe*, no. 1429, when the garments of priests were 'defiled' in much the same way, 'in mockery of a tonsure'; cf. Wickham, *Courts and Conflicts*, 218.

[64] *Reg. Sutton*, iv, 118: 'episcopalis auctoritas contemptum prout ipsi filii Belial attestatione funeste vocis proprie ediderunt'.

[65] Miller, 'To "frock" a cleric', esp. 279-84; Miller, 'Knights, bishops and deer parks', 218-19.

[66] *Reg. Sutton*, iv, 120.

[67] The archdeacons were to write back to Sutton, assuring him that his orders had been executed. Had any failed to do so, it is likely there would be a record of the bishop's reprimand.

[68] Southern, *Robert Grosseteste*, 235-7. Southern estimated that the Lincoln diocese, where Grosseteste was bishop 1235-53, contained c.2,000 parishes.

[69] *Reg. Sutton*, v, 113-14. This was nevertheless wider publication than the average excommunication.

immune from guilt. The text then described the new attack, in highly rhetorical and damnatory language. Exclamations of 'But behold!' ('Set ecce') and 'What more?' ('Quid plura?') highlight that the text is a record of a spoken declaration. Condemnatory adverbs were used: 'irreverently'; 'presumptuously'; 'wickedly'; 'atrociously'; 'heinously', 'foully'.[70] The sacrilegious invaders apparently dragged the clergy from the cemetery, and struck them on their heads and other parts of their bodies, and in the monastery they poked certain priests and clerics with knives and swords up to their bare flesh ('usque ad nudam carnem'). They had also inflicted various 'indignities', and otherwise wounded priests. Miller's analysis of the motive behind and meaning of the attacks on the clerics' clothing is informative, fully bringing out the symbolism of the particular character of this assault. It might be added, however, that the way the acts are described in the public excommunication is extreme almost to the point of being misleading. The hoods and sleeves were 'beheaded' and 'amputated' ('sumitatibus capitorum... clericorum... enormiter amputatis et manicis collobiorum... detrunccatis turpiter et decisis'). A listener not paying adequate attention might well have misunderstood the events; this is certainly the effect of skim-reading the sentence. Thus whilst the humiliation of this attack was a spectacle in its own right, the excommunication sought to make it sound as horrific as possible, again to influence perception of it, particularly by those who had not witnessed it first hand.

The somewhat hysterical body of the sentence is matched by the final denunciation. The bishop was obliged to punish those who had committed such 'enormous sacrilege' and 'so wicked a crime', which mocked Christ, violated ecclesiastical liberty, scorned episcopal authority, and brought the priestly and lesser order into ignominy.[71] All and each of the (as yet unnamed) sacrilegious malefactors was denounced to be

> anathematized, excommunicated, sequestered, and set far apart from the body of Christ, the bond of the church, and the communion of the faithful, so that they may receive their lots with Cain the fratricide and Dathan and Abiron, who were swallowed alive for their crimes.[72]

They had incurred this 'divine malediction' *ipso facto,* and the malefactors were 'dressing themselves in it as clothing, drinking it as water, and letting it penetrate to the marrow of their bones' (Ps. 108:18).

For late thirteenth-century England, this sentence is unusually curse-like, even if it pales in comparison to both earlier and later maledictions. Cain and Dathan

---

[70] 'irreverenter'; 'temere'; 'nequiter'; 'atrociter'; 'enormiter'; 'turpiter'.

[71] Rosalind Hill, the register's editor, has in this section mistranscribed 'vindictam' as 'vindicamus' (*Reg. Sutton,* iv, 118, 120), as the microfilm reveals. I am grateful to David d'Avray for confirming that the text cannot be construed with 'vindicamus'.

[72] *Reg. Sutton,* iv, 118.

and Abiron were frequently associated with curses and maledictions. Dathan and Abiron, who in the book of Numbers (16:12-15, 25-34) were swallowed alive for opposing Moses's authority, were particularly apt in this case because, like St John's usurpation of Thomas Sutton's role, they had intruded themselves into the priesthood.[73] Before dooming the malefactors to the fate of the Biblical villains, the sentence recalls Psalm 108, the 'cursing psalm'.[74] The verse of the psalm quoted denounces an unnamed malefactor for cursing: 'He loved to curse; let curses come upon him'. It thus turns the curses expressed by the evil-doer back on his head.[75] The excommunication implies that the treatment of the clergy perpetrated at Long Crendon and Notley was tantamount to cursing the church. The words used in this excommunication, in conjunction with multiple priests throwing their candles to the ground as a symbol of the souls' condemnation and the audience declaring 'fiat! fiat!' at the end of the sentence, could well have made this ceremony terrifying. Even if this excommunication is acknowledged to be in many ways exceptional, it nevertheless demonstrates that elements of cursing remained in this period.[76]

If this excommunication was more damnatory than average, this was surely because of the context of this particular dispute. The crimes committed were shocking, and such ridiculing of the clerical order evidently provoked outrage, but such acts were not unique.[77] By this time, however, around late September 1293,[78] the quarrel over the prebend of Thame had been ongoing for a year. The Suttons had not succeeded in securing the prebend. The bishop's previous excommunications had been ignored. As a result, there is a tangible sense of desperation—and perhaps a genuine desire to curse (against the theology of this period)—in the sentence pronounced after the Long Crendon and Notley attacks. Excommunication and rituals associated with it (such as clamours and maledictions) have long been associated with the social environment in which they were used. Thus Little observed that a simple 'I excommunicate you' might be used,

> But where there are attempts to heighten the drama... as with liturgical robes and candles, and to pile up multiple curses... more than likely there is a social setting in which authority is both weak and insecure.[79]

Little was here was discussing weak authority in the context of the years around 1000, after the disintegration of the Carolingian empire and the supposed collapse

---

[73] Baldwin, *Masters, Princes and Merchants*, 172; Little, *Benedictine Maledictions*, 65–8; Jaser, *Ecclesia maledicens*, 178–84; Genevieve Steele Edwards, 'Ritual excommunication', 84–5, 93.
[74] See 53–4.   [75] Little, *Benedictine Maledictions*, 64.   [76] See Chapter 1, 45–55.
[77] Comparable incidents can be found in episcopal registers, but are not treated with the same severity.
[78] The precise date of the sentence is unknown, but it is included in the register amongst entries from the last week of September 1293.
[79] Little, *Benedictine Maledictions*, 117.

of public justice that followed it. In the absence of a political power maintaining peace and justice, clergy could no longer rely on lay power to protect them. Clamours, maledictions, and excommunications were thus symptoms of powerless clergy attempting to protect themselves by invoking God to curse their persecutors. Charlotte Lewandowski has argued that during the anarchy of Stephen's reign, when excommunication and anathema was often used, 'the language of excommunication became increasingly elaborate in order to reflect the limited transmission of...documents in a violent and uncertain political environment'.[80] Christian Jaser has further observed that ritual excommunication forms peaked, then rapidly declined, in the twelfth century because local property disputes were more likely to be pursued in papal and royal courts. Self-defence of ecclesiastical property was less necessary and elaborate excommunications consequently less in demand.[81]

It is hardly possible to argue that there was any kind of anarchy or collapse of justice in 1293; Edward I's reign is seen as a period in which important developments in public justice took place. Far from the lay power being unable to keep the peace, the system of law enforcement had developed for the most part effectively.[82] However, if secular power was not absent in 1293, it was apparently uncooperative. Oliver Sutton had reason to feel that there was 'no hope of justice from men'.[83] Sutton had appealed to the king and sheriff for help on multiple occasions, but to no avail. Nor was there any help to be sought from ecclesiastical authority: there was neither a pope nor an archbishop to step in on the bishop's behalf. God Himself was the only remaining source of potential assistance. This political context, and the bishop's personal involvement in the case, must at least partially account for the unusual force of the anathema here, which betrays a level of desperation about lack of earthly remedy.

It is necessary now to turn to how secular justice was dealing with the matter, for the king had in fact done something about the August Thame attack. At the beginning of September (thus probably before the attacks at Long Crendon and Notley) a commission was sent to the sheriff of Oxford, ordering him to assemble a jury. On 7 October the inquest took place. The case found in favour of St John's adherents: certain knights did indeed go to Thame, and entered the church's court with horses and arms, but they did not break the bishop's fences or commit any of the offences alleged. They did this in the name of Edward St John, 'by a provision granted to Edward by the pope'.[84] The significance of this is, first, that the Suttons continued to be frustrated in their attempts to receive redress and secure the prebend. Second, the results of the inquest indicate that attempts to influence the

---

[80] Lewandowski, 'Cultural expressions of episcopal power', 97, and in ch. 2 as a whole. E.g. in *Councils & Synods* I, ed. Whitelock, Brett and Brooke, 786.
[81] Jaser, *Ecclesia maledicens*, 319–20. [82] See Prestwich, *Edward I*, ch. 10.
[83] Little, 'Anger in monastic curses', 29–31.
[84] *Calendar of Inquisitions Miscellaneous*, i, no. 1640.

publica fama may have failed. The jury seemingly believed that the attack was less serious than the bishop alleged and, moreover, that it was justified in the circumstances. It was to secure what was rightfully St John's. They were not convinced his claim was invalid, though pressure may have been brought to bear on the jurors through St John's considerable connections. Another attempt, in November, to have the king's men remove the force occupying the church was once again unsuccessful.[85] The sheriff reported that he found no force there, while St John himself asserted that he was the prebendary.[86] If, as the inquest and subsequent events imply, the neighbourhood (and the king) favoured St John, this further explains the vigour of the excommunication sentences. These secular proceedings also reveal how partisan and exaggerated a picture the excommunications give. Yet this was the version being pronounced throughout the diocese of Lincoln, and for many it might have been the only account they heard.

At first sight, depositions made in early 1294 at Canterbury imply that the bishop's narrative had by then become part of the public consciousness. John de Scalleby described how the church had been broken and set alight, how clerics had been injured and mass celebrated in the polluted church, and how Thomas Sutton's ministers had been violently ejected, and how St John's men were now nefariously detaining the church.[87] Others recounted a similar story in equally condemnatory words.[88] Several of these witnesses claimed that the facts they presented were public and notorious around Thame. 'It is notorious around Oxford that St John intruded himself into the church of Thame', said John Sutton.[89] However, their evidence is problematic, and not necessarily representative of public opinion. John de Scalleby was Oliver Sutton's registrar, and would have been the one to write the excommunication sentence in the register. Henry de Nassington, another witness, was the bishop's official; others were members of his *familia*.[90] Thus, although the events at Thame must have been known to many in the diocese of Lincoln only via the bishop's excommunications, there is no independent witness, important in legal proceedings, who we can suggest learned of events only via the excommunications. It is impossible from the extant evidence to know the extent to which the narrative was accepted by those unconnected with the case, even if these witnesses asserted that St John's 'intrusion' was indeed common knowledge (and interpreted as such) around Thame.[91]

Those who spoke for St John implied the opposite. One of his witnesses merely stated that the latter's induction took place on 12 August, and that he had been in

---

[85] Request in *Reg. Sutton*, iv, 132.   [86] *SCC*, 573, 610.   [87] *SCC*, 590.
[88] *SCC*, 593, 594, 596.   [89] *SCC*, 600 (the editors' calendar of the testimony).
[90] *SCC*, 575 n.11, 594, nn. 3–4.
[91] Those who had personally witnessed the attack, including one of the clerks who was himself injured, refer to the violent occupation, but in notably less graphic detail than those more closely related to the bishop (*SCC*, 582). Nevertheless, their testimony does confirm that the substance of the August excommunication was correct.

possession of the church some days before this, as was public and notorious in the area. Here it was Thomas Sutton who was described as molesting and disturbing Edward St John.[92] The subjectivity of the witnesses in these proceedings meant they all towed their own party's line, even if they often claimed that their version was common knowledge. Since no decision was ever reached by the court, we cannot know how their accounts were judged. Once again, however, divisions amongst churchmen and their (lay and ecclesiastical) factions were aired in public, for everyone to hear and discuss.[93]

The bishop's own efforts to bring his enemies to justice meanwhile continued. Investigations were launched into the names of those who had perpetrated the August attack.[94] Letters were also sent to various clergy in the area, telling them to regard Thomas Sutton as the true prebendary. The parishioners of Thame were to be urged not to communicate with the attackers in any way, and were reminded that communicating with excommunicates would cause them to be infected and defiled by the stain of contagion. Presumably some of them had been helping St John provide the occupiers with victuals. Trading, dealing, eating, and drinking with the malefactors were all prohibited. Parishioners were forbidden to hear divine services in the profaned church, polluted by extraction of blood.[95] Both letters rehearsed the earlier arguments concerning Thomas's peaceful collation and possession before the malicious, unjust, violent, and sacrilegious invasion. We are also reminded at this juncture that Thame's wealth was at the heart of this dispute. The bishop had added to the list of offences that the occupiers were 'usurping and thieving' the prebend's oblations and profits. On the other side, when a female parishioner was compelled to go to the dependent chapel to be churched after childbirth (indicating that the bishop's orders were being obeyed at least by some), the vicar took the resulting oblations on Thomas Sutton's authority.[96] As the editors of the Canterbury court records note, 'this is probably intended to show that Thomas had possession of the revenues of the church and was regarded by the vicar as being in possession'.[97] Being seen to perform the usual functions of the prebendary was probably also the motive behind the same vicar's collection of four shillings of oblations from a chapel of the prebend on Christmas Day. He did so with eight armed men, who were later received by Thomas Sutton himself. St John's witnesses, predictably, complained that Thomas's men had despoiled the prebend.[98]

As a result of the investigations initiated by Bishop Sutton, fifteen men were named as the 'principal authors' of the August attack. This allowed fourteen

---

[92] *SCC*, 582.   [93] See Chapter 4, 167–71, and esp. Chapter 5, 192–5, 198–212.
[94] *Reg. Sutton*, iv, 135–6.
[95] *Reg. Sutton*, iv, 136–8. These orders were fulfilled on 22 November, when the archdeacon of Buckingham warned St John's men to leave the church, prohibited them from celebrating divine services, and began to proceed against the delinquents 'by way of notoriety': *SCC*, 597.
[96] *SCC*, 597.   [97] *SCC*, 597 n. 6.   [98] *SCC*, 584–5.

laymen to be excommunicated, and one chaplain to be suspended, by name. On 15 December, Oliver Sutton ordered all eight of his archdeacons to publish the sentence in every church and chapel on every Sunday and feast day, and in all chapters and convocations of clergy. The bishop himself and the archdeacon of Buckingham published the sentence at Wycombe (*c.*13 miles from Thame) on 19 December, dressed in sacerdotal robes, and with many priests assisting in white stoles. Strangely, it was not, on this occasion, pronounced in English as well as Latin.[99] This excommunication was given the same striking publicity as that following the Long Crendon and Notley incidents. One of St John's witnesses knew of the denunciation 'from the widespread report of many people', admitting that it was public and notorious in Wycombe, Thame, and the surrounding area that such a sentence had been promulgated and published.[100] Its contents laid far more emphasis on the legal aspects of the sentence, however. Thus the earlier general sentence was done 'as justice urged' ('justicia suadente'), the names discovered through legitimate means, and the wrongdoers' 'contumacy and manifest offences' were noted. The excommunication's validity was being emphasized by describing how excommunication had been incurred automatically by the nature of the crimes, and for the contumacious refusal of the guilty to submit to the bishop's authority. The previous excommunications, from which they had not sought absolution, were mentioned as having been published 'far and wide in our diocese'. The language used in this excommunication is less remarkable than the previous sentence, which fits into a pattern in which general excommunications with unknown perpetrators used the harshest language. Nevertheless, the sentence related much of the same information as earlier excommunications and included various damnatory asides. It again referred to Psalm 108.[101]

The original general sentence had thus borne fruit: the names of the sinners had been discovered through investigations, allowing excommunication *nominatim*. This was how, in this period, general sentences functioned. Here a distinction may be drawn between thirteenth-century and earlier practice. General sentences certainly can imply the impotence of those using them, who were left to call upon God to punish unknown malefactors. But in this period administrative structures allowed enquiries into who was responsible to yield results. In this, if not in every case, the process worked.[102] However, the December sentence illuminates the value in another way, for it was a matter of contention in the Canterbury court as a result of an appeal made against it by Edward St John.

---

[99] *Reg. Sutton*, iv, 153–4. One unlettered witness described the ceremony but said that he had not understood the words because they were in Latin. His deposition shows that when the excommunications of March and August were announced in English, this was important in ensuring those sentences were understood. Why it was not pronounced in English in December is unclear (*SCC*, 585). See also Chapter 1, 48–9, for this witness's testimony.

[100] 'ex relatu wlgari multorum'.   [101] *Reg. Sutton*, iv, 150–2.

[102] See Hill, 'General excommunications', for this process.

We know, therefore, that St John was perturbed by it. Yet he was not himself one of those named, and it is this fact that demonstrates certain advantages to *not* naming people in sentences of excommunication.

The Wycombe excommunication came to be of importance in court proceedings for two reasons. First, it had been pronounced after St John's appeal, made on 18 December, to the apostolic see and the court of Canterbury. He argued that the sentence should therefore never have been pronounced. In fact, because he was not named, St John's contention held little weight. Second, after Christmas, St John requested a copy of the sentence, which he never received. The court of Canterbury thus sought to ascertain whether the bishop knew of the appeal before he pronounced the excommunication, and why St John had never received a written copy of it.[103] Unfortunately, the court never reached a decision on either point, and witnesses gave conflicting evidence on both matters. It is unclear whether Oliver Sutton knew of the appeal before 19 December. It is certain only that the bishop was told of a second appeal made by St John on 27 December.[104] The second question, though unresolved, reveals some interesting aspects of how excommunication was used.

Edward St John was arguing that the law required that he be provided with a copy of the excommunication. He was referring to *Cum medicinalis*, which stipulated that an excommunicator must 'write down expressly the reason' for a sentence and make a copy available on request.[105] St John claimed that the bishop had refused to do this when he was asked on 28 December.[106] The witnesses differ in their narratives of what took place. St John and his witnesses said that the bishop refused to give a copy 'against justice';[107] others said that he had been willing to provide a copy;[108] some did not know whether he had been asked and refused;[109] the witnesses for Oliver Sutton said that he had no obligation to make a copy. It is the latter argument that is most interesting. The bishop was not obliged to give a copy of the sentence he pronounced at Wycombe because St John was not named in it. The more technical argument made was that the bishop had only *published* a sentence, but had not himself excommunicated anyone.[110] The excommunication had been incurred *ipso facto*, so the law itself was the excommunicator. This provided the legal loophole that the bishop himself had not given

---

[103] For a similar issue regarding copies in the Cantilupe-Pecham dispute, see Douie, *Archbishop Pecham*, 224.
[104] *SCC*, 583.
[105] See also Chapter 1 above. Council of Lyon (1245), in Tanner, *Decrees*, i, 291–2, cc. 21, 19. This was paralleled in the secular sphere, though apparently later (Thierry Dutour associates it with the fourteenth century), when everyone had the right to demand a copy: Dutour, 'L'élaboration', 147.
[106] *SCC*, 579–80.   [107] *SCC*, 584.   [108] *SCC*, 591, 595.   [109] *SCC*, 585–6.
[110] *SCC*, 594, 595: he had not issued the sentence 'set solummodo pupplicavi...sentenciam ab aliis et a canone prius latam'. See also 588 n. 4, and 597–8, where a third witness makes the same argument.

a judgement and could thus argue that the law required nothing more from him. He was willing to provide a copy when the law required him to do so.[111]

What is significant here is that Edward St John was arguing that Oliver Sutton was using excommunication illegally, but in fact, because of the peculiar rules governing *ipso facto* excommunications, he was not.[112] The issue was not merely one of copies. Walter of Bedwyn, a witness for St John at Canterbury, complained that the detainers of the church, and all communicating with them, were excommunicated specially and by name, and publicly and solemnly announced excommunicated, 'not warned, not confessed, absent not through contumacy, without reasonable cause, and against the statutes of the general council... and against justice', at the instance or provocation of Thomas Sutton. The Suttons were 'pretending' that St John had no right to the prebend.[113] The fact that this excommunication was a *lata sententia* invalidated these complaints. When the malefactors had perpetrated their attacks, they had automatically incurred excommunication. Unusually, no specific *latae sententiae* were invoked, but it was presumably felt that it was obvious that these acts incurred excommunication. The perpetrators had injured clerics and were repeatedly condemned as sacrilegious (both covered by *Si quis suadente*), and it was asserted that they had violated ecclesiastical liberty and desecrated a church. The bishop had acted with reasonable cause and justly, 'as the order of law and the nature and character of the business required'.[114] Thus the acts had merited excommunication, and there was no need for warning, citation, or contumacy before a sentence was promulgated, because the *ipso facto* nature of the excommunication circumvented all these legal processes. Moreover, before the December sentence in which the malefactors were named, they had been given plenty of opportunity to make amends through the publication of the general sentences. These men had been excommunicated since August (so were now contumacious); the publication of their names was merely the result of an investigation into who had been the culprits. Technically, they were not being excommunicated, but were merely being denounced as excommunicates. Equally, the bishop himself had not, in legal terms, issued a sentence of excommunication. The excommunication was *a jure*.[115]

The Thame dispute demonstrates how *latae sententiae* allowed clergy deeply involved in disputes to anathematize their opponents, legally, without ever having recourse to anything resembling an impartial judge. In this particular case, the resulting excommunications give the impression that cursing was very much in

---

[111] SCC, 594: quando dicta copia petebatur dominus episcopus paratus erat omnem copiam petitam facere ad quam tenebatur de iure.

[112] Although the court never reached a decision.   [113] SCC, 583.   [114] SCC, 590-1.

[115] One witness seems to have been arguing that the sentence had been pronounced not by the bishop, but by others. This too was a valid argument, since the investigation had been conducted by the archdeacons. It had been they who proceeded against the malefactors, making them—if anyone—the official excommunicators.

the minds of those who performed the ritual ceremony. In any case, these sentences demonstrate how *ipso facto* sentences were enormously advantageous in certain circumstances. None of the excommunications pronounced during this dispute involved law courts. The excommunications were published immediately and with limited legal procedure. They were, however, completely in accordance with canon law. Edward St John may have been aggrieved by a perceived lack of judicial process, but it was not necessary in the circumstances. Canon law allowed immediate denunciation. The sequence of events here was not at all exceptional. *Ipso facto* excommunications proliferated in the thirteenth century, so that a great many offences resulted in instant excommunication. The advantage of such sentences, of course, was that those who offended the church could be disciplined—by which the sinner was warned and cited to appear in court—without need for the longer process otherwise required before someone could be excommunicated.

The complaint of Edward St John is notable because he was not named in the sentence. Since he was never personally denounced, he had no grounds for complaint. For the same reason, he had no reason to fear that the secular arm would be invoked against him or that he would be refused legal hearing. In fact, none of these possible consequences of excommunication appear to have happened to anyone involved in the Thame affair, although St John's supporters attempted to argue that both the Suttons were excommunicated (on papal authority for opposing Edward's provision) and that Oliver's collation of Thomas was invalid as a result.[116] St John thus had no reason to fear these tangible repercussions of excommunication. He had, however, almost certainly incurred excommunication for providing help and favour to those who occupied the church, who had also been excommunicated in August. One of the bishop's witnesses in fact noted that Oliver could have excommunicated him, but had deferred to St John out of kindness.[117]

It is often noted that excommunication in thirteenth-century England (and elsewhere) was overused and ineffective.[118] Without the help of the secular arm, it is assumed, it was something of a damp squib. Why then was St John so concerned about a sentence which could have resulted in neither this nor in legal consequences? He might have been concerned for his soul, since he had indeed incurred excommunication, but had simply not been publicly denounced as an excommunicate. However, since he was arguing that the sentence was invalid, and that the Suttons themselves were excommunicates, it is unlikely that he harboured fears about his soul. If he had, resigning his claim and seeking absolution would have been the best course of action. It is also unlikely that St John would have been

---

[116] *SCC*, 603, 605, 606. London, TNA, C85 does not appear to contain any writs that could relate to this dispute.
[117] *SCC*, 595.   [118] These comments are discussed in the Introduction, at 5–11.

ostracized by anyone he considered important, for he had many powerful supporters. His appeal was perhaps the result of ignorance. He may not have realized that he had not been included in the bishop's December sentence and that he had no grounds to appeal it. If he was unaware of its precise contents, this would explain his eagerness to obtain a copy. He knew that people had been named (for the first time in the dispute), after he had lodged an appeal, and perhaps assumed that he had been included. The fact that he was not, and that he was not even implicated in the 19 December excommunication at issue, provides the possibility that the bishop was being clever, not kind. Witnesses were unclear whether or not the bishop knew of St John's appeal of 18 December when he denounced the attackers the following day. It is certainly plausible that he had not been aware of it. Yet it is notable that Sutton's sentence included no clause which implicated St John in any way. It was perfectly standard to add in such sentences that those who provided help and counsel to those named were bound by the same excommunication. Earlier sentences in this dispute had done so.[119] If he had been mentioned or incriminated in any capacity following his appeal, St John's complaints might have held some weight, and denunciations would have had to be deferred while the appeal was pending. Oliver Sutton had completely avoided any wrongdoing. He could publish excommunication, and have it published, without breaking any rules or infringing any appeals.

In a case such as this, excommunication was not about having people arrested or preventing them being heard in court; it was about publicizing the illicit way in which a would-be usurper had gone about asserting his right to an ecclesiastical benefice. Removing any mention of St John was unlikely to be detrimental to Oliver Sutton's aim of using excommunication for publicity, since it must have been well known by now that the attack had been made in St John's name. St John was therefore almost certainly aggrieved about this damning indictment of his supporters' sacrilege, but he could do nothing to stop it being pronounced repeatedly throughout the entire diocese of Lincoln. Undoubtedly the bishop wanted to punish the wrongdoers by name, but he also needed the community's support, in terms of shunning the excommunicates but also regarding the wider issue of who rightly held the benefice. Massimo Vallerani has observed (discussing ecclesiastical courts) that 'that which counted was not the fact reconstructed by the parties, but the fact perceived in the parish and the negative *fama* of those behaviours, or of the person'.[120] Excommunication was about winning over the people. The automatic nature of the sentence, far from being a disadvantage, was of much use in this case. The law allowed the bishop, highly partisan in this instance, to use the sanction in this way.

---

[119] A cynical possibility is that the sentence, copied into the bishop's register later, had such references removed.
[120] Vallerani, *Medieval Public Justice*, 38.

The depositions concerning these ecclesiastical matters were made in February and March 1294. But between them and the events they described, further events had taken place, which resulted in an inquisition made before the king's bench. This time, it was St John who judged that appealing to secular justice was the best course of action. Certain members of the local community, whether influenced by Sutton's pronouncements or not, had taken action against Edward St John. The latter's complaint was that his adherents, who had been occupying the church of Thame since August, were being besieged inside the church. A multitude of armed men had been gathered by Oliver and Thomas Sutton, and had obstructed the royal highway around Thame with dykes and fences, preventing victuals from reaching St John and his men so that they were dying of hunger. This indicates that Thomas Sutton also had local support, and it is possible that some of this was generated by the bishop's excommunications, though he could have simply hired these musclemen. On 3 February, following St John's complaint, the king ordered an escheator to investigate the purported siege, to destroy the ditches and impediments (if he found them), and to attach those who had conducted the siege so that they appear before him three weeks after Easter to answer for their transgressions. The escheator was also to investigate how the writ ordering removal of the lay force inside the church had been executed by the sheriff, by impanelling a jury and going to the church himself.[121]

The inquest found that events had taken place broadly as St John described. Thomas Sutton had reportedly given permission for around a hundred armed men to blockade the church, and had later received the ringleaders.[122] The bailiff, by not interfering, had also consented. Although the highway was no longer obstructed (but was still not as it had been before), the two Suttons and eleven named men were cited to appear before the king to defend themselves against the accusations and the charge that they had acted against the king's peace and 'in contempt of the lord king of twenty thousand pounds'. While claiming the common bridge had been destroyed by a flood, they did not deny the blockade, but argued that it had been necessary and indeed authorized. Thus 'they did not blockade the aforesaid church unless it was that they were guarding the... felons... according to the law and custom of England'. They put emphasis on the fact that their actions were to maintain the king's peace. The men inside the church were dangerous criminals; one of them had murdered a man from Thame who had been guarding the church; the coroner had ordered the siege.[123]

There is an interesting overlap between secular and ecclesiastical jurisdictions here. Although the Suttons argued that the immediate cause of the blockade was

---

[121] *SKB*, iii, 11–12.   [122] They were named by the jurors.
[123] The siege in some ways resembles watches over churches in which felons had sought sanctuary, although having committed sacrilege and as excommunicates, the besieged were forbidden to seek sanctuary. See Jordan, 'A fresh look at sanctuary', esp. 21–5. And see above, 154–5.

the murder committed by its occupiers, the church was clearly being guarded before this (the victim was one of those protecting it). The significance of this is that by depriving St John's men of victuals, Sutton's men were in fact enforcing excommunication. The December sentence had specifically prohibited interaction with those inside the church by buying selling, eating, drinking, or providing fire or water. In an extreme manner, blockading the church enforced the bishop's order. It is therefore interesting that they did not give this explanation. Excommunication may not have been behind their actions, of course, but in other situations strict enforcement of excommunication resulted in similar complaints of starvation.[124] Possibly, the men judged that such a justification for barricading St John's men would hold little weight with the king. Stressing the occupiers' disturbance to the peace was a better line to take. This connection between how secular and canon law would deal with such a situation is noteworthy: treatment of felons, particularly outlaws, was much like that of excommunicates.[125] The similarities here, and the fact that enforcing excommunication was not used as an excuse, also emphasize that the protagonists in this two-year disagreement were tactically selecting and using legal procedures.[126]

The bishop's excommunications had conceivably been more successful at influencing public understanding of events by this point. His sentences may have manipulated the functioning of other legal systems, if perception of facts was altered by them. Following a grand jury on 8 July, all those accused were pardoned. Oliver and Thomas Sutton had earlier been released *sine die* on the grounds that they could not answer about ordering a crime until the crime itself had been proved.[127] This outcome indicates that the arguments of the accused were accepted. Since, unlike witnesses in the ecclesiastical court, jurors were not presented to the court by either party, their evidence was in one sense more likely to be impartial. Certainly, if the witnesses at the court of Canterbury are believed, the dispute over Thame was a matter of much discussion.[128] The excommunications defaming St John and his agents had been promulgated throughout the diocese for a considerable amount of time and were likely themselves to have been matters for discussion. This is an important and hitherto unrecognized value of the ecclesiastical sanction, though the point should not be pushed too far. It is difficult to find indisputable evidence, and it must be admitted that the pardon could have had more to do with the desire of the king, who was about to go to war, to settle the quarrel than the jury's impression. That is, perhaps the king rather than the bishop was manipulating legal systems.

---

[124] See Chapter 4, 118–19.
[125] Summerson, 'Structure of law enforcement', esp. 315. Felons seeking sanctuary were also starved out: Jordan, 'A fresh look at medieval sanctuary', 24–5.
[126] Hyams, *Rancor and Reconciliation*, 191–2.   [127] *SKB*, iii, 16–18.
[128] Depositions repeatedly note that facts were public and notorious; numerous witnesses confessed to only knowing facts through *publica fama*, rumours, or *ex relatu*.

The end of the Thame dispute is anti-climactic. This is partly because its resolution, after all the legal appeals, appears to have been conducted by the king through mediation rather than judgement. As a result, there are far fewer documents for the last phase. Much must have been going on behind the scenes that we cannot know. It seems unlikely that the various settlements were unrelated. On 26 June, Oliver Sutton ordered those who had incurred excommunication for 'diverse enormities' over the prebend to be absolved.[129] On 6 July, the king ordered the sheriff of Oxford to take all the appurtenances of the prebend, spiritual and temporal, into the king's hands. Neither party was to touch it until the king decided to whom it should be given. Religious services were to continue.[130] Some sort of arrangement was presumably reached, because on 25 July, in the presence of the king, Oliver Sutton agreed to confer a prebend worth 110 marks on Edward St John.

St John also felt that his reputation had been damaged, presumably via the bishop's excommunications. The bishop was therefore to write a letter preserving St John's reputation ('pro conservatione fame').[131] Securing a similar letter from the bishop may have been behind his earlier complaint about the December excommunication at the Canterbury court. A fortnight after the bishop's audience with the king in London, St John, now also in the king's presence, agreed to treat with the bishop and others about the dispute.[132] At both audiences with the king, a number of important men were present, including St John's influential father, John of St John.[133] On 1 October, the sheriff was finally ordered not to involve himself in the prebend of Thame any further and to restore the church and its appurtenances to Thomas Sutton, since the discords had been 'wholly settled before the king in the *curia regis*'.[134] Shortly afterwards, the king, 'at the instance' of Oliver Sutton, pardoned in parliament those who had been accused of blockading the church of Thame.[135] The murderers of St John's yeoman, who had been killed at the start of the dispute, were pardoned a few days later.[136]

Though the king's mediation was evidently successful, with both sides having cause to be happy with the outcome, the settlement was not as easy as his orders imply. There was a final bout of violence: when the sheriff sent his bailiff to take the prebend into the king's hands, the bailiff was murdered. Amongst those accused of this murder was Henry le Drye, who was also one of those indicted for blockading the church, so this killing was presumably perpetrated by Sutton's supporters. The event does not appear to have jeopardized the settlement of the

---

[129] *Reg. Sutton*, v, 12; Lincolnshire Archives, Register of Oliver Sutton, f. 103v (the full text was not printed by Hill).
[130] It is unclear when the church had been reconciled. See *Reg. Sutton,* iv, 152, 168.
[131] *CCR 1288–96*, 390.   [132] *CCR 1288–96*, 391.
[133] See *SCC,* 567 n.4, and Miller, 'Knights, bishops and deer parks', 214–18.
[134] *CCR 1288–96*, 370; Prynne, *Records,* 607–8.   [135] *SKB*, iii, 17–18.
[136] *CPR 1292–1301*, 97, 116.

dispute more generally and the accused all pleaded not guilty.[137] It indicates, however, that Sutton's supporters were not confident that the king would resolve the disagreement in their favour. After all, while matters were being dealt with the king had himself handed his household at Oxford to St John, exposing his connection with St John and potential favouritism.[138] The murder is also a final reminder of the strength of feeling of those involved in this case. Both Edward St John and Thomas Sutton had supporters who were willing to go to great lengths to help their attempts to secure this benefice.

The excommunications were the last part of the Thame dispute to be resolved. The matter was only laid to rest once everyone had been absolved. In March 1295, with Easter approaching, Thomas Sutton, prebendary of Thame, was instructed to grant absolution to those who wished to seek it and to give them a suitable penance. The difficult cases were reserved to the bishop.[139] Thomas de Lewknor, Edward St John's key clerical supporter, was absolved in August. The absolution was witnessed by several important figures, including the bishop of Winchester, in the king's wardrobe in the archbishop of York's house in London.[140] The place of absolution and those present indicate that political pressure may have forced the bishop to absolve Lewknor, and that this was not simply a case of Lewknor's remorse causing him to humbly seek absolution. There is no mention that he was given any penance as a condition of the absolution.[141] The final absolution did not occur until 14 July 1297, when it was at last ordered that William of Fotheringay, a clerk who had been included in the excommunication of 19 December 1293 as one of the principal authors of the attack on the church of Thame, was to be absolved, on the condition that he recognized his excesses and made satisfaction, and received pardon from those he had injured. Specifically, William had helped and consented to the notorious intrusions and illicit detentions, and had 'inflicted a ridiculous injury' on a monastic lay brother. His penance was to perambulate the church of Thame,[142] while divinities were being celebrated, reciting the seven penitential psalms, the fifteen psalms, and the litany, on every Sunday from 25 July until Christmas. He was humbly to abstain from entry into the church at these times.[143] Although quite a lengthy penance, it could have been far more severe, for it did not involve public beatings.[144] The relative leniency of the penance is remarkable. It is remarkable considering the severity of the excommunication sentences, and all the more so considering that it remained in the consciousness of the bishop's household long after it had been resolved. In 1298, all the documents

---

[137] It is not clear precisely how the case was concluded.   [138] *CCR 1288–96*, 358.
[139] *Reg. Sutton*, v, 65–6; Lincolnshire Archives, Register of Oliver Sutton, f. 119r.
[140] *Reg. Sutton*, v, 111–12; Lincolnshire Archives, Register of Oliver Sutton, f.131r.
[141] *Reg. Sutton*, v, 111–12; f. 131r; see also vi, 34–5, where a letter patent testified this absolution.
[142] If he was nearby, otherwise he could perform it outside the parish church where he happened to be.
[143] *Reg. Sutton*, vi, 15–16.
[144] Possibly because he was a clerk: Hill, 'Public penance', 223–4. This penance is mentioned on 219.

concerning the Thame affair were sent to the bishop of Salisbury.[145] It was possibly when this was being done that small faces (looking generally displeased) were drawn alongside most of the entries in the register concerning Thame. While the manuscript has some marginal notation, there is not a great deal. The faces were evidently drawn later than the original entries were written, added presumably to mark out the letters concerning Thame.[146] St John and his claim were not forgotten.

*

The diverse sources that convey the various strategies used by the disputants illuminate our understanding of society and legal processes in late thirteenth-century England. Though legal institutions and arguments featured prominently in the events of 1292–94, so too did violence. Both claimants and their supporters took matters into their own hands at the same time as they appealed to higher jurisdictional authorities. If the twelfth century onwards can be viewed as an 'age of law', this characterization should not be overemphasized. Just as in the earlier Middle Ages, resort to legal institutions was only one tactic amongst several of settling a dispute.[147] The Thame case enables an understanding of how these approaches interacted, and of how actions were presented in different contexts. As in earlier periods traditionally viewed as less 'judicial', the disagreement was resolved through negotiation, not a legal judgement.

Excommunication was only one aspect of the Thame dispute. But it was an important one. The sentences pronounced were unusually vehement and unusually widely promulgated. They show that the support of the church and its severest sanction was desirable as a way to attempt to influence public opinion. Here excommunication was being used justly, yet it was being used to the advantage of one party in a legal conflict. Oliver Sutton was not impartial, and, alongside violence and lawsuits, excommunication was one strategy used as a means of strengthening the position of the excommunicator.[148] The Thame excommunications did not cause St John and his men to desist (nor did St John's against the Suttons). In the end, Thomas Sutton's claim was upheld, but it can hardly be argued that St John's attempts to assert his claim to the prebend were ill advised. He ended up with a far richer benefice than he otherwise would have. He might even be taken as the 'winner'.

The excommunications pronounced during this dispute did not drive those sentenced straight back to the bosom of the church, but the efficacy, purpose, and value of excommunication went far beyond this. The sentences' importance was not limited to their ability to coerce St John and his supporters. As well as

---

[145] *Reg. Sutton*, vi, 116. [146] The marginal faces are not generally mentioned in Hill's edition.
[147] Davies and Fouracre, *Settlement of Disputes*, 'Conclusion', 237–8.
[148] Kaeuper, *War, Justice, and Public Order*, 142; Geary, *Living with the Dead*, 147–8.

showing, once again, that excommunications could be maledictory and *ex parte* while being imposed in accordance with the law, this case serves to emphasize the adaptability of ecclesiastical sanctions. Excommunication was not imposed by unthinking judges governed by canonical procedures, but was affected by the circumstances of those who wielded the power to excommunicate and what they wanted to achieve. It responded to events, then subsequently influenced them. In turn, implementation was affected by those against whom it was used and the behaviour of the wider community, at the same time as excommunication sought to influence that behaviour. Thus those who used excommunication, the people sentenced, and the wider community all had an impact upon the way in which excommunications panned out (and the cases in which they were used more generally). Understanding a sentence's full impact thus requires an exploration of its particular context, for excommunication was a living institution that was tailored to situations and involved interaction between churchmen, excommunicates, and communities.

7

Ecclesiastical Broadcasting in the Thirteenth Century

The Origins of the Great Curse

At the turn of the thirteenth century, a new practice sprung up whereby *ipso facto* sentences of excommunication were to be publicized on a regular basis in parish churches. It is clear that, amongst the various matters dealt with in ecclesiastical legislation, *ipso facto* sentences were treated with particular seriousness. For the remainder of the Middle Ages a great deal of emphasis was placed, in legislation and pastoral manuals, upon regular publication of what would come to be known as the Great Sentence or Great Curse. In 1195, a legatine council held at York anathematized perjurers and ordered 'every priest' to solemnly excommunicate them three times a year. Five years later, the council of Westminster, for the Canterbury province, was vaguer on publication but condemned more offences: sorcerers, perjurers, arsonists, 'atrocious thieves', and robbers were to be solemnly excommunicated 'every year'. Diocesan synods for Canterbury and Salisbury dioceses in the second decade of the century continued the trend, ordering thrice yearly publication of a list similar to that of the 1200 council. The most influential council was that of Oxford held by Stephen Langton in 1222, which began by declaring seven automatic sentences that were to be pronounced four times a year in every parish church.

It is well known that English provincial and diocesan legislation proliferated in the thirteenth century, to such an extent that there was little innovation beyond the early years of the fourteenth century, and indeed none in terms of statutes from the closing decades of the thirteenth. Most of these statutes, whether produced at the diocesan or provincial level, sought to ensure regular publication of *ipso facto* excommunications. The manuscript survival of these councils and synods indicates that the statutes remained in use for the rest of the Middle Ages.[1] The statutes' excommunications and accompanying provisions for publication were, therefore, extremely influential. Langton's Oxford sentences and John Pecham's 1281 Lambeth sentences were included *verbatim* in Lyndwood's *Provinciale*. The Middle English Great Sentence (which varied) was based upon

---

[1] Cheney, 'Statute-making', 150.

the thirteenth-century innovations, though inevitably the lists increased in length as new offences were added.

The importance attached to *ipso facto* sentences and their publication by English bishops in this golden age of ecclesiastical legislation is undeniable. In all, twenty-nine sets of statutes between 1195 and 1289 required clergy to publicize sentences.[2] Appendix I, which lists automatic sentences and their publication requirements, shows this clearly: the dioceses of Bath and Wells, Canterbury, Carlisle, Chichester, Coventry and Lichfield, Durham, Exeter, Lincoln, Norwich, Salisbury, Winchester, and York all produced statutes that ordered regular publication of *latae sententiae*. So too did provincial and legatine councils held at Oxford, London, Reading, and Lambeth. Ely might in fact be included in the list since its diocesan legislation 1239 × 1256 repeated three of the Oxford sentences and implied that it intended the original Oxford provisions be adhered to; it is not included in the appendix because it did not reiterate the publication provisions.[3] Hereford and Rochester produced no surviving statutes.[4] Thus only the dioceses of London and Worcester are outliers, in that they did produce legislation, but it did not emphasize the necessity of publishing *ipso facto* excommunications. Nevertheless, legislation produced by four provincial councils of course applied to the whole southern province, while archidiaconal statutes for London did include a list to be published.

These *latae sententiae* and the requirements that they be publicized locally are significant for a number of reasons. The offences that incurred immediate excommunication without need for judicial process tell us the particular concerns of the clergymen who pronounced them. Since councils tended to repeat legislation, a note of caution must be sounded here, yet many bishops were selective about which sentences they included, while others added clauses or clarifications to existing excommunications. The reasons given for insisting upon regular publication, not only in statutes but also in individual mandates and pastoral works, indicate that ensuring awareness of *ipso facto* excommunications was no fringe aspect of the cure of souls. Pastorally-minded bishops evidently viewed their duty to publicize such excommunications as a key part of their duty as shepherds to their flocks. Historians have failed to acknowledge the important place afforded to automatic sentences in this context. Moreover, there is plenty of evidence to suggest that *ipso facto* sentences were indeed published in parish churches with great frequency; publication provisions were not unthinkingly copied without

---

[2] Their importance is perhaps further shown by the fact that one copyist of Richard Poore's 1217 × 1219 diocesan statutes, which did not include a list of sentences, added John Pecham's 1279 list of excommunications to Poore's otherwise still useful constitutions. Cheney, *English Synodalia*, 49, 61. France experienced a similar synodal age: Mazel, *L'évêque et le territoire*, 322–6.

[3] *C&S*, 520–1.

[4] It is possible that they once existed; Cheney considered it possible that statutes have been lost: Cheney, 'Statute-making', 155.

attempts to observe or enforce them. The statutes do not merely tell us what the *Ecclesia Anglicana* considered most condemnation-worthy; men and women throughout England were well-informed about the same. Sentences of excommunication pronounced in parish churches were a means of broadcasting ecclesiastical rights, above all, alongside other contemporary concerns.

A New Practice

Before discussing the transgressions that these lists of sentences condemned, it ought to be stressed that this was a new practice. In England, its origins coincide precisely with the beginning of the 'chief period of activity' in English ecclesiastical legislation.[5] This was also the period when episcopal administration and diocesan organization were developing quickly, so that the feasibility of regular local pronouncements likewise increased, for channels of communication and plentiful documents were necessary conditions for routine pronouncement of specific material generated by bishops.[6] No provisions of this sort occurred before 1195 except in a council held by Eadmer, archbishop of Canterbury, in 1102, which ordered that an excommunication against those committing sodomitical sins ('sodomiticum flagitium facientes') should be renewed 'in all churches through the whole of England and on every Sunday'.[7] As Christian Jaser has observed, Pope Callixtus II's 1119 Reims council ordered pronouncement of an excommunication against infringers of the peace of God every Sunday, while Lateran III (1179) ordered a sentence against those who provided Saracens with weapons to be repeated frequently in coastal cities.[8] Gathering *ipso facto* sentences into lists for regular iteration was a new phenomenon at the turn of the thirteenth century and perhaps originated in England.[9] The first list of offences (as opposed to a single sin) to be publicized was produced in 1200.[10] The seminal council, however, was Langton's 1222 provincial council at Oxford. This may be, in turn, regarded as the starting point of the period in which was produced 'the legislation [that] exceeds in bulk and importance all that was produced in other periods of the Middle Ages'.[11] William Lyndwood, who wrote the *Provinciale*, an influential treatise on English canon law, in the 1430s, assumed the 1222 council as the

---

[5] Cheney, 'Statute-making', 150; Cheney, 'Legislation of the medieval English Church', I, 196.

[6] Cheney, *English Bishops' Chanceries*; Hamilton Thompson, 'Diocesan organisation'; Kemp, 'Informing the archdeacon'.

[7] *Councils and Synods* I, ed. Whitelock, Brett and Brooke, ii, 678–9.

[8] Jaser, *Ecclesia maledicens*, 364.

[9] Jaser, at least, cites no earlier examples, nor have I found any.

[10] *Councils and Synods* I, ed. Whitelock, Brett and Brooke, 1065; Papal sentences were similarly gathered into lists from the thirteenth century, for instance by Hostiensis. See Jaser, *Ecclesia maledicens*, 362.

[11] Cheney, 'Legislation of the medieval English Church', I, 218, and II, 389–90.

limit of legal memory.¹² Legislation produced in the twelfth century was largely ignored in the later Middle Ages, though the Westminster offences did not die off completely in later decades and centuries.¹³ The basis for the Great Curse, pronounced in parish churches throughout England for hundreds of years, was therefore firmly created in the early decades of the thirteenth century.

This trend for routine declaration of *latae sententiae* was, of course, related to the proliferation of such sentences in the twelfth and thirteenth centuries. By 1200, the concept of automatic excommunication, despite some initial qualms expressed by canonists (not least Gratian), was accepted.¹⁴ It was then perhaps inevitable that ecclesiastical authorities would add to the list of acts that incurred excommunication the moment they were committed, and this they certainly did. Grouping the sentences together and publicizing them was a natural and indeed necessary next step. Declaring that assaulting a clergyman rendered a person immediately excommunicated—a provision intended both to protect clergy and to signify their separation from the rest of society—was pointless if nobody was made aware of it. There was a clear pastoral need (discussed below) as well as the more practical, self-interested, desire to demonstrate the power of the church.

Christian Jaser notes that there was a particularly strong, and early, tradition in England, but that it was not unique.¹⁵ In the same period, the papacy initiated a similar practice, known as the 'General Process', whereby the list of papal *latae sententiae* was solemnly pronounced by the pope on Maundy Thursday, the Ascension, and the Consecration of St Peter's Basilica. It is unknown precisely when the practice began, but a letter of Honorius III implies that it was under his predecessor, Innocent III. The Maundy Thursday ritual (*Bulla in Coena Domini*) continued until 1770.¹⁶ Like the English practice, regular papal pronouncement of general sentences began in the early thirteenth century and continued, with many additions and amendments, for centuries. The key difference was that the papal ceremony was a single grand event with the pope placed centre-stage. In England, the intention was that each parish priest was holding such a ceremony in his own church. Many parallels of intention and practice can be drawn between the two traditions, but there are also important differences. Agostino Paravicini Bagliani has described the papal rite as having a 'purely political character'.¹⁷

---

¹² Cheney, 'William Lyndwood's *Provinciale*', 164.

¹³ Cheney, 'Legislation of the medieval English Church', I, 214 and *passim*.

¹⁴ See Introduction, 14–17.

¹⁵ Jaser, '*Ostensio Exclusionis*', 365. It certainly seems that there was no such strong tradition in France, at least in the earlier period. Further research may well add to occasional comparable practices on the continent (e.g. the Statutes of Cambrai, 1238–1248, ordered parish priests to excommunicate those who conspired against their priests or prelates three times a year, at Christmas, Easter, and All Saints: *Statuts Synodaux* IV, ed. Avril, 62). H.C. Lea gives examples from Le Mans (1248) and Bamburg (1491): *Studies in Church History*, 458. Beaulande, *Malheur*, 58, notes French synodal *latae sententiae*.

¹⁶ Jaser, *Ecclesia maledicens*, 374, 523–4; Paravicini Bagliani, 'Il rito pontificio di scomunica', 215–16; Paravicini Bagliani, 'Bonifacio VIII, la loggia di giustizia', 392.

¹⁷ Paravicini Bagliani, 'Bonifacio VIII, la loggia di giustizia', 409.

Though certainly political, the English one can by no means be described as purely so.

Offences Condemned

Lists of *ipso facto* sentences were a means of broadcasting crimes that were categorically condemned in order to influence the attitude of parishioners. A great many acts were covered by automatic excommunication. Many more offences than those under discussion here seemingly (the language is sometimes ambiguous) incurred excommunication *ipso facto*. Yet not all were intended to be fulminated regularly. As is evident in Appendix I, there were three main traditions (not mutually exclusive) of lists to be promulgated separately from their statutes: the Westminster/Salisbury clause, the Oxford sentences (later augmented by John Pecham), and sentences belonging to the northern province, used by Durham and York. Condemning these particular offences was rarely innovative, as such. Precedents for condemnation of each type of wrongdoing, some of which can be found in Anglo-Saxon law codes, for instance, are far too numerous to discuss here.[18] The novelty was the use of automatic excommunication in conjunction with publication provisions.

The significance lies in what crimes were deemed worthy of regular public reiteration, and where. There are several caveats to make about overinterpreting this evidence, however. First, there is a great deal of overlap between statutes—much was simply lifted from earlier councils. Moreover, even inclusions or omissions of individual sentences only tell us so much, for they might often have simply been the result of what manuscript was being copied. There were no 'official' texts: only some manuscripts of Salisbury I (reissued as Durham I when Richard Poore moved dioceses) condemn invocation of demons, for instance. At some point, this was either added or removed by a transcriber, affecting any copies that subsequently stemmed from it. Second, the fact that certain excommunications stopped being issued in statutes does not mean they disappeared from use. Appendix I shows that the Westminster/Salisbury tradition was gradually replaced by the Oxford sentences (despite only minor overlap in content), while the northern province's sentences had little traction beyond it. However, many of the Westminster/Salisbury crimes resurfaced (along with many new ones) in Middle English texts of the Great Curse, such as that recorded by John Mirk.[19] Later medieval texts of the Great Sentence varied a great deal and were certainly not dependent on decisions made by thirteenth-century bishops as

---

[18] Hamilton, 'Remedies for "great transgressions"', 98.
[19] Sorcery, usury, not paying tithes, forgery of money and seals, and so on. John Mirk, *Quatuor Sermones*, 57–60. See also Pattwell, 'A sentence of cursing', 131–3.

is the focus here. Most importantly, when transgressions were omitted from lists or apparently fell out of favour, it did *not* mean that people were no longer excommunicated for committing them. All the offences in the appendix could result in excommunication, anywhere, and at any time. The geographical and temporal differences related only to decisions about which offences were publicly recited to the laity on a frequent basis.

Local concerns are nonetheless evident. Fornication, adultery, and prostitution, for instance, occur only in the London archdeaconry list. These sins would land an individual in hot water with the church throughout Christendom and throughout the Middle Ages. What is interesting, therefore, is that only in London were these sins thought worthy of publication. Though the London statutes are the only surviving archidiaconal statutes, it is difficult not to conclude that such offences were more common, or at least evident, in the city. It is interesting, similarly, that only in the diocese of Winchester was pilfering from shipwrecks, apparently a sufficiently big problem that condemning the practice three times a year, in coastal areas and on the Isle of Wight, was deemed necessary. As William Campbell has recently cautioned, it is important not to see pastoral care in England as homogenous. It varied from diocese to diocese.[20]

The frequency with which infringing churches' liberties and other offences were condemned in thirteenth-century English legislation is represented in Table 1.[21] Grouping these excommunications and conveying their sense in short phrases is not a science; the simple chart is intended merely to give a rough idea of sorts of offences condemned, and in how many thirteenth-century English councils.[22] It does not convey that some offenders were condemned with one word (for example, 'sorcerers') always alongside other offenders in a single list, while other offences consisted of whole paragraphs detailed in a separate clause. Some of the distinctions might appear arbitrary—perjury, broadly defined, appears several times—but reflect the different phrasings that proliferated. Appendix I provides details of these crimes, which sentences were borrowed by synods and how they were altered, as well as frequency of publication and numbers of extant manuscripts. The number of councils is not everything: some were a great deal more influential and more widely transmitted than others, so that the prominence of certain offences is far greater when extant manuscripts are taken into account (discussed below).

---

[20] Campbell, *Landscape of Pastoral Care*; 'Theologies of reconciliation'.
[21] Cf. Beaulande, *Malheur*, 107–8.
[22] For instance, Reading and Lambeth c. 2 added public thieves and plunderers to those who disturbed the king's peace, so it is included twice in the chart.

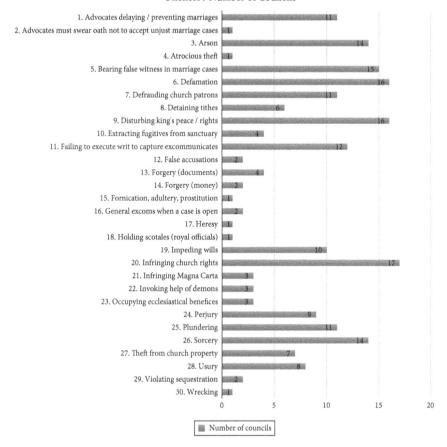

Offences / Number of Councils

#	Offence	Number of councils
1	Advocates delaying / preventing marriages	11
2	Advocates must swear oath not to accept unjust marriage cases	1
3	Arson	14
4	Atrocious theft	1
5	Bearing false witness in marriage cases	15
6	Defamation	16
7	Defrauding church patrons	11
8	Detaining tithes	6
9	Disturbing king's peace / rights	16
10	Extracting fugitives from sanctuary	4
11	Failing to execute writ to capture excommunicates	12
12	False accusations	2
13	Forgery (documents)	4
14	Forgery (money)	2
15	Fornication, adultery, prostitution	1
16	General excoms when a case is open	2
17	Heresy	1
18	Holding scotales (royal officials)	1
19	Impeding wills	10
20	Infringing church rights	17
21	Infringing Magna Carta	3
22	Invoking help of demons	3
23	Occupying ecclesiastical benefices	3
24	Perjury	9
25	Plundering	11
26	Sorcery	14
27	Theft from church property	7
28	Usury	8
29	Violating sequestration	2
30	Wrecking	1

The table makes clear that the first priority was protecting the church's rights, possessions, and members. As Helmholz noted, the first *lata sententia*, *Si quis suadente*, separated clergy from the secular world 'by creating a special immunity from violence in the clergy'.[23] This remained the preoccupation of *latae sententiae*: if grouped together, clauses that protected clergy outnumber other concerns by a large margin. The limited number of areas that fell under ecclesiastical jurisdiction, notably marriage, defamation, and sanctuary, also feature prominently; marriage evidently caused particular anxiety. Safeguarding the (king's) peace and bearing false witness were also key concerns of thirteenth-century archbishops and bishops. As the chart makes clear, the excommunications pronounced at the 1222 Council of Oxford (1, 5, 6, 7, 9, 11, and 20 above) were by

---

[23] Helmholz, 'Si quis suadente', 425; Fossier, *Bureau de âmes*, 415–16.

far the most significant *latae sententiae* publicized in medieval England.[24] Even here, though, there is variation—advocates impeding marriages and the rights of church patrons (Oxford cc. 4 and 6) were apparently not considered big problems everywhere. By contrast, Oxford c. 1 (*Qui malitiose ecclesias*) was never omitted and usually placed first in lists. Local legislation often, indeed, added a clause emphasizing the rights of the local church—'especially the church of Salisbury' and so on.

The Oxford sentences were taken up by so many diocesan and later provincial synods, later forming the basis for the Great Sentence, that they quickly appear commonplace to anyone familiar with this legislation. But their initial declaration was in fact striking, unprecedented, and somewhat provocative. The opening clause (of the entire council) was a clear statement that anyone who infringed ecclesiastical liberties, whether these liberties belonged to a monastery, cathedral, or merely a parish church, was condemned by the church. The statement was so short and stark that it would surely have been easy to remember and understand, especially since it almost always came first in any list of such sentences. It offered a general statement of ecclesiastical liberty, while at the same time made clear that it covered specific and individual rights as much as 'the freedom of the church'. The clause implied no specific accusations about who or what, specifically, might have been Langton's target. People at all levels of society were accused of incurring the sentence—the excommunication affected peasants as much as the king. Nevertheless, the king and his officials were often implicated, and it is certainly plausible that Langton intended to assert that governmental infringements against ecclesiastical liberty would not be tolerated.

Fifty-seven years later, Archbishop John Pecham made any implication that royal officials were the target of *Qui malitiose ecclesias* explicit, exacerbating ecclesiastical tensions with the crown. Extending the clause at his provincial council at Reading (1279), Pecham emphasized that liberties, great and small, were protected by the excommunication, and also clarified the ways in which temporal possessions and rights counted as ecclesiastical rights alongside the spiritual. His next clarification addressed a key issue in the struggle between ecclesiastical and secular jurisdiction: writs of prohibition. Such writs sought to prevent the progress of cases held in court Christian, on the grounds that they rightly belonged to secular courts. The practice frequently hindered ecclesiastical justice.[25] Although the excommunication covered anyone who sought such writs, it was clearly aimed at Edward I's officials. Though the Oxford clause had always been interpreted broadly—Pecham was merely articulating usage—the king did

---

[24] Manuscript transmission, discussed at page 280–2, shows their prominence even more clearly.
[25] Douie, *Archbishop Pecham*, 113–18; Flahiff, 'Writ of prohibition' (parts I and II).

not respond happily to the challenge. The archbishop was forced to revoke three of his excommunications in parliament.[26]

Pecham had the last laugh: the excommunication, whatever Edward I's objections, was pronounced four times a year for the rest of the Middle Ages.[27] At his council in Lambeth (1281), Pecham reiterated the excommunications as before, spelling out in addition that he did not approve of any other disturbances not mentioned, but merely wished particularly to castigate those he highlighted. He further added that those who used false exemptions to impede or evade ecclesiastical discipline were equally bound by the sentence. It had value as a practical protection of ecclesiastical property, rights, and jurisdiction, and also served as a quarterly reminder to the people of England that they, and the king, imperilled their souls if they dared treat the church as anything but sacrosanct.

It is worth noting, however, that Pecham's clarifications blunted the rhetorical impact of Langton's pithy sentence. In one respect he improved the clause by specifying and publicizing particularly common and destructive abuses of ecclesiastical liberty. He certainly sought to bring royal officials to heel. Proclaiming that they incurred excommunication for their actions throughout the country was one way of doing this. It is also true, however, that his clarifications and additions removed some of the clarity, memorability, and broad coverage of the excommunication. It was less effective propaganda, and indeed John Mirk's fourteenth-century sentences did not include the additions. Priests may have not bothered to include them each time they denounced the *ipso facto* sentences. By the late Middle Ages, lists of *ipso facto* sentences could include over seventy different clauses.[28] They needed to be concisely expressed.[29]

The next excommunication (*Qui pacem et tranquillitatem*) had a quite different emphasis. It protected the king and his rights, and, perhaps most importantly, his peace. This was also one of the more popular Oxford sentences, taken up by bishops even when others from 1222 were not. Statutes of the diocese of Salisbury (1238 × 1244), reacting against a supposed plot of 1238 to assassinate Henry III, added those who plotted the king's death or any sedition.[30] This addition, though specific to the diocese, received wider influence via inclusion in the popular priests' manual of William of Pagula.[31] The original canon was also expanded by Pecham at Reading. The archbishop added that it should be understood to

---

[26] *C&S*, 855–7.
[27] Though many historians have focused on Edward I's 'victory', in 1925 Hilda Johnstone observed that 'So far from losing the fight ... [Pecham] was left in possession of the field', 'Archbishop Pecham', 172–3.
[28] Pickering, 'Notes on the sentence of cursing', 232.
[29] Already in the fourteenth century, Berengar Fredol compiled a list of over a hundred sentences: Jaser, *Ecclesia maledicens*, 362. It is difficult not to conclude that there came to be too many to remember or heed. By the time the Roman practice was halted in the late eighteenth century, the sentence was considered far too long, lasting an hour and a half. Paravicini Bagliani, 'Bonifacio VIII, la loggia di giustizia', 405; Jaser, *Ecclesia maledicens*, 522–3.
[30] See Powicke, 'Murder of Henry Clement'; Carpenter, *Henry III*, 205.   [31] See Appendix II.

include not only those 'stirring up the horror of wars', but also public thieves and plunderers ('latrones'). As Pecham's additions make clear, though the clause protected the king's rights, its primary aim was to maintain a peaceful kingdom. It was the church's duty to maintain peace, and the peace of the church and the kingdom were inseparable.[32] Nevertheless, the excommunication ensured that English parishioners understood that the church did not support attempts to limit the king's rights unjustly. The king also had a protected status, and ecclesiastical legislation decreed that anyone who challenged this was automatically condemned by the church. In practice, however, the clause was invoked rarely, probably because royal justice dealt with such matters. Unlike *Qui malitiose ecclesias*, which was in quotidian use at the same time as it made a public statement, *Qui pacem et tranquillitatem* may be viewed primarily as an ideological statement.

Of the remaining five Oxford sentences, c. 5, which condemned those who defamed good and honest men (*Crimen imponunt alicui*), was the most commonly invoked. R. H. Helmholz has discussed the excommunication and its use in detail in the introduction to the Seldon Society's *Select Cases on Defamation*. He observes that, like the other sentences Langton pronounced, there are no clear precedents for the excommunication. 'The Council of Oxford was making its own decision about a legal rule.' The defamation sentence was both broader and narrower than 'formal canon law'—broader because it provided laypeople a remedy for an essentially secular wrong; narrower because it focused on a crime being imputed rather than simply anything that damaged reputations.[33]

Oxford clauses 3–6 perhaps above all emphasized ecclesiastical jurisdiction. The importance of valid marriages was emphasised in 3 and 4. Marriage was a sacrament; illicit acts concerning it were not mere secular infringements but endangered the souls of those who disrespected the holy state. The sixth excommunication here is a little puzzling. Considering bishops were often excluded from influencing appointments to benefices, protecting the rights of patrons in this way was potentially against their interests.[34] Perhaps this was why it was the least popular of the Oxford sentences, omitted in six statutes.

The seventh excommunication, *Contempnunt exequi domini*, is particularly worthy of comment because its chief value perhaps lay in the requirement for quarterly promulgation. Those who, for profit, out of hatred, or otherwise maliciously refused (*contempnunt*) to carry out the king's mandate against excommunicates (i.e. writs ordering their capture) were *ipso facto* excommunicated. First, regular reiteration of this clause would have reminded the faithful of the consequences (albeit not automatic) of remaining excommunicate: arrest and imprisonment by the secular arm. If the threat of excommunication was to work as a

---

[32] Ambler, *Bishops in the Political Community*, ch. 3.
[33] *Select Cases on Defamation*, ed. Helmholz, xiv–xix.
[34] Swanson, *Religion and Devotion*, 53.

deterrent, it would do no harm to constantly remind people of the temporal as well as the spiritual consequences of the sanction. Second, since it was royal officials, usually sheriffs, who were tasked with arresting contumacious excommunicates when bishops so requested (via the royal chancery), the archbishop was publicly criticizing and defaming such officials.[35] It undermined, throughout the kingdom and on a frequent basis, kings' claims that royal officials could not be excommunicated. Whatever problems clergy faced when trying to enforce the sentence against individuals, the propaganda value was significant. It stated that royal officials who scorned the keys of the church deserved to be bound by a sentence of excommunication, just like everyone else. Edward I objected to the sentence when Pecham reiterated it at Reading. The archbishop was forced to assert in parliament that 'ministers of the king should not be excommunicated, even if they do not obey the king's mandate by not capturing excommunicates'.[36] However, like the other Reading sentences Pecham was made to revoke, the excommunication was repeated at Lambeth and continued to be part of the list of excommunications so often read out locally. Logan has stated that the excommunication was 'meaningless' when repeated in 1281, because of this revocation.[37] It might instead be argued that the revocation was meaningless, since it did not result in the sentence's removal. Pecham's 1279 reversal in parliament was nothing but a short-lived symbolic victory of Edward I over his archbishop. In the long term, it altered nothing.

In 1279 Pecham added sentences to Langton's original list, thus augmenting the core upon which the Great Curse was based. He took three sentences from the papal legate Ottobuono's 1268 London council. Reading c. 11 viii, condemning those who took bribes to prevent legal cases being settled, was based on a canon from 1268 (which had not originally been given publication provisions).[38] Pecham split c. 12 of Ottobuono's council into two parts (Reading c. 11 ix and x); both excommunications were often cited. *Quicumque de domibus* (ix) dealt explicitly with temporal possessions, condemning those who removed anything from clerics' houses, manors, granges, or other property. Like Pecham's expansion of *Qui malitiose ecclesias*, it emphasized that ecclesiastical persons, rights, and property enjoyed special and protected status, regardless of whether some might seem 'worldly'. *Quicumque abstrahunt violenter* (x) stressed the sanctity of ecclesiastical ground, sentencing those who violently removed fugitives from churches and cemeteries, or who prevented the seekers of sanctuary from being supplied with victuals. *Quicumque de domibus* was another of the sentences to which the king objected in 1279, on the grounds that royal punishment sufficed. The king thus claimed that, since secular jurisdiction would deal with such matters, there was no

---

[35] For this procedure, see Logan, *Excommunication and the Secular Arm*, particularly ch. 3. See above Chapter 4, 176–7, for complaints that the procedure was undermined by royal officials.
[36] C&S, 857.   [37] Logan, *Excommunication and the Secular Arm*, 103.   [38] C&S, 775–6.

need for ecclesiastical sanctions. Pecham probably disagreed, but again a large part of the value here lay in the publicity given to this condemnation. The sentence came to be of significance again during the troubles following *Clericis laicos*, when the king himself, along with his officials, stood accused of incurring it for confiscating clerical property. Archbishop Winchelsey ordered all his bishops to pronounce the sentence alongside Boniface VIII's *Clericis laicos* in September 1297, leaving no doubt that the king himself, as well as his men, was implicated.

The final excommunication in the Great Sentence's core—though a latecomer only brought into lists of sentences by Pecham—was that pronounced against infringers of Magna Carta.[39] Magna Carta was, of course, a document that addressed a great many matters, of which the liberty of the English church was merely one. The church was, however, given pride of place in the charter's first clause. David d'Avray is right to argue that Stephen Langton and other prelates who had studied theology at Paris or Oxford supported the principle of placing limitations on the crown's autonomy.[40] The church symbolically stood behind the charter as a whole when, in 1225, it provided excommunication as the means of the charter's enforcement. Nonetheless, it is equally clear that churchmen supported the charter because it protected their own rights (in the first clause, but also elsewhere).[41] In 1253 a form of excommunication was pronounced and recorded, then subsequently promulgated widely. This text very clearly prioritized the liberty of the church.[42] Although it covered Magna Carta and the Forest Charter as a whole, its first clause closely resembles *Qui malitiose ecclesias*. Only in the second clause are the charters mentioned, in the phrase 'all those who violate, infringe or diminish ecclesiastical liberties or the ancient, approved customs of the realm, and especially the liberties and free customs which are contained in the charters of common liberties and of the forest'. It is hardly surprising that, on occasion, the 'Magna Carta' excommunication was not recognized as such in manuscript rubrics, but was rather described as an excommunication against infringers of ecclesiastical liberties.[43]

Pecham included the excommunication in his 1279 list because there was no doubt by then that the excommunication was here to stay. It therefore deserved a place alongside the other key English *latae sententiae*. Pecham's only innovation was to order in addition that Magna Carta was to be posted in churches twice a year.[44] In this case Edward's objection appears to have had permanent effects, but

---

[39] For the following see my 2016 article: Hill, 'Magna Carta'.   [40] d'Avray, 'Magna Carta'.
[41] Carpenter, 'Archbishop Langton', 1056–7; Carpenter, *Magna Carta*, 122–3.
[42] *C&S*, 477–8.
[43] For example London, BL Harley MS 3911, fos. 163r–166v; BL Cotton MS Faustina A IV, fos. 23v–25v; BL Stowe MS 937, fos. 135r–138v; the calendar of Godfrey Giffard's register: *Reg. G. Giffard*, 38; BL Royal MS 9 A II does not include the excommunication, but describes the charter as 'Carta regis Henrici de libertatibus Anglicane ecclesie que vocatur magna carta' (f. 15).
[44] Clanchy, *From Memory to Written Record*, 266.

like the other excommunications revoked by Pecham, the Magna Carta sentence remained in force.

Publication Provisions

Ecclesiastical legislation demonstrates the ever-present desire to publicize these sentences. Frequency of publication varied from diocese to diocese. Langton's 1222 list was to be published four times a year in parish churches. A quarterly pronouncement remained the most common expectation, followed as it was in the influential councils at Reading and Lambeth. Many councils ordered pronouncements three times a year, however, as appears to have been the earlier practice in the Westminster/Salisbury tradition. The 1268 legatine council even demanded weekly promulgation of his excommunications, though once Pecham incorporated them into his list they too fell under the four times a year banner. While four times a year persisted as the standard for the Great Sentence, followed by Pagula (c.1320), Lyndwood (1430s), *Jacob's Well* (early fifteenth century), and Mirk's *Quatuor Sermones* (early fifteenth century), the matter was apparently never completely settled, for Mirk's *Instructions* suggested 'twies or thries in the yere'.[45] Again it ought to be stressed that it was probably only from *circa* the late twelfth century that the infrastructure necessary for such an enterprise was available. Copies of lists needed to be readily available and transmitted; this required episcopal administration and chanceries.

The days chosen to pronounce the sentences, whether three or four times in the year, were presumably intended to be days when most laity were likely to be present in church. Several councils mentioned that 'major' or 'solemn' feast days should be chosen. Others named specific days (see Appendix I for details), but these were not generally the biggest feast days. There are no clear patterns, but perhaps the greatest consideration here was that the days were evenly spaced through the year. They were therefore unlike the feasts prescribed for the papal *general process* (Maundy Thursday, the Ascension of Christ, the Consecration of St Peter's basilica), which were chosen as the most solemn days.[46] The most crucial and potentially challenging aspect of these regular iterations of the excommunications, perhaps, was simply ensuring that parish clergy did as instructed. This may have been why John Pecham ordered that the days of publication would be the Sundays following celebration of rural chapters. This would allow senior clergy

---

[45] Appendix II; William Lyndwood, *Provinciale*, 161; Carruthers, '*Great curse*', 52; John Mirk, *Quatuor Sermones*, 56; John Mirk, *Instructions*, 104.

[46] Maundy Thursday was also appropriate because of the tradition of reconciliation of sinners on that day—the ceremony was all the more striking for this contrast. Jaser, *Ecclesia maledicens*, 374–8. Jaser plausibly rejects the tortured explanations provided in the Ordo Romanus XIII; Paravicini Bagliani, 'Il rito pontificio di scomunica', 217–25.

to remind their subordinates, again demonstrating the control bishops had over their dioceses by the end of the thirteenth century.[47]

The papal ceremony developed into an impressively staged production, eventually performed in a specially constructed loggia.[48] The intention in England that the sentence be pronounced in every parish church, presumably simultaneously, necessitated far less imposing spectacles. The crowds would be smaller, the attire less spectacular, and the clergy present fewer. Yet the ceremonies that were to be enacted in parish churches were nevertheless meant to be solemn and dramatic. The Council of Oxford did not itself specify this, but Langton's use of the 'Auctoritate Dei' formula indicates it.[49] Other councils required that candles and bells be used when making the pronouncements. Versions of the Great Curse also make this clear.[50]

Specific efforts, separate from legislation, were also occasionally made to ensure that *ipso facto* sentences were pronounced in parish churches. These orders might be responses to particular events. The 1255 orders to have the Magna Carta excommunication and the charter itself published followed Innocent IV's confirmation of the sentence the previous year.[51] In 1297, Winchelsey ordered sentences to be published in reaction to the papal bull *Clericis laicos*. The pope's excommunication was to be pronounced, but alongside it *Si quis suadente* and *Quicumque de domibus*, both of which were then being infringed.[52] It is less obvious why other mandates specifically concerned with automatic excommunications were sent at particular times.

Such mandates tend to be more informative about how these sentences were to be published, in particular revealing the importance of using the vernacular.[53] They stress the necessity of lay comprehension more than the general orders in statutes. When Richard of Gravesend, dean of Lincoln, ordered the Magna Carta sentence to be published in 1255, following papal confirmation, he ordered that it be pronounced in both English and French, distinctly and plainly. Moreover, this was to be done not only in churches but also in county and hundred courts, and other public meeting places.[54] The chroniclers confirm that the 1253 sentence was

---

[47] The two versions of the statutes for the archdeaconry of London, the only place where rural chapters are specified, have the Fridays following the feasts of St Michael, Epiphany, Easter, and St John the Baptist, and the Fridays following the feasts of St Michael, Christmas, Easter week, and the Ascension (C&S, 328, 330). On rural chapters see *Reg. Sutton*, iii, xxx–xxxii. On episcopal control see Mazel, *L'évêque et le territoire*, 306–22.

[48] See Jaser, 'Ostensio exclusionis', esp. 377–9; Jaser, *Ecclesia maledicens*, 404ff.; Paravicini Bagliani, 'Bonifacio VIII, la loggia di giustizia'.

[49] See Chapter 1 for this formula, 51, 53.

[50] For the Great Curse, and the dates expected for publication, see Wordsworth and Littlehales, *Old Service-Books*, 272.

[51] *Ann. Burton*, 318–2. [52] *C&S*, 1173–6.

[53] Only in 1435 was a Middle English version officially circulated, by Archbishop Chichele: *Register of Henry Chichele*, ed. Jacob, iii, 257–8. This followed the 1279 Reading list.

[54] *Ann. Burton*, 320–2; substantially the same letter, sent to William of Kilkenny, bishop-elect of Ely, is in Cambridge, University Library MS. EDC 1/B/95. I owe this reference to Nicholas Vincent.

publicized after its first recital in May, and indicate that the orders were carried out with due solemnity.[55] Godfrey Giffard ordered certain sentences—including *Qui malitiose ecclesias*, the Magna Carta sentence, and *Quicumque de domibus*—to be pronounced in 1270, ordering them to be explained to both the lettered and the laity, in the (presumably English, possibly also Welsh and French) vernacular.[56] Oliver Sutton, bishop of Lincoln, executed Winchelsey's 1297 mandate to publish *Quicumque de domibus, Si quis suadente, Clericis laicos,* and a sentence against those who occupied ecclesiastical benefices through lay force,[57] dressed in alb and stole, after he had preached his sermon, with clergy assisting. He explained in English what he was doing, and why, before reciting the sentences.[58] The following year, Winchelsey himself stated that the sentences should be explained in English one by one ('seriatim'), so that notice reached everyone.[59] Sutton confirmed that he had duly published the sentences in accordance with this mandate, and had 'explained them each in English'.[60] Simon of Ghent similarly urged vernacular publication of *Clericis laicos* in 1301.[61] In 1302, a papal sentence against invaders of church goods was to be pronounced yearly in each archdeaconry of the diocese of Salisbury, explained in English 'so that notice reaches everyone'. The bishop ordered a yearly report to be made confirming the order was carried out.[62] Winchelsey's 1309 orders to publish *ipso facto* sentences as set out in earlier statutes similarly noted that they should be published 'distinctly and intelligibly in the vernacular'.[63]

Why publish *latae sententiae*?

It is obvious that publication of these sentences was partly intended to deter people from committing crimes that harmed the church. They elevated the church and clergy, advertising the fact that those who infringed their protections were excluded from society and indeed salvation. The statutes of Durham II (1241 × 1249) explicitly stated a duty to protect the liberty of the church: 'Because the English church is in many ways deformed with oppressions of her liberties in many articles, which we cannot ignore without concern for eternal salvation, we promulgate a sentence of excommunication against those who presume to attempt such things'.[64] The statutes of Wells (1258?) referred to the Oxford sentences as being 'against disturbers of the liberties of the church', and similarly noted the

---

[55] *C&S*, 475–7.   [56] *Concilia Magnae Britanniae et Hiberniae*, ed. Wilkins, ii, 22, 23.
[57] Cf. Appendix I: York I, c. 41 i, Durham II, c. 50 ii.
[58] *Reg. Sutton*, vi, 24–7. Vernacular explanations of excommunications were far from new, cf. *Pontifical romano-germanique*, i, 311 (a formula from c.906). See also Edwards, 'Ritual excommunication', 66–8.
[59] *C&S*, 1193, 1194, 1195 (*in vulgari, in anglico, in anglico*).   [60] *Reg. Sutton*, vi, 187–8.
[61] *Reg. Gandavo*, i, 65–6.   [62] *Reg. Gandavo*, i, 70–2.   [63] *C&S*, 1275.   [64] *C&S*, 434.

importance of ensuring that the order to frequently renew them be obeyed.[65] Ottobuono's 1268 *ipso facto* sentences also noted that the excommunications were intended to prevent the dangers that threatened the church.[66] Winchelsey's 1309 mandate included a long preamble in which various oppressions, evils, and disturbances suffered by the church were described.[67] The priesthood was in a worse condition than it had been under Pharoah. The archbishop noted that the statutes of Langton and the papal legates intended to reform the state of the church and clergy 'oppressed by serious burdens and innumerable and intolerable injuries against ecclesiastical liberty', once again ordering quarterly publication of their excommunications.[68] Bishops clearly intended to curb infringements of ecclesiastical liberties via this publicity.

The ritual ceremony, enacted throughout the year, hoped to deter infringements by provoking fear. Thus Grosseteste described the 1222 sentences as intended 'to terrify the malicious and restrain their malice'.[69] This description was adopted in Winchester III (1262 × 1265) to introduce the list of sentences.[70] Winchelsey explained that it was necessary that sentences be pronounced with due solemnity, using candles and bells, 'so that [the sentence] might be more feared on account of this solemnity, to which laymen pay more attention than the consequences of these sentences'.[71] Another reason to make the decision to censure offences with a *lata sententia*—considering that many of the crimes were surely grounds for excommunication *ab homine*—was perhaps because absolution of *latae sententiae* was reserved to the archbishops, or indeed the pope.[72] Langton, for instance, may have been seeking greater control by making his office the only source of absolution. Indeed, at Paris in 1200, Eudes de Sully had grouped together excommunications which required absolution from the pope into a single constitution, in a catalogue resembling lists of *ipso facto* sentences.[73] Moreover, there were indeed complaints about illicit absolutions from automatic sentences, implying there was a reason to reserve absolution to higher clergy.[74]

However, though bishops no doubt understood the publicity value for protecting their own interests, publication was also required by the law and was necessary in order to ensure that souls were not recklessly endangered. Self-interest was not the only motive for ensuring that these automatic excommunications were well known. Once crimes had been covered with a *lata sententia*, the law required that the fact be well publicized. This related to the rules governing use of

---

[65] *C&S*, 625.   [66] *C&S*, 764.

[67] By this time, the age of statutes was over and mandates were the typical way that archbishops ordered their suffragans to execute practices.

[68] *C&S*, 1274–7.   [69] *C&S*, 275.   [70] *C&S*, 722.   [71] *C&S*, 1194, 1195.

[72] Jaser, 'Ostensio exclusionis', 371; Jaser, *Ecclesia maledicens*, 360, 387–9, 520. See also Longere, 'Les eveques et l'administration'.

[73] *Statuts Synodaux*, I, ed. Pontal, 62.

[74] *Reg. Urban IV*, iii, no. 1562; *C&S*, 898–99, cf. *Reg. Epp. Pecham*, iii, 909–10. See also below, 77.

excommunication generally, as well as to the specific workings of *latae sententiae*. Since the normal requirements regarding warning prior to excommunication could not apply to *ipso facto* sentences, the solution to this offered by the canonists was to decree that all crimes incurred *ipso facto* should be publicized. Publication served as due warning.

How important a factor the legal requirement to publicize these sentences was for the English clergy is impossible to tell. Certainly, the mantra that ignorance should not provide an excuse was often repeated in relation to the need to publicize such sentences.[75] Though the refrain was pertinent in this context, it hardly applied specifically to excommunications *latae sententiae*.[76] Nevertheless, the rules regarding excommunication, particularly as promulgated by the councils held at the Lateran (1215) and in Lyon (1245), were noted in English legislation.[77] It might be assumed that the legislating bishops knew the law and accordingly ordered regular publication of sentences. This conclusion is strengthened by the proximity of the rule requiring sufficient warning to orders for the publication of *latae sententiae* in various statutes. Langton's diocesan statutes (1213 × 1214), for example, note the requirement for canonical warning (c. 49). The clause went on immediately to order the thrice-yearly pronouncement of *ipso facto* sentences. Langton thus perhaps had in mind the requirement that excommunication be accompanied by ample warning when he legislated to ensure wide promulgation of his sentences, in both his diocesan and provincial statutes.[78] The Statutes of Salisbury I reveal a similar proximity.[79] The legal requirement that *latae sententiae* be made widely known in lieu of specific warnings is important, but there is little to prove that this was a major concern for the clergy of thirteenth-century England.

The pastoral obligation to publicize automatic sentences, by contrast, comes across clearly in statutes and episcopal documents. There was a moral imperative here: souls were at stake. The thirteenth-century English episcopate was famously obsessed with providing adequate pastoral care for the faithful.[80] Perhaps inspired by Lateran IV and its clear preoccupation with cure of souls, diocesan reforms

---

[75] To cite merely one example, *Reg. Gandavo*, i, 184–5. The phrase was used in many other contexts, not least sheltering heretics: Sackville, 'Church's institutional response to heresy', 128.

[76] Fossier, *Bureau de âmes*, 292–9, discusses the ignorance doctrine. Secular ordinances also explained the need for publication with the phrase 'lest anyone is able to profess ignorance': Dutour, 'L'élaboration', 152. Ian Forrest notes that the doctrine that ignorance did not provide an excuse led bishops to assume communication of material had been effective, but doubts whether, in reality, promulgation led to the knowledge desired. Promulgation ticked a box but did not necessarily achieve perfect knowledge amongst the populace: *Trustworthy Men*, 432.

[77] See Gibbs and Lang, *Bishops and Reform*, 124–5.

[78] *C&S*, 33. Recited verbatim also in statutes of an unknown bishop: *C&S*, 192–3.

[79] *C&S*, 76 (c. 51).

[80] See Robert Brentano's comparison with Italian bishops of the same period: *Two Churches*, 174–237, particularly 220–1; also Boyle, 'Robert Grosseteste and the pastoral care'; Gibbs and Lang, *Bishops and Reform*, 164; Denton, *Robert Winchelsey*, 40.

were enacted, chiefly through the statutes already discussed.[81] Since excommunication imperilled the soul, it was important that it was taken seriously. If *latae sententiae* were not brought to the attention of Christ's flock, souls were put at risk. Ignorance of the law in this context was dangerous. There is a great deal of evidence that bishops understood the pastoral significance of excommunications incurred *ipso facto*.

Many of the statutes and mandates that ordered their regular reiteration placed their orders firmly in the context of concern for souls. Knowledge of automatic excommunications became a crucial part of clerical education, so that parish priests were able to relate them to their parishioners. This they were expected to do thoroughly and clearly, in the vernacular, so that laymen understood them. Diocesan statutes from Exeter even expected priests to learn them by heart.[82] Lists of sentences were included not only in legislation but also in pastoral manuals.

When Pecham then introduced his sentences at Reading in 1279, he explained why it was necessary that they be published:

> Because it is not possible to avoid evil unless it is known, but there are many sentences of excommunication, by which wicked men are struck down...we order all the priests of the province of Canterbury openly to set forth the sentences of excommunication which follow, to the people entrusted to them, on all Sundays immediately following the celebration of the rural chapter, lest henceforth through ignorance they are plunged into the pit of such great danger.[83]

Seven years later, the Statutes of Exeter II similarly made clear the imperative to publish such sentences: 'So that we take care for the salvation of our subordinates more cautiously, lest they incur sentences of excommunications brought *ipso facto* through ignorance in any way, we have decided to insert the sentences of excommunications....'[84]

Pecham's 1281 Council of Lambeth clarifies that the archbishop considered *ipso facto* excommunications fundamental information for the laity. He ordered that two of his constitutions be published four times a year. The first of these was the *Ignorantia sacerdotum*, a syllabus of Christian knowledge that parish priests should explain to their parishioners. It included, amongst other things, the creed, the sacraments, lists of principal virtues and vices, and the Ten Commandments.[85] It was a basic catalogue of the most vital elements of pastoral care. Historians have made much of this clause (while pointing out that in itself it was not particularly educational), but there has been far too little discussion of the fact

---

[81] Lateran IV is often credited with increasing the role and importance of pastoral care in parish life. See for example Boyle, 'Fourth Lateran Council', 30–1; Boyle, '*Oculus Sacerdotis*', 81.
[82] *C&S*, 625–6, 1057–9.   [83] *C&S*, 848.   [84] *C&S*, 1057.   [85] *C&S*, 900–5.

that it was paired with the following clause, containing *ipso facto* excommunications.[86] Pecham evidently considered both clauses to be of equal importance: they were to be published at the same time. Indeed, later medieval tracts on religious instruction typically included the Great Sentence alongside the basic knowledge set out by Pecham (as he intended). Moreover, Niamh Pattwell points out that as well as being one of the items more frequently included in these manuals, the General Sentence was sometimes the only Middle English item in them.[87] A Latin tract titled 'Modus pronunciandi sententias excommunicationum' did not, in fact, only describe how to pronounce excommunications, but provided various material that priests ought to repeat to their parishioners often. About half of it consists of *latae sententiae*; the remainder is general information such as how to baptize (in the vernacular) in an emergency, rules about contracting marriage and paying tithes, how to revere the host, and so on.[88] Automatic excommunications were a crucial part of the knowledge that had to be explained to the populace. The *Ignorantia Sacerdotum* should not be decoupled from the list of excommunications with which it was paired and travelled alongside.[89]

The clearest indication of pastoral concerns regarding automatic excommunication is found in a 1277 mandate of Walter Bronescombe. The bishop of Exeter wrote to his subordinates, quoting Ezekiel 3:18–19, to explain at length their duties:[90]

> Among the other anxieties of pastoral care which rest upon us, the reason for the coming of our Redeemer, Who came not only for the sake of the just but for all who had died, unceasingly arouses the duty of our office and diligently summons us to watch over the safety of souls, wholesomely to preserve in health the sheep of the flock entrusted to us, and by the remedy of salvation to lead back those to the path of truth who have strayed in error so that they may be cured, lest—which God forbid—they perish through our dissimulation and we be punished by God's judgement for our negligence on their account [Ezek. 3:18-19]. Indeed, certain of our parishioners through a certain very great ignorance of letters do not know the statutes of the canons and the traditions of the holy fathers, and have frequently fallen under sentences of excommunication... which we relate with sorrow, and unwisely believe that they may do what is unlawful; in order

---

[86] On the *Ignorantia Sacerdotum*, see Pantin, *English Church*, 194–5; Boyle, 'Oculus sacerdotis', 82; Douie, *Archbishop Pecham*, 134–42; Denton, 'Competence of the parish clergy', 273–5; Haines, *Ecclesia Anglicana*, 133–7, and his notes.

[87] Pickering, 'Notes on the sentence of cursing', 230; Pattwell, 'A sentence of cursing', 121–2.

[88] I hope to publish this tract in future. It is contained, for example, in Cambridge, Corpus Christi College, MS 255, fos. 206va-209va.

[89] Moreover, G.R. Owst found that the *Ignorantia sacerdotum* generally was accompanied by the articles of excommunication in most manuscripts: Owst, *Preaching in Medieval England*, 296; cf. Wordsworth and Littlehales, *Old Service-Books*, 270.

[90] Sutton quoted the chapters before publishing automatic sentences in 1297: *Reg. Sutton*, vi, 24–7.

that the snare of such sentences may be with circumspection avoided and the blindness of ignorance shut out, we command you... that you should have the articles set out below, on account of which sentence of excommunication is incurred *ipso facto*, published by the parish priests in every collegiate and parish church on every Sunday... You are to enjoin on every rector, vicar, and parish priest of such churches that each of them should, within a month, have the contents of the present letter clearly posted up in a prominent place in their churches, under threat of a penalty to be assessed at the judgement of the ordinary.[91]

Some months later, Bronescombe referred to his earlier mandate, quoting Gregory the Great: 'For there is no excusing the shepherd if the wolf eats the sheep without the shepherd's knowledge'.[92] His sentiments were echoed in 1310, when William Greenfield, archbishop of York, ordered publication of *ipso facto* sentences on Sundays and feast days throughout his diocese, lest blood be required from the hands of himself or his subordinates as a result of their negligence.[93]

It is hardly surprising, therefore, that lists of automatic excommunications were also a key component of pastoral manuals. As early as *c*.1216, Thomas of Chobham urged priests to learn which sentences were incurred *ipso facto* in their own dioceses.[94] Subsequently, manuals provided lists. In England, Robert Grosseteste's *Templum Dei*, a short manual set out almost as a series of diagrams, proved influential. It contained a list of sentences incurred *ipso facto* (interestingly, a list that bore little relation to the English traditions), followed by lists of reserved absolutions, exceptions to *Si quis suadente*, and various other excommunication-related information.[95] In the fourteenth century, William of Pagula provided extensive lists. In his *Oculus sacerdotis* (*c*.1320), he included two lists. The first contains ninety *ipso facto* sentences extracted from papal and English councils. The second (Appendix II), requiring quarterly publication, contained thirty-four sentences. Pagula's concern here was explicitly pastoral care. This is not to argue that he did not care about politics—he certainly did[96]—but this manual was written so that parish priests would be able to minister to their charges.

A note of caution about pastoral imperatives must, however, be sounded. It is clear that, though a great deal of offences incurred automatic excommunication, not all were publicized equally. The principle was not consistently applied. For

---

[91] *Reg. Bronescombe*, no. 1222.
[92] *Reg. Bronescombe*, no. 1229; Gregory the Great, *Registrum Epistolarum*, ed. Norberg, iii, esp. 52; The phrase was incorporated into the *Liber extra*, X 5.41.10.
[93] *Reg. Greenfield*, i, no. 300.   [94] Chobham, *Summa*, 250–1.
[95] Robert Grosseteste, *Templum Dei*, VII.3–13. The list is generally papal sentences, copied from Serlo.
[96] 'Mirror of King Edward III', in Nederman, *Political Thought*, 63–139.

instance, some diocesan synods chose to promote only some of the seven Oxford sentences, even though all were applicable to them. One possible explanation for singling out certain sentences for publicity was that they were deemed most often incurred (and indeed an argument for not overwhelming listeners with too much information could also be made). William of Pagula's shorter list of only thirty-four that required quarterly publication consisted explicitly of excommunications of more frequent occurrence.[97] Pagula acknowledged that a full list included far too many sentences to read out.[98] It was better to focus on sentences people were most likely to incur. Elsewhere, bishops' commitment must have varied.

It is, therefore, probably going too far to make arguments based on absence of publicity. Sophie Ambler contends that no automatic sentence was promulgated against infringers of the Provisions of Oxford in 1258, mostly basing her argument on the fact that our only evidence is very late. However, she also reasons that because the Provisions were never (apparently) published, no excommunication was pronounced. That is, she argues that the pastoral imperatives to publish *latae sententiae*, as I have previously set out, make it unlikely that a sentence would be pronounced then not extensively disseminated. Yet other such *ipso facto* sentences certainly were pronounced but not subsequently widely publicized, regardless of the potential danger to souls this posed. The Provisions did not obviously affect the majority of the population, who would therefore not be in danger of incurring any sentence thus pronounced. Most importantly, the Provisions were quickly annulled by the papacy. There was hardly time to urge publication, especially given that the episcopate was disunited, and the kingdom in turmoil.[99] Even the Magna Carta excommunication was not widely disseminated until the 1250s, though it was originally pronounced in 1225.[100] It is certainly plausible that a sentence supporting the Provisions might be declared, even if, in practice, no such sentence was pronounced. Certainly, excommunication was used by the Montfortian bishops during the period of reform and rebellion, so that the

---

[97] Boyle, '*Oculus sacerdotis*', 87–90.

[98] In fact, fifty items in the longer list were clauses of Magna Carta and the Forest Charter. It is interesting that, in a different part of his work, in which he advised on confession, Pagula urged priests to check whether their charges had incurred any automatic sentences. Though many of the clauses of the charters were unlikely to affect the average layperson, c. 23 on false weights and measures might. Pagula singled it out for mention in this section. It is perhaps not a coincidence that using false weights and measures came to be part of the Great Sentence separate from the charters.

[99] The 1258 involvement of Richard Gravesend, who was tasked with publicizing the Magna Carta in 1255, does support Ambler's argument, however.

[100] Ambler argues, citing my 'Magna Carta': 'Since the Provisions of Oxford were never published, to employ a broad sentence would be to place countless souls in jeopardy, since many might violate the Provisions and fall under the sentence in ignorance. This was a danger of which the bishops, who had made such great efforts to publicize the charters throughout the 1250s with this very concern in mind, were acutely aware. It is possible, then, that later chroniclers superimposed onto the Oxford parliament either the bishops' sentence in support for the Provisions of Westminster in 1259 or that of 1265.' *Bishops in the Political Community*, 110.

chroniclers who later asserted that an excommunication had been pronounced in 1258 were not suggesting an unlikely scenario.

In *latae sententiae*, politics and pastoral care were deeply intertwined: the political ideologies expressed in *ipso facto* sentences had to be disseminated by clergy responsible for their flocks, so that faithful Christians did not unwittingly endanger their souls. Bishops' motives were not unselfish here: they would themselves be answerable to God if souls were lost as a result of their negligence. Deterring infringement of ecclesiastical rights and publicly implicating royal government were also attractive incentives. Nevertheless, the pastoral obligation to publicize *latae sententiae* is crucial, having widespread and long-lasting consequences. Various politically charged sentences, and perhaps most surprisingly Magna Carta, were brought to the attention of the English laity.

Implementation

The emphasis on publicizing excommunications in legislation and elsewhere does not mean that orders were obeyed. Parish priests might have been negligent in performing their duties. Some were probably unable to read. Despite the emphasis on vernacular pronouncement, the texts that circulated in thirteenth-century England were all in Latin.[101] They might have been unaware of the sentences they were supposed to pronounce regularly, despite the efforts of bishops and compilers of priests' manuals. Legislation also differed from diocese to diocese, so that conflicting provisions may have been confusing; which, then, should be followed? It would be foolish to argue that they were published, without fail, in every parish church as often as required. Yet, though there are difficulties when it comes to assessing execution of publication provisions, there is nevertheless reason to conclude that they were indeed widely disseminated. Increasingly bureaucratized diocesan governance undoubtedly played a role here, ensuring promulgation through developed networks.[102]

The argument for enforcement of orders to publish *ipso facto* excommunications is first supported by the high number of surviving manuscripts containing them. The extant manuscripts date from the thirteenth to the fifteenth centuries, so manuscript (MS) evidence by its nature does not concern merely the thirteenth century. The prevalence of manuscripts proves the enduring usefulness of, in particular, the Councils of Oxford (1222), London (1268), Reading (1279),

---

[101] Archbishop Chichele circulated an English text of the excommunications in 1435: *Register of Henry Chichele*, ed. Jacob, iii, 257–8.
[102] For these developments see Mazel, *L'évêque et le territoire*, ch. 5.

and Lambeth (1281).[103] The legislation of these councils survives in far more copies. Indeed, on the basis of manuscript transmission, Table 1 is somewhat misleading, for whilst it shows that the excommunication of wreckers was pronounced only in a single council, it does not show that it also survives in only one manuscript. The excommunication was therefore of relatively little significance.[104] By contrast, the seven Oxford sentences appear in copies of the thirteenth-century statutes in well over 200 MSS and made it beyond England;[105] violating sanctuary or ecclesiastical immunity appears in almost 200, plundering in about 150, arson in around 140, infringing Magna Carta is in at least 110, sorcery in about seventy, and perjury and usury each in just over fifty.

Copies of thirteenth-century legislation are far from the full story, however, for the excommunications circulated in other contexts too. In the later medieval Great Sentence some of the earlier excommunications resurfaced.[106] Thus while coin clipping was condemned in only two thirteenth-century councils (eight MSS), it was included in various versions of the Great Curse.[107] Heresy, given short shrift in the thirteenth century (one council, one MS) unsurprisingly came to be included in the quarterly sentence in the era of Wycliffism and Lollardy.[108] William of Pagula's *Oculus sacerdotis* (c. 1320, Appendix II) contained papal general sentences (*Si quis suadente*, forging bulls, providing arms to Saracens etc.) as well as ones specific to England, and possibly provided the basis for many lists in the later Middle Ages. A full classification of manuscripts of the Great Sentence in the late Middle Ages, assessing the number of occurrences of each offence, would be fruitful. Significant progress has been made by Niamh Pattwell, and previously by Oliver Pickering. Pattwell nevertheless urges further study: 'The sentence of cursing has much to contribute to the study of religious writing and manuscripts of the late Middle Ages'.[109] What is certain, and most important here, is that the Oxford sentences, with orders that they be published in parish churches four times a year,[110] survive in many hundreds of manuscripts and incunabula. They were included in the *Oculus sacerdotis* (c. fifty extant MSS) and Pagula's *Summa summarum* (c. eleven MSS), John Mirk's *Instructions for Parish Priests* (two MSS containing the Great Sentence), and Lyndwood's *Provinciale* (c. fifty-five MSS). All of these texts, and Mirk's *Quatuor Sermones* (of which there are no

---

[103] However, whilst acknowledging the possibility that statutes surviving in only few MSS were hardly used, Cheney argued instead that lack of MSS indicates they were used so heavily they fell apart. 'Statute-making', 150.
[104] Appendix I provides MS information.
[105] Gwynn, 'Provincial and Diocesan Decrees of the Diocese of Dublin'.
[106] Further supporting Cheney's point about MSS falling apart in 'Statue-making, 150'.
[107] See the tables provided in Pattwell, 'A sentence of cursing', 132 (no. 17.1). The tables provided in this article show that variations amongst thirteenth-century conciliar excommunications continued to be represented in later iterations.
[108] See Forrest, 'William Swinderby', 263–4.
[109] Pattwell, 'A sentence of cursing', quotation 130; Pickering, 'Notes on the sentence of cursing'.
[110] There is some variation in frequency, see page 271.

known surviving MS copies), were printed in the late fifteenth and early sixteenth centuries.[111] If there was any failure to pronounce these excommunications in the thirteenth, fourteenth, and fifteenth centuries, it is unlikely to have been because of a lack of available copies.[112]

Evidence specific to the thirteenth and early-fourteenth centuries gives further cause for optimism. Clergy who failed to publish these sentences were supposed to be punished. Salisbury II thus ordered prelates and priests to observe the promulgation of sentences if they wished to avoid punishment.[113] Archdeacons appear to have been tasked with punishing priests found negligent.[114] When Richard of Gravesend decreed publication of the Magna Carta sentence, and the charter itself, in 1255, he ordered anyone who wished to 'cast off that burden from his shoulders' to come to Richard at Lincoln (where he was dean) to explain their presumption.[115] At Lambeth, Pecham went so far as to order local archdeacons 'diligently to inquire' about the publication he had ordered, and to compel them, 'disciplining with canonical penalty', to supply what might have been presumptuously omitted.[116] Similarly, in 1309 Winchelsey assured his suffragans that he would inquire into publication, punishing those found negligent. Every year, the bishops were to send letters patent confirming execution of his mandate. Subsequent letters sent by Winchelsey demonstrate that he was particularly anxious to ensure his orders were carried out.[117] Greenfield's 1310 order to publish *ipso facto* sentences demanded confirmation that his mandates had been executed.[118]

Such orders, particularly Winchelsey's, might be taken as indications that clergy had thus far been negligent. Winchelsey did experience problems in forcing his subordinates to publish the *Clericis laicos* excommunications of 1297; it is clear from entries in his register that many did not carry out publication as they ought to have done. However, this was a fraught situation, probably not representative of general practice.[119] In general, there is little to suggest that clergy were punished for failing to ensure publication, even if no firm conclusions can be drawn from absence of evidence. It is clear that punishment would have been issued at an administrative level for which records do not survive in this period, so lack of evidence is to be expected. On the other hand, if failure to pronounce sentences was an endemic problem, it remains surprising that there is

---

[111] Boyle, 'The *Oculus Sacerdotis*', 94–5; Cheney, 'William Lyndwood', 178–80; John Mirk, *Instructions*, 12.

[112] We would expect, of course, that a higher proportion of thirteenth-century manuscripts fell apart through use, but their existence is implied by the later survivals. It is also probable that the excommunications were copied onto single sheets, which would not survive.

[113] C&S, 387.

[114] C&S, 337. If this general sentence were to be published in some churches, but not all, this would generate 'scandal and opprobrium'.

[115] Ann. Burton, 322.   [116] C&S, 907.   [117] C&S, 1275–6.

[118] Reg. Greenfield, i, no. 300.

[119] Reg. Winchelsey, i, 154–9; C&S, 1192–6; Reg. Gandavo, i, 17–21.

no indication of it in episcopal registers, as there was when *Clericis laicos* was insufficiently promulgated.

In fact, there is evidence that commands to publish these excommunications were fulfilled. We could never hope to find records of individual parishes confirming execution of mandates in this period, but higher clergy seem to have taken their duties seriously. Oliver Sutton of Lincoln, therefore, certainly did as required by his primate in 1297, as did the bishop of Salisbury. Sutton also ensured that the Magna Carta excommunication was pronounced throughout his diocese in 1299.[120] On 24 April 1300, the bishop of Durham ordered weekly publication of an *ipso facto* sentence against those who disturbed or violated the rights, liberties, jurisdictions, or possessions of the bishop or church of Durham. It was to be pronounced in the cathedral and 'every other regular and parish church and chapel of our whole diocese, every Sunday and feast day' until Pentecost (5 June). His official confirmed that the sentence had been carried out in the cathedral and explained in English. It was then 'constantly asserted' that the mandate should be executed throughout the diocese.[121] Winchelsey's 1309 order to his bishops was certainly carried out by Simon of Ghent, bishop of Salisbury. Ghent was informed of Winchelsey's mandate by the bishop of London, and duly ordered his dean to have it observed by all his subjects. The dean was to provide well-written copies and distribute them everywhere so that no one could be ignorant or remiss. He was to write back to the archbishop. Since Winchelsey had ordered yearly returns, a year later Ghent wrote once again to his four archdeacons, ordering them to have rectors, vicars, and chaplains make copies so that in due course each church would have a copy.[122]

The above examples concern special mandates rather than the routine yearly pronouncements, which there was no reason to include in episcopal registers (early visitations do not seem to have asked whether the regular pronouncements were carried out).[123] However, rather than express doubt that the quarterly sentences were pronounced, bishops appear to have assumed it. When certain malefactors incurred *Qui malitiose ecclesias* in 1277, the bishop of Exeter reminded them of the excommunications recently published throughout the city and diocese of Exeter.[124] In 1295, Winchelsey ordered the bishop of Chichester to excommunicate certain malefactors who had entered the archbishop's liberty at Lindfield and harassed the archbishop's subjects there. He noted that those guilty could not pretend ignorance of the law because it was known to all that such

---

[120] *Reg. Sutton*, vi, 24–7, 158, 187–8; *Reg. Gandavo*, i, 65–6 'the canon of Boniface VIII was recently published so often through the whole province of Canterbury that these things can and should be hidden to no Catholic'. Cf. *Reg. Winchelsey*, i.364.
[121] *Records of Antony Bek*, ed. Fraser, no. 66.   [122] *Reg. Gandavo*, i, 378–82.
[123] Later ones (e.g. 1458) did, however, and there are examples of negligent priests: *Visitations Of Churches Belonging To St. Paul's Cathedral*, ed. Simpson, 74–5, 105.
[124] *Reg. Bronescombe*, no. 1229. Cf. no. 1222.

actions would incur the penalties stipulated in *Qui malitiose ecclesias,* 'which we believe to be published four times a year in every church'.[125] Similar optimism was harboured by John le Romeyn, archbishop of York, who remarked that the sentences were published throughout the year in every church when denouncing those who had fallen into *Crimen imponunt alicui.*[126] Likewise, Archbishop Wickwane, when Richard de Vescy and his accomplices incurred sentences for their armed attack on a church, ordered them to be denounced 'because such malefactors are solemnly bound by a sentence of excommunication twice a year, in accordance with the synodal statute'.[127]

In 1292, certain parishioners in Ecton, Northamptonshire, were excommunicated because they snatched the sheet ('cedula') from which a chaplain was reciting the general sentence of excommunication, and the candles held by his assistants. This sentence, the record matter-of-factly notes, was that 'according to the form given at the Council of Oxford, to be solemnly promulgated at every general synod four times a year... following the English custom'.[128] The only reason we know of the sentence published here is because of the ensuing violence when the chaplain was attacked. There is nothing to indicate that his publication was exceptional. Not only did he have access to the text, the incident suggests that reading from a single sheet copied separately from books of statutes might have been common; it would certainly have been easier. It is interesting that the chaplain was using the Oxford sentences, and not, apparently, the updated version promulgated by Pecham. It might show that innovations took some time to filter down to parish level, though it is possible that this was just shorthand for the *ipso facto* sentences (the excommunications continued to be closely associated with Langton's council). It is worth noting that the practice fell into abeyance in the fifteenth century: Henry Chichele complained about neglect in 1435. However, this prompted renewed efforts, including an English translation, to have the sentences published as they should be.[129]

Chronicle evidence confirms publication of the more politically charged excommunications such as Magna Carta and *Clericis laicos.* Matthew Paris observed that in 1253, Grosseteste had the Magna Carta excommunication pronounced in all the parishes of his diocese 'the multitude of which can scarcely be estimated'.[130] This he had done unceasingly through the whole year, not only in

---

[125] *Reg. Winchelsey,* i.16–18. See also Forrest, *Trustworthy Men,* 342.
[126] *Reg. le Romeyn,* i, 261–2.
[127] 'per synodale statutum', *Register of William Wickwane,* ed. Brown, no. 329. The twice a year assertion is a little puzzling, however.
[128] *Reg. Sutton,* iv, 35.
[129] *Register of Henry Chichele,* ed. Jacob, iii, 253–8; *Register of Thomas Spofford,* ed. Bannister, 198–201; 198–201; *Register of John Stafford,* ed. Holmes, ii, 170–2; Owst, *Preaching in Medieval England,* 296 n. 5.
[130] R.W. Southern estimated 2,000: *Robert Grosseteste,* 235–7.

churches, but wherever men gathered.[131] Two years later, Gravesend's mandate was carried out, and the sentence was pronounced in councils, synods, churches, and wherever men gathered.[132] In 1269, the Magna Carta sentence, *Si quis suadente*, and *Quicumque abstrahunt violenter* were pronounced in parliament by nine bishops, and the sentence was subsequently published by all the parish priests of London.[133] The bishop of Carlisle obeyed orders to publish the *Clericis laicos* sentence in 1297.[134] We know, however, that Winchelsey did not succeed in persuading all his suffragans to do this, so that the Bury St Edmund's chronicler must be wrong in his assertion that the sentence 'was fulminated by each and every bishop in their dioceses'.[135] Pecham, in 1282, held a procession at Lewes in Sussex, dressed in pontificals, then preached in the great church, and finally recited the sentences of his predecessors in English before the people ('audiente populo'), urging his audience in future to 'abstain' from such crimes more prudently.[136]

Finally, the regularity with which people fell into these sentences demonstrates that they were well known, at least amongst the clergy. At the Council of Lambeth, Pecham expressed anger and concern that certain clergy were absolving *de facto* those whom they could not absolve *de jure*. That is, they were absolving excommunicates bound by sentences reserved to the archbishop. Pecham specifically mentioned the sentences pronounced in the Council of Oxford and against those who detained tithes.[137] In fact, his complaint indicates that laymen themselves were aware of the sentences, since such excommunicates were clearly being absolved in the confessional rather than through any sort of legal process.[138] Therefore, either they were being asked by clergy whether they had done anything that would incur one of these automatic sentences, or they knew they had incurred excommunication and specifically sought absolution. If the latter, they might have been seeking an 'easy' absolution from less scrupulous clergy. The former possibility is made less likely by the fact that only diligent clergy would be so thorough in confession, which does not fit with Pecham's description of clergymen willing to offer illicit absolutions. These sentences were supposed to be reserved cases.

The frequency with which these excommunications were incurred varies a great deal. Several of the Oxford sentences were frequently invoked by bishops. Others

---

[131] *CM*, v, 377–8, 395, 400; *Flores Historiarum*, ii, 385–6.
[132] *CM*, v, 500–1; *Ann. Burton*, 320–2; *Oxenedes*, 201–2.
[133] *De Antiquis Legibus Liber*, ed. Stapleton, 122–3. Helmholz notes that *Si quis suadente* was regularly read out in the later Middle Ages: 'Si quis suadente', 432.
[134] *Guisborough*, 313–14.   [135] *Chron. Bury*, 140–1; *Reg. Winchelsey*, 154–9.
[136] Lewes annals transcribed by Blaauw, 'On the early history of Lewes Priory', 33: 'ab antecessoribus suis datas sententias' must refer to these automatic sentences. His warning is also much like Sutton's in 1297 and one given by Simon of Ghent in 1312: *Reg. Gandavo*, i, 184–5. Cf. also a letter about the liberties of Canterbury being infringed by people from Lewes the same year: *Reg. Pecham*, ii, 59.
[137] *C&S*, 898–9; in 1264, Urban IV complained, in much the same terms, about illegal absolutions from *latae sententiae*: *Reg. Urban IV*, iii, 1562.
[138] See Chapter 2 for absolution in the penitential forum 68–78.

were cited far less often.¹³⁹ Whether offences were committed by unknown malefactors or by known individuals, an infringement of an *ipso facto* sentence meant that it would be proclaimed on Sundays and feast days for several weeks. Thus even more exposure was given to certain crimes via this route. A cursory perusal of any episcopal register will quickly yield an infringer of ecclesiastical rights excommunicated by authority of the Council of Oxford. *Qui malitiose ecclesias* might be incurred in many ways, from pursuing a case against the bishop of St Asaph in the king's court, to compelling the archbishop's tenants to repair Rochester Bridge.¹⁴⁰ After the Council of Lambeth, Pecham's additions were also sometimes invoked, as when tithes were appropriated from the church of Immingham (county and diocese of Lincoln), in 1291.¹⁴¹ Indeed the prevalence of *Qui malitiose ecclesias* more than explains the infrequency of the Magna Carta sentence's use. Though Magna Carta was certainly useful in certain situations, in the quotidian running of parishes and dioceses there was already an established law with which to sentence malefactors. The church in fact gained no more protection from the charter than it did from the Council of Oxford.¹⁴²

The other sentences occur less frequently, but they were certainly incurred (with examples in episcopal registers from the second half of the century). *Qui pacem et tranquillitatem* was not routinely invoked, and seems to have been incurred mostly by the Welsh, who were repeatedly excommunicated for breaking the peace and infringing the king's rights, as well as for violating the rights of the church. Here its use perhaps related to the fact that their offences lay outside the jurisdiction of routine royal justice.¹⁴³ It was occasionally cited elsewhere, as when archbishop Boniface's official was assaulted in 1252. The archbishop excommunicated the perpetrators of this deed on the grounds that they had fallen into both *Si quis suadente* and *Qui malitiose ecclesias*, but also mentioned that they had broken the king's peace (apparently not specifying, however, that this in itself incurred excommunication).¹⁴⁴ The bishop of Salisbury ordered his archdeacons to publicize the sentence in the 1280s, possibly in response to infringements of it.¹⁴⁵ A marriage case in 1296 prompted a renewal of Oxford c. 3 on false marriage testimony for three Sundays or feast days, so that those who had acted contrary to the canon should know that they were ensnared.¹⁴⁶ An interesting case held in the court of Canterbury further demonstrates that *latae sententiae* were well known. Two men mutually accused one another of having fallen into automatic excommunications. Oliver de Brocton, a clerk, accused Adam Mulgars of incurring *Si*

---

¹³⁹ It is worth noting that the Oxford and later sentences include identifiable phrasing, whereas 'perjury' and so on can far less easily be attributed to knowledge of promulgated lists.
¹⁴⁰ *Reg. Epp. Pecham*, i, 250–1, ii, 408–9.   ¹⁴¹ *Reg. Sutton*, iii, 77–8.
¹⁴² Pecham equates the two sentences in *Reg. Epp. Pecham*, iii, 909–10.
¹⁴³ *CPR 1258–66*, 103; *Foedera*, I.i.399–400, I.ii.536–7; *Reg. Epp. Pecham*, ii, 422–3, 477.
¹⁴⁴ *CM*, vi, 222–5 (see above 192–5). For further examples: *Reg. Gandavo*, i, 237–40, 494–6; *Reg. Winchelsey*, ii, 268–72, *Reg. Epp. Pecham*, i, 324, 352.
¹⁴⁵ Hill, *Ecclesiastical Letter-Books*, 116–17.   ¹⁴⁶ *Reg. Winchelsey*, i, 110–1.

quis suadente for assualting him, and asked that Adam be denounced and shunned. Adam, however, made a counter-claim that Oliver was defaming him, citing *Crimen imponunt alicui*. The case shows how such sentences were invoked, and that they were common knowledge, even if the protagonists may have sought advice for their cases.[147] Some select further examples of the other Oxford sentences can be found through the references cited below.[148] *Quicumque de domibus* was particularly important in the late 1290s (in relation to the *Clericis laicos* commotion), but was also used routinely, as for instance in early 1296, when various Lincolnshire parishioners were excommunicated for stealing ash-trees from the churchyard of Kingerby.[149]

Reception

That the core *ipso facto* excommunications were common knowledge in the late thirteenth century seems to me undeniable. How the masses received and understood them is another matter. As Ian Forrest has argued, it is important not to assume that publicly disseminated information was taken as it was intended. It might be misunderstood or ignored.[150] In practical terms, it is impossible to determine how far these pronouncements worked as a deterrent. It is possible that fear of hell prevented some from committing offences. Others may have felt concern after the fact and turned themselves in to the ecclesiastical authorities. However, though parishioners will have witnessed or been involved in investigations to find out the names of unknown malefactors who had incurred one of these sentences, it seems more than likely that some of them gambled upon never being discovered. They were excommunicated, but if nobody knew about it then they could live normally, perhaps intending to seek absolution on their deathbeds.

It is also possible that the concept of *ipso facto* excommunication was not grasped by the laity. Certainly, pains were taken to explain the immediate danger to souls, particularly through the ceremony in which candles were symbolically extinguished. Still, the idea of immediate excommunication with no individual to impose a sentence is conceptually difficult, conceivably leading to a misconception that such offences *could* lead to excommunication if discovered. Priests asking in

---

[147] *SCC*, 387-97.
[148] *Reg. Pontissara*, ii, 615-7, 767-8 (*Crimen imponunt alicui*). Many more cases can be found in *Select Cases on Defamation*, ed. Helmholz; *Reg. Sutton*, iii, 21-2 (c. 3 on marriage testimony); *Reg. Epp. Pecham*, i, 35-6 (*Crimen imponunt alicui*); *Reg. Epp. Pecham*, ii, 606-8 (*Contempnunt exequi domini*). The number of *Qui malitiose ecclesias* cases is overwhelming. Interestingly, in 1292 Oliver Sutton pronounced a general sentence for 'atrocious theft', citing the council of Oxford even though Oxford did not include this particular sentence. It perhaps indicates that all English *ipso facto* sentences were associated with Langton's council: *Reg. Sutton*, iv, 8-9.
[149] *Reg. Sutton*, v, 146; cf. *Reg. Sutton*, iii, 172-4, vi, 33-4. In the fourteenth century, a new *ipso facto* sentence that specifically protected trees was introduced.
[150] Forrest, *Trustworthy Men*, 341.

confession whether excommunication had been incurred for any reason would have helped dispel any such delusion, but this required diligent priests. Moreover, while the offences listed were simple enough at face value, as discussed in Chapter 4, there was room for differing interpretations and opinions about what precisely incurred excommunication in a specific case.[151] Maliciously infringing ecclesiastical rights, for instance, was a statement that invited interpretation.

The practical efficacy is thus debatable, but the significance lies instead in the public broadcasting of ecclesiastical concerns through these quarterly pronouncements in parish churches. What the excommunications lacked in specificity they made up for with clarity about the overarching concerns of the *Ecclesia Anglicana*. The emphasis was firmly placed upon protecting ecclesiastical rights, jurisdiction, property, goods, and income. The clergy and their privileges were placed in an elevated position, protected by God. Nobody was left in any doubt about that. At the same time as the king's peace and his rights were guaranteed by excommunication, he and his men were implicated in several of the excommunications, and of course Magna Carta held the king to account. Whatever immunities were claimed by the king and royal officials, the more prominent message was that they were subject to spiritual sanctions like everyone else.

How the general populace felt about these reminders is impossible to say, but the pronouncements could well have backfired. The 1292 attack on the chaplain of Ecton while he was reading from his list of sentences suggests that they could have caused resentment. However, there are a multitude of possible motives for this attack, such as personal animosity towards the chaplain and a particularly solemn occasion on which to attack and humiliate him.[152] In the later Middle Ages, the sentences were criticized as self-serving. In the late fourteenth century, a text called the 'Great Sentence of curs expounded' based a diatribe against the church on the practice. Amounting to almost seventy printed pages, the tract (possibly written by a follower of John Wyclif) painstakingly expounded the Great Sentence.[153] In 1528, a treatise complained that when priests read out the sentences, there was so much emphasis on ecclesiastical rights and privileges 'that the people be greatly offended therby, and thynke great parcialite in them, and iuge them rather to be made of a pryde and couetise of the church; than of any charite to the people, whereby many doo rather dyspyse them than obey them.'[154] Martin Luther similarly criticized the papal general sentence in the 1520s.[155] It should be noted that the formulae were far harsher—more akin to cursing—than used in the

---

[151] Chapter 4, 172–6.

[152] *Reg. Sutton*, iv, 35. Andrew Miller links the Ecton attack to the Thame affair (Chapter 6), but the link seems to me tenuous. The attack took place in early September 1292, before there is any indication of the St Johns' designs upon the Thame benefice. Ecton is *c.*45 miles from Thame, even if it was an 'important' church for Thomas Sutton. '*Carpe Ecclesiam*', 308–9.

[153] Pickering, 'Notes on the sentence of cursing', 240; Forrest, 'William Swinderby', 263–4; *Select English works of John Wyclif*, ed. Arnold, iii, 267–337.

[154] *Monumenta Ritualia*, ed. Maskell, ii, clxxiv.   [155] Jaser, *Ecclesia maledicens*, 402–4.

thirteenth century, but nevertheless the idea that clergy were being good shepherds, informing the laity for their own good, was a tough sell. Mirk's *Quatuor Sermones* tried to persuade listeners that clergy did not desire to curse them; the pronouncement was for their own benefit. *Jacob's Well* similarly suggested parishioners should be glad to hear the sentences. 'The Great Sentence of Cur Expounded', by contrast, questioned the desire to curse.[156] Thus while the English Church made clear its priorities, whether this benefitted its reputation amongst the laity is questionable.

Conclusions

The practice of publishing *ipso facto* excommunications quarterly illuminates many of the tensions inherent in excommunication. To work as a deterrent, the ceremony needed to emphasize the hellish consequences of incurring a sentence. At the same time, bishops were bound by the law and pastoral care to publish the sentences, however uncharitable they appeared. The fact that excommunication was a penalty, and often a self-interested one, appears at odds with the argument that chastising the faithful was an important part of pastoral care. But protecting their own interests and saving souls were, in this context, deeply interwoven. High medieval clergy would have seen no hypocrisy here. Perhaps *ipso facto* sentences were ultimately a flawed concept, but that ship had sailed. There was obvious incentive to defend rules that were highly valued and at risk of being broken with this type of excommunication. Offences protected by *latae sententiae* required regular publication, but this requirement must also have been a strong incentive to protect offences with automatic sanction. As with the publicity afforded *nominatim* sentences, this publicity was a double-edged sword. Ecclesiastical rights and values were constantly broadcast. Just as importantly, in the absence of sentences against individuals the consequences of excommunication were emphasized regularly via the ritual ceremony that implied damnation for excommunicates. However, this ceremony risked appearing harsh rather than merciful. Rather than increase respect for the church and its members, it perhaps caused some of the faithful to judge their preoccupation with temporal rights and goods and their frivolous and opportunistic use of this most severe penalty.

---

[156] John Mirk, *Quatuor Sermones*, 57: 'see that no man nor woman say that I curse hem for hit longyth not to me but to shewe the poyntis and the articles of the sentence of cursyng / For I do you wel to wyte / who so doth ageynst ony of these poyntis that I shal you shewe / he is acursyd in the ded of doying of the pope / archbysshop bsysshop and of al holy chirche'. *Jacob's Well* also suggested parishioners should be glad to hear the sentences: Carruthers, '*Great Curse*', 52; *Select English works of John Wyclif*, iii, 336.

Conclusion

Excommunication was a powerful but volatile sanction. Dependent upon the responses and attitudes of the wider population, its results were by no means guaranteed. There can be no question, however, that it formed a significant part of life for medieval Christians. For churchmen and laymen, whether they were imposing, suffering, enforcing, or questioning excommunication, the sanction was ever-present in their social and spiritual lives. Promulgation of excommunications, and the expectation that those under the ban be excluded from social intercourse, meant that the censure touched those who were never sanctioned as well as those who were. Excommunication was not, therefore, merely a sanction that was imposed upon others by senior members of the ecclesiastical hierarchy. Achieving a viable three-way relationship between excommunicator, excommunicate, and community was crucial, but extremely challenging. Excommunication's impact was felt in political struggles and in daily parish interactions alike, affecting everyone living in thirteenth-century England one way or another. The study of such a multifaceted sanction—one that sought to change behaviour by threatening spiritual, social, and legal repercussions—shows the strengths and limitations of the institutional church. For the historian, excommunication is fruitful and complicated to study because it intersects with so many different spheres. It provides a window into beliefs, attitudes to the church, and social and political behaviours.

At the heart of excommunication lay the tension between its ostensible medicinal purpose and its actual social modus operandi. In many ways, it is this that sets it apart from other comparable penalties used in the Middle Ages and beyond. There was frequently tension between making the sanction as effective as possible and ensuring that it was neither punitive nor irreversible. This is immediately evident when one considers how the consequences of dying excommunicated are presented in our sources. Although by the thirteenth century excommunication can only have led to purgatory (otherwise posthumous absolution would not have been possible), churchmen had a clear incentive to emphasize the idea that hell was the ultimate destination for those who refused to make amends. If excommunication did not damn an excommunicate, its strength was severely diminished. As a result, legal texts, *exempla*, and the ceremony of excommunication implied (or expressly stated) that excommunicates would end up in hell. The dramatic ritual, so familiar to the faithful, retained links to cursing. Whatever neat distinctions were devised by clerical elites, maintaining ambiguity in this instance was advantageous to the church.¹ The majority of clergy and the laity—no distinction ought to be made here—were encouraged to associate excommunication with the inferno.

The evidence indicates that the serious effects of excommunication upon the soul and the afterlife were believed in thirteenth-century England. Qualms about dying excommunicate are the biggest indication of this. Yet reactions varied. An image in the Becket Leaves—the front cover—encapsulates the range of reactions: amongst those who are witnessing Thomas Becket pronounce his sentence, throwing a candle to the ground, there is a man in a green hat recognizably cowering in fear.² Others are making gestures of blessing. To the modern eye, however, the latter appear to be making gestures of contempt. The different reactions shown here, albeit anachronistically interpreted, fit with the medieval reality. The sanction was to a degree dependent on the personal piety of the person sentenced: exclusion from church and the sacraments would of course be more effective on those who cherished these religious rites. Others would be less concerned, not least because the importance of making absolution available to anyone who wished to repent (which again related to the medicinal intent behind excommunication) removed the urgency to seek reconciliation. Absolution could be relatively safely delayed until it suited the excommunicate. Temporal concerns and motivations might trump the spiritual under these conditions. If this was an 'age of faith', the healthy did not necessarily prioritize their souls. Still others reacted not merely apathetically but derisively. There is no indication that such people were heretics; they merely did not believe that their own sentences were valid. They bought into the system as a whole. But the ability of individuals to accept a process in principle, yet nevertheless to maintain that it does not apply in their case, is evident. Such a human tendency is surely in evidence throughout history; attitudes towards the medieval church and its judgments were no exception.

Nonetheless, excommunicates faced considerable temporal repercussions too. The ability to function in society was, in theory, severely curtailed. Sentences made excommunicates vulnerable to mistreatment, urging their fellows to cut them off from all social contact. In military conflicts it legitimized attacks that were otherwise, if not questionable, certainly not laudable. To fight against those separated from God was quite different to combat with unsanctioned Christians. Reputations could be damaged, not merely from the fact that the excommunicate had been excluded from the church, but via public pronouncements that detailed their offences and explained how deplorable such people were. Though rules governed how and when sentences could be imposed, there were no such strict rules regarding how they were implemented. Thus the solemnity of

---

¹ Such advantageous ambiguity was not, of course, limited to excommunication. Cf. indulgences.
² See printed edition: *The Becket Leaves*, ed. Backhouse and de Hamel, f. 2.

ritual pronouncements could be turned up or down. The language used to condemn could be strong or simply informative; the length of denunciations could vary. Perhaps most significantly, how extensively a sentence might be publicized varied considerably. Though excommunication had always been a public matter, increased administrative networks from the twelfth century potentially increased the ability of those who could use the sanction to ensure local publication was performed.

The different ways in which excommunication functioned meant that the particular circumstances of the individual and the specifics of each case mattered a great deal. Some were quickly reined in by the sanction while others persisted in their contumacy. In twenty-first-century England and Wales, over 40 per cent of marriages end in divorce. The increase in divorces following the 1969 Divorce Reform Act suggests that, as divorce has become more common, it probably has less stigma attached.[3] Yet assessing an individual's experience of the process is impossible without a great many more details. Do the couple have children? Was the decision mutual? How old are the couple (and their children)? What is their financial situation? Is either member of the couple or their families religious? Is divorce common amongst their social circle or those with whom they work? All these questions and many more deeply affect what it 'means' to get divorced. Medieval excommunication is just as complex. Though modern divorce and medieval excommunication are wildly different phenomena, neither can be adequately analyzed through statistics or generalizations. The experience of both depends not only on the individuals involved but upon their circumstances and the attitudes of their friends and neighbours. It is, of course, impossible to know all the circumstances of a medieval excommunicate. The point that requires emphasis, nevertheless, is that there is no one-size-fits-all when it comes to the personal experience of this sanction. For some it was perhaps not too considerable a burden, so that they were able to live with their sentences; for others it will have induced a prompt change in behaviour.

Excommunication reveals, as Ian Forrest has recently shown elsewhere, how dependent the church was upon the general population.[4] Susan Reynolds argued that 'lay society and government depended in a mass of different ways on the collective activities of a wide range of people'; the same is true for ecclesiastical society and government, not least where excommunication was concerned. Just as Reynolds found in lay contexts, these activities could be in support of or in opposition to institutions.[5] The church was not able to force parishioners or indeed members of its own hierarchy to exclude those under the ban, either by persuasion or by coercion. The treatment of excommunicates in thirteenth-

---

[3] https://www.ons.gov.uk/peoplepopulationandcommunity/birthsdeathsandmarriages/divorce/bulletins/divorcesinenglandandwales/2019#number-of-divorces-and-rates [accessed 18/9/21].
[4] Forrest, *Trustworthy Men*.   [5] Reynolds, *Kingdoms and Communities*, 332.

century England does not suggest the 'persecuting society' presented by R. I. Moore.[6] Sometimes communal judgments aligned with those of churchmen using excommunication, but the church was not so masterful that it had full control over how sentences played out. Sometimes it was advantageous for people to enforce sentences. They might even do so too forcefully. But they might be enforcing a sentence for their own ends as much as because they had been ordered to do so. While comparisons with other societies show that communal shunning is possible in close-knit societies, it is common for religious sanctions to be greeted with dissent and consequent disobedience. This is particularly true when social sanctions were imposed by elite members of a group who lived separately from the communities supposed to carry out this shunning. Clergy who typically lived amongst the people, that is to say parish priests, did not have the right to excommunicate. The 'solidarities' within the Christian community were diverse; failing to toe the church's line was not necessarily a shunnable offence.

Once again the medicinal nature of excommunication is crucial here. As a 'cure', for the individual and not just society, the sanction was designed to be temporary. Unlike exile or banishment, excommunication did not remove those separated from the community from the sight and minds of its remaining members. It proved difficult to convince people to alter their behaviour towards those with whom they lived. Excommunication was a temporary state imposed for a wide variety of offences, making 'othering' difficult. Thus while excommunication relied, to a large extent, upon clergy and laity playing the game, they did not always do so. This was a negotiation, not a strictly one-sided relationship. This does not mean that excommunications were never enforced: when ecclesiastical sentiment was in line with the flow of public sentiment the mechanism could be effective. How excommunicates were supposed to be treated was common knowledge. But the relationship between excommunication and its theoretical consequences was not automatic. The doctrine that excommunicates were infectious spiritual lepers was repeatedly questioned.

The fact that excommunications were up for debate demonstrates that solidarities were complicated and not easily governed by the pronouncements of churchmen. Laity made up their own minds about such pronouncements, often finding them unjust. Clergy, too, frequently fell on opposite sides of disputes. All sorts of conflicting loyalties, differing interpretations and values, convictions, and senses of injustice are revealed by reactions to excommunications. The communal enforcement expected in the institution of excommunication allows us to witness the people, clerical and lay, voting with their feet. Groups and individuals reached their own conclusions. Certainly, no automatic respect was felt towards those who wielded the sword of excommunication, whatever procedures and safeguards were

---

[6] Moore, *Formation of a Persecuting Society*.

put in place that sought to ensure just sentences. Studies of excommunication in places where anti-clericalism and heretical sects were well known and targeted by the church might profit from comparing these attitudes at a time and a place where there were no such undertakings. Questioning ecclesiastical authority was not the preserve only of those who had had larger doubts about the institutional church.

Positing a definite timeline of excommunication's development is challenging. Within thirteenth-century England, the source material does not suggest any significant changes across the century; the richness of chronicle commentary for the first half of the century is not matched in the second, while episcopal registers only reveal practice in the second half.[7] Changes may be occluded by these imbalances. Over the longer durée, despite a considerable increase of available source material, it can be suggested there is more continuity than previous studies have perhaps suggested. The earlier maledictions did not die out; excommunication was not completely 'tamed' and did not become a purely legal sanction. Nevertheless, bureaucratization did result in important changes. It perhaps enabled more widespread use of excommunication, in this sense fitting into Moore's thesis of a society that had ever more tools of persecution available. Here, however, these developments may also have highlighted flaws in the mechanism. Gregory VII curbed the infectiousness of excommunication with his exceptions, realizing that both souls and ecclesiastical authority were at risk when sentences were disregarded. More routine usage might have contributed to disregard, but increasing oversight in localities might have simply made contempt more evident. Systematization of rules and procedures associated with excommunication was logical in the circumstances but conflicted with language of infection and contagion. As Reynolds argued, contradictions were thus exposed.[8] The 'naturalness' of the ostracism that the church hoped to harness was undermined by codification and mitigations. There was a tension here between practicality and the spirit of the sanction. Practically, mitigations were necessary: without limits put on contagion, there was a risk that everyone would 'catch' excommunication. Not only was this a danger to souls, but it risked making the church look weak. Yet, like interdict, mitigating the severity of excommunication did not make it more effective.[9] Exceptions and complicated rules undermined the simplicity and intelligibility of a sanction that sought to convince that those under the ban were dangerous.

At the same time, however, the ever-growing diocesan administration increased the publicity value of excommunication. Ensuring that clergy made regular denunciations must have become easier, and there were probably more and better trained clergy as time progressed. Excommunication had always been an ideal

---

[7] Registers appear earlier but without general memoranda.
[8] Reynolds, *Kingdoms and Communities*, 338.   [9] Clarke, *Interdict*, 262–4.

means to distribute information. Sentences were meant to be publicized, publication fitted into the mass, and vernaculars were used. As diocesan administration became more sophisticated and effective, so too did the system of denunciation. The promulgation of information here was not only a matter of bureaucracy, however. Denunciation was supposed to be solemn and striking, with clergy in ceremonial dress, making use of visual and audio effects created by candles and bells. Whether general communications about offences the church censured, or condemnations of specific acts or people, churchmen could use excommunication to promulgate their messages. In theory, denunciations merely informed the masses of a sentence that had been pronounced, but in fact they might have influenced how wider events and actions were perceived. They might have affected public perception of one side or the other in a conflict. In this sense, excommunication was a propaganda tool.

Excommunication as a means of mass communication was perhaps a blunt instrument—there was no room for nuance or argument in a denunciation that certain people or types of offender were out of the church—but it was an important means by which forceful condemnations could be disseminated throughout society. The potential gains for clergy employing this were considerable. Rivals might be discredited, causes undermined, disinformation or at least exaggerations spread. The value attached to making information known to the populace is evident through excommunication. Laymen recognized it too, benefitting from its influence when clerics used excommunication on their behalf. For excommunication's mechanisms, spreading knowledge was indispensable. But the importance of extensive publicity in medieval politics more generally, the desire to influence public opinion, has been underestimated. The public nature of the information spread in thirteenth-century England via excommunication might profitably lead to consideration of the practice of politics in public in further studies.

The publicity that was so crucial a part of excommunication was a valuable tool, but also perhaps proved its biggest liability. Excommunication, like other institutions—interdict and inquisition spring to mind—could prove effective but could backfire. While publicizing excommunications had its advantages, it also shone a spotlight upon potential abuses. Thus if a sentence was deemed unjust or unnecessary in the circumstances, the potential misuse was amplified. Only a tiny proportion of medieval people had any say in what sort of crimes incurred excommunication. Only a few more were able to influence individual judgements.[10] Public excommunications that sought to convince the masses to enforce sentences highlighted the frequently self-serving nature of excommunication. Lists of *latae sententiae* risked provoking contempt or disrespect by appearing

---

[10] There is little sense that consent of publics was sought, in interesting contrast to inquisitions recently discussed by John Sabapathy: 'Making public knowledge'.

self-interested. The same problem of excommunication being used for the temporal advantage of clergy was evident in specific circumstances. Sentences might persuade people as a churchman intended, or they might bring that churchman, and by extension potentially the church as a whole, into disrepute. Indeed, one type of abuse was overly enthusiastic promulgation of a sentence beyond what the sanction required. Clergy using it against one another was especially problematic. Such occasions encouraged the public to discuss and debate sentences, sometimes necessitating that people pick a side. Ambiguous *latae sententiae* similarly opened the door to public consideration of ecclesiastical proclamations. Such debate did not require printing presses or coffee houses. The effects such discussions had upon the way excommunications played out was in fact quite considerable. It is going much too far to suggest a latent democracy here, but certainly all of adult society had a role to play in the functioning of the church's most severe sanction.

Excommunication was worth employing. The desired effects were by no means guaranteed, but it was too promising and too useful to neglect. Limits of ecclesiastical authority meant that clergy were not completely in control of how excommunication would be received and acted upon, but this unpredictability did not render excommunication ineffectual. Even a sentence initially ignored might quickly become effective if circumstances and attitudes altered. Similarly, while use of excommunication could show churchmen to be self-serving and only human, the publicity associated with excommunication was too valuable a political tool to relinquish.

The wider effects of excommunication were thus considerable. Sentences sought to convince the populace to shun excommunicates, or to take a particular side, so that they encouraged public debate. Whether or not such debate went as churchmen intended, excommunication increased the political awareness of the laity. This might mean that papal and episcopal decisions were questioned, so it was not always to the church's benefit, but its historical significance is substantial. The spiritual repercussions of the sentence and its contagiousness meant that all members of society had to be informed equally. The reach of the sanction is shown by variable reactions to it. Whether people were disapproving, ignoring, resisting, or responding more positively to excommunication, they had to form an opinion and were engaging with the concept. Excommunication enabled the church to penetrate deeply and regularly into the lives of medieval people, but not predictably, and not without unintended consequences.

APPENDIX 1

Ipso facto excommunications promulgated via thirteenth-century English ecclesiastical legislation, with provisions for their regular pronouncement

Council / no. of extant MSS	Date	Type of offender automatically excommunicated	Publication provisions	C&S
Legatine council, York / 3	1195	[13] Perjurers	3×/yr	i.1051
Westminster / 3	1200	[7] Sorcerers (*sorciarii*), perjurers [swearing] on the gospels, arsonists, atrocious thieves, robbers (*raptores*)	Every year	i.1065
Canterbury I (Cant. dioc.) / 4	1213 × 1214	[49] Sorcerers, witnesses perjuring on the gospels, arsonists, usurers, plunderers (*publici raptores*), those who impede wills, those who detain tithes	3×/yr: Christmas, Pentecost, Assumption of Mary	ii.33
Salisbury I / Durham I (Salis. & Durh. diocs) / 7	1217 × 1219 (1228 × 1236)	[52] Sorcerers, witnesses perjuring on the gospels, arsonists, usurers, plunderers, those who impede wills, (in 5 MSS) invoking help of demons, and (in 3 of these MSS) abusing the sacraments	3×/yr: Three major feasts. 2 MSS specify Christmas and Pentecost; one of these also the Assumption of Mary	ii.76 (201)
OXFORD (Cant. province) / *c.* 70	1222	[1] Those who maliciously deprive churches of their rights and liberties [2] Those who disturb the peace of the king and realm, or strive to detain the king's rights [3] Those who knowingly procure false testimony or witnesses in marriages cases [4] Advocates who maliciously raise objections to prevent or delay marriages	Every year in episcopal synods, 4×/year in parish churches	ii.106–7, 125

Continued

Continued

Council / no. of extant MSS	Date	Type of offender automatically excommunicated	Publication provisions	C&S
		[5] Those who maliciously or for profit make defamatory accusations [6] Those who maliciously defraud true patrons of collations to their vacant churches [7] Those who maliciously or for profit refuse to execute the king's mandate to arrest contumacious excommunicates		
Winchester I (Winch. dioc.) / 1	1224	[70] Those who for gain obstruct sailors in danger of shipwrecks from avoiding the danger of death [72] Those who give false testimony	3×/yr on the Isle of Wight and in coastal areas on the mainland 4×/yr in parish churches	ii.136
Synodal statutes for unknown diocese / c. 30	1222 × 1225	[62] *Westminster* [7], adds usurers, atrocious thieves, intruders, forgers, those who impede wills	3 or 4×/yr	ii.150–1
Canterbury II (Cant. dioc.) / 3	1222 × 1228	[52] *Salisbury I* [52]	3×/yr: Three major feasts	ii.165–6
Constitutions of an unknown bishop / 1	1225 × 1230	[70] *Canterbury I* [49]	3×/yr: Christmas, Pentecost, Assumption of Mary	ii.192
Coventry (Cov. and Lichfield dioc.) / 11	1224 × 1237	[14] *Oxford* [3] [5]	Every Sunday	ii.213
Exeter I (Ex. dioc.) / 1	1225 × 1237	[8] *Salisbury I* [52], incl. those invoking the help of a demon. Omits usurers; *Oxford* [1] and [2] given in full, the remaining Oxford sentences summarized as 'and also all those who the	3×/yr	ii.230–1

Lincoln (Linc. dioc.) / c. 25	1239?	Council of Oxford instructs to be excommunicated' [9] Perjurers swearing on the gospels	4×/yr	ii.275–6
Statutes for London archdeaconry / 7	c.1229 × 1241	[46] *Oxford [1]-[7]* Renewed (in writing?) every year in every church	ii.332
		[7] *Oxford [1]-[6]*; Detainers of tithes, usurers, arsonists, sorcerers, forgers of bulls and coin clippers, notorious fornicators, adulterers and prostitutes, and their defenders	4×/yr: First Sunday of Advent, first Sunday of Lent, Trinity Sunday, the Sunday within the octave of the Assumption of Mary. The statutes also order that tithe-detaining be publicly forbidden on pain of excommunication (so not an *ipso facto* sentence) in every church annually for three Sundays following the Nativity of John the Baptist	
Norwich (Nor. dioc.) / 5 N.B. These statutes have a complicated manuscript tradition (*C&S*, 344–5)	1240 × 1243	[57] MSS AC: *Oxford [1]-[7]* MS D: one long clause, protecting ecclesiastical customs, noting many authorities MS E: all heretics, sorcerers, money forgers. The text then resembles the gist of *Oxford [1]-[7]*, though disordered and with additions. Amongst these are included detainers of tithes, and forgers of papal letters, charters, or seals.	Every year in episcopal synods and 4×/yr in parish churches. MS E only: Sunday after the feast of St Michael, Sunday in the middle of Lent, Trinity Sunday, Sunday following the feast of St Peter in Chains	ii.355–7
	1238 × 1244			ii.387

Continued

Continued

Council / no. of extant MSS	Date	Type of offender automatically excommunicated	Publication provisions	C&S
Salisbury II (Salis. dioc.) / 2		[59] *Oxford [1]*, adds 'the church of Salisbury and other catholic churches'; *Oxford [2]*, adds 'and plot his death or any sedition'; *Oxford [3]-[7]*; Those who despoil the church of Salisbury of tithes, revenues, pasture, liberties, etc.	Every month in churches, after the gospel on Sundays or solemn days	
Durham II (Durh. dioc.) / 4	1241 × 1249	[50] i. *Oxford [2]*, omits the king's rights; *Oxford [1]*, adds or who lays hands on ecclesiastical goods ii. Those who intrude themselves into ecclesiastical benefices by violence and occupy them with lay force; especially those who infringe or disturb the liberties of the church of Durham iii. All arsonists, burglars (*fractores*) of churches, sorcerers/witches (*veneficos/as*), users of magical incantations iv. *Oxford [3]* [4], with minor changes v. *Oxford [5]* vi. Forbids advocates of the city or diocese to provide their services in cases and consistories unless they swear an oath that they will not accept a case which they know to be unjust, especially in a matrimonial case	4×/yr: Greater feasts of the year; to be diligently and faithfully explained	ii.434–5
'Durham peculiars' (York dioc., see C&S 435–6) / 1	1241 × 1249?	[35] *Salisbury I [52]*, adds forgers	3×/yr: Three greater feasts	ii.442
Chichester I (Chich. dioc.) / 1	1245 × 1253	[72] *Oxford [1]* [73] *Oxford [3]* [74] *Oxford [4]* [75] *Salisbury I [52]*, adds violators of immunity of churches and detainers of tithes and other dues; omits Sorcerers, perjurers [76] *Oxford [5]*	4×/yr: Solemn days through whole bishopric	ii.466

York I, with later additions (York dioc.) / 5	1261 × 1276	[77] *Oxford* [6] [78] *Oxford* [7]		After every synod in 'every deanery nearest the chapter'; to be explained in every article	ii.495–6
	1269?	[39] Anyone who impedes the executors or administrators of wills, assigned by the archbishop or his officials			
	1241 × 1276	[40] *London* [12], omits extraction of fugitives			
		[41] i. *Durham II* [50] *i*, adds especially the sacrosanct church of York. *Durham II* [50] *ii*. shortened, and omits clause on Durham liberties			
	Before 1276	[41] ii. Those who violate the archbishop's sequestration (*sequestra*); *Oxford* [7] though phrased differently			
	1241 × 1276	[41] *Durham II* [50] *iii*. adds and those procuring them and those who violate the immunity of the church			
		[42] i. Forbids a general excommunication to be pronounced for injuries, whenever someone against whom he has an action can be determined, unless there is a clear need			
		ii. Those who, for hatred or profit etc., make false accusations for which the punishment, if the accused were judicially convicted, would be death, exile, loss of limb, disinheritance, or spoliation of goods			
		iii. If anyone proposes something to further defame, which impedes custom, they should be canonically punished			
Salisbury III (Customs of Salisbury dioc.) / 1	1228 × 1256	[15] 'General excommunication' (that of Salisbury I or II, perhaps?)		3×/yr in every church	ii.514
Wells (Bath & Wells dioc.) / 2	1258?	[80] *Oxford* [1]–[3]		3×/yr: on major solemnities by anyone having care of a parish	ii.625–6
Carlisle (Carlisle dioc.) / 1	1258 × 1259	[81] *Oxford* [1]–[3]		3×/yr: on major solemnities by anyone having care of a parish	ii.629
	1262 × 1265				ii.722–3

Continued

Continued

Council / no. of extant MSS	Date	Type of offender automatically excommunicated	Publication provisions	C&S
Winchester III (Winch. dioc.) / 6		[103] *Oxford [1]–[7]*, adds 'and especially the church of Winchester or others of the diocese' to [1]	3×/yr in every church of the diocese	ii.762–4
LONDON (Legatine Council held by Ottobuono) / c. 70	1268	[12] Those who extract fugitives from churches, cemeteries, or cloisters, or by violence remove another's property deposited there, or help such people. Those who burn churches or break into them. Those who consume or remove anything from houses, manors, granges, or other places pertaining to ecclesiastical persons or their churches	Every Sunday in cathedral and college churches and others, by their chaplains and rectors, with a crowd of parishioners and the faithful present	
Durham III (Durh. dioc.) / 2	1276	[10] *Oxford [1] [2] [5]*; Anyone who impedes the executors or administrators of wills; *York [41] ii*, not verbatim; *Oxford [7]* worded differently (as *York I [41] ii*); *Durham II [50] iii*.	3×/yr: Major feasts	ii.820
READING (Cant. province) / c. 40	1279	[11] i. *Oxford [1]*, adds clarification that it included all who sent writs of prohibition in cases which pertained to the ecclesiastical forum ii. *Oxford [2]*, adds clarification that it included those stirring up the horror of wars and public thieves and plunderers iii–vi. *Oxford [3]–[6]* vii. *Oxford [7]*, adds or who impede capture or procure unjust liberation viii. Those who receive anything to impede peace or settlement of litigation (based on *London [27]*) ix. *London [12]* on removal of things from ecclesiastical houses, manors etc. (abbreviated) x. *London [12]* on removal of fugitives from sanctuary (abbreviated)	4×/yr: To be explained openly to the people, in greater and lesser churches, on the Sundays following rural chapters	ii. 848–50

		xi. Those who infringe Magna Carta, confirmed many times by the apostolic see	
LAMBETH (Cant. province) / c. 60; printed 1504	1281	[10] i. *Reading [11] i*, expanded considerably, asserting that it protected both temporal and spiritual possessions, and liberties great and small. See Glossary ii–xi. *Reading [11] ii–xi*	4×/yr: Once every quarter of the year, on a solemn day or many. These provisions are specified in the previous clause (the *Ignorantia sacerdotum*)	ii. 900–1, 905–7
Exeter II (Ex. dioc.) / 12	1287	[56] *Oxford [1]–[7]*; *Reading [11] viii–xi*	3×/yr: First Sunday of Advent, Sunday in Lent, Sunday before the feast of St Peter in chains. In every parish church, with crowd present, and on the said feast of St Peter in Exeter cathedral	ii.1057–8
Chichester II (Chich. dioc.) / 1 (3 known to have existed)	1289	[39] i. *York [41]* ii. *York [41] ii* iii. *York [41] iii* [40] i. *York [42] i* ii. *York [42] ii* iv. *York [42] iii*	4×/yr: Third Sunday of Advent, Sunday in the middle of Lent; Sunday before the feast of the Nativity of John the Baptist; Sunday before the feast of St Michael; to be explained in every article, in the mother tongue.	ii.1089–90

APPENDIX II

William of Pagula's *Oculus sacerdotis* (*c*.1320), Dextera Pars

The following text is a transcription of a section of the *Oculus sacerdotis*, instructing parish priests to regularly publicise certain *ipso facto* sentences of excommunication, from BL Royal MS 8 C II (*R1*), fos. 85vb-87ra.[1] It has been checked against BL Royal MS 8 B XV (*R2*), fos. 52r-54r and BL Harley MS 1307 (*H*), fos. 41v-43v. Both Royal MSS are fourteenth-century, the Harleian MS fourteenth or fifteenth-century. *R2* does not contain marginal numeration; *H* uses arabic numerals but numbers the clauses differently. Abbreviations are expanded silently. When the text from *R1* is not used, its reading is given in footnotes. Select variant readings from the other two manuscripts are also noted. Cues to the apparatus are placed before lemmata. Minor variations, including plurals used instead of singulars or vice versa, are not noted.[2] Cc. i-xi follow the 1281 Council of Lambeth (*C&S*, 900-1) and individual references are not provided. From c. xii, canon law references in the text have been expanded and capitalised for clarity, so 'de sen. ex.' becomes 'De sententia excommunicationis', and incipits of canons have been italicized. Modern-style canon law references are provided in brackets.

§ Sentences of excommunication to be frequently published by parish priests on Sundays and feast days

[f. 85vb] Ultimo debet sacerdos parochialis frequenter diebus dominicis [3]et aliis diebus festivis solempnibus intra missarum solempnia publicare excommunicaciones latas in [4]consilio Oxon' et de Lameth Pecham, et excommunicaciones a canone latas [5]frequenter occurentes, ne per ignoranciam velamen excommunicacionis ab aliquo pretendatur et debet publicare sub hac forma:

[i.] Auctoritate dei patris omnipotentis et filii et spiritus sancti et gloriose dei genitricis [6]semperque virginis marie et beatorum apostolorum petri et pauli, omniumque apostolorum ac martirum et confessorum atque virginum omniumque sanctorum dei, denuncio excommunicatos omnes illos qui ecclesias quascumque suo iure maliciose privare presumunt aut per maliciam libertates earumdem infringere vel perturbare contendunt; ubi tria genera hominum excommunicantur, videlicet: – auferentes ab ecclesiis sua iura; – item infringentes ecclesiasticas libertates – quod non solum intelligitur de generalibus libertatibus universalis ecclesie, verum etiam [7]de [8]specialibus, tam spiritualibus quam temporalibus,

---

[1] In the first part (*Oculus sacerdotis*) a longer list of *ipso facto* excommunications is provided. In *R1* this longer list is on fos. 67ra-73rb. For the *Oculus sacerdotis* and its three parts, see Boyle, 'The Oculus sacerdotis'.

[2] For instance, 'all those are excommunication who do X' vs 'he is excommunicated who does X'.

[3] vel *H*.   [4] conciliis *H*.   [5] frequencius *H*.   [6] semperque virginis *om. H*.

[7] de specialibus...temporalibus] de temporalibus tam spiritualibus quam corporalibus *H*.

[8] *Cor. from* spiritualibus *in R1. R2: has* de temporalibus tam spiritualibus quam corporalibus.

exquo intelliguntur [9]excommunicati omnes illi qui impetrant litteras a quacumque curia laicali ad impediendum processum iudicum ecclesiasticorum in causis, que per sacros canones ad forum ecclesiasticum pertinere [10]noscuntur, quod nullatenus possunt nec consueverunt per seculare iudicium termi-[f. 86ra]-nari: – item omnes illos qui false et maliciose [11]episcopalem aut archiepiscopalem processum impediunt aut subiter fugiunt disciplinam.

ii. [12]Item denuncio excommunicatos omnes illos qui pacem et tranquillitatem domini regis et regni (fo. 70va) auctoritate opere vel consilio perturbant et in mortem eius vel sedicionem aliquam machinantur, et qui iura domini regis iniuste detinere contendunt, exquo intelliguntur excommunicati non solum guerrarum [13]suscitantes [14]errorem, verum etiam publici latrones omnes, pariter et predones et quicumque iusticiam regni temere inpugnantes.

iii. Item omnes illos qui scienter falsum perhibent testimonium vel perhiberi procurant vel qui tales testes scienter producunt ad impediendum iustum matrimonium vel ad exheredacionem alicuius procurandam.

iiii. Item advocatos omnes qui in causis matrimonialibus opponunt excepciones maliciose vel opponi procurant vel in quibuscumque causis ut processus cause diucius suspendatur.

v. Item omnes illos qui gratia, lucri vel odii seu favoris vel alia quacumque de causa alicui maliciose crimen [15]opponunt, cum infamatus non sit [16]apud bonos et graves, ut sic saltem ei purgacio indicatur vel alio modo gravetur.

vi. Item omnes illos qui vacante ecclesia maliciose opponunt vel opponi procurant questionem de iure patronatus ut sic verum patronum a collatione illius [17]ecclesie saltem impediant illa vice.

vii. Item omnes illos qui maliciose contempnunt exequi mandatum domini regis de excommunicatis capiendis vel eorum impediunt capcionem seu procurant iniustam eorum liberacionem contra decretum ecclesiastice discipline.

viii. Item excommunicantur in consilio sancte memorie Octob[oni] omnes illi qui pro impedimento pacis seu pro conpensacione litigancium quicquam recipiunt donec ipsum sic receptum restituerint donatori et tantumdem exsolverint pauperibus errogandis.

[ix.] Item [18]excommunicantur per eundem quicumque de domibus, maneriis vel [19]grangiis seu locis aliis archiepiscoporum, episcoporum vel aliarum personarum ecclesiasticarum contra ipsorum voluntatem, vel custodum rerum earumdem, auferunt aliquid vel consumunt vel iniuriose contractant qua sentencia excommunicationis ligantur, nec [20]absolvuntur donec de iniuriis satisfacerint competenter.

[x.] tem excommunicantur ab eodem quicumque abstra[h]unt [21]violenter aliquem ad ecclesiam vel cymiterium seu ad claustrum [22]fugientem vel qui ei victum neccesarium prohibent exhiberi vel qui res [23]alienas in locis eisdem depositas violenter asportant vel asportari faciunt, [f. 86rb] vel qui asportacionem talem nomine suo factam vel a familiaribus suis ratam habuerint, vel qui ad hoc publice vel occulte dederint consilium, auxilium vel consensum.

xi. Item excommunicati sunt ab omnibus archiepiscopis et episcopis Anglie omnes illi qui veniunt aut faciunt contra magnam cartam, que sentencia per sedem apostolicam est

---

[9] R2, H: excommunicantur R1.   [10] R2, H: nascantur R1.
[11] episcopalem aut archiepiscopalem R2, H: episcopale aut archiepiscopale R1.
[12] H is so highly abbreviated – 'It' den' ex. o. i. q^{li}' – that denuncio *has been added in superscript*.
[13] R2, H: succitantes R1.   [14] cf. C&S, 849 n.a.   [15] impoununt H.   [16] inter H.
[17] R2, H: om. R1.   [18] R2, H: excommunicatur R1.   [19] R2, H: grangeis R1.
[20] absolvantur R2 *(perhaps correctly)*.   [21] violenter om. H.   [22] confugientem H.
[23] alienas om. H.

pluries confirmata. In constitutiones provincie de Lameth Pecham c. *Eisdem temporibus*. In Const. [24]Oxon' c. i. et in Const' Octob[oni] c. *Ad cautelam* et c. *Cum partes*. Unde in magna carta sunt xxxv articuli et in carta de foresta sunt xv, et omnes illi articuli notantur in speculo prelatorum[25] titulo xx.

xii. Item excommunicantur omnes illi qui in clericos vel religiosos vel conversos et nondum professos manus [26]iniecerint temere violentas vel nomine suo factum ratum habuerint precipiunt vel sibi mandant. Extra 'De sententia excommunicationis', *Non dubium* etc. [X.5.39.5], *Mulieres ac parochianos* etc. [X.5.39.6; X.5.39.9], *Porro* etc. [X.5.39.7], *Religioso* etc. [VI.5.11.21], *Cum quis*, li. vi. [VI.5.11.23] xvii. q. [27]iiii. c. *Siquis suadente* [C.17, q.4, c.29].

xiii. Item excommunicantur quicumque scienter in gradibus consanguinitatis vel affinitatis constitutione canonica interdictis aut cum monialibus de facto matrimonium contraxerit, necnon religiosi seu moniales vel clerici in sacris ordinibus constituti de facto matrimonia contrahentes, et prelati ecclesiarum tamdiu debent denunciare illos quos eis constiterit taliter contraxisse publice excommunicatos seu a suis subditis faciant denunciari donec [28]suum humiliter recognoscant errorem, separentur ab invicem, et absolucionis beneficium meruerunt optinendum. In Const' Extravag' pape Clementis v, 'De consanguinitate et affinitate', c. *Eos qui*, li vi [Clem. 4.1.1].

xiv. Item excommunicantur falsarii litterarum domini pape cum fautoribus et defensoribus suis et qui huius falsas litteras [29]impetraverint et qui usi fuerint scienter huius falsis litteris. Extra 'De crimine falsi', *Ad falsariorum* etc. [X.5.20.7], *Dura* [X.5.20.4].

xv. Item excommunicantur violatores, raptores et incendiarii ecclesiarum sive religiosorum locorum et omnes eis consentientes. xi. q. iii, *Canonica* [C.11, q.3, c.107], xvii. q. iiii, *Omnes* [C.17, q.4, c.5], xxiii. q. ult' *Pessimam* [C.23, q.8, c.32], Extra 'De sententia excommunicationis', *Conquesti* etc. [X.5.39.22], *Tua nos* [X.5.39.19].

xvi. Item excommunicantur symoniaci. i. q. i. *Reperiuntur* [C.1, q.1, c.7].

xvii. Item heretici defensores, receptores et fautores eorumdem hereticorum. Extra 'De hereticis', c. *Sicut ait* etc. [X.5.7.8] [30]*Excommunicamus* i et ii [X.5.7.13; X.5.7.15].

xviii. Item excommunicantur omnes qui faciunt statuta edita consuetudines contra ecclesiasticam libertatem et stacionarii et etiam scriptores huius statutorum et qui huius statuta vel consuetudines fecerint observari, nisi ea infra mensem fecerint revocari vel secundum ea presumpserint iudicare vel in publicam formam scribere taliter iudicata. Extra 'De sententia excommunicationis', *Noverit* [X.5.39.40].

[f. 86va] xix. Item excommunicantur qui per se vel per alios spoliant ecclesias bonis suis vel iniuste prosequuntur electores seu consanguineos eorum gravant pro eo quod electores noluerunt eligere illum in prelatum pro quo rogabantur sive inducebantur. Extra 'De electione', *Sciant cuncti* li.vi [VI.1.6.12].

xx. Item excommunicantur illi qui per vim vel per metum extorquent absolutionem a sententia excommunicationis seu extorquent revocacionem excommunicationis vel suspensionis seu interdicti. Extra 'De hiis que vi metusve causa fiunt', c. *Absolutionis* li.vi. [VI.1.20.1].

xxi. Item excommunicantur illi qui habent temporale dominium et subditis suis interdicunt ne prelatis aut clericis seu personis ecclesiasticis quicquam vendant aut aliquid

---

[24] *R2, H*: Exon' *R1*.

[25] Another of Pagula's works. In fact, part I of the *Oculus sacerdotis* also contains abbreviations of Magna Carta and the Forest Charter (fos. 71ra-73ra in *R1*).

[26] *R2, H*: iniecerat *R1*.   [27] *R2, H*: iii *R1*.   [28] *R2, H*: suam *R1*.

[29] *R2, H*: impetraverit *R1*.   [30] excommunicatus *H*.

emant ab eisdem necque ³¹eisdem bladum molant nec panem coquant aut alia obsequia eis exhibere presumant. Extra 'De immunitate etc.', *Eos qui* li.vi. [VI.3.24.5].

xxii. Item excommunicantur illi qui scienter tradiderint ecclesiastice sepulture hereticos seu credentes erroribus eorum defensores ac fautores eorum. Extra 'De hereticis', *quicumque* li.vi. [VI.5.2.2].

xxiii. Item excommunicatur ille qui manus violentas iniecerit in illum qui ingressus fuerit religionem ³²quamvis nec tacite neque expresse fuerit professus. Extra 'De sententia excommunicationis', li.vi. c. *Religioso* [VI.5.11.21].

xxiiii. Item excommunicatur ille qui ab homine vel a canone est excommunicatus et propter mortis periculum vel aliud inpedimentum legitimum vel absolvatur ab eo qui alias de iure non potest eum absolvere si postea cessante periculo seu impedimento contempserit quam cito commode poterit se presentare illi a quo de iure deberet absolvi ipsius mandatum ³³suscepturus et satisfacturus prout iusticia suadebit, vel qui a sede apostolica vel eius legato fuerit absolutus et sibi iniungatur ut penitenciam recipiat a suo ordinario et passis iniuriam satisfaciat, si hoc cum primum commode poterit non curaverit adimplere, ³⁴in eandem excommunicationis sententiam recidit ipso iure. Extra 'De sentencia excommunicationis', c. *Eos qui* li. vi. [VI.5.11.22], In Const' Extravag' pape Clementis v. 'De penis', c. *Si quis* ¶ ult'. [Clem.5.8.1 (last para.)].

xxv. Item excommunicatur quicumque cuiuscumque status seu conditionis vel gradus etiam si pontificali prefulgeat dignitate executor seu quivis alius fecerit corpus defuncti exenterari seu membrati dividi. In Const' Extravag' pape Bonifacii viii. c. *Detestande* [*Extravagantes communes* 3.6.1].

xxvi. Item excommunicantur qui scienter tempore interdicti in casibus non concessis a iure in cymiteriis ³⁵corpora defunctorum etiam publice excommunicatos aut nominati interdictos [f. 86rb] vel usurarios manifestos sepelierint. In Const' Extravag' pape Clementis v. 'De sepultura', c. *Eos* [Clem. 3.7.1].

xxvii. Item excommunicantur quicumque fecerint statuta scripserint seu dictaverint quod solvantur usure vel quod usure solute non repetantur nec restituantur. Item excommunicantur qui huius statuta hactenus edita de libris communitatum ipsarum si super hoc peccatem habuerint non deleverint infra iii menses. In Const' Extrav' pape Clementis v. 'De usuris', c. *Gravi* [Clem. 5.5.1].

xxviii. Item excommunicantur religiosi qui clericis aut laycis ministrant sacramentum eukaristie vel unctionis extreme vel matrimonium inter aliquos solempnizant non habita super hiis ³⁶parochialis presbiteri licentia speciali aut qui excommunicatos a canone vel a sententiis per statuta provincialia aut synodalia promulgatis aliquid absolverint preter quam in casibus a iure ³⁷expressis vel ³⁸per privilegia sedis apostolice concessis eisdem seu a pena et a culpa de facto absolverint. In Const' Extravag' pape Clementis v. 'De privilegiis', c. *Religiosi* [Clem. 5.7.1].

xxix. Item excommunicantur illi qui capiunt viros ecclesiasticos et captos detinent donec sua beneficia ³⁹resignent aut citatos ab homine vel a iure ad sedem apostolicam et etiam procurantes huius capcionem sunt excommunicati. In Const' Extravag' pape Clementis v. 'De penis', c. *Multorum* [Clem. 5.8.2.].

xxx. Item excommunicantur qui in loco supposito interdicto quamquam cogerint divina officia celebrare aut qui tempore interdicti per campanarum pulsacionem populos publice

---

³¹ R1: ipsis R2, H.   ³² H: quam n/uⁱ R1: R2 unclear.   ³³ suscepturus et receupturus H.
³⁴ *om.* R1.   ³⁵ corpora defunctorum etiam *om.* H.
³⁶ licencia *crossed out after* paroch' in R1.   ³⁷ promissis H.   ³⁸ *om.* R1.
³⁹ resignant R2, H.

excommunicatos seu interdictos evocaverint ad audiendas missas seu fecerint evocari aut qui suis subiectis publice excommunicatis seu interdictis [40]preceperint ne exeant de ecclesiis dum in ipsis missarum solempnia celebrantur vel a celebrantibus moniti fuerint ut exeant necnon excommunicati publice interdicti qui in ipsis ecclesiis nominatim a celebrantibus moniti ut exeant remanere presumpserint nec possunt absolvi nisi per sedem apostolicam. In Const' Extrav' pape Clementis v. 'De sententia excommunicationis', c. *Gravis* [Clem. 5.10.2.].

xxxi. Item excommunicantur clerici arma deferentes et se furibus et predonibus ac aliis malefactoribus sociantes rapinas et furta precipientes nec possunt absolvi nisi prius ad arbitrium episcopi dyocesani satisfecerint de premissis. In Const' Ottob' c. *Quoniam in armis* [C&S, 751, c. 4].

xxxii. Item excommunicantur qui impediunt seu [41]impediri procurant ultimas voluntates defunctorum presertim in hiis que de iure vel consuetudine legari possunt.

xxxiii. Item excommunicantur quicumque qui impediunt vel perturbant seu faciant perturbari aut impediri iustam seu consuetam testi liberam factionem alicuius [42]solute mulieris vel coniugate [f. 87ra] proprie vel alterius. In Const' de Lameth Bonifacii c. *Contingit*. ¶ *Item testimentis* et ¶ *Statuimus* [C&S, 681-2].

xxxiiii. Item excommunicantur quicumque [43]recipit plura beneficia curata et ea retinuerit absque dispensatione sedis apostolice vel assecutus per modum institutionis vel commendationis seu custodie vel unum beneficium [44]titulo instititionis aliud titulo commendationis seu custodie preter illum modum quem consitutio Gregoriana edita in consilio Lugd' permittit. In Const' Radig' Pecham c. i. ¶ *Huic quoque* [C&S, 840; VI.1.16.3].

Multi sunt alii casus in quibus quis est excommunicatus ipso facto et illi casus notantur in speculo prelatorum in secunda parte ti. xxi.

---

[40] precepit *R1, R2, H*. [41] *R2, H:* impedire *R1*. [42] *R2, H:* solucite *R1*. [43] om. *H*.
[44] nomine *H*.

Bibliography

Canon law references are to the *Corpus Iuris Canonici*, ed. E. Friedberg, 2 vols. (Leipzig, 1879). Gratian's *Decretum* in the form 'C.1, q.1, c.1' or 'D.1, c.1.' *Liber Extra (Decretales Gregorii IX)* in the form 'X 1.1.1.' *Liber Sextus* (of Boniface VIII) in the form 'VI 1.1.1.' *Clementines* (of Clement V) in the form 'Clem. 1.1.1.'

Footnotes provide author surname and short title for secondary works, short title and editor for primary sources. Abbreviations for select primary sources precede their full references in the bibliography.

Abbreviations

BL	British Library
CYS	Canterbury and York Society
EHR	*English Historical Review*
HR	*Historical Research*
JEH	*Journal of Ecclesiastical History*
JMH	*Journal of Medieval History*
RS	Rolls Series
SCH	*Studies in Church History*
TCE	*Thirteenth Century England*
TNA	The National Archives

Manuscript Sources

Cambridge, University Library
EDC 1/B/95.

Cambridge, Corpus Christi College
MS 255 (*Modus pronunciandi*).

Lincolnshire Archives
Episcopal Register I: Register of Oliver Sutton (consulted on microfilm: *Church, authority and power in medieval and early modern Britain: the episcopal registers.* Part 2).

London, British library
Additional 15236 (excommunication formula).
Additional 11284 (*Speculum laicorum*).
Cotton Faustina A IV (cartulary of St Neots priory).
Harley 1307 (*Oculus sacerdotis*).
Harley 3911 (cartulary of Holm Cultram abbey).
Royal 8 B XV (*Oculus sacerdotis*; excommunication formula).
Royal 8 C II (*Oculus sacerdotis*).

Royal 9 A II (statute book).
Royal 11 A XIV (excommunication formula).
Stowe 937 (cartulary of Pipewell abbey).

London, The National Archives
C85 (writs *de excommunicato capiendo*).
SC1 (Ancient correspondence of the chancery and the exchequer).

Oxford, Bodleian Library
Bodley 91 (Boniface of Savoy's 1263 excommunication).

York, Borthwick Institute
Abp Register 6 (Thomas Corbridge (1300–1304)).

Printed Sources

The 1258-9 Special Eyre of Surrey and Kent, ed. A.H. Hershey (Surrey Record Society 38, 2004).

'A plea roll of Edward I's army in Scotland, 1296', ed. C.J. Neville, in *Miscellany of Scottish History Society XI* (Edinburgh, 1990).

A Formulary of the Papal Penitentiary in the Thirteenth Century, ed. H.C. Lea (Philadelphia, PA, 1892).

Ann. Burton: Annales Monasterii de Burton, 1004–1263, *Ann. Mon.* i.

Ann. Dunstable: Annales Prioratus de Dunstaplia A.D. 1–1297, *Ann. Mon.* iii.

Ann. Mon.: Annales Monastici, ed. H.R. Luard, 5 vols. (RS, 1864–1869).

Ann. Tewksbury: Annales Monasterii de Theokesberia, *Ann. Mon.* i.

Ann. Worcester: Annales Prioratus de Wigornia, A.D. 1–1377, *Ann. Mon.* iv.

Annales Londonienses, in *Chronicles of the Reigns of Edward I and Edward II*, ed. W. Stubbs, i, (RS, 1882).

Annales Monasterii de Oseneia, 1016–1347, Ann. Mon. iv.

Annales Monasterii de Waverleia, A.D. 1–1291, Ann. Mon. ii.

Annales Monasterii de Wintonia, 519–1277, Ann. Mon. ii.

The Annals of Dunstable Priory, trans. David Preest, ed. H. R. Webster (Woodbridge, 2018).

Aquinas, *Summa Theologiae*: Thomas Aquinas, *Summa Theologiae* in *Opera Omnia iussu Leonis XIII*, xii (Rome, 1906).

The Becket Leaves, ed. J. Backhouse and C. de Hamel (London, 1988).

Bonaventure, *Commentaria in quatuor libros sententiarum magistri Petri Lombardi*, in *Opera Omnia*, iv, ed. P. Bernardini (Quaracchi, 1889).

Bracton De legibus et consuetudinibus Angliae, ed. G.E. Woodbine, trans. with revisions and notes by S.E. Thorne, 4 vols. (Cambridge, Mass., 1968–77).

Bullarium franciscanum romanorum pontificum constitutiones, epistolas, ac diplomata continens tribus ordinibus minorum, clarissarum et poenitentium, etc., ed. J. H. Sbaraleae, ii, (Rome, 1761).

C&S: Councils and Synods with other documents relating to the English Church, II, A.D. 1205–1313, ed. F.M. Powicke and C.R. Cheney, 2 vols. (Oxford, 1964).

Cal. Pap. Reg.: Calendar of Entries in the Papal Registers relating to Great Britain and Ireland, i: 1198–1304 (London, 1893).

Calendar of Inquisitions Miscellaneous preserved in the Public Record Office, i (London, 1916).

Catalogue of Romances in the Department of Manuscripts, ed. J.A. Herbert, iii (London, 1910).

CCR: *Calendar of the Close Rolls Preserved in the Public Record Office* (London, 1900–).
Chanter, *Summa*: Peter the Chanter, *Summa de Sacramentis et Animae Consiliis*, ed. J-A. Dugauquier, A. M. Namurcensia, vol.16 (Paris, 1963).
Chobham, *Summa*: *Thomas de Chobham Summa Confessorum*, ed. Revd. D. Broomfield (Louvain, 1968).
Chron. Bury: *The Chronicle of Bury St Edmunds, 1212–1301*, ed. A. Gransden (London, 1964).
Chronica Magisteri Rogeri de Hovedene, ed. W. Stubbs, 4 vols. (RS, 1868–71).
The Chronicle of Pierre de Langtoft in French Verse, ed. T. Wright, 2 vols. (RS, 1866–8).
The Chronicle of William de Rishanger of the Barons' Wars, ed. J.O. Halliwell (Camden Soc., 1840).
Chronicon Petroburgense, ed. T. Stapleton (Camden Soc. 47, 1849).
CM: Matthew Paris, *Chronica Majora*, ed. H.R. Luard, 7 vols. (RS, 1872–83).
Coggeshall: *Chronicon Anglicanum Radulphi Coggeshall*, ed. J. Stevenson, 2 vols. (RS, 1875).
Concilia Magnae Britanniae et Hiberniae, ed. D. Wilkins, 4 vols. (London, 1737).
Corpus Iuris Canonici, ed. E. Friedberg, 2 vols. (Leipzig, 1879).
The Correspondence of Thomas Becket, Archbishop of Canterbury 1162–1170, ed. A. J. Duggan, 2 vols. (Oxford, 2000).
Cotton: *Bartholomæi de Cotton, Historia Anglicana, A.D. 449–1298*, ed. H.R. Luard (RS, 1859).
Councils and Synods with other documents relating to the English Church, I, *A.D. 871–1204*, ed. D. Whitelock, M. Brett, and C.N.L. Brooke, 2 vols. (Oxford, 1981).
Coventry: *Memoriale Fratri Walteri de Coventria*, ed. W. Stubbs, vol. 2 (RS, 1873).
CPR: *Calendar of the Patent Rolls Preserved in the Public Record Office* (1892–)
CR: *Close Rolls of the Reign of Henry III*, 14 vols. (London, 1902–1938).
CRR: *Curia Regis Rolls*, 20 vols. (1922–2006).
De Antiquis Legibus Liber: Cronica Maiorum et Vicecomitum Londoniarum, ed. T. Stapleton, (Camden Soc., 34, 1846).
Diplomatarium Norvegicum, ed. C.R. Unger and H.J. Huitfelt, vii (Oslo, 1867).
Diplomatic Documents Preserved in the Public Record Office, vol. 1: *1101–1272*, ed. P. Chaplais (London, 1964).
Documents Illustrating the Crisis of 1297–98 in England, ed. M. Prestwich (Camden Soc., 4th ser., 24, 1980).
Documents of the Baronial Movement of Reform and Rebellion, 1258–1267, ed. R.F. Treharne and I.J. Sanders (Oxford, 1973).
English Episcopal Acta 35: Hereford 1234–1275, ed. J. Barrow (Oxford, 2009).
Fasti Ecclesiae Anglicanae 1066–1300, iii: (Lincoln, 1977).
Fine Rolls: *Calendar of the Fine Rolls of the Reign of Henry III*, http://www.finerollshenry3.org.uk, (accessed 18/9/2021).
Flamborough, *Liber Poenitentialis*: Robert of Flamborough, *Liber Poenitentialis: A Critical Edition with Introduction and Notes*, ed. J.J.F. Firth (Toronto, 1971).
Flores Historiarum, ed. H.R. Luard, 3 vols. (RS, 1890).
Foedera: *Foedera, Conventiones, Litterae et cujuscumque generis Acta Publica*, ed. T. Rymer, new edn. ed. A. Clarke and F. Holbrooke, 4 vols. (London, 1816–69).
Friars' Tales: Thirteenth-Century exempla *from the British Isles*, ed. and trans. David Jones (Manchester, 2011).
Gerald of Wales, *Gemma Ecclesiastica*, in *Giraldi Cambrensis Opera*, ed. J.S. Brewer, ii (London, 1862).
Gervase: *The Historical Works of Gervase of Canterbury*, ed. W. Stubbs, vol. 2. (RS, 1880).

Gesta Abbatum Monasterii Sancti Albani, ed. H.T. Riley, 3 vols. (RS, 1867–9).
Gregory the Great, *Registrum Epistolarum Libri I–VII*, ed. D. Norberg (Corpus Christianorum Series Latina, 140, Turnhout, 1982).
Grosseteste Epistolae: Roberti Grosseteste episcopi quondam Lincolniensis epistolae, ed. H.R. Luard (RS, 1861).
Grosseteste Letters: The Letters of Robert Grosseteste, Bishop of Lincoln, ed. F.A.C. Mantello and J. Goering (London, 2010).
Guisborough: The Chronicle of Walter of Guisborough, ed. H. Rothwell (Camden Soc., 3rd ser., 84, 1957).
Heidemann: Papst Clemes IV., Eine Monographie: Das Vorleben des Papstes und sein Legationregister, ed. J. Heidemann (Münster, 1903).
History of the Dukes of Normandy and the Kings of England by the Anonymous of Béthune, trans. Janet Shirley, notes by Paul Webster (London, 2021).
History of William Marshal, ed. A.J. Holden, trans. S. Gregory, notes by D. Crouch, 2 vols. (London, 2004).
Index exemplorum: A Handbook of Medieval Religious Tales, ed. F.C. Tubach, (Helsinki, 1981).
Jacob's Well: An English Treatise on the Cleansing of Man's Conscience, ed. A. Brandeis (Early English Text Society, 115, 1900).
John Mirk, *Instructions for Parish Priests*, ed. G. Kristensson (Lund, 1974).
John Mirk, *Quatuor Sermones*, reprinted from the first edition printed by William Caxton (Roxburghe Club, London, 1883).
Lanercost: Chronicon de Lanercost, ed. J. Stevenson (Maitland Club, 1839).
The Letters and Charters of Cardinal Guala Bicchieri, papal legate in England 1216–1218, ed. N. Vincent (CYS 83, 1996).
Letters of Innocent III: The Letters of Pope Innocent III (1198–1216) concerning England and Wales. A Calendar with an appendix of texts, ed. C.R. Cheney and M.G. Cheney (Oxford, 1967).
Liber Albus, Liber Custumorum, et Liber Horn, ed. H.T.M. Riley, 3 vols. (RS, 1859).
The Life of St Hugh of Lincoln, ed. and trans. D.L. Douie and D.H. Farmer, 2 vols. (Oxford, 1961–85).
Martène, *Thesaurus: Thesaurus Novus Anecdotorum*, ed. E. Martène and U. Durand, vol. ii (Paris, 1717).
Melrose: Chronica de Mailros, ed. J. Stevenson (Bannatyne Club, Edinburgh, 1835).
Monumenta Ritualia Ecclesiae Anglicanae, ed. W. Maskell, 3 vols. (2nd edn., Oxford, 1882).
Odoricus Raynaldus, *Annales ecclesiastici ab anno MCXCVIII ubi desinit Cardinalus Baronius*, ed. J.D. Mansi, iv, (Lucca, 1749).
Oxenedes: Chronica Johannis de Oxenedes, ed. H. Ellis (RS, 1859).
Parliament Rolls: The Parliament Rolls of Medieval England, 1275–1504, ed. C. Given-Wilson, vols. i-ii: *Edward I (1275–1294; 1294–1307)*, ed. P. Brand (Woodbridge, 2005).
Patrologiae Latinae cursus completus, ed. J.P. Migne *(Innocentii papae III opera omnia* (Paris, 1858) = vols. 214–217).
Peñafort, *De Poenitentia: Summa Sancti Raymundi de Peniafort Barcinonensis, De Poenitentia et Matrimonio cum Glossis Iohannis de Friburgo*, 1603 (Rpr. Farnborough, 1967).
Peter of Cornwall, *Book of Revelations*, ed. R. Easting and R. Sharpe (Toronto, 2013).
Potthast, A., *Regesta Pontificum Romanorum*, 2 vols. (Berlin, 1874–5).
Le Pontifical romain au moyen-âge, III: Le Pontifical de Guillaume Durand, ed. M. Andrieu, Studi e Testi 88 (Vatican, 1940).

Le Pontifical romano-germanique du dixième siècle, 3 vols., Studi e Testi 226, 227, 269 (Vatican, 1963–72).
PR: Patent Rolls of the Reign of Henry III, 2 vols. (London, 1901–3).
Prynne, *Records*: Prynne, W., *The Third Tome of our Exact Chronological Vindication of the Supreme Ecclesiastical Jurisdiction of our ... English Kings* (London, 1668).
Records of Antony Bek, Bishop and Patriarch, 1283–1311, ed. C.M. Fraser (Suretees Soc. 162, 1952).
Reg. Bronescombe: *The Register of Walter Bronescombe, Bishop of Exeter 1258–1280*, ed. O.F. Robinson, 3 vols. (CYS 82, 87, 94, 1995–2003).
Reg. Cantilupe: *Registrum Thome Cantilupo, episcopi Herefordensis (A.D. 1275–1282)*, ed. R.G. Griffiths, intro W.W. Capes (CYS 2, 1906).
Reg. Clement IV: *Les Registres de Clément IV*, ed. E. Jordan (Paris, 1945).
Reg. Epp. Pecham: *Registrum epistolarum fratris Iohannis Peckham, archiepiscopi Cantuariensis*, ed. C. Trice-Martin, 3 vols. (RS, 1882–85).
Reg. G. Giffard: *Register of Bishop Godfrey Giffard, 1268–1301*, ed. J.W. Willis-Bund, (Worcestershire Historical Soc., Oxford, 1902).
Reg. Gandavo: *Registrum Simonis de Gandavo, diocesis Saresbiriensis, A.D. 1297–1315*, ed. C.T. Flower and M.C.B. Dawes, 2 vols. (CYS 40–1, 1934).
Reg. Gray: *The Register or Rolls of Walter Gray, lord Archbishop of York*, ed. J. Raine (Surtees Soc. 56, 1872).
Reg. Greenfield: *The Register of William Greenfield, Lord Archbishop of York 1306–1315*, ed. W. Brown and A.H. Thompson, 5 vols. (Surtees Soc. 145, 149, 151–3, 1939–40).
Reg. Gregory IX: *Les Registres de Grégoire IX*, ed. L. Auvray et al., 4 vols. (Paris, 1896–1955).
Reg. Halton: *The Register of John de Halton, Bishop of Carlisle, A.D. 1292–1324*, ed. W.N. Thompson, 2 vols. (CYS 12, 13, 1913).
Reg. Innocent IV: *Les Registres d'Innocent IV*, ed. É. Berger, 4 vols. (Paris, 1884–1921).
Reg. Langton: *The Register of Walter Langton, Bishop of Coventry and Lichfield, 1296–1321*, ed. J.B. Hughes, 2 vols. (CYS 91, 97, 2001–7).
Reg. le Romeyn: *The Register of John le Romeyn, Lord Archbishop of York, 1286–1296*, ed. W. Brown, 2 vols. (Surtees Soc. 123, 128, 1913–17).
Reg. Pecham: *The Register of John Pecham, Archbishop of Canterbury, 1279–1292*, ed. F.N. Davis and D. Douie, 2 vols. (CYS 64–65, 1968–9).
Reg. Pontissara: *Registrum Johannis de Pontissara, episcopi Wyntoniensis, A.D. 1282–1304*, ed. C. Deedes, 2 vols. (CYS 19, 30, 1915–24).
Reg. Sutton: *The Rolls and Register of Bishop Oliver Sutton, 1280–1299*, ed. R.M.T. Hill, 8 vols. (Lincoln Record Soc. 39, 43, 48, 52, 60, 64, 69, 76, 1948–75).
Reg. Swinfield: *Registrum Ricardi Swinfield, episcopi Herefordensis, A.D. 1282–1317*, ed. W.W. Capes (CYS 6, 1909).
Reg. Urban IV: *Les Registres d'Urbain IV*, ed. J. Guiraud and S. Clémencet, 4 vols. (Paris, 1899–1958).
Reg. W. Giffard: *The Register of Walter Giffard, Lord Archbishop of York, 1266–1279*, ed. W. Brown (Surtees Soc. 109, 1907).
Reg. Winchelsey: *Registrum Roberti Winchelsey, Cantuariensis Archiepiscopi, A.D. 1294–1313*, ed. R. Graham, 2 vols. (CYS 51–52, 1952–6).
Register of Henry Chichele, Archbishop of Canterbury 1414–1443, ed. E.F. Jacob, 4 vols (CYS 44–7, 1941–45).
The Register of John Stafford, Bishop of Bath and Wells, 1425–1443, ed. T. S. Holmes, 2 vols. (Somerset Record Soc. 31–2, 1915–16).

The Register of Thomas of Corbridge, Lord Archbishop of York, 1300–1304, ed. A. Hamilton Thompson, 2 vols. (Surtees Soc. 138, 141, 1925–28).
The Register of Thomas Spofford, Bishop of Hereford (1422–1448), ed. A. T. Bannister (CYS 23, 1917).
The Register of William Wickwane, Lord Archbishop of York 1279–1285, ed. W. Brown (Surtees Soc. 114, 1907).
Les Registres d'Alexandre IV (1254–1261), ed. C. Bourel de la Roncière et al., 3 vols. (Paris, 1895–1959).
Les Registres de Grégoire X, ed. J. Guiraud, 3 vols. (Paris, 1892–1906).
Registrum Antiquissimum: The Registrum Antiquissimum of the Cathedral Church of Lincoln, i-ii, ed. C.W. Foster (Lincoln Record Soc. 27–28, 1931–33).
Robert Grosseteste, *Templum Dei*, edited from *MS 27 of Emmanuel College, Cambridge*, by J. Goering and F.A.C. Mantello (Toronto, 1984).
Robert of Gloucester: The Metrical Chronicle of Robert of Gloucester, ed. W.A. Wright, 2 vols. (RS, 1887).
Rotuli Hugonis de Welles, episcopi Lincolniensis A.D. 1209–1235, ed. W.P.W. Phillimore and F.N. Davis, 3 vols. (CYS 1, 3, 4, 1907–9).
Rotuli Litterarum Clausarum in Turri Londinensi asservati, ed. T. D. Hardy, 2 vols. (London, 1833–4).
Rotuli Ricardi Gravesend, diocesis Lincolniensis, ed. F.N. Davis, additions by C.W. Foster and A. Hamilton Thompson (CYS 31, 1925).
Royal Letters: Royal and other historical letters illustrative of the reign of Henry III, ed. W.W. Shirley, 2 vols. (RS, 1862–6).
'Saint Austin at Compton', in *Saints' Lives in Middle English Collections*, ed. E. Gordon Whatley, A. B. Thompson, and R. K. Upchurch (Kalamazoo, MI, 2004).
SCC: *Select Cases from the Ecclesiastical Courts of the Province of Canterbury c.1200–1301*, ed. N. Adams and C. Donahue Jr. (Seldon Soc. 95, 1981).
Select Cases on Defamation to 1600, ed. R.H. Helmholz (Seldon Soc. 101, 1985).
Select Charters and Other Illustrations of English Constitutional History from the Earliest Times to the Reign of Edward the First, ed. W. Stubbs, 9th edn. (Oxford, 1913).
Select English works of John Wyclif, III: *Miscellaneous Works*, ed. T. Arnold (Oxford, 1871).
SKB: *Select Cases in the Court of the King's Bench under Edward I*, ed. G.O. Sayles, 3 vols. (Seldon Soc. 55, 57, 58, 1936–39).
SLI: *Selected Letters of Pope Innocent III concerning England (1198–1216)*, ed. C.R. Cheney and W.H. Semple (London, 1953).
The Song of Lewes, ed. and trans. C.L. Kingsford (Oxford, 1890).
Speculum laicorum, edition d'une collection d'exempla, composée en Angleterre à la fin du XIIIe siècle, ed. J. Th. Welter, *Thesaurus Exemplorum*, fasc. 5 (Paris, 1914).
Statutes of the Realm, i (London, 1810).
Les Statuts Synodaux Français du XIIIe Siècle, I: *Les Statuts de Paris et le Synodal de l'Ouest*, ed. O. Pontal (Paris, 1971).
Les Statuts Synodaux Français du XIIIe Siècle, IV: *Le Statuts Synododaux de l'Ancienne Province de Reims*, ed. J. Avril (Paris, 1995).
Stephen of Bourbon, *Anecdotes Historiques, Légendes et Apologues: Tirés du Recueil inédit d'Étienne de Bourbon*, ed. A. Lecoy de la Marche (Paris, 1887).
Tanner, *Decrees: Decrees of the Ecumenical Councils*, ed. and trans. Norman P. Tanner, 2 vols. (London, 1990).
Thomas Wright's Political Songs of England, from the Reign of John to that of Edward II, ed. P. Coss (Cambridge, 1996).

Visitations of Churches Belonging to St Paul's Cathedral in 1297 and in 1458, ed. W. Sparrow Simpson (Camden Soc., new ser. 55, 1895).
Willelmi Rishanger Chronica et Annales, ed. H.T. Riley (RS, 1865).
William Lyndwood, *Provinciale* (Oxford, 1679).
Wykes: Chronicon vulgo dictum Chronicon Thomae Wykes, 1066–1288, in *Ann. Mon.* iv.

Secondary works

Allen, Richard, 'The earliest known list of excommunicates from ducal Normandy', *JMH* 39 (2013), 394–415.
Ambler, S.T., 'The Montfortian bishops and the justification of conciliar government', *HR* 85 (2012), 193–209.
Ambler, S.T., 'Magna Carta: its confirmation at Simon de Montfort's parliament of 1265', *EHR* 130 (2015), 801–30.
Ambler, S.T., *Bishops in the Political Community of England, 1213–1272* (Oxford, 2017).
Ambler, S.T., *The Song of Simon de Montfort: England's first revolutionary and the death of chivalry* (London, 2019).
Antonopolou, Zoé, 'Continuité et ruptures dans la vie politique Byzantine: de l'ostracisme à l'excommunication', *Byzantion: Revue Internationale des Études Byzantines* 72 (2002), 325–46.
Arnold, John, *Belief and Unbelief in Medieval Europe* (London, 2005).
Austin, J.L., *How to do Things with Words* (2nd edn. Oxford, 1975).
Bachrach, D.S., 'The Ecclesia Anglicana goes to war: prayers, propaganda, and conquest during the reign of Edward I of England, 1272-1307', *Albion* 36 (2004), 393–406.
Baldwin, John W., *Masters, Princes and Merchants: The Social Views of Peter the Chanter and His Circle* (Princeton, 1970).
Baldwin, John W. 'Master Stephen Langton, future Archbishop of Canterbury: The Paris Schools and Magna Carta', *EHR* 123 (2008), 811–46.
Barner-Barry, Carol, 'Rob: Children's tacit use of peer ostracism', *Ethology and Sociobiology* 7 (1986), 133–145 (281–93).
Barton, Richard E., 'Enquête, exaction and excommunication: experiencing power in Western France, c.1190–1245', in *Anglo-Norman Studies XLIII*, ed. S.D. Church (Woodbridge, 2021), 177–96.
Barrow, Julia, 'The clergy in English dioceses, 900–1066', in *Pastoral Care in Late Anglo-Saxon England*, ed. F. Tinti (Woodbridge, 2005), 17–26.
Beaulande, Véronique, *Le malheur d'être exclu? Excommunication, réconciliation et société à la fin du Moyen Âge* (Sorbonne, 2006).
Beaulande, Véronique, 'La force de la censure: l'excommunication dans les conflits de pouvoir au sein des villes au XIIIe siècle', *Revue historique* 110 (2008), 251–78.
Beaulande-Barraud, Véronique, 'Contester l'excommunication à la fin du Moyen Âge: contestation, résistance, indifférence, XIIIe–XVe siècles', in *La contestation (Moyen Âge et Temps modernes)*, ed. G. Lecuppre (Paris, 2016), 251–73.
Bezzina, Edwin, 'The consistory of Loudun, 1589-1602: seeking an equilibrium between utility, compassion and social discipline in uncertain times', in *Dire l'Interdit: The Vocabulary of Censure and Exclusion in the Early Modern Tradition*, ed. Raymond A. Mentzer, Françoise Moreil and Philippe Chareyre (Leiden, 2010), 239–71.
Birkett, Helen, 'News in the Middle Ages: News, communication, and the launch of the third crusade in 1187–1188', *Viator* 49 (2018), 23–61.

Blaauw, W.H., 'On the early history of Lewes priory, and its seals, with extracts from a MS chronicle', *Sussex Archaeological Collections* 2 (1849), 7-37.
Blair, John, *The Church in Anglo-Saxon Society* (Oxford, 2005).
Bonfil, Robert, *Rabbis and Jewish Communities in Renaissance Italy*, trans. Jonathan Chipman (Oxford, 1990).
Boyle, L.E., 'The *Oculus Sacerdotis* and some other works of William of Pagula', *Transactions of the Royal Historical Society*, 5th ser., 5 (1955), 81-110.
Boyle, L.E., 'A study of the works attributed to William of Pagula, with special reference to the *Oculus sacerdotis* and *Summa summarum*' (Oxford University D.Phil. thesis, 1956).
Boyle, L.E., 'Robert Grosseteste and pastoral care', in *Pastoral Care, Clerical Education and Canon law, 1200-1400* (London, 1981).
Boyle, L.E., 'The Fourth Lateran Council and manuals of popular theology', in *The Popular Literature of Medieval England*, ed. T.J. Heffernan (Knoxville, Tenn., 1985), 30-43.
Brand, P., 'Boreham, Hervey of (b. before 1228?, d. 1277), administrator and justice', (2008) *ODNB* https://doi.org/10.1093/ref:odnb/37540 (accessed 18/9/21).
Brentano, Robert, *Two Churches: England and Italy in the Thirteenth Century. With an additional essay by the author* (Berkeley, CA, 1988).
Brown, David C., 'The keys of the kingdom: excommunication in colonial Massachusetts', *New England Quarterly* 67 (1994), 531-66.
Brown, E.A.R., 'Moral imperatives and conundrums of conscience: reflections on Philip the Fair of France', *Speculum* 87 (2012), 1-36.
Brown, E.A.R., 'The faith of Guillaume de Nogaret, his excommunication and the fall of the knights Templar', in *Cristo e il potere. Teologia, antropologia e politica*, ed. L. Andreani and A. Paravicini Bagliani (Florence, 2017), 157-81.
Brunner, Melanie, 'Disorder, debts and excommunication: Pope John XXII and the reform of the order of Grandmont', *JMH* 36 (2010), 341-58.
Bryan, Lindsay, 'Scandala is heaved sunne', *Florilegium* 14 (1995-6), 71-86.
Bryan, Lindsay, '*Periculum animarum*: bishops, gender and scandal', *Florilegium* 19 (2002), 49-73.
Bryan, Lindsay, 'From stumbling block to deadly sin: the theology of scandal', in *Scandala*, ed. G. Jaritz (Krems, 2008), 7-17.
Bührer-Thierry, Geneviève, and Stéphane Gioanni (eds), *Exclure de la communauté chrétienne: sens et pratiques sociales de l'anathème et de l'excommunication (IVe-XIIe Siècle)* (Turnhout, 2015).
Burger, Michael, *Bishops, Clerks, and Diocesan Governance in Thirteenth-Century England: Reward and Punishment* (Cambridge, 2012).
Burton, D.W., 'Politics, propaganda and public opinion in the reigns of Henry III and Edward I' (Oxford University D.Phil. thesis, 1985).
Burton, D.W., 'Requests for prayers and royal propaganda under Edward I', *TCE iii: Proceedings of the Newcastle-upon-Tyne Conference 1989*, ed. P.R. Coss and S.D. Lloyd (Woodbridge, 1991), 25-36.
Campbell, G.J. 'The attitude of the monarchy toward the use of ecclesiastical censures in the reign of St. Louis', *Speculum* 35 (1960), 535-55.
Campbell, William H., 'Theologies of reconciliation in thirteenth-century England', in *SCH 40: Retribution, Repentance and Reconciliation*, ed. K. Cooper and J. Gregory (Woodbridge, 2004), 84-94.
Campbell, William H., *The Landscape of Pastoral Care in Thirteenth-Century England* (Cambridge, 2019).

Carpenter, D.A., 'The fall of Hubert de Burgh', *Journal of British Studies* 19 (1980), 1–17. Rpt. *The Reign of Henry III*, 45–60.
Carpenter, D.A., 'What happened in 1258?', in *War and Government in the Middle Ages: Essays in Honour of J.O. Prestwich*, ed. J. Gillingham and J.C. Holt (Woodbridge, 1984), 106–119. Rpt. *The Reign of Henry III*, 183–97.
Carpenter, D.A., 'King, magnates and society: the personal rule of Henry III, 1234-1258', *Speculum* 60 (1985), 39–70. Rpt. *The Reign of Henry III*, 75–106.
Carpenter, D.A., *The Minority of Henry III* (London, 1990).
Carpenter, D.A., 'Simon de Montfort: the first leader of a political movement in history', *History* 76 (1991), 3–23. Rpt. *The Reign of Henry III*, 219–39.
Carpenter, D.A., 'English peasants in politics, 1258-1267', *Past & Present* 136 (1992), 3–42. Rpt. *The Reign of Henry III*, 309–48.
Carpenter, D.A., *The Reign of Henry III* (London, 1996).
Carpenter, D.A., 'Archbishop Langton and Magna Carta: His Contribution, His Doubts and His Hypocrisy', *EHR* 126 (2011), 1041–65.
Carpenter, D.A., 'Henry III and the Sicilian affair', *Henry III Fine Rolls Project: Fine of the Month,* February 2012: http://www.finerollshenry3.org.uk/redist/pdf/fm-02-2012.pdf (accessed 18/9/2021).
Carpenter, D.A., 'Magna Carta 1253: the ambitions of the church and the divisions within the realm', and 'More light on Henry III's confirmation of Magna Carta in 1253', *HR* 86 (2013), 179–95.
Carpenter, D.A., *Magna Carta* (London, 2015).
Carpenter, D.A., *Henry III: The Rise to Power and Personal Rule, 1207–1258* (London, 2020).
Carruthers, Leo, 'The *Great Curse*: Excommunication, canon law and the judicial system in late medieval society, through the eyes of an English preacher', *Anglophonia* 29 (2011), 45–59.
Cazel, F.A., 'The legates Guala and Pandulf', in *TCE ii: Proceedings of the Newcastle-upon-Tyne Conference 1987*, ed. P.R. Coss and S.D. Lloyd (Woodbridge, 1988), 15–21.
Challet, Vincent and Ian Forrest, 'The masses', in *Government and Political Life in England and France, c.1300–c.1500*, ed. C. Fletcher, J-P. Genet, and J. Watts (Cambridge, 2015), 279–316.
Chareyre, Phillippe, ' "Maudit est celui qui fait l'œuvre du seigneur lâchement": les pasteurs face á la censure', in *Dire l'Interdit: The Vocabulary of Censure and Exclusion in the Early Modern Tradition*, ed. R.A. Mentzer, F. Moreil, and P. Chareyre (Leiden, 2010), 65–102.
Cheney, C.R., 'Legislation of the medieval English church', *EHR* 50 (1935), 193–224.
Cheney, C.R., *English Bishops' Chanceries, 1100–1250* (Manchester, 1950).
Cheney, C.R., *From Becket to Langton: English Church Government 1170–1213* (Manchester, 1956).
Cheney, C.R., *English Synodalia of the Thirteenth century* (Oxford, 1968).
Cheney, C.R., *Medieval Texts and Studies* (London, 1973).
Cheney, C.R., 'Magna Carta Beati Thome: another Canterbury forgery', in *idem*, Medieval Texts and Studies, 78–110.
Cheney, C.R., 'Statute-making in the English Church in the thirteenth century', in *idem*, *Medieval Texts and Studies,* 138–57.
Cheney, C.R., 'William Lyndwood's *Provinciale*', in *idem*, *Medieval Texts and Studies*, 158–84.
Cheney, C.R., *Pope Innocent III and England* (Stuttgart, 1976).
Cheney, C.R., *The Papacy and England, twelfth to fourteenth centuries* (London, 1982).

Cheney, C.R., 'King John and the papal interdict', in idem, *The Papacy and England*, Essay IX.

Cheney, C.R., 'King John's reaction to the interdict on England', in idem, *The Papacy and England*, Essay X.

Cheney, C.R., 'A recent view of the general interdict on England', in idem, *The Papacy and England*, Essay XI.

Cheney, C.R., 'The alleged deposition of King John', in idem, *The Papacy and England*, Essay XII.

Cheney, C.R., *Episcopal Visitation of Monasteries in the Thirteenth Century* (2nd edn., Manchester, 1983).

Church, Stephen, *King John: England, Magna Carta and the Making of a Tyrant* (London, 2015).

Clanchy, M. T., *From Memory to Written Record: England 1066-1307* (3rd edn., Oxford, 2013).

Clanchy, M. T., *England and its Rulers, 1066-1272* (4th edn., Oxford, 2014).

Clarke, Peter D., 'Central authority and local powers: the apostolic penitentiary and the English Church in the fifteenth century', *HR* 84 (2001), 416-42.

Clarke, Peter D., 'Innocent III the interdict and medieval theories of popular resistance', in *Pope, Church and City: Essays in Honour of Brenda Bolton*, ed. F. Andrews, C. Egger, and C. M. Rousseau (Leiden, 2004), 77-97.

Clarke, Peter D., *The Interdict in the Thirteenth Century: A Question of Collective Guilt* (Oxford, 2007).

Clarke, Peter D. and Patrick Zutschi, *Supplications from England and Wales in the Registers of the Apostolic Penitentiary, 1410-1503*, i: 1410-1464 (CYS 103, 2012).

Crawfield, Sally, 'Differentiation in the later Anglo-Saxon burial ritual on the basis of mental or physical impairment: a documentary perspective', in *Burial in Later Anglo-Saxon England, c.650-1100*, ed. Jo Buckberry and A. Cherryson (Oxford, 2010).

Creed, Gerald W., 'Reconsidering community', in *The Seductions of Community: Emancipations, Oppressions, Quandaries*, ed. G.W. Creed (Oxford, 2006), 3-22.

Crouch, David, *Tournament* (London, 2005).

Crouch, David, *William Marshal* (3rd edn., Abingdon, 2016).

Davies, Wendy, and Paul Fouracre (eds), *The Settlement of Disputes in Early Medieval Europe* (Cambridge, 1986).

D'Avray, D.L., '"Magna Carta": Its background in Stephen Langton's academic Biblical exegesis and its episcopal reception', *Studi Medievali*, 3rd ser., 38 (1997), 423-38.

D'Avray, D.L., *Medieval Marriage Sermons: Mass Communication in a Culture without Print* (Oxford, 2001).

D'Avray, D.L., *Medieval Religious Rationalities: A Weberian Analysis* (Cambridge, 2010).

Demangel, Stéphanie, 'L'excommuniation du roi et l'éboration d'une théocratie séculière en France', *Revue du droit canonique* 49 (1999), 323-49.

Denholm-Young, N., 'The tournament in the thirteenth century', in *Studies in Medieval History presented to Frederick Maurice Powicke*, ed. R.W. Hunt, W.A. Pantin, and R.W. Southern (Oxford, 1948), 240-68.

Denton, J.H., 'The crisis of 1297 from the Evesham chronicle', *EHR* 93 (1978), 568-79.

Denton, J.H., *Robert Winchelsey and the Crown 1294-1313: A study in the defence of ecclesiastical liberty* (Cambridge, 1980).

Denton, J.H., 'The competence of the parish clergy in thirteenth-century England', in *The Church and Learning in Later Medieval Society: Essays in Honour of R.B. Dobson*, ed. C.M. Barron and J. Stratford (Donington, 2002), 273-85.

Douglas, Mary, *Purity and Danger: An Analysis of the Concept of Pollution and Taboo* (London, 1966, 2004 Routledge edn.).

Douie, Decima L., *Archbishop Pecham* (Oxford, 1952).

Dresch, Paul, 'Outlawry, exile and banishment: reflections on community and justice', in *Legalism: Community and Justice*, ed. F. Pirie and J. Scheele (Oxford, 2014), 97–124.

Duggan, Anne J., 'Diplomacy, status, and conscience: Henry II's penance for Becket's murder', in *Forschungen zur Reichs-, Papst- und Landesgeschichte. Peter Herde zum 65. Geburtstag von Freunden, Schülern und Kollegen dargebracht*, ed. K. Borchardt and E. Bünz (Stuttgart, 1998), vol. I, 265–90.

Duggan, Anne J., 'Henry II, the English Church and the Papacy, 1154–76', in *Henry II: New Interpretations*, ed. C. Harper-Bill and N. Vincent (Woodbridge, 2007), 154–183.

Dutour, Thierry, 'L'élaboration, la publication et la diffusion de l'information à la fin du Moyen Âge (Bourgogne ducale et France royale)', in *Haro! Noël! Oyé! Pratiques du cri au Moyen Âge*, ed. Didier Lett and Nicholas Offenstadt (Paris, 2003), 141–55.

Edwards, G.R., 'Purgatory: "Birth" or evolution?', *JEH* 36 (1985), 634–46.

Edwards, J.G., 'Confirmatio cartarum and the baronial grievances in 1297', *EHR* 58 (1943), 147–71.

Edwards, Genevieve Steele, 'Ritual excommunication in medieval France and England, 900–1200', (Stanford University PhD thesis, 1997).

Elliott, Dyan, 'Violence against the dead: the negative translation and *damnatio memoriae* in the Middle Ages', *Speculum* 92 (2017), 1020–55.

Erikson, Kai T., *Wayward Puritans: A Study in the Sociology of Deviance* (London, 1966).

Finkelstein, Louis, *Jewish Self-Government in the Middle Ages* (Westport, 1924).

Finucane, R.C., 'The Cantilupe-Pecham controversy', in *St. Thomas Cantilupe, Bishop of Hereford*, ed. M. Jancey (Hereford, 1982), 103–23.

Flahiff, G.B., 'The writ of prohibition to court Christian in the thirteenth century: part I', *Mediaeval Studies* 6 (1944), 261–313.

Flahiff, G.B., 'The writ of prohibition to court Christian in the thirteenth century: part II', *Mediaeval Studies* 7 (1945), 229–90.

Flanagan, M.T., 'Ó Máelmuaid, Ailbe [Albinus O'Molloy] (d. 1223)', *ODNB*: https://doi.org/10.1093/ref:odnb/20758 (accessed 18/9/2021).

Flanagin, D.Z., 'Extra ecclesiam salus non est—sed quae ecclesia?: Ecclesiology and authority in the later Middle Ages', in *A Companion to the Great Western Schism (1378–1417)*, ed. J. Rolle-Koster and T. M. Izbicki (Leiden, 2009), 333–374.

Forrest, Ian, 'Defamation, heresy and late medieval social life', in *Image, Text and Church, 1380–1600. Essays for Margaret Aston*, ed. L. Clark, M. Jurkowski and C. Richmond (Toronto, 2009), 142–61.

Forrest, Ian, 'William Swinderby and the Wycliffite attitude to excommunication', *JEH* 60 (2009), 246–69.

Forrest, Ian, 'The transformation of visitation in thirteenth-century England', *Past & Present* 221 (2013), 3–38.

Forrest, Ian, 'Trust and doubt: the late medieval bishop and local knowledge', *SCH* 52, ed. F. Andrews, C. Methuen and A. Spicer (London, 2016), 215–19.

Forrest, Ian, *Trustworthy Men: How Inequality and Faith Made the Medieval Church* (Woodstock, 2018).

Forrest, Ian, and Christopher Whittick, 'The thirteenth-century visitation records of the diocese of Hereford', *EHR* 131 (2016), 737–62.

Fossier, Arnaud, 'Le for "interne" de l'église (XIIe-XIVe siècle): entre ordre public et salut des âmes', in *Intus et Foris: Un catégorie de la pensée médiévale?*, ed. M. Guag, M-P. Halary and P. Moran (Paris-Sorbonne, 2013), 59–69.

Fossier, Arnaud, *Le Bureau de âmes. Écritures et pratiques administratives de la Pénitencerie Apostolique (XIIIe-XVIe siécle)*, Bibliothèque des Écoles françaises d'Athènes et de Rome 378 (Rome, 2018).
Foxhall Forbes, Helen, *Heaven and Earth in Anglo-Saxon England: Theology and Society in an Age of Faith* (Farnham, 2013).
Franklin, R.M., 'Basset, Fulk (*d.* 1259)', *ODNB* https://doi.org/10.1093/ref:odnb/1638, (accessed 18/9/2021).
Gallant, Thomas, 'Peasant ideology and excommunication for crime in a colonial context: the Ionian islands (Greece), 1817-1864', *Journal of Social History* 23 (1990), 485–512.
Geary, Patrick, *Living with the Dead in the Middle Ages* (London, 1994).
Gelin, Marie-Pierre, 'Gervase of Canterbury, Christ Church and the archbishops', *JEH* 60 (2009), 449–63.
Gibbs, M., and J. Lang, *Bishops and Reform, 1215–1272, with special reference to the Lateran Council of 1215* (Oxford, 1934).
Gilson, J.P., 'The Parliament of 1264', *EHR* 16 (1901), 499–501.
Goebel, Julius Jr., *Felony and Misdemeanor: A Study in the History of Criminal Law, with an introduction by Edward Peters* (Philadelphia, 1976).
Goering, Joseph, 'The internal forum and the literature of penance and confession', in *The History of Medieval Canon Law in the Classical Period, 1140–1234, from Gratian to the Decretals of Pope Gregory IX*, ed. W. Hartmann and K. Pennington (Washington, D.C., 2008), 379–428.
Graham, Rose, 'An interdict on Dover, 1298-9', *Archaeological Journal* 78 (1921), 227–32.
Gransden, Antonia, 'Some late thirteenth-century records of an ecclesiastical court in the archdeaconry of Sudbury', *Bulletin of the Institute of Historical Research* 32 (1959), 62–69.
Gray, J.W., 'Archbishop Pecham and the decrees of Boniface', *SCH* 2, ed. G.J. Cushing (London, 1965), 215–19.
Gray, J.W., 'The Church and Magna Charta', *Historical Studies: Papers Read Before the Irish Conference of Historians*, VI (1968), 23–38.
Groot, Roger D., 'The Jury of Presentment before 1215', *American Journal of Legal History* 26 (1982), 1–24.
Gruter, Margaret, and Roger D. Masters (eds), *Ostracism as a Social and Biological Phenomenon*, Special issue of *Ethology and Sociobiology*, vol. 7 (1986) Issues 3–4.
Gruter, Margaret, and Roger D. Masters, 'Ostracism as a social and biological phenomenon: An introduction', *Ethology and Sociobiology* 7 (1986), 1–10 (149–158).
Gruter, Margaret, 'Ostracism on trial: the limits of individual rights', *Ethology and Sociobiology* 7 (1986), 123–131 (272–279).
Guesnet, François, 'Jews of medieval Poland-Lithuania (1650-1815)', in *The Cambridge History of Judaism, 7: The Early Modern World, 1500–1815*, ed. J. Karp and A. Sutcliffe (Cambridge, 2017), 798–830.
Gundacker, Jay, 'Absolutions and acts of disobedience: excommunication and society in fourteenth-century Armagh', *Traditio* 64 (2009), 183–212.
Gurevitch, Aron, *Medieval Popular Culture: Problems of Belief and Perception*, trans. M. Bale and P.A. Hollingsworth (Cambridge, 1988).
Gurevitch, Aron, *Historical Anthropology of the Middle Ages* (Cambridge, 1992).
Gwynn, Aubrey, 'Provincial and diocesan decrees of the diocese of Dublin during the Anglo-Norman period', *Archivium Hibernicum* 11 (1944), 31–117.
Haines, R.M., 'Education in English ecclesiastical legislation of the later Middle Ages', in *SCH* 7, ed. G.J. Cuming and D. Baker (London, 1971), 161–75.

Haines, R.M., *Ecclesia Anglicana: Studies in the English Church of the Later Middle Ages* (Toronto, 1989).
Hamilton, Sarah, *The Practice of Penance, 900–1050* (Woodbridge, 2001).
Hamilton, Sarah, 'Penance in the age of Gregorian Reform', in *SCH* 40, ed. K. Cooper and J. Gregory (Woodbridge, 2004), 47–73.
Hamilton, Sarah, 'Remedies for "great transgressions": penance and excommunication in late Anglo-Saxon England', in *Pastoral Care in Late Anglo-Saxon England*, ed. F. Tinti (Woodbridge, 2005), 83–105.
Hamilton, Sarah, 'The Anglo-Saxon and Frankish Evidence for Rites for the Reconciliation of Excommunicants', in *Recht und Gericht in Kirche und Welt um 900*, ed. Wilfried Hartmann (Berlin, 2007), 169–96.
Hamilton, Sarah, 'Absoluimus uos uice beati petri apostolorum principis: episcopal authority and the reconciliation of excommunicants in England and Francia c. 900–c.1150', in *Frankland: The Franks and the World of the Early Middle Ages. Essays in Honour of Dame Jinty Nelson*, ed. P. Fouracre and D. Ganz (Manchester, 2008), 209–41.
Hamilton, Sarah, 'Inquiring into adultery and other wicked deeds: episcopal justice in tenth-century and early eleventh-century Italy', *Viator* 41 (2010), 21–43.
Hamilton, Sarah, *Church and People in the Medieval West, 900–1200* (Abingdon, 2013).
Hamilton, Sarah, 'Interpreting diversity: excommunication rites in the tenth and eleventh centuries', in *Understanding Medieval Liturgy: Essays in Interpretation*, ed. H. Gittos and S. Hamilton (Aldershot, 2015), 125–58.
Hamilton, Sarah, 'Law and liturgy: Excommunication records 900–1050', in *Using and Not Using the Past after the Carolingian Empire*, ed. S. Greer, A. Hicklin, and S. Esders (London, 2019), 282–302.
Hamilton Thompson, A., 'Diocesan organization in the middle ages: archdeacons and rural deans', *Proceedings of the British Academy* 39 (1943), 153–94.
Hanley, Catherine, *Louis: The French Prince Who Invaded England* (London, 2016).
Haring, N.M., 'Peter Cantor's view on ecclesiastical excommunication and its practical consequences', *Mediaeval Studies* 11 (1949), 100–12.
Harper-Bill, Christopher, 'John and the Church of Rome', in *King John: New Interpretations*, ed. S.D. Church (Woodbridge, 1999), 289–315.
Harriss, G.L., *King, Parliament, and Public Finance in Medieval England to 1369* (Oxford, 1975).
Hartman, Abigail, 'Poetry and the cause of Simon de Montfort after the Battle of Evesham: And the violent take it by force', *The Mediaeval Journal* 9.2 (2019), 41–61.
Helmholz, R.H., 'The Writ of Prohibition to Court Christian before 1500', *Mediaeval Studies* 43 (1981), 297–314.
Helmholz, R.H., 'Excommunication as a legal sanction: the attitudes of the medieval canonists', *Zeitschrift der Savigny-Stiftung für Rechtsgeschichte: Kanonistische Abteilung* 68 (1982), 202–18.
Helmholz, R.H., 'The early history of the Grand Jury and the canon law', *University of Chicago Law Review* 50 (1983), 613–27.
Helmholz, R.H., '"Si quis suadente" (c.17 q.4 c.29): Theory and practice', in *Proceedings of the Seventh International Congress of Canon Law, Cambridge 23–27 July 1984*, ed. P. Linehan (Monumenta Iuris Canonici, Series C, vol. 8, B.A.V., 1988), 425–38.
Helmholz, R.H., 'Excommunication in twelfth century England', *Journal of Law and Religion* 11 (1994–95), 235–53.
Helmholz, R.H., 'Excommunication and the Angevin leap forward', *Haskins Society Journal* 7 (1995), 133–49.

Helmholz, R.H., *The Spirit of Classical Canon Law* (London, 1996).
Helmholz, R.H., 'Canonical "juries" in medieval England', in *Ins Wasser geworfen und Ozeane durchquert: Festschrift für Knut Wolfgang Nörr*, ed. M. Ascheri et al. (Köln, 2003), 403–18.
Helmholz, R.H., *The Oxford History of the Laws of England*, i: *The Canon Law and Ecclesiastical Jurisdiction from 597 to the 1640s* (Oxford, 2004).
Helmholz, R.H., 'Scandalum in the medieval canon law and in the English ecclesiastical courts', *Zeitschrift der Savigny-Stiftung für Rechtsgeschichte: Kanonistische Abteilung* 96 (2010), 258–74.
Hertz, Deborah, 'Judaism in Germany (1650–1815), in *The Cambridge History of Judaism, 7: The Early Modern World, 1500–1815*, ed. J. Karp and A. Sutcliffe (Cambridge, 2017), 737–762.
Hicks, Leonie, 'Exclusion as exile: spiritual punishment and physical illness in Normandy c. 1050-1300', in *Exile in the Middle Ages*, ed. L. Napran and E. van Houts (Turnhout, 2004), 135–58.
Hill, F.G., 'The church and Magna Carta: the 1253 sentence of excommunication and the freedom of the English church' (UCL MA thesis, 2012).
Hill, F.G., 'Magna Carta, canon law and pastoral care: excommunication and the church's publication of the charter', *HR* 89 (2016), 636–50.
Hill, F.G., 'Excommunication and politics in thirteenth-century England' (UEA PhD thesis, 2016).
Hill, F.G., '*Damnatio eternae mortis* or *medicinalis non mortalis*: the ambiguities of excommunication in thirteenth-century England', in *TCE xvi: Proceedings of The Cambridge Conference, 2015*, ed. A.M. Spencer and C. Watkins (Woodbridge, 2017), 37–53.
Hill, F.G., 'General excommunications of unknown malefactors: conscience, community and investigations in England, c. 1150–1350', in *SCH 56*, ed. R. McKitterick, A. Spicer, and C. Methuen (Cambridge, 2020), 93–113.
Hill, R.M.T., *Ecclesiastical Letter-Books of the Thirteenth Century* (1937).
Hill, R.M.T., 'Public penance: some problems of a thirteenth-century bishop', *History* 36 (1951), 213–26.
Hill, R.M.T., 'The theory and practice of excommunication in Medieval England', *History* 42 (1957), 1–11.
Hill, R.M.T., 'Belief and practice as illustrated by John XXII's excommunication of Robert Bruce', in *SCH 8*, ed. G.J. Cuming and Derek Baker (Cambridge, 1972), 135–8.
Holt, J.C., *Magna Carta* (2nd edn., Cambridge, 1992).
Hoskin, Philippa, 'Natural Law, protest and the English episcopate 1257-1265', in *TCE xv: Authority and Resistance in the Age of Magna Carta, Proceedings of the Aberystwyth and Lampeter Conference 2013*, ed. J. Burton, P. Schofield and B. Weiler (Woodbridge, 2015), 83–97.
Hoskin, Philippa, '"By Force and Arms": Lay invasion, the writ de vi laica amovenda and tensions of State and Church in the thirteenth and fourteenth centuries', in *Petitions and Strategies of Persuasion in the Middle Ages: The English Crown and the Church, c.1200–c.1550*, ed. T. W. Smith and H. Killick (Woodbridge, 2018), 148–163.
Huizing, Peter, 'The earliest development of excommunication latae sententiae by Gratian and the earliest decretists', *Studia Gratiana* 3 (1955), 277–320.
Hurnard, Naomi D., 'The jury of presentment and the Assize of Clarendon', *EHR* 56 (1941), 374–410.

Huysmans, Ortwin, 'Excommunication under discussion in the early twelfth-century diocese of Liège: A comparative inquiry into the opinions of Lambert of St.-Hubert and Sigebert of Gembloux', *Trajecta* 23 (2014), 37-64.
Hyams, Paul, 'Nastiness and wrong, rancor and reconciliation', in *Conflict in Medieval Europe: Changing perspectives on society and culture*, ed. W.C. Brown and P. Górecki (Aldershot, 2003), 195-218.
Hyams, Paul, *Rancor and Reconciliation in Medieval England* (London, 2003).
Hyland, F.E., *Excommunication: Its Nature, Historical Development and Effects* (Washington, D.C., 1928).
Jaritz, Gerhard, 'Varieties of scandalum', in *Scandala*, ed. G. Jaritz (Krems, 2008), 44-55.
Jaser, Christian, 'Usurping the spiritual sword: performative and literary alienations of ritual excommunication', in *Ritual Dynamics and the Science of Ritual, III: State, Power, and Violence*, section III, ed. G. Schwedler and E. Tounta (Wiesbaden, 2010), 505-42.
Jaser, Christian, 'Ritual excommunication: an "Ars Oblivionalis"?, *Memory and Commemoration in Medieval Culture*, ed. E. Brenner, M. Cohen, M. Franklin-Brown (Farnham, 2013), 119-139.
Jaser, Christian, *Ecclesia maledicens: Rituelle und zeremonielle Exkommunikationsformen im Mittelalter* (Tübingen, 2013).
Jaser, Christian, 'Ostensio exclusionis: Die päpstliche Generalexkommunikation zwischen kirchenrechtlicher Innovation und zeremoniellem Handeln', in *Die Päpste: Amt und Herrschaft in Antike, Mittelalter und Renaissance*, ed. B. Schneidmüller et al. (2016), 357-83.
Jasper, Detlev, 'The deposition and excommunication of emperors and kings: a collection of historical examples from the Investiture Conflict', in *Canon Law, Religion, and Politics: 'Liber Amicorum' Robert Somerville*, ed. U-R. Blumenthal et al. (Catholic University of America, 2012), 199-214.
Jégou, Laurent, 'La sepulture de l'âne. Le sort réservé aux corps des excommuniés', in *Exclure de la Communauté Chrétien*, ed. G. Bührer-Thierry and S. Gioanni (Turnhout, 2015), 197-212.
The Jewish Encyclopedia: a descriptive record of the history, religion, literature, and customs of the Jewish people (London, 1901-06).
Johnstone, Hilda, 'Archbishop Pecham and the Council of Lambeth of 1281', in *Essays in Medieval History Presented to Thomas Frederick Tout*, ed. A.G. Little and F.M. Powicke (Manchester, 1925), 171-88.
Jordan, W.C., 'Christian excommunication of the Jews in the Middle Ages: a restatement of the issues', *Jewish History* 1 (1986), 31-38.
Jordan, W.C., 'A fresh look at medieval sanctuary', in *Law and the Illicit in Medieval Europe*, ed. R. M. Karras, J. Kaye and A. E. Matter (Pennsylvania, 2008), 17-32.
Jørgensen, Torstein, 'Excommunication – an act of expulsion from heaven and earth', in *The Creation of Medieval Northern Europe: Christianisations, Social Transformations, and Historiography: Essays in Honour of Sverre Bagge*, ed. L. Melve and S. Sønnesyn (Oslo, 2012), 58-69.
Kabir, Ananya Jahanara, *Paradise, Death and Doomsday in Anglo-Saxon Literature* (Cambridge, 2001).
Kaeuper, Richard W., *War, Justice, and Public Order: England and France in the Later Middle Ages* (Oxford, 1988).
Kaplan, Yosef, *Religion, Politics and Freedom of Conscience: Excommunication in Early Modern Jewish Amsterdam* (Amsterdam, 2010).

Kaplan, Yosef, 'Discipline, dissent, and communal authority in the western Sephardic diaspora', *The Cambridge History of Judaism, v. 7: The Early Modern World, 1500-1815*, ed. J. Karp and A. Sutcliffe (Cambridge, 2018), 378-406.

Karn, Nicholas, 'Textus Roffensis and its uses', in *Textus Roffensis: Law, Language, and Libraries in Early Medieval England*, ed. B. O'Brien and B. Bombi (Turnhout, 2015), 47-67.

Katz, Jacob, *Tradition and Crisis: Jewish Society at the end of the Middle Ages*, trans. Bernard Dov Cooperman (New York, 1993).

Kemp, Brian, 'Informing the archdeacon on ecclesiastical matters in twelfth-century England', in, *Medieval Studies in Honour of Dorothy M. Owen*, ed. M.J. Franklin and C. Harper-Bill (Woodbridge, 1995), 131-49.

Keygnaert, Frederik, 'Misbruik en devaluatie van excommunicatie in het Merovingische rijk', *Jaarboek voor Middeleeuwse Geschiedenis* 12 (2009), 7-39.

Keygnaert, Frederik, 'The Prohibition of Church Services in Cambrai (1095-1107): The Local Interdict as Church Weapon in the Investiture Controversy', *Trajecta* 24 (2015), 243-264.

Keygnaert, Frederik, 'The meaning of ecclesiastical exclusion in the archdiocese of Reims, c. 1100. The legal difference between excommunication, anathema and interdict', in *Proceedings of the Fourteenth International Congress of Canon Law, Toronto, 5-11 August 2012*, ed. J. Goering, S. Dusil, and A. Thier (Vatican, 2016), 767-77.

Knaake, J.K.F. et al., *D. Martin Luthers Werke* (Weimar, 1883).

Knowles, C.H., *Simon de Montfort, 1265-1965* (London, 1965).

Knowles, C.H., 'Resettlement of England after the barons' war', *Transactions of the Royal Historical Society*, 5th Ser. 32 (1982), 25-41.

Kramer, Susan R., 'Understanding contagion: The contaminating effect of another's sin', in *History in the Comic Mode*, ed. R. Fulton and B.W. Holsinger (Chichester, 2007), 145-157.

Lange, Tyler, *Excommunication for Debt in Late Medieval France: The Business of Salvation* (Cambridge, 2016).

Lawrence, C.H., *St Edmund of Abingdon: A Study in Hagiography and History* (Oxford, 1960).

Lea, H.C., *Studies in Church History: The Rise of the Temporal Power—Benefit of Clergy—Excommunication—the Early Church and Heresy* (Philadelphia, 1883).

Lecuppre, Gilles, 'Le scandale: de l'exemple pervers à l'outil politique (XIIIe-XVe siècle)', *Cahiers de recherches medievales et humanistes* 25 (2013), 181-91.

Le Goff, Jacques, *The Birth of Purgatory*, trans. Arthur Goldhammer (London, 1984).

Lemeneva, Elena M., '"Do not scandalize thy brother": scandal as preached on by Jacobus de Voragine and other thirteenth-century sermon-writers', in *Scandala*, ed. G. Jaritz (Krems, 2008), 18-32.

Leveleux-Teixeira, Corinne, 'Le droit canonique médiéval et l'horreur du scandale', *Cahiers de recherches médiévales et humanistes* 25 (2013), 193-211.

Lewandowski, Charlotte, 'Cultural expressions of episcopal power, 1070-*c*.1150' (Birmingham University PhD thesis, 2012).

Lipman, Vivian D., 'Anatomy of medieval Anglo-Jewry', *Transactions (Jewish Historical Society of England)* 21 (1962-1967), 64-77.

Little, Lester K., 'La morphologie des malédictions monastiques', *Annales. Economies, sociétés, civilisations* 34 (1979), 43-60.

Little, Lester K., *Benedictine Maledictions: Liturgical cursing in Romanesque France* (London, 1993).

Little, Lester K., 'Anger in monastic curses' in *Anger's Past: The Social Uses of an Emotion in the Middle Ages*, ed. B. Rosenwein (London, 1998), 9–35.

Liu, Hui, 'Matthew Paris and John Mansel', in *TCE xi: Proceedings of the Gregynog Conference 2005*, ed. B. Weiler, J. Burton, P. Schofield, and K. Stöber (Woodbridge, 2007), 159–73.

Lloyd, Simon, '"Political crusades" in England, c.1215-17 and c.1263-5', in *Crusade and Settlement: Papers Read at the First Conference of the Society for the Study of Crusades and the Latin East*, ed. P.W. Edbury (Cardiff, 1985), 113–20.

Logan, F.D., *Excommunication and the Secular Arm: A Study in Legal Procedure from the Thirteenth to the Sixteenth Century* (Toronto, 1968).

Logan, F.D., 'Excommunication', *Dictionary of the Middle Ages*, ed. J.R. Strayer et al., 13 vols. (New York, 1982–88), vi.

Longère, Jean, 'Les évêques et l'administration du sacrement de pénitence aux XIIIe siècle: les cas réservés', in *Papauté, Monachisme et Théories Politiques II: Etudes d'histoire médiévale offertes à Marcel Pacaut* (Lyon, 1994), 537–50.

Lukes, Steven, *Émile Durkheim: His Life and Work* (Harmondsworth, 1973).

Macfarlane, Alan, 'History, anthropology and the study of communities', *Social History* 2 (1977), 631–52.

Maciejewski, Jacek, 'Making war and enormities: violence within the church in the diocese of Cracow at the beginning of the 14th century', in *Ecclesia et Violentia: Violence against the Church and Violence within the Church in the Middle Ages*, ed. R. Kotechi and J. Maciejewski (Newcastle-upon-Tyne, 2014), 141–65.

Macy, G., *The Theologies of the Eucharist in the early scholastic period: a study of the salvific function of the sacrament according to the theologians, c.1080–c.1220* (Oxford, 1984).

Maddicott, J.R., 'The Crusade Taxation of 1268-70 and the development of Parliament', in *TCE ii: Proceedings of the Newcastle-upon-Tyne Conference 1987*, ed. P.R. Coss and S.D. Lloyd (Woodbridge, 1988), 93–117.

Maddicott, J.R., *Simon de Montfort* (Cambridge, 1994).

Maddicott, J.R., *Origins of the English Parliament, 924–1327* (Oxford, 2010).

Maddicott, J.R., 'The Oath of Marlborough, 1209: Fear, government and popular allegiance in the reign of King John', *EHR* 126 (2011), 281–318.

Maddicott, J.R., 'Politics and people in thirteenth-century England', in *TCE xiv: Proceedings of the Aberystwyth and Lampeter Conference 2011*, ed. J. Burton, P. Schofield and B. Weiler (Woodbridge, 2013), 1–13.

MaGuire, Michael R., and Michael J. Raleigh, 'Behavioral and physiological correlates of ostracism', *Ethology and Sociobiology* 7 (1986), 39–52 (187–200).

Malkopoulou, Anthoula, 'Ostracism and democratic self-defense in Athens', *Constellations* 24 (2017) 623–636.

Mansfield, Mary C., *The Humiliation of Sinners: Public Penance in Thirteenth-Century France* (London, 1995).

Masschaele, James, 'The public space of the marketplace in medieval England', *Speculum* 77 (2002), 383–421.

Mazel, Florian, *L'evêque et le territoire: L'invention médiévale de l'espace (Ve-XIIIe siècle)* (Paris, 2016).

Meens, Rob, 'The uses of excommunication in missionary contexts (sixth-eighth centuries)' in *Exclure de la Communauté Chrétienne*, ed. G. Bührer-Thierry and S. Gioanni (Turnhout, 2015), 143–56.

Melve, Leidulf, 'The public debate during the Baronial Rebellion', in *TCE xii: Proceedings of the Gregynog Conference 2007*, ed. J. Burton, P. Schofield and B. Weiler (Woodbridge, 2009), 45–59.

Melve, Leidulf, '"Even the very laymen are chattering about it": the politicization of public opinion, 800-1200', *Viator* 44 (2013), 25–48.

Melve, Leidulf, 'Public debate, propaganda, and public opinion in the Becket controversy', *Viator* 48 (2017), 79–102.

Mentzer, Raymond A., Françoise Moreil and Philippe Chareyre (eds), *Dire l'Interdit: The Vocabulary of Censure and Exclusion in the Early Modern Tradition* (Leiden, 2010).

Mentzer, Raymond A., 'Marking the taboo: excommunication in French reformed churches', in *Sin and the Calvinists: Morals Control and the Consistory in the Reformed Tradition*, ed. R. Mentzer (Sixteenth-Century Essays and Studies 32, 1994), 97–128.

Meyer, Hannah, 'Making sense of Christian excommunication of Jews in thirteenth-century England', *Jewish Quarterly Review* 100 (2010) 598–630.

Milani, Giuliano, 'An ambiguous sentence: Dante confronting his banishment', in *Images and Words in Exile*, ed. E. Brilli, L. Fenelli, and G. Wolf (Florence, 2015), 138–51.

Milani, Giuliano, 'Ban and the bag', in *Images of Shame: Infamy, Defamation and the Ethics of Oeconomia*, ed. C. Behrmann (Berlin, 2016), 119–40.

Miller, A.G., '*Carpe Ecclesiam*: Households, Identity & Violent Communication ('Church' & 'Crown' under King Edward I)' (University of California, Santa Barbara, PhD thesis, 2003).

Miller, A.G., 'Knights, bishops and deer parks: episcopal identity, emasculation and clerical space in medieval England', in *Negotiating Clerical Identities: Priests, Monks and Masculinity in the Middle Ages*, ed. J. D. Thibodeaux (London, 2010), 204–37.

Miller, A.G., 'To "frock" a cleric: the gendered implications of mutilating ecclesiastical vestments in medieval England', *Gender and History* 24 (2012), 271–91.

Monter, E.W., 'Consistory of Geneva', *Bibliotèque d'Humanisme et Renaissance* 38 (1976), 467–84.

Moore, R.I., *The Formation of a Persecuting Society: Authority and Deviance in Western Europe 950-1250* (2nd edn., Oxford, 2007).

Moorman, John R.H., *Church Life in England in the Thirteenth Century* (Cambridge, 1946).

Morgan, Marjorie M., 'The excommunication of Grosseteste in 1243', *EHR* 57 (1942), 244–50.

Morris, Colin, *The Papal Monarchy: The Western Church from 1050 to 1250* (Oxford, 1989).

Murphy, Margaret, 'Ecclesiastical censures: an aspect of their use in thirteenth century Dublin', *Archivium Hibernicum* 44 (1989), 89–97.

Murray, Alexander, 'Piety and impiety in thirteenth-century Italy', in *SCH* 8, ed. G. J. Cuming and D. Baker (Cambridge, 1972).

Murray, Alexander, *Suicide in the Middle Ages*, 2 vols (Oxford, 1998-2000).

Murray, Alexander, 'Excommunication and conscience in the Middle Ages', in *idem, Conscience and Authority in the Medieval Church* (Oxford, 2015), 163–97 (Originally published 1991 as John Coffin Memorial Lecture).

Murray, Alexander, 'Confession as a historical source', *Conscience and Authority in the Medieval Church* (Oxford, 2015), 49–86.

Napran, Laura, 'Marriage and excommunication: the comital house of Flanders', in *Exile in the Middle Ages*, ed. L. Napran and E. van Houts (Turnhout, 2004), 69–80.

Nederman, C. J., *Political Thought in Early 14th-Century England* (Turnhout, 2002).

Nemo-Pekelman, C., 'Scandale et vérité dans la doctrine canonique médiévale (XIIe–XIIIe siècles)', *Revue historique de droit français et étranger* 84/5 (2007), 491–504.

Owst, G.R., *Preaching in Medieval England: An Introduction to Sermon Manuscripts of the Period c.1350-1450* (Cambridge, 1926).
Page, William (ed.), *The Victoria History of the County of Gloucester*, ii (London, 1907).
Pantin, W.A., *The English Church in the Fourteenth Century* (Cambridge, 1955).
Paravicini Bagliani, Agostino, 'Bonifacio VIII, la loggia di Giustizia al Laterano e i processi generali di scomunica', *Rivista di Storia della Chiesa in Italia* 59 (2005), 377–428.
Paravicini Bagliani, Agostino, 'Il rito di scomunica, da Gregorio VII a Innocenzo III', *idem, Il Potere del Papa. Corporeità, autorappresentazione, simboli* (Florence, 2009), 215-26.
Parker, Robert, *Miasma: Pollution and Purification in early Greek Religion* (Oxford, 1983, rpr. 1996).
Parkes, Henry, 'Questioning the authority of Vogel and Elze's Pontifical Romano-Germanique', in *Understanding Medieval Liturgy: Essays in Interpretation*, ed. S. Hamilton and H. Gittos (Farnham, 2016), 75–101.
Pattwell, Niamh, 'A sentence of cursing in Pembroke College, Cambridge MS 285', *Leeds Studies in English*, new ser. 35 (2004), 121–36.
Pavlac, Brian A., 'Excommunication and territorial politics in high medieval Trier', *Church History* 60 (1991), 20-36.
Pavlac, Brian A., 'The curse of Cusanus: excommunication in fifteenth century Germany', in *Nicholas of Cusa and his Age: Intellect and Spirituality*, ed. T. M. Izbicki and C. M. Bellitto (Leiden, 2002), 199–213.
Péricard, Jacques, 'L'excommunication dans le royaume franc. Quelques remarques sur la législation canonique et ses contournements (v^e-ixe siècle)', in *Exclure de la Communauté Chrétienne*, ed. G. Bührer-Thierry and S. Gioanni (Turnhout, 2015), 21–37.
Pickering, O.S., 'Notes on the sentence of cursing in Middle English or, a case for the Index of Middle English Prose', *Leeds Studies in English*, n.s. 12, (1981), 229–44.
Pollock, Frederick and F.W. Maitland, *The History of English Law before the Time of Edward I* (2nd edn., Cambridge, 1911).
Powicke, F.M., 'The Bull "Miramur plurimum" and a Letter to Archbishop Stephen Langton, 5 September 1215', *EHR* 44 (1929), 87–93.
Powicke, F.M., *King Henry III and Lord Edward: the community of the realm in the thirteenth century*, 2 vols. (Oxford, 1947).
Powicke, F.M., *The Thirteenth Century, 1216–1307* (2nd edn., Oxford, 1962).
Powicke, F.M., 'The murder of Henry Clement and the pirates of Lundy Island', in *idem, Ways of Medieval Life and Thought* (Oxford, 1967), 38–68.
Prestwich, M., *War, Politics and Finance Under Edward I* (London, 1972).
Prestwich, M., 'The Piety of Edward I', in *England in the Thirteenth Century*, ed. W. M. Ormrod (Woodbridge, 1986), 120-8.
Prestwich, M., *Edward I* (London, 1988).
Prestwich, M., *English Politics in the Thirteenth Century* (Basingstoke, 1990).
Price, Douglas A., 'The abuses of excommunication and the decline of ecclesiastical discipline under Queen Elizabeth', *EHR* 57 (1942), 106–115.
Reuter, T., 'Contextualising Canossa: excommunication, penance, surrender, reconciliation', in *idem, Medieval Polities and Modern Mentalities*, ed. J. L. Nelson (Cambridge, 2006), 147–66.
Reuter, T., '*Velle sibi fieri in forma hac*: symbolic acts in the Becket dispute', in *idem, Medieval Polities and Modern Mentalities*, 167–90.
Reynolds, Andrew, *Anglo-Saxon Deviant Burial Customs* (Oxford, 2009).

Reynolds, Roger E., 'Rites of separation and reconciliation in the early Middle Ages', in *Segni e riti nella chiesa altomedievale occidentale 11–17 aprile 1985*, Settimane di Studio de centro Italiano di studi sull'alto Medioevo XXXIII (Spoleto, 1987), 405–33.

Reynolds, Susan, *Kingdoms and Communities in Western Europe, 900–1300* (Oxford, 1984).

Reynolds, Susan, 'Social mentalities and the case of medieval scepticism', *Transactions of the Royal Historical Society*, 5th ser., 41 (1991), 21–41; rpr. in *Ideas and Solidarities*, Essay I.

Reynolds, Susan, *Ideas and Solidarities of the Medieval Laity: England and Western Europe* (Aldershot, 1995).

Rider, Catherine, 'Lay religion and pastoral care in thirteenth-century England: the evidence of a group of short confession manuals', *JMH* 36 (2010), 327–340.

Ridgeway, H., 'The ecclesiastical career of Aymer de Lusignan, bishop elect of Winchester, 1250-1260', in *The Cloister and the World: Essays in Medieval History in Honour of Barbara Harvey*, ed. J. Blair and B. Golding (Oxford, 1996), 148–77.

Rieder, Paula M., 'The implications of exclusion: the regulation of churching in medieval Northern France', *Essays in Medieval Studies* 15 (1999), 71–80.

Rosemblieh, Émilie, 'Limiter la contagion de l'excommunication: la vaine tentative de réformer les peines canoniques encourues ipso facto à l'époque du concile de Bâle (1431-1449)', in *Normes juridiques et pratiques judiciaires du Moyen Âge à l'époque contemporaine*, ed. B. Garnot (Dijon, 2007), 61–69.

Rosenwein, Barbara (ed.), *Anger's Past: The Social Uses of an Emotion in the Middle Ages* (London, 1998).

Rosser, Gervase, 'Sanctuary and social negotiation in medieval England', in *The Cloister and the World: Essays in Medieval History in Honour of Barbara Harvey*, ed. J. Blair and B. Golding (Oxford, 1996), 57–79.

Rubin, Miri, *Corpus Christi: The Eucharist in Late Medieval Culture* (Cambridge, 1991).

Sabapathy, John, 'Making public knowledge—Making knowledge public: the territorial, reparative, heretical, and canonisation enquiries of Gui Foucois (ca. 1200-1268)', *Journal for the History of Knowledge* 1 (2020), 1–21.

Sackville, Lucy, 'The Church's institutional response to heresy in the thirteenth century', in *A Companion to Heresy Inquisitions*, ed. D. S. Prudlo (Leiden, 2019), 108–40.

Sartore, Melissa, *Outlawry, Governance, and Law in Medieval England* (New York, 2013).

Sayers, Jane E., *Papal Government and England during the Pontificate of Honorius III (1216-1227)* (Cambridge, 1984).

Sayers, Jane E., *Innocent III: Leader of Europe 1189–1216* (London, 1994).

Sayers, Jane E., 'Peter's Throne and Augustine's Chair: Rome and Canterbury from Baldwin (1184–90) to Robert Winchelsey (1297–1313)', *JEH* 51 (2000), 249–66.

Schmitz-Esser, Romedio, *The Corpse in the Middle Ages: Embalming, Cremating, and the Cultural Creation of the Dead Body*, trans. Albrecht Classen and Carolin Radtke (Turnhout, 2020).

Schmugge, Ludwig, 'Towards the medieval conscience: the activities of the papal penitentiary', in *New Approaches to the History of late Medieval and early Modern Europe*, ed. T. Dahlerup and P. Ingesman, (Historisk-filosofiske Meddelelser 104, Copenhagen, 2009), 208–30.

Sère, Bénédicte, and Jörg Wettlaufer (eds), *Between Punishment and Penance: The Social Usages of Shame in the Middle Ages and Early Modern Times* (Florence, 2013).

Shatzmiller, Joseph, 'Jews "separated from the communion of the faithful in Christ" in the Middle Ages', in *Studies in Medieval Jewish History and Literature*, ed. I. Twersky (London, 1979), 307–14.

Shatzmiller, Joseph, 'Christian "excommunication" of Jews: some further clarifications', in *Schlomo Simonsohn Jubilee Volume: Studies on the History of the Jews in the Middle Ages and Renaissance Period* (Tel Aviv, 1993), 245-55.
Smail, Daniel Lord, 'Hatred as a social institution in late-medieval society', *Speculum* 76 (2001), 90-126.
Smail, Daniel Lord, *The Consumption of Justice: Emotions, Publicity, and Legal Culture in Marseille, 1264-1423* (London, 2003).
Snyder, Susan Taylor, 'Orthodox fears: anti-inquisitorial violence and defining heresy', in *Fear and its Representations in the Middle Ages and Renaissance*, ed. A. Scott and C. Kosso (Turnhout, 2002), 92-104.
Southern, R.W., *Robert Grosseteste* (Oxford, 1986).
Stacey, R. C., 'Crusades, crusaders and the baronial *Gravamina* of 1263-1264', in *TCE iii: Proceedings of the Newcastle-upon-Tyne Conference 1989*, ed. P. R. Coss and S. D. Lloyd (Woodbridge, 1991), 137-50.
Starn, Randolph, *Contrary Commonwealth: The Theme of Exile in Medieval and Renaissance Italy* (Berkeley CA., 1982).
Stewart, Susan, 'Outlawry as an instrument of justice in the thirteenth century', in *Outlaws in Medieval and Earl Modern England. Crime, Government and Society, c.1066-c.1600*, ed. J.C. Appleby and P. Dalton (Farnham, 2009), 37-54.
Strayer, J.R., 'The Political Crusades of the Thirteenth Century', in *idem, Medieval Statecraft and the Perspectives of History* (Princeton, N.J., 1971), 123-58.
Strickland, Matthew, 'Robert, Fitzwalter (d. 1235)', *ODNB* https://doi.org/10.1093/ref:odnb/9648 (accessed 18/9/2021).
Summerson, H.R.T., 'The structure of law enforcement in thirteenth-century England', *American Journal of Legal History* 23 (1979), 313-27.
Summerson, H.R.T., 'The criminal underworld of Medieval England', *Journal of Legal History* 17 (1996), 197-224.
Swanson, R.N., *Church and Society in Late Medieval England* (Oxford, 1989).
Swanson, R.N., *Religion and Devotion in Europe, c.1215-c.1515* (Cambridge, 1995).
Sweetinburgh, S., 'Caught in the cross-fire', in *Cathedrals, Communities and Conflict in the Anglo-Norman World*, ed. P. Dalton, C. Insley, and L. Wilkinson (Woodbridge, 2011), 187-202.
Tanner, Norman and Sethina Watson, 'Least of the laity: the minimum requirements for a medieval Christian', *JMH* 32 (2006), 395-423.
Thomas, Keith, *Religion and the Decline of Magic: Studies in Popular Beliefs in Sixteenth and Seventeenth Century England* (London, 1971).
Töbelmann, Paul, 'Excommunication in the Middle Ages: a meta-ritual and the many faces of its efficacy', in *The Problem of Ritual Efficacy*, ed. W.S. Sax, J. Quack and J. Weinhold (Oxford, 2010), 93-112.
Todd, Margo, '"None to haunt, frequent, nor intercommon with them": the problem of excommunication in the Scottish kirk', in *Dire l'Interdit: The Vocabulary of Censure and Exclusion in the Early Modern Tradition*, ed. R. A. Mentzer, F. Moreil and P. Chareyre (Leiden, 2010), 219-35.
Thompson, E.P., *Whigs and Hunters: The Origin of the Black Act* (London, 1975).
Treharne, E.M., 'A unique Old English formula for excommunication from Cambridge, Corpus Christi College 303', *Anglo-Saxon England* 24 (1995), 185-211.
Treharne, R.F., *The Baronial Plan of Reform, 1258-1263* (Manchester, rpr. 1971).
Turner, R.V., 'William de Forz, Count of Aumale: an early thirteenth-century English baron', *Proceedings of the American Philosophical Society* 115 (1971), 221-49.

Turner, R.V., *King John: England's Evil King?* (Stroud, 2005).
Tyerman, C., *England and The Crusades, 1095-1588* (London, 1988).
Ullmann, Walter, *The Growth of Papal Government in the Middle Ages* (London, 1955).
Ullmann, Walter, *Principles of Government and Politics in the Middle Ages* (London, 1961).
Vale, Malcolm, 'St John, Sir John de (*d.* 1302)', *ODNB* https://doi.org/10.1093/ref:odnb/24499 (accessed 18/9/2021).
Valente, Claire, 'Simon de Montfort, Earl of Leicester, and the utility of sanctity in thirteenth-century England', *JMH* 21 (1995), 27-49.
Vallerani, Massimo, *Medieval Public Justice*, trans. Sarah Rubin Blanshei (Washington, 2012).
Van Cleve, T.C., *The Emperor Frederick II of Hohenstaufen: Immutator Mundi* (Oxford, 1972).
Van Houts, Elisabeth, 'The vocabulary of exile and outlawry in the North Sea area around the first millennium', in *Exile in the Middle Ages*, ed. L. Napran and E. van Houts (Turnhout, 2004), 13-28.
Vecchio, Silvana, 'Légitimité et efficacité de la malédiction dans la réflexion théologique médiévale', in *Le Pouvoir des Mots au Moyen Âge*, ed. N. Bériou, J-P. Boudet and I. Rossier-Catach (Turnhout, 2014), 349-61.
Vincent, Nicholas, 'Master Alexander of Stainsby, bishop of Coventry and Lichfield, 1224-1238', *JEH* 46 (1995), 615-40.
Vincent, Nicholas, *Peter des Roches: An Alien in English Politics, 1205-1238* (Cambridge, 1996).
Vincent, Nicholas, *The Holy Blood: Henry III and the Westminster Blood Relic* (Cambridge, 2001).
Vincent, Nicholas, 'Some pardoners' tales: the earliest English indulgences', *Transactions of the Royal Historical Society*, 6th ser., 12 (2002), 23-58.
Vincent, Nicholas, 'Stephen Langton, Archbishop of Canterbury', in *Étienne Langton: Prédicateur, Bibliste, Théologien* (Turnhout, 2010), 51-123.
Vincent, Nicholas, 'King John's diary and itinerary', *The Magna Carta Project*: http://www.magnacartaresearch.org/read/itinerary (accessed 18/9/2021).
Vincent, Nicholas, 'A New Letter of the Twenty-Five Barons of Magna Carta', *The Magna Carta Project*: http://magnacartaresearch.org/read/feature_of_the_month/Jul_2015_2 (accessed 18/9/2021).
Vincent, Nicholas, *Magna Carta: Origins and Legacy* (Oxford, 2015).
Vise, Melissa, 'The women and the inquisitor: peacemaking in Bologna, 1299', *Speculum* 93 (2018), 357-86.
Vodola, E., *Excommunication in the Middle Ages* (Berkeley, CA, 1986).
Vodola, E., 'Sovereignty and tabu: evolution of the sanction against communication with excommunicates. Part 1: Gregory VII, in *The Church and Sovereignty, c.590-1918: Essays in Honour of Michael Wilks*, ed. D. Wood (*SCH Subsidia* 9, 1991), 35-55.
Vodola, E., 'Sovereignty and tabu: evolution of the sanction against communication with excommunicates. Part 2: Canonical collections', in *Studia in Honorem Eminentissimi Cardinalis Alphonsi M. Stickler*, ed. R. C. Lara (Rome, 1992), 581-98.
Warren, W.L., *King John* (new edn., London, 1997).
Watkins, Carl, 'Sin, penance and purgatory in the Anglo-Norman realm: the evidence of visions and ghost stories', *Past & Present* 175 (2002), 3-33.
Watkins, Carl, *History and the Supernatural in Medieval England* (Cambridge, 2007).
Weiler, Björn, 'Henry III and the Sicilian business: a reassessment', *HR* 74 (2001), 127-50.

Weiler, Björn, 'Symbolism and politics in the reign of Henry III', in *TCE ix: Proceedings of the Durham Conference 2001*, ed. M. Prestwich, R. Britnell, and R. Frame (Woodbridge, 2003), 15–41.
Weiler, Björn, *Henry III of England and the Staufen Empire, 1216–1272* (Woodbridge, 2006).
Weiler, Björn, *Kingship, Rebellion and Political Culture, England and Germany, c.1215–1250* (Basingstoke, 2007).
Weiler, Björn, 'Matthew Paris on the writing of history', *JMH* 35 (2009), 254–78.
Whalen, Brett Edward, *The Two Powers: The Papacy, the Empire, and the Struggle for Sovereignty in the Thirteenth Century* (Philadelphia, P.A., 2019).
Whatley, E. Gordon, 'John Lydgate's Saint Austin at Compton: the poem and its sources', in *Anglo-Latin and its Heritage: Essays in Honour of A. Rigg on his 64th birthday*, ed. S. Achard and G. R. Wieland (Turnhout, 2001), 191–227.
Whatley, E. Gordon, Anne B. Thompson, and Robert K. Upchurch (eds), *Saints' Lives in Middle English Collections Saints' Lives in Middle English Collections* (Kalamazoo, MI, 2004).
White, Stephen D., 'The politics of anger', in *Anger's Past: The Social Uses of an Emotion in the Middle Ages*, ed. B. Rosenwein (London, 1998), 127–52.
Wickham, Chris, 'Gossip and resistance among the medieval peasantry', *Past & Present* 160 (1998), 3–24.
Wickham, Chris, 'Conclusion' to *The Moral World of the Law*, ed. P. Coss (Cambridge, 2000).
Wickham, Chris, *Courts and Conflict in Twelfth-Century Tuscany* (Oxford, 2003).
Wickham, Chris, 'Fama and the law in twelfth-century Tuscany', in *Fama: The Politics of Talk and Reputation in Medieval Europe* ed. T. Fenster and D. L. Smail (London, 2003), 15–26.
Williams, Kipling D., *Ostracism: The Power of Silence* (London, 2001).
Willis-Bund, J.W. and William Page (eds), *The Victoria History of the County of Worcester*, ii (London, 1906).
Winroth, Anders, *The Making of Gratian's Decretum* (Cambridge, 2004).
Wood, Andy, *The Memory of the People: Custom and Popular Senses of the Past in Early Modern England* (Cambridge, 2013).
Woolf, Jeffrey R., *The Fabric of Religious Life in Medieval Ashkenaz (1000–1300): Creating Sacred Communities* (Leiden, 2015).
Woolf, Jeffrey R., 'Communal and religious organisation', *The Cambridge History of Judaism, 6: The Middle Ages: The Christian World*, ed. R. Chazan (Cambridge, 2018), 380–92.
Wordsworth, Christopher, and Henry Littlehales, *The Old Service-Books of the English Church* (London, 1904).
Work, James A., 'Echoes of the Anathema in Chaucer', *Proceedings of the Modern Language Association* 47 (1932), 419–30.
Zimmer, Eric, *Harmony and Discord: An Analysis of the Decline of Jewish Self-Government in 15th Century Central Europe* (New York, 1970).

Index

For the benefit of digital users, indexed terms that span two pages (e.g., 52–53) may, on occasion, appear on only one of those pages.

Medieval names are listed by Christian name; all others by surname.

abbesses 13 n.86, 106, *see also* nuns
Abbo of Fleury 6–7
abbots 13–14, 49, 63, 76, 95, 112–13, 122–3, 153–4, 181, 190–1, 211 n.156, 218, *see also* monks
Abelard, *see* Peter Abelard
abjuration of the realm 108–9, 142, 154–5
absolution 1, 13–14, 19, 22–3, 35–7, 39–40, 52, 60, 68–78, 97, 114–17, 119–20, 122–3, 128, 156–7, 160, 212–19, 223–4, 228–9, 251–2, 255–7, 291
    deathbed (*in articulo mortis*) 13–14, 60–8, 90–1, 99–100, 115, 287–8, 307
    on false pretences 65
    in penitential forum 69, 71–5, 285
    posthumous 38–42, 60–1, 64, 91, 93, 290–1
    power to impose 119–20
    proactive 67–8, 71, 73–5, 82–4
    provided illicitly 34, 77, 285, 306
    provisional (*ad cautelam*) 13–14
    reserved 69, 79–80, 210–11, 274, 278, 285
    rite of 49 n.95, 213
    satisfaction as precondition for 23, 40, 60–4, 67–8, 76–7, 82–3, 91–2, 223–4, 234
    unhealthy 79–80
Adam le Warner 1, 62–3, 65–6
adultery 23–4, 145–6, 164 n.136, 264–6, Appendix I
Agen, bishop of 219
aggravation of excommunication 43 n.66, 129, 158–9, 188–9, 200–1, 208
Alexander IV, pope 84–6, 124–5, 168–9, 201, 219–22
Alexander Stainsby, bishop of Coventry and Lichfield 113, 174–5
Alfonso X, king of Castile 121, 123
Alice Clement, nun 113, 166–7
Amaury de Montfort 64–5
Ambler, Sophie 170–1, 279–80
Amish, the 148–50
anathema 7–8, 33–4, 42–4, 46, 49–50, 52–5, 64–5, 70, 79–80, 88, 106 n.16, 110 n.51, 168, 177–8, 228, 231, 240, 243–5, 250–1, 259

anger 41–5, 56, 58, 139, 144, 173, 178–9, 188–9, 195–6, 202, 218–19, 222, 289
Anglo-Saxon
    conversion 37–8
    law codes 108–9, 263
Anglo-Scottish wars 53–4, 67–8, 76–7, 123–4, 144–5, 197–8, 222
animals
    excommunication of 36–7
    ostracism amongst 104–5
    theft of 24–5, 178–9, 220
Ankerwic 166–7
Anonymous of Béthune 127–8, 161–2
anti-clericalism 204–5
Antony Bek, bishop of Durham 107 n.26, 220, 283
apostasy, *see* monks and nuns
Apostolic See, *see* papacy
Aquinas, *see* Thomas Aquinas
archdeacons, archdeaconries 13–14, 20, 54, 112–13, 141–2, 167–8, 188–90, 197, 209–11, 217–18, 220–1, 231–2, 238, 240, 242, 247–8, 264, 272–3, 282–3, 286–7
Arlot, papal nuncio 85–6
Armagh, archbishop of 6–7
    archbishop-elect of 208
Arnold, John 63–4, 172
arson 67–8, 259, 265–6, 280–1, Appendix I
articles of the faith 97
Asgarby 62–3
assault of clerics, *see Si quis suadente*
Auch, archbishop of 224
audiences witnessing excommunications 36, 47–50, 185–95, 197, 200–1, 215–16, 239, 242–4
Augustine of Canterbury 37–40
Augustine of Hippo 6–7, 32
Austin, J.L. 47
Aymer de Lusignan, bishop of Winchester 192–5, 199 n.81, 221–2

bailiffs 22, 116–17, 181, 215–18, 253
Bangor, bishop of 76–7

334 INDEX

banishment, *see* exile
baptism 24–5, 157, 276–7
barons 84–6, 120–1, 127–8, 159–60, 225
   rebellious 3–4, 60–2, 65, 78–9, 85–6, 88–9, 95–7, 118, 124–5, 128–31, 134–5, 159–62, 164, 173–4, 200, 202–4, 221–2, 226–7
Barton, Richard 9–10
Basing 233–4
Bath and Wells 181, 260
battle 87–90, 97–8, *see also* Evesham, Lewes, Lincoln
Beaulande, Véronique 2–3, 7 n.46, 9–10, 23–4, 52, 55, 60, 99–100, 114–15, 123, 147–8, 165–6, 189–90, 198–9, 218–19
Becket, *see* Thomas Becket
Bedford
   archdeacon of 240
   castle of 82–3, 134, 202–3
Belial, sons of 131, 193–7, 230, 239–40
bells 45–50, 56–7, 187–9, 193, 236, 272, 274, 294–5, 307–8
Berwick 233–4
bible 54
   Old Testament 54–5
   Genesis, 1:28 42
   Numbers 54, 243–4
   Numbers, 16:30 35–6
   Deuteronomy 54–5
   Psalms 54–5, 256–7
   Psalm 51 213
   Psalm 108 42, 53–5, 243–4, 247–8
   Isaiah 5:22–3 170
   Jeremiah 22:19 36
   Ezekiel 3:18–19 140, 277–8
   New Testament 30–1, 99–100
   Matthew 6:24 80 n.100
   Matthew 10:28 163–4
   Matthew 18 32 n.15
   Matthew 18:15–17 104
   Matthew 18:17 30–1, 65, 182
   Matthew 18:18 92–3
   Romans 12:14 30–1
   1 Corinthians 5 104–5
   1 Corinthians 5:5 30–1, 41, 57, 70
biblical figures
   Ananias and Sapphira 54
   Caiaphas 54
   Cain 54, 243–4
   Dathan and Abiron 52–4, 243–4
   Judas 54
   Moses 54, 243–4
   Pontius Pilate 54
binding and loosing, *see* keys

bloodshed, on consecrated ground 25, 154, 195–6, 230, 239–41, 247
Bodmin 158–9
Bologna 166, 172
Bonaventure 30–1
Boniface of Savoy, archbishop of Canterbury 47–8, 80–1, 92, 168–70, 192–6, 217–18, 226–7, 286–7
Boniface VIII, pope 66–7, 80, 118, 168, 176, 269–70, *see also Clericis laicos* and *Liber Sextus*
books 24, 49, 227–8
Bordeaux, archbishop of 178–9, 223–4
Boulogne 162–4
Bourges, archbishop of 131
Bracton, *see* Henry Bracton
Brand, Paul 119
bread 36–7
Bristol 124–5
   mayor and burgesses of 123–4
Brixton, hundred of 194–5
Buckingham 190, 220–1, 238
   archdeacon of 240, 247–8, 247 n.95
burial 24, 36–7, 41–2, 61–5, 68, 87, 115, 152–3, 208–11, 307
Burton, annals of 188–9
Bury St Edmund's, chronicle of 80, 220, 284–5
Bytham, castle of 133–4

Callixtus II, pope 261–2
Calvinists 6–7
Cambrai 52–3
Campbell, William 264
candles 24, 34–5, 45–50, 52–7, 84, 133, 187–8, 193, 227–8, 236, 238, 243–4, 272, 274, 284, 287–8, 291, 294–5
Canon law 3–5, 10–12, 15–16, 30–2, 34, 36, 41, 43–4, 58, 93–5, 105–6, 109–10, 154, 156–7, 173, 187–8, 203–4, 251, 254, 261–2, 268, 274–5, 289
   Ad vitanda 109–10, 143–4
   Cum medicinalis 32–6, 249–50
   Quoniam multos 109–10
   studies of 2–3
   see also *Clementine*, Gratian, *Liber Extra*, *Liber Sextus*
canonists 15–16, 29, 53, 110–11, 150, 158, 172–3, 213–14, 262, 274–5
canons 22–4, 118, 123–4, 161–2, 170, 200–1, 217–18
Canterbury, prior of 49, 95
   archbishop of 231–2, *see also* Eadmer, Stephen Langton, Edmund of Abingdon, Boniface of Savoy, John Pecham, Robert Winchelsey, Henry Chichele

INDEX 335

Christ Church priory and monks 116, 162, 206–12
church of 204–5
city of 207–11
diocese of 260
official, archbishop's 181
province of 190, 209, 216–17
see also Court of the Arches
Carlisle, bishop of 76, 284–5, *see also* John de Halton
canons of 161–2
diocese of 260
Carolingian Empire 244–5
Carpenter, David 85, 88–9
catholic reformers 7–8
Challet, Vincent 149–50
Channel Islands 227–8
Charlemagne 6–7
charters 24, 25, 63, 121, 128, 206–7, *see also* Magna Carta, Forest Charter
Cheney, C.R. 129–31
Chester
bishop of 117, 204
see also Ranulf, earl of Chester
Chichester, diocese of 181, 260, 283–4
bishop of 97, 181, 193, 208, 283–4
Christina of Heyford, nun 22–3, 25
chronicles 78–82, 164–5, 173
Church, Stephen 128
churches
doors of 185 n.1, 187–8, 189 n.22, 213–16
fortification of 242
occupation of 167
reconciliation of 239–40, 255 n.130
vacant 24–5, 168–9, 233–4, 305
churching 121–2, 247
Cinque Ports 226–7
Clarke, Peter 23–4, 61, 64, 69, 99–100, 149–50, 158, 160–2, 165–6, 180–1, 209–10
Claybrook 242
Clement IV, pope (Gui Fouquois) 60–1, 65, 97–8, 124–5, 134–5, 162–4, 176, 190–1, 225–7
Clement V, pope 67–8, 76, see also *Clementine*
Clementine 306–8
Clericis laicos 66–7, 80, 92, 95, 176, 178–9, 222–3, 269–70, 282–7
Clermont, bishop of 223–4
Close Rolls 76, 81–2, 213
coin clipping 281–2, Appendix I
confession 11–12, 69, 81, 97–8, 105–6, 146–7, 285, 287–8
Conrad IV of Germany 84–5

conscience 31, 35–6, 66–78, 85, 93–5, 97–9, 166–7, 199–200, 219–20, 235–6
Contempnunt exequi domini 126, 176–8, 268–9, 287 n.149, Appendix I, 305, *see also* secular arm
contumacy 12, 22–4, 31–2, 35–6, 43–4, 52, 66, 78, 86–7, 91, 140, 144–7, 157–60, 188–9, 192, 207–10, 247–8, 250, 269–70, 292
convocations 140, 208, 240, 247–8, *see also* councils
corpses of excommunicates 36, 38, 64, 307
do not decay 37–8, 42
exhumation of 61–2, 64–5
see also burial
councils 242, 284–5
papal
Reims (1119) 261–2
Lateran II (1139) 16–17
Lateran III (1179) 261–2
Lateran IV (1215) 31–5, 69, 180, 275–6
Lyon I (1245) 32–5, 43, 109–10, 249 n.105, 275
Lyon II (1274) 228
Vienne (1311) 6–7, 109–10
legatine
York (1195) 259, 261–262, Appendix I
London (1268) 16–17, 64–5, 216–17, 260, 269–71, 273–4, Appendix I, 305–6, 308
provincial
Meaux (845) 33–4
Westminster (1102) 261–2
Westminster (1200) 259, 261–4, 271, Appendix I
Oxford (1222) 16–17, 173, 176–8, 214, 227–8, 259–68, 272–4, 278–82, 284–7, Appendix I, 304–6
Merton (1258) 177–8
Reading (1279) 16–17, 222, 260, 266–71, 276, 280–1, Appendix I, 308
Lambeth (1281) 16–17, 34, 173, 177–8, 259–60, 267–9, 271, 276–7, 280–2, 285–6, 304–6, Appendix I, 304–6
diocesan Appendix I *passim*
Canterbury I (1213 x 1214) 259, 275
Salisbury I (1217 x 1219) (Durham I) 259, 263–4, 275
Unknown diocese (1222 x 1225) 177–8
Coventry and Lichfield (1224 x 1237) 105–6
Salisbury II (1238 x 1244) 267–8, 282
Durham II (1241 x 1249) 273–4
Ely (1239 x 1256) 260
Salisbury (1257) 214
Wells (1258?) 34 n.27, 273–4
Winchester II (*c*. 1247) 177–8

councils (*cont.*)
  Winchester III (1262 x 1265) 274
  Exeter II (1287) 34–5, 34 n.27, 187–8, 276
Court of the Arches, Canterbury 140, 217–18, 233–4, 236–7, 246–7, 249–51, 253, 255, 286–7
Coventry and Lichfield, bishop of 117, *see also* Alexander Stainsby
  diocese of 260
  dean of 117
Crimen imponunt alicui 173, 265–6, 268, 283–4, 286–7, 287 n.149, Appendix I, 305
cross
  held erect during excommunication ceremony 49
  crusader, worn on clothing 96, 132, 134–5
Crowland chronicle 120–1, 131–3, 173–4
crusade 88–9, 96, 130–6, 159–60
Cuddesdon 234, 238
  deanery of 238
Curia Regis Rolls 63, 112–14
curse 4–5, 30–3, 36–7, 41–4, 46–7, 51–7, 96, 140, 240, 242–5, 250–1, 257–8, 288–9, 293–4

D'Avray, David 11, 270
Daffyd, prince of North Wales 169–70
damnation, *see* hell
deans 13–14, 20, 35–6, 63–4, 74, 117, 161–2, 170, 190, 194, 204–5, 217–18, 242, 272–3, 282–3
debt 24, 110–11, 117, 147, 165–6
Decem Librarum 232–4
defamation 198–212, 217, 228–9, 265–6, 268, *see also* reputation
demons 36, 70
  invocation of 263–6, Appendix I
Denton, Jeffrey 8 n.47, 92, 176
deposition 129–31, 134, 167–8, 202
divorce 292
Dominicans 30–1, 166, 210–11, 234
Dover 61, 162–4, 195–6, 225–7
Dresch, Paul 6–7
dress, solemn 48–50, 49 n.95, 96, 193, 238, 242, 244, 247–8, 272–3, 284–5
  defiled 242–3, 247–8
Dublin 116–17
  archbishop of, *see* Henry of London
Dunstable
  annals of 59, 86, 91–2, 133, 211 n.155
  priory of 59
  citizens of 59, 91–2, 158–9
Durandus, *see* pontificals

Durham, priory of 118
  bishop of 216–17, *see also* Richard Poore, Antony Bek
  diocese of 260, 263–4
Durkheim, Émile 149

Eadmer, archbishop of Canterbury 261–2
early modern period 6–8, 11, 147–8, 151
Easter, *see* feast days
Ecton 227–8, 284, 288–9
Edmund of Abingdon, archbishop of Canterbury 47–8, 82–4, 97, 175, 201–2, 204–12
Edmund, son of Henry III of England 84–5
Edward I, king of England 53–5, 66–8, 76–7, 80, 95, 119–21, 176, 178–81, 197–8, 216–17, 221–3, 231–2, 237–9, 245, 253, 255–6, 266–71
Edward II, king of England 67–8
Edward St John 23–58 *passim*
Edwards, Genvieve Steele 4–5, 7–8, 45–6, 53
Eleanor de Montfort 121–2
Eleanor of Provence, queen of England 121–2
Ely
  disinherited at 97, 170–1
  diocese of 260
Eucharist 47–8, 70, 132, 147, 215–16, 276–7, 307
Eudes de Sully, bishop of Paris 274
Eustace de Bingham 23, 124–5
Eustace of Lynn, official of Canterbury 192–5
Evesham, Battle of (1265) 60–2, 64–5, 96, 135, 162–3, 170–1, 226
excommunicates
  corpses of, *see* corpses
  inheritance of 113
  loss of legal rights 14–15, 20, 68, 70–1, 111–14
  number of 6–7, 18–22
  runaway 106, 124–5, 141–2
  sentences annulled 19
  sentences appealed 19, 95, 168, 248–9, 251–2
  status or profession of individual 22
excommunication
  ab homine 13–14, 47–8
  absolution from, *see* absolution
  abuse of 5–10, 138
  aggravation of, *see* aggravation
  audiences witnessing, *see* audience
  by name (*nominatim*) 17–18, 200, 250–1, 289
  causes of 23–5, 144–8, 152–3, 263–71, Appendix I *passim*, Appendix II *passim*
  communal enforcement of 138–9, 148–65, 185, 229, 292–4

contagiousness of 61, 103–7, 124–5, 136, 138–40, 143, 146–9, 157–8, 160, 162–3, 167–8, 175, 187–8, 247, 293–4
 exceptions to 109–11, 142–4, 294
dying excommunicated 1, 40, 57, 60–8, 87, 113, 170–1, 290–1
eagerness to avoid 78–86
early modern, *see* early modern period
efficacy of 5–10, 56, 58, 99–100, 103, 128–9, 182, 186, 228–9, 231, 257–8, 290
endured temporarily 95–6, 98–100
exception of 111–14, 150, 177–80
formulae 51–7
 'auctoritate dei' formula 51, 53, 272
general sentences of 24, 45, 70, 178–9, 186, 197, 200, 220–1, 238, 248–9, 285–7
 king excepted from 181, 221 n.212, 237–40, 242–3
ignorance of 34, 106–7, 187–8, 275–8, 275 n.76
ipso facto, *see* lata sententia
as insult 121–3
lata sententia 14–17, 19, 44–5, 56–7, 66–78, 82–5, 94, 98–9, 109–10, 113–14, 121, 123–4, 143–4, 153, 156–7, 172–6, 182, 185, 189–90, 200, 222–3, 227–8, 231, 249–52, 260–89, 295–6, Appendix I *passim*, Appendix II *passim*. See also *Clericis laicos*, *Contempnunt exequi domini*, *Crimen imponunt alicui*, *Quicumque abstrahunt violenter*, *Quicumque de domibus*, *Qui malitiose ecclesias*, *Qui pacem et tranquillitatem*, *Si quis suadente*
medicinal nature of 11–13, 23, 30–5, 55–7, 99–100, 108–9, 138, 142–3, 151, 291, 293
 lack of medicinal intent 41–5, 207, 210–11
minor 13, 109, 139, 146–7, 157–9, 187–8, 210–11
mnemonic poems on 106 n.16, 110 n.51
mocking of 87, 96
mutual sentences of 96–7, 169–72, 194–5, 205–6, 229, 234–5, 295–6
overused 2, 5–10, 128, 138, 147–8, 156–7, 182
power to impose 13–14, 156
solemn ritual of 4–5, 45–51, 57–8, 274, 289–91, 294–5
unjust 13–14, 42, 65–6, 92–9, 103, 140–1, 153, 164–72, 182, 201–3
unpublicised 1, 128–9
warnings required 31–2, 34–5, 44, 207, 275
written copies required 4, 34–5, 199–200, 249–51
exempla, *see* miracle stories
exemptions, *see* privileges

Exeter diocese 260
exile 107–8, 127–8, 141–3, 148–9, 171, 202–3, 226–7, 293

Falkes de Bréauté 79, 94–5, 108–9, 117, 119–20, 134, 141–2, 166, 202–4, 213
fama, *see also* reputation 85, 216–17, 219–20, 234–8, 245–6, 252, 255
Fawler 155
fealty, absolution from 129
fear 78–86, 90–1, 98–100, 237
 (lack of) 251–2, 291
feast days 47, 49–50, 114–15, 185–6, 188–9, 193, 197, 207–8, 214–16, 236, 238, 240, 247–8, 272 n.47, 278, 283, 285–7, Appendix I
 All Saints 262 n.15
 Ascension Day 209–10, 262–3, 271–2
 Consecration of the Basilica of St Peter 262–3, 271–2
 Christmas 262 n.15
 Easter 114–15, 147, 253, 256–7, 262 n.15
 Feast of Fools 172–3
 Holy Trinity 190–1
 Maundy Thursday 47–8, 262–3, 271–2
 Palm Sunday, vigil of 63
 Pentecost 190–1, 283
Ferns, bishop of, *see* Ailbe
flagellation, *see* penance, public
Flores Historiarum 202, 226–7
food, *see* supplies
fora, internal (penitential) and external 12, 69, 74–5, 77–8, 231, *see also* absolution
forest 74–5, 116–17, 177–8
Forest Charter 270
forgery 206–7, 263 n.19, 265–6, Appendix I, 306
fornication 22–3, 25, 104, 111, 145–6, 214 n.173, 264–6, Appendix I
Forrest, Ian 10 n.64, 138–9, 149–50, 152, 168, 195, 287, 292–3
Fossier, Arnaud 69
Fotheringay, castle of 133
Franciscans 36–7, 79–82, 96, 170–1, 210–11, 218, 234
Frederick II, German emperor 2, 58, 80–2, 129–30, 165–6, 190, 202, 204, 228
fugitives 25, 108–9, 141–2, 154–5, 265–6, 269–70
 see also sanctuary
Fulk Basset, bishop of London 92, 170
Fulk de Cantilupe 159

Gascony 121, 135, 222–4
Geoffrey of Buckland, dean of St Martin's-le-Grand 161–2
Gerald of Wales 6–7, 36–7

Glastonbury, abbot of 181
Godfrey Giffard, bishop of Worcester 118, 272–3
  register of 122–3, 181, 214–15
Goff, Jacques le 38–9
gossip, *see* rumour
Gratian, *Decretum* 15–16, 33–5, 46–7, 61 n.10, 93, 93 n.168, 105, 106 n.17, 109 n.44, 129, 130 n.155, 154 n.76, 172 n.173, 187–8, 225 n.230, 262, 306
Great Curse 259–64, 266, 269–71, 272 n.50, 279 n.98, 281–2, 288–9, Appendix II
Great Malvern priory 118, 181, 190, 216
Great Sentence, *see* Great Curse
Gregorian reform 153
Gregory the Great, pope 81, 278
Gregory VII, pope 87, 109–10, 129, 294
Gregory IX, pope 35–6, 58, 76–7, 80–3, 142–3, 174–5, 177–9, 190, 202, 211 n.155
Gregory X, pope 62
Gruter, Margaret 104–5, 148–50
Guala, papal legate 76–7, 88–9
Gui Fouquois, papal legate, *see* Clement IV
Guillaume de Nogaret 199–200, 204

Haakon IV, king of Norway 165–6
Hackington 206–7
Hamilton, Sarah 4–5, 31–2, 45–6, 48, 51, 119–20
Hardy, Thomas 53–4
Hartman, Abigail 96
hell 11–12, 29–30, 32–40, 42, 46–50, 52–3, 55–63, 68, 78–9, 87, 89–92, 97–100, 132, 242–4, 287, 289–91
Helmholz, Richard 2–9, 29–30, 32–3, 46–7, 165, 169–70, 173, 265–6, 268
Henry Bracton, *De legibus* 105, 112
Henry Chichele, archbishop of Canterbury 284
Henry II, king of England 214–15
Henry III, king of England 41–2, 49–50, 79–86, 88–9, 94–5, 97–8, 116–23, 126–7, 141–2, 164, 170, 173–81, 190–1, 202–3, 219–22, 232–3, 267–8
Henry IV, German emperor 129–30, 195, 214–15
Henry of London, archbishop of Dublin 116–17, 119, 217
Henry of Sandford, bishop of Rochester 178–9, 220
Hereford
  bishop of 112, 193, *see also* Thomas Cantilupe
  chapter of 205
  dean of 205–6
  diocese of 47, 98, 260
herem 6–7, 45–6, 93 n.169, 104–5, 110 n.46, 150–3, 165, 169 n.159, 213 n.162

heresy, heretics 3–4, 6–7, 16–17, 82–3, 97–9, 105 n.9, 115, 130, 140, 143–4, 147, 151, 165–6, 172, 204–5, 226, 265–6, 275 n.75, 281–2, 288–9, 291, 293–4, 306, 307
Hervey de Boreham 119
Hill, Rosalind 5–6, 21, 73–4, 103–4, 123–5, 188–9, 214–15, 231–2
Holy Land 131, 135, 214–15
Honorius III, pope 161–2, 202–3, 262–3
Honyburn 106
host, *see also* Eucharist 47–8, 215–16, 246–7
Hubert de Burgh 82–3, 89, 132, 220
Hugh de Lacy, earl of Ulster 119–20
Hugh of Lincoln (St), bishop of Lincoln 5 n.21
Hugh of Wells, bishop of Lincoln, register of 161–2
humiliation, *see* shame
Huntingdon, archdeacon of 217–18, 240

Ignorantia sacerdotum 276–7
Immingham 285
indulgences 66, 134–5, 193, 202–3, 291 n.1
Innocent III, pope 3–4, 38–9, 61 n.10, 94–5, 94 n.172, 106, 110–11, 127–32, 159–60, 173–4, 200, 262–3
Innocent IV, pope 32–4, 81, 109–10, 165–6, 201–2, 212 n.157, 217–18, 223–4, 272
inquests, *see* investigations
insanity 25
interdict 13, 23–4, 43, 61, 67–8, 80–1, 85, 99–NaN, 114, 116–18, 127–9, 135, 138–9, 157–62, 165–8, 180–1, 189 n.23, 191 n.39, 209–11, 213, 221–2, 225–7, 294–6, 306–8
investigations 24, 45, 64, 70, 74–5, 98, 125, 152, 155, 159–60, 167–8, 209–10, 224, 236–8, 247–50, 253, 287
Isle of Wight 216 n.188, 264
Isabella de Mortimer 22–4

Jacob's Well 56–7, 271, 288–9
Jaser, Christian 2–5, 29–30, 36, 45–6, 46 n.79, 46 n.80, 47–8, 55 n.131, 71, 96 n.185, 244–5, 261–3, 271 n.46
Jewish excommunication, *see herem*
Jews 143–4, 150–1, 180
Johannes Andreae 29
John, king of England 3–4, 78–9, 82, 88, 127–32, 159–62, 164, 173–4, 221
John de Beaupré, knight 91–2
John Bromyard 37–8
John Comyn 197–8
John de Halton, bishop of Carlisle 103, 107, 188–9

John Lydgate 37–9
John Mansel 232–3
John Mirk 263–4, 267, 271, 281–2, 288 n.152
John Pecham, archbishop of Canterbury 15–17, 34, 54, 66 n.40, 77, 93–4, 118–19, 173, 177–8, 178 n.208, 181, 189 n.26, 196–7, 217–18, 222, 259–60, 263, 266–72, 276–7, 282, 284–6, 304–6, 308
John of Pontoise, bishop of Winchester
  register of 124–5, 167, 190, 214
John le Romeyn, archbishop of York 220, 283–4
  register of 52
John of St John 231–2, 255
John de Stonegrave 125, 160
John Wyclif 281–2, 288–9
Jordan 'salsarius' 208–10
Judgement Day 37, 39 n.53, 146–7
judicial process 4–5, 29–32, 43–4, 58, 62–3, 73–5, 77, 93, 236, 250–1, 257–8, 260–1, 285
Juliana Box 1, 107, 145–6
Julianus Pomerius 105

Kaplan, Yosef 151
Karn, Nicholas 51
Kattedy priory 145
Katz, Jacob 93 n.169, 151–2
Kenilworth, siege of 49 n.94, 96
Keygnaert, Frederik 7–8
keys of St Peter 13 n.87, 34–5, 98, 140, 218, 268–9
king's bench 123–4, 125 n.127, 253
Kingerby 286–7
Kramer, Susan 157–8

Lambeth, palace of 192
  see also councils
Lanercost, chronicle of 49, 53–4, 170–1, 197–8
Lange, Tyler 114–15
Lawrence, C. H. 206–7, 211–12
Lea, H.C. 7–8
Leicester, earl of, see Simon de Montfort
Leighton Manor 168
Lent 63, 75–6, 214–15, 237
Leopold V, duke of Austria 86
lepers, leprosy 31 n.8, 64–5, 105–7, 122–3, 138, 143–4, 293
Lewandowski, Charlotte 130, 244–5
Lewes 284–5
  Battle of (1264) 96, 119, 134–5, 225
  prior 19 n.104
  Song of 134–5
Liber Extra 34–5, 39 n.49, 61 n.10, 71–2, 93 n.165, 94 n.172, 109, 109 n.40, 111 n.55, 115 n.73, 151 n.52, 157 n.89, 172 n.173, 278 n.92, 306

Liber Sextus 32, 157 n.89, 306–7
Lichfield, dean of 117
Lincoln 234, 282
  archdeacon of 141–2, 242
  Battle of (1217) 62, 88–90, 132–3
  bishops of 156, see also Hugh of Wells, Robert Grosseteste, Richard Gravesend, Oliver Sutton
  cathedral of 230, 233–6
  dean and chapter of 35–6, 62–3, 282
  diocese of 18–21, 232–3, 240–1, 246, 252, 260
  official of bishop 246
Little, Lester 46–7, 53–4, 244–5
Llywelyn the Great, prince of Wales 94–5, 98 n.194, 129, 166, 190–1
Logan, Donald 2–3, 23–4, 29–30, 45, 91, 126, 268–9
Lollards, Lollardy 281–2
London 140, 145–6, 161–2, 208, 213, 216–17, 226–7, 255–7, 284–5
  annals of 216–17, 226–7
  bishop of 19 n.104, 124–5, 162–3, 217, 283, see also Fulk Basset
  diocese of 260
  mayor 127, 140–1
  statutes of 34 n.27, 189 n.25, 260, 264, 272 n.47, 287 n.149, see also councils
Long Crendon 241–4
Louis the Pious, king of France 6–7
Louis VII, king of France 88
Louis, prince (later king Louis VIII) of France 49 n.95, 88–9, 95–6, 120, 131–2, 134, 141–2, 161–2, 173–4, 214–15
Louis IX, king of France 76–7, 81–3, 135
Lucca, bishop of 130
Lusignans 194
Luther, see Martin Luther
Lyndwood, William, *Provinciale* 259–62, 271, 281–2

Maddicott, John 97–8, 128–9
Madoc, Welsh prince 119–20
Magna Carta 3–4, 16 n.102, 47–51, 55–7, 82–4, 127, 170–1, 175, 189 n.22, 190–1, 228, 265, 270–3, 279–86, 288, Appendix I, 305–6
Maidstone 192, 206–7, 209
malediction, see curse
Malton, canons of 123–4
Mansfield, Mary 69 n.51, 199 n. 76, 200–1, 216
Marini Sanuti 6–7
marketplaces 22–3, 214–16, 214 n.173, 229
Marlborough, rector of St Mary's 199–200
  oath of, see oaths

marriage 23–4, 94 n.172, 112–13, 121–2, 145–6, 265–6, 268, 276–7, 286–7, 287 n.149, 292, Appendix I, 305, 306, 307
Martin IV, pope 66 n.40, 76–7
Martin Luther 87, 204–5, 288–9
Martin, papal legate 80–1
mass 38, 98, 114–15, 147, 158–9, 188, 188 n.16, 221, 230, 239–41, 246, 294–5, 307–8
Masters, Roger D. 104–5
Matthew Paris 41–4, 47–8, 56–8, 65–6, 79–82, 84–8, 92, 108–9, 121–3, 126–7, 141–2, 165–6, 168–70, 174–6, 192–5, 201–2, 204–5, 207, 211 n.155, 228, 284–5
Meens, Rob 9–10
meidung (shunning), Amish 148–50
Melrose, chronicle of 88, 161–2
Melve, Leidulf 195
merchants 106, 140–1, 211
Middle English 37–9, 53, 56–7, 259–60, 263–4, 276–7, 288–9
Milani, Giuliani 195–6
Miller, Andrew 231–2, 242–3
Minety 167–8
miracle stories 4–5, 36–41, 70, 78, 81–2, 86–90, 105–6
misfortune 78, 86–90, 132
monks 1–2, 42–3, 49–50, 73, 79–80, 87, 91–2, 116, 118–19, 122–3, 126–7, 141–2, 153–4, 161–2, 167, 181, 190, 206–12, 216–18
  apostasy of 23–4
Montfortian' bishops 162–4, 170–1, 279–80
Moore, R.I. 105, 144, 292–4
Moorman, J.H. 60
Moray, bishop of 74
Murray, Alexander 4–5, 8–9, 30, 32–3, 87, 90, 93–4, 115, 152–3

Newark castle 86
Nicholas from Wallingford 115, 146–7
Nicholas IV, pope 66 n.40, 233–6
Northampton 84, 119–20, 204
Norwich 61–2, 118
  bishop of 51, 72, 127–8
  diocese of 71–2, 260
Notley 241–4, 247–8
Nuneaton, chaplain of 242
nuns 22–3, 25, 106, 113, 166–7
  abduction of 214–15
  apostasy of 23–4, 113, 145, 166–7

oath 23, 96–7, 224, 241–2, 265–6
  of Marlborough (1209) 128–9

officials
  ecclesiastical 13–14, 20, 117, 181, 192, 207–8, 217, 238, 242, 246, 283, 286–7
  royal 117, 178–80
  privilege protecting from excommunication 116–17, 177–80, 217, 220, 268–9, 288
Oliver Sutton, bishop of Lincoln 34, 48, 66–7, 221, 231–57, 272–3, 283
  familia of 246
  register of 18–25, 49–50, 73–4, 154 n.71, 214–15, 235–6, 246, 256–7
Osbert Giffard 214–15
Osney
  abbey of 190–1
  annals of 64–5
ostracism 103–12, 115–26, 139–57, 164–5, 173, 179–80, 182, 186–8, 217–18, 292–4
  failure of 127–8, 138–82, 186–7, 198–9, 208–9, 228–9
Otto, papal legate 190–1, 207–8, 228
Otto IV, German emperor 3–4, 129–30
Ottobuono, papal legate 16–17, 64–5, 96–7, 135, 162–3, 226, 269–70, 273–4, 305
outlawry, outlaws 6–7, 80, 92, 94–5, 108–9, 111–12, 123–4, 141–2, 187–8, 216–17, 253–4
Oxford 22, 188–91, 193–4, 215–16, 234–6, 238, 241, 246, 255–6, 270
  archdeacon of 238, 240
  Provisions of, *see* Provisions
  St Frideswide's 190–1
  St Mary's 238
  schools of 25, 178–9, 188–9, 193, 234, 238, 270
  sheriff of 238, 245–6, 255
  statutes of, *see* councils

Pandulf, papal legate 45–6, 133
papacy 7–8, 16–17, 65–6, 78–81, 97, 121–2, 129–31, 161–2, 165–6, 169–71, 175–6, 201–2, 221–2, 228, 231–2, 234–5, 237, 239–40, 262–3, 279–80
  absolution reserved to 69, 71–2, 274
  general excommunication ('general process') of 7–8, 47–8, 262–3, 271–2, 288–9
  registers of 3–4
paralysis 25, 81–2
Paravicini Bagliani, Agostino 262–3
Paris 270
  bishop of 76–7, 274
parish priests 13–14, 34–5, 45, 68, 70, 156, 158–9, 185–90, 228, 262–3, 276–8, 280, 284–5, 292–3, 304
parliament rolls 217

parliament 117, 217–18, 238–9, 255, 266–9, 284–5
pastoral care 12–13, 17–18, 40, 81–2, 106–7, 109–10, 142–4, 156–7, 187–8, 259–62, 264, 275–80, 289
Pattwell, Niamh 276–7, 281–2
Pavlac, Brian 9–10
Peace of God 261–2
penance 12, 38, 60–1, 69, 71–2, 75, 82–3, 91, 97–8, 223–4
  public 22–3, 75–6, 91, 188, 200–1, 213–16, 218–19, 256–7
penitentiary, papal 69, 71–4, 77, 221–2
perjury 23, 62–3, 74, 81–2, 84–6, 259, 264–6, 280–1, Appendix I, 305
Peter Abelard 31
Peter the Chanter 72 n.68, 172–3
Peter of Cornwall 70
Peter des Roches, bishop of Winchester 82–3, 95, 127–8, 174–5, 220
Philip II 'Augustus', king of France 3–4, 130–1, 177 n.202
Philip IV the 'Fair', king of France 199–200
Pickering, dean of 218
Pickering, Oliver 281–2
Poitevins 194–5
pontificals 51–2
  romano-Germanic 51–2
  William Durandus 46, 54–5
preaching 36, 56–7, 81–2, 105–6, 109, 134–5, 161–2, 209, 213, 219, 272–3, 284–5
Prestwich, Michael 82–3
privileges 9, 67, 77 n.92, 80–3, 116–17, 127, 177–9, 220, 223–4, 307
processions 49, 208–11, 214–16, 284–5
propaganda 134–5, 194–5, 197–8, 202, 221, 227, 267–9, 294–6
prostitution 264–6, Appendix I
Provisions of Oxford (1258) 49–50, 97–8, 134–5, 170–1, 221–2, 279–80
provisions, papal 65–6, 233–6, 245–6
Prynne, William 76–7
psalms, see bible
public denunciations 21, 47, 58, 67, 185–229, 234–6, 238–43, 247–8, 251–2, 254, 271–3, 291–2, 294–6
  failure to execute 186–7, 189–90
  prevention of 225–8, 241–2
  revenge for 228
public opinion 92, 164–6, 168–72, 182, 185, 193–5, 197–9, 207, 210–12, 222, 225, 228–9, 231, 235–42, 246–8, 252, 254, 257–8, 287–9, 292–6
purgatory 32–3, 38–40, 57, 60–1, 290–1

Quicumque abstrahunt violenter 154–5, 269–70, 284–5, Appendix I, 305
Quicumque de domibus 66, 75, 269–70, 272–3, 286–7, Appendix I, 305
Qui malitiose ecclesias 15–16, 44, 62–3, 173, 176, 193–4, 265–70, 272–3, 283–8, 287 n.149, Appendix I, 304–5
Qui pacem et tranquillitatem 94–5, 120–1, 173–6, 197–8, 265–8, 286–7, Appendix I, 305

Ralph Chenduit 87
Ralph de Honilane, vintner 140, 145–6, 157–8
Ranulf, earl of Chester 49–50, 89, 120–1, 133
Raymond of Peñafort 13 n.84, 34 n.25, 73 n.74, 110–11, 173 n.177
Raymond VII, Count of Toulouse 82–3
Reformation 6–8, 23–4, 147–8, 165–6
Reginald of Cornhill 159
Reims 200–1, 261–2
relics 49
Renaissance 6–7
reputation 186–7, 198–205, 208, 211–12, 218–22, 229, 235, 255, 291–2
Reynolds, Roger E. 45–6
Reynolds, Susan 150 n.48, 292–4
Richard I, king of England 86
Richard of Gravesend, dean then bishop of Lincoln 162 n.126, 272–3, 282, 284–5
Richard Marshal, earl of Pembroke 174–6
Richard Poore, bishop of Salisbury, bishop of Durham 260 n.2, 263–4
Richard de Scholand 1, 64
Robert the Bruce 49, 188–9, 197–8
Robert Fitzwalter 127–8
Robert of Flamborough 105–6, 110, 213
Robert of Gloucester, chronicle of 96
Robert Grosseteste, bishop of Lincoln 35–6, 49–50, 65–6, 81–2, 93–4, 97, 111, 116–17, 122, 130, 228, 232–3, 274, 278, 284–5
Robert Winchelsey, archbishop of Canterbury 47–8, 61–2, 64, 71–2, 80, 92, 119–20, 140–1, 145–6, 157–8, 162, 195–6, 216–17, 269–70, 272–4, 282–5
  register of 71–2
Rochester 212
  bishop of 208, see also Henry of Sandford
  diocese of 260
Roger of Wendover 78–9, 88–90, 95–6, 128–33, 159–62, 175–6, 200, 212, 221
Rome 93–4, 141–2, 159, 193–4, 209
Rosser, Gervase 154–5
rumour 120–1, 129–30, 200, 216–17, 221–2, 229, 235
Ryedale, dean of 218

sacraments 38, 60, 97–8, 147, 158–60, 162–3, 264, 268, 276–7, 307
  exclusion from 13, 31, 90–1, 98–9, 103, 109, 114–15, 157, 210–11, 291
  see also baptism, Eucharist, penance, marriage, confession
sacrilege 64, 67–8, 96, 154, 193–4, 226, 230, 239–43, 247, 250, 252
St Albans 87
  abbot and convent of 49, 76, 79–80, 211 n.155, 216–18
  historical writing at 84, 87, 175–6, 202, *see also* Matthew Paris, Roger of Wendover, and *Flores Historiarum*
St Asaph
  bishop of 285–6
  diocese of 47
St Mary le Bow 193
St Mary's abbey, York 76
St Oswald's Priory 118, 181
St Paul's cathedral 133, 155, 170, 217–18
  dean of 170, 204–5
St Swithun's, Winchester 49–50, 167, 178–9
St Thomas's priory, Southwark 192–5
Salisbury
  bishop of 286–7, *see also* Richard Poore, Simon of Ghent
  cathedral 190–1
  church of 265–6
  dean of 283
  diocese of 259–60, 263, 272–3
  earl of 49–50, 133
  statutes of, *see* councils
sanctuary, violation of 24–5, 154–5, 253 n.123, 265–6, 269–70, 280–1, 305, see also *Quicumque abstrahunt violenter*
Satan 41, 70, 195–7, 230, 239–40
Savoyards 194
scandal 11–12, 170, 195–6, 199–201, 203–12, 216–17, 219–23
Scarborough 218
scepticism 36–7, 87, 90–1, 97–9
Schism, Great Western 3–4, 109–10, 169–70
Schmugge, Ludwig 69
secular arm 1–3, 19–21, 23–4, 70–1, 91, 103, 112–13, 124–7, 135, 145–7, 160, 176–80, 251–2, 268–9, see also *Contempnunt exequi domini*
sermons, *see* preaching
services, ecclesiastical 24, 98, 114–15, 158–63, 167–8, 208–10, 243, 247, 255, 307–8
Sewal de Bovill, archbishop of York 65–6, 93, 168–9, 201–2, 204

shame 11–12, 30–1, 64–5, 68, 77–8, 107, 119, 122, 149, 199–200, 202, 208–9, 212–16, 218–19, 242
sheriffs 76, 120, 126, 146–7, 176–8, 181, 209, 220–1, 238–9, 245–6, 253, 255–6, 268–9
shipwrecks 264–6, 281–2, Appendix I
Shoreham, dean of 64
Si quis suadente 16–17, 23–5, 66, 71–2, 74, 126–7, 141–2, 153–4, 172–3, 176, 193–4, 215–16, 226, 250, 265–6, 272–3, 278, 281–2, 284–7, 306
Sicilian business 79–80, 84–6, 219–20
Simon de Montfort, earl of Leicester 64–5, 96–8, 119, 121–3, 134–6, 162–4, 170–1, 190–1, 212, 223–7
Simon Langton, archdeacon of Canterbury 161 n.112, 209–11
Simon of Ghent, bishop of Salisbury 75, 106, 146–7, 155, 167–8, 190–1, 257, 272–3, 283
slander, *see* reputation
sodomy 144, 261–2
sorcery 144, 214 n.173, 259, 263 n.19, 264–6, 280–1, Appendix I
Southern, Richard 242
Southmalling, Sussex 74–5
Southwark, dean of 194
Spaldwick 234
Sparsholt 155
Speculum laicorum 36–7, 39
Stamford, dean of 217–18
statutes, ecclesiastical, *see* councils
Stephen Langton, archbishop of Canterbury 16–17, 16 nn.101–2, 84, 120–1, 127–8, 159, 162, 166, 176–8, 200, 202–5, 213, 259–62, 266–75, 284
Stephen of Bourbon 105–6
Stephen of Seagrave 80–1, 174–5
Stephen, King of England 130, 244–5
Stubbs, William 207
suicide 115, 152–3
Summerson, Henry 154–5
Sundays, *see* feast days
supplies, deprivation of 105–6, 118–19, 123–4, 155, 181, 247, 253–4, 269–70
synods, *see* councils

taxatio (1291) 232–3
taxation 23–4, 59, 79–81
Taylor Snyder, Susan 166
Temple church, London 41–2
Tewksbury, annals of 135
Thame 48–9, 53–4, 230–58

theft 22–5, 70, 259, 265–6, 287 n.149, Appendix I
of church property 23–4, 41–4, 95–6, 153–4,
196–7, 265–6, 306
theologians 4, 29–32, 35, 39–43, 93–4, 172–3
theology 33, 39–40, 54–5, 57–8, 79–80, 94–5, 244
Thomas Aquinas, *Summa Theologiae* 30–1
Thomas Becket 15–16, 16 n.102, 49, 51, 201–2,
214–15, 291
Thomas Cantilupe, bishop of Hereford 54, 74–5,
93–4, 190, 205–6
Thomas of Chobham 46, 93, 105, 107, 121–2,
141–2, 214–15, 278
Thomas de Lewknor 231–4, 256–7
Thomas fitz Adam 116–17, 217
Thomas Sutton, archdeacon of
Northampton 230–58 *passim*
Thomas Wykes 163–4, 226–7
Thorney, abbot of 63
Titchfield, abbot of 112–13
tithes 14 n.88, 23–5, 38, 40, 110–12, 153–4,
215–16, 263 n.19, 265–6, 276–7, 285–6
Töblemann, Paul 10
Todd, Margo 147–8
tourneying 64 n.31, 84, 120–1, 172–3
trees 24, 70, 75, 153–4, 196–7, 287 n.150
Treharne, Elaine 4–5, 31–2
Turner, R.V. 128

Urban II, pope 129–30
Urban IV, pope 77, 135, 179
Usk castle 174
usury 81, 214 n.173, 263 n.19, 265–6, 280–1,
Appendix I, 307

Vallerani, Massimo 252
Van Cleve, T.C. 202
Velascus, papal penitentiary 221–2
vernacular 47, 53, 185–6, 188–9, 230, 236,
239–40, 272–3, 276–7, 280, 283–5, 294–5,
see also Middle English
Vincent, Nicholas 175–6, 193
Vise, Melissa 166
Vodola, Elisabeth 2–5, 12, 15–16, 29–30, 32–3,
54–5, 109–14, 150, 176–80

Waddesdon 234, 238
Walter of Coventry, continuator of 88, 206
Walter Bronescombe, bishop of Exeter 277–8,
283–4
register of 91, 213
Walter de Cantilupe, bishop of Worcester 134–5,
162–3, 226–7
Walter Giffard, archbishop of York 160, 203–4,
216–17

Waltham, abbot of 76
war crimes 67–8, 76–7
Warren, W.L. 128
Waverley, annals of 211
Weiler, Björn 10 n.65, 122, 168–9, 175–6,
195
Welsh wars 66, 76–7, 190–1, 195–8, 286–7
language, *see* vernacular
Wendover 238
Roger of, *see* Roger of Wendover
Westminster
abbot of 95, 181
archdeacon of 128
statutes, ecclesiastical, *see* councils
sacristan of 196–7
Statute of (1275) 223
Wickham, Chris 239
William I, king of England 177
Willian de Forz, earl of Aumale 49–50,
120–1, 133
William Greenfield, archbishop of York
278, 282
William of Malmesbury 6–7
William Marshal 41–4, 53–4, 63–4, 82–3, 86,
89–90, 132
History of 89–90, 132
William Marshal (II) 42
William of Pagula 267–8, 271, 278–9, 281–2,
304–8
William Rishanger 97
William Wickwane, archbishop of
York 283–4
Williams, Kipling D. 104–5, 107–8, 148
wills 22–5, 64, 113, 140, 145–6, 265–6,
Appendix I
Wilton, abbess of 106
Wiltshire, archdeacon of 167–8
Winchester
bishop of 162–3, 167, 190–1, 226–7, *see also*
Peter des Roches, Aymer de Lusignan,
John of Pontoise
diocese of 260
mayor and bailiffs 220
official of 49–50, 88–9, 178–9, 220
palace of 122
prior of 126–7, 167
witness depositions 48–9
see also Court of the Arches
women
cannot excommunicate 13–14
excommunication of 20–2
public penance of 213–15
Worcester 95
annals of 190 n.30

Worcester (*cont.*)
  bishop of 49, 76–7, 113, 118, *see also* Walter de Cantilupe, Godfrey Giffard
  Cathedral Priory 161–2
  diocese of 190, 260
writs 209
  de excommunicato capiendo, *see* secular arm and *Contempnunt exequi domini*
  de vi laica amovenda 237–9, 245–6, 253
  novel disseisin 238–9
  of prohibition 179, 266–7

Wyclif, *see* John Wyclif
Wycombe 247–50

Yoder, Andy 148–9
York, diocese 260
  archbishops of, *see* Sewal de Bovill, John le Romeyn, Walter Giffard, William Wickwane, John le Romeyn, William Greenfield

Zutschi, Patrick 69